KB

Religious Law

Library of Congress Classification
2008

Prepared by the Cataloging Policy and Support Office
Library Services

LIBRARY OF CONGRESS
Cataloging Distribution Service
Washington, D.C.

This edition cumulates all additions and changes to class KB through Weekly List 2008/33, dated August 13, 2008. Additions and changes made subsequent to that date are published in weekly lists posted on the World Wide Web at

<http://www.loc.gov/aba/cataloging/classification/weeklylists/>

and are also available in *Classification Web*, the online Web-based edition of the Library of Congress Classification.

Library of Congress Cataloging-in-Publication Data

Library of Congress.
Library of Congress classification. KB. Religious law / prepared by the Cataloging Policy and Support Office, Library Services. — 2008 ed.
p. cm.
"This edition cumulates all additions and changes to class KB through Weekly List 2008/33, dated August 13, 2008. Additions and changes made subsequent to that date are published in weekly lists posted on the World Wide Web at <http://www.loc.gov/aba/cataloging/classification/weeklylists/> and are also available in Classification Web, the online Web-based edition of the Library of Congress classification." — T.p. verso.
Includes index.
ISBN-13: 978-0-8444-1223-8
1. Classification, Library of Congress. 2. Classification—Books—Religious law and legislation. 3. Classification—Books—Ecclesiastical law. 4. Religious law and legislation—Classification. 5. Canon law—Classification. 6. Islamic law—Classification. 7. Jewish law—Classification. I. Library of Congress. Cataloging Policy and Support Office. II. Title. III. Title: Religious law.
Z696.U5K25 2008   025.4'62084—dc22   2008038087

For sale by the Library of Congress Cataloging Distribution Service,
101 Independence Avenue, S.E., Washington, DC 20541-4912.
Product catalog available on the Web at **www.loc.gov/cds.**

PREFACE

Subclass KB, *Religious Law*, is currently in the process of being developed by Jolande E. Goldberg, law classification specialist in the Cataloging Policy and Support Office. Subclasses KBR, *History of Canon Law*, and KBU, *Law of the Roman Catholic Church. The Holy See*, the first two subclasses to be completed, were published in 2000. The 2004 edition included, in addition to those two subclasses, three new subclasses that were developed between 2000 and 2004: KB, *Religious Law in General. Comparative Religious Law. Jurisprudence*; KBM, *Jewish Law. Halakah*; and KBP, *Islamic Law. Sharī'ah. Fiqh*. This 2008 edition includes additions and changes that have been made to these subclasses between 2004 and 2008. For this edition, Arabic script has been provided for many of the proper names and Arabic terms in subclass KBP, in addition to their Latin counterparts. Future editions of KB will incorporate additional subclasses until all of the KB subclasses have been completed.

Classification numbers or spans of numbers that appear in parentheses are formerly valid numbers that are now obsolete. Numbers or spans that appear in angle brackets are optional numbers that have never been used at the Library of Congress but are provided for other libraries that wish to use them. In most cases, a parenthesized or angle-bracketed number is accompanied by a "see" reference directing the user to the actual number that the Library of Congress currently uses, or a note explaining Library of Congress practice.

Access to the online version of the full Library of Congress Classification is available on the World Wide Web by subscription to *Classification Web*. Details about ordering and pricing may be obtained from the Cataloging Distribution Service at

<http://www.loc.gov/cds/>

New or revised numbers and captions are added to the L.C. Classification schedules as a result of development proposals made by the cataloging staff of the Library of Congress and cooperating institutions. Upon approval of these proposals by the weekly editorial meeting of the Cataloging Policy and Support Office, new classification records are created or existing records are revised in the master classification database. Weekly lists of newly approved or revised classification numbers and captions are posted on the World Wide Web at

<http://www.loc.gov/aba/cataloging/classification/weeklylists/>

Kent Griffiths, assistant editor of classification schedules, is responsible for creating new classification records, maintaining the master database, and creating index terms for the captions.

The Library of Congress gratefully acknowledges the assistance and support of the Advisory Committee on LC Law Classification during the development of the major classes of religious law presented in this volume. From the University of California at Berkeley School of Law, Professor Laurent Mayali, Director, Robbins Collection, and Thomas H. Reynolds, Associate Director of the Library (now retired), provided funding and other support that enabled the law classification specialist to conduct an in-depth study of the Robbins Collection on Canon and Roman law, which laid the groundwork for subclasses KBR and KBU. The Library also wishes to extend its thanks to those law libraries who have generously contributed staff resources to the development of the schedules on Jewish law (KBM) and Islamic law (KBP): M. Kathleen Price, Director and Professor of Law, and Professor Noah Feldman of New York University Law School Library and Faculty; Professor Harry S. Martin, Librarian and Professor of Law, Harvard Law School Library; the Islamic Legal Studies Program at Harvard Law School, in particular Professor Frank Vogel, Director, Peri Bearman, Associate Director, Lesley Wilkins, Bibliographer of the Islamic World, and Aron Zysow, Research Associate. The Library also extends its thanks to Professor Michel Theriault, Université Saint-Paul, Faculté de Droit Canonique, for his critique and encouragement during the final drafting stage of the schedules. Recognition is also due to Oberstudienrat Helmut Hoerr, Bad Homburg/Germany, and Dario C. Ferreira, Senior Legal Research Analyst and Librarian (Law-Romance Languages), Law Library of Congress, for reviewing and editing the Latin portions of the text.

In addition, the Library would like to express its gratitude to William Kopycki, University of Pennsylvania, for his assistance in providing the Arabic script for subclass KBP.

Barbara B. Tillett, Chief
Cataloging Policy and Support Office

August 2008

Religious Law in General. Comparative Religious Law. Jurisprudence

Jewish Law. Halakhah

Islamic Law. Shari'ah. Fiqh

History of Canon Law

Law of the Roman Catholic Church. The Holy See

OUTLINE

KB1-4855	Religious law in general. Comparative religious law. Jurisprudence
KB2-4	Bibliography
KB7-68	Periodicals
KB68	Annuals. Annuaires
KB70.A-Z	Monographic series. By title, A-Z
KB73	Collections. Compilations (General and comprehensive)
KB74-78	Auxiliary sciences
KB90.A-Z	Encyclopedias. Law dictionaries. Terms and phrases. Vocabularies. By author or title, A-Z
KB100.A-Z	Proverbia. Legal maxims. Brocardica juris. Regulae juris. By author or title, A-Z
KB122	Biography (Collective)
KB130	Legal research. Legal bibliography. Methods of bibliographic research
KB150	Conferences. Symposia
KB160	General works. Treatises
KB162-250	Legal systems compared
KB270-280	Theory, philosophy, and science of religious law
KB400-4855	Interdisciplinary discussion of subjects
KB400	Ritual law. Religious observances and rituals
KB410	Law reform and policies. Criticism
KB479	Private law (General)
KB480-482	Private international law. Conflict of laws
KB491	Civil law (General)
KB524-530	Persons
KB531-619	Domestic relations. Family law
KB622-628.5	Guardianship. Guardian and ward
KB632-636.2	Inheritance and succession
KB636.3	Gifts. Charitable gifts. Donations
KB640-726	Property. Res in commercio
KB810-962.8	Obligations. Contracts and transactions
KB1270-1278	Labor laws and legislation
KB1468-1550	Social laws and legislation. Welfare. Charities
KB1572-1690	Courts and procedure
KB2000-2035	Public law. The State
KB2101-2862	Constitutions and religion. Constitutional and administrative law
KB2870	Civil service. Employees of state, communal agencies, and religious corporations
KB3000-3034	Police and public safety
KB3040.5-3056	Public property. Government property
KB3075-3096.5	Public health

OUTLINE

	Religious law in general. Comparative religious law. Jurisprudence
	Interdisciplinary discussion of subjects - Continued
KB3098-3121.7	Medical legislation
KB3122	Veterinary medicine and hygiene. Veterinary public health
KB3123-3123.5	Animal protection. Animal welfare. Animal rights
KB3124-3125	Birth control. Family planning
KB3127-3135	Environmental law
KB3137-3183	Cultural affairs
KB3190-3429	Economic law
KB3440-3500.7	Transportation and communication
KB3515-3522	Professions. Intelligentsia
KB3526-3694	Public finance
KB3709-3726	Government measures in time of war, national emergency, or economic crisis
KB3735-3780	Military law
KB3790-4855	Criminal law and procedure
KBM1-4855	Jewish law. Halakah
	Halakah
KBM523.6	Even ha-ʻezer law (General)
KBM523.72	Ḥoshen mishpaṭ law (General)
KBM523.8-4855	Mishpat Ivri
KBM523.8	Bibliography
KBM523.82	Monographic series
KBM523.9	Legal education. Study and teaching
KBM524	General works
KBM524.12-524.26	The concept of Jewish law
KBM524.3	Sources of Jewish law (Mishpat Ivri)
KBM524.32-.34	Methodology of law development
KBM524.36	Influence of other legal systems on Jewish law
KBM524.38	Law reform and policies. Criticism
KBM524.4.A-Z	Concepts applying to several branches of the law, A-Z
KBM524.42	Private law
KBM524.43	Conflict of laws. Plurality of laws conflict
KBM524.5	Assistance in emergencies
KBM524.6-530	Persons
KBM531-619	Domestic relations. Family law
KBM622-628.5	Guardian and ward. Apotropos
KBM632-636.2	Inheritance and succession
KBM636.3	Gifts. Charitable gifts. Donations
KBM639-1424	Dinei mamonot
KBM1468-1547	Social laws and legislation

Jewish law. Halakah
Mishpat Ivri - Continued
KBM1572-1942 Courts and procedure
KBM2000-2024 Public law. The state and the Jewish community. Kehillah
KBM2070-2614 Constitutional law. Constitutional principles of the Jewish community
KBM2711-2840 Administrative law and process of communal agencies
KBM2970 Civil service. Employees of communal agencies
KBM3000-3036.5 Police and public safety
KBM3040.5-3073 Public property. Communal property. Restraints on private property
KBM3075-3097 Public health
KBM3098-3122 Medical legislation
KBM3124-3125 Birth control. Family planning
KBM3127-3134 Environmental law
KBM3137-3183 Cultural affairs
KBM3190-3436 Economic law
KBM3440-3504.5 Transportation and communication
KBM3515-3519 Professions
KBM3526-3695 Public finance
KBM3709-3729 Measures in time of war, national emergency, or economic crisis
KBM3738-3785 Community defense. Military law
KBM3790-4855 Criminal law and procedure

KBP1-4860 Islamic law. Sharīʻah. Fiqh
KBP2.2-8 Bibliography
KBP9.5 Monographic series
KBP10-14.5 Societies. Associations
KBP15 Congresses. Conferences
KBP18 Academies. Institutes
KBP40 Encyclopedias. Dictionaries
KBP40.2 Maxims. Quotations
KBP40.5 Directories
KBP41 Legal research
KBP42-43 Legal education. Study and teaching
KBP50-69 History, development and application of Islamic law
KBP70-75.4 Biography
KBP100-136.8 Sources
KBP144 General works
KBP173.25-.6 Islamic law and other disciplines or subjects
KBP174-190.5 Observances and practice of Islam
KBP250-420 Schools of thought. Islamic legal schools. Madhāhib

Islamic law. Sharī'ah. Fiqh - Continued
KBP425-466.3 Uṣūl al-fiqh. Jurisprudence and theory of law. Science of legal reasoning
KBP469 Influence of other legal systems on Islamic law
KBP470 Law reform. Criticism. Tanẓīm
KBP480-485 Conflict of laws. Tanāzu' al-qawānīn
KBP490-4860 Furū' al-fiqh. Substantive law. Branches of law
KBP490.2-.95 General works. Treatises
KBP491-497.95 Particular genres
KBP500-509.8 General concepts
KBP524-638 Aḥwāl shakhṣīyah
KBP639-1154 Mu'āmalāt
KBP1155-1194 Intellectual and industrial property
KBP1234-1259 Unfair competition
KBP1270-1467 Labor laws and legislation
KBP1468-1569 Social laws and legislation
KBP1572-1942 Courts and procedure
KBP2000-2035 Public law. The state and Islam
KBP2101-2612 Constitution of the state. Constitutional law
KBP2730-2968 Government and administration. Siyāsah. Administrative process
KBP2970 Civil service. Employees of communal agencies
KBP3000-3037 Police and public safety
KBP3040.5-3072 Public property. Government property
KBP3075-3096.5 Public health
KBP3098-3121.5 Medical legislation
KBP3122 Veterinary medicine and hygiene. Veterinary public health
KBP3123-3123.5 Animal protection. Animal welfare. Animal rights
KBP3124-3125 Birth control. Family planning
KBP3127-3135 Environmental law
KBP3137-3183.3 Cultural affairs
KBP3190-3437 Economic law
KBP3440-3512 Transportation and communication
KBP3515-3521 Professions. Intelligentsia
KBP3526-3705 Public finance
KBP3709-3727 Government measures in time of war, national emergency, or economic crisis
KBP3738-3785 Military law
KBP3790-4860 Criminal law and procedure

KBR2-4090 History of canon law
KBR2-19 Bibliography
KBR21 Annuals. Annuaires. Yearbooks

OUTLINE

	History of canon law - Continued
KBR22	Monographic series
KBR27-41.7	Official acts of the Holy See
KBR42-54.5	Decisions of ecclesiastical tribunals and courts, and related materials
KBR56	Encyclopedias. Law dictionaries. Terms and phrases. Vocabularia
KBR64	Directories
KBR74-83	Auxiliary sciences
KBR100.A-Z	Proverbia. Legal maxims. Brocardica juris. Regulae juris
KBR105.A-Z	Formularies. Clauses and forms. Formularia
KBR122-124	Collective biography of canonists or jurists
KBR127-129.5	Trials
KBR130-132	Legal research. Legal bibliography. Methods of bibliographic research
KBR133-134	Legal education. Study and teaching
KBR136-148	Societies. Associations. Academies, etc.
KBR150	Conferences. Symposia
KBR160	General works
KBR190-2154.5	Sources
KBR2155-2157	Canon law and other disciplines or subjects
KBR2160-2204.5	Canonical jurisprudence. Canonical science
KBR2205-2206.3	Influence of other legal systems on Canon law
KBR2207	Law reform and policies. Criticism
KBR2208.A-Z	General concepts and principles, A-Z
KBR2224-2295	Ius ecclesiasticum privatum
KBR2310-3026	Constitution of the Church
KBR3040-3070	The teaching office of the church. Magisterium. De ecclesiae munere docendi
KBR3077-3165	Sacraments. Administration of sacraments. De sacramentis et administratione
KBR3180-3182	Sacramentals. Sacramentalia
KBR3184-3256	Other acts of divine worship. De ceteris actibus Cultus Divini
KBR3264-3280	Social work of the Church. Public welfare. Caritas
KBR3320-3460	Church property. Church economics and finance. Administration
KBR3500-3774	Penal (Criminal) law. De lege poenali
KBR3780-3983	Judiciary. Ecclesiastical courts and procedure. De processibus
KBR4000-4090	Church and state relationships. De relationibus inter ecclesiam et status. Ius publicum ecclesiae

OUTLINE

KBU2-4820	Law of the Roman Catholic Church. The Holy See
KBU2-19	Bibliography
KBU21	Annuals. Annuaires. Yearbooks
KBU22	Monographic series
KBU25-26	Official gazette of the Holy See
KBU26.8-41.5	Official acts of the Holy See
KBU42-54.5	Decisions of ecclesiastical tribunals and courts, and related materials
KBU56	Encyclopedias
KBU56.5	Dictionaries. Terms and phrases. Vocabularies
KBU64	Directories
KBU102	Form books. Clauses and forms
KBU127-129.5	Trials
KBU130-132	Legal research. Legal bibliography. Methods of bibliographic research
KBU133	Legal education. Study and teaching
KBU136-148	Societies. Associations. Academies, etc.
KBU149	Academies. Institutes
KBU150	Conferences. Symposia
KBU160	General works
KBU180.A-Z	Works on diverse aspects of a particular subject and falling within several branches of the law. By subject, A-Z
KBU195-1565	Collections. Compilations. Selections
KBU2155-2157	Canon law and other disciplines or subjects
KBU2160-2204	Canonical jurisprudence. Theory and science of canon law
KBU2205-2206	Influence of other legal systems on canon law
KBU2207	Law reform and policies. Criticism
KBU2208.A-Z	Concepts applying to several branches of the law, A-Z
KBU2210-2212	The codes of canon law
KBU2215-2308	General norms and principles. De normis generalibus
KBU2310-3026	Constitution of the Church
KBU3040-3070	The teaching office of the Church. Magisterium. De ecclesiae munere docendi
KBU3075-3165	Sacraments. Administration of sacraments. De sacramentis et administratione
KBU3180-3182	Sacramentals. Sacramentalia
KBU3184-3256	Other acts of divine worship. De ceteris actibus Cultus Divini
KBU3264-3280	Social work of the Church. Public welfare. Caritas
KBU3282-3310	Medical ethics and legislation. Church policy
KBU3320-3460	Church property. Church economics and finance
KBU3500-3774	Sanctions in the Church. Criminal law. De sanctionibus in Ecclesia. De lege poenali
KBU3780-3985	Courts and procedure. De processibus

Religious law in general. Comparative religious law. Jurisprudence

Class here comparative studies on different religious legal systems, as well as intra-denominational comparisons (e.g. different Christian religious legal systems)

Further, class here comparative studies on religious legal systems with other legal systems, including ancient law

For comparison of a religious legal system with the law of two or more jurisdictions, see the religious system (e.g. Islamic law compared to Egyptian and Malaysian law, see KBP)

Comparisons include both systematic-theoretical elaborations as well as parallel presentations of different systems

For influences of a religious legal system on the law of a particuar jurisdiction, see the jurisdiction

For works on law and religion see BL65.L33

Bibliography

For personal bibliography or bibliography relating to a particular religious system or subject, see the appropriate KB subclass

2 Bibliography of bibliography. Bibliographical concordances

4 Indexes for periodical literature, society publications, collections, etc.

Periodicals

For KB8-KB68, the book number, derived from the main entry, is determined by the letters following the letter for which the class number stands, e.g. KB11.I54, Dine Yisrael

7 General

Jewish

8 A - Archiu

8.3 Archiv - Archivz

e.g.

8.3.R37 Archives d'histoire du droit oriental

9 Archiw - Az

9.3 B

e.g.

9.3.U43 Bulletin/International Association of Jewish Lawyers and Jurists

10 C

11 D

e.g.

11.I54 Dine Yisrael: shanaton le-mishpat ‘Ivri ule-mishpahah be-Yi’srael

12 E - Etuder

12.3 Etudes - Ez

13 F

14 G

15 H

Periodicals
Jewish -- Continued

16 I
e.g.
16.T87 'Iture kohanim
17 J - Jewisg
17.2 Jewish
The book number is determined by the second word of the main entry
e.g.
17.2.L39 Jewish Law Annual
17.2.L395 Jewish lawyer
17.3 Jewisha - Journak
17.4 Journal
The book number is determined by the second word of the main entry
e.g.
17.4.O34 Journal of halacha and contemporary society
17.5 Journala - Jz
e.g.
17.5.U84 Justice/International Association of Jewish Lawyers and Jurists
18 K
18.3 L
19 M
e.g.
19.E37 Mehkere mishpat
19.3 N
e.g.
19.3.A88 National Jewish Law Review
19.3.E94 Newsletter/International Association of Jewish Lawyers and Jurists
20 O
20.3 P
21 Q
21.3 R
22 S
e.g.
22.E43 Selected topics in Jewish Law
22.H46 Shenaton ha-mishpat ha-'Ivri shel ha-Makhon le-heker ha-mishpat ha-'Ivri
22.3 T
23 U
23.3 V
24 W
24.3 X

Periodicals
Jewish -- Continued
25 Y
25.3 Z
Islamic
26 A
e.g.
26.R33 Arab law quarterly
26.U97 Aux sources de la sagesse: revue islamique trimestrielle
27 B
27.3 C
28 D
29 E - Etuder
30 Etudes
The book number is determined by the second word of the main entry
e.g.
30.2.D4 Etudes de Droit Musulman
30.2.D57 Etudes d'Islamologie: Droit Musulman
30.3 Etudet - Ez
31 F
32 G
32.3 H
e.g.
32.3.A68 Ḥaqq: sharīʻah wa-qānūn
33 I
e.g.
33.R77 Irsyad hukum
33.S578 Islamic law and society
33.S58 The Islamic Quarterly
33.S585 The Islamic Review
34 J - Journak
34.2 Journal
The book number is determined by the second word of the main entry
e.g.
34.2.O35 Journal of Islamic and comparative law
34.2.O354 Journal of Islamic law & culture
34.3 Journala - Jz
34.4 K
35 L
e.g.
35.A94 Law majallah
36 M - Majallas

Periodicals
Islamic -- Continued
36.3 Majallat
The book number is determined by the second word of the main entry
e.g.
36.3.A43 Majallat al-fiqh al-Islāmī
36.3.A433 Majallat al-fiqh al-Mālikī wa-al-turāth al-qaḍāʻī bi-al-Maghrib
36.3.A435 Majallat al-ḥuqūq wa-al-sharīʻah
36.3.K85 Majallat Kullīyat al-Fiqh
36.3.K855 Majallat Kullīyat al-Sharīʻah wa-al-Qānūn
36.4 Majallata - Mz
e.g.
36.4.O83 The Moslem World
37 N
37.2 O
37.3 Q
38 R - Revud
38.3 Revue
The book number is determined by the second word of the main entry
e.g.
38.3.A43 Revue al-Ulum al-Qanuniya Wal-Iqtiṣadiya
38.3.D47 Revue des Etudes Islamiqiues
38.3.D85 Revue du Monde Musulman
38.4 Revuea - Rz
39 S
e.g.
39.H37 Shari'ah: the Islamic law journal
39.T83 Studia Islamica
40 T
e.g.
40.R35 Traite de Droit Musulman Compare
41 U
e.g.
41.C58 UCLA journal of Islamic and Near Eastern Law
42 V
43 W
44 X - Y
45 Z
Christian
Including all Christian denominations
46 A - Archiu
46.2 Archiv - Archivz
e.g.

	Periodicals
	Christian
	Archiv - Archivz -- Continued
46.2.R34	Archiv für evangelisches Kirchenrecht
46.2.R345	Archiv für katholisches Kirchenrecht
46.2.R38	Archivum Historiae Pontificiae
47	Archiw - Az
48	B
	e.g.
48.U44	Bulletin of Medieval Canon Law
49	C
	e.g.
49.A87	Catholic Historical Review
49.O47	Commentarium pro religiosis et missionariis
49.O475	Communications
49.O53	Concilium
50	D
	e.g.
50.E923	Deutsche Zeitschrift für Kirchenrecht
50.E925	Deutsches Archiv für Erforschung des Mittelalters
50.I75	Il diritto ecclesiastico
50.3	E
	e.g.
50.3.P48	Ephemerides Juris Canonici
50.3.P484	Ephemerides Theologicae Lovaniensis
50.3.V36	Evangelische Kirche
51	F
52	G
52.2	H
52.3	I
	e.g.
52.3.U82	Ius canonicum
52.3.U823	Ius Ecclesiae: rivista internazionale di diritto canonico
52.4	J - Journak
52.5	Journal
	The book number is determined by the second word of the main entry
	e.g.
52.5.O32	Journal du droit canon et de la jurisprudence canonique
52.5.O33	Journal of Church and State
52.5.O356	Journal of law and religion
53	Journala - Jz
53.2	K
	e.g.
53.2.I73	Kirche und Recht
54	L

Periodicals
Christian -- Continued
54.3 M
e.g.
54.3.O55 Il monitore ecclesiastico
55 N
e.g.
55.E34 Nederlands Archiv voor Kerkgeschiedenis
56 O
e.g.
56.R54 Orientalia Christiana Periodica
56.S75 Ostkirchliche Studien
57 P
e.g.
57.R93 Praxis juridique et religion
58 Q
59 R - Revist
59.3 Revista
The book number is determined by the second word of the main entry
59.4 Revistaa - Revud
59.5 Revue
The book number is determined by the second word of the main entry
e.g.
59.5.D42 Revue de droit canonique
59.7 Revuea - Rz
60 S
e.g.
60.T83 Studia canonica
60.T85 Studia Gratiana
61 T
62 U
62.3 V
63 W
64 X - Y
65 Z - Zeitschrifs
66 Zeitschrift
The book number is determined by the second word of the main entry
e.g.
66.D47 Zeitschrift der Savigny-Stiftung für Rechtsgeschichte: Kanonistische Abteilung
66.F873 Zeitschrift für Kirchengeschichte
66.F874 Zeitschrift für Kirchenrecht
67 Zeitschrifta - Zz

68 Annuals
L'Année canonique see KBR21
Annuarium historiae conciliorum see KBR21
68.D35 Daimon: annuario di diritto comparato delle religioni
70.A-Z Monographic series. By title, A-Z
Cutter numbers listed below are provided as examples
For works related to a particular denomination, see the appropriate KB subclass
70.A55 Annali di storia dell' esegesi
Canon law studies (The Catholic University of America) see KBR22
70.J88 Jus ecclesiasticum
70.K57 Kirchenrechtliche Abhandlungen
70.M43 Medieval Studies
Monumenta iuris canonici see KBR22
70.S82 Staatskirchenrechtliche Abhandlungen
Studia et documenta juris canonici see KBR22
73 Collections. Compilations (General and comprehensive)
Auxiliary sciences
74 General works
78.A-Z Archaeology. Symbolism in law. By author or title, A-Z
Subarrange each author by Table K4
Class here general and comparative works on legal symbolism (including works on concepts represented by schemata or stemmata such as "arbores"), present in the sources of different legal systems
Cutter numbers listed below are provided as examples
For works on legal symbolism relating to a particular legal system, see the appropriate K subclass, e.g. KBR78; KJ78; KJA78; KL78, etc.
78.C65 Conrat, Max (1848-1911) (Table K4)
78.C65A3-.C65A39 Individual works. By title
e.g. Arbor iuris des frühen Mittelalters
78.E58 Eis, Helko (1936-) (Table K4)
78.E58A3-.E58A39 Individual works. By title
e.g. Zur Rezeption der kanonischen Verwandschaftsbäume Johannes Andrae's
Cf. KBR1775.A3A+ Giovanni d'Andrea. Super arboribus consanguinitatis et affinitatis
78.S25 Schadt, Hermann (Table K4)
78.S25A3-.S25A39 Individual works. By title
e.g. Die Darstellungen der Arbores consanguinitatis und der Arbores Affinitatis: Bildschemata in juristischen Handschriften

90.A-Z Encyclopedias. Law dictionaries. Terms and phrases. Vocabularies. By author or title, A-Z
Subarrange each author by Table K4
Cutter numbers listed below are provided as examples
For works of pre-Tridentinum (before 1545) periods relating to both Roman and canon law (e.g. Johannes, de Erfordia, ca. 1250-ca. 1325. Tabula utriusque iuris) see KBR56
90.C34 Calvinus, Johannes (d. 1614) (Table K4)
90.C34A3-.C34A39 Individual works. By title
e.g. Lexicon iuridicum juris caesarei simvl, et canonici, feudalis item ... leges ac magistratus romanos, et caetera ...
90.S25 Scot, Alexander (fl. 1591) (Table K4)
90.S25A3-.S25A39 Individual works. By title
e.g. Vocabularium utriusque iuris
90.V52 Vicat, Béat Philippe, 1715-1770? (Table K4)
90.V52A3-90.V52A39 Individual works. By title
e.g. Vocabularium juris utriusque ex variis ante editis
100.A-Z Proverbia. Legal maxims. Brocardica juris. Regulae juris. By author or title, A-Z
Subarrange each author by Table K4
Cutter numbers listed below are provided as examples
100.B37 Bartocetti, Vittorio (Table K4)
100.D84 Dueñias, Pedro de (16th cent.) (Table K4)
100.D84A3-.D84A39 Individual works. By title
e.g. Regularium utriusque juris...liber primus
100.P43 Peck, Pierre (1529-1589) (Table K4)
100.R44 Regulae juris tam civilis quam canonici (Fallentiae regularum juris) (Table K21)
100.S25 Schwartz, Meinradus. Commentarium in regulas juris (Table K4)
100.S45 Selectissimarum regularum juris ex utroque iure collectarum (Table K21)
122 Biography (Collective)
Legal research. Legal bibliography. Methods of bibliographic research
130 General
132 Systems of citation. Legal abbreviations. Modus legendi abbreviaturas in utroque iure
Including early works
133 Legal education. Study and teaching
Including works on study and teaching of both Roman and canon law comparatively, e.g. Johannes Jacobus Canis (d. 1490), De modo studendi in utroque iure; Bartolomé Cartagena (fl. 1608), Enchiridion iuris utriusque

150 Conferences. Symposia
160 General works. Treatises
Legal systems compared
Interdenominational comparative studies
For comparison by subject, see the subject in KB400+
162 Sources (Collective and selective)
Class here broad collections for the comparative study of the various systems, including early editions
Law of different Christian denominations
165.A-Z Eastern churches and Roman Catholic Church. By author or title, A-Z
Subarrange each author by Table K4
170.A-Z Roman Catholic Church and Protestant Church. By author or title, A-Z
Subarrange each author by Table K4
e.g.
170.F74 Friedberg, Emil (1837-1910) (Table K4)
170.R52 Richter, Aemilius Ludwig (1808-1864) (Table K4)
170.S35 Schilter, Johann (1632-1705) (Table K4)
170.S36 Schulte, Joh. Friedrich von (1827-1914) (Table K4)
Law of Christian denominations and other religious systems
180.A-Z Jewish law. By author or title, A-Z
Subarrange each author by Table K4
e.g.
180.S38 Sessa, Giuseppe (fl. 1715) (Table K4)
185.A-Z Islamic law. By author or title, A-Z
Subarrange each author by Table K4
190 Jewish law and Islamic law
Interdisciplinary comparative studies. Religious legal systems compared with other legal systems
Including ancient (historic/defunct) systems
For comparison by subject, see the subject in KB400+
Cf. KL147+ Ancient legal systems compared
197 General
Sources (Collective and selective)
Class here broad collections for the comparative study of the various systems, including early editions
197.2 General
198 Iuris civilis fontes et rivi
200 Mosaicarum et Romanarum legum collatio (398-438) (Table K20b)
Jewish law, Roman law, and civil law
201 Fellenberg, Daniel (d. 1801) (Table K3)
202 Mayer, Samuel (1807-1875) (Table K3)

Legal systems compared
Interdisciplinary comparative studies. Religious legal systems compared with other legal systems
Jewish law, Roman law, and civil law
Mayer, Samuel (1807-1875) -- Continued
202.A3A-.A3Z Individual works. By title
e.g. Die Rechte der Israeliten, Athener und Römer
Mosaicarum et Romanarum legum collatio see KB200
206 Müller, David Heinrich (1846-1912) (Table K3)
206.A3A-.A3Z Individual works. By title
e.g. Die Gesetze Hammurabis und ihr Verhältnis zur Mosaischen Gesetzgebung sowie zu den XII Tafeln; Das syrisch-römische Rechtsbuch und Hammurabi
210 Rubin, Simon (Table K3)
210.A3A-.A3Z Individual works. By title
e.g. Das talmudische Recht auf den verschiedenen Stufen seiner Entwicklung mit dem Römischen verglichen
211 General works by other authors
Class here general works comparing Jewish law, Roman law, and civil law by authors other than those listed above
Canon law, Roman law, and civil law
215 General works
For pre-Tridentine (pre-1545) genre see KBR2150.5+
Canon law (Occidental) and Roman law
For general works, see KB215
For comparisons by subject, see the subject in KB400+
For pre-Tridentine comparison by subject, see the period and author in KBR
Authors of encyclopedic works
Class here authors who produced comprehensive analytical treatises arranged by subject that compare different systems or categories of law, including related works such as court decisions, consilia, etc.
230 De Luca, Giovanni Battista (1614-1683) (Table K3 modified)
230.A3A-.A3Z Individual works. By title, A-Z
Including unannotated and annotated editions, translations, particular manuscript editions, and textual criticism
(230.A3M35) Mantissa decisionum Sanctae Rotae Romanae ad theatrum veritatis et justitiae
see KBR44.5.D42
230.A3S86 Summa sive compendium Theatri veritatis & justitiae

Legal systems compared
Interdisciplinary comparative studies. Religious legal systems compared with other legal systems
Canon law, Roman law, and civil law
Canon law (Occidental) and Roman law
Encyclopedic works
De Luca, Giovanni Battista (1614-1683)
Individual works. By title -- Continued
230.A3T45 Theatrum veritatis et justitiae
For the Decisiones ad Theatrum veritatis Cardinalis De Luca see KBR44.5.D42
(230.A3T73) Tractatus de officiis venalibus vacabilibus Romanae Curiae
see KBR2420
237 Toschi, Domenico (1535-1620) (Table K3)
240.A-Z Other authors or titles, A-Z
240.C68 Costa, Emanuel (d. 1564) (Table K4)
240.C68A3-.C68A39 Individual works. By title
e.g. Omnia quae quidem extant in ius canonicum et civile opera
240.G32 Gabrielli, Antonio (d. 1555) (Table K4)
240.G32A3-.G32A39 Individual works. By title
e.g. Communes conclusiones
240.G37 Garcia, Fortunius (1494-1534) (Table K4)
240.G37A3-.G37A39 Individual works. By title
e.g. De ultimo fine juris canonici et civili
240.L35 Lancelotti, Giovanni Paolo (1522-1590) (Table K4)
240.L35A3-.L35A39 Individual works. By title
e.g. De comparatione iuris pontificii et caesarei et utriusque interpretandi ratione
240.M35 Mansfeld, Carolus von (d. 1661) (Table K4)
240.M35A3-.M35A39 Individual works. By title
e.g. Utriusue iuris concors discordia
240.M36 Petrus Maurocensus (Table K4)
240.M36A3-.M36A39 Individual works. By title
e.g. Concordantiae iuris civilis et canonici
240.S24 Ioannes Baptista de S. Blasio (Table K4)
240.S24A3-.S24A39 Individual works. By title
e.g. Contradictiones iuris civilis cum canonico
240.T73 Tractatus universi iuris, duce, & auspice Gregorio XIII
243.A-Z Canon law (Occidental) and common law. By author or title, A-Z
Subarrange each author by Table K4
With or without inclusion of civil law

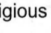

Legal systems compared
Interdisciplinary comparative studies. Religious legal systems compared with other legal systems
Canon law, Roman law, and Civil law -- Continued
245.A-Z Canon law (Greek-Byzantine and post-schismatic) and Roman law. By author or title, A-Z
Subarrange each author by Table K4
250 Islamic law and secular law
Including comparison of Islamic law with secular legal systems such as civil law, common law, etc.
For comparison by subject, see the subject in subclass KBP
For works on the influence of Islamic law on a specific country or region see the country or region
Islamic law and Jewish law see KB190
Islamic law and canon law see KB185.A+
Islamic law and the law of several "Islamic" jurisdictions see KBP
255.A-Z Other religious systems compared to secular legal systems, A-Z
255.B34 Bahai
International law and religious legal systems
For general works, see KZ1276
259 International law and Jewish law
260 International law and Islamic law
265 International law and Christian law
Theory, philosophy, and science of religious law
270 General works. Treatises
Interdisciplinary discussion of concepts and principles
280 Natural law and religious law
For natural law and divine law as a source of law for a particular religious system, see the religious system, e.g. KBR2190, Natural law as a source of canon law
Interdisciplinary discussion of subjects
Including interdenominational comparisons of subjects, and comparative studies on subjects falling under different legal systems (including religious and jurisdictional) not otherwise provided for
400 Ritual law. Religious observances and rituals
410 Law reform and policies. Criticism
479 Private law (General)
Private international law. Conflict of laws
480 General works
481 Public order. Ordre public
482 Choice of law
491 Civil law (General)
Persons

Interdisciplinary discussion of subjects
Persons -- Continued
524 General works
Personality. Legal capacity and disability
524.7 General works
524.72 Birth. Unborn child. Nasciturus
524.8 Death
Including absent and missing persons. Presumption of death
525 Legal minority. Legal majority
Women
526 General works
528.A-Z Special topics, A-Z
529 Insane persons. People with mental disabilities
Slaves
Including male and female slaves
529.3 General works
529.5.A-Z Special topics, A-Z
529.5.C45 Children
529.5.E52 Emancipation
529.5.M35 Manumission
529.5.P38 Patronage
529.7.A-Z Other types of persons, A-Z
529.7.H47 Hermaphrodites
529.72 Citizenship
530.A-Z Special topics, A-Z
Domestic relations. Family law
531 General works
Marriage
Including marriage age
542 General works
Betrothal
543 General works
543.3 Dower. Nuptial gifts
Impediments to marriage
544 General works
544.2 Consanguinity and affinity
Cf. KB78.A+ Symbolism in law
546 Celebration of marriage. Consummation
546.2 Mixed marriage. Intermarriage
546.4 Multiple marriage. Polygamy. Polyandry
546.5 Temporary marriage
546.6 Same-sex marriage
Husband and wife. Rights and duties
547 General works
549 Legal status of married women

Interdisciplinary discussion of subjects
Domestic relations. Family law
Marriage -- Continued
Dissolution of marriage. Matrimonial actions
555 General works
Defective marriage and invalid marriage
556 General works
557.A-Z Special topics, A-Z
Divorce
558 General works
559.A-Z Grounds for divorce, A-Z
560 Reconciliation
562 Procedure
567 Settlement of claims from defective or dissolved marriage
568.A-Z Special topics, A-Z
568.U56 Unmarried cohabitation
Marital property and regime
569 General works
579.A-Z Special topics, A-Z
Consanguinity. Affinity. Kinship
Cf. KB544+ Impediments to marriage
583 General works
Parent and child
587 General works
589 Children
Parental power
598 General works
602 Custody. Access to children
609 Adoption
610 Fosterage
612 Illegitimacy
Paternity and maternity
Including patrilineal and matrilineal descendants and ascendants
616.5 General works
619.A-Z Special topics, A-Z
Guardianship. Guardian and ward
622 General works
625 Guardianship over minors
627 Guardianship over adults
628 Interdiction
628.5.A-Z Special topics, A-Z
Inheritance and succession
Including legal causes of inheritance, e.g. consanguinity, affinity, etc.

Interdisciplinary discussion of subjects
Inheritance and succession -- Continued
632 General works
633 Decedents' estates. Shares
Including claims against, and partititon and distribution of, estate
634 Qualification as heir. Legal sharers. Order of succession
634.6 Exclusion from inheritance
Including slave quality, homicide, infidelity, apostasy, etc.
Wills. Testamentary succession
635 General works
635.2 Legacies. Testamentary bequests. Distribution of estate
636 Unworthiness of heir. Disinheritance
636.2 Gifts mortis causa
636.3 Gifts. Charitable gifts. Donations
Including donation for life and donation for the surviving party
Property. Res in commercio
640 General works
Things. Types of property
642.3 Fungibles. Non-fungibles
Including fungibles such as measured, weighed, or counted things
Real (Immovable) property see KB683+
643 Personal (Movable) property
644.A-Z Other, A-Z
Possession and ownership. Real rights (Jura in re)
Including owner and possessor
647.A-Z Types of possession, A-Z
Acquisition (original and derivative) and transfer of possession and ownership
648 General works
651 Dispossession
Acquisition and loss of ownership
655 General works
656 Occupation
658 Treasure troves
663 Acquisition of fruits and parts of things
673 Loss of ownership
Including abandonment and dereliction
674 Co-ownership. Joint ownership
For co-ownership of land see KB694
675 Protection of ownership. Claims and actions resulting from ownership
Real (Immovable) property. Land law
Including land ownership and tenancy
683 General (Comparative)

Interdisciplinary discussion of subjects
Property. Res in commercio
Real (Immovable) property. Land law -- Continued
686 Terres communes. Group lands. Commons for use without shares in ownership
Acquisition and loss of ownership
687.5 General works
687.6 Occupancy of waste land by cultivator
694 Co-ownership of land. Customary co-ownership
For communal property see KB686
Rights incident to ownership of land
695 General works
697 Underground. Minerals, metals and other resources
698 Riparian rights. Water rights. Underground water
699 Hunting and fishing rights
700 Adjoining landowners
Rights as to the use of another's land
706 General works
708 Commonage and pasture. Grazing rights
Servitudes
709 General works
710 Real servitudes
e.g. right of way (passage), right to draw water, etc.
713 Personal servitudes
715 Usufruct
716 Right of pre-emption
717 Hypothecation
726 Pledges. Contracts of pledging
Including both pledges of personal property and pledges of rights
737 Land register. Registration of land titles
Obligations. Contracts and transactions
810 General (Comparative)
811 Debtor and creditor
816 Transfer and assumption of obligations
817 Extinction of obligation
Including acquittance, payment, performance, settlement, etc.
Bankruptcy. Discharge of debt according to secular law see KBM1942
823 Confusion of rights
823.5.A-Z Special topics, A-Z
Nonperformance. Culpa
Including dolus and negligence
824 General works
825.5 Culpa in contrahendo
826 Breach of contract

Interdisciplinary discussion of subjects
Obligations. Contracts and transactions
Nonperformance. Culpa -- Continued
827.5 Default
Delicts (Torts) and damages
Class here works on wrongful acts and damages, including lost profits and damages for pain and suffering
834 General works
839 Delict liability
Including dolus and negligence
840.A-Z Individual torts and damages, A-Z
840.E58 Environmental damages
Unjust enrichment
854 General works
855 Restitution
857.A-Z Special topics, A-Z
Concepts and principles of contract law
858 General works
858.3 Liberty of contract. Party autonomy
858.5.A-Z Types of contracts, A-Z
859 Security. Secured and fiduciary transactions
For particular transactions, see KBM877.2; KBM881.3; KBM894
Intention. Declaration of intention
860 General works
861 Agency
Including unauthorized representation (Falsus procurator)
864 Mandate
866.5 Risk
Void and voidable contracts and transactions. Nullity
867 General works
867.3 Mistake. Error
867.5 Fraud. Duress. Threat
Unconscionable transactions. Illegal contracts
868 General works
868.2 Usurious contracts
Formation of contract
Including commercial contracts
869 General works
Offer and acceptance
Including withdrawal of offer and right of rescission
869.3 General works
869.34.A-Z Special topics, A-Z
870 Clauses. Terms. Conditions
872 Stipulations
872.5 Formalities

Interdisciplinary discussion of subjects
Obligations. Contracts and transactions -- Continued
Parties to contract
873 General works
873.3 Third parties
873.8 Cancellation of contract
Individual contracts and transactions
Including commercial contracts
874 Sale
879 Exchange of monetary assets or rights. Barter
Pecuniary transaction without countervalue
879.23 General works
Donations. Gifts see KB636.3
Lease. Landlord and tenant
880 General works
881.3 Liens of the landlord
884.A-Z Types of property, A-Z
Land lease see KB884.R43
884.R43 Real property. Land lease
889 Fiduciary transactions. Trust and trustee
890 Loan for use. Commodatum
891 Personal loans. Mutuum
Contract for service and labor. Master and servant
892 General works
892.5 Dependent work. Hire and lease. Locatio conductio
892.8.A-Z Special topics, A-Z
Contract for work and labor
Class here works on contracts concluded by independent contractor or artisan
Including liability and warranty
893 General works
893.3.A-Z Particular contracts or tasks, A-Z
898.5 Life annuity
899 Aleatory contracts. Natural obligations
900 Suretyship. Debtor and guarantor
Including suretyship for the person and for the claim
929 Brokerage
930 Auctioneers
930.3 Warehousing
931 Freight forwarders and carriers. Carriage of passengers and goods
940.A-Z Banks and banking. Banking transactions, A-Z
962.8 Commodity exchanges. Produce exchanges
Maritime contracts. Maritime law
970 General works

Interdisciplinary discussion of subjects
Obligations. Contracts and transactions
Individual contracts and transactions
Maritime contracts. Maritime law -- Continued
971 Affreightment. Carriage of goods at sea and inland waters
976 Carriage of passengers at sea and inland waters
979 Average. Havarie grosse
Including special average (collision at sea)
981 Salvage
998.A-Z Insurance law. Hazards, risks, and damages, A-Z
Associations. Corporations
Including religious brotherhoods
1040 General works
Partnerships. Personal companies
Including unlimited and limited (liability) partnerships and liability
1043 General works
1048 Artisans' partnership
1049.A-Z Other, A-Z
1120.A-Z Cooperative societies, A-Z
Intellectual and industrial property
1155 General works
1160 Copyright
1194 Patent law and trademarks
1234 Unfair competition
Labor laws and legislation
1270 General works
1278.A-Z Special topics, A-Z
1278.C45 Child and youth labor
1278.W65 Women's labor
Youth labor see KB1278.C45
Social laws and legislation. Welfare. Charities
1520 General works
1528 The poor and destitute
1534.A-Z People with disabilities, A-Z
Including physically, mentally, and emotionally disabled people
1536 Homeless persons
War-related and conflict-related groups of beneficiaries
1537 General works
1539.A-Z Particular groups, A-Z
1540 Children. Youth
1550.A-Z Special topics, A-Z
Courts and procedure
Administration of justice. Organization of the judiciary

Interdisciplinary discussion of subjects
Courts and procedure
Administration of justice. Organization of the judiciary -- Continued
1572 General works
Courts and tribunals
Including courts of both civil and criminal jurisdiction
1580 General works
1582 Regular courts
1588.2.A-Z Tribunals and courts of special jurisdiction, A-Z
1593.A-Z Other public bodies with judicial functions, A-Z
The legal profession. Court personnel
Including legal education
1600 General works
Biography see KB122
1610 Judges
Notaries see KB1846+
1620.A-Z Other, A-Z
Procedure in general
1650 General works
Procedural principles
1651 Due process of law
1655 Parties to action
Including plaintiff (claimant) and defendant
Pretrial procedures
1660 General works
1662.A-Z Particular, A-Z
Procedure at trial
1663 General works
1664 Jurisdiction. The competent court. Competence in subject matter and venue
Actions and defenses. Litigation
1666 General
1667.A-Z Particular, A-Z
1668.A-Z Particular proceedings, A-Z
Compromise see KB1668.S48
1668.I68 Intervention
1668.S48 Settlement out of court. Compromise
Evidence. Burden of proof
1672 General works
Witnesses. Testimony
1675 General works
1676 Privileged witnesses. Expert testimony
1676.7 Documentary evidence
1677.A-Z Special topics, A-Z

Interdisciplinary discussion of subjects
Courts and procedure
Procedure in general
Procedure at trial
Evidence. Burden of proof
Special topics, A-Z -- Continued
1677.O23 Oath
Including oath of witnesses and parties
1677.O73 Ordeal
1677.P74 Presumption
Judicial decisions
1679 General works
1679.3 Judicial opinions. Advisory opinions
Remedies
1686 General works
1687 Appellate procedures
1690 Execution of judgment
Particular procedures
Matrimonial actions see KB555+
1807 Procedure in parent and child cases
Criminal procedure
see KB4601+
1815.A-Z Other particular procedures, A-Z
1829 Arbitration
Notaries. Notarial practice and procedure
1846 General works
1847 Legal instruments. Certification
Registration. Recording
1850 General works
Civil register
1854 General works
Registration of civil status
1856 General works
1857 Family names
1860 Marriage
1862 Birth and death
For absence and presumption of death see KB524.8
Land registers see KB737
Interdiction see KB628
1880 Interitance (Probate court) procedures
Insolvency
1885 General works
Execution for payment due. Procedure
1888 General works
1913 Detention of debtor

Interdisciplinary discussion of subjects
Courts and procedure
Insolvency
Execution for payment due. Procedure -- Continued
1925.A-Z Special topics, A-Z
1926 Remedies
1932 Suspension. Accord and satisfaction
1942 Bankruptcy
Public law. The State
Including works on philosophy and theory of state and religion with or without comparisons to two or more countries
For works on public law and religion in a particular country see the country
Cf. BL65.S8 Religion in relation to the state
2000 General works
2015 Sovereignty questions
Rule of law. God's rule
2020 General works
2035 Compatibility of democratic government and religion
Constitutions and religion. Constitutional and administrative law
2101 General works
2200.A-Z Special topics, A-Z
Particular principles
Including historic concepts
2250.3 Secular authority and duties of leaders
Rule of law see KB2020+
2270 Separation and delegation of powers
2275 Ethics in government. Conflict of interests
2300 Privileges, prerogatives, and immunities of rulers
Sources and relationships of laws
2340 Customary law and observances
Individual and state
2430 General works
Human rights. Civil and political rights
2460 General works
2462 Dignity
Equality before the law
2465 General works
2467.A-Z Groups discriminated against, A-Z
2467.5 Sex discrimination
2468.A-Z Special subjects, A-Z
Freedom
2469 General works
2470 Freedom of expression
2472 Freedom of religion. Freedom of worship

Interdisciplinary discussion of subjects
Constitutions and religion. Constitutional and administrative law
Individual and state
Human rights. Civil and political rights
Freedom -- Continued
Freedom of thought and speech
2474 General works
2476 Freedom of information
2478 Prohibition of censorship
2483 Freedom of assembly, association, and demonstration
2484 Due process of law
Particular rights
2484.5 Life. Right to life
Including works on reproductive choices
For right to die see KB3121.7
2485.5 Right of asylum
Right to be free from torture and other cruel, inhumane, or degrading treatment see KB4541
2486 Right to resistance against political authority or ideology
2490 Control of subversive activities or groups
Organs of government. Organs of state power and state administration
2500 General works
2510 Legislature. Legislative (law making) power and process
Heads of state
2530 General works
Kings, princes, or traditional rulers
2532 General works
2535.A-Z Special topics, A-Z
2535.D96 Dynastic rules. Legal status of dynasty
Legal status of dynasty see KB2535.D96
2535.S92 Succession
2540 Presidents
Prerogatives and powers
2550 General works
2554 Crown privilege
2558 Treatymaking power
2564 War and emergency powers
The Executive branch. Government and administration
2577 General works

Interdisciplinary discussion of subjects
Constitutions and religion. Constitutional and administrative law
Organs of government. Organs of state power and state administration
The Executive branch. Government and administration -- Continued
Eminent domain. Nationalization. Expropriation. Public restraint on private property
Including land under customary co-ownership, and including incorporation of derelict, undeveloped (unexploited) and unoccupied land (terres vacantes et sans maître), and including procedure
2824 General works
2829 Categories of land. Agricultural, grazing, hunting, and forest land
2862.A-Z By region or country, A-Z
2870 Civil service. Employees of state, communal agencies, and religious corporations
Police and public safety
3000 General works
3022 Control of individuals
3034 Control of social activities
Public property. Government property
3040.5 General works
Water resources
Including rivers, lakes, watercourses, underground water, etc.
3046 General works
3046.7 Water rights
Cf. KB698 Riparian rights (Property)
Protection against pollution see KB3131
3054 National preserves
3055.A-Z Other, A-Z
3056 Public lands. Public land law
Including land development, rural planning (village settlement), etc.
For co-ownership of land and customary co-ownership see KB694
Public health
3075 General works
Contagious and infectious diseases. Parasitic diseases
3080 General works
3082.A-Z Particular diseases, A-Z
3082.A53 AIDS
3082.S47 Sexually transmitted diseases. Venereal diseases
Venereal diseases see KB3082.S47

Interdisciplinary discussion of subjects
Public health
Contagious and infectious diseases. Parasitic diseases -- Continued
Public health measures
Including compulsory measures
3084 General works
3086.A-Z Immunization. Vaccination. By disease, A-Z
3087 Quarantine
Environmental pollution see KB3130+
3088.A-Z Other public health hazards and measures, A-Z
3089 Drinking water standards
Drug laws. Drugs of abuse
Including recreational drugs
3090 General works
3092 Narcotics. Opium legislation
3096.5 Tobacco use. Smoking
Medical legislation
3098 General works
The health professions
3100 Physicians
3103.A-Z Other, A-Z
3103.H42 Healers
Auxiliary medical professions. Paramedical professions
3104 General works
3104.3.A-Z Particular, A-Z
3104.3.M53 Midwives
3104.3.N87 Nurses and nursing
Hospitals and other medical institutions or health services
3110 General works
3110.3.A-Z Particular, A-Z
3110.3.56 Blood banks
Biomedical engineering. Medical technology
Including human experimentation in medicine
3115 General works
3115.5 Genetic engineering
For artificial insemination see KB3117
3116 Transplantation of organs, tissues, etc.
Including donation of organs, tissues, etc.
3117 Human reproductive technology
Including artificial insemination and fertilization in vitro
Cf. KB616.5+ Paternity and maternity (Family law)
3119.A-Z Special topics, A-Z
Abortion, Voluntary see KB3125.A36
3119.C57 Circumcision
For female circumcision see KB3119.F45

Interdisciplinary discussion of subjects
Medical legislation
Special topics, A-Z -- Continued
Experiments with the human body see KB3115+
3119.F45 Female circumcision
3119.M43 Medical instruments and apparatus. Medical devices
3119.P42 Plastic surgery
Eugenics. Sterilization and castration
3121 General (Comparative)
3121.5.A-Z Special topics, A-Z
3121.7 Euthanasia
Including works on right to die and living will
3122 Veterinary medicine and hygiene. Veterinary public health
Animal protection. Animal welfare. Animal rights
Class here works on treatment and prevention of cruelty to animals
Cf. HV4701+ Social pathology
3123 General works
3123.3 Slaughtering of animals
3123.5.A-Z Special topics, A-Z
3123.5.M88 Mutilation
Birth control. Family planning
3124 General (Comparative)
3125.A-Z Special topics, A-Z
3125.A36 Abortion, Forced, for population control
Including voluntary abortion
Environmental law
For civil liability see KB840.E58
3127 General (Comparative)
3128 Organization and administration
3129 Environmental planning. Conservation of environmental resources
Environmental pollution
3130 General works
3130.5 Air pollution
Including noxious gases, automobile emission control, etc.
For tobacco smoking see KB3096.5
3131 Water and groundwater pollution
Including pollutants and sewage control
Pollutants
3131.5 General works
3132 Radioactive substances
3132.5 Noise
Wilderness preservation
Including natural monuments, parks, deserts, and forests
3134 General works

Interdisciplinary discussion of subjects
Environmental law
Wilderness preservation -- Continued
3134.6 Plant protection
3135 Wildlife conservation
Including game, birds, and fish
Cultural affairs
3137 General works
3137.5 Freedom of science and the arts. Academic freedom
3137.7 Cultural policy
3137.8 Language
Including purity, regulation of use, etc.
Education
Including religious education
3138 General works
Students
3139 General works
3139.3 Obligation of parents to educate their children
3140 Teachers. School functionaries (General)
For particular teachers see the level of instruction, e.g. KB3147 university teachers
Elementary education
Including teachers
3141 General works
3142 Rural schools
3143 Education of children with disabilities
Including children with physical and mental disabilities, and children with social disabilities (e.g. orphans, outcasts, paupers, etc.)
3146 Secondary education
3147 Higher education. Universities
Including teachers and students
Science and the arts
Including public policies in research
3160 General works
3161 Public institutions. Academies
3165.A-Z Branches and subjects, A-Z
Language see KB3137.8
The arts
Including censorship
3168 General works
3169 Fine arts
Performing arts
3170 General works
3171 Music. Musicians
3172 Theater

Interdisciplinary discussion of subjects
Cultural affairs
Science and the arts
The arts
Performing arts -- Continued
3173 Motion pictures
Public collections
3176 General works
3177 Archives. Historic documents
3179 Libraries
Including librarians
3182.5 Museums and galleries
3183 Historic buildings and monuments. Shrines. Architectural landmarks
Including sites of archaeological importance
Economic law
Including theories and concepts
3190 General works
3210 Prices and price control. Just price
3220 Control of contracts and combinations in restraint of trade. Competition rules
For unfair competition see KB1234
Money, currency, and foreign exchange control see KB3534
Standards. Norms
3254 General works
3257 Weights and measures. Containers
Standardization
3259 General works
3264 Norms and standards for conservation of raw or scarce materials
Price norms see KB3210
3268 Labeling
Class here general works. For the labeling of particular goods or products, see the good or product
Regulation of industry, trade, and commerce
3272 General works
3280 Advertising
Primary production. Extractive industries
Agriculture. Forestry. Rural law
3295 General (Comparative)
Co-ownership of land see KB694
Land settlement. Village settlement see KB3056
3299 Conservation of agricultural and forestry lands
3314 Agricultural cooperatives. Grazing associations
3334 Apiculture. Beekeeping

Interdisciplinary discussion of subjects
Economic law
Regulation of industry, trade, and commerce
Primary production. Extractive industries
Agriculture. Forestry. Rural law -- Continued
3335 Horticulture
3336 Forestry
Including timber laws and game laws
3340 Fishery
For conservation and ecological aspects see KB3135
3344 Mining and quarrying
Including metallurgy
3377 Food processing industries. Food products
Class here works on trade practices, sanitation, and quality inspection
International trade
3405 General (Comparative)
3410 Export trade
Domestic trade
3415 General works
3418 Retail trade. Government retail trade
Including conditions of trading and holiday legislation
Artisans
3426 General works
3427 Apprentises
3429 Guilds and other cooperative associations. Corporate representation
Transportation and communication
Class here comparative works
3440 General works
Communication. Mass media
3482 General (Comparative)
3483 Freedom of communication. Censorship
3491 Radio communication
Including radio and television broadcasting
Press law. Publishers and publishing. Journalists
3500 General works
Freedom of the press and censorship see KB3483
3500.3 Right to information
3500.7 Press and criminal justice
Professions. Intelligentsia
3515 General (Comparative)
3521.A-Z Individual professions, A-Z
Health professions see KB3100+
Teachers see KB3140

Interdisciplinary discussion of subjects
Professions. Intelligentsia -- Continued
3522 Professional ethics
For ethics of a particular profession, see the profession
Public finance
3526 General (Comparative)
3534 Money
National and local revenue
3540 General (Comparative)
Taxation
3541 General (Comparative)
3556.A-Z Taxation of particular activities, A-Z
3558 Tax administration. Revenue service
Including collection and enforcement
For financial courts see KB3682
3572.A-Z Classes of taxpayers or lines of business, A-Z
Income tax
3573 General works
3591.A-Z Classes of taxpayers or lines of business, A-Z
3592 Corporation tax
3616 Property tax. Taxation of capital
3621 Estate, inheritance, and gift taxes
3623 Capital gains tax
Excise taxes. Taxes on sales, services, and transactions
3627 General works
3640.A-Z Particular, A-Z
3640.B35 Banking transactions
3670 Real property tax. Land tax
Business tax
3674 General works
3679.A-36679.Z Classes of taxpayers or lines of business, A-Z
3680.A-Z Other taxes, A-Z
3681 Customs. Tariff
3682 Tax and customs courts and procedure
Tax and customs crimes and delinquency. Procedure
3693 General works
3694.A-Z Individual offenses, A-Z
3694.T39 Tax evasion and avoidance
Government measures in time of war, national emergency, or economic crisis
3709 General works
3725.A-Z Particular measures, A-Z
3726 Criminal provisions
Military law
For emergency and wartime legislation see KB3709+

Interdisciplinary discussion of subjects -- Continued
For jīhad see KBP182+
For the law of war and neutrality see KZ6378+
3735 General works
Organized forces. The armed forces
3738 General works
3739 Obligation to serve
Military criminal law and procedure
Cf. KB4470 Crimes against national defense
3758 General works
3760.A-Z Individual offenses, A-Z
Courts and procedure
3770 General works
3780 Military discipline. Law enforcement. Procedure
Including works on superior orders and enforcement
Criminal law and procedure
For criminology and penology see HV6001+
3790 Reform of criminal law, procedure, and execution
3791 General (Comparative)
Class here works on crimes, procedure, and punishment discussed together
Theory of punishment see KB3950+
Relationship of criminal law to other subjects or phenomena
3817 General works
3818 Criminal law and society
Cf. HV6115+ Social pathology
3821 Interpretation and construction. Legal hermeneutics
3823.A-Z Terms and phrases, A-Z
Concepts and principles
3824 General works
3838 Personal applicability. Immunities
Criminal offense. Criminal act
3840 General works
Form of criminal act
3852 General works
3854 Attempt
For active repentance see KB4023.A25
Justification of otherwise prohibited acts
3855 General works
3856 Self-defense or defense of another
3857 Necessity
3858 Preservation of life
3859 Duty to act (Legal authority or duty)
3861 Consent of the injured party. Assumption of risk
3867 Criminal intent. Mens rea

Interdisciplinary discussion of subjects
Criminal law and procedure
Criminal offense. Criminal act -- Continued
Criminal liability. Guilt. Culpability
3878 General works
Capacity. Limited capacity and incapacity
3882 General works
3884 Insane persons. People with mental or emotional disabilities
3886 Minors
Including infants, juveniles, etc.
3886.5 Slaves
3892.A-Z Special topics, A-Z
3896 Ignorance or mistake of law
3897 Exculpating circumstances
e.g. Duress
3902 Error
Including error about fact, error about grounds for justification or excusation, error in persona, etc.
3922 Perpetrators (Principles and accessory). Complicity
Crimes and punishment
3946 General works
Theory of punishment. Measure of punishment
3950 General works
3952 Retaliation. Talion
3954 Safeguarding the social and political order
3980.A-Z Particular penalties, A-Z
Banishment. Exile see KB3993.B35
3980.B43 Beheading. Decapitation by the sword
3980.B78 Crucifixion
Decapitation by the sword see KB3980.B43
3980.F57 Flagellation. Whipping
Flogging see KB3980.F57
Lashing see KB3980.F57
3980.M87 Mutilation
3980.S85 Stoning
Whipping see KB3980.F57
Preventive or coercive measures. Measures of rehabilitation
3982 General works
3993.A-Z Special topics, A-Z
3993.B35 Banishment. Exile
Exile see KB3993.B35
3993.I47 Imprisonment. Protective custody
3993.I54 Infamy
Protective custody see KB3993.I47

Interdisciplinary discussion of subjects
Criminal law and procedure
Crimes and punishment
Sentencing and determining the measure of punishment. Gradation

4012 General works
4023.A-Z Special topics, A-Z
4023.A25 Active repentance
Cf. KB3854 Attempt
4023.A35 Aggravating and extenuating circumstances
4034 Pardon
4038 Limitation of actions
Individual criminal offenses
4048 General works
Homicide
Including murder and manslaughter
4050 General works
4058 Euthanasia
Including assisting suicide
4070 Crimes against incohate life
Including causing an abortion
Crimes against physical inviolability
4074 General works
4076 Battery. Battery with deadly consequences
Crimes against personal freedom
4116 General works
4120 Extortionate kidnapping
4121 Kidnapping for sale. Slave traffic
4147 Defamation
4172 Sodomy
Crimes against property
Including works on things extra commercium
4230 General works
4235 Theft. Larceny
Including works on family theft
4250 Embezzlement
4254 Robbery
4256 Destruction of property and conversion
4258 Fraud
Offenses against public order and convenience
4305 General works
4330 Crimes against security of legal and monetary transactions and documents
Including forgery and counterfeiting
4351.A-Z Other, A-Z
Crimes involving danger to the community. Terrorism

Interdisciplinary discussion of subjects
Criminal law and procedure
Crimes and punishment
Individual criminal offenses
Crimes involving danger to the community. Terrorism -- Continued
4351.5 General works
4354 Arson
4364 Poisoning wells or soil
4368 Biological terrorism
Including spreading communicable diseases, morbific agents, or parasites
4377 Crimes aboard aircraft. Air piracy
Crimes affecting traffic
4380 Dangerous interference with rail, ship, or air traffic
4384 Dangerous interference with street traffic. Motor vehicle offenses
Offenses against the government. Offenses against the peace. Political offenses
4415 General works
High treason and treason
4417 General works
4442 Espionage
4447.A-Z Special topics, A-Z
4470 Crimes against national defense
4514 Crimes involving communal employees. Corruption. Bribery
Including omission of official acts
Crimes against humanity
4538 General works
4540 Genocide
4541 Torture
4543 Crimes against foreign states, supranational institutions, or international institutions
4545 War crimes
Criminal procedure
For works on reform of criminal procedure see KB3790
For works on both criminal law and criminal procedure see KB3791
4601 General (Comparative)
Administration of criminal justice. Courts see KB1572+
Procedural principles
4624 Accusation principle (no prosecution ex officio)
4630.A-Z Parties to action, A-Z
4630.A25 Accused. Person charged. Defendant
4630.A253 Accusers

Interdisciplinary discussion of subjects
Criminal law and procedure
Criminal procedure
Procedural principles
Parties to action, A-Z -- Continued
Defendant see KB4630.A25
4630.D43 Defense
Person charged see KB4630.A25
4630.V52 Victim. Victim's family
Pretrial procedures
4632 General works
4636 Investigation. Examination
For techniques of criminal investigation see HV8073
4648 Time periods. Deadlines
4650 Compulsory measures against the accused. Securing of evidence
Procedure at trial
4664 General works
4666 Jurisdiction
Including competence in subject matter and venue
4667.A-Z Special topics, A-Z
Trial
4673 General works
Evidence. Burden of proof
Including admission of evidence, confession, and retraction of confession
4675 General works
4687 Physical examination
For forensic medicine see RA1001+
4689 Electronic listening and recording devices
Including wiretapping
4692 Witnesses
Including qualification and number of witnesses, etc.
4700 Expert testimony
Cf. RA1001+ Medical jurisprudence
4709.A-Z Other, A-Z
4709.A45 Alibi
4709.C57 Circumstantial evidence
4709.D63 Documentary evidence
4709.O28 Oath
4709.R48 Retraction of evidence
Including oath of witnesses and parties
4709.T47 Testimony of the accused
4710 Particular proceedings
e.g. proceedings against absentees and fugitives

Interdisciplinary discussion of subjects
Criminal law and procedure
Criminal procedure
Procedure at trial
Trial -- Continued
4720 Procedure for juvenile delinquency
Judicial decisions. Judgment
Including judicial discretion (opportunity and equity)
4738 General works
4742.A-Z Particular, A-Z
4742.A27-Z Acquittal
4742.C66 Conviction
4742.57 Dismissal
4753 Correction or withdrawal of faulty decisions (errors)
4754 Res judicata
4768.A-Z Special procedures A-Z
4770 Remedies
Execution of sentence
4795 General works
Exile. Banishment. Punitive deportation see KB3993.B35
Pardon see KB4034
4855 Victimology. Victims of crimes

Jewish law. Halakhah
Class here comprehensive and comparative works on the development and principles of Jewish law (Halakhah) as well as the application of such principles to Mishpat Ivri.
The parenthesized numbers between <KBM1> and <KBM523.5>, introduced from Class BM (Judaism), represent sources and subjects common to Judaism and Jewish law. They are intended to provide an alternative arrangement for those institutions who wish to integrate these materials in KBM in a single file.
At the Library of Congress, the primary sources such as the talmudic and post-talmudic literature, and the works on history and codification of Jewish law (Halakhah) are classed in BM495-BM523.5. The Tanakh (Hebrew Bible) is classed in the range BS701-BS1830.

KBM

<1> Periodicals on Judaism
For periodicals on Jewish law (Halakhah) see BM520
For law periodicals see KB8+
Cf. KBM520 Periodicals on Jewish law (Halakhah)

Bibliography
For bibliography on mishpat Ivri see KBM523.8
For bibliography on Jews and Judaism see Z6366+
For bibliography on Jewish law (Halakhah) see Z6374.L4
Cf. KBM520.32 Bibliography on Jewish law (Halakhah)

<21> Societies (Judaism). Associations (Judaism)
For Jewish law societies see BM520.45
Cf. KBM520.45 Jewish law societies

<30> Congresses on Judaism. Conferences on Judaism
For Jewish law conferences see BM520.46
Cf. KBM520.46 Jewish law conferences

Collected works on Judaism
Several authors
<40> General works
<42> Addresses, essays, lectures
<43> Extracts form several authors
<44> Pamphlet collections
<45> Individual authors
<50> Encyclopedias and dictionaries on Judaism
For dictionaries on Israeli law, see KMK26
For encyclopedias and dictionaries on Jewish law (Halakhah) see BM520.4
For Hebrew language and multilingual law dictionaries see K50+
Cf. KBM520.4 Encyclopedias and dictionaries on Jewish law (Halakhah)

Directories on Judaism
For directories on Jewish law (Halakhah) see BM520.42
Cf. KBM520.42 Directories on Jewish law (Halakhah)
<55> General
By region or country
<60> United States
<65.A-Z> Other regions or countries, A-Z
Research
For legal research. Methods of research on Jewish law (Halakhah) see BM520.43
Cf. KBM520.43 Methods of research on Jewish law (Halakhah)
<66> Information services
<67> Computer network resources
Including the Internet
Study and teaching of Judaism
Cf. KBM523.9 Legal education
Cf. KBM3138 Education (Mishpat Ivri)
<70> General works
<71> General special
By region or country
United States
<75> General works
<77.A-.W> By state, A-W
<80.A-Z> By city, A-Z
<85.A-Z> Other regions or countries, A-Z
For Talmudic academies in Babylonia and Palestine (through 11th century) see BM502
Cf. KBM502 Talmudic academies in Babylonia and Palestine
Biography
<88> Collective
Individual see BM755.A+
By school
<90.A-Z> American (United States), A-Z
<95.A-Z> Other, A-Z
Religious education of the young. Sabbath schools
<100> Periodicals. Societies. Serials
<101> Congresses. Conferences
<102.A-Z> Biography, A-Z
<103> General works
<105> Textbooks
Cf. BM573 Juvenile works on the principles of Judaism
<107> Stories, etc.
<108> Teacher training
<109.A-Z> Special types of schools, A-Z
<109.C6> Congregational Hebrew School

Study and teaching of Judaism
Religious education of the young. Sabbath schools
Special types of schools, A-Z -- Continued
<109.H4> Heder
<109.T3> Talmud Torah
<110.A-Z> Individual schools. By place, A-Z
Entertainment exercises, etc.
<125> General works
<127.A-Z> Special days, A-Z
<135> Social life, recreation, etc., in the synagogue. Camps
History of Judaism
Cf. KBM520.5+ History of halakhah
For history of halakhah see BM520.5+
For constitutional history of the Jewish community see KBM2085+
Cf. DS101+ History of the Jews
General
<150> Early through 1800
<155> 1801-1950
<155.2> 1951-2000
<155.3> 2001-
<156> Handbooks, manuals, etc.
<157> General special
<160> Addresses, essays, lectures
By period
Cf. DS121+ History of the Jews by period
To 70
Cf. BS1192.5 Theology of the Tanakh (Hebrew Bible)
<165> General works
<170> General special
<173> Addresses, essays, lectures
<175.A-Z> Particular movements, sects, etc., A-Z
Including history and general principles
<175.A1> General works
<175.A2> Unidentified sects
<175.E8> Essenes. Isiyim
<175.H36> Hasideans. Hasidim (Talmudic era)
<175.P4> Pharisees. Perushim
<175.Q6> Qumran community. Kat Midbar Yehudah
<175.S2> Sadducees. Zedukim. Tsadoḳim
Samaritans. Shomronim see BM900+
<175.T5> Therapeutae
<175.Z3> Zadokites. Benei Zadok
<175.Z4> Zealots (Party). Kanna'im
<176> 586 B.C. - 70 A.D.
Including the Hellenistic period (323-30 B.C.)

History of Judaism
By period -- Continued
<177> 70-500
Including the period of the redaction of the Talmud
For history and development of the Talmud see BM501.15+
Cf. KBM501.15+ History and development of the Talmud
500-1500
<180> General works
<182> Ashkenazim. Sephardim
Including works on the development of each and on the relations between the two
Cf. DS133+ Jewish diaspora
Cf. DS135.E8+ History of Jews in Eastern Europe
Cf. DS135.S7+ History of Jews in Spain
Karaites
Including history and general principles
<185> General works
Liturgy and ritual
<185.3> General works
<185.4.A-Z> Special liturgical books. By title, A-Z
Haggadah
<185.4.H35> Texts. By date
<185.4.H353A-.H353Z> Criticism. By author
Seder berakhot le-khol ha-shanah
<185.4.S43> Texts. By date
<185.4.S433A-.S433Z> Criticism. By author
Siddur
<185.4.S53> Texts. By date
<185.4.S533A-.S533Z> Criticism. By author
1500-
<190> General works
By period
<193> 1500-1800
<194> Haskalah (ca. 1780-ca.1880)
<195> 1800-1948
<195.2> 1948-

History of Judaism
By period
1500- -- Continued
Specific movements, sects, etc.
Class here works on the history and general principles of the movements
For works on a specific topic within the context of a particular movement, see the topic
For biography see BM750+
For works on individual congregations see BM201+
Cf. KBM201+ Individual congregations

<196> General works
<197> Reform Judaism. Progressive Judaism
<197.5> Conservative Judaism
<197.6> Orthodox Judaism
<197.7> Reconstructionist Judaism
<197.8> Humanistic Judaism

Hasidism. Hasidim
For comprehensive works on Jewish mysticism see BM723+
Cf. BM532 Hasidic tales and legends

General works
<198> Through 1994
<198.2> 1995-
<198.3> History
<198.4.A-Z> By region or country, A-Z

By sect
<198.5> Belz
<198.52> Bratslav
<198.53> Guardian-of-the-Faithful
<198.54> Habad. Lubavitch
<198.55> Satmar
<198.56.A-Z> Other sects, A-Z
<198.56.B62> Bobov
<198.56.B87> Buhusi
<198.56.G87> Gur
<198.56.K37> Karlin
<198.56.S83> Stefanesti
<198.56.Z35> Zanz

Hasideans
see BM175.H36
Cf. KBM175.H36 Hasideans

<198.8> Mitnaggedim
<199.A-Z> Other specific movements, sects, etc., A-Z
e. g.
<199.S3> Sabbathaians

History of Judaism -- Continued
By region or country
Including history of individual synagogues
<201> America
North America
<203> General works
United States
<205> General works
By region
<208> New England
<211> South
<214> Central
<218> West
<221> Pacific coast
<223.A-.W> By state, A-W
<225.A-Z> By city, A-Z
Subarrange each city by Table KBM2
Canada
<227> General works
<228.A-Z> By province, A-Z
<229.A-Z> By city, A-Z
Subarrange each city by Table KBM2
Mexico
<230> General works
<231.A-.W> By state, A-W
<232.A-Z> By city, A-Z
Subarrange each city by Table KBM2
Central America
<233> General works
Belize
<234> General works
<235.A-Z> Local, A-Z
Subarrange each locality by Table KBM2
Costa Rica
<236> General works
<237.A-Z> Local, A-Z
Subarrange each locality by Table KBM2
El Salvador
see BM246+
Cf. KBM246+ El Salvador
Guatemala
<238> General works
<239.A-Z> Local, A-Z
Subarrange each locality by Table KBM2
Honduras
<240> General works

History of Judaism
By region or country
Central America
Honduras -- Continued
<241.A-Z> Local, A-Z
Subarrange each locality by Table KBM2
Nicaragua
<242> General works
<243.A-Z> Local, A-Z
Subarrange each locality by Table KBM2
Panama
<244> General works
<245.A-Z> Local, A-Z
Subarrange each locality by Table KBM2
Salvador. El Salvador
<246> General works
<247.A-Z> Local, A-Z
Subarrange each locality by Table KBM2
West Indies
<248> General works
Bahamas
<250> General works
<251.A-Z> Local, A-Z
Subarrange each locality by Table KBM2
Cuba
<252> General works
<253.A-Z> Local, A-Z
Subarrange each locality by Table KBM2
Haiti
<254> General works
<255.A-Z> Local, A-Z
Subarrange each locality by Table KBM2
Jamaica
<256> General works
<257.A-Z> Local, A-Z
Subarrange each locality by Table KBM2
Puerto Rico
<258> General works
<259.A-Z> Local, A-Z
Subarrange each locality by Table KBM2
<260.A-Z> Other islands, A-Z
South America
<261> General works
Argentina
<262> General works
<263.A-Z> Local, A-Z
Subarrange each locality by Table KBM2

History of Judaism
By region or country
South America -- Continued
Bolivia
<264> General works
<265.A-Z> Local, A-Z
Subarrange each locality by Table KBM2
Brazil
<266> General works
<267.A-Z> Local, A-Z
Subarrange each locality by Table KBM2
Chile
<268> General works
<269.A-Z> Local, A-Z
Subarrange each locality by Table KBM2
Columbia
<270> General works
<271.A-Z> Local, A-Z
Subarrange each locality by Table KBM2
Ecuador
<272> General works
<273.A-Z> Local, A-Z
Subarrange each locality by Table KBM2
Guianas
<274> General works
Guyana
<276> General works
<277.A-Z> Local, A-Z
Subarrange each locality by Table KBM2
Suriname
<278> General works
<279.A-Z> Local, A-Z
Subarrange each locality by Table KBM2
French Guiana
<280> General works
<281.A-Z> Local, A-Z
Subarrange each locality by Table KBM2
Paraguay
<282> General works
<283.A-Z> Local, A-Z
Subarrange each locality by Table KBM2
Peru
<284> General works
<285.A-Z> Local, A-Z
Subarrange each locality by Table KBM2
Uruguay
<286> General works

History of Judaism
By region or country
South America
Uruguay -- Continued
<287.A-Z> Local, A-Z
Subarrange each locality by Table KBM2
Venezuela
<288> General works
<289.A-Z> Local, A-Z
Subarrange each locality by Table KBM2
Europe
<290> General works
Great Britain. England
<292> General works
<294.A-Z> By English county, A-Z
By English city, A-Z
London
<294.8> General works
<295.A-Z> Individual synagogues or congregations, A-Z
<296.A-Z> Other, A-Z
Subarrange each city by Table KBM2
Scotland
<297> General works
<298.A-Z> By political division, A-Z
<299.A-Z> By city, A-Z
Subarrange each city by Table KBM2
Northern Ireland
<300> General works
<301.A-Z> By political division, A-Z
<302.A-Z> By city, A-Z
Subarrange each city by Table KBM2
Wales
<303> General works
<304.A-Z> By political division, A-Z
<305.A-Z> By city, A-Z
Subarrange each city by Table KBM2
Ireland (Republic)
<306> General works
<306.2.A-Z> By political division, A-Z
<306.3.A-Z> By city, A-Z
Subarrange each city by Table KBM2
Austria
<307> General works
<308.A-Z> By political division, A-Z
<309.A-Z> By city, A-Z
Subarrange each city by Table KBM2
Belgium

History of Judaism
By region or country
Europe
Belgium -- Continued
<310> General works
<311.A-Z> By political division, A-Z
<312.A-Z> By city, A-Z
Subarrange each city by Table KBM2
France
<313> General works
<314.A-Z> By political division, A-Z
<315.A-Z> By city, A-Z
Subarrange each city by Table KBM2
Germany
<316> General works
<317.A-Z> By political division, A-Z
<318.A-Z> By city, A-Z
Subarrange each city by Table KBM2
Greece
<319> General works
<320.A-Z> By political division, A-Z
<321.A-Z> By city, A-Z
Subarrange each city by Table KBM2
Italy
<322> General works
<323.A-Z> By political division, A-Z
<324.A-Z> By city, A-Z
Subarrange each city by Table KBM2
Netherlands
<325> General works
<326.A-Z> By political division, A-Z
<327.A-Z> By city, A-Z
Subarrange each city by Table KBM2
Portugal
<328> General works
<329.A-Z> By political division, A-Z
<330.A-Z> By city, A-Z
Subarrange each city by Table KBM2
Russia. Soviet Union. Russia (Federation)
For former Soviet Republics in Europe see BM376.A+
For former Soviet Republic in Central Asia see BM399+
Cf. KBM376.A+ Other European countries
Cf. KBM399+ Central Asia
<331> General works
<332.A-Z> By political division, A-Z

History of Judaism
By region or country
Europe
Russia. Soviet Union. Russia (Federation) -- Continued
<333.A-Z> By city, A-Z
Subarrange each city by Table KBM2
Finland
<334> General works
<335.A-Z> By political division, A-Z
<336.A-Z> By city, A-Z
Subarrange each city by Table KBM2
Poland
<337> General works
<338.A-Z> By political division A-Z
<339.A-Z> By city, A-Z
Subarrange each city by Table KBM2
Scandinavia
<340> General works
Denmark
<342> General works
<343.A-Z> By political division, A-Z
<344.A-Z> By city, A-Z
Subarrange each city by Table KBM2
Iceland
<345> General works
<346.A-Z> By political division, A-Z
<347.A-Z> By city, A-Z
Subarrange each city by Table KBM2
Norway
<348> General works
<349.A-Z> By political division, A-Z
<350.A-Z> By city, A-Z
Subarrange each city by Table KBM2
Sweden
<351> General works
<352.A-Z> By political division, A-Z
<353.A-Z> By city, A-Z
Subarrange each city by Table KBM2
Spain
<354> General works
<355.A-Z> By political division, A-Z
<356.A-Z> By city, A-Z
Subarrange each city by Table KBM2
Switzerland
<357> General works
<358.A-Z> By political division, A-Z

History of Judaism
By region or country
Europe
Switzerland -- Continued
<359.A-Z> By city, A-Z
Subarrange each city by Table KBM2
Turkey
<360> General works
<361.A-Z> By political division, A-Z
<362.A-Z> By city, A-Z
Subarrange each city by Table KBM2
Balkan states
<363> General works
Bulgaria
<364> General works
<365.A-Z> By political division, A-Z
<366.A-Z> By city, A-Z
Subarrange each city by Table KBM2
Romania
<370> General works
<371.A-Z> By political division, A-Z
<372.A-Z> By city, A-Z
Subarrange each city by Table KBM2
Yugoslavia (to 1992)
For successor states see BM376.A+
Cf. KBM376.A+ Successor states
<373> General works
<374.A-Z> By political division, A-Z
<375.A-Z> By city, A-Z
Subarrange each city by Table KBM2
<376.A-Z> Other European countries, A-Z
Subarrange each country by Table KBM2a
<376.H8> Hungary
<376.L5> Lithuania
<376.S56> Slovakia
<376.U38> Ukraine
Asia
<377> General works
Southwest Asia. Middle East
<379> General works
Turkey in Asia
<381> General works
<382.A-Z> By Turkish vilayet, region, etc., A-Z
<383.A-Z> By city, A-Z
Subarrange each city by Table KBM2
Armenia
<384> General works

History of Judaism
By region or country
Asia
Southwest Asia. Middle East
Armenia -- Continued
<385.A-Z> By political division, A-Z
<386.A-Z> By city, A-Z
Subarrange each city by Table KBM2
Iraq. Mesopotamia
<386.4> General works
<386.5.A-Z> By political division, A-Z
<386.5.B33> Babylonia
<386.6.A-Z> By city, A-Z
Subarrange each city by Table KBM2
Palestine
Cf. KBM165+ Ancient history of Judaism
<387> General works
<388.A-Z> By political division, A-Z
<389.A-Z> By city, A-Z
Subarrange each city by Table KBM2
Israel (The modern state)
<390> General works
<391.A-Z> By political division, A-Z
<392.A-Z> By city, A-Z
Subarrange each city by Table KBM2
Arab countries
For Iraq see BM386.4+
For Arab countries in other regions, e. g. Africa see BM432+
Cf. KBM386.4+ Iraq
Cf. KBM432+ Arab countries in other regions, e. g. Africa
<393> General works
<394.A-Z> By country, A-Z
Subarrange each country by Table KBM2a
<394.S27> Saudi Arabia
<394.S95> Syria
<394.Y4> Yemen
Iran
<396> General works
<397.A-Z> By political division, A-Z
<398.A-Z> By city, A-Z
Subarrange each city by Table KBM2
Central Asia
<399> General works
Afghanistan
<400> General works

History of Judaism
By region or country
Asia
Central Asia
Afghanistan -- Continued
<402.A-Z> By political division, A-Z
<403.A-Z> By city, A-Z
Subarrange each city by Table KBM2
<404.A-Z> Other, A-Z
Subarrange each country by Table KBM4
Including former Soviet Republics in Central Asia
South Asia. Southeast Asia
<405> General works
Pakistan
<405.4> General works
<405.5.A-Z> By political division, A-Z
<405.6.A-Z> By city, A-Z
Subarrange each city by Table KBM2
India
<406> General works
<409.A-Z> By political division, A-Z
<410.A-Z> By city, A-Z
Subarrange each city by Table KBM2
<410.3> Burma. Myanmar
<410.5> Sri Lanka
Indochina
<411> General works
<412.A-Z> By country, A-Z
Subarrange each country by Table KBM2a
<412.C3> Cambodia
<412.L3> Laos
<412.V5> Vietnam
<414> Malaysia
Indonesia
<415> General works
<416.A-Z> By political division, A-Z
<417.A-Z> By city, A-Z
Subarrange each city by Table KBM2
Philippines
<418> General works
<419.A-Z> By political division, A-Z
<420.A-Z> By city, A-Z
Subarrange each city by Table KBM2
<421.A-Z> Other countries, A-Z
Subarrange each country by Table KBM2a
East Asia
<422> General works

History of Judaism
By region or country
Asia
East Asia -- Continued
China
<423> General works
<424.A-Z> By political division, A-Z
<425.A-Z> By city, A-Z
Subarrange each city by Table KBM2
Japan
<426> General works
<427.A-Z> By political division, A-Z
<428.A-Z> By city, A-Z
Subarrange each city by Table KBM2
<431.A-Z> Other countries, A-Z
Subarrange each country by Table KBM2a
Africa
<432> General works
Egypt
<434> General works
<435.A-Z> By political division, A-Z
<436.A-Z> By city, A-Z
Subarrange each city by Table KBM2
<437> South Africa
<440.A-Z> Other regions or countries, A-Z
Subarrange each country by Table KBM2a
<440.A8355> Africa, North
<440.E8> Ethiopia
<440.M8> Morocco
Australia
<443> General works
<444.A-Z> By political division, A-Z
<445.A-Z> By city, A-Z
Subarrange each city by Table KBM2
New Zealand
<446> General works
<446.2.A-Z> By political division, A-Z
<446.3.A-Z> By city, A-Z
Subarrange each city by Table KBM2
Islands of the Pacific
<447> General works
<449.A-Z> By individual island or group of islands, A-Z
Subarrange each island by Table KBM2
Sources
For collections, compilations, and selections see BM495+
For discussion of sources of Jewish law see KBM524.3
Cf. KBM495+ Collections. Compilations. Selections

Sources -- Continued
Tanakh. Hebrew Bible
Alternative classification for Tanakh, not applied at the Library of Congress
For Library of Congress collections see BS701+
<450> Complete text of the Tanakh (Table KBM9)
<452> Pentateuch. Ḥumash (Table KBM9)
<453> Genesis. Be-reshit (Table KBM9)
<454> Exodus. Shemot (Table KBM9)
<455> Leviticus. Ṿa-yiḳra (Table KBM9)
<456> Numbers. Ba-midbar (Table KBM9)
<457> Deuteronomy. Devarim (Table KBM9)
<460> Prophets and writings. Nakh (Table KBM9)
<461> Prophets. Nevi'im (Table KBM9)
<462> Joshua. Yehoshuʻa (Table KBM9)
<463> Judges. Shofṭim (Table KBM9)
<464> Samuel. Shemu'el (Table KBM9)
<464.7> Samuel, 1st. Shemu'el 1 (Table KBM10)
<464.8> Samuel, 2nd. Shemu'el 2 (Table KBM10)
<465> Kings. Melakhim (Table KBM9)
<465.7> Kings, 1st. Melakhim 1 (Table KBM10)
<465.8> Kings, 2nd. Melakhim 2 (Table KBM10)
<468> Isaiah. Yeshaʻyahu (Table KBM9)
<469> Jeremiah. Yirmeyahu (Table KBM9)
<470> Ezekiel. Yeḥezḳel (Table KBM9)
<471> Minor prophets. Tere ʻaśar (Table KBM9)
<471.7> Hosea. Hosheʻa (Table KBM10)
<471.76> Joel. Yo'el (Table KBM10)
<471.77> Amos. ʻAmos (Table KBM10)
<471.78> Obadiah. ʻOvadyah (Table KBM10)
<471.79> Jonah. Yonah (Table KBM10)
<471.8> Micah. Mikhah (Table KBM10)
<471.86> Nahum. Naḥum (Table KBM10)
<471.87> Habakkuk. Ḥabaḳuḳ (Table KBM10)
<471.88> Zephaniah. Tsefanyah (Table KBM10)
<471.89> Haggai. Hagai (Table KBM10)
<471.9> Zechariah. Zekharyah (Table KBM10)
<471.96> Malachi. Mal'akhi (Table KBM10)
<472> Hagiographa. Writings. Ketuvim (Table KBM9)
<473> Psalms. Tehilim (Table KBM9)
<474> Proverbs. Mishle (Table KBM9)
<475> Job. Iyov (Table KBM9)
<476> Five Scrolls. Ḥamesh megilot (Table KBM9)
<476.6> Song of Songs. Shir ha-shirim (Table KBM10)
<476.66> Ruth. Rut (Table KBM10)
<476.7> Lamentations. Ekhah (Table KBM10)
<476.76> Ecclesiastes. Ḳohelet (Table KBM10)

Sources
Tanakh. Hebrew Bible
Complete text of the Tanakh
Hagiographa. Writings. Ketuvim
Five Scrolls. Ḥamesh megilot -- Continued
<476.8> Esther. Ester (Table KBM10)
<477> Daniel, Ezra, Nehemiah. Daniyel, ‘Ezra, Neḥemyah (two or three published together) (Table KBM9)
<477.7> Daniel. Daniyel (Table KBM10)
<477.8> Ezra. ‘Ezra (Table KBM10)
<477.9> Nehemiah. Neḥemyah (Table KBM10)
<478> Chronicles. Divre ha-yamim (Table KBM9)
<478.7> Chronicles, 1st. Divre ha-yamim 1 (Table KBM10)
<478.8> Chronicles, 2nd. Divre ha-yamim 2 (Table KBM10)
Pre-Talmudic literature (non-Biblical)
<480> Collections. Compilations. Selections
<485> History and criticism
Particular texts or groups of texts
For Letter of Aristeas see BS744.A7
Apocrypha and apocryphal books
Including the Pseudepigrapha
Alternative classification for Apocrypha, not applied at the Library of Congress
For Library of Congress collections see BS1691+
Collections
<486> Polyglot. Texts in Hebrew, Aramaic, or Greek. By date
<486 .2.A-486.2.Z> Other languages. By language, A-Z, and date
<486.3> Selections
<486.4> History and criticism. Commentaries
<486.5.A-Z> Individual books, A-Z
Subarrange each by Table KBM11
Dead Sea scrolls
Texts
<487.A05> Facsimiles. By date
<487.A1> Original language. By date
Translations
<487.A2> Hebrew. By date
<487.A3> English. By date
<487.A4> French. By date
<487.A5> German. By date
<487.A6A-.A6Z> Other languages. By language, A-Z, and date
<487.A62> Periodicals
<487.A7> History and criticism
Language see PJ4901+
<488.A-Z> Individual scrolls, A-Z
For Biblical texts, see Subclass BS

Sources
Pre-Talmudic literature (non-Biblical)
Particular texts or groups of texts
Dead Sea scrolls
Individual scrolls, A-Z -- Continued
<488.A15> 4QInstruction (Table KBM3)
<488.C6> Copper Scroll (Table KBM3)
Genesis Apocryphon see BS1830.G4+
Habakkuk commentary see BS1635.H26+
<488.M3> Manual of discipline (Table KBM3)
<488.N48> New Jerusalem Scroll (Table KBM3)
<488.R85> Rule of the congregation (Table KBM3)
<488.S47> Serekh shirot olat ha-Shabbat (Table KBM3)
Songs of the Sabbath sacrifice
see BM488.S47
Cf. KBM488.S47 Songs of the Sabbath sacrifice
<488.T44> Temple scroll (Table KBM3)
<488.T5> Thanksgiving Psalms. Thanksgiving scroll (Table KBM3)
<488.W3> War of the Sons of Light against the Sons of Darkness (Table KBM3)
Selections of scrolls from individual caves
Cave 4
Texts
<488.5.A05> Facsimiles. By date
<488.5.A1> Original language. By date
Translations
<488.5.A2> Hebrew. By date
<488.5.A3> English. By date
<488.5.A4> French. By date
<488.5.A5> German. By date
<488.5.A6A-.A6Z> Other languages. By language, A-Z, and date
<488.5.A7-Z> History and criticism
Cave 11
Texts
<488.8.A05> Facsimiles. By date
<488.8.A1> Original language. By date
Translations
<488.8.A2> Hebrew. By date
<488.8.A3> English. By date
<488.8.A4> French. By date
<488.8.A5> German. By date
<488.8.A6A-.A6Z> Other languages. By language, A-Z, and date
<488.8.A7-Z> History and criticism
Elephantine papyri see PJ5208.E4+

Sources -- Continued
Rabbinical literature
Including the Mishnah, Talmud Yerushalmi, Talmud (Bavli), baraita, Tosefta, and Midrash
For the codes see BM520.82+
Cf. KBM520.82+ The codes
Collections. Compilations. Selections
<495> Several authors
<495.5> Individual authors
Works about the sources
<496.A1> Periodicals. Societies. Serials
General works
<496.A4-Z> Early works through 1900
<496.5> 1901-2000
<496.6> 2001-
<496.8> Publication and distribution
<496.9.A-Z> Special topics, A-Z
For special topics in Talmudic literature see BM509.A+
For special topics in the midrash see BM518.A+
<496.9.A2> Abraham
<496.9.A4> Adam
<496.9.A45> Allegory
<496.9.A48> Angels
<496.9.A5> Animals
Cf. KBM3122 Veterinary medicine and hygiene in mishpat Ivri
<496.9.A68> Asceticism
<496.9.A7> Astrology
<496.9.A72> Astronomy
<496.9.B57> Boethusians
<496.9.B6> Botany. Plants
<496.9.B87> Burning bush
<496.9.C3> Caesarean section
<496.9.C34> Cain
<496.9.C45> Census
<496.9.C47> Ceramics
<496.9.C5> Christians
<496.9.C57> Circumcision
Cf. BM705 Berit milah (religious and ritual aspects)
Cf. KBM3119.C57 Circumcision in mishpat Ivri
<496.9.C67> Creation
<496.9.C76> Crown of God
<496.9.D5> Dialectic
<496.9.D73> Dream interpretation
<496.9.E27> Economics
Cf. DS140.5 Economic conditions (Jewish diaspora)
Cf. KBM3190+ Economic law in mishpat Ivri

KBM

Sources
Rabbinical literature
Special topics, A-Z -- Continued

<496.9.E3> Education
Cf. BM70+ Study and teaching of Judaism
Cf. KBM70+ Study and teaching of Judaism
Cf. KBM3138+ Education in mishpat Ivri
Cf. LC701+ Jewish education
Cf. LC3551+ Education of Jews

<496.9.E4> Elijah, the Prophet

<496.9.E8> Eschatology

<496.9.E9> Evil eye

Gehenna see KBM496.9.H4

<496.9.G4> Geography

<496.9.G63> Gods

<496.9.H35> Haman

<496.9.H4> Hell. Gehenna

<496.9.H47> Hermaphroditism
Cf. KBM529.7.H47 Hermaphroditism in Mishpat Ivri

<496.9.H54> Hides and skins

<496.9.H57> Historiography

<496.9.H84> Human anatomy
Cf. KBM3115+ Biomedical engineering in mishpat Ivri

<496.9.H85> Humanism

<496.9.I5> Image of God

<496.9.I53> Incense

<496.9.I6> Iran

<496.9.I8> Isaac

<496.9.J4> Jerusalem

<496.9.J48> Jews

<496.9.J67> Jordan

<496.9.K5> Kings and rulers
Cf. KBM2129+ Kingship in Mishpat Ivri

<496.9.L18> Laban

<496.9.L2> Labor. Working class
Cf. HD6305.J3 Jews in labor
Cf. KBM1270+ Labor law and legislation in mishpat Ivri

<496.9.M3> Mathematics

Measures see KBM3257+

<496.9.M47> Messiah

<496.9.M58> Mnemonic devices

<496.9.M6> Moses

<496.9.M87> Mysticism

<496.9.N3> Names
Cf. KBM529.8 Personality rights in mishpat Ivri

<496.9.N37> Narration

Sources
Rabbinical literature
Special topics, A-Z -- Continued
<496.9.N4> Natural history
<496.9.P25> Palestine
<496.9.P3> Parables
Plants
see BM496.9.B6
Cf. KBM496.9.B6 Botany
<496.9.P64> Politics
<496.9.P75> Prophets
<496.9.P8> Psychology
<496.9.R33> Rain
<496.9.R66> Rome
Rulers
see BM496.9.K5
Cf. KBM496.9.K5 Kings and rulers
<496.9.S24> Sabbath
<496.9.S38> Saul, King of Israel
<496.9.S43> Scapegoat
<496.9.S44> Science
Cf. KBM3160+ Science and the arts in mishpat Ivri
<496.9.S48> Sex
Cf. BM720.S4 Sex (Jewish religious and ritual aspects)
Cf. KBM4180+ Offenses against marriage, family, and family status in mishpat Ivri
<496.9.S55> Ships
Cf. KBM970.97 Ships and ship owners in mishpat Ivri
Skins
For hides and skins see BM496.9.H54
Cf. KBM496.9.H54 Hides and skins
<496.9.S93> Suffering of God
<496.9.S95> Supererogation
<496.9.T5> Titus, Emperor of Rome
Weights and measures see KBM3257+
<496.9.W7> Women
Cf. KBM526+ Women in mishpat Ivri
Working class
see BM496.9.L2
Cf. KBM496.9.L2 Labor

Sources
Rabbinical literature -- Continued
Talmudic literature
Class Talmudic literature in general in the range for Talmud (Bavli), BM499-BM504.7
For works limited to Talmud (Bavli) see BM499+
For individual orders and tractates see BM506+
Cf. KBM499+ Talmudic literature
Cf. KBM499+ Talmud (Bavli)
Cf. KBM506+ Individual orders and tractates
For works limited to Mishnah see BM497+
For works limited to Talmud Yerushalmi see BM498+
For individual minor tractates see BM506.4.A+
Cf. KBM497+ Mishnah
Cf. KBM498+ Talmud Yerushalmi
Cf. KBM506.4.A+ Individual minor tractates
Mishnah
Original language (Hebrew and Aramaic)
<497> Complete texts. By date
<497.2> Selections. By editor or date
<497.5.A-Z> Translations. By language, A-Z
Under each language:
.x Complete texts. By date
.x2 Selections. By editor or date
Cf. KBM506.A+ Individual tractates
For individual tractates see BM506.A+
Works about the Mishnah
<497.7> Early works through 1900
<497.8> 1901-2000
<497.85> 2001-
Talmud Yerushalmi. Jerusalem Talmud. Palestinian Talmud
Original language (Hebrew and Aramaic)
<498> Complete texts. By date
<498.2> Selections. By editor or date
<498.5.A-Z> Translations. By language, A-Z
Under each language:
.x Complete texts. By date
.x2 Selections. By editor or date
Cf. KBM506.A+ Individual tractates
For individual tractates see BM506.A+
Works about the Talmud Yerushalmi
<498.7> Early works through 1900
<498.8> 1901-2000
<498.9> 2001-
Talmud. Talmud Bavli. Babylonian Talmud
Original language (Hebrew and Aramaic)

Sources
Rabbinical literature
Talmudic literature
Talmud. Talmud Bavli. Babylonian Talmud
Original language (Hebrew and Aramaic) -- Continued
<499> Complete texts. By date
<499.2> Selections. By editor or date
<499.5.A-Z> Translations. By language, A-Z
Under each language:
.x Complete texts. By date
.x2 Selections. By editor or date
For individual tractates see BM506.A+
Cf. KBM506.A+ Individual tractates
Works about the Talmud (Bavli)
Including works on both the Talmud (Bavli) and Talmud Yerushalmi
<500> Periodicals. Societies. Serials
<500.2> Collected works. Selections
<500.5> Concordances. Subject dictionaries. Indexes, etc.
Hebrew language, Talmudic see PJ4901+
Aramaic language
Talmud Yerushalmi see PJ5251+
Talmud (Bavli) see PJ5301+
<501> General works
History and development of the Talmud
Cf. BM177 History of Judaism, 70-500
<501.15> Collective biography of Talmudists (General)
Under each group of Talmudists include collective biography
For the evaluation of individual Talmudists see BM502.3.A+
For the biography of individual Talmudists see BM755.A+
Cf. KBM502.3.A+ Evaluation of individual Talmudists
<501.17> Soferim
<501.2> Tannaim
<501.25> Beth Hillel and Beth Shammai
<501.3> Amoraim
For Baraita see BM507+
For Tosefta see BM508+
Cf. KBM507+ Baraita
Cf. KBM508+ Tosefta
<501.4> Saboraim
<501.5> Geonim
<501.6> "Rishonim" (Early authorities)

Sources
Rabbinical literature
Talmudic literature
Talmud. Talmud Bavli. Babylonian Talmud
Works about the Talmud (Bavli)
History and development of the Talmud
"Rishonim" (Early authorities) -- Continued

<501.7> North African and Spanish scholars
Cf. BM545+ Maimonides

<501.8> French and German scholars
e. g. Rashi, 1040-1105 and his school; Tosafists

<501.9> "Aharonim" (Later authorities, 16th century to date)

<502> Talmudic academies in Babylonia and Palestine (through 11th century)

<502.3.A-Z> Criticism and evaluation of individual Talmudists, A-Z
For biography see BM755.A+

<502.3.A2> Abba Arika, 3rd cent.

<502.3.A36> Akiba ben Joseph, ca. 50-ca. 132

<502.3.E38> Eleazer ben Azariah

<502.3.E4> Eliezer ben Hyrcanus

<502.3.G35> Gamaliel II, fl. 80-110

<502.3.H35> Ḥanina, Segan ha-Kohanim, 1st cent.

<502.3.H55> Hillel, 1st cent. B.C. - 1st cent. A.D.

<502.3.I8> Ishmael ben Elisha, 2nd cent.

<502.3.J67> Jose the Galilean

<502.3.J68> Joshua ben Ḥananiah, 1st cent.

<502.3.M44> Meir, 2nd cent.

<502.3.P36> Papa, ca. 300-375

<502.3.R3> Rabbah bar Bar Ḥana, 3rd cent.

Rav, 3rd cent.
see BM502.3.A2
Cf. KBM502.3.A2 Abba Arika, 3rd cent.

<502.3.S34> Samuel ben Naḥman, 3rd/4th cent.

<502.3.S37> Samuel of Nehardea, ca. 177-257

<502.3.S5> Simeon bar Yoḥai, 2nd cent.

<502.3.T37> Tarfon

<502.3.U44> Ulla I, 3rd cent.

Study and teaching of the Talmud

<502.5> General works

<502.7> Hadran

Individual institutions
see BM90+
Cf. KBM90+ By school

<503> Evidences. Authority. Oral tradition. Authoritative explication of oral law
Cf. BM529 Tradition (Judaism)

Sources
Rabbinical literature
Talmudic literature
Talmud. Talmud Bavli. Babylonian Talmud
Works about the Talmud (Bavli) -- Continued

<503.3> Apologetics
For controversial works against the Jews, including works against the Talmud see BM585+
Cf. BM648 Apologetic works

<503.5> Introductions
Methodology
For legal methodology see KBM524.32+
<503.6> General works
<503.7> Hermeneutics
<503.8> Pilpul
<503.9> Textual criticism
Commentaries
<504> General works
<504.2> Novellae (Hidushim)
<504.3> Theology of the Talmud
<504.5> Addresses, essays, lectures
<504.7> Juvenile works
For Aggada see BM516+
Cf. BM530+ Jewish myths and legends
Cf. KBM516+ Aggada

<506.A-Z> Individual orders and tractates of the Mishnah, the Talmud Yerushalmi, and the Talmud (Bavli), A-Z
Subarrange each by Table BM1

Minor tractates (not part of the Mishnah)
<506.2> Collections. Compilations. Selections
<506.3> Works on the minor tractates
<506.4.A-Z> Individual minor tractates, A-Z
Abadim (Avadim)
<506.4.A15> Original texts (Hebrew or Aramaic). By date
<506.4.A15A-.A15Z> Translations. By language, A-Z
<506.4.A16> Selections. By date
<506.4.A17> Criticism. Commentaries, etc.
Avadim
see BM506.4.A15+
Cf. KBM506.4.A15+ Abadim
Avot de-Rabbi Nathan
<506.4.A94> Original texts (Hebrew or Aramaic). By date
<506.4.A94A-.A94Z> Translations. By language, A-Z
<506.4.A942> Selections. By date
<506.4.A943> Criticism. Commentaries, etc.
Derekh ereẓ

Sources
Rabbinical literature
Talmudic literature
Talmud. Talmud Bavli. Babylonian Talmud
Minor tractates (not part of the Mishnah)
Individual minor tractates, A-Z
Derekh ereẓ -- Continued

<506.4.D4> Original texts (Hebrew or Aramaic). By date
<506.4.D4A-.D4Z> Translations. By language, A-Z
<506.4.D5> Selections. By date
<506.4.D6> Criticism. Commentaries, etc.

Evel
see BM506.4.S4+
Cf. KBM506.4.S4+ Semaḥot

Gerim
<506.4.G4> Original texts (Hebrew or Aramaic). By date
<506.4.G4A-.G4Z> Translations. By language, A-Z
<506.4.G42> Selections. By date
<506.4.G43> Criticism. Commentaries, etc.

Kallah
<506.4.K3> Original texts (Hebrew or Aramaic). By date
<506.4.K3A-.K3Z> Translations. By language, A-Z
<506.4.K32> Selections. By date
<506.4.K33> Criticism. Commentaries, etc.

Kallah rabbati
<506.4.K35> Original texts (Hebrew or Aramaic). By date
<506.4.K35A-.K35Z> Translations. By language, A-Z
<506.4.K352> Selections. By date
<506.4.K353> Criticism. Commentaries, etc.

Kutim
<506.4.K8> Original texts (Hebrew or Aramaic). By date
<506.4.K8A-.K8Z> Translations. By language, A-Z
<506.4.K82> Selections. By date
<506.4.K83> Criticism. Commentaries, etc.

Mezuzah
<506.4.M48> Original texts (Hebrew or Aramaic). By date
<506.4.M48A-.M48Z> Translations. By language, A-Z
<506.4.M482> Selections. By date
<506.4.M483> Criticism. Commentaries, etc.

Semaḥot. Evel
<506.4.S4> Original texts (Hebrew or Aramaic). By date
<506.4.S4A-.S4Z> Translations. By language, A-Z
<506.4.S42> Selections. By date
<506.4.S43> Criticism. Commentaries, etc.

Soferim
<506.4.S6> Original texts (Hebrew or Aramaic). By date
<506.4.S6A-.S6Z> Translations. By language, A-Z

Sources
Rabbinical literature
Talmudic literature
Talmud. Talmud Bavli. Babylonian Talmud
Minor tractates (not part of the Mishnah)
Individual minor tractates, A-Z
Soferim -- Continued
<506.4.S62> Selections. By date
<506.4.S63> Criticism. Commentaries, etc.
Tsitsit
see BM506.4.Z5+
Cf. KBM506.4.Z5+ Ẓiẓit
Ẓiẓit
<506.4.Z5> Original texts (Hebrew or Aramaic). By date
<506.4.Z5A-.Z5Z> Translations. By language, A-Z
<506.4.Z52> Selections. By date
<506.4.Z53> Criticism. Commentaries, etc.
Baraita
<507> Collections
<507.2> Works on the Baraita
<507.5.A-Z> Individual baraitot, A-Z
Baraita de-Melekhet ha-Mishkan
see BM507.5.E6+
Cf. KBM507.5.E6+ Baraita on the Erection of the tabernacle
Baraita on the Aboth (Abot)
<507.5.A2> Original texts (Hebrew or Aramaic). By date
<507.5.A2A-.A2Z> Translations. By language, A-Z
<507.5.A3> Selections. By date
<507.5.A4> Criticism. Commentaries, etc.
Baraita of Rabbi Ada
<507.5.A5> Original texts (Hebrew or Aramaic). By date
<507.5.A5A-.A5Z> Translations. By language, A-Z
<507.5.A6> Selections. By date
<507.5.A7> Criticism. Commentaries, etc.
Baraita on the Erection of the tabernacle
<507.5.E6> Original texts (Hebrew or Aramaic). By date
<507.5.E6A-.E6Z> Translations. By language, A-Z
<507.5.E7> Selections. By date
<507.5.E8> Criticism. Commentaries, etc.
Baraita of the Forty-nine rules
<507.5.F5> Original texts (Hebrew or Aramaic). By date
<507.5.F5A-.F5Z> Translations. By language, A-Z
<507.5.F6> Selections. By date
<507.5.F7> Criticism. Commentaries, etc.
Baraita of Rabbi Ishmael (Yishma'el)
<507.5.I7> Original texts (Hebrew or Aramaic). By date

Sources
Rabbinical literature
Talmudic literature
Talmud. Talmud Bavli. Babylonian Talmud
Baraita
Individual baraitot, A-Z
Baraita of Rabbi Ishmael (Yishma'el) -- Continued
<507.5.I7A-.I7Z> Translations. By language, A-Z
<507.5.I8> Selections. By date
<507.5.I9> Criticism. Commentaries, etc.
Baraita de-Melekhet ha-Mishkan see KBM507.5.E6+
Baraita of the Mystery of the calculation of the calendar
<507.5.M7> Original texts (Hebrew or Aramaic). By date
<507.5.M7A-.M7Z> Translations. By language, A-Z
<507.5.M8> Selections. By date
<507.5.M9> Criticism. Commentaries, etc.
Baraita de-Niddah
<507.5.N4> Original texts (Hebrew or Aramaic). By date
<507.5.N4A-.N4Z> Translations. By language, A-Z
<507.5.N5> Selections. By date
<507.5.N6> Criticism. Commentaries, etc.
Baraita of Rabbi Phinehas ben Jair
Including sayings on Messianic times and on Sotah IX.15
<507.5.P4> Original texts (Hebrew or Aramaic). By date
<507.5.P4A-.P4Z> Translations. By language, A-Z
<507.5.P5> Selections. By date
<507.5.P6> Criticism. Commentaries, etc.
Baraita on Salvation
<507.5.S2> Original texts (Hebrew or Aramaic). By date
<507.5.S2A-.S2Z> Translations. By language, A-Z
<507.5.S3> Selections. By date
<507.5.S4> Criticism. Commentaries, etc.
Baraita of Samuel
<507.5.S6> Original texts (Hebrew or Aramaic). By date
<507.5.S6A-.S6Z> Translations. By language, A-Z
<507.5.S7> Selections. By date
<507.5.S8> Criticism. Commentaries, etc.
Baraita of the Thirty-two rules
<507.5.T4> Original texts (Hebrew or Aramaic). By date
<507.5.T4A-.T4Z> Translations. By language, A-Z
<507.5.T5> Selections. By date
<507.5.T6> Criticism. Commentaries, etc.
Tosefta
<508.A-Z> Editions. By editor, A-Z

Sources
Rabbinical literature
Talmudic literature
Talmud. Talmud Bavli. Babylonian Talmud
Tosefta -- Continued
<508.12> Selections. By editor or date
<508.13.A-Z> Translations. By language, A-Z
Under each language:
.x Complete texts. By date
.x2 Selections. By editor or date
<508.15> Concordances. Subject dictionaries, indexes, etc.
<508.2> Works on the Tosefta
<508.5.A-Z> Individual orders and tractates, A-Z (Table KBM1)
<509.A-Z> Special topics, A-Z
For list of Cutter numbers see BM496.9.A+
Cf. KBM496.9.A+ Special topics in rabbinical literature
Midrash
<510> Original language (Hebrew or Aramaic)
<511-513> Translations
<514> Works about the midrash
<515> Halakhic midrashim. Midreshei halakhah
Including collections and works about the halakhic midrashim
Aggada
Including Talmudic Aggada
<516.A-Z> Texts. By author or title, A-Z
Under each:
.x Original. By date
.x2A-.x2Z Translations. By language, A-Z and date
.x3 Criticism, commentaries, etc.
<516.5> Works about the Aggada
<517.A-Z> Individual midrashim, A-Z
Abba Guryon
<517.A1> Original texts (Hebrew or Aramaic). By date
<517.A1A-.A1Z> Translations. By language, A-Z
<517.A12> Selections. By date
<517.A13> Criticism. Commentaries, etc.
Abkir (Avkir)
<517.A2> Original texts (Hebrew or Aramaic). By date
<517.A2A-.A2Z> Translations. By language, A-Z
<517.A22> Selections. By date
<517.A23> Criticism. Commentaries, etc.
Aggadat Bereshit
<517.A3> Original texts (Hebrew or Aramaic). By date
<517.A3A-.A3Z> Translations. By language, A-Z

Sources
Rabbinical literature
Midrash
Individual midrashim, A-Z
Aggadat Bereshit -- Continued
<517.A32> Selections. By date
<517.A33> Criticism. Commentaries, etc.
Aggadat Ester
<517.A34> Original texts (Hebrew or Aramaic). By date
<517.A34A-.A34Z> Translations. By language, A-Z
<517.A35> Selections. By date
<517.A36> Criticism. Commentaries, etc.
Al yithalel
<517.A4> Original texts (Hebrew or Aramaic). By date
<517.A4A-.A4Z> Translations. By language, A-Z
<517.A5> Selections. By date
<517.A6> Criticism. Commentaries, etc.
Alef bet
see BM517.A63+ KBM517.A63+
Alef bet de-Rabbi Akiva
see BM517.O8+ KBM517.O8+
Aleph beth
<517.A63> Original texts (Hebrew or Aramaic). By date
<517.A63A-.A63Z> Translations. By language, A-Z
<517.A632> Selections. By date
<517.A633> Criticism. Commentaries, etc.
'A'seret ha-dibrot
<517.A7> Original texts (Hebrew or Aramaic). By date
<517.A7A-.A7Z> Translations. By language, A-Z
<517.A8> Selections. By date
<517.A9> Criticism. Commentaries, etc.
Avkir
see BM517.A2+ KBM517.A2+
Bamidbar rabbah
see BM517.M68+ KBM517.M68+
Baraita of Rabbi Eliezer
see BM517.P7+ KBM517.P7+
Baraita of Rabbi Phinehas ben Jair (Genesis)
see BM517.T3+ KBM517.T3+
Bereshit rabati
<517.B7> Original texts (Hebrew or Aramaic). By date
<517.B7A-.B7Z> Translations. By language, A-Z
<517.B72> Selections. By date
<517.B73> Criticism. Commentaries, etc.
Bereshit rabbah
see BM517.M65+ KBM517.M65+
Bereshit zuta

Sources
Rabbinical literature
Midrash
Individual midrashim, A-Z
Bereshit zuta -- Continued
<517.B8> Original texts (Hebrew or Aramaic). By date
<517.B8A-.B8Z> Translations. By language, A-Z
<517.B82> Selections. By date
<517.B83> Criticism. Commentaries, etc.
Devarim rabbah see KBM517.M69+
Devarim zuta
<517.D4> Original texts (Hebrew or Aramaic). By date
<517.D4A-.D4Z> Translations. By language, A-Z
<517.D42> Selections. By date
<517.D43> Criticism. Commentaries, etc.
Divrei ha-yamim shel Moshe
<517.D5> Original texts (Hebrew or Aramaic). By date
<517.D5A-.D5Z> Translations. By language, A-Z
<517.D6> Selections. By date
<517.D7> Criticism. Commentaries, etc.
Eikhah rabbah
see BM517.M74+ KBM517.M74+
Eleh ezkerah. Ma'a'seh 'a'sarah haruge malkhut
<517.E5> Original texts (Hebrew or Aramaic). By date
<517.E5A-.E5Z> Translations. By language, A-Z
<517.E52> Selections. By date
<517.E53> Criticism. Commentaries, etc.
Eser galuyyot
<517.E6> Original texts (Hebrew or Aramaic). By date
<517.E6A-.E6Z> Translations. By language, A-Z
<517.E62> Selections. By date
<517.E63> Criticism. Commentaries, etc.
Esfah
<517.E7> Original texts (Hebrew or Aramaic). By date
<517.E7A-.E7Z> Translations. By language, A-Z
<517.E72> Selections. By date
<517.E73> Criticism. Commentaries, etc.
Esther rabbah
see BM517.M76+ KBM517.M76+
Midrash ha-gadol
see BM517.M5+ KBM517.M5+
Ḥamesh Megillot
see BM517.M7+ KBM517.M7+
Ḥaserot vi-yeterot
see BM517.T2+ KBM517.T2+
Iyov
<517.I7> Original texts (Hebrew or Aramaic). By date

Sources
Rabbinical literature
Midrash
Individual midrashim, A-Z
Iyov -- Continued
<517.I7A-.I7Z> Translations. By language, A-Z
<517.I8> Selections. By date
<517.I9> Criticism. Commentaries, etc.
Kohelet
<517.K5> Original texts (Hebrew or Aramaic). By date
<517.K5A-.K5Z> Translations. By language, A-Z
<517.K6> Selections. By date
<517.K7> Criticism. Commentaries, etc.
Kohelet rabbah
see BM517.M75+ KBM517.M75+
Konen
<517.K8> Original texts (Hebrew or Aramaic). By date
<517.K8A-.K8Z> Translations. By language, A-Z
<517.K82> Selections. By date
<517.K83> Criticism. Commentaries, etc.
Ma'a'seh 'a'sarah haruge malkhut
see BM517.E5+ KBM517.E5+
Ma'a'seh Torah
<517.M2> Original texts (Hebrew or Aramaic). By date
<517.M2A-.M2Z> Translations. By language, A-Z
<517.M22> Selections. By date
<517.M23> Criticism. Commentaries, etc.
Mekhilta of Rabbi Ishmael
<517.M4> Original texts (Hebrew or Aramaic). By date
<517.M4A-.M4Z> Translations. By language, A-Z
<517.M42> Selections. By date
<517.M43> Criticism. Commentaries, etc.
Mekhilta of Rabbi Simeon ben Yoḥai
<517.M45> Original texts (Hebrew or Aramaic). By date
<517.M45A-.M45Z> Translations. By language, A-Z
<517.M46> Selections. By date
<517.M47> Criticism. Commentaries, etc.
Midrash ha-gadol
<517.M5> Original texts (Hebrew or Aramaic). By date
<517.M5A-.M5Z> Translations. By language, A-Z
<517.M52> Selections. By date
<517.M53> Criticism. Commentaries, etc.
Special parts
Genesis
<517.M55> Texts. By date
Translations
<517.M55A3> English. By date

Sources
Rabbinical literature
Midrash
Individual midrashim, A-Z
Midrash ha-gadol
Special parts
Genesis
Translations -- Continued
<517.M55A32-.M55A49> Other languages, alphabetically. By date
<517.M55A5-.M55Z> Criticism. Commentaries, etc.
Exodus
<517.M56> Texts. By date
Translations
<517.M56A3> English. By date
<517.M56A32-.M56A49> Other languages, alphabetically. By date
<517.M56A5-.M56Z> Criticism. Commentaries, etc.
Leviticus
<517.M57> Texts. By date
Translations
<517.M57A3> English. By date
<517.M57A32-.M57A49> Other languages, alphabetically. By date
<517.M57A5-.M57Z> Criticism. Commentaries, etc.
Numbers
<517.M58> Texts. By date
Translations
<517.M58A3> English. By date
<517.M58A32-.M58A49> Other languages, alphabetically. By date
<517.M58A5-.M58Z> Criticism. Commentaries, etc.
Deuteronomy
<517.M59> Texts. By date
Translations
<517.M59A3> English. By date
<517.M59A32-.M59A49> Other languages, alphabetically. By date
<517.M59A5-.M59Z> Criticism. Commentaries, etc.
Midrash rabbah
<517.M6> Original texts (Hebrew or Aramaic). By date
<517.M6A-.M6Z> Translations. By language, A-Z
<517.M62> Selections. By date
<517.M63> Criticism. Commentaries, etc.
Special parts
Pentateuch
<517.M64> Texts. By date

Sources
Rabbinical literature
Midrash
Individual midrashim, A-Z
Midrash rabbah
Special parts
Pentateuch -- Continued
Translations
<517.M64A3> English. By date
<517.M64A32-.M64A49> Other languages, alphabetically. By date
<517.M64A5-.M64Z> Criticism. Commentaries, etc.
Genesis. Bereshit rabbah
<517.M65> Texts. By date
Translations
<517.M65A3> English. By date
<517.M65A32-.M65A49> Other languages, alphabetically. By date
<517.M65A5-.M65Z> Criticism. Commentaries, etc.
Exodus. Shemot rabbah
<517.M66> Texts. By date
Translations
<517.M66A3> English. By date
<517.M66A32-.M66A49> Other languages, alphabetically. By date
<517.M66A5-.M66Z> Criticism. Commentaries
Leviticus. Vayikra rabbah
<517.M67> Texts. By date
Translations
<517.M67A3> English. By date
<517.M67A32-.M67A49> Other languages, alphabetically. By date
<517.M67A5-.M67Z> Criticism. Commentaries, etc.
Numbers. Bamidbar rabbah
<517.M68> Texts. By date
Translations
<517.M68A3> English. By date
<517.M68A32-.M68A49> Other languages, alphabetically. By date
<517.M68A5-.M68Z> Criticism. Commentaries, etc.
Deuteronomy. Devarim rabbah
<517.M69> Texts. By date
Translations
<517.M69A3> English. By date
<517.M69A32-.M69A49> Other languages, alphabetically. By date
<517.M69A5-.M69Z> Criticism. Commentaries, etc.

Sources
Rabbinical literature
Midrash
Individual midrashim, A-Z
Midrash rabbah
Special parts -- Continued
Five Scrolls. Ḥamesh Megillot

<517.M7> Texts. By date
Translations
<517.M7A3> English. By date
<517.M7A32-.M7A49> Other languages, alphabetically. By date
<517.M7A5-.M7Z> Criticism. Commentaries, etc.

Song of Solomon. Shir ha-shirim rabbah
<517.M72> Texts. By date
Translations
<517.M72A3> English. By date
<517.M72A32-.M72A49> Other languages, alphabetically. By date
<517.M72A5-.M72Z> Criticism. Commentaries, etc.

Ruth. Ruth rabbah
<517.M73> Texts. By date
Translations
<517.M73A3> English. By date
<517.M73A32-.M73A49> Other languages, alphabetically. By date
<517.M73A5-.M73Z> Criticism. Commentaries, etc.

Lamentations. Eikhah rabbah
<517.M74> Texts. By date
Translations
<517.M74A3> English. By date
<517.M74A32-.M74A49> Other languages, alphabetically. By date
<517.M74A5-.M74Z> Criticism. Commentaries, etc.

Ecclesiastes. Kohelet rabbah
<517.M75> Texts. By date
Translations
<517.M75A3> English. By date
<517.M75A32-.M75A49> Other languages, alphabetically. By date
<517.M75A5-.M75Z> Criticsm. Commentaries, etc.

Esther. Esther rabbah
<517.M76> Texts. By date
Translations
<517.M76A3> English. By date
<517.M76A32-.M76A49> Other languages, alphabetically. By date

Sources
Rabbinical literature
Midrash
Individual midrashim, A-Z
Midrash rabbah
Special parts
Five Scrolls. Ḥamesh Megillot
Esther. Esther rabbah -- Continued

<517.M76A5-.M76Z> Criticism. Commentaries, etc.

Mishle. Proverbs

<517.M77> Original texts (Hebrew or Aramaic). By date
<517.M77A-.M77Z> Translations. By language, A-Z
<517.M78> Selections. By date
<517.M79> Criticism. Commentaries, etc.

Otiyyot de-Rabbi Akiva

<517.O8> Original texts (Hebrew or Aramaic). By date
<517.O8A-.O8Z> Translations. By language, A-Z
<517.O82> Selections. By date
<517.O83> Criticism. Commentaries, etc.

Panim a ḥerim le-Esther

<517.P1> Original texts (Hebrew or Aramaic). By date
<517.P1A-.P1Z> Translations. By language, A-Z
<517.P12> Selections. By date
<517.P13> Criticism. Commentaries, etc.

Peli'ah

<517.P2> Original texts (Hebrew or Aramaic). By date
<517.P2A-.P2Z> Translations. By language, A-Z
<517.P22> Selections. By date
<517.P23> Criticism. Commentaries, etc.

Pesikta

<517.P3> Original texts (Hebrew or Aramaic). By date
<517.P3A-.P3Z> Translations. By language, A-Z
<517.P32> Selections. By date
<517.P33> Criticism. Commentaries, etc.

Pesikta de-Rav Kahana

<517.P34> Original texts (Hebrew or Aramaic). By date
<517.P34A-.P34Z> Translations. By language, A-Z
<517.P35> Selections. By date
<517.P36> Criticism. Commentaries, etc.

Pesikta rabbati

<517.P4> Original texts (Hebrew or Aramaic). By date
<517.P4A-.P4Z> Translations. By language, A-Z
<517.P42> Selctions. By date
<517.P43> Criticism. Commentaries, etc.

Peṭirat Aharon

<517.P5> Original texts (Hebrew or Aramaic). By date
<517.P5A-.P5Z> Translations. By language, A-Z

Sources
Rabbinical literature
Midrash
Individual midrashim, A-Z
Peṭirat Aharon -- Continued
<517.P52> Selections. By date
<517.P53> Criticism. Commentaries, etc.
Peṭirat Mosheh
<517.P6> Original texts (Hebrew or Aramaic). By date
<517.P6A-.P6Z> Translations. By language, A-Z
<517.P62> Selections. By date
<517.P63> Criticism. Commentaries, etc.
Pirkei de-Rabbi Eliezer
<517.P7> Original texts (Hebrew or Aramaic). By date
<517.P7A-.P7Z> Translations. By language, A-Z
<517.P72> Selections. By date
<517.P73> Criticism. Commentaries, etc.
Proverbs see KBM517.M77+
Midrash rabbah see KBM517.M6+
Ruth rabbah see KBM517.M73+
Samuel see KBM517.S4+
Shemot rabbah see KBM517.M66+
Shemu'el. Samuel
<517.S4> Original texts (Hebrew or Aramaic). By date
<517.S4A-.S4Z> Translations. By language, A-Z
<517.S42> Selections. By date
<517.S43> Criticism. Commentaries, etc.
Shir ha-shirim
<517.S45> Original texts (Hebrew or Aramaic). By date
<517.S45A-.S45Z> Translations. By language, A-Z
<517.S46> Selections. By date
<517.S47> Criticism. Commentaries, etc.
Shir ha-shirim rabbah see KBM517.M72+
Shoḥerṭov see KBM517.M77+
Shoḥerṭov see KBM517.S4+
Shoḥerṭov see KBM517.T5+
Sifra. Torat Kohanim
<517.S6> Original texts (Hebrew or Aramaic). By date
<517.S6A-.S6Z> Translations. By language, A-Z
<517.S62> Selections. By date
<517.S63> Criticism. Commentaries, etc.
Sifrei
<517.S7> Original texts (Hebrew or Aramaic). By date
<517.S7A-.S7Z> Translations. By language, A-Z
<517.S72> Selections. By date
<517.S73> Criticism. Commentaries, etc.
Special parts

Sources
Rabbinical literature
Midrash
Individual midrashim, A-Z
Sifrei
Special parts -- Continued
Numbers

<517.S74>	Texts. By date
	Translations
<517.S74A3>	English. By date
<517.S74A32-.S74A49>	Other languages, alphabetically. By date
<517.S74A5-.S74Z>	Criticism. Commentaries, etc.
	Deuteronomy
<517.S75>	Texts. By date
	Translations
<517.S75A3>	English. By date
<517.S75A32-.S75A49>	Other languages, alphabetically. By date
<517.S75A5-.S75Z>	Criticism. Commentaries, etc.
	Sifrei zuta
<517.S85>	Original texts (Hebrew or Aramaic). By date
<517.S85A-.S85Z>	Translations. By language, A-Z
<517.S86>	Selections. By date
<517.S87>	Criticism. Commentaries, etc.
	Ta'ame ḥaserot vi-yeterot
<517.T2>	Original texts (Hebrew or Aramaic). By date
<517.T2A-.T2Z>	Translations. By language, A-Z
<517.T22>	Selections. By date
<517.T23>	Criticism. Commentaries, etc.
	Tadshe
<517.T3>	Original texts (Hebrew or Aramaic). By date
<517.T3A-.T3Z>	Translations. By language, A-Z
<517.T32>	Selections. By date
<517.T33>	Criticism. Commentaries, etc.
	Tanḥuma. Yelammedenu
<517.T35>	Original texts (Hebrew or Aramaic). By date
<517.T35A-.T35Z>	Translations. By language, A-Z
<517.T36>	Selections. By date
<517.T37>	Criticism. Commentaries, etc.
	Tanna de-vei Eliyahu
	In two parts: (1) Seder Eliyahu rabbah; (2) Seder Eliyahu zuta
<517.T4>	Original texts (Hebrew or Aramaic). By date
<517.T4A-.T4Z>	Translations. By language, A-Z
<517.T42>	Selections. By date
<517.T43>	Criticism. Commentaries, etc.

Sources
Rabbinical literature
Midrash
Individual midrashim, A-Z -- Continued

	Tehillim
<517.T5>	Original texts (Hebrew or Aramaic). By date
<517.T5A-.T5Z>	Translations. By language, A-Z
<517.T52>	Selections. By date
<517.T53>	Criticism. Commentaries, etc.
	Temurah
<517.T6>	Original texts (Hebrew or Aramaic). By date
<517.T6A-.T6Z>	Translations. By language, A-Z
<517.T7>	Selections. By date
<517.T8>	Criticism. Commentaries, etc.
	Torat Kohanim see KBM517.S6+
	Va-yekhullu
<517.V2>	Original texts (Hebrew or Aramaic). By date
<517.V2A-.V2Z>	Translations. By language, A-Z
<517.V22>	Selections. By date
<517.V23>	Criticism. Commentaries, etc.
	Ṿa-yiḳra rabbah see KBM517.M67+
	Va-yissa'u
<517.V4>	Original texts (Hebrew or Aramaic). By date
<517.V4A-.V4Z>	Translations. By language, A-Z
<517.V42>	Selections. By date
<517.V43>	Criticism. Commentaries, etc.
	Va-yosha'
<517.V5>	Original texts (Hebrew or Aramaic). By date
<517.V5A-.V5Z>	Translations. By language, A-Z
<517.V52>	Selections. By date
<517.V53>	Criticism. Commentaries, etc.
	Vayikra rabbah see KBM517.M67+
	Ve-hizhir
<517.V6>	Original texts (Hebrew or Aramaic). By date
<517.V6A-.V6Z>	Translations. By language, A-Z
<517.V7>	Selections. By date
<517.V8>	Criticism. Commentaries, etc.
	Yalkut ha-Makhiri
<517.Y2>	Original texts (Hebrew or Aramaic). By date
<517.Y2A-.Y2Z>	Translations. By language, A-Z
<517.Y22>	Selections. By date
<517.Y23>	Criticism. Commentaries, etc.
	Yalkut Shimoni
<517.Y3>	Original texts (Hebrew or Aramaic). By date
<517.Y3A-.Y3Z>	Translations. By language, A-Z
<517.Y32>	Selections. By date
<517.Y33>	Criticism. Commentaries, etc.

Sources
Rabbinical literature
Midrash
Individual midrashim, A-Z -- Continued
Yelammedenu see KBM517.T35+
Yesha'yah
<517.Y4> Original texts (Hebrew or Aramaic). By date
<517.Y4A-.Y4Z> Translations. By language, A-Z
<517.Y5> Selections. By date
<517.Y6> Criticism. Commentaries, etc.
Yonah
<517.Y7> Original texts (Hebrew or Aramaic). By date
<517.Y7A-.Y7Z> Translations. By language, A-Z
<517.Y8> Selections. By date
<517.Y9> Criticism. Commentaries, etc.
Midrash zuta
<517.Z8> Original texts (Hebrew or Aramaic). By date
<517.Z8A-.Z8Z> Translations. By language, A-Z
<517.Z82> Selections. By date
<517.Z83> Criticism. Commentaries, etc.
<518.A-Z> Special topics, A-Z
For list of Cutter numbers see BM496.9.A+
Cf. KBM496.9.A+ Special topics in rabbinical literature
Halakhah
Class here works on Jewish law (Halakhah) including works limited to the ritual aspects of Jewish law
For works limited to mishpat Ivri see KBM523.8+
<520> Periodicals. Serials
Including yearbooks
For law periodicals see KB7+
For legal monographic series see KBM523.82
Collected works
<520.2> Several authors
<520.3> Individual authors
<520.32> Bibliography
For bibliography on mishpat Ivri see KBM523.8
For bibliography of Jewish law (Halakhah) see Z6374.L4
<520.4> Encyclopedias. Dictionaries
Including encyclopedias and dictionaries limited to mishpat Ivri
For dictionaries on Israeli law, see KMK26
For Hebrew language, and multilingual, law dictionaries see K50+
Yearbooks. Annuals see KB8+
<520.42> Directories
<520.43> Legal research. Methods of research on Jewish law
Including information services and computer network resources

Halakhah -- Continued
<520.45> Law societies. Associations
<520.46> Conferences. Symposia
Including papers presented at the conference or symposium
History
Cf. DS114+ History of the Jews
For history of Judaism see BM150+
For constitutional history of the Jewish community see KBM2085+
Cf. KBM150+ History of Judaism
<520.5> General (Comparative)
By period
To 500
Including the period of the redaction of the Talmud
For works on the history and development of the Talmud see BM501.15+
Cf. KBM501.15+ Works on the history and development of the Talmud
<520.52> General works
Special topics
see the topic
500-1500
<520.53> General works
Special topics
see the topic
1500-1800
<520.54> General works
Special topics
see the topic
1800-1948
<520.55> General works
Special topics
see the topic
1948-
<520.56> General works
Special topics
see the topic
<520.6> Philosophy (General)
Cf. KBM524.12+ Concept of Jewish law
Sources. Halakhic portions of the Hebrew Bible, Talmudic literature, and Midrash see BM450+
Cf. KBM450+ Tanakh. Hebrew Bible
Commandments. Mitsvot
<520.7> General works

Halakhah
Commandments. Mitsvot -- Continued
<520.73> Noahide Laws. Sheva‘ mitzvot bene Noaḥ
Cf. BP605.N63 Noahides. Noachide movement
Cf. KBM524.15 Relationship of Jewish law to natural law and international law
Cf. KBM529.7.N65 Legal status of non-Jews under halakhah
<520.75> Ten Commandments. ‘Aśeret ha-dibrot
Class here works on the precepts of the Ten Commandments in Judaism
Cf. BS1281+ Texts and criticism of the Ten commandments
<520.8> Six hundred and thirteen commandments. Taryag mitsvot
Codes. Restatements of halakhah. Posekim
For excerpts or selections based on a particular subject, see the subject
For works on codification see BM521
Cf. KBM521 Works on codification
Alfasi, Isaac ben Jacob, 1013-1103. Halakhot
<520.82.A2> Original texts. By date
<520.82.A21-.A219> Translations. By language
Subarrange by translator
<520.82.A3-Z> Criticisms, commentaries, etc.
Maimonides, Moses, 1135-1204 (Moses ben Maimon). Mishneh Torah
<520.84.A2> Original texts. By date
<520.84.A21-.A219> Translations. By language
Subarrange by translator
<520.84.A3-Z> Criticism, commentaries, etc.
Jacob ben Asher, ca. 1269-ca. 1340. Arba‘ah ṭurim
<520.86.A2> Original texts. By date
<520.86.A3-.A39> Original selections. By date
<520.86.A4-.A49> Translations. By language
Subarrange by translator
Special parts
Oraḥ ḥayim
<520.86.A52> Texts
<520.86.A53> Criticism, commentaries, etc.
Yoreh de‘ah
<520.86.A54> Texts
<520.86.A55> Criticism, commentaries, etc.
Even ha-‘ezer
<520.86.A56> Texts
<520.86.A57> Criticism, commentaries, etc.
Ḥoshen mishpaṭ
<520.86.A58> Texts

Halakhah
Codes. Restatements of halakhah. Posekim
Jacob ben Asher, ca. 1269-ca. 1340. Arba'ah ṭurim
Special parts
Ḥoshen mishpaṭ -- Continued
<520.86.A59> Criticism, commentaries, etc.
<520.86.A6-Z> Criticism, commentaries, etc.
Karo, Joseph ben Ephraim, 1488-1575 (Caro, Joseph). Shulhan 'arukh
<520.88.A2> Original texts. By date
<520.88.A3-.A39> Original selections. By date
<520.88.A4-.A49> Translations. By language
Subarrange by translator
Special parts
Oraḥ ḥayim
<520.88.A52> Texts
<520.88.A53> Criticism, commentaries, etc.
Yoreh de'ah
<520.88.A54> Texts
<520.88.A55> Criticism, commentaries, etc.
Even ha-'ezer
<520.88.A56> Texts
<520.88.A57> Criticism, commentaries, etc.
Ḥoshen mishpaṭ
<520.88.A58> Texts
<520.88.A59> Criticism, commentaries, etc.
<520.88.A6-Z> Criticism, commentaries, etc.
<520.9> Other codes (after Shulḥan 'arukh)
<521> General works
Class here works on Jewish law (Halakhah) including works on codification
For general works limited to mishpat Ivri see KBM524
Responsa
For responsa on a particular subject, see the subject
For responsa arrangement applied at LC see BM522+
Alternative classification for Responsa
This classification of responsa is not applied at the Library of Congress
<521.15> Collections. Compilations. Selections
Class here responsa of authors from different periods or of authors whose period cannot be determined
By period
To 1040
Including the geonim
<521.2> Collected
<521.25> Individual. By author or title

Halakhah
Responsa
Alternative classification for Responsa, not applied at the Library of Congress
By period
1040-1500
Including the rishonim
<521.3> Collected
<521.35> Individual. By author or title
1500-1800
Including the aḥaronim
<521.4> Collected
<521.45> Individual. By author or title
1800-1948
<521.5> Collected
<521.55> Individual. By author or title
1948-
<521.6> Collected
<521.65> Individual. By author or title
By movement
Class here responsa issued by modern rabbinical assemblies
<521.7> Conservative
<521.8> Reform
<521.85> Orthodox
<523> Works on Responsa. History. Criticism
General and comparative works on specific areas of the law as defined by Shulḥan 'arukh
Including responsa and treatises on a single section
Oraḥ ḥayim law
<523.2> General works
<523.3.A-Z> Special topics, A-Z
Avot melakhot
see BM523.3.P7; KBM523.3.P7
Bein ha-shemashot
see BM523.3.T9; KBM523.3.T9
<523.3.B4> Benediction. Berakhah
Berakhah
see BM523.3.B4; KBM523.3.B4
Bet keneset see BM653+
Festivals. Ḥagim. Mo'adim see BM690+
Fringes. Zizith see BM657.F7
Ḥagim see BM690+
<523.3.I5> International date line
Cf. KBM524.4.T54 Time
Mo'adim see BM690+
Phylacteries. Tefillin see BM657.P5

Halakhah
General and comparative works on specific areas of the law as defined by Shulḥan ʻarukh
Oraḥ ḥayim law
Special topics, A-Z
<523.3.P7> Prohibited work. Avot melakhot
Cf. KBM3419 Conditions of trading
Cf. KBM3455 Carriage of goods and passengers
Sabbath. Shabbat see BM685
Shabbat see BM685
Synagogue. Bet keneset see BM653+
Tefillin see BM657.P5
<523.3.T9> Twilight. Bein ha-shemashot
Work see BM523.3.P7
Cf. KBM523.3.P7 Prohibited work. Avot melakhot
Zizith see BM657.F7
Yoreh deʻah law
<523.4> General works
<523.5.A-Z> Special topics, A-Z
Avelut see BM712
ʻAvodat elilim
see BM523.5.I3; KBM523.5.I3
<523.5.B4> Benevolence. Gemilut ḥasadim
Biḳur ḥolim see BM729.V5
Legal (civil) aspects see KBM3119.C57
Circumcision. Berit milah
Religious and ritual aspects see BM705
Dietary laws. Kashrut see BM710
Gemilut ḥasadim
see BM523.5.B4; KBM523.5.B4
Giluaḥ
see BM523.5.S53; KBM523.5.S53
<523.5.H3> Hallah
<523.5.I3> Idolatry. ʻAvodat elilim
Interest. Ribit see KBM955.4
Kashrut see BM710
Kibud av va-em
see BM523.5.R4; KBM523.5.R4
Mourning. Avelut see BM712
Pidyon ha-ben see BM720.R4
Purity. Ṭohorah see BM702+
Redemption of the firstborn. Pidyon ha-ben see BM720.R4
<523.5.R4> Respect to parents and teachers. Kibud av va-em
Cf. KBM3140+ Teachers in mishpat Ivri
Ribit see KBM955.4
<523.5.S5> Shaatnez

Halakhah
General and comparative works on specific areas of the law as defined by Shulḥan ʻarukh
Yoreh deʻah law
Special topics, A-Z -- Continued
<523.5.S53> Shaving. Giluaḥ
Slaughter of animals see BM720.S6+
Ṭohorah see BM702+
Visiting the sick. Biḳur ḥolim see BM729.V5
<523.5.W5> Wine and winemaking. Yayin
Yayin
see BM523.5.W5; KBM523.5.W5
523.6 Even ha-ʻezer law (General)
For works on religious and ritual aspects of special topics, see the topic in subclass BM
For works on legal (civil) aspects of special topics, see the topic in KBM523.8+
For agunahs see KBM550.5
For common law marriage see KBM546.17
For divorce (legal (civil) aspects) see KBM558+
For divorce (religious and ritual aspects) see BM713.5
For marriage (legal (civil) aspects) see KBM542+
For marriage (religious and ritual aspects) see BM713
For parent and child (legal (civil) aspects) see KBM587+
For parent and child (religious and ritual aspects) see BM725+
523.72 Ḥoshen mishpaṭ law (General)
For special topics, see the topic, e. g. Dinei mamonot, see KBM639+
Mishpat Ivri
Class here works on that part of halakhah which corresponds to concepts of contemporary legal systems and the rules governing relationships and interactions in modern society
For the law of a particular jurisdiction, see the jurisdiction, e. g. KMK, Israel
For periodicals see KB8+
523.8 Bibliography
523.82 Monographic series
Encyclopedias. Dictionaries
see BM520.4
Cf. KBM520.4 Encyclopedias. Dictionaries
Yearbooks. Annuals see KB8+
Directories
see BM520.42
Cf. KBM520.42 Directories

Mishpat Ivri -- Continued
Legal research. Methods of research on Jewish law
see BM520.43
Cf. KBM520.43 Halakhah
523.9 Legal education. Study and teaching
Law societies. Associations
see BM520.45
Cf. KBM520.45 Law societies. Associations
Conferences. Symposia
see BM520.46
Cf. KBM520.46 Conferences. Symposia
History
see BM520.5+
Cf. KBM520.5+ History
524 General works
The concept of Jewish law
524.12 Law and justice
524.13 Equity
524.14 Ethics. Morality of law. Public policy
Cf. KBM3098.5 Medical ethics
524.15 Relationship of Jewish law to natural law and international law
e. g. John Seldon, De iure naturali et gentium juxta disciplinam Ebræorum
Cf. BM520.73 Noahide laws
Cf. KBM520.73 Noahide laws
524.17 Legal positivism and contemporary Jewish law
Including dichotomy of halakhah
Divine law and secular authority to set and define law. Legal order. Respect for law
Cf. KBM2020+ Rule of law
524.2 General works
524.22 Rights and duties. Sanctions
524.24 Validity, nullity, and effectiveness of law
Including status of non-Jewish law (Dina de-malkhuta dina)
524.26 Legal certainty
524.3 Sources of Jewish law (Mishpat Ivri)
Including custom (minhag), oral law and its authoritative explication, and tradition; including legislation (takanot; communal ordinance, rules and regulations, etc.)
For Rabbinical literature see BM495+
For Tanakh (Hebrew Bible) see BS701+
Cf. KBM450+ Tanakh. Hebrew Bible
Methodology of law development
Including law integration, approximation, harmonization, etc.
524.32 Legal hermeneutics. Interpretation and construction
524.33 Legal semantics. Legal language

KBM

Mishpat Ivri
Methodology of law development -- Continued
524.34 Asmakhta
524.36 Influence of other legal systems on Jewish law
For comparisons of Jewish law with other legal or religious legal systems, including ancient systems, see KB190 and KB202+
524.38 Law reform and policies. Criticism
524.4.A-Z Concepts applying to several branches of the law, A-Z
Including diverse aspects of a particular subject falling within several branches of the law
524.4.C38 Causation. Gerama
Including proximate cause
524.4.C65 Computers
524.4.E65 Equality
524.4.F52 Fictions
524.4.G66 Good faith
524.4.K55 Ḳinyanim
524.4.P74 Privacy, Right of
524.4.T54 Time
524.4.T73 Trees
Cf. BM538.A4 Agriculture and Judaism
524.4.W75 Wrongful act, Prohibition of benefitting from. Isur hana'ah
524.42 Private law
Class here general works on all aspects of private law
524.43 Conflict of laws. Plurality of laws conflict
524.44 Civil law in general
524.5 Assistance in emergencies
Persons
524.6 General (Comparative)
Natural persons
Personality. Capacity and incapacity
524.7 General works
525 Minors. Ḳeṭanim
Women
526 General (Comparative)
528.A-Z Special topics, A-Z
529 Insane persons. People with mental disabilities. Shoṭeh
529.3 Slaves
529.7.A-Z Other types of natural persons, A-Z
Androginos see KBM529.7.H47
Goyim see KBM529.7.N65
529.7.H47 Hermaphrodites. Androginos. Persons of uncertain gender
529.7.N65 Non-Jews. Goyim. Gentiles
Persons of uncertain gender see KBM529.7.H47
529.7.U53 Unborn children. Fetus. 'Ubar

Mishpat Ivri
Persons
Natural persons
Personality. Capacity and incapacity -- Continued
529.8 Personality rights
Including personal names
Cf. CS3010 Jewish personal names
529.83 Jewishness. Mihu Yehudi. Who is a Jew?
For Jewishness under Israeli citizenship law see KMK1+
Conversion. Giyur
For religious aspects of conversion see BM645.C6
For legal aspects of conversion see KBM2448
530 Juristic persons. Corporations. Associations. Foundations
Domestic relations. Family law
531 General works
531.5 Ḥerem de-Rabenu Gershom
Marriage. Nissu'in
Cf. BM713 Jewish rites and customs of marriage
542 General works
Betrothal. Tenaim. Erusin
Including pre-betrothal arrangements (shiddukhin)
543 General works
543.5 Betrothal of girls under age of Bat Mitzvah. Child marriage
Impediments to marriage
544 General (Comparative)
544.2 Consanguinity and affinity. Incest
Including matrilineal and patrilineal ascendants and descendants
Cf. KBM583+ Domestic relations
544.5 Restrictions on cohanim. Ḥalal
544.6 Bigamy
544.7 Adultery
544.8 Mamzerim. Questionable mamzerim. Safeḳ mamzerim
Cf. KBM546.2 Marriage to non-Jews
Performance of marriage
Cf. BM713 Jewish marriage rites and customs
546 General works
546.13 Ketubah
Cf. KBM572 Ketubah as an economic document
546.14 Ḥuppah
546.15 Ḳiddushin
546.16 Consummation. Bi'ah
546.17 Irregular and de facto marriages. Yadu'a ba-tsibur. Marriage by reputation. Unmarried cohabitation. Concubinage. Pilegesh. Common law marriages

Mishpat Ivri
Domestic relations. Family law
Marriage. Nissu'in -- Continued
546.18 Validity and effect of civil marriages
546.2 Interfaith marriage. Marriage to non-Jews
546.3.A-Z Marriage of members of Jewish sects, A-Z
546.3.E86 Ethiopian Jews
546.3.K37 Karaites
546.3.S36 Samaritans
546.4 Multiple marriage. Polygamy
Cf. KBM562.7 Heter me'ah rabanim
546.5 Temporary marriage
Cf. HQ803 Temporary marriage (General)
Levirate marriage and ḥalitsah. Yibum see KBM563
Husband and wife. Rights and duties
547 General works
548 Matrimonial domicile. Choice of residence
548.3 Duty of husband to support wife. Mezonot
549 Family name
Legal status of married women
Including duties and obedience of wife towards husband
For marital property see KBM569
550 General works
550.5 Agunahs (Women who are barred from remarriage)
Including women whose husbands are missing and women whose husbands refuse to divorce them (de facto agunahs)
552 Sexual behavior within marriage
Cf. BM720.S4 Sex (Jewish rites and customs)
553.A-Z Special topics, A-Z
Matrimonial actions. Dissolution of marriage
555 General works
556 Defective marriage. Void or voidable marriage. Ḳidushe ṭa'ut. Mistake
Agunahs (Women whose husbands refuse to deliver a geṭ) see KBM550.5
Divorce. Gerushim
Cf. BM713.5 Jewish rites and customs
558 General works
Particular grounds for divorce
559 General works
559.3 Misconduct by wife. Rebellious wife. Moredet
559.6 Misconduct by husband
559.65 Impotence
Grounds for compelling a divorce
559.7 General works

Mishpat Ivri
Domestic relations. Family law
Matrimonial actions. Dissolution of marriage
Divorce. Gerushim
Particular grounds for divorce
Grounds for compelling a divorce -- Continued
559.8 Adultery
Cf. KBM544.7 Impediments to marriage
560 Reconciliation. Pursuit of Shelom bayit. Condonation
Procedure. Sidur ha-geṭ
562 General works
562.3 Geṭ. Bill of divorce
Cf. KBM549 Family name
562.4 Procedure if husband refuses to deliver a get. Heter me'ah rabanim
Including coercion (Kefiyah. Geṭ me'uśeh)
562.5 Use of non-Jewish courts as kefiyah
For use of non-Jewish courts to compel issuance of a get in specific countries, see the country, e. g. KFN5126.5
Status of women whose husbands refuse to divorce them (De facto agunahs) see KBM550.5
562.7 Procedure if wife refuses to accept a get
Including Heter me'ah rabanim
Cf. KBM562.4 Procedure if husband refuses to deliver a get
562.8 Initiation of divorce proceedings by wife
563 Levirate marriage. Ḥalitsah. Yibum
567 Settlement of economic claims from defective or dissolved marriages
Including alimony, dowry, payment of ketubah, etc.
Quasi-matrimonial relationships. Unmarried cohabitation see KBM546.17
Marital property and regime
569 General works
570 Statutory regimes. Takkanot ha-Ḳahal. Communal ordinances
572 Antenuptial contracts. Ketubah as an economic document
Cf. KBM546.13 Performance of marriage
573 Separation of property
574 Community of property
Property questions arising from unmarried cohabitation see KBM546.17
Consanguinity. Affinity. Kinship. Yiḥus
Cf. KBM544.2 Impediments to marriage
583 General works

Mishpat Ivri
Domestic relations. Family law
Consanguinity. Affinity. Kinship. Yiḥus -- Continued
584 Support
Parent and child
Cf. BM523.5.R4 Respect for parents
Cf. BM725+ Religious duties of parents
587 General works
Children
Including children from defective marriages, divorced marriages, etc.
589 General works
589.3 Non-Jewish children of Jews
Jewishness see KBM529.83
Parental power
598 General works
602 Custody. Access to children
Including parental kidnapping
Education see KBM3139.3
606 Property management
607 Parental power of mother
608 Stepchildren
609 Adoption. Raising a child not one's own
Illegitimacy. Mamzerut
612 General works
613 Mamzer. Legal status of a child of an incestuous or adulterous relationship
Paternity and maternity
Including patrilineal and matrilineal descendants and ascendants
616.5 General works
619.A-Z Special topics, A-Z
619.A77 Artificial insemination. Assisted reproduction. Surrogate motherhood
Cf. KBM3117 Public health
Mamzer see KBM613
619.P38 Paternity, Proof of
Including child of an adulterous relationship (Mamzer)
Surrogate motherhood see KBM619.A77
Guardian and ward. Apotropos
Including curatorship
622 General works
625 Guardianship over minors
Guardianship over adults
627 General works
Guardianship in marriage see KBM572

Mishpat Ivri
Guardian and ward. Apotropos -- Continued
628 Interdiction
628.5.A-Z Special topics, A-Z
Inheritance and succession
Including legal causes of inheritance, e. g. consanguinity, affinity, marriage, etc.
632 General works
Decedents' estates. Shares
Including claims against estate, and partition and distribution of estate
633 General works
633.2.A-Z Special topics, A-Z
Qualification as heir. Legal sharers
633.5 General works
Order of succession
634 General works
634.3.A-Z Special topics, A-Z
634.6 Exclusion from inheritance
Including slave quality, homicide, infidelity, apostasy, domicile, etc.
634.7 Liability. Debts of estate
Wills. Testamentary succession
635 General works
635.2 Legacies. Testamentary bequests. Distribution of estate
635.4 Executors and administrators of estate
636 Unworthiness of heir. Disinheritance
636.2 Gifts mortis causa
636.3 Gifts. Charitable gifts. Donations
Including donation for life and donation for the surviving party
Dinei mamonot
639 General works
Property. Res in commercio
640 General (Comparative)
Things. Types of property
642.3 Fungibles. Non-fungibles
Including fungibles such as measured, weighed, or counted things
Real (Immovable) property see KBM683+
643 Personal (Movable) property
644.A-Z Other, A-Z
Possession and ownership
Including owner and possessor
646 General works
Acquisition and transfer of possession and ownership
Including original and derivative acquisition
648 General works

Mishpat Ivri
Dinei mamonot
Property. Res in commercio
Possession and ownership
Acquisition and transfer of possession and ownership -- Continued
651 Dispossession
652 Possessory actions
Acquisition and loss of ownership
655 General works
656 Occupation
657 Lost property
658 Treasure troves
663 Acquisition of fruits and parts of things
672 Loss of ownership
Including abandonment and dereliction
674 Co-ownership. Joint ownership
For co-ownership of land see KBM694
675 Protection of ownership. Claims and actions resulting from ownership
Real (Immovable) property. Land law
683 General (Comparative)
685.5 Collective patrimony
Acquisition and loss of ownership
Including vendor and purchaser
687.5 General works
687.6 Occupation of waste land by cultivator
694 Co-ownership of land. Customary co-ownership of land
Cf. KBM698 Rights to water
Rights incident to ownership of land
695 General works
696 Air and space above ground
697 Underground. Minerals, metals, and other resources
698 Riparian rights. Water rights. Underground water
699 Hunting and fishing rights
Adjoining landowners
700 General works
701.A-Z Special topics, A-Z
Rights as to the use of another's land
706 General works
708 Commonage and pasture. Grazing rights
Servitudes
709 General works
710 Real servitudes
e. g. Right of way (passage); right to draw water
713 Personal servitude
715 Usufruct

Mishpat Ivri
Dinei mamonot
Property. Res in commercio
Real (Immovable) property. Land law -- Continued
716 Right of pre-emption
Pledges. Contracts of pledging
726 General works
728 Pledges of personal property
730 Pledges of rights
731 Retention to secure a claim
Class here general works
For particular rights in rem (lien), see KBM77.2; KBM81.3; KBM94
Land register. Registration of land titles
737 General works
743.A-Z Special topics, A-Z
745 Effect of registration
758 Cadastral surveys. Cadaster
Inheritance and succession see KBM632+
Obligations. Contracts and transactions
801 General (Comparative)
811 Debtor and creditor
812 Plurality of debtor and creditor. Joint obligations
Types of obligations
814 Civil and natural (aleatory) obligations
Cf. KBM899+ Aleatory contracts
814.5 Obligations to give
815 Obligations to do or refrain from doing
816 Transfer and assumption of obligations
Extinction of obligation
817 General works
Performance. Payment. Settlement. Acquittance
818 General works
820 Special rules as to payment of money debts
Bankruptcy. Discharge of debt according to secular law see KBM1942
822 Compensation for maintenance and improvement
822.5 Enforcement
823 Confusion of rights
823.5.A-Z Special topics, A-Z
Rescission see KBM869.3+
Withdrawal see KBM869.3+
Nonperformance
824 General works
824.5 Culpa
Including dolus and negligence
826 Breach of contract

Mishpat Ivri
Dinei mamonot
Obligations. Contracts and transactions
Nonperformance -- Continued
827.5 Default
Damages
For damages (compensation), including lost profits and damages for pain and suffering, see the particular torts under KBM842-853
For delict liability (liability for wrongful acts) see KBM834+
Delicts. Torts
Class here works on wrongful acts and damages
834 General works
Liability
Including dolus and negligence
839 General works
839.7 Liability for the torts of others
Individual torts and damages
Including lost profits and damages for pain and suffering
842 Violation of freedom
Physical injuries
842.2 General works
842.3 Accidents
842.6 Death by wrongful act
Violation of integrity
842.7 General works
842.8 Libel and slander
843 Violation of privacy
Immoral transactions see KBM868+
846 Deceit. Forgery. Misrepresentation
846.2 Usurpation of another's property. Theft
Breach of contract see KBM826
848 Sports. Sport fields or installations
852.4 Liability for environmental damage
For environmental crimes see KBM4351.5
853.A-Z Other liabilities, A-Z
853.E47 Emotional distress
853.F57 Fire
Unjust enrichment
854 General works
855 Restitution
857.A-Z Special topics, A-Z
Concepts and principles of contract law
858 General works
858.3 Liberty of contract. Party autonomy
858.5.A-Z Types of contracts, A-Z

Mishpat Ivri
Dinei mamonot
Obligations. Contracts and transactions
Concepts and principles of contract law
Types of contracts, A-Z -- Continued
858.5.O68 Option
859 Security. Secured and fiduciary transactions
For particular transactions, see KBM877.2; KBM881.3 KBM894
Intention. Declaration of intention
860 General works
Agency
861 General works
861.2 Criminal liability of agents and principals
Including agency for a criminal purpose (shaliaḥ li-devar 'averah)
862 Unauthorized representation. Falsus procurator
864 Mandate
866 Form requirements. Notice. Time of effectiveness
866.5 Risk
Void and voidable contracts and transactions. Nullity
867 General works
867.3 Mistake. Error
867.5 Fraud. Duress. Threat
Unconscionable transactions. Illegal contracts
868 General works
868.2 Usurious contracts
Formation of contracts
Including commercial contracts
869 General works
Offer and acceptance
Including withdrawal of offer and right of rescission
869.3 General works
869.55 Contracts by adhesion
869.6 Declaration of consent. Implied consent (conclusive act or gesture)
870 Clauses. Terms. Conditions
872 Stipulations
Cf. KBM869.3+ Right of rescission
872.5 Formalities
Parties to contract
873 General works
873.3 Third parties
873.8 Cancellation of contract
Individual contracts and transactions
Sale
874 General (Comparative)

Mishpat Ivri
Dinei mamonot
Obligations. Contracts and transactions
Individual contracts and transactions
Sale -- Continued
875 Warranty
876 Defects of goods sold
Including right of rescission
Modes of sale
Conditional sale
877 General works
877.2 Retention of ownership
877.3 Sale on credit
878.A-Z Other, A-Z
878.R47 Resale
Exchange of monetary assets or rights. Barter
879 General works
879.2.A-Z Special topics, A-Z
Pecuniary transaction without countervalue
Donations. Gifts see KBM636.3
879.23 Loan of non-fungibles
Lease. Landlord and tenant
880 General works
881.3 Liens of the landlord
884.A-Z Types of property, A-Z
Land lease see KBM884.R43
884.R43 Real property. Land lease
Fiduciary transactions. Trust and trustee
889 General works
Deposit see KBM896
890 Loan for use
891 Personal loans
Contract for service and labor. Master and servant
892 General works
892.3 Independent work. Professions
Dependent work. Hire and lease
892.5 General works
892.6 Servants and employees
Including rent and wage
892.7.A-Z Particular groups, A-Z
Contract for work and labor
Class here works on contracts concluded by independent contractor or artisan
893 General works
893.3.A-Z Particular contracts or tasks, A-Z
893.5 Liability and warranty
894 Security. Liens

Mishpat Ivri
Dinei mamonot
Obligations. Contracts and transactions
Individual contracts and transactions -- Continued
896 Deposit
Aleatory contracts. Natural obligations
899 General works
899.3 Gambling. Betting. Lotteries
900 Suretyship. Debtor and guarantor
Including suretyship for the person and for the claim
Commercial law. Commercial transactions
920 General works
Merchant and business enterprise
921 General works
923 Accounting
924 Agency and prokura
Including commercial employees, traveling salespeople, etc.
Commercial sale
926 General works
926.2.A-Z Particular, A-Z
926.2.C65 Consignation
926.2.D43 Default of buyer
926.2.F87 Futures
926.3.A-Z Special modes of selling, A-Z
926.3.F72 Franchises
926.3.T73 Traveling salespeople
926.5.A-Z Particular products or goods, A-Z
927 Commercial agents
928 Consignment. Commission merchant
929 Brokerage
930 Auctioneers. Auctions
930.3 Warehousing
931 Freight forwarders and carriers. Carriage of passengers and goods
Negotiable instruments. Titles of credit
937 General works
937.3 Possession, ownership, and transfer
938 Bills of exchange
Banks and banking
940 General (Comparative)
Banking transactions
951 General works
Loans. Credit
955 General works
955.2 Free loan societies. Gemach
955.4 Interest

Mishpat Ivri
Dinei mamonot
Obligations. Contracts and transactions
Commercial law. Commercial transactions
Banks and banking -- Continued
961.5 Commercial investments
962.8 Commodity exchanges. Produce exchanges
Maritime contracts. Maritime law
970 General works
970.97 Ships and ship owners. Ship masters
971 Affreightment. Carriage of goods at sea and inland waters
976 Carriage of passengers at sea and inland waters
Average
978 General works
979 Havarie grosse
980 Collision at sea
981 Salvage
984.5 Maritime courts
985 Marine insurance
Insurance law
998 General works
1020.A-Z Particular hazards, A-Z
1030 Particular risks and damages
Associations. Corporations
1040 General works
Partnerships. Personal companies
Including commercial partnerships
1043 General works
1043.3 Partners
Unlimited commercial partnership
1045 General works
1045.4 Equal shares
1045.6 Liability
Limited partnership
Including limited liability partnership
1047 General works
1047.4 Capital. Profits
1047.6 Liability
1048 Artisans' partnership
Silent partnership
1049 General works
1049.3 Silent partner
1049.4 Capital. Profits
1049.7 Termination. Dissolution
Stock companies. Incorporated business associations
1050 General works

Mishpat Ivri
Dinei mamonot
Obligations. Contracts and transactions
Commercial law. Commercial transactions
Associations. Corporations
Stock companies. Incorporated business associations
-- Continued
Corporate finance
1061 General works
1062 Capital stock
1064 Securities. Stocks. Bonds. Trust investments
1085 Termination. Dissolution. Liquidation
Cooperative societies
1120 General works
1131 Membership
1133.A-Z Types of cooperatives, A-Z
1134 Termination. Dissolution. Liquidation
Combinations. Industrial trusts
1137 General works
1138 Consortium
1139 Joint ventures
1147 Corporate reorganization
Insolvency and bankruptcy see KBM1885+
Intellectual and industrial property
1155 General works
1156 Principles
Copyright
1160 General works
1160.6 Scope of protection
1185 Author and publisher
1194 Patent law and trademarks
Unfair competition
1234 General works
1235 Public policy
1237 Advertising
1250 Rebates and premiums
Labor laws and legislation
1270 General works
Labor contract and employment
1279 General works
1295 Formation of contracts
1302 Void and voidable contracts. Immoral contracts
1303 Extinction of employment
1330 Wages
Protection of labor
1408 General works
1422 Child and youth labor

Mishpat Ivri
Dinei mamonot
Labor laws and legislation
Labor contract and employment
Protection of labor -- Continued
1424 Women's labor
Social laws and legislation
1468 Social reform and policies
1469 General works
Social insurance. Social security
1472 General works
1476 Coverage and benefits
1483 Health insurance
1495 Worker's compensation
1508 Old age, survivors, and disability insurance
1512 Unemployment insurance
Social service. Welfare
1520 General works
Social service beneficiaries
1528 The poor and destitute
1529 Older people
1530 Pensioners
1531 Large families
People with disabilities
Including people with physical, mental, and social disabilities
1532 General works
1534.A-Z Beneficiaries, A-Z
1534.B54 Blind
1534.D42 Deaf-mute
1534.S38 Severely disabled people
1536 Homeless persons
War-related and conflict-related groups of beneficiaries
1537 General works
1538 Refugees
1539 Soldiers. Prisoners. Ransoming of captives. Pidyon shevuyim
Including ex-prisoners and veterans
Children. Youth
1542 General works
Measures and provisions
1545 General works
1546 Protection of children in public
1547 Protection of children against obscenity
Courts and procedure
Administration of justice. Organization of the judiciary
1572 General works

Mishpat Ivri
Courts and procedure
Administration of justice. Organization of the judiciary -- Continued
1574 The judiciary and foreign relations
1575 Relationships with secular courts
Courts and tribunals
1580 General works
1582 Rabbinical Courts. Bet din
Ad hoc bet din see KBM1619
1586 Appeal from one court to another
Sanhedrin
1587 General works
1587.5 Proposals for restoration of the Sanhedrin
1588 Courts of special jurisdiction. Special tribunals. Arbitration
1593.A-Z Other public bodies with judicial functions, A-Z
1595 Court decorum and discipline
The legal profession. Court personnel
1600 General works
Judges. Dayyanim
1610 General works
1611 Women judges
1612 Independence of judges
1614 Ethics and discipline
1619 Arbitrators. Appointment of judges for an ad hoc bet din
Notaries see KBM1846+
Auxiliary personnel
1620 General works
1623 Court administration. Court records
1624 Bailiffs. Gabai or Shammash. Sheliaḥ bet din
Cf. BM659.A+ Religious functionaries
Experts and expert witnesses
1626 General works
1628.A-Z Special topics, A-Z
1630 Practice of law. Attorneys
Class here works on the practice of law before Jewish courts
For works on Jewish lawyers in a particular place see the law of the jurisdiction, e.g. KF299.J4
For the status under Jewish law of Jewish lawyers practicing in non-Jewish courts see KBM3522
Procedure in general
Including civil procedure
1650 General works
Procedural principles
1651 Due process of law
Parties to action

Mishpat Ivri
Courts and procedure
Procedure in general
Procedural principles
Parties to action -- Continued
1655 General works
1657 Litigants
Including third parties
Pretrial procedures
1660 General works
1662.A-Z Particular, A-Z
1662.S86 Summons. Hazmanah
1662.T56 Time periods. Deadlines
Including default and restitution
Procedure at trial
1663 General works
1664 Jurisdiction. Competence in subject matter and venue. The competent court
Actions and defenses. Types of proceedings
1666 General works
1667.A-Z Particular, A-Z
Evidence. Burden of proof
1672 General works
Witnesses. Testimony
1675 General works
1676 Privileged witnesses (Confidential communication). Expert testimony
1676.5 Testimony by a single witness. ʻEd eḥad
1676.7 Documentary evidence
1677.A-Z Special topics, A-Z
1677.H37 Ḥazaḳah
Oaths see KBM1677.S53
Presumptions see KBM1677.H37
1677.S53 Shevuot
Judicial decisions
1679 General works
1679.3 Judicial opinions. Advisory opinions
1679.5 Judicial errors. Mistakes
Including correction of judicial errors
1680.A-Z Particular decisions, A-Z
Remedies
1686 General works
1687 Appellate procedure
1690 Execution of judgment
1804 Particular procedures
1829 Arbitration
Notaries. Notarial practice and procedure

Mishpat Ivri
Courts and procedure
Notaries. Notarial practice and procedure -- Continued
1846 General works
1846.5 Jewish scribes. Soferim
Cf. BM659.S3 Practical Judaism
1847 Legal instruments. Certification
1850 Registration. Recording
1880 Inheritance (Probate court) procedure
Insolvency
1885 General works
1888 Execution
Including attachment and garnishment
1926 Remedies
1942 Bankruptcy
Public law. The state and the Jewish community. Kehillah
Class here comparative works on relationships between the Jewish community (kehillah) and governments (the state), and other ethnic or religious communities, as well as works on the internal governance of the Jewish community. For works on the status of Jews in a particular jurisdiction, or discussions of the state's legal and political institutions in halakhah, see the jurisdiction
Cf. BM538.S7 Judaism and state
2000 General works
Philosophy and theory
2015 Questions of sovereignty
Rule of law
For works on divine law and secular authority see KBM524.2+
Cf. KBM524.24 Dina de-malkhuta dina
2020 General works
Obedience to the law issued by secular authorities
2021 General works
2022 Obligation of paying taxes to secular authority
2023 Bribery of officials of secular authority
2024 Criminal laws
Constitutional law. Constitutional principles of the Jewish community
Including internal self-government
2070 General works
Constitutional history
Cf. BM520.5+ History of Halakhah
Cf. BM520.52 Constitutional history
Cf. KBM150+ History of Judaism
Cf. KBM520.5+ History of Halakhah
2085 General works

Mishpat Ivri
Constitutional law. Constitutional principles of the Jewish community
Constitutional history -- Continued
Biblical period, through ca. 135 C.E.
2090 General works
2095 To establishment of the first monarchy
Including the periods of the Avot through Shoftim (Patriarch and judges)
2100 First Commonwealth. Bayit rishon
Including the House of Saul and David
2104 Second Commonwealth. Bayit sheni, to 135 C.E.
Class here works from the destruction of the First Commonwealth through the Bar Kokhba Rebellion (132-135)
Diaspora
2106 General works
2107 Exilarch. Resh galuta
Constitutional principles
Kingship
2129 General works
2130 House of David. Bet David
2200.A-Z Special topics, A-Z
Class here works on topics not otherwise provided for
2200.R33 Rabbis. Rabbinate
Concepts and principles
Including historic concepts
2240 Legitimacy
2250 Legality
2250.3 Duties and responsibilities of leaders
Rule of law see KBM2020+
2275 Ethics in government. Conflict of interests
2300 Privileges, prerogatives, and immunities of rulers
Sources and relationships of the law
2340 Customary law
Relationship of the Jewish community (Kehillah) to the secular state
2370 General works
2380 Cooperation of the Jewish community and state government
2385 Concurring and exclusive jurisdiction
2387 Jews leading, serving, or employed by the state
2400 Relations with non-Jews
Relationship of the individual to the Jewish community and state
2430 General works

Mishpat Ivri
Constitutional law. Constitutional principles of the Jewish community
Relationship of the individual to the Jewish community and state -- Continued
Membership in the Jewish community
Cf. KBM529.83 Jewishness
2447 General works
2448 Conversion to Judaism. Giyur
2450.A-Z Particular groups, A-Z
Human rights. Civil and political rights
Including civil duties
2460 General works
2462 Human dignity
Equality before the law. Legal and social equality
Including positions of the Jewish community on civil rights under secular states and governmental entities
2465 General works
2467.A-Z Particular groups, A-Z
2467.B32 Ba'ale teshuvah. Jews returning to Orthodox Judaism
2467.C48 Children. Youth
2467.C64 Converts to Judaism
2467.D58 Disabilities, People with
Including people with physical, mental, and social disabilities
2467.G37 Gays. Lesbians
Jews returning to Orthodox Judaism see KBM2467.B32
Lesbians see KBM2467.G37
2467.N64 Non-Jews
People with disabilities see KBM2467.D58
2467.P64 The poor
Youth see KBM2467.C48
2467.5 Sex discrimination
2468.A-Z Special subjects, A-Z
Culture see KBM2468.L36
2468.L36 Language and culture
Including rights of speakers of linguistic minorities within the Jewish community
Freedom
2469 General works
2470 Freedom of expression
2472 Freedom of religion. Freedom of worship
Cf. KBM4418 Heresy
Freedom of thought and speech
2474 General works

Mishpat Ivri
Constitutional law. Constitutional principles of the Jewish community
Relationship of the individual to the Jewish community and state
Human rights. Civil and political rights
Freedom
Freedom of thought and speech -- Continued
2476 Freedom of information
2478 Prohibition of censorship
2483 Freedom of association
2484 Due process of law
Particular rights
2484.5 Right to life
Including works on reproductive choices and death penalty
2486 Right to resistance against political authority. Civil disobedience
2490 Control of subversive activities or groups
Organs of government and administration
2500 General works
Legislative power and process. Communal legislation. Takkanot ha-kahal
2510 General works
2510.4.A-Z Special topics, A-Z
2532 Jewish communal leaders
Including Nagid, Parnas, etc.
For Resh galuta see KBM2107
The executive branch
2577 General works
2612.A-Z Special boards, councils, bureaus, task forces, etc. By name, A-Z
Jewish councils see KBM2612.J83
2612.J83 Judenrat. Jewish councils in occupied Europe, 1939-1945
2614.A-Z Special topics, A-Z
Administrative law and process of communal agencies
2711 General works
2724 Autonomy. Rulemaking power
2732 Acts of government or communal agencies
2757 Enforcement. Administrative sanctions
Indemnification for acts performed by government. Public restraint on private property
2824 General works
2840 Government liability. Liability of communal agencies
2970 Civil service. Employees of communal agencies
Police and public safety

Mishpat Ivri
Police and public safety -- Continued
3000 General works
3002 Licenses, concessions, permits
3007 Police force
Including communal-sponsored patrols, militias, etc.
3009 Public safety
Including control of hazardous materials and processes
3016 Fire prevention and control
3022 Control of individuals
Control of social activities
3034 General works
3034.5 Vacationing
Including campgrounds, hostels, outdoor swimming facilities, etc.
Sport activities
3035 General works
3035.5 Mass events
3036.A-Z Particular sports, A-Z
3036.S65 Soccer
3036.5.A-Z Other, A-Z
3036.5.D45 Demonstrations. Processions
3036.5.G35 Gambling
Including lotteries, games of chance, etc.
Games of chance see KBM3036.5.G35
Lotteries see KBM3036.5.G35
Processions see KBM3036.5.D45
3037 Emergency management. Disaster control. Disaster relief
Public property. Communal property. Restraints on private property
Cf. KBM2824+ Indemnification
3040.5 General works
3042 Records management. Access to records
3044.7 Roads and highways
Water resources
Including rivers, lakes, watercourses, underground water, etc.
3046 General works
3046.5 Common use
Architectural landmarks and historic monuments see KBM3183
3055.A-Z Other, A-Z
Public land law
Agrarian land policy see KBM3293
City planning and redevelopment
3062 General works
3065 Assessment of utilities
Including sanitation

Mishpat Ivri
Public property. Communal property. Restraints on private property
Public land law -- Continued
Building and construction
Including administrative control and procedure
Cf. KBM3402 Building and construction industry
3067 General works
3069 Adjoining landowners
3071 Building safety and control
3072.A-Z Special topics, A-Z
3072.R65 Roofs. Ma'akeh
3073 Public works
Including public works contracts
Public health
3075 General (Comparative)
Burial and cemetery laws. Disposal of the dead
Cf. BM712 Jewish funeral rites
3078 General works
3078.5 Burial society. Ḥevra kaddisha
Contagious and infectious diseases. Parasitic diseases
3080 General works
3082.A-Z Diseases. Agents. Parasites, A-Z
3082.A53 AIDS
3082.S47 Sexually transmitted diseases. Venereal diseases
3082.T82 Tuberculosis
Venereal diseases see KBM3082.S47
Public health measures
Including compulsory measures
3084 General works
Immunization. Vaccination
3085 General works
3086.A-Z Diseases, A-Z
3086.S62 Smallpox
3087 Quarantine
Environmental pollution see KBM3130+
3088.A-Z Other public health hazards and measures, A-Z
3088.R43 Refuse disposal
3088.S77 Street cleaning
3089 Drinking water standards
Food laws see KBM3377+
Drug laws
3090 General works
3092 Narcotics
Including psychopharmaca
3096.5 Tobacco use. Smoking

Mishpat Ivri
Public health -- Continued
3097 Alcoholic beverages
Cf. BM538.H43 Relation of Judaism to health and medicine
Medical legislation
3098 General works
3098.5 Jewish medical ethics
The health professions
Class here works on education, licensing, and liability
Physicians
Including works on medical personnel in general
3100 General works
3100.5 Malpractice
3103.A-Z Other, A-Z
3103.D45 Dentists. Refuat shinayim
3103.H42 Healers
Including herbalists, homeopaths, naturopaths, etc.
3103.P79 Psychologists. Psychotherapists
Auxiliary medical professions. Paramedical professions
3104 General works
3105 Nurses and nursing
3106 Midwives
3107 Physical therapists
3108.A-Z Health organizations. By name, A-Z
3108.H36 Hatsalah
3108.M33 Magen David adom
3108.R43 Red Cross
Cf. KBM3037 Emergency management. Disaster relief
Hospitals and other medical institutions or health services
3110 General works
3111 Health resorts and spas
3112 Blood banks
3113 Institutions for the mentally ill and/or developmentally disabled
Including group homes
3114.A-Z Other health organizations, institutions, or services, A-Z
3114.D39 Day care centers for infants and children
3114.E43 Emergency medical services
Nursing homes see KBM3114.O42
3114.O42 Old age homes. Nursing homes
Including invalid adults
Biomedical engineering. Medical technology
Including human experimentation in medicine
3115 General (Comparative)

Mishpat Ivri
Medical legislation
Biomedical engineering. Medical technology -- Continued
3115.5 Genetic engineering
For artificial insemination see KBM3117
3116 Transplantation of organs, tissues, etc.
Including donation of organs, tissues, etc.
3117 Human reproductive technology
Including artificial insemination and fertilization in vitro
Cf. KBM619.A77 Domestic relations
3119.A-Z Special topics, A-Z
3119.A36 Abortion
Cf. KBM4070 Criminal law
3119.A88 Autopsy
3119.C57 Circumcision
Cf. BM705 Berit milah
3119.D43 Death, Definition of
Experiments with the human body see KBM3115+
3119.M43 Medical instruments and apparatus. Medical devices
3121 Eugenics. Sterilization and castration
3121.7 Euthanasia
Including works on right to die and living will
3122 Veterinary medicine and hygiene
Animal protection. Animal welfare. Animal rights
Including prevention of cruelty to animals
3123 General works
3123.2 Animal experimentation and research
Birth control. Family planning
3124 General works
3125.A-Z Special topics, A-Z
3125.A36 Abortion, Forced, for population control
Voluntary abortion see KBM3119.A36
Environmental law
For civil liability for environmental damages see KBM852.4
3127 General works
3129 Environmental planning. Conservation of environmental resources
Environmental pollution
3130 General works
3130.5 Air pollution
Including noxious gases, automobile emission control, etc.
Smoking see KBM3096.5
3131 Water and groundwater pollution
Including pollutants and sewage control
Pollutants
3131.5 General works

Mishpat Ivri
Environmental law
Environmental pollution
Pollutants -- Continued
3132 Radioactive substances
3132.5 Noise
Including traffic noise and noise control
3134 Wilderness preservation
Including natural monuments, parks, and forests
Cultural affairs
3137 General works
3137.5 Freedom of science and the arts. Academic freedom
3137.7 Cultural policy. Encouragement of science and the arts
Language
Including purity, regulation of use, etc.
3137.9 Hebrew language
3137.92.A-Z Other languages, A-Z
Education
Cf. BM70+ Study and teaching of Judaism
3138 General (Comparative)
3138.55 School government
Students
3139 General works
3139.3 Right of children to education. Obligation of parents to educate their children
3139.4 Compulsory education
Teachers. School functionaries
For particular teachers, see the level of instruction, e.g. KBM3141 Elementary teachers
Cf. BM523.5.R4 Respect for parents and teachers
Cf. KBM523.5.R4 Respect to parents and teachers
3140 General works
3140.5 Education and training
3140.7 Disciplinary power
3140.9 Preschool education
3141 Elementary education
Including teachers
Education of disabled children
3143 General works
3143.4 Socially disabled children
Including children of converts to Judaism, and Ba'ale teshuvah
3143.6 Physically and mentally disabled children
3144.5 Vocational education
Including teachers
3146 Secondary education
Higher education

Mishpat Ivri
Cultural affairs
Education
Higher education -- Continued
3147 General works
3147.5 Universities and colleges offering secular studies
3147.6 Schools and departments of Jewish studies
3147.7.A-Z Yeshivot. Rabbinical seminaries. By name, A-Z
3147.8 Teachers' training institutes and seminaries
3152 Teachers
3153 Students
3156.A-Z Universities and institutions. By name, A-Z
3158.5 Adult education
3159 Physical education. Sports
For liability for sports accidents see KBM848
Cf. KBM3035+ Sports activities
Science and the arts
Including public policies in research
3160 General works
3161 Public institutions. Academies
3165.A-Z Branches and subjects, A-Z
Language see KBM3137.9+
The arts
3168 General works
3169 Fine arts
Performing arts
3170 General works
3171 Music. Musicians
3172 Theater
3173 Motion pictures
Public collections
3176 General works
3177 Archives. Historic documents
3179 Libraries
Including librarians
3182.5 Museums and galleries
3183 Historic buildings and monuments. Architectural landmarks
Including sites of archaeological importance
Economic law
Including theories and concepts
3190 General works
3210 Prices and price control
3217 Community-owned business enterprises
Control of contracts and combinations in restraint of trade. Competition rules
For unfair competition see KBM1234+

Mishpat Ivri
Economic law
Control of contracts and combinations in restraint of trade.
Competition rules -- Continued
3220 General works
3242 Monopolies. Antitrust law
3247 Damages (Private law) and indemnification (Public law)
Standards. Norms
For particular products, see the product
3254 General works
3255 Quality control
Weights and measures. Midot. Containers
3257 General works
3258.A-Z By instrument, A-Z
Standardization
3259 General works
Price norms see KBM3210
3268 Labeling
Class here general works; for the labeling of particular goods or products, see the product
Regulation of industry, trade, and commerce
3272 General works
3273 Licensing
3276 Consumer protection
3280 Advertising
Primary production. Extractive industries
Agriculture. Forestry. Rural law
3293 Land policy legislation
Including mitzvah connected to the land
Cf. BM538.A4 Agriculture and Judaism
Cf. BM720.S2 Sabbatical year
Cf. KBM524.4.T73 Trees in Mishpat Ivri
3295 General works
Collective farming. Agricultural cooperatives
3316 General works
3317 Producers and marketing cooperatives
Livestock industry and trade
3327 General works
3328.A-Z Particular, A-Z
Milk production. Dairy farming
3329 General works
3329.5.A-Z Products, A-Z
3333 Viticulture
3334 Apiculture. Beekeeping
3335 Horticulture
3336 Forestry
Including timber laws and game laws

KBM

Mishpat Ivri
Economic law
Regulation of industry, trade, and commerce
Primary production. Extractive industries -- Continued
3340 Fishery
Mining and quarrying
Including metallurgy
3344 General works
3345 Public restraint on property rights and positions. Government rights
Manufacturing industries
Including heavy and light industries
3372 General works
3373.A-Z Types of manufacture, A-Z
3373.L57 Liturgical objects. Tashmishe ḳodesh
Cf. BM657.A+ Jewish liturgical objects
Tashmishe ḳodesh see KBM3373.L57
Food processing industries. Food products
Class here works on trade practices, economic assistance, labeling, sanitation, and quality inspection
Including regulation of adulteration and food additives
Cf. BM710 Jewish dietary laws
3377 General works
3378 Labeling
3379 Purity
3380 Cereal products
3381 Fruits and vegetables
3382 Confectionary industry
3383 Meat and meat products
3384 Poultry products
3388 Dairy products
3392 Fish. Seafood
Beverages
3395 Brewing
3397 Winemaking
3400.A-Z Related industries and products, A-Z
3402 Building and construction industry
For building laws see KBM3067+
3405 Trade with non-Jews
Trade within the Jewish community
3415 General works
3416 Wholesale trade
Retail trade
Cf. KBM3429 Artisans
3418 General works

Mishpat Ivri
Economic law
Regulation of industry, trade, and commerce
Trade within the Jewish community
Retail trade -- Continued
3419 Conditions of trading
Including licensing
For holiday and Sabbath legislation, see the jurisdiction
Cf. BM523.3.P7 Prohibited work
3420.A-Z Modes of trading, A-Z
Fairs see KBM3420.M37
3420.M34 Mail-order and Web-based businesses
3420.M37 Markets. Fairs
3420.P43 Peddling
Web-based businesses see KBM3420.M34
3421 Cooperative retail trade
3422.A-Z Products, A-Z
3422.A88 Automobiles
3422.D52 Diamonds
3422.M48 Metals
Metals, Precious see KBM3422.P73
3422.P73 Precious metals
Secondhand trade
3423 General works
3423.5.A-Z Types of trade, A-Z
3423.5.A82 Auction houses
3423.5.C64 Consignment shops. Pawnbrokers
Pawnbrokers see KBM3423.5.C64
Service trades
3424 General works
Old age homes see KBM3114.O42
3424.5 Hotels, taverns, and restaurants
Artisans
3426 General works
3427 Apprentices
3428 Licensing and registration
3429 Associations and societies
3430.A-Z Crafts, A-Z
Energy policy. Power supply
Including publicly and privately owned utilities
3431 General works
3432 Particular sources of power
3436 Nuclear energy
Transportation and communication
3440 General works
Road traffic. Automotive transportation
3442 General works

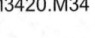

Mishpat Ivri
Transportation and communication
Road traffic. Automotive transportation -- Continued
3448 Traffic regulations and enforcement
Including highway safety
3455 Carriage of goods and passengers
For holiday and Sabbath legislation, see the jurisdiction
Cf. BM523.3.P7 Prohibited work
3459 Railroads
3467 Aviation. Air law
3469 Space law
3471 Water transportation
Communication. Mass media
3482 General works
3483 Freedom of communication . Censorship
Postal services
3485 General works
3485.7 Non-governmental delivery of letters
3487 Telecommunication. Telephone
Radio communication
Including radio and television broadcasting
3491 General works
3495 Broadcasting
Including programming
Press law
3500 General works
Censorship see KBM3483
3500.3 Right to information
Publishers and publishing
3503 General works
3504 Community-operated publishing activities
3504.5 Bookdealers
Libel and slander see KBM842.8
Professions
3515 General works
Individual professions
Economic and financial advisors
3517 Accountants
3518 Auditors
Engineering and construction
3519 Engineers
Other professions, see the subject

Mishpat Ivri
Professions
Individual professions -- Continued
3522 Lawyers
Class here works on the status under Jewish law of Jewish lawyers practicing in non-Jewish courts
For works on Jewish lawyers in a particular place see the law of the jurisdiction, e.g. KF299.J4
For works on the practice of law before Jewish courts see KBM1630
Public finance
3526 General works
Money
Including control of circulation
3534 General works
3537 Gold trading and gold standard
Communal taxation and fundraising
Including revenue raising by the Jewish community for communal purposes
Cf. KBM2022 Obligation of paying taxes to secular authority
3540 General works
Taxation and tax exemption as a measure of social and economic policy. Fairness. Equality
3556.A-Z Taxation of particular activities, A-Z
3557 Tax saving. Tax avoidance
For tax planning relating to a particular tax, see the tax
3558 Tax administration. Administration of fundraising
3572.A-Z Classes of taxpayers or lines of business, A-Z
Income tax. Taxation based on current income
3573 General works
3576 Assessment
Taxable income. Exemptions
3578 General works
3578.5.A-Z Particular, A-Z
Capital gains see KBM3578.5.P75
3578.5.P75 Profits. Capital gains
Deductions
3579 General works
3580 Charitable or educational gifts and contributions
Expenses and losses
3582 General works
3582.3.A-Z Kinds of expenses, A-Z
3582.3.B88 Business expenses
3582.3.E38 Educational expenses
3584 Salaries and wages
Including fringe benefits, non-wage payments, etc.

Mishpat Ivri
Public finance
Communal taxation and fundraising
Income tax. Taxation based on current income -- Continued
3592 Income from corporations or business associations
Wealth tax. Property tax. Taxation of capital
Including fundraising based on individual assets
3616 General works
3617 Tax valuation
3619 Assessment
3620 Taxable property. Exemptions
3621 Estate, inheritance, and gift taxes
3623 Capital gains tax
Surtaxes
3624 General works
3625 Excess profits tax
Including war profits tax
3626 Taxation per capita. Poll tax. Taxation independent of income, wealth, or expenses
Excise taxes. Taxes on transactions
3627 General works
3640.A-Z Commodities, services, and transactions, A-Z
3640.K66 Kosher food. Kosher meat
Kosher meat see KBM3640.K66
3640.R48 Retail trade
Local finance
3655 General works
3660 Taxation and fundraising
For particular topics see KBM3540+
Tax and customs crimes and delinquency. Procedure
3693 General works
3695.A-Z Individual offenses, A-Z
Measures in time of war, national emergency, or economic crisis
3709 General works
Particular measures
3710 Requisition of private property for community use
3712 Control of property. Confiscations
3714 Control of unemployment. Manpower control
3717 Insolvent debtors. Wartime and crisis relief
Special levies, war taxes, etc. see KBM3624+
3720 Economic recovery measures. Expropriation and nationalization
3724 Rationing. Price control

Mishpat Ivri
Measures in time of war, national emergency, or economic crisis -- Continued
Damage compensation
Including compensation for damages resulting from actions taken by communal authorities
For damages inflicted by non-Jews upon the Jewish community, see the particular institution
Cf. KBM2020+ Rule of law
3727 General works
3728.A-Z Particular claims, A-Z
Confiscations see KBM3728.R47
3728.P47 Personal damages. Property loss or damages
Property loss or damages see KBM3728.P47
3728.R47 Requisitions. Confiscations
3729.A-Z Particular victims, A-Z
Community defense. Military law
For emergency and wartime legislation see KBM3709+
Cf. BM538.P3 Peace and war in Judaism
Organized defense forces. Patrols. Militias. The armed forces
3738 General works
Obligation to serve
3739 General works
3740.A-Z Special topics, A-Z
3740.C65 Conscientious objection
3740.M54 Milḥemet Mitzvah. War declared by a king
3749 Auxiliary services during war or emergency
3752 Civil defense
Military criminal law and procedure
3758 General works
3758.5 Illegality and justification. Superior orders
3760.A-Z Individual offenses, A-Z
3760.D46 Desertion
3760.D73 Draft evasion
3760.I53 Incitement. Mutiny
3760.I56 Insubordination
Malingering see KBM3760.S44
Mutiny see KBM3760.I53
3760.S32 Sabotoging weapons, equipment, or means of defense
3760.S44 Self-mutilation. Malingering
3770 Courts and procedure
Military discipline. Law enforcement. Procedure
Including all branches of the armed forces
3780 General works
3782 Superior orders. Enforcement of orders
3785.A-Z Other, A-Z

Mishpat Ivri -- Continued
Criminal law and procedure
For criminology and penology see HV6001+
3790 Reform of criminal law and procedure
For punishment for violation of a specific legal or religious principle, see the subject in BM or KBM
For criminology and penology see HV6001+
Criminal law and procedure
Including criminal law and criminal procedure discussed together
3800 General works
3810 Criminal law in the Ḥumash. Doraita
3811 Rebelliousness
Philosophy of criminal law
3812 General works
Theories of punishment. Criminal policy see KBM3950+
Relationship of criminal law to other disciplines, subjects, or phenomena
3817 General works
3818 Criminal law and society
Cf. HV6115+ Social pathology
3819 Criminal law and psychology
Cf. HV6080+ Criminal psychology
3821 Interpretation and constuction. Legal hermeneutics
3823.A-Z Terms and phrases, A-Z
Drugs see KBM3823.F67
3823.F67 Force and coercion. ‘Onés
Including drugs and hypnosis
Hypnosis see KBM3823.F67
‘Onés see KBM3823.F67
Concepts and principles
Applicability and validity of the law
3825 General works
3826 Nulla poena sine lege. Nullum crimen sine lege
3835 Conflict of laws
Including violation of secular laws
3838.3 Personal applicability. Immunities
Criminal offense. Criminal act
3840 General works
3851 Causation. Proximate cause
3853 Omission
3854 Attempt. Preparation
Justification of otherwise prohibited acts
3855 General works
3856 Self-defense or defense of another
3857 Necessity

Mishpat Ivri
Criminal law and procedure
Criminal law
Criminal offense. Criminal act
Justification of otherwise prohibited acts -- Continued
3858 Preservation of life. Pikku’aḥ nefesh
3859 Duty to act (Legal authority or duty)
3861 Consent of the injured party
3867 Criminal intent. Mens rea. Kaṿanah
3868 Warning by witnesses and acknowledgment by offender
3874 Negligence and wantonness
Including foresight and standard of conduct
Criminal liability. Guilt
3878 General works
Capacity
3880 General works
Incapacity and limited capacity
3882 General works
3884 Insane persons. People with mental or emotional disabilities
3886 Minors. Ḳeṭanim
Including infants, juveniles, and young adults
3892.A-Z Special topics, A-Z
3892.D58 Distemper. Passion
3892.I58 Intoxication
Passion see KBM3892.D58
3897 Exculpating circumstances
3900 Superior orders and justification or excusation
Including Divre ha-rav and Divre ha-talmid
3902 Error
Including error about fact, error about grounds for justification or excusation, and error about extenuating circumstances, error in persona, etc.
Forms of the criminal act
3920 Perpetrators and accomplices
3940 Compound offenses and compound punishment
Punishment
3946 General works
3948 In Ḥumash. Doraita
Theory and policy of punishment
3950 General works
3952 Retaliation. Retribution
3954 Safeguarding the social and political system
3956 General and special prevention
Including education, rehabilitation, etc.
Penalties

Mishpat Ivri
Criminal law and procedure
Criminal law
Punishment
Penalties -- Continued
3962 General works
Capital punishment
3964 General works
3964.1 Stoning. Seḳilah
3964.2 Decapitation. Herev
3964.3 Burning. Serefah
3964.4 Strangulation. Ḥinuḳ
3964.5 Being tossed into a pit due to lack of admissible evidence
3965 Execution other than after formal proceedings
Including assassination by order of Bet din
Cf. KBM1582 Bet din (General)
3970 Imprisonment
3976 Fines. Knasim
3978 Reprimand
3980.A-Z Other penalties, A-Z
3980.F55 Flogging. Makot
Makot see KBM3980.F55
3980.M87 Mutilation
Measures entailing deprivation of liberty
Including commitment to medical, psychiatric, or other therapeutic facilities
3982 General works
3992 Protective custody
Including dangerous or habitual criminals
3995 Protective surveillance
Other measures
3997 Expulsion. Banishment. Deportation. Ḥerem
Including exile to a city of refuge
Cf. KBM4826+ Criminal law
4002 Prohibition against practicing a profession
4004 Loss of civil rights. Infamy. Disenfranchisement
4006 Property confiscation
4010 Forfeiture
4012 Sentencing and determining the measure of punishment
4038 Limitation of actions
Individual offenses
Offenses against the person
Homicide
4050 General works
4052 Murder

Mishpat Ivri
Criminal law and procedure
Criminal law
Individual offenses
Offenses against the person
Homicide -- Continued
4054 Manslaughter
4056 Assisting suicide. Killing on request
Euthanasia see KBM3121.7
4070 Crimes against inchoate life. Illegal abortion
Including ethical, social, medical, and eugenic aspects
Cf. KBM3119.A36 Medical legislation
Crimes against physical inviolability
4074 General works
4076 Battery
4077 Wife abuse. Husband abuse
4096 Criminal aspects of surgical and other medical treatment
Cf. KBM3115+ Medical legislation
Crimes against personal freedom
Cf. KBM842+ Individual torts and damages
4116 General works
4118 False imprisonment
4120 Extortionate kidnapping
4121 Kidnapping for sale. Slave traffic
4125 Abduction
Cf. KBM4188 Parental kidnapping
Crimes against dignity and honor see KBM842.7+
Violation of personal privacy and secrets see KBM843
Offenses against religious tranquility and the peace of the dead
4170 General works
4172 Blasphemy
4174 Disturbing a religious observance
4176 Disturbing the peace of the dead
Including cemeteries and funerals
Offenses against marriage, family, and family status
4180 General works
4182 Incest
4184 Adultery
Including Sotah ritual
Cf. KBM544.2 Domestic relations
Bigamy see KBM544.6
Multiple marriage. Polygamy see KBM546.4
4188 Abduction of a minor from legal custodian. Parental kidnapping

Mishpat Ivri
Criminal law and procedure
Criminal law
Individual offenses
Offenses against marriage, family, and family status -- Continued
4190 Abandonment, neglect, or abuse of a child
4192 Breach of duty of support
Offenses against sexual integrity
4200 General works
4202 Rape
4224 Pandering and pimping. Prostitution
Offenses against private and public property
4230 General works
4234 Theft. Larceny and embezzlement. Genevah. Gezelah
4256 Destruction of property and conversion
4258 Fraud
4264 Extortion
4266 Breach of trust
4268 Usury
Cf. KBM868.2 Usurious contracts
4270 Defeating rights of creditors
Offenses against the national economy
4286 General works
4290 Violation of price regulations
Including price fixing, hoarding, discrimination, overselling and underselling prices established by government, etc.
4292 Foreign exchange violations
Offenses against public order and convenience
Including aggravating circumstances
4305 General works
4307 Inciting insubordination
4309 Rowdyism. Vandalism
4310 Inciting crime
4320 Disrupting the peace of the community
4330 Crimes against security of legal and monetary transactions and documents
Including forgery and counterfeiting
Cf. KBM846 Torts
4351.5 Crimes involving danger to the community
Including terrorism, crimes against the environment, and arson
Crimes affecting traffic
4380 Dangerous interference with rail, ship, or air traffic

Mishpat Ivri
Criminal law and procedure
Criminal law
Individual offenses
Offenses against public order and convenience
Crimes affecting traffic -- Continued
4384 Dangerous interference with street traffic. Motor vehicle offenses
Including driving while intoxicated or improper driving
4396 Crimes aboard aircraft. Air piracy
4398 Riots
Crimes against public health
4400 General works
4404 Illicit use of, possession of, and traffic in narcotics
4406 Gambling
Offenses against the peace. Political offenses
4415.7 General works
4418 Idolatry. Heresy. Apikoros
4432 Endangering the welfare of the community
4442 Informing. Malshinim. Collaborating
Endangering the administration of justice. Obstruction of justice
4484 False testimony. Perjury
4496 False accusation
4498 Bringing false complaint
4500 Thwarting criminal justice
4507 Prosecuting innocent persons
4510 Contempt of court
Crimes against communal employees
4514 General works
Corruption
Including omission of official acts
4516 General works
4520 Bribery. Shoḥad
4538 Crimes against humanity
4545 War crimes
For works on both criminal law and criminal procedure see KBM3800+
Criminal procedure
4610 General works
4612 Dine nefashot. Capital punishment. Trial by little or great Sanhedrin
4613 Criminal proceeding by a formal Rabbinical court (Beis din)
Including proceedings that are criminal in nature even if not denominated as criminal

Mishpat Ivri
Criminal law and procedure
Criminal procedure -- Continued
4613.5 Other de facto proceedings
Including proceedings involving individuals acting in an informal or underground manner
4616 Sociology of criminal procedure
Courts see KBM1580+
Procedural principles
4620 Due process of law
4621 Duty to warn accused before commission of the crime
Cf. KBM4630.W56 Witnesses as accusers
4630.A-Z Parties to action, A-Z
4630.A25 Accused. Person charged. Defendant
Avenger see KBM4630.V52
4630.C74 Criminal judge
Defendant see KBM4630.A25
4630.D43 Defense attorney. Public defender
'Edim see KBM4630.W56
Person charged see KBM4630.A25
Procurator see KBM4630.S73
Public defender see KBM4630.D43
4630.S73 State prosecutor. Procurator
Including accusers other than witnesses
4630.V52 Victim. Avenger
Including victim's family
4630.W56 Witnesses. 'Edim
Pretrial procedures
4632 General works
4634 Penal report. Charges brought against a person. Accusation by witnesses
4636 Investigation
For techniques of criminal investigation see HV8073+
4646 Summonses, service of process, and subpoena. Wanted notice
4648 Time periods. Deadlines
4650 Compulsory measures against the accused. Securing of evidence
Including arrest and detention before trial
Procedure at trial
4664 General works
4666 Jurisdiction
Including competence in subject matter and venue
4668 Action. Complaint. Formal charge
4670 Exclusion and challenge of court members
Time periods and deadlines see KBM4648

Mishpat Ivri
Criminal law and procedure
Criminal procedure
Procedure at trial -- Continued
Limitation of actions see KBM4038
Trial
4673 General works
Evidence. Burden of proof
4675 General works
Admission of evidence
4679 General works
4681 Confession. Self-incrimination. Entrapment
4687 Physical examination
Including blood tests, urine tests, etc.
For forensic medicine see RA1001+
4689 Electronic listening and recording devices
Including wiretapping
4690 Previous testimony, police records, etc.
Witnesses
4692 General works
4696 Privileged witnesses (confidential communication)
4698.A-Z Other witnesses, A-Z
4700 Expert testimony
Cf. RA1001+ Medical jurisprudence
4702 Testimony of the accused
4704 Documentary evidence
4705 Circumstantial evidence
4706 Alibi
4709.A-Z Other, A-Z
4720 Procedure for juvenile delinquency
Judicial decisions
4736 General works
4738 Judgment
For punishment see KBM4012
4740 Judicial discretion
Including opportunity and equity
4744 Acquittal
4746 Conviction
4750 Dismissal
4753 Correction or withdrawal of faulty decisions (errors)
4754 Res judicata
4767 Civil suits of victims in connection with criminal proceedings
Including reparation (compensation to victims of crimes)
Special procedures
4769 Criminal proceedings by an irregular court
Post-conviction remedies

KBM

Mishpat Ivri
Criminal law and procedure
Criminal procedure
Post-conviction remedies -- Continued
4790 General works
4792 Reopening a case. New trial
Execution of sentence
4795 General works
Capital punishment see KBM3964+
4798 Imprisonment
4820 Sale as slave as punishment for convicted criminals
Exile. Banishment. Punitive deportation
4826 General works
4826.5 ʻIre miḳlaṭ. Cities of refuge. Asylum
Cf. BS1199.A8 Right of asylum
4845 Criminal registers
4855 Victimology. Victims of crimes

Islamic law. Sharīʻah. Fiqh. شريعة. فقه

Class here works on concepts, doctrines and schools of Islamic law, not related to any given jurisdiction (country or organization)

Further, class here comparative works on Islamic legal principles as present in the law of two or more jurisdictions (e.g. Islamic countries) or comparative works on laws and legal acts affecting Muslims in two or more jurisdictions

For comparison of the Islamic legal system with another legal or religious legal system see KB

<1> Periodicals

For Islamic law periodicals see KB26+

Bibliography

Including international and national bibliography

2.2 Bibliography of bibliography. Bibliographical concordances

2.3 General bibliography

2.4 Indexes for periodical literature, society publications, collections, etc.

Subject bibliography

Including manuscripts

For subject bibliography on Islam see Z7835.M6

3 General (Collective)

Individual subjects and topics

see the subject

3.3 Personal bibliography.

Including bio-bibliography

Catalogs, inventories, and guides to manuscripts and early or rare book collections in public libraries or archives. By name of the library or archive

Including university, museum, or mosque libraries, and other institutional libraries or archives

4 General (Collective)

4.2.A-Z North American, A-Z

Including United States and Canada

5.A-Z Central and South American, A-Z

6.A-Z European, A-Z

7.A-Z Asian and Pacific, A-Z

8.A-Z African, A-Z

<9> Annuals. Yearbooks

For legal yearbooks see KB26+

9.5 Monographic series

Societies. Associations

10 International

National

11 North American

Including United States and Canada

12 Central and South American

13 European

Societies. Associations
National -- Continued
14 Asian and Pacific
14.5 African
15 Congresses. Conferences
18 Academies. Institutes
Court decisions (including advisory opinions). Maḥākim sharʻīyah. محاكم شريعة
see the Islamic court in the appropriate K subclass for the country
40 Encyclopedias. Dictionaries
For dictionaries of Islamic law as applied in a particular country, see the K subclass for the country
For Arabic dictionaries, not limited by subject, see class P
For dictionaries on the Qur'ān or ḥadīth, see (KBP133) and (KBP135.2)
For dictionaries on uṣūl al-fiqh see KBP427
40.2 Maxims. Quotations
40.5 Directories
41 Legal research
Legal education. Study and teaching
Including all periods
For Islamic schools of law (Madhāhib) see KBP250+
42 General works
43.A-Z By region or country, A-Z
Under each:

.x	*General works*
.x2A-.x2Z	*Institutions of learning. By name, A-Z*

Including historic regions and jurisdictions (e.g. during Ottoman rule)
<44-48> Religious education
see BP44+
Historiography
Cf. BP49+ Islam
<49> General works
<49.5> Biography of scholars and historians
Including non-Muslim scholars
For other biography (collective and individual) see BP70+
For biography of legal scholars (collective and individual) including non-Muslim scholars see KBP253
The legal profession see KBP1572
Law and lawyers in literature
see class P

History, development and application of Islamic law
Including contemporary theoretical and polemic literature on application (taṭbīq. تطبيق الشريعة) of sharīʻah and works on codification
Cf. BP50+ Islam
50 General works
Auxiliary sciences
53.5 Legal archaeology. Symbolism in law
54 Chronology
54.5 Genealogy
By period
55 Early period (from origins through 11th century)
56 Middle period (to ca. 1920)
Including the Ottoman Empire
60 Late period (ca. 1920-)
By region or country
Cf. BP63+ Islam
62 General
e.g. Islamic countries in different regions
Asia
63 General
63.3 Middle East
64 Africa
65 Europe
66 Pacific Area
Including Australia and New Zealand
The Americas
67 North America
Including United States and Canada
68 Central and South America
69.A-Z Countries, A-Z
Biography
For bio-bibliography see KBP3.3
Collective biographies
<70> General
For biography of legal scholars (collective and individual) including non-Muslim scholars see KBP253
<72> Martyrs
<73> Women
By region or country
74.12 General
e.g. Islamic countries in different regions
Asia
74.2 General
74.3 Middle East
74.4 Africa

Biography
Collective biographies
By region or country -- Continued
74.5 Europe
74.6 Pacific Area
Including Australia and New Zealand
The Americas
74.7 North America
Including United States and Canada
74.8 Central and South America
74.9.A-Z Countries, A-Z
Biography of Muḥammad, Prophet, d. 632
The numbers <KBP75>-<KBP75.4> are provided as an optional arrangment for libraries using this classification. The Library of Congress uses the numbers BP75+
For other individual legal biography, including profession or qualification (e.g. qāḍī; quḍāt) see KBP250+
For companions,Ṣaḥābah (collective) see KBP255
<75-75.29> By language
<75.3> Historiography. History and criticism of biographies
<75.4> Biographers of Muḥammad (Collective)
Sources
For sources of fiqh see KBP449+
Qur'ān. Koran. القرأن
The numbers <KBP100>-<KBP133.5> are provided as an optional arrangement for libraries using this classification. The Library of Congress uses the numbers BP100+
Cf. BP100+ Islam. Sacred books
Texts. By language
Arabic
Including facsimiles or originals; and including typographical reproductions of the text entirely in non-Roman or ancient type, or transliterated into Roman characters
Cf. BP100+ Islam
Entire work
<100> Texts. By date
<100.2> Rearrangements of the entire Qur'ān
Including chronological and topical rearrangements
<100.22> Variant readings of the Qur'ān
<100.3> Works on manuscripts
<101> Selections. By date
Including selections arranged by topic
For abrogated verses, see <KBP130.3>
History and criticism
see <KBP130.1>

Sources
Qur'ān. Koran. القرأن
Texts. By language -- Continued
<102-127> Other languages (Translations)
Subarrange each language as follows:
.12 Entire work (including editions with or without comment). By date
.2 Selections (including two or more selected surahs, and including editions with or without comment). By date
Including parallel presentations of Arabic text and translation
<128.15-129.83> Individual parts and chapters
Subarrange each by Table K20b
Cf. BP128.15+ Islam
Works on the Qur'ān
<130> General works
Including theological-topical essays on the Qur'ān
Criticism
<130.1> General works
<130.2> Principles of criticism. Hermeneutics
<130.3> Abrogation. Abrogated verses (collected). Nāsikh wa-al-mansūkh. ناسخ والمنسوخ
Cf. <KBP136.78> Abrogated hadith
For naskh (theory of abrogation) see KBP463
<130.32> Revelation. Asbāb al-nuzūl. اسباب النزول
<130.4> Exegesis. Interpretation. Commentary
Cf. BP130.4 Islam
Theological-topical essays on the Qur'ān
see <KBP130>
<133> Dictionaries. Concordances. Indexes, etc.
For philological studies on the Qur'an see PJ6696.A6+
Cf. BP133 Islam
<133.5> Study and teaching of the Qur'ān
Hadith. Traditions. Sunna. حديث. سنة
Including statements of companions
The numbers <KBP135.A1>-<KBP136.8> are provided as an optional arrangment for libraries using this classification. The Library of Congress uses the numbers BP135+
Collections. Compilations
<135.A1> General
Cf. BP135.A1 Islam
By compiler
Cf. BP135.A12+ Islam
<135.A12> Bukhārī, Muḥammad ibn Ismā'īl, 810-870. البخاري, محمد بن اسماعيل (Table K20b)

Sources
Hadith. Traditions. Sunna. حديث. سنة
Collections. Compilations
By compiler -- Continued

<135.A13> Abū Dā'ūd Sulaymān ibn al-Ashʻath al-Sijistānī, 817 or 18-889. ابو داود سليمان بن الاشعث السجستاني (Table K20b)

<135.A14> Muslim ibn al-Ḥajjāj al-Qushayrī, ca. 821-975. مسلم بن الحجاج القشيري (Table K20b)

<135.A15> Tirmidhī, Muḥammad ibn ʻĪsá, d. 892. الترمزي, محمد بن عيس (Table K20b)

<135.A16> Nasā'ī, Aḥmad ibn Shu'ayb, 830 or 31-915. النسائي, احمد بن شعيب (Table K20b)

<135.A17> Ibn Mājah, Muḥammad ibn Yazīd, d. 887. ابن ماجة, محمد بن يزيد (Table K20b)

<135.A2> Other compilations
Subarrange by author
Cf. BP135.A2 Islam

Selections. Extracts, etc.
Cf. BP135.A3 Islam

<135.A3> General

Abrogated hadith (Collected)
see (KBP135.3)

<135.2> Dictionaries. Concordances. Indexes, etc.
For dictionaries on a particular collection, see the collection
For philological studies see PJ6696.A6+
Cf. BP135.2 Islam

<135.3> Particular hadith genre
Including aḥkām al-ḥadīth collections, collections of mawḍūʻāt, nāsikh or mansūkh collections, "Forty hadith", etc.

Study and teaching. ʻUlūm al-ḥadīth. علوم الحديث

<135.6> History
Cf. BP135.6+ Islam

<135.62.A-Z> By region or country, A-Z
Including collective biography of commentators and scholars
For individual biography see BP80.A+
Cf. BP135.62.A+ Islam

<135.65> General works. Treatises

Appreciation. Excellence. Authority. Credibility
Including biography
Cf. BP136.4+ Islam

<136.4> General works

Sources
Hadith. Traditions. Sunna. حديث. سنة
Appreciation. Excellence. Authority. Credibility -- Continued
Isnād. Ascription and chain of transmission. Transmitters.
ʻIlm al-rijāl. علم الرجال
For works on an individual transmitter present in a particular collection, see the collection, e.g. <KBP135.A12> Bukhārī, Muḥammad ibn Ismāʻīl
<136.42> Establishment of authoritativeness of transmitters
<136.5> Quality of the transmission of the tradition
<136.78> Abrogating hadith and abrogated hadith
For (collected) instances of abrogated hadith see <KBP135.3>
For naskh (theory of abrogating) see KBP463
Cf. BP136.78 Islam
<136.79> Asbāb al-wurūd. اسباب الورود
<136.8> Commentaries on the hadith
Cf. BP136.8 Islam
144 General works
Class here general contemporary introductions to Islamic law
Including visual aids, maps, charts, etc.
For general works on Islam see BP160+
Islamic law compared with other religious legal systems see KB190; KB195
Islamic law and other disciplines or subjects
For Islamic law and mysticism (Sufism) see <KBP188.5>+
For Islam and international law see KB260
For Islamic law and women see KBP526+
For Islam and human or civil rights see KBP2460+
For Islam and mass media, communication, etc. see KBP3482+
173.25 Islamic law and society
<173.6> Islam and the state
For works on the compatibility of Islam and democratic government see KBP2035
Cf. BP173.6 Islam
Observances and practice of Islam
Class here works on legal aspects of observances and practice of Islam
Cf. BP174+ Islam
<174> General works
The five duties of a Muslim. Pillars of Islam
<176> General works
<177> Profession of faith
<178> Prayer
<179> Fasting. Ṣawm. صوم

KBP

Observances and practice of Islam
The five duties of a Muslim. Pillars of Islam -- Continued
<180> Zakat. Zakāh. Almsgiving. زكاة
Cf. KBP3620+ Taxation
<181> Pilgrimage to Mecca. Ḥajj. حج
Cf. KBP187.2+ Mecca
Jihād. Inner conflict (Conflict of conscience). جهاد
For jihād as conflict between nations see KBP2416
182 General (Table KBP2)
182.2.A-Z Special topics, A-Z
Subarrange each by Table KBP3
<182.5> Symbols and symbolism
For symbolism in law see KBP53.5
ʻIbādāt. Ritual law. Worship. عبادات
184 General (Table KBP2)
184.12 Nīyah. Purity of intention. نية
Prayer
Including times and call to prayer, conditions, traditions, and obligatory elements of prayer
Cf. KBP178 Pillars of Islam (Prayer)
184.3 General works
184.32.A-Z Kinds of prayer, A-Z
184.32.F74 Friday prayer
Funeral procession prayer see KBP184.55
184.32.G75 Group prayer. Public worship
Public worship see KBP184.32.G75
184.32.R34 Rain prayer
184.32.T72 Traveler's prayer
184.33.A-Z Special topics, A-Z
184.33.C67 Corruption of prayer
184.33.M58 Mistakes in prayer
Ritual purity. Ṭahārah. طهارة
Including stipulations and requirements for purity and purifying agents (e.g. water)
184.4 General works
Impurity
Including alcoholic beverages (intoxicants; khamr); alcoholic preparations (e.g. perfumes), tobacco, etc.
Cf. KBP4045 Ḥadd crimes
184.42 General works
184.43 Acceptable impurity
Purification
184.44 General works
184.45 Istinjāʼ. استنجاء
Including various types of purification (e.g. for female pilgrims)

Observances and practice of Islam
'Ibādāt. Ritual law. Worship. عبادات
Ritual purity. Ṭahārah. طهارة -- Continued
Ablutions. Wuḍū'. وضوء
Including duties, traditions, customs, peculiarities, etc.
184.46 General works
184.47.A-Z Other special topics, A-Z
184.47.C45 Childbirth
184.47.M45 Menstruation
184.47.M68 Mosques
184.47.P72 Prayer (Ablutions (cleansing) before prayer)
184.47.P82 Public baths
Taghsīl (Ritual bathing of the corpse). تغسيل see KBP184.55
Fasting. Ṣawm. Seclusion. صوم
Including laws and rules for fasting (obligatory fasting, traditions, customs, kinds of fasting, etc.)
Cf. KBP179 Pillars of Islam
184.5 General works
184.54.A-Z Special topics, A-Z
Feast of breaking the Ramadan fast see KBP184.54.I32
184.54.I32 'Īd al-Fiṭr. Feast of breaking the Ramadan fast. عيد الفطر
184.54.R35 Ramadan fast
184.55 Funeral rites
Including burial service (tadfīn) (تدفين), ritual bathing of the corpse (taghsīl) (تغسيل), shroud (takfīn) (تكفين), funeral procession prayers, etc.
Blood sacrifices. Ritual slaughtering
184.6 General works
184.62.A-Z Special topics, A-Z
184.62.L43 Legitimacy
184.62.S23 Sacrificial animal
184.62.S74 Stipulations
Muslim pilgrims and pilgrimages. Duty of pilgrimage
Cf. (KBP187.52) Non-Meccan shrines and sanctuaries, etc.
184.7 General works
184.72 Laws, requirements, time, and place for major and minor pilgrimages
184.73.A-Z Elements of the major and minor pilgrimages, A-Z
184.8 Circumcision
Cf. KBP3119.C57 Medical legislation
184.9.A-Z Other subjects, A-Z
184.9.A27 Abstinence (Mandatory) from alcohol
184.9.B45 Blood as food or medicine
Burial service see KBP184.55

KBP

Observances and practice of Islam
‘Ibādāt. Ritual law. Worship. عبادات
Other subjects, A-Z -- Continued
184.9.C45 Clothing and dress. Ḥijāb. حجاب
184.9.D54 Dietary laws
Including food and forbidden food, eating customs, etc.
Dress see KBP184.9.C45
184.9.D74 Drinking
184.9.F34 Faith
Intoxicants see KBP184.42
184.9.J38 Jewelry
Khamr. خمر see KBP184.42
184.9.P45 Penance
Perfume see KBP184.42
184.9.P56 Photography. Painting
Ritual bathing of the corpse see KBP184.55
184.9.S38 Sex. Sexual etiquette
Shroud see KBP184.55
Tadfīn. تدفين see KBP184.55
Taghsīl. تغسيل see KBP184.55
Takfīn. تكفين see KBP184.55
Tobacco see KBP184.42
184.9.T72 Travel
Cf. KBP184.32.T72 Traveler's prayer
184.9.V68 Vows
Water see KBP184.4+
184.9.W55 Wine
Cf. KBP184.42 Ritual purity
Liturgical objects, memorials, etc. Minbars
Cf. BP184.95+ Islam
<184.95> General works
<184.96.A-Z> Special objects, A-Z
<185> Religious functionaries. Imams. Religious legal scholars. ‘Ulamā’. علماء
Cf. BP185+ Islam
Mass media and telecommunication see KBP3482
Cf. BP185.7+ Islam
<186-186.9> Calendar. Sacred times. Fasts and feasts
Cf. BP186+ Islam
<186> General works
<186.15> Fridays. al-Jum‘ah. الجمعة
<186.2> New Year's Day (The first of Muḥarram). محرم
<186.3> ‘Āshūrā’ (The tenth of Muḥarram). العاشوراء
<186.34> Mawlid al-Nabī. مولد النبي
<186.36> Laylat al-Mi‘rāj. ليلة المعراج

Observances and practice of Islam

Calendar. Sacred times. Fasts and feasts -- Continued

<186.38> Laylat al-Barā'ah (Berat gecesi). Night of mid-Shaʻbān. ليلة البراءه

<186.4> Ramadan. Ramaḍān. رمضان

<186.43> Laylat al-Qadr. ليلة القدر

<186.45> ʻĪd al-Fiṭr. Fast-breaking at the end of Ramaḍān. عيد الفطر

<186.6> ʻĪd al-Aḍḥā (Day of sacrifice). عيد الاضحى

<186.9.A-Z> Other, A-Z

Veneration. Relics, etc.

Including superstitious practices

<186.97> General works

<186.97.A-Z> Special topics, A-Z

<186.97.A58> Amulets

<186.97.T65> Tombs, Visitation of

Visitation of tombs see KBP186.97.T65

Sacred places

Cf. BP187+ Islam

<187> General works

<187.2-.4> Mecca

<187.52-.55> Non-Meccan shrines, sanctuaries, etc. Mazārāt. Ḥaram. مزارات. حرم

<187.62-.69> Mosques. Monasteries

Sufism. Mysticism

Cf. BP188.45+ Islam

<188.5> History

<188.9> General works

<189.4> Biography

Including Saints, etc.

Sufi. Ṣūfī. صوفي

<189.5> General works

<189.585> Saint worship

<189.68> Monasticism. Ṣūfī orders

<190> Communal religious activities

For endowments, charitable uses, foundations, waqf (وقف) see KBP637+

<190.5.A-Z> Topics not otherwise provided for, A-Z

Schools of thought. Islamic legal schools. Madhāhib. مذاهب

Class here scholarly works, including works on both uṣūl al-fiqh and furūʻ al-fiqh (أصول الفقه، فروع الفقه) combined, with or without ʻIbādāt (عبادات)

For works limited to ʻibādāt (عبادات) see KBP184+

For works limited to furūʻ al-fiqh (فروع الفقه) see KBP490.2+

250 General (Collective and comparative)

253 Biography. Biographical dictionaries

Schools of thought. Islamic legal schools. Madhāhib. مذاهب -- Continued

Unaffiliated authors

Class here authors not affiliated with a particular school

Early period (1st and 2nd cent. A.H.)

Including companions and successors

255 General (Collective)

260.A-Z Individual authors, A-Z

260.A23 ʻAbd Allāh ibn al-ʻAbbās, d. 688?. عبد الله ابن العباس (Table K4)

260.A28 Abū ʻUbaydah Maʻmar ibn al-Muthanná al-Taymī, 728?-824?. أبو عبيدة معمر بن المثنى التيمي (Table K4)

260.I267 Ibn Rāhwayh, Isḥāq ibn Ibrāhīm, 778?-852? ابن راهويه, اسحاق بن ابراهيم (Table K4)

260.L39 Layth ibn Saʻd, 713-791. ليث بن سعد (Table K4)

260.N39 Naẓẓām, Ibrāhīm ibn Sayyār, 760?-845. النظام، ابراهيم ابن سيار (Table K4)

Middle period (to ca. 1920)

270 General (Collective)

275.A-Z Individual authors, A-Z

275.A35 Aḥmad bin ʻAlī Saʻīd, d. 1717. أحمد بن علي سعيد (Table K4)

275.I245 Ibn al-Qaṭṭān al-Fāsī, ʻAli ibn Muḥammad, 1166 or 7-1230. ابن القطان الفاسي، عل بن محمد (Table K4)

275.I26 Ibn al-Tilimsānī, ʻAbd Allāh ibn Muḥammad, 1171 or 2-1246 or 7. ابن التلمساني، عبد الله بن محمد (Table K4)

275.K39 Kawtharī, Muḥammad Zāhid ibn al-Ḥasan. الكوثري، محمد زاهد بن الحسن (Table K4)

275.M39 Māwardī, ʻAlī ibn Muḥammad, 974?-1058. الماوردي، علي بن محمد (Table K4)

275.R39 Rāzī, Fakhr al-Dīn ibn ʻUmar, 1149 or 50-1210. الرازي، فخر الدين بن عمر (Table K4)

275.S26 Ṣanʻānī, Muḥammad ibn Ismāʻīl, 1688-1768. صنعاني, محمد بن اسماعيل (Table K4)

275.S438 Shawkānī, Muḥammad ibn ʻAlī, 1759-1839. شوكاني, محمد بن علي (Table K4)

275.S55 Sijilmāsī, Aḥmad ibn Mubārak, d. 1743. السجلماسي، احمد بن مبارك (Table K4)

275.W37 Waṣābī, ʻUlwāh ibn Muḥammad al-Ḥibrī, 14th cent. الوصابي، علواة بن محمة الحبري (Table K4)

Late period (ca. 1920-)

280 General (Collective)

Schools of thought. Islamic legal schools. Madhāhib. مذاهب
Unaffiliated authors
Late period (ca. 1920-) -- Continued
283.A-Z Individual authors, A-Z
Subarrange each by Table K4
e. g.
283.A28 Abū Iṣba‘, ‘Abd al-Hādī Idrīs. أبو أصبع، عبد الهادي ادريس (Table K4)
283.F37 Farfūr, Walī al-Dīn Muḥammad Ṣāliḥ. الفرفور، ولي الدين محمد صالح (Table K4)
283.H36 Ḥammād, Miṣbāḥ al-Mutawallī al-Sayyid. حماد، مصباح المتولي السيد (Table K4)
283.I25 Ibn al-Ṣiddīq, Aḥmad, 1902-1960. ابن الصديق، أحمد (Table K4)
283.M35 Mālikī, ‘Alawī ibn ‘Abbās, 1909-1971. المالكي، علوي بن عباس (Table K4)
283.M37 Mar‘ashlī, Muḥammad ‘Abd al-Raḥmān. المرعشلي، محمد عبد الرحمن (Table K4)
283.Q37 Qāsimī, Mujāhidulislām, 1936-. القاسمي، مجاهد الاسلام (Table K4)
283.R34 Raḥmānī, Khālid Saifullāh. الرحمانى, خالد سيف الله (Table K4)
283.R59 Rizvī Amjad ‘Alī A‘ẓamī (Table K4)
283.S234 Sa‘dī, ‘Abd al-Raḥmān ibn Nāṣir. السعدي، عبد الرحمن بن ناصر (Table K4)
283.S34 Schacht, Joseph. (Table K4)
Schools and authors affiliated with a particular school
Sunnī schools
285 General (Collective and comparative)
Including works on several schools or on several authors belonging to different Sunnī (السني) schools (branches), and including biography
For works comparing Sunnī law (السني) with Shī‘ī law (الشيعي) see KBP420
290 Biographical dictionaries. Ṭabaqāt
Ḥanafī. Ḥanafīyah. طبقات، الحنفي، الحنفية
295 General works on school or authors (collective)
Including histories
300.A-Z Individual authors, A-Z
300.A234 ‘Abd al-Ḥaqq ibn Sayf al-Dīn Dihlavī, 1551-1642. عبد الحق بن سيف الدين دهلقي (Table K4)
300.A265 Abū al-Layth al-Samarqandī, Naṣr ibn Muḥammad, d. 983? ابو الليث السمرقندي، نصر بن محمد (Table K4)
300.A268 Abū al-Sa‘ūd Muḥammad ibn Muḥammad, 1492 or 3-1574 or 5. ابو السعود محمد بن محمد (Table K4)

Schools of thought. Islamic legal schools. Madhāhib. مذاهب
Schools and authors affiliated with a particular school
Sunnī schools
Ḥanafī. Ḥanafīyah. طبقات، الحنفي، الحنفية
Individual authors, A-Z -- Continued

300.A2688 Abū al-Su‘ūd, Muḥammad, d. 1758 or 9. ابو السعود, محمد (Table K4)

300.A272 Abū Ḥanīfah, d. 767 or 8. ابو حنيفة (Table K4)

300.A275 Abū Sharḥbīl (Table K4)

300.A278 Abū Yūsuf Ya‘qūb, 731 or 2-798. ابو يوسف يعقوب (Table K4)

300.A28 Abū Zayd al-Dābūsī, ‘Abd Allāh ibn ‘Umar, 977 or 8-1038 or 9. ابو زيد الدابوسي، عبد الله بن عمر (Table K4)

300.A37 Afghanī, ‘Abd al-Ḥakīm, 1835 or 6-1908 or 9. الأفغاني، عبد الحكيم (Table K4)

300.A39 Akhsīkathī, Muḥammad ibn Muḥammad, d. 1247. الاخسيكثي، محمد بن محمد (Table K4)

300.A42 Akmal al-Dīn al-Bābartī, Muḥammad ibn Maḥmūd, 1310 or 11-1384 or 5. اكمل الدين البابرتي، محمد بن محمود (Table K4)

300.A43 ‘Alī, 1117 or 8-1196 or 7. علي (Table K4)

300.A44 Ali Çelebi, Kınalızade, 1510-1571. على چلب، كيناليزاده (Table K4)

300.A45 ‘Ālim ibn ‘Alā’, d. 1384 or 5. عالم بن علاء (Table K4)

300.A88 ‘Attābī, Aḥmad ibn Muḥammad, d. 1190 or 91. العتابي، احمد بن محمد (Table K4)

300.A96 ‘Aynī, Badr al-Dīn Maḥmūd ibn Aḥmad, 1361-1451. العيني، بدر الدين محمود بن احمد (Table K4)

300.A97 A‘ẓimī, Niẓamuddīn, 1910- (Table K4)

300.B34 Bahā’ al-Dīn Zādah, Muḥammad ibn Bahā’ al-Dīn, d. 1545. بهاء الدين زادة، محمد بن بهاء الدين (Table K4)

300.B37 Baqqālī, Muḥammad ibn Abī al-Qāsim, 1096 or 7-1166 or 7. البقالي، محمد بن ابي القاسم (Table K4)

300.B39 Bazdawī, ‘Alī ibn Muḥammad, 1010-1089. البزدوي، علي بن محمد (Table K4)

300.B43 Bedreddin, Şeyh, 1358?-1420. بدر الدين، شيخ (Table K4)

300.B57 Birgivî, Mehmet Efendi, ca. 1522-1573. البرغوي، محمد افندي (Table K4)

300.B573 Birjandī, ‘Abd al-‘Alī ibn Muḥammad ibn Ḥusayn, 16th cent. البرجندي، عبد العلي بن محمد بن حسين (Table K4)

300.B847 Bukhārī, ‘Abd al-‘Azīz ibn Aḥmad, d. 1329 or 30. البخاري، عبد العزيز بن احمد (Table K4)

Schools of thought. Islamic legal schools. Madhāhib. مذاهب
Schools and authors affiliated with a particular school
Sunnī schools
Ḥanafī. Ḥanafīyah. طبقات، الحنفي، الحنفية
Individual authors, A-Z -- Continued

300.B85 Bukhārī, Ṭāhir ibn Aḥmad, 1090-1147. البخاري، طاهر بن احمد (Table K4)
300.D35 Dāmaghānī, Ḥusayn ibn Muḥammad, 1007-1085. الدامغاني، حسين بن محمد (Table K4)
300.F36 Fanārī, ‘Alī ibn Yūsuf, d. 1497 or 8. الفناري، علي بن يوسف (Table K4)
300.F362 Fanārī, Ḥasan ibn Muḥammad Shāh, 1436 or 7-1481 or 2. الفناري، حسن بن محمد شاه (Table K4)
300.F363 Fanārī, Muḥammad ibn Ḥamzah, 1350 or 51-1430 or 31. الفناري، محمد بن حمزة (Table K4)
300.F37 Faraḍī, Maḥmūd ibn Abī Bakr, 1246 or 7-1300. الفرضي، محمود بن ابي بكر (Table K4)
300.G528 Ghaznawī, Aḥmad, d. 1196 or 7. الغزنوي، احمد (Table K4)
300.G53 Ghaznawī, ‘Umar ibn Isḥaq, 1304 or 5-1371 or 2. الغزنوي، عمر بن اسحق (Table K4)
300.H33 Ḥaddād, Abū Bakr ibn ‘Alī, d. 1397 or 8. الحداد، ابو بكر بن علي (Table K4)
300.H35 Ḥalabī, Ibrāhīm ibn Muḥammad, d. 1549 or 50. الحلبي، ابراهيم بن محمد (Table K4)
300.H369 Ḥaṣīrī, Jamāl al-Dīn, 1151 or 2-1238 or 9. الحصيري، جمال الدين (Table K4)
300.H37 Ḥaṣkafī, Muḥammad ibn ‘Alī, ca. 1616-1670. الحصكفي، محمد بن علي (Table K4)
300.H39 Haytham ibn Sulaymān, 9th/10th cent. هيثم بن سليمان (Table K4)
300.H55 Hilāl al-Ra’y, d. 859 or 60. هلال الرأي (Table K4)
300.H59 Hızır Bey, 1407-1458. خضر بك (Table K4)
300.H87 Hüsrev, Molla, d. 1480. خسرو، ملا (Table K4)
300.I224 Ibn Abī al-‘Izz, ‘Alī ibn ‘Alī, 1330 or 31-1389 or 90. ابن ابي العز، علي بن علي (Table K4)
300.I225 Ibn Abī al-Wafā’ al-Qurashī, ‘Abd al-Qādir ibn Muḥammad, 1297-1373. ابن ابي الوفاء القرشي، عبد القادر بن محمد (Table K4)
300.I226 Ibn Abī ‘Āṣim al-Ḍaḥḥāk, Aḥmad ibn ‘Amr, 822-900. ابن أبي عاصم الضحاك، أحمد بن عمر (Table K4)
300.I23 Ibn al-‘Adīm, Kamāl al-Dīn ‘Umar ibn Aḥmad, 1192-1262. ابن العديم، كمال الدين عمر بن أحمد (Table K4)
300.I234 Ibn al-Jarrāḥ, Wakī‘, 746-812. ابن الجراح، وكيع (Table K4)

Schools of thought. Islamic legal schools. Madhāhib. مذاهب
Schools and authors affiliated with a particular school
Sunnī schools
Ḥanafī. Ḥanafīyah. طبقات، الحنفي، الحنفية
Individual authors, A-Z -- Continued

300.I237 Ibn al-Sāʻātī, Aḥmad ibn ʻAlī, 1254-1294 or 5. ابن الساعاتي، أحمد بن علي (Table K4)

300.I2372 Ibn al-Shiḥnah, ʻAbd al-Barr ibn Muḥammad, 1447 or 8-1515 or 16. ابن الشحنة، عبد البر بن محمد (Table K4)

300.I23724 Ibn al-Shiḥnah, Ibrāhīm ibn Muḥammad, d. 1477 or 8. ابن الشحنة، ابراهيم بن محمد (Table K4)

300.I238 Ibn al-Thaljī, Muḥammad ibn Shujāʻ, 797 or 8-879 or 80. ابن الثلجي، محمد بن شجاع (Table K4)

300.I239 Ibn Al-Turkumānī, ʻAlī ibn Ūthmān, 1284 or 5-1349. ابن التركماني، علي بن عثمان (Table K4)

300.I24 Ibn Amīr Ḥājj, Muḥammad ibn Muḥammad. 1421 or 2-1474 or 5. ابن أمير حاج، محمد بن محمد (Table K4)

300.I243 Ibn Balabān, ʻAlī, 1276 or 7-1339. ابن بلبان، علي (Table K4)

300.I25 Ibn Ḥabīb, Ṭāhir ibn al-Ḥasan, ca. 1339-1405 or 6. ابن حبيب، طاهر بن الحسن (Table K4)

300.I257 Ibn Makkī, ʻAlī ibn Aḥmad, d. 1201 or 2. ابن مكي، علي بن أحمد (Table K4)

300.I258 Ibn Malak, ʻAbd al-Laṭīf ibn ʻAbd al-ʻAzīz, d. 1398 or 9. ابن ملك، عبد اللطيف بن عبد العزيز (Table K4)

300.I26 Ibn Nujaym, ʻUmar ibn Ibrāhīm, d. 1596 or 7. ابن نجيم، عمر بن ابراهيم (Table K4)

300.I2615 Ibn Nujaym, Zayn al-Dīn ibn Ibrāhīm, d. 1563. ابن نجيم، زين الدين بن ابراهيم (Table K4)

300.I264 Ibn Quṭlūbughā, al-Qāsim ibn ʻAbd Allāh, 1399 or 1400-1474 or 5. ابن قطلوبغا، القاسم بن عبد الله (Table K4)

300.I267 Ibn Ṭūlūn, Shams al-Dīn Muḥammad ibn ʻAlī, 1485?-1546. ابن طولون، شمس الدين محمد بن علي (Table K4)

300.I27 Ibn Wahbān, ʻAbd al-Wahhāb ibn Aḥmad, d. 1366 or 7. ابن وهبان، عبد الوهاب بن أحمد (Table K4)

300.I43 Imām'zādah, Muḥammad ibn Abī Bakr, 1097 or 8 - 1177 or 8. امام زاده، محمد بن أبي بكر (Table K4)

300.I47 ʻImrānī, Yaḥyá ibn Abū al-Khayr, 1095 or 6-1163. عمراني، يحيى بن أبو الخير (Table K4)

300.I95 Izmīrī, Muḥammad ibn Walī, d. 1751 or 2. الازميري، محمد بن ولي (Table K4)

Schools of thought. Islamic legal schools. Madhāhib. مذاهب
Schools and authors affiliated with a particular school
Sunnī schools
Ḥanafī. Ḥanafīyah. طبقات، الحنفي، الحنفية
Individual authors, A-Z -- Continued

300.J37 Jaṣṣāṣ, Aḥmad ibn ʻAlī, 917-982. الجساس، أحمد بن علي (Table K4)

300.J87 Jurjānī, ʻAlī ibn Muḥammad, al-Sayyid al-Sharīf, 1340-1413. الجرجاني، علي بن محمد، السيد الشريف (Table K4)

300.K34 Kāfiyajī, Muḥammad ibn Sulaymān, d. 1474. الكافيجي، محمد بن سليمان (Table K4)

300.K35 Kākī, Muḥammad ibn Muḥammad, d. 1348 or 9. الكاكي، محمد بن محمد (Table K4)

300.K365 Karābīsī, Asʻad ibn Muḥammad, d. 1174. الكرابيسي، اسعد بن محمد (Table K4)

300.K366 Kardarī, Ibn al-Bazzāz, d. 1424. الكردري, أبن البزاز (Table K4)

300.K368 Karkhī, ʻUbayd Allāh ibn al-Ḥusayn, 873 or 4-952. الكرخي، عبيد الله بن حسين (Table K4)

300.K37 Karmānī, Muḥammad ibn Mukarram, d. ca. 1478. الكرماني، محمد بن مكرم (Table K4)

300.K376 Kāsānī, Abū Bakr ibn Masʻūd, d. 1191. الكاساني، ابو بكر بن مسعود (Table K4)

300.K378 Kāshgharī, Sadīd al-Dīn, 13th cent? الكشغاري، سديد الدين (Table K4)

300.K45 Kemalpaşazade, 1468 or 9-1534. كمالپشازاده (Table K4)

300.K532 Khabbāzī, ʻUmar ibn Muḥammad, 1231 or 2-1292. الخبازي، عمر بن محمد (Table K4)

300.K537 Khaṣṣāf, Aḥmad ibn ʻUmar, d. 874 or 5. الخصاف، احمد بن عمر (Table K4)

300.K538 Khaṭīb al-Tamartāshī, Muḥammad ibn ʻAbd Allāh, 1532 or 3-1595 or 6. خطيب التمرتاشي، محمد بن عبد الله (Table K4)

300.K54 Khiṭāʼī, ʻUthmān, 15th cent. خطائي، عثمان (Table K4)

300.K549 Khwājah'zādah, Muṣṭafá ibn Yūsuf, d. 1487 or 8. خواجهزاده، مصطفى بن يوسف (Table K4)

300.K87 Kūrānī, Aḥmad ibn Ismāʻīl, 1410 or 11-1487 or 8. الكوراني، احمد بن اسماعيل (Table K4)

300.L36 Lāmishī, Maḥmūd ibn Zayd, 11th/12th/ cent. اللامشي، محمود بن زيد (Table K4)

300.L85 Lu'lu'ī, al-Ḥasan Ibn Ziyād, d. 819 or 20. اللؤلؤي، الحسن بن زياد (Table K4)

300.M338 Maḥbūbī, Maḥmūd ibn ʻUbayd Allāh, d. 1344 or 5. إلمحبوبي، محمود بن عبيد الله (Table K4)

Schools of thought. Islamic legal schools. Madhāhib. مذاهب
Schools and authors affiliated with a particular school
Sunnī schools
Ḥanafī. Ḥanafīyah. طبقات، الحنفي، الحنفية
Individual authors, A-Z -- Continued

300.M34 Maḥbūbī, ʻUbayd Allāh ibn Masʻūd, d. 1346 or 7. المحبوبي، عبيد الله بن مسعود (Table K4)

300.M345 Mahmut Esat bin Emin, 1857-1917. محمود اسعد بن امين (Table K4)

300.M35 Makkī, Muḥammad ibn Muḥammad, d. 1480. المكي، محمد بن محمد (Table K4)

300.M36 Manbijī, ʻAlī ibn Zakarīyā, d. 1287 or 8. المنبجي، علي بن زكريا (Table K4)

300.M365 Maqdisī, ʻAlī ibn Ghānim, 1514-1596. المقدسي، علي بن غانم (Table K4)

300.M37 Marghīnānī, ʻAlī ibn Abī Bakr, d. 1196 or 7. المرغيناني، علي بن ابي بكر (Table K4)

300.M372 Marghīnānī, Maḥmūd ibn Aḥmad, 1156 or 7-1219 or 20. المرغيناني، محمود بن احمد (Table K4)

300.M374 Marīsī, Bishr ibn Ghayāth, d. 833. المريسي، بشر بن غياث (Table K4)

300.M38 Māturīdī, Muḥammad ibn Muḥammad, d. 944 or 5. الماتريدي، محمد بن محمد (Table K4)

300.M39 Mawṣilī, ʻAbd Allāh ibn Maḥmūd, 1202 or 3-1284. الموصلي، عبد الله بن محمود (Table K4)

300.M835 Muḥammad ʻAbd al-Ḥayy, 1848-1886 or 7 محمد عبد الحي (Table K4)

300.M84 Muʻīn al-Dīn Farāhī, d. 1501 or 2. معين الدين فراهي (Table K4)

300.M85 Mullā al-Aḥsāʼī, Abū Bakr ibn Muḥammad ibn ʻUmar. ملا الحسائي، ابو بكر بن محمد بن عمر (Table K4)

300.M88 Muṭarrizī, Nāṣir ibn ʻAbd al-Sayyid, 1144-1213. المطرزي، ناصر بن عبد السيد (Table K4)

300.N33 Nābulusī, ʻAbd al-Ghanī ibn Ismāʻīl, 1641-1731. النابلسي، عبد الغني بن اسماعيل (Table K4)

300.N37 Nasafī, ʻAbd Allāh ibn Aḥmad, d. 1310. النسفي، عبد الله بن احمد (Table K4)

300.N373 Nasafī, Maymūn ibn Muḥammad, d. 1115. النسفي، ميمون بن محمد (Table K4)

300.N374 Nasafī, Muḥammad ibn Muḥammad, 1203 or 4-1288 or 9. النسفي، محمد بن محمد (Table K4)

300.N375 Nasafī, ʻUmar ibn Muḥamad, 1068?-1142. النسفي، عمر بن محمد (Table K4)

300.N39 Nāẓirzādah, Muḥammad ibn Sulaymān, 17th cent. ناظرزاده, محمد بن سليمان (Table K4)

Schools of thought. Islamic legal schools. Madhāhib. مذاهب
Schools and authors affiliated with a particular school
Sunnī schools
Ḥanafī. Ḥanafīyah. طبقات، الحنفي، الحنفية
Individual authors, A-Z -- Continued

300.Q23 Qāḍī Khān, al-Ḥasan ibn Manṣūr al-Ūzjandī al-Farghānī, d. 1196. قاضي خان، الحسن بن منصور الاوزجندي (Table K4)

300.Q27 Qāriʼ al-Hidāyah, ʻAlī, d. 1426. قارئ الهداية (Table K4)

300.Q38 Qudūrī, Aḥmad ibn Muḥammad, 972 or 3-1037. القدوري، احمد بن محمد (Table K4)

300.Q53 Quhandizī, ʻAlī ibn Muḥammad, d. 1267 or 8. قهندزي، علي بن محمد (Table K4)

300.S227 Saʻdī Chalabī, Saʻd Allāh ibn ʻĪsá, d. 1538 or 9. سعدي چلبي، سعد الله بن عيسى (Table K4)

300.S23 Ṣadr al-Shahīd, ʻUmar ibn ʻAbd al-ʻAzīz, 1090 or 91-1141. صدر الشهيد، عمر بن عبد العزيز (Table K4)

300.S242 Ṣaghānī, al-Ḥasan ibn Muḥammad, 1181-1252. الصغاني، الحسن بن محمد (Table K4)

300.S243 Saghnāqī, al-Ḥusayn ibn ʻAlī, d. 1311 or 12. الصغناقي، الحسين بن علي (Table K4)

300.S245 Sajāwandī, Sirāj al-Dīn Muḥammad ibn Muḥammad, 12th cent. السجاوندي، سراج الدين محمد بن محمد (Table K4)

300.S247 Sakkākī, Yūsuf ibn Abī Bakr, b. 1160. السكاكي، يوسف بن ابي بكر (Table K4)

300.S25 Salāmat ʻAlī K͟hān, 18th cent. سلامت علي خان (Table K4)

300.S258 Samarqandī, ʻAlāʼ al-Dīn Muḥammad ibn Aḥmad, d. 1144? السمرقندي، علاء الدين محمد بن احمد (Table K4)

300.S26 Samarqandī, Muḥammad ibn Yūsuf, d. 1160 or 61. السمرقندي، محمد بن يوسف (Table K4)

300.S27 Sarakhsī, Muḥammad ibn Aḥmad, 11th cent. السرخسي، محمد بن احمد (Table K4)

300.S277 Sarrūjī, Aḥmad ibn Ibrāhīm, ca. 1239-ca. 1310. السروجي، احمد بن ابراهيم (Table K4)

300.S29 Ṣaymarī, Abū ʻAbd Allāh Ḥusayn ibn ʻAlī, d. 1044. الصيمري، ابو عبد الله حسين بن علي (Table K4)

300.S49 Shāshī, Aḥmad ibn Muḥammad, d. 955 or 6. الشاشي، احمد بن محمد (Table K4)

300.S53 Shaybānī, Muḥammad ibn al-Ḥasan, ca. 750-804 or 5. الشيباني، محمد بن الحسن (Table K4)

KBP

Schools of thought. Islamic legal schools. Madhāhib. مذاهب
Schools and authors affiliated with a particular school
Sunnī schools
Ḥanafī. Ḥanafīyah. طبقات، الحنفي، الحنفية
Individual authors, A-Z -- Continued

300.S54 Shaykhʹzādah, Muḥammad ibn Muṣṭafá, d. 1544 or 5. شيخزاده، محمد بن مصطفى (Table K4)

300.S576 Shumunnī, Aḥmad ibn Muḥammad ibn Muḥammad, 1399-1468. الشموني، احمد بن محمد بن محمد (Table K4)

300.S58 Shurunbulālī, Ḥasan ibn ʻAmmār, 1585 or 6-1659. الشرنبلالي، حسن بن عمار (Table K4)

300.S59 Sinan Paşa, 1440-1486. سنن پاشا (Table K4)

300.S593 Sindī, Raḥmat Allāh ibn ʻAbd Allāh, ca. 1523-1585. السندي، رحمة الله بن عبد الله (Table K4)

300.S84 Sughdī, ʻAlī ibn al-Ḥusayn, d. 1068 or 9. سغدي، علي بن الحسين (Table K4)

300.T335 Taftāzānī, Masʻūd ibn ʻUmar, 1322-1389? التفتزاني، مسعود بن عمر (Table K4)

300.T34 Ṭaḥāwī, Aḥmad ibn Muḥammad, 852?-933. الطحاوي، أحمد بن محمد (Table K4)

300.T367 Ṭarābulusī, Ibrāhīm ibn Mūsá, 1439 or 40-1516 or 17. الطرابلسي، ابراهيم بن موسى (Table K4)

300.T37 Ṭaraṣūṣī, Ibrāhīm ibn ʻAlī, 1320-ca. 1356. الطرصوصي، ابراهيم بن علي (Table K4)

300.T375 Ṭāshkubrīʹzādah, Aḥmad ibn Muṣṭafá, 1495-1561. الطاشكبريزاده، أحمد بن مصطفى (Table K4)

300.T87 Ṭūrī, Muḥammad ibn al-Ḥusayn, fl. 1726. الطوري، محمد بن الحسين (Table K4)

300.T875 Ṭūsī, ʻAlī ibn Muḥammad, d. 1472 or 3. الطوسي، علي بن محمد (Table K4)

300.U76 Ūshī, ʻAlī ibn ʻUthmān, 12th cent. الأوشي، علي بن عثمان (Table K4)

300.U78 Ustarūshanī, Muḥammad ibn Maḥmūd, d. 1234 or 5. الاستروشني، محمد بن محمود (Table K4)

300.V36 Vankulu Mehmet Efendi, d. 1592. ونكولو، محمد أفندي (Table K4)

300.W35 Walwālījī, ʻAbd al-Rashīd ibn Abī Ḥanīfah, 1074 or 5-ca. 1145. الولواليجي، عبد الرشيد بن أبي حنيفة (Table K4)

300.Z35 Zamakhsharī, Maḥmūd ibn ʻUmar, 1075-1144. الزمخشري، محمود بن عمر (Table K4)

300.Z39 Zaylaʻī, ʻAbd Allāh ibn Yūsuf, d. 1360 or 61. الزيلعي، عبد الله بن يوسف (Table K4)

300.Z394 Zaylaʻī, ʻUthmān ibn ʻAlī, d. 1342 or 3. الزيلعي، عثمان بن علي (Table K4)

Schools of thought. Islamic legal schools. Madhāhib. مذاهب
Schools and authors affiliated with a particular school
Sunnī schools -- Continued
Ḥanbalī. Ḥanbalīyah. Ḥanābilah. الحنبلي الحنبلية. الحنابلة

305 General works on school or authors (collective)
Including histories

310.A-Z Individual authors, A-Z

310.A33 Adamī, Aḥmad ibn Muḥammad, d. ca. 1348 or 9. الأدمي، أحمد بن محمد (Table K4)

310.B33 Badrān, 'Abd al-Qādir, d. 1927. بدران، عبد القادر (Table K4)

310.B346 Ba'lī, 'Abd al-Raḥmān ibn 'Abd Allāh, 1698 or 9-1778 or 9. البعلي، عبد الرحمن بن عبد الله (Table K4)

310.B347 Ba'lī, 'Alī ibn Muḥammad. البعلي، علي بن محمد (Table K4)

310.B35 Ba'lī, Muḥammad ibn Abī al-Fatḥ, 1247 or 8-1309 or 10. البعلي، محمد بن أبي الفتح (Table K4)

310.B39 Baghdādī, 'Abd al-Raḥīm ibn 'Abd Allāh, d. 1341 البغدادي, عبد الرحيم بن عبد الله (Table K4)

310.B84 Buhūtī, Manṣūr ibn Yūnus, d. 1641. البهوتي، منصور بن يونس (Table K4)

310.G43 Ghassānī, 'Abd al-Raḥmān ibn Razīn, d. 1258. الغساني, عبد الرحمن بن رزين (Table K4)

310.H854 Ḥujāwī, Mūsá ibn Aḥmad, d. 1560. الحجاوي، موسى بن أحمد (Table K4)

310.I254 Ibn al-Bannā', al-Ḥasan ibn Aḥmad, 1005 or 6-1079. ابن البناء، الحسن بن أحمد (Table K4)

310.I256 Ibn al-Farrā', Abū Ya'lá Muḥammad ibn al-Ḥusayn, 990-1066. ابن الفراء، أبو يعلى محمد بن الحسين (Table K4)

310.I263 Ibn al-Mibrad, Yūsuf ibn Ḥasan, 1436 or 7-1503. ابن المبرد، يوسف بن حسن (Table K4)

310.I2633 Ibn al-Najjār, Taqī al-Dīn Muḥammad ibn Aḥmad, 1492 or 3-1564 or 5. ابن النجار, تقي الدين محمد بن أحمد (Table K4)

310.I2636 Ibn 'Aqīl, Abū al-Wafā' 'Alī, d. 1119. ابن عقيل، أبو الوفاء علي (Table K4)

310.I2638 Ibn Balabān, Muḥammad ibn Badr al-Dīn, 1597 or 8-1672 or 3. ابن بلبان، محمد بن بدر الدين (Table K4)

310.I2639 Ibn Baṭṭah, 'Ubayd Allāh ibn Muḥammad, 917-997. ابن بطة، عبيد الله محمد (Table K4)

310.I264 Ibn Ḍūyān, Ibrāhīm ibn Muḥammad, 1858 or 9-1934 or 5. ابن ضويان، ابراهيم بن محمد (Table K4)

KBP

Schools of thought. Islamic legal schools. Madhāhib. مذاهب
Schools and authors affiliated with a particular school
Sunnī schools
Ḥanbalī. Ḥanbalīyah. Ḥanābilah. الحنبلي الحنبلية. الحنابلة
Individual authors, A-Z -- Continued

310.I265 Ibn Ḥamdān, Aḥmad ibn Ḥamdān, 1206 or 7-1295 or 6. ابن حمدان، أحمد بن حمدان (Table K4)

310.I2653 Ibn Ḥanbal, Aḥmad ibn Muḥammad, 780-855. ابن حنبل، أحمد بن محمد (Table K4)

310.I266 Ibn Hubayrah, Yaḥyá ibn Muḥammad, d. 1165. ابن هبيرة، يحيى بن محمد (Table K4)

310.I27 Ibn Mufliḥ al-Maqdisī, Muḥammad, d. 1362. ابن مفلح المقدسي, محمد (Table K4)

310.I277 Ibn Qāsim, ʻAbd al-Raḥmān ibn Muḥammad. ابن قاسم، عبد الرحمن بن محمد (Table K4)

310.I28 Ibn Qayyim al-Jawzīyah, Muḥammad ibn Abī Bakr, 1292-1350. ابن قيم الجوزية، محمد بن أبي بكر (Table K4)

310.I285 Ibn Qudāmah, Muwaffaq al-Dīn ʻAbd Allāh ibn Aḥmad, 1147-1223. ابن قدامة، موفق الدين عبد الله بن أحمد (Table K4)

310.I2855 Ibn Qundus, Abū Bakr ibn Ibrāhīm, ca. 1406-ca. 1456. ابن قندس، أبو بكر بن ابراهيم (Table K4)

310.I2864 Ibn Shihāb, al-Ḥasan ibn Shihāb, ca. 946-1037. ابن شهاب، الحسن بن شهاب (Table K4)

310.I2867 Ibn Sunaynah, Muḥammad ibn ʻAbd Allāh, 1140 or 41-1219. ابن سنينة، محمد بن عبد الله (Table K4)

310.I287 Ibn Rajab, ʻAbd al-Raḥmān ibn Aḥmad, 1336-1393. ابن رجب، عبد الرحمن بن أحمد (Table K4)

310.I2878 Ibn Taymīyah, ʻAbd al-Salām ibn ʻAbd Allāh, 1193 or 4-1254 or 5. ابن تيمية، عبد السلام بن عبد الله (Table K4)

310.I288 Ibn Taymīyah, Aḥmad ibn ʻAbd al-Ḥalīm, 1263-1328. ابن تيمية، أحمد بن عبد الحليم (Table K4)

310.I2885 Ibn Taymīyah, Muḥammad ibn al-Khuḍr, 1147-1225. ابن تيمية، محمد بن الخضر (Table K4)

310.I294 Ibn ʻUbaydān, ʻAbd al-Raḥmān ibn Maḥmūd, 1276 or 7-1333. ابن عبيدان، عبد الرحمن بن محمود (Table K4)

310.J35 Jammāʻīlī, ʻAbd al-Ghanī ibn ʻAbd al-Wāḥid, 1146-1203. الجماعيلي، عبد الغني بن عبد الواحد (Table K4)

310.J37 Jarrāʻī, Abū Bakr ibn Zayd, 1422-1478. الجراعي، أبو بكر بن زيد (Table K4)

Schools of thought. Islamic legal schools. Madhāhib. مذاهب
Schools and authors affiliated with a particular school
Sunnī schools
Ḥanbalī. Ḥanbalīyah. Ḥanābilah. الحنبلي الحنبلية. الحنابلة
Individual authors, A-Z -- Continued

310.J57 Jirāʻī, Abū Bakr ibn Zayd, 1422-1478. الجراعي، أبو بكر بن زيد (Table K4)

310.K35 Kalwadhānī, Maḥfūẓ ibn Aḥmad, 1041-1116. الكلوذاني، محفوظ بن أحمد (Table K4)

310.K37 Karmī, Marʻī ibn Yūsuf, d. 1623 or 4. الكرمي، مرعي بن يوسف (Table K4)

310.M87 Mushayqiḥ, Khālid ibn ʻAlī ibn Muḥammad. المشيقح، خالد بن علي بن محمد (Table K4)

310.S24 Saffārīnī, Muḥammad ibn Muḥammad, 1702 or 3-1774. السفاريني، محمد بن محمد (Table K4)

310.S89 Ṣuwayyigh, ʻAbd al-Muḥsin ibn ʻAbd al-ʻAzīz الصويغ، عبد المحسن بن عبد العزيز (Table K4)

310.U39 ʻUkbarī, al-Ḥusayn ibn Muḥammad, 11th cent. العكبري، الحسين بن محمد (Table K4)

310.Z83 Zubayrī, ʻAbd Allāh ibn ʻAbd al-Raḥmān al-Ḥamūd al-Ḥanbalī. الزبيري، عبد الله بن عبد الرحمن الحمود الحنبلي (Table K4)

Mālikī. Mālikīyah. المالكي، المالكية

315 General works on school or authors (collective)
Including histories

320.A-Z Individual authors, A-Z

320.A24 ʻAbd al-Wahhāb, 972 or 3-1031 or 2. عبد الوهاب (Table K4)

320.A393 Akhḍarī, ʻAbd al-Raḥmān ibn Muḥammad, 1512 or 13-1575. الأخضري، عبد الرحمن بن محمد (Table K4)

320.B35 Bājī, Sulaymān ibn Khalaf, 1012 or 3-1081? الباجي، سليمان بن خلف (Table K4)

320.B36 Ballūṭī, Mundhir ibn Saʻīd, 886-966. البلوتي، منذير بن سعيد (Table K4)

320.B37 Baqqūrī, Muḥammad ibn Ibrāhīm, d. 1307 or 8. البقوري، محمد بن ابراهيم (Table K4)

320.B87 Burzulī, Abū al-Qāsim ibn Aḥmad, 1340-1440. البرزلي، أبو القاسم بن أحمد (Table K4)

320.F35 Falaysī, Muḥammad ibn ʻAbd al-Raḥmān, fl. 17th cent. الفليسي، محمد بن عبد الرحمن (Table K4)

320.F36 Fandlāwī, Yūsuf ibn Dūnās, d. 1148 or 9. الفندلاوي، يوسف بن دوناس (Table K4)

Schools of thought. Islamic legal schools. Madhāhib. مذاهب
Schools and authors affiliated with a particular school
Sunnī schools
Mālikī. Mālikīyah. المالكي، المالكية
Individual authors, A-Z -- Continued

320.G48 Ghalāwī, Muḥammad al-Nābighah ibn ʻUmar, d. 1828. الغلاوي، محمد النابغة بن عمر (Table K4)

320.G87 Gursīfī, ʻUmar ibn ʻAbd al-ʻAzīz, d. 1799 or 1800. گرسيفي، عمر بن عبد العزيز (Table K4)

320.H34 Ḥajwī, Muḥammad ibn al-Ḥasan. حجوي, محمد بن الحسن (Table K4)

320.H35 Ḥalūlū, Aḥmad ibn ʻAbd al-Raḥmān, 15th cent. الحلولو، أحمد بن عبد الرحمن (Table K4)

320.H37 Ḥasanī, Muḥammad ibn Laḥsan. الحسني، محمد بن لحسن (Table K4)

320.I23 Ibn Abī Zayd al-Qayrawānī, ʻAbd Allāh ibn ʻAbd al-Raḥmān, 10th cent. ابن أبي زيد القيرواني، عبد الله بن عبد الرحمن (Table K4)

320.I25 Ibn al-Ḥājib, ʻUthmān ibn ʻUmar, 1175-1249. ابن الحاجب، عثمان بن عمر (Table K4)

320.I26 Ibn al-Ḥājj, al-Ṭālib ibn Ḥamdūn, d. 1856 or 7. ابن الحاج، الطالب بن حمدون (Table K4)

320.I2625 Ibn Daqīq al-ʻĪd, Muḥammad ibn ʻAlī, 1228-1302. ابن دقيق العيد، محمد بن علي (Table K4)

320.I263 Ibn Nāṣir al-Dīn, Muḥammad ibn ʻAbd Allāh, 1375-1438. ابن ناصر الدين، محمد بن عبد الله (Table K4)

320.I265 Ibn Saʻdūn, Yaḥyá ibn ʻUmar, 1093 or 4-1172. ابن سعدون، يحيى بن عمر (Table K4)

320.I267 Ibn Wahb, ʻAbd Allāh, 742 or 3-812 or 13. ابن وهب، عبد الله (Table K4)

320.I93 ʻIyāḍ ibn Mūsá, 1083-1149. عياد بن موسى (Table K4)

320.J37 Jashtīmī, Abū Zayd ʻAbd al-Raḥmān ibn ʻAbd Allāh, 1771-1853. حشتيمي, ابو زيد عبد الرحمن بن عبد الله (Table K4)

320.K43 Khalīl ibn Isḥāq al-Jundī, d. 1365? خليل بن اسحاق الجندي (Table K4)

320.L37 Laqānī, Ibrāhīm ibn Ibrāhīm, d. 1631 or 2. اللقاني، ابراهيم بن ابراهيم (Table K4)

320.M35 Mālik ibn Anas, d. 795. مالك بن أنس (Table K4)

320.M38 Mawwāq, Muḥammad ibn Yūsuf, d. 1491 or 2. مواق, محمد بن يوسف (Table K4)

320.M84 Muḥammad ibn ʻAbd Allāh, Sultan of Morocco, d. 1790. محمد بن عبد الله، سلطان المغرب (Table K4)

Schools of thought. Islamic legal schools. Madhāhib. مذاهب
Schools and authors affiliated with a particular school
Sunnī schools
Mālikī. Mālikīyah. المالكي، المالكية
Individual authors, A-Z -- Continued

320.Q27 Qarāfī, Aḥmad ibn Idrīs, d. 1285. القرافي، أحمد بن ادريس (Table K4)

320.S26 Saḥnūn, ‘Abd al-Salām ibn Sa‘īd, 776 or 7-854. السحنون، عبد السلام بن سعيد (Table K4)

320.S53 Shāṭibī, Ibrāhīm ibn Mūsá, d. 1388. الشاطبى، ابراهيم بن موسى (Table K4)

320.S64 Sijilmāsī, Muḥammad ibn Abī al-Qāsim, d. 1800 سجلماسي، محمد بن ابي القاسم (Table K4)

320.T39 Tāwudī, Muḥammad, 1699 or 1700-1795. التاودي، محمد (Table K4)

320.W37 Waqashī, Abū al-Walīd Hishām ibn Aḥmad, d. 1096. الوقشي، أبو الوليد هشام بن أحمد (Table K4)

Shāfi‘ī. Shāfi‘īyah. الشافعي، الشافعية

325 General works on school or authors (collective)
Including histories

330.A-Z Individual authors, A-Z

330.A28 Abū Shujā‘ al-Iṣfahānī, Aḥmad ibn al-Ḥusayn, b. ca. 1042. أبو شجاع الاصفهاني، أحمد بن الحسين (Table K4)

330.A57 Anṣārī, Zakarīyā ibn Muḥammad, ca. 1423-ca. 1520. الأنصاري, زكريا بن محمد (Table K4)

330.A73 Ardabīlī, Yūsuf ibn Ibrāhīm, d. 1396 or 7. أردبيلي, يوسف بن ابراهيم (Table K4)

330.B36 Banbī, Muḥammad ibn Ḥasan, 1398 or 9-1460 or 61. البنبي، محمد بن حسن (Table K4)

330.B393 Bayḍāwī, ‘Abd Allāh ibn ‘Umar, d. 1286? البيضاوي عبد الله بن عمر (Table K4)

330.F57 Fīrūzābādī al-Shīrāzī, Abū Isḥāq Ibrāhīm ibn ‘Alī ibn Yūsuf, cal 1003-1083. الفيروزابادي الشيرازي، أبو اسحاق ابراهيم ين علي بن يوسف (Table K4)

330.I22 Ibn al-Bārizī, Hibat Allāh ibn Najm al-Dīn, 1247-1338. ابن البارزي، هبة الله بن نجم الدين (Table K4)

330.I24 Ibn al-Dahhān, Muḥammad ibn ‘Alī, d. 1193. ابن الدهان، محمد بن علي (Table K4)

330.I244 Ibn al-Daybā‘, ‘Abd al-Raḥmān ibn ‘Alī, 1461-1537. ابن الديباع، عبد الرحمن بن علي (Table K4)

330.I26 Ibn al-Mulaqqin, ‘Umar ibn ‘Alī, 1323-1401. ابن الملقن، عمر بن علي (Table K4)

330.I2625 Ibn Daqīq al-‘Īd, Muḥammad ibn ‘Alī, 1228-1302. ابن دقيق العيد، محمد بن علي (Table K4)

Schools of thought. Islamic legal schools. Madhāhib. مذاهب
Schools and authors affiliated with a particular school
Sunni schools
Shāfiʻī. Shāfiʻīyah. الشافعي، الشافعية
Individual authors, A-Z -- Continued

330.I263 Ibn Imām al-Kāmilīyah, Muḥammad ibn Muḥammad, 1406-1469 or 70. ابن امام الكاملية، محمد بن محمد (Table K4)

330.I265 Ibn Surayj, Aḥmad ibn ʻUmar, 863-918. ابن سريج، أحمد بن عمر (Table K4)

330.I43 Imām al-Ḥaramayn al-Juwaynī, ʻAbd al-Malik ibn ʻAbd Allāh, 1028-1085. امام الحرمين الجويني, عبد الملك بن عبد الله (Table K4)

330.I47 ʻImrānī, Yaḥyá ibn Abū al-Khayr, 1095 or 6-1163. العمراني، يحيى بن أبو الخير (Table K4)

330.K45 Khalīfī, ʻAbd al-ʻAzīz ibn Ṣāliḥ. خليفي، عبد العزيز بن صالح (Table K4)

330.N39 Nawawī, 1233-1277. النووي (Table K4)

330.R39 Raymī, Muḥammad ibn ʻAbd Allāh, d. 1389 or 90 الريمي، محمد بن عبد الله (Table K4)

330.S53 Shāfiʻī, Muḥammad ibn Idrīs, 767 or 8-820. الشافعي، محمد بن ادريس (Table K4)

330.S54 Shaʻrānī, ʻAbd al-Wahhāb ibn Aḥmad, 1493 (ca.)-1565 or 6. الشعراني، عبد الوهاب بن أحمد (Table K4)

330.S93 Subkī, Tāj al-Dīn ʻAbd al-Wahhāb ibn ʻAlī, ca. 1337-1370. السبكي، تاج الدين عبد الوهاب بن علي (Table K4)

330.S95 Sulamī, ʻIzz al-Dīn ʻAbd al-ʻAzīz ibn ʻAbd al-Salām, ca. 1182-1262. السلمي، عز الدين عبد العزيز بن عبد السلام (Table K4)

Ẓāhirī. Ẓāhirīyah. الظاهري، الظاهرية

335 General works on schools or authors (collective)
Including histories

340.A-Z Individual authors, A-Z
Subarrange each author by Table K4

Mixed. Comparative see KBP290

Shīʻī schools. Shīʻah. شيعة

350 General (Collective and comparative)
Including works on several schools (branches); or on several authors belonging to different Shīʻī schools (branches); and including biography
For works comparing Shīʻī law with Sunnī law see KBP420

Ismāʻīlī. أسماعيلي

355 General works on school or authors (collective)
Including histories

Schools of thought. Islamic legal schools. Madhāhib. مذاهب
Schools and authors affiliated with a particular school
Shīʻī schools. Shīʻah. شيعة
Ismāʻīlī. أسماعيلي -- Continued
360.A-Z Individual authors, A-Z
Subarrange each author by Table K4
Jaʻfarīs. Ithnaʻasharis. الجعفريون. الاثناء عشريون
365 General works on school or authors (collective)
Including histories
370.A-Z Individual authors, A-Z
370.A57 Anṣārī, Murtaḍá ibn Muḥammad Amīn, 1799 or 1800-1864. الانصاري، مرتضى بن محمد امين (Table K4)
370.B34 Baḥrānī, Muḥammad Ṣanqūr ʻAlī. البحراني، محمد صنقور علي (Table K4)
370.B85 Bujnūrdī, Ḥasan ibn ʻAlī Aṣghar al-Mūsawī. البجنوردي، حسن بن علي اصغر الموسوي (Table K4)
370.B87 Burūjirdī, Ḥusayn al-Ṭabāṭabāʼī. البروجردي، حسين الطباطبايي (Table K4)
370.H35 Ḥāʼirī, ʻAlī ibn ʻAbd al-Ḥusayn, b. 1883 or 4. الحايري، علي بن عبد الحسين (Table K4)
370.H353 Ḥāʼirī, al-Burūjirdī, Bahāʼ al-Dīn, 1891 or 2-1969 or 70. حجتي البروجردي، بهاء الدين (Table K4)
370.I263 Ibn al-Muṭahhar al-Ḥillī, al-Ḥasan ibn Yūsuf, 1250-1325. أبن المطهر الحلي، الحسن بن يوسف (Table K4)
370.I267 Ibn al-Shahīd al-Thānī, al-Ḥasan, 1551 or 2-1602-3. أبن الشهيد الثاني، الحسن (Table K4)
370.I27 Ibn Bābawayh al-Qummī, Muḥammad ibn ʻAlī, 918 or 19-991 or 2. ابن بابويه القمي, مجمد بن علي (Table K4)
370.I28 Ibn Fahd, Aḥmad ibn Muḥammad, 1356 or 7-1437 or 8. ابن فهد, أحمد بن محمد (Table K4)
370.K49 Khurāsānī, Muḥammad Kāẓim, 1839 or 40-1911. الخراساني، محمد كاظم (Table K4)
370.M33 Madanī, ʻAlī ibn Jaʻfar, d. 825. مدني, علي بن جعفر (Table K4)
370.M83 Mufīd, Muḥammad ibn Muḥammad, d. 1022. مفيد، محمد بن محمد (Table K4)
370.M84 Muḥaqqiq al-Ḥillī, Jaʻfar ibn al-Ḥasan, 1205 or 6-1277. محقق الحلي, جعفر بن الحسن (Table K4)
370.R34 Raḥmatī, Muḥammad. الرحمتي، محمد (Table K4)
370.S52 Shahīd al-Awwal, Muḥammad ibn Makkī, 1333 or 4-1380. الشهيد الاول، محمد بن مكي (Table K4)
370.S53 Shahīd al-Thānī, Zayn al-Dīn ibn ʻAlī, 1506-1559. الشهيد الثاني، زين الدين بن علي (Table K4)

Schools of thought. Islamic legal schools. Madhāhib. مذاهب
Schools and authors affiliated with a particular school
Shīʻī schools. Shīʻah. شيعة
Jaʻfarīs. Ithnaʻasharis. الجعفريون. الاثناء عشريون
Individual authors, A-Z -- Continued
370.S58 Sīstānī, ʻAlī al-Ḥusaynī. سيستاني، علي الحسيني (Table K4)
370.S87 Surūr, Muḥammad. سرور, محمد (Table K4)
370.T329 Ṭabāṭabāʼī al-Ḥakīm, Muḥammad Saʻīd. طباطبايئي الحكيم, محمد سعيد (Table K4)
370.T33 Ṭabāṭabāʼī al-Ḥakīm, Muḥsin ibn Mahdī. الطباطبايئي الحكيم، محسن بن مهدي (Table K4)
370.T54 Ṭihrānī, Muḥammad Taqī ibn ʻAbd al-Raḥīm, d. 1832 or 3. الطهراني، محمد تقي بن عبد الرحيم (Table K4)
370.T88 Ṭūsī, Muḥammad ibn al-Ḥasan, 995-1067?. طوسي، محمد بن الحسن (Table K4)
Zaydī. Zaydīyah. زيدي. زيدية
375 General works on school or authors (collective)
Including histories
380.A-Z Individual authors, A-Z
Subarrange each author by Table K4
380.Z39 Zayd ibn ʻAlī, d. 740. زيد بن علي (Table K4)
ʻIbāḍī. اباضي
390 General works on school or authors (collective)
Including histories
395.A-Z Individual authors, A-Z
395.A24 Aḥmad ibn Saʻīd ibn Khalfān, d. 1907. احمد بن سعيد بن خلفان (Table K4)
395.A45 ʻĀmir ibn Khamīs, ca. 1067-1157. أمر بن خامس (Table K4)
395.A87 Aṭṭafayyish, Muḥammad ibn Yūsuf, 1820 or 21-1914. عطفيش، محمد بن يوسف (Table K4)
395.I26 Ibn Sayʻīd, Yaḥyá. أبن سعيد، يحيى (Table K4)
395.J36 Jannawnī, Yaḥyá ibn al-Khayr. الجناوني، يحيى بن الخير (Table K4)
395.K43 Kharūṣī, Saʻīd ibn Khalaf. خروصي، سعيد بن خلف (Table K4)
395.S25 Sālimī, ʻAbd Allāh ibn Ḥumayyid, b. ca. 1871. السالمي، عبدالله بن حميد (Table K4)
395.S29 Sayyābī, Sālim ibn Ḥammūd. سيابي، سالم بن حمود (Table K4)
395.S55 Shiqṣī al-Rustāqī, Khamīs. الشقصي الرستاقي (Table K4)
395.T49 Thamīnī, ʻAbd al-ʻAzīz ibn Ibrāhīm, 1720-1808. الثميني، عبدالعزيز بن ابراهيم (Table K4)

Schools of thought. Islamic legal schools. Madhāhib. مذاهب
Schools and authors affiliated with a particular school -- Continued
400.A-Z Other schools, A-Z
420 Mixed. Comparative
Class here works comparing Sunnī and Shīʻī schools and authors, and works comparing Sunnī law with Shīʻī law
Uṣūl al-fiqh. Jurisprudence and theory of law. Science of legal reasoning. اصول الفقه
425 Bibliography
427 Encyclopedias. Dictionaries
Biography
see the school or individiual author, KBP250+
430 Epistemology. Theory of knowledge
440.2-.95 General works. Treatises (Table KBP1)
Add number in table to KBP440
Subdivide works by individual authors further by Table K4
Including works on derivation of furūʻ from uṣūl
Concepts of uṣūl al-fiqh
442 Maqāṣid al-sharīʻah. Maṣlaḥah. Object and objective of law. Law and justice. مقاصد الشريعة. مصلحة
444 Akhlāqīyah. Mores of Islam. Ethics. اخلاقية
Rule of law see KBP2020+
445 Dichotomy of fiqh (derived by legal scholarship) and siyāsah (of the ruler). سياسة
446 Qisṭ. Equity. قسط
447 Ḥukm. Legal qualification. حكم
Class here works on legal qualification for facts and acts such as wājib (واجب) (obligation), ibāḥah (اباحه) (permission), fasād (فساد) or buṭlān (validity and invalidity), ʻillah (علة) (cause), sabab (سبب) (occasions), etc.
448.A-Z Other topics, A-Z
ʻAdl. عدل see KBP524.7+
448.A74 ʻAql. Reason. عقل
448.B53 Bidʻah. Innovation
448.F35 Falsehood
448.H37 Ḥaqq. Truth. حق
448.I38 Iḥtiyāṭ. Precaution
Innovation see KBP448.B53
Precaution see KBP448.I38
Reason see KBP448.A74
Truth see KBP448.H37
Sources of fiqh
Including instances of application
Class here discussions on textual and rational sources

Uṣūl al-fiqh. Jurisprudence and theory of law. Science of legal reasoning. اصول الفقه
Sources of fiqh -- Continued
449 Qur'ān. Koran. القرآن
Including works on the Qur'ān (القرآن) in relation to hadith (الحديث)
450 Hadith. Sunna. الحديث. السنة
For particular hadith genre see <KBP135.3>
451 Ijmā'. Consensus. اجماع
Other sources
Including disputed sources
452 Qiyāṣ. Analogical deduction. قياس
453 Ijtihād. Ijtihād al-ra'y. Rational deduction and derivation of law from scriptural sources for lack of a definitive revelation. اجتهاد. اجتهاد الراي
453.2 Ra'y. Opinion. Individual reasoning. Sound judgment. راي
454 Taqlīd. Relying upon opinion of another. Legal conformism
454.3 Istiḥsān. Scholarly discretion in breach of strict analogy. استحسان
455 'Urf. 'Ādāt. Custom. عرف. عادات
456 Istiṣlāḥ. Maṣlaḥah. Ratio utilitatis. استصلاح. مصلحة
457 Istiṣḥāb. Presumption of preference. استصحاب
457.3 Sadd al-dharā'ī'. سد الذرائع
458.A-Z Non-traditional sources of law, A-Z
458.L35 Lā'iḥah (Amendments). Regulations. By-laws. لائحة
458.N59 Niẓām. Decree law of Muslim rulers. نظام
458.Q36 Qānūn. Code. Statute. قانون
458.T74 Tribal law
458.Y37 Yāsā. ياسا
Cf. KBP2535.Y37 Dynastic rules
460 Ta'āruḍ al-adillah. Conflict of sources. تعارض الادلة
Interpretation and grammar. Logic. Words
461 General works
462.A-Z Terms, A-Z
462.A57 Amr 'āmm. امر عام
462.I78 Istithnā'. Exceptions. استثناء
462.K45 Khāṣṣ. خاص
462.M35 Majāz. Metaphor. مجاز
463 Naskh. Theory of abrogation. نسخ
Cf. <KBP136.78> Hadith
465 Ikhtilāf. Theory of ikhtilāf. Scholarly legal disagreement. اختلاف
466 Jadal. Rules of legal disputation. جدل
Theory of the fatwa see KBP491+
466.3.A-Z Other, A-Z

469 Influence of other legal systems on Islamic law
Including Jewish law, early canon law, etc.
For the influence of Islamic law on other legal systems, see the legal system or jurisdiction
470 Law reform. Criticism. Tanẓīm. تنظيم
Including reform of administration of justice and courts
Conflict of laws. Tanāzu‘ al-qawānīn. تنازع القوانين
Class here works on conflict of laws, e.g. secular law and Islamic law, or indigenous (tribal or customary) law and Islamic law, etc.
Including plurality of laws conflict
For works on conflict rules of branches other than private law (e.g. criminal law), see the subject
480 General works
481 Public order
Choice of law
Including indigenous (tribal or customary) law and Islamic law
482 General works
485.A-Z Particular branches and subjects of the law, A-Z
Furū‘ al-fiqh. Substantive law. Branches of law. فروع الفقه
490.2-.95 General works. Treatises (Table KBP1)
Add number in table to KBP490
Class here general works on furū‘ al-fiqh (فروع الفقه)
For works on the derivation of furū‘ from uṣūl see KBP440.2+
For broad and comprehensive works on both furū‘al-fiqh and uṣū al-fiqh, with or without ‘ibādāt see KBP250+
For general works limited to uṣūl al-fiqh (اصول الفقه) see KBP440.2+
Particular genres
For Ijmā‘ see KBP451
For Ikhtilāf, scholarly legal disagreement see KBP465
Fatwas
491 General. Theory of the fatwa. Muftis
Official fatwas
Class here individual or collected fatwas issued by government bodies and other public organizations
For fatwas of inter-governmental (regional) organizations, see the organization in the appropriate region, e.g. KME, Middle East
492 General (Collective and comparative)
493 Individual
For contemporary fatwas issued by government bodies and other public organizations, see the jurisdiction
494.2-.95 Private fatwas (Table KBP1)
Add number in table to KBP494
Subdivide works by individual authors further by Table K4
496 Ḥiyal. Legal artifices. حيال

Furūʻ al-fiqh. Substantive law. Branches of law. فروع الفقه
Particular genres -- Continued
496.3 Shurūṭ. Forms. شروط
497.2-.95 Furūq Ashbāh wa-naẓā'ir, qawā'id. فروق اشباه و نطائر، قواعد (Table KBP1)
Add number in table to KBP497
General concepts
For ethics of the law see KBP444
500 Ignorance of the law
For error, see KBP867.3; KBP3902
Applicability. Validity of the law
501 General works
501.3 Validity of pre-Islamic law
501.5 ʻAẓīmah/Rukhṣah. Strict or lenient application of the law. عظيمة/رخصة
Qiyāṣ. Interpretation and deduction. قياس see KBP452
502.2 Waraʻ. Extreme scrupulousness. ورع
Legal status see KBP524.7+
Adāllah. Probity. أدالة see KBP524.6
502.4 Rights
Including immaterial, non-proprietary rights
Things see KBP642.3+
504 Legal implications of acts and facts
Class here works on legal effects of various psychological states beyond error or ignorance, e.g. fear (khawf) (خوف), forgetfulness (nisyān) (نسيان), confusion (waswasah) (وسوسة), etc.
Illegal and unlawful acts see KBP868
504.5 Nīyah. Intention. نية
Cf. KBP184.12 Purity of intention
Cf. KBP860+ Contracts
Agency. Power of attorney see KBP861+
Mandate see KBP864
505 Conditions. Terms
Including suspensive conditions and retroactivity
506 Time periods. Waqt. وقت
Limitation of actions. Taqādum. Muddah al-qānūnīyah lil-daʻwá. تقادم. مدة القانونية للدعوى
507 General works
508 Delay
Exercise of rights. Protection of rights
509 Self-defense. Difāʻ ʻan al-nafs. Necessity. Ḍarūrah. دفاع عن النفس. ضرورة
Cf. KBP3856 Penal (Criminal) law
Evidence
see KBP1672 ; KBP1771
509.8.A-Z Other, A-Z

Furū' al-fiqh. Substantive law. Branches of law
‘Ibādāt. Ritual law. Worship. عبادات see KBP184+
Aḥwāl shakhṣīyah. أحوال شخسية
524 General (Table KBP2)
Subdivide works by individual authors further by Table K4
Persons. Ashkhāṣ. Afrād. أشخاص. أفراد
524.6 General (Table KBP2)
Subdivide works by individual authors further by Table K4
Personality. Legal capacity and disability. Ahlīyah. ‘Adam al-kaf'. أهلية/ عدم الكفء
Including capacity to acquire rights and duties (ahlīyat al-wujūb) (أهلية الوجوب) and capacity to fulfill obligations (ahlīyat al-adā') (أهلية الأداء), and including limited capacity and heightened capacity (‘adl) (عدل)
524.7 General (Table KBP2)
524.72 Birth. Unborn child. Nasciturus. Janīn. جنين
524.8 Death
Including absent (ghā'ib) (غايِب) and missing person (mafqūd) (مفقود) and presumption of death
Legal minority. Legal majority. Rushd. رشد
525 Minors. Ṣabīy. Ṣaghīr. Children. Ṭifl. صبي. صغير. طفل
525.5 Adults. Mukallaf. Person of age. Bālīgh. مخلف. باليغ
525.6.A-Z Special topics, A-Z
525.6.B84 Bulūgh. Puberty. بلوغ
Puberty see KBP525.6.B84
Women. Nisā'. Mar'ah. نساء. مرءة
Class here works on legal status of Muslim women (qawānīn al-khaṣṣah bi-al-nisā') (قوانين الخصة بالنساء) under all legal aspects
For legal status of a married woman or widow (arāmil; thayyib) (أرامل ؛ ثيب) see KBP550+
526.2-.95 General (Table KBP1)
Add number in table to KBP526
528.A-Z Special topics, A-Z
528.B54 Bikr. Virginity. بكر
Dress see KBP528.H54
Equality see KBP528.K33
528.H54 Ḥijāb. Dress. حجاب
Cf. KBP184.9.C45 Ritual law
528.K33 Kafā'ah. Equality. كفاءة
528.P74 Pregnancy. حمل
Virginity see KBP528.B54

Furūʻ al-fiqh. Substantive law. Branches of law. فروع الفقه
Aḥwāl shakhṣīyah. أحوال شخصية
Persons. Ashkhāṣ. Afrād. أشخاص. أفراد
Personality. Legal capacity and disability. Ahlīyah. ʻAdam al-kafʼ. أهلية/ عدم الكفء
529 Insane persons. Majnūn. People with mental disabilities. Maʻtūh. مجنون. معتوه
For interdiction (ḥajr) (حجر) see KBP628
For institutional care of the mentally ill see KBP3113
Slaves. Raqīq. Male slave. ʻAbd. Female slave. Amah. رقيق. عبد. أمة
Including slaves and slavery before Islam
529.3 General (Table KBP2)
529.5 Emancipation
Including kitābah (contractual emancipation) (كتابة), tadbīr (emancipation depending on death) (تدبير), istīlād (claiming a child) (استيلاد), umm walad (أم ولد), etc.
529.52 Patronage. Walāʼ. ولاء
529.53 Manumission. ʻItq or Iʻtāq. عتق، اعتاق
529.54 Children of a female slave
529.6 Non-Muslims. Dhimmīyūn. Ḥarbīyūn. ذميون. حربيون
Cf. KBP2449 Constitutional law
529.7.A-Z Other groups of persons, A-Z
529.7.H47 Hermaphrodites
Non-Muslims. Dhimmīyūn. Ḥarbīyūn. ذميون. حربيون see KBP529.6
529.7.P48 People with physical disabilities and illness (maraḍ) (مرض)
529.72 Citizenship
Cf. KBP2430+ Individual and state
529.8 Personality rights
Including personal names
529.83 Privacy, Right of
Juristic persons. Corporations. Associations see KBP1040+
Charitable trusts and uses. Endowments. Waqf. وقف see KBP637+
Public waqf (e.g. in social welfare) see KBP1522
Domestic relations. Family law
540.2-.95 General (Table KBP1)
Add number in table to KBP540
Subdivide works by individual authors further by Table K4
Marriage. Nikāḥ. Zawāj. نكاح. زواج
542.2-.95 General (Table KBP1)
Add number in table to KBP542

Furūʻ al-fiqh. Substantive law. Branches of law. فروع الفقه
Aḥwāl shakhṣīyah. أحوال شخصية
Domestic relations. Family law
Marriage. Nikāḥ. Zawāj. نكاح. زواج -- Continued
Betrothal. Khuṭūbah. خطوبة
543.2 General works
543.952 Antenuptial contract. Offer and acceptance. Consent. Riḍá. رضى
Including stipulations
Cf. KBP572 Marital property and regime
Dower. Mahr. مهر
Including nuptial gifts (ṣadūqah) (صدوقة)
543.953 General works
543.9532.A-Z Special topics, A-Z
Guardianship over the betrothed. Wālī. والي
543.954 General works
543.955 Marriage age. Child marriage
Including both bridegroom and bride
543.956.A-Z Special topics, A-Z
543.957 Equal status of bridegroom. Kafāʼah. كفاءة
543.958 Witnesses. Shuhūd. شهود
Impediments to marriage
Including non-marriageable persons (maḥārim) (مهارم)
544.2 General works
544.955 Consanguinity. Qarābah. Qurbah. Affinity. Sabab. قرابة. قربة. سبب
Including matrilineal and patrilineal ascendants or descendants, and quasi-consanguinity, such as relationship by nursing (raḍāʻ) (رضاع)
ʻIddah. Waiting period. عدة see KBP566
545 Premarital examination
Performance of marriage
Witnesses see KBP543.958
Certification. Registration. Recording of marriage see KBP1860
546.16 Consummation. Dukhūl. دخول
546.17 De-facto marriage. Unmarried cohabitation. Concubinage
546.2 Validity and effect of marriage. Valid (ṣaḥīḥ) (صحيح) marriage
For defective (voidable or correctable) marriage and (void) non-marriage see KBP556+
546.952 Interfaith marriage. Marriage to a non-Muslim. Zawāj bayna Muslim wa-ghayr Muslimah. زواج بين مسلم وغير مسلمة
Cf. HQ1031 Family. Marriage. Home

Furūʻ al-fiqh. Substantive law. Branches of law. فروع الفقه
Aḥwāl shakhṣīyah. أحوال شخسية
Domestic relations. Family law
Marriage. Nikāḥ. Zawāj. نكاح. زواج -- Continued
546.954 Multiple marriage. Polygamy. Polyandry. Taʻaddud al-zawjāt. تعدد الزوجات
546.955 Muta. Mutʻah. Misyār. Temporary marriage. Companionate marriage. متعة. مسيار
Cf. HQ803 Family. Marriage. Home
Concubinage see KBP546.17
Husband and wife. Zawj. Zawjah. Rights and duties. زوج. زوجة
547.2 General works
548 Matrimonial domicile (Maskan). Choice of residence. مسكن
548.3 Duty of husband to support wife
Legal status of married women. Ḥuqūq wa-qawānīn al-mutazawwijāt. حقوق وقوانين المتزوجات
Including disciplinary authority of the husband and obedience of the wife towards husband, and including status of widows (arāmil) (ارامل)
550.2-.95 General (Table KBP1)
Add number in table to KBP550
553.A-Z Special topics, A-Z
553.F73 Freedom, Personal
553.P38 Paternal ancestry
Personal freedom see KBP553.F73
553.P76 Property regime
Matrimonial actions. Dissolution of marriage
555.2-.95 General (Table KBP1)
Add number in table to KBP555
Defective (fāsid) (فاسد) marriage and invalid or void (bāṭil) (باطل) marriage
556.2 General works
557 Annulment. Faskh. فسخ
557.3 Invalidity of originally valid marriage
Including apostasy from Islam of a spouse
Divorce. Ṭalāq divorce. طلاق
Including conditions and legal effect of divorce
558.2-.95 General (Table KBP1)
Add number in table to KBP558
Grounds for divorce
559.2-.95 General (Table KBP1)
Add number in table to KBP559
559.952 Discord. Shiqāq. شقاق
559.953 Disobedience. Nushūz. نشوز
559.958 Zināʼ. Unlawful intercourse. زناء

Furūʻ al-fiqh. Substantive law. Branches of law. فروع الفقه
Aḥwāl shakhṣīyah. أحوال شخسية
Domestic relations. Family law
Marriage. Nikāḥ. Zawāj. نكاح. زواج
Matrimonial actions. Dissolution of marriage -- Continued
560 Rajʻah. Retaining the repudiated wife. Reconciliation. رجعة
Procedure
Including procedure for both husband and wife
Repudiation (Ṭalāq) of wife by husband. طلاق
562.2-.95 General (Table KBP1)
Add number in table to KBP562
562.953 Revocable divorce. Ṭalāq rajʻī. Final (Irrevocable) divorce. Ṭalāq bāʼ in. طلاق رجعي. طلاق بائن
Variant forms of repudiation
562.954 Conditional repudiation. Taʻlīq al-ṭalāq. تعليق الطلاق
563 Tafwīḍ. Wife has the power to repudiate herself. تفويض
563.2 Mubāraʻah. Divorce with mutual waiving of financial obligations. مبارعة
563.4 Khulʻ. Divorce for a consideration/ compensation. خلع
563.6 Ẓihār. ظهار
564 Īlāʼ. Oath of abstinence by husband. Separation from marital bed. ايلاء
564.2.A-Z Other, A-Z
564.2.L52 Liʻān. Husband's oath on wife's unchastity. لعان
565 Tafrīq. Dissolution of marriage pronounced by qāḍī. تفريق
Including both husband and wife's right of rescission (age), impotence or incurable diseases of husband, etc.
566 ʻIddah. Waiting period. عدة
Including status of a woman (muʻtaddah) (معتدة) during ʻiddah (عدة)
567 Settlement of claims from dissolved marriage
Including alimony (nafaqah) (نفقة) and dower (mahr) (مهر)
Concubinage. De-facto marriage. Unmarried cohabitation see KBP546.17
Marital property and regime
569.2-.95 General (Table KBP1)
Add number in table to KBP569

KBP

Furū' al-fiqh. Substantive law. Branches of law. فروع الفقه
Aḥwāl shakhṣīyah. أحوال شخسية
Domestic relations. Family law
Marital property and regime -- Continued
572 Marriage (Antenuptial) contracts. 'Uqūd al-zawāj. عقود الزواج
Consanguinity. Qarābah. Affinity. Sabab. قرابة. سبب
Including civil and social responsibilities for relatives
For consanguinity and affinity as marriage impediments see KBP544.955
583.2-.95 General (Table KBP1)
Add number in table to KBP583
584 Support. Alimony. Nafaqah. نفقة
Parent and child. Wālid. Walad. والد. ولد
587.2 General works
Parental power
598.2 General works
602 Custody. Access to children
Including parental kidnapping
602.5 Ḥiḍānah. Care for the child. حضانة
609 Adoption. Kafālah. كفالة
610.2 Fosterage. Relationship by nursing. Raḍā'. رضاع
Cf. KBP544.955 Consanguinity
Illegitimate children. Children resulting from unlawful intercourse. Filius nullius. Walad al-zinā'. ولد الزناء
612 General (Table KB 10)
612.5.A-Z Special topics, A-Z
Paternity. Nasab. النسب
616.5 General (Table KBP2)
Illegitimate children see KBP612+
619.A-Z Special topics, A-Z
Artificial insemination see KBP619.T34
Assisted reproduction see KBP619.T34
Foundling see KBP619.L34
619.I75 Ithbāt al-nasab. Proof of paternity. Qiyāfah. Physiognomy. اثبات النسب. قيافة
619.L34 Laqīṭ. Foundling. لقيط
Paternity, Proof of see KBP619.I75
Physiognomy see KBP619.I75
Qiyāfah. قيافة see KBP619.I75
619.T34 Talqīḥ basharī. Artificial insemination. Assisted reproduction. تلقيح بشري
Cf. KBP3117 Human reproductive technology
Guardianship. Guardian and ward. Walī. Qāṣir. ولي. قاصر
Including curatorship

Furū‘ al-fiqh. Substantive law. Branches of law. فروع الفقه
Aḥwāl shakhṣīyah. أحوال شخصية
Domestic relations. Family law
Consanguinity. Qarābah. Affinity. Sabab. قرابة. سبب
Guardianship. Guardian and ward. Walī. Qāṣir. ولي. قاصر -- Continued
622.2-.95 General (Table KBP1)
Add number in table to KBP622
625 Guardianship over minors
Guardianship over adults
627.2 General works
Guardianship in marriage see KBP543.954+
628 Interdiction. Ḥajr. حجر
Including procedure, and including six categories of maḥājīr (محاجير), e.g. children, people with mental disabilities, slaves, bankrupts, patients, and consorts
628.5.A-Z Special topics, A-Z
Inheritance and succession. Mīrāth. Tawrīth. Farā’iḍ. ميراث. توريث. فرائض
Including legal causes of inheritance, e.g. consanguinity (qarābah) (قرابة), affinity (sabab) (سبب), marriage, and decedent's estate (tarikah) (تركة)
632.2-.95 General (Table KBP1)
Add number in table to KBP632
Decedents' estates. Tarikah. Shares. تركة
Including claims against, and partition and distribution of, estate (taqsīm al-tarikah) (تقسيم التركة)
633.2-.95 General (Table KBP1)
Add number in table to KBP633
633.952.A-Z Special topics, A-Z
633.952.A84 ‘Awl. Decrease of share. عول
Claims against, and partition and distribution of, estate see KBP633.952.T37
Decrease of share see KBP633.952.A84
633.952.R33 Radd. Return. رد
Return see KBP633.952.R33
633.952.T37 Taqsīm al-tarikah. Claims against, and partition and distribution of, estate. تقسيم التركة
Qualification as heir. Wārith. Legal sharers. Dhawū al-furūḍ. وارث. ذوو الفروض
Including agnates (‘aṣabah) (العصبة), cognates (dhawū al-arḥām) (ذوو الارحام), Patronage/clientship (mawlá al-muwālat) (مولى الموالات), etc.
633.955 General works
Order of succession

Furū' al-fiqh. Substantive law. Branches of law. فروع الفقه
Aḥwāl shakhṣīyah. أحوال شخصية
Inheritance and succession. Mīrāth. Tawrīth. Farā'iḍ. ميراث. توريث. فرائض
Qualification as heir. Wārith. Legal sharers. Dhawū al-furūḍ. وارث. ذوو الفروض
Order of succession -- Continued
634.2-.95 General (Table KBP1)
Add number in table to KBP634
634.953.A-Z Special topics, A-Z
634.953.J35 Janīn. Unborn children. جنين
634.953.L67 Lost or missing persons
Missing persons see KBP634.953.L67
Unborn children see KBP634.953.J35
634.953.W34 Walad al-li'ān. ولد اللعان
Cf. KBP564.2.L52 Li'an (لعان). Husband's oath on wife's unchastity
Walad al-mulā'anah. ولد الملاعنة see KBP634.953.W34
634.953.W35 Walad al-zinā'. ولد الزناء
Cf. KBP612+ Illegitimate children
634.954 Surviving spouses
634.955 Natural parents
634.956 Exclusion from inheritance
Including partial exclusion (ḥajb al-nuqṣān) (حجب النقصان) and complete exclusion (ḥajb al-ḥirmān) (حجب الحرمان) in favor of an heir with a stronger legal position
634.957 Liability. Debts of estate
Wills. Testamentary succession. Waṣīyah. وصية
635.2-.95 General (Table KBP1)
Add number in table to KBP635
635.952 Legacies. Testamentary bequests. Distribution of estate
635.954 Executors and administrators of estate. Waṣīy. Munaffidh al-waṣīyah. وصي. منفذ الوصية
636 Impediments to inheritance. Mawānī. مواني
Including slave quality, homicide, infidelity, apostasy, difference of religion or domicile, etc.
636.2 Gifts mortis causa
636.3 Gifts. Charitable gifts. Ṣadaqah. Donations. Hibah. صداقة. هبة
Including donation for life ('umrá) (عمرى) and donation for the surviving party (ruqbá) (رقبى)
Waqf. Endowments. Charitable uses. Foundations. وقف
Including supervisor (nāẓir) (ناظر)

Furū‘ al-fiqh. Substantive law. Branches of law. فروع الفقه
Aḥwāl shakhṣīyah. أحوال شخصية
Waqf. Endowments. Charitable uses. Foundations. وقف -- Continued
637.2-.95 General (Table KBP1)
Add number in table to KBP637
Subject and object of waqf
637.955 General works
638 Particular beneficiaries of waqf
For waqf for social welfare see KBP1522
Mu‘āmalāt. معاملات
639.2-.95 General (Table KBP1)
Add number in table to KBP639
Property. Māl. Res in commercio. مال
640.2-.95 General (Table KBP1)
Add number in table to KBP640
Things. ‘Ayn. Types of property. عين
642.3 Fungibles. Mithlī. Non-fungibles. Qīmī. المثلي
Including fungibles such as measured (makīl) (مكيل), weighed (mawzūn) (موزون), or counted (ma‘dūd mutaqārib) (معدود متقارب) things
Real (Immovable) property see KBP683+
643 Personal (Movable) property. Māl manqūl. مال منقول
644.A-Z Other, A-Z
Possession and ownership. Yad. Milk
Including owner (mālik) (مالك) and possessor (dhū al-yad) (ذو اليد)
646.2 General works
647.A-Z Types of possession, A-Z
Acquisition (original and derivative) and transfer of possession and ownership (milk) (ملك)
648.2 General works
651 Dispossession
652 Possessory actions
Acquisition and loss of ownership
655.2 General works
656 Occupation. Istīlā’. استيلاء
657 Lost property
658 Treasure troves. Luqāṭah. لقاطة
659 Accessions
Including commixtion, confusion, and specification
663 Acquisition of fruits and parts of things, and proceeds. Istighlāl. الاتغلال
673 Loss of ownership
Including abandonment and dereliction

Furū' al-fiqh. Substantive law. Branches of law. فروع الفقه
Mu'āmalāt. معاملات
Property. Māl. Res in commercio. مال
Possession and ownership. Yad. Milk -- Continued
674 Co-ownership. Joint ownership. Sharikat māl. Mushā'. Ishtirāk. شركة مال. مشاع. اشتراك
For co-ownership of land see KBP694
675 Protection of ownership. Claims and actions resulting from ownership. Māl manqūl. مال منقول
Real (Immovable) property. 'Aqār. Land law. عقار
Including land ownership and tenancy
683.2-.95 General (Table KBP1)
Add number in table to KBP683
686 Terres communes. Group lands. Commons for use without shares in ownership
Acquisition and loss of ownership
687.5 General (Table KBP2)
687.6 Occupancy of wasteland by cultivator. Iḥyā' al-mawāt. احياء الموات
694 Co-ownership of land. Customary co-ownership
For communal property see KBP686
Cf. KBP698 Rights to water
Rights incident to ownership of land
695.2 General works
696 Air and space above ground
697 Underground. Minerals, metals and other resources
698 Riparian rights. Water rights. Underground water
699 Hunting and fishing rights
Adjoining landowners
700.2 General works
701.A-Z Special topics, A-Z
Rights as to the use of another's land
706.2 General works
708 Commonage and pasture. Grazing rights
Servitudes
709.2-.95 General (Table KBP1)
Add number in table to KBP709
710 Real servitudes
e.g. right of way (passage), right to draw water
713 Personal servitudes
715 Usufruct. Muzāra'ah. Manfa'ah. مزاوعة. منفعة
716 Right of pre-emption. Shuf'ah. شفعة
Pledges. Rahn. Contracts of pledging. رهن
726.2-.95 General (Table KBP1)
Add number in table to KBP726
728 Pledges of personal property
730 Pledges of rights

Furū‘ al-fiqh. Substantive law. Branches of law. فروع الفقه
Mu‘āmalāt. معاملات
Property. Māl. Res in commercio. مال -- Continued
Retention to secure a claim. Ḥabs. حبس
731.2-.95 General (Table KBP1)
Add number in table to KBP731
Particular rights in rem (lien)
see KBP877.2; KBP881.3; KBP894
737 Land register. Registration of land titles. Tawthīq ‘aqārī. Tasjīl ‘aqārī. توثيق عقاري. تسجيل عقاري
759.A-Z Other, A-Z
Inheritance and succession see KBP632+
Obligations. Dhimmah. Contracts and transactions. ذمة
810.2-.95 General (Table KBP1)
Add number in table to KBP810
811 Debtor and creditor. Dā’in wa-madyūn. Aṣīl. دائن ومديون. اصيل
812 Plurality of debtor and creditor. Joint obligations
Types of obligations
814 Civil and natural (aleatory) obligations
Cf. KBP899 Aleatory contracts
814.5 Obligation to give
815 Obligation to do or refrain from doing
Transfer and assumption of obligations. Ḥawālah. حوالة
816 General (Table KBP2)
816.7 Iqrār. Assumption of debt. اقرار
Extinction of obligation
817 General works
Performance. Īfā’. Payment. Qaḍā’. Compromise. Ṣulḥ. افاء. قضاء. صلح
817.2 General works
817.3 Counterclaim. Muqāṣṣah. مقصة
Cf. KBP1667.T33 Procedure at trial
817.5 Acquittance. Waiver. Ibrā’. Substituted performance. Taṣyīr. ابراء. تسير
820 Special rules as to payment of money debts
822 Compensation for maintenance and improvement
822.5 Enforcement
823 Confusion of rights
823.5.A-Z Special topics, A-Z
Rescission see KBP869.3+
Withdrawal see KBP869.3+
Nonperformance
Including breach of contract
824.2 General works
825.5 Culpa in contrahendo
Damages see KBP842+

KBP

Furū‘ al-fiqh. Substantive law. Branches of law. فروع الفقه
Mu‘āmalāt. معاملات
Obligations. Dhimmah. Contracts and transactions. ذمة
Delicts. Torts. Ta‘addiyāt. تعديات
834.2-.95 General (Table KBP1)
Add number in table to KBP834
Liability. Extra-contractual liability. Ḍamān. ضمان
Including dolus and negligence (mistake)
839 General (Table KBP2)
839.7 Liability for the torts of others
e.g. a slave
Individual torts and damages
842 Violation of freedom
Physical injuries. Crimes against the person
Including liability of payment of blood money (dīyah) (دية) in place of retaliation, and ghurrah (غرة) for causing an abortion
Cf. KBP3976 Qiṣāṣ punishment. قصاص
842.2 General (Table KBP2)
842.6 Death (unintentional) by wrongful act
842.8 Destruction of property. Itlāf. اتلاف
Immoral transactions see KBP868+
846 Deceit. Forgery. Misrepresentation
846.2 Usurpation of another's property. Ghaṣb. غصب
Breach of contract see KBP824+
853.A-Z Other torts and liabilities, A-Z
Unjust enrichment. Faḍl māl bi-lā ‘iwaḍ. فضل مال بلا عوض
854.2-.95 General (Table KBP1)
Add number in table to KBP854
855 Restitution
Including restitution to the poor
856 Bay‘ al-dayn bi-al-dayn. Prohibition of exchange of obligation for obligation. بيع الدين بالدين
857.A-Z Special topics, A-Z
Concepts and principles of contract law
858 General (Table KBP2)
858.3 Liberty of contract. Party autonomy
858.5.A-Z Types of contracts, A-Z
858.5.K45 Khiyār. Option
Option see KBP858.5.K45
859 Security. Secured and fiduciary transactions
For particular transactions, see KBP877.2; KBP881.3; KBP894
Nīyah. Intention. نية
Cf. KBP184.12 Ritual law
860.2 General works

Furū‘ al-fiqh. Substantive law. Branches of law
Mu‘āmalāt. معاملات
Obligations. Dhimmah. Contracts and transactions. ذمة
Concepts and principles of contract law
Nīyah. Intention. نية
Agency
861 General works
861.3 Authorization. Idhn. اذن
862 Unauthorized agent. Falsus procurator. Fuḍūlī. فضولي
864 Mandate
866 Form requirements. Notice. Time of effectiveness
866.5 Risk. Gharar. غرر
Void and voidable contracts and transactions. Nullity
867 General (Table KBP2)
867.3 Mistake. Error. Khaṭa’. Ghalṭah. خطاء. غلطة
867.5 Fraud. Duress. Ikrāh. Threat. Tahdīd. اكراه. تحديد
Unconscionable transactions. Illegal contracts. ‘Uqūd ghayr sharī‘ah. عقود غير شريعة
868 General (Table KBP2)
868.2 Usurious contracts. Ribā
Formation of contract
Including commercial contracts
869 General (Table KBP2)
Offer and acceptance. Ījāb and qabūl. ايجاب. قبول
Including withdrawal of offer (rujū‘) (رجوع) and right of rescission (sharṭ al-khiyār) (شرط الخيار)
869.3 General (Table KBP2)
869.55 Contracts by adhesion
869.6 Declaration of consent. Riḍá. Implied consent (conclusive act or gesture). Ishārah ma‘hūdah. رضى. اشارة محدودة
870 Clauses. Terms. Conditions
872 Stipulations
Cf. KBP869.3+ Right of rescission
872.5 Formalities
Parties to contract
873 General (Table KBP2)
873.3 Third parties
873.8 Cancellation of contract. Faskh. فسخ
Individual contracts and transactions
Sale. Bay‘. بيع
874.2-.95 General (Table KBP1)
Add number in table to KBP874
875 Warranty
876 Defects of goods sold
Including right of rescission

Furū' al-fiqh. Substantive law. Branches of law. فروع الفقه
Mu'āmalāt. معاملات
Obligations. Dhimmah. Contracts and transactions. ذمة
Individual contracts and transactions
Sale. Bay'. بيع -- Continued
Modes of sale
Conditional sale
877 General (Table KBP2)
877.2 Retention of ownership
877.3 Sale on credit. Bay' al-'īnah. بيع العينة
877.4 Salam contract
Including contract of manufacture (istiṣnā') (استسناع)
878.A-Z Other, A-Z
878.A93 Auctions. Muzāyadah. مزيدة
878.R47 Resale
Including waḍī'ah (with rebate) (وضيعة) and murābaḥah (with surcharge) (مرابحة)
Exchange of monetary assets or rights. Mu'āwaḍah mālīyah. معاوضة مالية
879 General (Table KBP2)
879.2.A-Z Special topics, A-Z
Money, Exchange of see KBP879.2.S27
Precious metals, Exchange of see KBP879.2.S27
879.2.S27 Ṣarf. Exchange of money and precious metals. صرف
Pecuniary transaction without countervalue. 'Iwaḍ. عوض
Donations (Hibah) (هبة). Gifts see KBP636.3
879.4 Loan of non-fungibles. Commodatum. 'Āriyah. عارية
Including return (rujū') (رجوع)
Lease. Landlord and tenant
880 General (Table KBP2)
881.3 Liens of the landlord
884.A-Z Types of property, A-Z
Land lease see KBP884.R43
884.R43 Real property. Land lease
Fiduciary transactions. Trust and trustee. Amānah. امانة
889.2-.95 General (Table KBP1)
Add number in table to KBP889
Waqf. Charitable uses see KBP637+
Waqf for social welfare see KBP1522
Waḍī'ah see KBP896
891 Personal loans. Loans for consumption. Mutuum. Qarḍ. متم. قرض
Contract for service and labor. Master and servant

Furū' al-fiqh. Substantive law. Branches of law. فروع الفقه
Mu'āmalāt. معاملات
Obligations. Dhimmah. Contracts and transactions. ذمة
Individual contracts and transactions
Contract for service and labor. Master and servant -- Continued
892 General (Table KBP2)
892.3 Independent work. Professions
Dependent work. Hire and lease. Ijārah. Locatio conductio. اجارة
892.5 General works
892.6 Servants and employees. Ajīr and Ajīr khāṣṣ. اجير. اجير خاص
Including rent (ujrah) (اجرة) and wage (ajīr) (اجير)
892.7.A-Z Particular groups, A-Z
Contract for work and labor
Class here works on contracts concluded by independent contractor or artisan (ajīr mushtarak) (اجير مشترك)
893 General works
893.3.A-Z Particular contracts or tasks, A-Z
Istiṣnā' see KBP877.4
893.5 Liability and warranty
894 Security. Liens. Ḥabs
895 Offer of reward. Ji'ālah. جعالة
896 Deposit. Waḍī'ah. وضيعة
899 Aleatory contracts. Ilqá bi-al-ḥajar. القى بالحجر
900 Suretyship. Kafālah. Debtor and guarantor. Aṣīl and kāfil. كفالة. اصيل. كافل
Including suretyship for the person (kafālah bi-al-nafs) (كفالة بالنفس) and for the claim (kafālah bi-al-māl) (كفالة بالمال)
Commercial law. Commercial transactions
920 General works
929 Brokerage
931 Freight forwarders and carriers. Carriage of passengers and goods
Negotiable instruments. Titles of credit
937 General works
937.3 Possession, ownership, and transfer
938 Bills of exchange. Suftajah. سفتجة
Including the difference between ḥawālah and suftajah
Banks and banking. Qānūn al-bunūk. قانون البنوك
940.2 General works
Banking transactions
951.2 General works
Loans. Credit. Qurūḍ. قروض
955 General (Table KBP2)

Furū‘ al-fiqh. Substantive law. Branches of law. فروع الفقه
Mu‘āmalāt. معاملات
Obligations. Dhimmah. Contracts and transactions. ذمة
Commercial law. Commercial transactions
Banks and banking. Qānūn al-bunūk. قانون البنوك
Banking transactions
Loans. Credit. Qurūḍ. قروض -- Continued
955.4 Mukhāṭarah. ‘Īnah. Interest device. مخاطرة. عينة
Commercial investments (Muqaradah) see KBP1049+
961 Noncash funds transfer
Including electronic funds transfer and bill paying services
962.8 Commodity exchanges. Produce exchanges
Maritime contracts. Maritime law. Qānūn al-baḥrīyah. قانون البحرية
970.2 General works
970.97 Ships and ship owners. Ship masters
971 Affreightment. Carriage of goods at sea and inland waters
976 Carriage of passengers at sea and inland waters
Average
978.2 General works
979 Havarie grosse
980 Collision at sea
981 Salvage. Shipwreck
984.5 Maritime courts
Insurance law. Qānūn al-ta’mīn. قانون التأمين
998.2 General works
1020.A-Z Particular hazards, A-Z
1030 Particular risks and damages
Associations. Sharikah. Corporations. ‘Āqilah. شركة. عقيلة
Including works on juristic persons in general
For waqf see KBP637+
1040.2-.95 General (Table KBP1)
Add number in table to KBP1040
Partnerships. Personal companies. Sharikat ‘aqd. شركة عقد
Including commercial partnerships
1043 General works
1043.3 Partners. Sharīk. شريك
Unlimited commercial partnership. Mufāwaḍah. مفاوضة
1045 General works
1045.4 Equal shares
1045.6 Liability

Furū‘ al-fiqh. Substantive law. Branches of law. فروع الفقه
Mu‘āmalāt. معاملات
Obligations. Dhimmah. Contracts and transactions. ذمة
Commercial law. Commercial transactions
Partnerships. Personal companies. Sharikat ‘aqd. شركة. عقيلة
Partnerships. Personal companies. Sharikat ‘aqd. شركة عقد -- Continued
Limited partnership. Sharikat ‘inān. شركة عنان
Including limited liability partnership
1047 General works
1047.4 Capital. Profits
1047.6 Liability
1048 Artisans' partnership. Sharikat al-ṣanā‘ī wa-al-taqabbul. شركة الصناعي والتقبل
Silent partnership. Muḍārabah. مضاربة
1049 General works
1049.3 Silent partner. Rabb al-māl. رب المال
1049.4 Capital. Profits
1049.7 Termination. Dissolution
Stock companies. Incorporated business associations
1050.2 General works
Stock corporations
1052.2 General works
Corporate finance
1061.2 General works
1062 Capital stock
1064 Securities. Stocks. Bonds. Trust investments
1085 Termination. Dissolution. Liquidation
1116 Multi-national corporations
Cooperative societies
1120.2 General works
1131 Membership
1133.A-Z Types of cooperatives, A-Z
Credit cooperatives see KBP1133.S35
1133.S35 Sharikat al-wujūh. Credit cooperatives. شركة الوجوه
1134 Termination. Dissolution. Liquidation
Combinations. Industrial trusts
1137 General works
1138 Consortium
1139 Joint ventures
1147 Corporate reorganization
Insolvency and bankruptcy see KBP1885+
1154.A-Z Other, A-Z
Intellectual and industrial property
1155 General works

Furūʻ al-fiqh. Substantive law. Branches of law. فروع الفقه
Intellectual and industrial property -- Continued
1156 Principles
Copyright
1160 General works
1160.6 Scope of protection
1185 Author and publisher
1194 Patent law and trademarks
Unfair competition
1234 General works
1235 Public policy
1237 Advertising
1250 Rebates and premiums
1259.A-Z Other, A-Z
Labor laws and legislation
1270 General works
Labor contract and employment
1279 General works
1295 Formation of contract
1300 Parties to contract
1302 Void and voidable contracts. Immoral contracts
1303 Extinction of employment
1330 Wages
Protection of labor
1408 General works
1422 Child and youth labor
1424 Women's labor
1467.A-Z Other, A-Z
Social laws and legislation
1468 Social reform and policies
1469 General works
Social insurance. Social security
1472 General works
1476 Coverage and benefits
1483 Health insurance
1495 Worker's compensation
1508 Old age, survivors and disability insurance
1512 Unemployment insurance
Social service. Welfare. Charities
1520 General works
1522 Waqf for social welfare. وقف
For waqf for charitable (private) uses see KBP637+
Social service beneficiaries
1528 The poor and destitute
1529 Older people
1530 Pensioners
1531 Large families

Furūʻ al-fiqh. Substantive law. Branches of law. فروع الفقه
Social laws and legislation
Social service. Welfare. Charities
Social service beneficiaries -- Continued
People with disabilities
Including people with physical, mental, and social disabilities
1532 General works
1534.A-Z Beneficiaries, A-Z
1534.B54 Blind
1534.D42 Deaf-mute
1534.S38 Severely disabled people
1536 Homeless persons
War-related and conflict-related groups of beneficiaries
1537 General works
1538 Refugees
1539 Soldiers. Prisoners of war
Including ex-prisoners and veterans
Children. Youth
1542 General works
Measures and provisions
1545 General works
1546 Protection of children in public
1547 Protection of children against obscenity
1569.A-Z Other, A-Z
Courts and procedure
1572 Aḥkām sulṭānīyah. Administration of justice. احكام سلطانية
Courts
Including sharīʻah (شريعة) courts (maḥākim) (محاكم) and siyāsah (سياسة) tribunals (regulatory) of both civil and criminal jurisdiction
1580 General works
Including niẓām al-qaḍāʼ (Court organization) (نظام القضاء)
1584 Single-judge court. Qāḍī court. قاضي
1585 Multiple-judge court
1586 Appeal from one court to another
Courts of special jurisdiction. Special tribunals
1588 General works
1588.3 Criminal or police court. Shurṭah. شرطة
1588.4 Maẓālim. Grievance court. مظالم
1588.7 Religious minority court. Ahl al-dhimmah. اهل الذمة
1591.2.A-Z Other courts of special jurisdiction, A-Z
1591.5 Supreme judicial authority
1593.A-Z Other public bodies with judicial functions, A-Z

Furūʻ al-fiqh. Substantive law. Branches of law. فروع الفقه
Courts and procedure
Courts -- Continued
1595 Court decorum and discipline. Duty of the qāḍī. Adab al-qāḍī. ادب القاضي
The legal profession
For biography see KBP70+
1600 General works
Legal education see KBP42+
Judges. Qāḍī. قاضي
1610 General works
1611 Women judges
1612 Independence of judges
1614 Ethics and discipline
1619 Arbitrator. Ḥakam. حكم
Including appointment
1619.3 Muḥtasib. Private prosecutor and his office (ḥisbah). المحتسب. الحسبة
Notaries see KBP1846+
Auxiliary personnel
1620 General works
1621 Assistant to the qāḍī. Clerk. Kātib. كاتب
1622 Agent/interpreter of the qāḍī. Amīn. امين
1622.2 Divider of inheritance. Qasīm. قسيم
1623 Administration. Court records. Dīwān. Minutes of proceedings. Maḥḍar. ديوان. محضر
1624 Bailiffs
Experts and expert witnesses
1626 General works
1628.A-Z Special topics, A-Z
Practice of law. Wakālah. وكالة
1630 General works
1637 Procurator. Attorney. Wakīl. وكيل
1648.A-Z Other, A-Z
Procedure in general
1650 General works
Procedural principles
1651 Due process of law
Parties to action. Khaṣm. خصم
1655 General works
1656 Privileged parties
1657 Litigants
Including plaintiff (claimant; muddaʻī) (مدعي) and defendant (muddaʻá ʻalayhī) (مدعى عليه)
Pretrial procedures
1660 General works
1662.A-Z Particular, A-Z

Furūʻ al-fiqh. Substantive law. Branches of law. فروع الفقه
Courts and procedure
Procedure in general
Pretrial procedures
Particular, A-Z -- Continued
Deadlines see KBP1662.T56
1662.S86 Summons
1662.T56 Time periods. Deadlines
Including default and restitution
Procedure at trial
1663 General works
1664 Jurisdiction. Competence in subject matter and venue. The competent court
Actions and defenses. Khuṣūmah. Litigation. خصومة
1666 General works
1667.A-Z Particular, A-Z
Counterclaim see KBP1667.T33
1667.F67 Form requirements
1667.L55 Limitation of actions
1667.L58 Lis pendens
(1667.R48) Res judicata
see KBP1681
Set-off see KBP1667.T33
1667.T33 Taḥāluf. Counterclaim. Set-off. تحالف
1668.A-Z Particular proceedings, A-Z
1668.C53 Change of parties. Death of party
Compromise see KBP1668.S88
Death of party see KBP1668.C53
1668.I68 Intervention
Out of court settlement see KBP1668.S88
Settlement out of court see KBP1668.S88
1668.S88 Ṣulḥ. Compromise. Settlement out of court. الصلح
Evidence. Bayyinah. Burden of proof. بينة
1672 General works
Witnesses. Testimony. Shahādah. شهادة
1675 General works
1676 Privileged witnesses. Confidential communication. Expert testimony
1676.7 Documentary evidence. Ṣakk. Wathīqah/wathā’iq. صك. وثيقة \ وثائق
1677.A-Z Special topics, A-Z
Conflict of equivalent testimony see KBP1677.T35
Oath see KBP1677.Y35
Presumptions see KBP1677.T35
Taḥāluf. تحالف see KBP1667.T33
1677.T35 Tahātur. Conflict of equivalent testimony. Presumptions. تهاتر

KBP

Furūʻ al-fiqh. Substantive law. Branches of law. فروع الفقه
Courts and procedure
Procedure in general
Procedure at trial
Evidence. Bayyinah. Burden of proof. بينة
Special topics, A-Z -- Continued
1677.W65 Women witnesses
1677.Y35 Yamīn. Oath. يمين
Including oath of witnesses and parties
Judicial decisions. Qaḍā'. Sijill. القضاء. السجل
1679 General works
1679.3 Judicial opinions. Advisory opinions
1680.A-Z Particular decisions, A-Z
1681 Res judicata
Remedies
1686 General works
1687 Appeal
Including Qāḍī al-Quḍāh (قاضي القضاة)
1690 Execution of judgment
Particular procedures
Matrimonial actions see KBP555+
1807 Procedure in parent and child cases
Interdiction in guardianship cases see KBP628
Criminal procedures see KBP4601+
1815.A-Z Other particular procedures, A-Z
Arbitration
1829 General works
1829.3.A-Z Special topics, A-Z
Notaries. Kātib. Notarial practice and procedure. كاتب
1846 General works
1847 Legal instruments. Certification
Registration. Recording
1850 General works
1852 Publicity
Civil register
1854 General works
Registration of civil status
1856 General works
1857 Family names
1860 Marriage
1862 Birth
1864 Death
For absence and presumption of death see KBP524.8
1865 Aliens. Stateless foreigners
Land registers see KBP737
Interdiction. Ḥajr. حجر see KBP628

Furū' al-fiqh. Substantive law. Branches of law. فروع الفقه
Courts and procedure -- Continued
1880 Inheritance (Probate court) procedures
1883 Execution of judgment and self-help
Insolvency
1885 General works
Execution for payment due. Procedure
1888 General works
1913 Detention of debtor
1925.A-Z Special topics, A-Z
1925.M85 Mulāzamah. ملازمة
1925.S87 Surety for the defendant
1926 Remedies
1932 Suspension. Accord and satisfaction
1942 Bankruptcy. Muflis. Iflās. المفلس. الافلاس
Public law. The Islamic state
Class here works on the legal philosophy and theory of the Islamic theocratic state, with or without comparisons to two or more Islamic countries
For works on public law and Islam in a particular country, see the country
For works on the political philosophy and theory of the Islamic theocratic state see JC49
Cf. BL65.S8 Religion in relation to the state
2000 General works
2015 Questions of sovereignty
International law and Islam see KB270+
Rule of law. God's rule
Cf. KBP2510+ Legislative power and process
2020 General works
Siyāsah and sharī'ah. Secular authority and sharī'ah. السياسة والشريعة see KBP2511
Dichotomy of siyāsah (السياسة) and fiqh (الفقه) see KBP445
2035 Compatibility of Islam and democratic government
Cf. BP173.6 Islam
Constitution of the state
Comparative constitutional history
Including periods of colonization in Africa and Asia
2101 General works
2200.A-Z Special topics, A-Z
2200.D86 Dustūr al-Madīnah. Constitution of Medina. دستور المدينة
Particular principles
Including historic concepts
2240 Legitimacy
2250 Legality

Furūʻ al-fiqh. Substantive law. Branches of law. فروع الفقه
Constitution of the state
Particular principles -- Continued
2250.3 Secular authority and duties of leaders
2255 Shūrá. Consultation. الشورى
Rule of law see KBP2020+
2270 Separation and delegation of powers
2275 Ethics in government. Conflict of interests
2300 Privileges, prerogatives, and immunities of rulers
2310.A-Z Other, A-Z
Sources and relationships of the law
2340 Customary law and observances. ʻUrf. العرف
Code and decree law. "King's law". Qānūn (القانون), niẓām (النظام) and fiqh (الفقه) see KBP445
2390 Territory
Foreign relations. Siyar. السير
2400 General works
2415 Neutrality
2416 Jihād. War. الجهاد
For jihād as a concept see KBP182+
Individual and state
Nationality and citizenship
2430 General works
2449 Non-Muslims. Dhimmīyūn. Ḥarbīyūn. الذميون. الحربيون
2450.A-Z Particular groups, A-Z
Non-Muslims. Dhimmīyūn. Ḥarbīyūn. الذميون. الحربيون see KBP2449
Human rights. Civil and political rights
2460 General works
2462 Dignity
Equality before the law
2465 General works
2467.A-Z Groups discriminated against, A-Z
2467.D58 Disabled. People with disabilities
Including physical, mental, and social disabilities, and minority disabled people
2467.5 Sex discrimination
2468.A-Z Special subjects, A-Z
Culture see KBP2468.L36
2468.L36 Language and culture
Freedom
2469 General works
2470 Freedom of expression
2472 Freedom of religion. Freedom of worship
Freedom of thought and speech
2474 General works

Furūʻ al-fiqh. Substantive law. Branches of law. فروع الفقه
Constitution of the state
Individual and state
Human rights. Civil and political rights
Freedom
Freedom of thought and speech -- Continued
2476 Freedom of information
2478 Prohibition of censorship
2483 Freedom of assembly, association, and demonstration
2484 Due process of law
Particular rights
2484.5 Life. Right to life
Including works on reproductive choices
2485.5 Right of asylum
Right to be free from torture and other cruel, inhuman, or degrading treatment or punishment see KBP4541
2486 Right to resistance against political authority or ideology
2490 Control of subversive activities or groups
Organs of government. Organs of state power and state administration
2500 General works
Legislative (law-making) power
2510 General works
2511 Siyāsah sharīʻah. Ruler's right to issue decrees within the limits of divine law. سياسة شريعة
2516 Legislative (law-making) process. Decree law versus ijtihād (اجتهاد)
Traditional leaders. Imams. Imām. Dynasty. امام
Including Caliph (Khalīfah) (خليفة); Sultan (Sulṭān) (سلطان); King (Malik) (ملك); Prince or ruler (Amīr) (امير), etc.
2532 General works
2535.A-Z Special topics, A-Z
Dynastic rules. Legal status of dynasty see KBP2535.Y37
2535.S92 Succession
2535.Y37 Yāsā. Dynastic rules. ياسا
Including legal status of dynasty
Cf. KBP458.Y37 Disputed sources of fiqh (فقه)
2540 Presidents
Prerogatives and powers
2550 General works
2554 Crown privilege
2558 Treatymaking power

Furū' al-fiqh. Substantive law. Branches of law. فروع الفقه
Constitution of the state
Organs of government. Organs of state power and state administration -- Continued
The executive branch
2577 General works
2580 Ministry. Wizārah. Viziers. Wazīr. The Cabinet. وزارة. وزير
2585 Council of ministers and other organs or bodies
2604 The Foreign Office
2612.A-Z Special boards, commissions, bureaus, task forces, etc., A-Z
Government and administration. Siyāsah. Administrative process. سياسة
2730 General works
2732 Acts of government
2754 Legal transactions. Government contracts
2757 Enforcement. Administrative sanctions
Eminent domain. Nationalization. Public restraint on private property
Including procedure
2824 General works
Expropriation or land apppropriation by the state for public utility's sake
Including land under customary co-ownership (collectivité)
2825 General works
2829 Categories of land
Including agricultural, grazing, hunting, and forest land
2840 Government liability
Including liability of communal agencies
Administrative organization
2860 General works
Local government. Municipal government
2920 General works
2938 Autonomy and rule-making power
Municipal public services. Public utilities
2955 General works
2956 Water. Sewage
2968.A-Z Other, A-Z
2970 Civil service. Employees of communal agencies
Police and public safety
3000 General works
Public safety
3009 General works
Hazardous articles and processes
Including transportation by land
3011 General works

Furūʻ al-fiqh. Substantive law. Branches of law. فروع الفقه
Police and public safety
Public safety
Hazardous articles and processes -- Continued
3012 Nuclear power. Reactors
3014.A-Z Poisons and toxic substances, A-Z
Control of individuals
3022 General works
3025 Particular groups
3033 Traveling and transit traffic. Tourism
Control of social activities
3034 General (Table KBP2)
3034.3 Ḥisbah. الحسبة
3037 Emergency management. Disaster control. Disaster relief
Public property. Government property
3040.5 General (Comparative)
3044.7 Roads and highways
Water resources
Including rivers, lakes, watercourses, underground water, etc.
3046 General works
3046.5 Common use
3046.7 Water rights
Cf. KBP698 Riparian rights (Property)
3047 Abutting property
Protection against pollution see KBP3131
3049 Development and conservation of water resources
3053 Shore protection. Coastal zone management
Land reclamation. Irrigation. Drainage see KBP3058
3054 National preserves
Architectural landmarks and historic monuments see KBP3183+
Continental shelf and its resources see KBP3347
Natural resources and mines see KBP3350
3055.A-Z Other, A-Z
Public lands. Public land law. Arāḍī al-dawlah. اراضي الدولة
3056 Land reform and land policy. Legislation on new land systems
Regional planning. Land development
3057 General works
3057.3 Public land acquisition legislation
For incorporation of derelict, undeveloped (unexploited) and unoccupied land (terres vacantes et sans maître) see KBP2824+
3058 Public irrigation zones
Rural planning and development zones
3059 General works

Furū‘ al-fiqh. Substantive law. Branches of law. فروع الفقه
Public property. Government property
Public lands. Public land law. Arāḍī al-dawlah. اراضي الدولة
Regional planning. Land development
Rural planning and development zones -- Continued
3060 Land settlement. Village settlement
Collective patrimony see KBP686
Co-ownership of land. Customary co-ownership see KBP694
3061 State land grants. Iqṭā‘. اقطاع
City planning and redevelopment
3062 General works
3065 Assessment of utilities
Including sanitation
Building and construction
Including administrative control and procedure
Cf. KBP3402 Building and construction industry
3067 General works
3069 Adjoining landowners
3071 Building safety and control
3072.A-Z Special topics, A-Z
Public health
For alcohol and alcoholic beverages see KBP184.42+
3075 General (Comparative)
3078 Burial and cemetery laws. Disposal of the dead
Contagious and infectious diseases. Parasitic diseases
3080 General works
3082.A-Z Diseases. Agents. Parasites, A-Z
3082.A53 AIDS
3082.S47 Sexually transmitted diseases. Venereal diseases
3082.T82 Tuberculosis
Venereal diseases see KBP3082.S47
Public health measures
Including compulsory measures
3084 General works
3086.A-Z Immunization. Vaccination. By disease, A-Z
Environmental pollution see KBP3130+
3088.A-Z Other public health hazards and measures, A-Z
3088.R43 Refuse disposal
3088.S77 Street cleaning
3089 Drinking water standards
Food laws (General)
see KBP3377+
Dietary laws
see KBP184+
Drug laws. Drugs of abuse

Furū' al-fiqh. Substantive law. Branches of law. فروع الفقه
Public health
Drug laws. Drugs of abuse -- Continued
3090 General works
3092 Narcotics. Opium legislation
3096.5 Tobacco use. Smoking
Medical legislation
3098 General works
The health professions
Class here works on education, licensing, ethics, and liability
Physicians
3100 General works
3100.5 Malpractice
3103.A-Z Other, A-Z
3103.H42 Healers
Auxiliary medical professions. Paramedical professions
3104 General works
3105 Nurses and nursing
3106 Midwives
3108.A-Z Health organizations. By name, A-Z
3108.R42 Red Crescent
3108.R43 Red Cross
Cf. KBP3037 Disaster relief
Hospitals and other medical institutions or health services
3110 General works
3112 Blood banks
3113 Institutions for the mentally ill
3114.A-Z Other health organizations, institutions, and services, A-Z
Biomedical engineering. Medical technology
Including human experimentation in medicine
3115 General (Comparative)
3115.5 Genetic engineering
For artificial insemination see KBP3117
3116 Transplantation of organs, tissues, etc.
Including donation of organs, tissues, etc.
3117 Human reproductive technology
Including artificial insemination and fertilization in vitro
Cf. KBP619.T34 Family law
3119.A-Z Special topics, A-Z
Abortion see KBP3125.A36
3119.B55 Blood transfusion
3119.C57 Circumcision
For female circumcision see KBP3119.F45
Cf. KBP184.8 Ritual laws
3119.C87 Cupping
Euthanasia see KBP4058
Experiments with the human body see KBP3115+

KBP

Furū' al-fiqh. Substantive law. Branches of law. فروع الفقه
Medical legislation
Special topics, A-Z
3119.F45 Female circumcision. Clitoridectomy
3119.M43 Medical instruments and apparatus. Medical devices
3119.P42 Plastic surgery
Eugenics. Sterilization and castration
3121 General (Comparative)
3121.5.A-Z Special topics, A-Z
3122 Veterinary medicine and hygiene. Veterinary public health
Animal protection. Animal welfare. Animal rights
Class here works on treatment and prevention of cruelty to animals
Cf. HV4701+ Animal rights as a social issue
3123 General works
3123.2 Animal experimentation and research
Including vivisection and dissection
3123.3 Slaughtering of animals
3123.5.A-Z Special topics, A-Z
3123.5.M88 Mutilation
Birth control. Family planning
3124 General (Comparative)
3125.A-Z Special topics, A-Z
3125.A36 Abortion
Cf. KBP4070 Illegal abortion (Penal law)
Environmental law
For criminal provisions see KBP4351.5+
3127 General (Comparative)
3128 Organization and administration
3129 Environmental planning. Conservation of environmental resources
Environmental pollution
3130 General (Comparative)
3130.5 Air pollution
Including noxious gases, automobile emission control, etc
3131 Water and groundwater pollution
Including pollutants and sewage control
Pollutants
3131.5 General works
3132 Radioactive substances
3132.5 Noise
Including traffic noise and noise control
3133.3.A-Z Other, A-Z
Wilderness preservation
Including natural monuments, parks, deserts, and forests
3134 General works
3134.6 Plant protection

Furūʻ al-fiqh. Substantive law. Branches of law. فروع الفقه
Environmental law
Wilderness preservation -- Continued
3135 Wildlife conservation
Including game, birds, and fish
Cultural affairs
3137 General (Comparative)
3137.9 Language
Including purity, regulation of use, etc.
Education
3138 General (Comparative)
3138.55 School government
Students
3139 General works
3139.3 Obligation of parents to educate their children
Teachers. School functionaries (General)
For particular teachers, see the level of instruction, e. g. KBP3152 University teachers
3140 General works
3140.5 Education and training of teachers
Including religious education
Elementary education
Including teachers
3141 General works
3142 Rural schools
Education of children with disabilities
3143 General works
3143.4 Children with social disabilities
Including orphans, outcasts, paupers, etc.
3143.6 Children with physical and mental disabilities
3144.5 Vocational education
Including teachers
3146 Secondary education
Higher education. Universities
For legal education see KBP42+
3147 General works
3152 Teachers
3153 Students
3156.A-Z Universities. By place, A-Z
3158 Adult education
3158.3.A-Z Special topics, A-Z
3159 Physical education. Sports
Science and the arts
3160 Public policy
Including research, and academies, institutes, etc.
3165.A-Z Branches and subjects, A-Z
Language see KBP3137.9

KBP

Furūʻ al-fiqh. Substantive law. Branches of law. فروع الفقه
Cultural affairs
Science and the arts -- Continued
The arts
Including censorship
3168 General works
3169 Fine arts
Performing arts
3170 General works
3171 Music. Musicians
3172 Theater
3173 Motion pictures
3175.A-Z Special topics, A-Z
Public collections
3176 General works
3177 Archives. Historic documents
3179 Libraries
Including librarians
3182.5 Museums and galleries
3182.7.A-Z Other, A-Z
Historic buildings and monuments. Architectural landmarks
Including sites of archaeological importance
3183 General
3183.3.A-Z Special topics, A-Z
Economic law
Including theories and concepts
3190 General (Comparative)
3206 Economic assistance
3210 Prices and price control
3217 Government business enterprises
Control of contracts and combinations in restraint of trade. Competition rules
3220 General works
Cartels
3225 General (Comparative)
3228.A-Z Industries, occupations, etc., A-Z
3237 Licensing contracts
3239 Standardized forms of contract
3242 Monopolies. Oligopolies. Antitrust law
3247 Damages (Private law) and indemnification (Public law)
3249 Small business
3250 Cooperative societies
3252.A-Z Other, A-Z
Money, currency, and foreign exchange control see KBP3534+

Furū' al-fiqh. Substantive law. Branches of law. فروع الفقه
Economic law -- Continued
Standards. Norms
For a particular product, see the product
3254 General (Comparative)
3255 Quality control
Weights and measures. Containers
3257 General works
3258.A-Z By instrument, A-Z
Standardization
3259 General works
Norms and standards for conservation of raw or scarce materials
Including recycling of refuse (metal, glass, paper, wood, etc.)
3264 General works
3265 Prohibition of industrial use of scarce materials
Price norms see KBP3210
3268 Labeling
Class here general works. For the labeling of particular goods or products, see the good or product
Regulation of industry, trade, and commerce
3272 General works
Ḥisbah. حسبة see KBP3034.3
3273 Licensing
3276 Consumer protection
3280 Advertising
Agriculture. Forestry. Rural laws
Primary production. Extractive industries
Land reform. Land use policy see KBP3056
Collective patrimony see KBP686
Co-ownership of land see KBP694
3295 General (Comparative)
3299 Conservation of agricultural and forestry lands
Including soil conservation, field irrigation, erosion control, etc.
3316 Collective farming. Agricultural cooperatives
Including grazing associations
Cf. KBP3059+ Rural planning and development
Marketing orders
3320 General works
3321 Economic assistance
Livestock industry and trade
3327 General works
3328.A-Z Particular, A-Z
Milk production. Dairy farming
3329 General works

Furūʻ al-fiqh. Substantive law. Branches of law. فروع الفقه
Economic law
Regulation of industry, trade, and commerce
Primary production. Extractive industries
Agriculture. Forestry. Rural laws
Milk production. Dairy farming -- Continued
3329.5.A-Z Products, A-Z
3334 Apiculture. Beekeeping
3335 Horticulture
3336 Forestry
Including timber laws and game laws
Fishery
For conservation and ecological aspects see KBP3135
3340 General works
3342.A-Z Particular fish or marine fauna, A-Z
Mining and quarrying
Including metallurgy
3344 General (Comparative)
3345 Public restraint on property rights and positions. Government rights
3347 Continental shelf and its resources
3350 Rights to mines and mineral resources
Including procedure and registration
3353 Mining industry and finance
Resources
Petroleum. Natural gas
3366 General works
3367 Oil and gas leases
3369.A-Z Other resources, A-Z
3371.A-Z Special topics, A-Z
Manufacturing industries
Including heavy and light industries
3372 General (Comparative)
3373.A-Z Types of manufacture, A-Z
Food processing industries. Food products
Class here works on trade practices, sanitation, and quality inspection
3377 General works
3379 Purity
Including regulation of adulteration and food additives
Cf. KBP184.9.D54 Ritual laws
3380 Cereal products
3381 Fruits and vegetables
3382 Confectionary industry
3383 Meat
3384 Poultry products

Furūʻ al-fiqh. Substantive law. Branches of law. فروع الفقه
Economic law
Regulation of industry, trade, and commerce
Food processing industries. Food products -- Continued
3386 Egg products
3388 Dairy products
3392 Fishery products. Seafood
3393 Oils and fats
Beverages
3396 Coffee
3399 Mineral waters
3401.A-Z Other, A-Z
3402 Building and construction industry
Including contracts and specifications
For building laws see KBP3067+
International trade
3405 General (Comparative)
3410 Export trade
Domestic trade
3415 General works
3416 Wholesale trade
Retail trade
Cf. KBP3429 Artisans
3418 General works
3419 Conditions of trading
Including holiday laws
3420.A-Z Special topics, A-Z
3422.A-Z Products, A-Z
3422.A88 Automobiles
3422.M48 Metals
Metals, Precious see KBP3422.P73
3422.P73 Precious metals
Secondhand trade
3423 General works
3423.5.A-Z Types of trade, A-Z
3423.5.A82 Auction houses
Service trades
3424 General works
3424.5 Hotels, taverns, and restaurants
Artisans
3426 General works
3427 Apprentices
3429 Guilds and other cooperative societies. Corporate representation
3430.A-Z Crafts, A-Z
Energy policy. Power supply
Including publicly and privately owned utilities

Furūʻ al-fiqh. Substantive law. Branches of law. فروع الفقه
Economic law
Energy policy. Power supply -- Continued
3431 General (Comparative)
3431.15 National, state, and local jurisdiction and supervision
Special topics
3431.2 Planning and conservation
3431.25 Licensing
3431.4 Corporate structure
3431.7 Engineering
Particular sources of power
3432 Electricity
3433 Gas. Natural gas
Water see KBP2956
3435 Heat. Steam distributed by central plant
3436 Nuclear energy
For protection from radiation see KBP3012
For ecological aspects see KBP3132
3437.A-Z Other sources of power, A-Z
Transportation and communication
3440 General works
Road traffic. Automotive transportation
3442 General works
Traffic regulations and enforcement
3448 General works
Carriage of passengers and goods
3455 General works
3458 Holiday laws
3459 Railroads
3466 Pipelines
3467 Air and space law
Water transportation
3470 General works
3478 Coastwise and inland shipping
Including carriage of passengers and goods, and including rafting
Cf. KBP971 Affreightment
3481.A-Z Special topics, A-Z
Communication. Mass media
3482 General (Comparative)
3483 Freedom of communication. Censorship
Telecommunication. Postal services
3485 General works
3487 Telecommunication
3491 Radio communication
Including radio and television broadcasting
Press law. Publishers and publishing

Furū' al-fiqh. Substantive law. Branches of law. فروع الفقه
Transportation and communication
Communication. Mass media
Press law. Publishers and publishing -- Continued
3500 General works
Freedom of the press and censorship see KBP3483
3500.3 Right to information
3504.3 Journalists. Domestic and foreign correspondents
3504.5 Bookdealers
3507 Press and criminal justice
3512 Special topics, A-Z
Professions. Intelligentsia
3515 General (Comparative)
Individual professions
Health professions see KBP3100+
Veterinarians see KBP3122
Lawyers see KBP1630+
3519 Engineering and construction. Engineers
3521.A-Z Other professions, A-Z
Public finance
3526 General (Comparative)
Money
Including control of circulation
3534 General (Comparative)
3537 Gold trading and gold standard
National and local revenue
3540 General (Comparative)
3540.3 Fees. Fines
Taxation
3541 General (Comparative)
Taxation and tax exemption as a measure of social and economic policy
3553 General works
3553.3 Investments
Including foreign investments
3555.A-Z Classes of taxpayers or lines of business, A-Z
3556.A-Z Taxation of particular activities, A-Z
Tax administration. Revenue service
3558 General (Comparative)
Collection and enforcement
3560 General works
Financial courts see KBP3682+
Tax avoidance see KBP3695
3570 Execution
3571.A-Z Special topics, A-Z
3572.A-Z Classes of taxpayers or lines of business, A-Z
Income tax

KBP

Furūʻ al-fiqh. Substantive law. Branches of law. فروع الفقه
Public finance
National and local revenue
Taxation
Income tax -- Continued
3573 General works
Taxable income. Exemptions
3578 General works
3578.5.A-Z Particular, A-Z
Capital gains see KBP3578.5.P75
3578.5.P75 Profits. Capital gains
Deductions
3579 General works
3580 Charitable or educational gifts and contributions
3582.3.A-Z Expenses and losses, A-Z
3588 Capital investment
Including foreign investment
3589.3.A-Z Sources of income, A-Z
3591.A-Z Classes of taxpayers or lines of business, A-Z
Corporation tax
3592 General (Comparative)
Nonprofit associations, nonprofit corporations, etc.
3593 General works
3593.5.A-Z Special topics, A-Z
Personal companies. Unincorporated business associations
3594 General works
3594.5.A-Z Special topics, A-Z
Cooperatives
3595 General works
3595.5.A-Z Special topics, A-Z
Stock companies. Incorporated business associations
3596 General works
3597.3 Assessment
3613.A-Z Lines of corporate business, A-Z
Drilling see KBP3613.M54
3613.M54 Mining. Drilling
Foreign corporations and stockholders
3614 General (Comparative)
3614.3 Special topics, A-Z
Multi-national corporations
3615 General (Comparative)
3615.3 Special topics, A-Z
Property tax. Taxation of capital
Including juristic persons and business enterprises
3616 General works

Furūʻ al-fiqh. Substantive law. Branches of law. فروع الفقه
Public finance
National and local revenue
Taxation
Property tax. Taxation of capital -- Continued
Real property tax see KBP3670+
Zakat. Zakāh. Prescribed giving. Almsgiving. زكاة
Including obligations, conditions, times, and requirements for almsgiving
3620 General works
3620.3.A-Z Kinds of taxable income, A-Z
3620.3.A54 Animals
3620.3.B84 Buildings
Commercial merchandise see KBP3620.3.M47
3620.3.C75 Crops and fruits
Fruits see KBP3620.3.C75
3620.3.M47 Merchandise, Commercial
3620.3.M48 Metals
3620.3.M55 Minerals
3620.3.M65 Money
3620.3.T72 Transactions
3621 Estate, inheritance, and gift taxes
3623 Capital gains tax
3624 Surtaxes
Excise taxes. Taxes on sales, services, and transactions
3627 General works
3640.A-Z Particular commodities, services, and transactions, A-Z
3640.B35 Banking transactions
Bonds see KBP3640.S42
3640.E96 Export-import sales
Import sales see KBP3640.E96
3640.R48 Retail trade
3640.S25 Sales
3640.S42 Securities and bonds
3640.S76 Stock exchange transactions
3663 Property tax. Taxation of capital
Including juristic persons and business enterprises
Real property tax. Land tax. Kharāj
3670 General works
3672 Capital gains tax
Including development gains
Business tax
3674 General works
3679.A-Z Classes of taxpayers or lines of business, A-Z
3680.A-Z Other taxes, A-Z

KBP

Furū' al-fiqh. Substantive law. Branches of law. فروع الفقه
Public finance
National and local revenue
Taxation
Other taxes, A-Z -- Continued
3680.J59 Jizyah. Poll tax. جزية
Poll tax see KBP3680.J59
3681 Customs. Tariff
Tax and customs courts and procedure
3682 General (Comparative)
3692.A-Z Special topics, A-Z
Tax and customs crimes and delinquency. Procedure
3693 General works
Individual offenses
3695 Tax evasion and avoidance
3698 Organized smuggling
3699 Forgery of seals, stamps, etc.
Procedure
General see KBP3693
3704.3.A-Z Special topics, A-Z
3705 Amnesty. Pardon
Government measures in time of war, national emergency, or economic crisis
3709 General works
Particular measures
3710 Military requisitions from civilians. Requisitioned land
For damages and compensation see KBP3727
3712 Control of property. Confiscations
Including enemy and alien property
Manpower control
3714 General works
3715 Compulsory and forced labor
3720 Economic recovery measures. Expropriation and nationalization
3724 Rationing. Price control
3725.A-Z Other, A-Z
3727 Damage compensation
Including compensation for damages resulting from actions taken by communal authorities
Military law
For jihād see KBP182+
For emergency and wartime legislation see KBP3709+
For the law of war and neutrality see KZ6378+
Organized defense forces. The armed forces
3738 General works
Obligation to serve
3739 General works

Furūʻ al-fiqh. Substantive law. Branches of law. فروع الفقه
Military law
Organized defense forces. The armed forces
Obligation to serve -- Continued
3740.A-Z Special topics, A-Z
3748.A-Z Particular services, A-Z
3748.M54 Militias. Patrols
Patrols see KBP3748.M54
Military criminal law and procedure
Cf. KBP4470 Crimes against national defense
3758 General works
3760.A-Z Individual offenses, A-Z
3760.D46 Desertion
3760.I53 Incitement. Mutiny
3760.I56 Insubordination
Malingering see KBP3760.S44
Mutiny see KBP3760.I53
3760.S32 Sabotaging weapons, equipment, or means of defense
3760.S44 Self-mutilation. Malingering
3770 Courts and procedure
Military discipline. Law enforcement. Procedure
Including all branches of the armed forces
3780 General works
3782 Superior orders. Enforcement of orders
3785.A-Z Other, A-Z
Criminal law and procedure
For criminology and penology see HV6001+
3790 Reform of criminal law, procedure, and execution
3791 General (Comparative)
Class here works on crimes, procedure, and punishment discussed together
Criminology and penology see HV6001+
Theory of punishment see KBP3950+
Relationship of criminal law to other subjects or phenomena
3817 General works
3818 Criminal law and society
Cf. HV6115+ Social pathology
3821 Interpretation and construction. Legal hermeneutics
3823.A-Z Terms and phrases, A-Z
3824.A-Z Concepts and principles, A-Z
3824.I55 Immunities. Personal applicability
Personal applicability see KBP3824.I55
Criminal offense. Criminal act
3840 General works
3851 Causation. Indirect causation. Tasbīb
Form of criminal act

KBP

Furūʻ al-fiqh. Substantive law. Branches of law. فروع الفقه
Criminal law and procedure
Criminal offense. Criminal act
Form of criminal act -- Continued
3852 General works
3854 Attempt
For active repentance (tawbah) see KBP4023.T38
Justification of otherwise prohibited acts
3855 General works
3856 Self-defense or defense of another
Including limits of self-defense
3857 Necessity
3858 Preservation of life
3859 Duty to act (Legal authority or duty)
3861 Consent of the injured party. Assumption of risk
3865.A-Z Other grounds for justification, A-Z
Criminal intent. Mens rea
3867 General works
3868 Deliberate intent. Tawbah. Qaṣd. توبة. قصد
3869 Quasi-deliberate intent. Shibh al-ʻamd. شبه العمد
3870 Khatā'. خطاء
Criminal liability. Guilt. Culpability
Cf. KBP834+ Tort liability
3878 General works
Capacity. Limited capacity and incapacity
3882 General works
3884 Insane persons. People with mental disabilities
3886 Minors
Including infants, juveniles, etc.
3886.5 Slaves
3892.A-Z Special topics, A-Z
3897.A-Z Exculpating circumstances, A-Z
Duress see KBP3897.I47
3897.I47 Ikrāh. Duress. اكراه
3902 Error
Including error about fact, error about grounds for justification or excusation, error in persona, etc.
3922 Perpetrators (Principals and accessories). Complicity
Crimes and punishment
3946 General works
Theory of punishment. Measure of punishment
3950 General works
3950.2 Safeguarding the social and political order (Siyāsah) (سياسة)
3951 Tashābuh. Resemblance of punishment to the committed act. تشابه

Furū‘ al-fiqh. Substantive law. Branches of law. فروع الفقه
Criminal law and procedure
Crimes and punishment
Theory of punishment. Measure of punishment -- Continued
3964 Ḥadd punishment (with scriptural authority proscribed). حد
3965 Ta‘zīr punishment (Discretionary punishment awarded by the qāḍī). تعزير
Qiṣāṣ punishment. قصاص
3975 General works
3976 Blood money. Dīyah. Compensation. Fines. دية
For settlement see KBP842.2
3979 Expiation. Kaffārah. كفارة
3980.A-Z Particular penalties, A-Z
3980.A46 Amputation of limbs
Banishment see KBP3997
3980.B43 Beheading. Decapitation by the sword
3980.C78 Crucifixion
Decapitation by the sword see KBP3980.B43
Exile see KBP3997
3980.F57 Flagellation. Whipping
Flogging see KBP3980.F57
Kaffārah see KBP3979
Lashing see KBP3980.F57
3980.M87 Mutilation
3980.S85 Stoning
Whipping see KBP3980.F57
3980.W68 Wounds, Surgical repetition of
Preventive or coercive measures. Measures of rehabilitation
3982 General works
3992 Protective custody. Imprisonment. Ḥabs. حبس
e. g. Imprisonment aiming at repentance (Tawbah) (توبة)
3995 Protective surveillance
3997 Exile. Banishment. Expulsion. Nafy. نفي
4004 Infamy
4006 Property confiscation
4011.A-Z Special topics, A-Z
Sentencing and determining the measure of punishment. Gradation
4012 General works
Circumstances (aggravating and extenuating) influencing measures of penalty
4020 General works
4023.A-Z Special topics, A-Z

Furū‘ al-fiqh. Substantive law. Branches of law. فروع الفقه
Criminal law and procedure
Crimes and punishment
Sentencing and determining the measure of punishment
Circumstances (aggravating and extenuating) incluencing measures of penalty
Special topics, A-Z
Active repentance see KBP4023.T38
Cf. KBP3854 Attempt
4023.K56 Kinship. Qarābah. قرابة
4023.T38 Tawbah. Active repentance
4034 Pardon. ‘Afw. عفو
4038 Limitation of actions. Taqādum. تقادم
Individual offenses. Jarā’im. جرائم
Ḥadd crimes. حد
4041 General works
4043 Zinā’. Unlawful intercourse. زناء
Cf. KBP4147 Defamation (Qadhf)
4044 Qadhf. False accusation of unlawful intercourse. قذف
4045 Shurb al-khamr. Drinking of wine. شرب الخمر
4046 Qaṭ‘ al-ṭarīq. Highway robbery with homicide. قطع الطريق
4046.2 Aggravated theft
Cf. KBP4235 Theft
Cf. KBP4254 Robbery
4047.A-Z Other, A-Z
Other offenses
Including crimes falling under the category of ta‘zīr (تعزير) or intentional qiṣāṣ (قصاص)
4048 General works
Homicide
Including murder and manslaughter
4050 General works
4054.5 Indirect homicide. Qatl bi-sabab. قتل بسبب
4058 Euthanasia
Including assisting suicide
4070 Crimes against inchoate life. Abortion without consent of father
Including causing an abortion
Cf. KBP842.2+ Torts
Crimes against physical inviolability
4074 General works
Battery
4076 General works
4076.5 Battery with deadly consequences
Crimes against personal freedom

Furūʻ al-fiqh. Substantive law. Branches of law. فروع الفقه
Criminal law and procedure
Crimes and punishment
Individual offenses. Jarā'im. جرائم
Other offenses
Crimes against personal freedom -- Continued
4116 General works
4120 Extortionate kidnapping
4121 Kidnapping for sale. Slave traffic
4125 Abduction
4147 Defamation
Including qadhf (accusation of sexual intercourse) (قذف)
Offenses against religious tranquility and the peace of the dead
4170 General
4172 Apostasy. Riddah. Idolatry. Blasphemy. ردة
4174 Disturbing a religious observance
4176 Disturbing the peace of the dead
Including cemeteries and funerals
Offenses against marriage, family, and family status
4180 General
4182 Incest
4184 Adultery
4186 Bigamy
(4188) Abduction of a minor from legal custodian. Parental kidnapping
see KBP602
4190 Abandonment, neglect, or abuse of a child
4192 Breach of duty of support
4194 Breach of duty of assistance to a pregnant woman
Abortion see KBP4070
Offenses against sexual integrity
4200 General
4202 Rape
4204 Lewd acts with persons incapable of resistance
4206 Abduction for lewd acts
4208 Lewd acts with children or charges
4216 Sodomy
Crimes against property
Including works on things extra commercium
4230 General works
4235 Theft. Larceny. Sariqah. سرقة
Including works on family theft and pickpocketing (ikhtilās) (اخلاس)
4250 Embezzlement. Khiyānah. خيانة
4254 Robbery. Nahb. نهب

Furū‘ al-fiqh. Substantive law. Branches of law. فروع الفقه
Criminal law and procedure
Crimes and punishment
Individual offenses. Jarā’im. جرائم
Other offenses
Crimes against property -- Continued
4256 Destruction of property and conversion
Usurpation of another's property (Ghasb) (غسب)
see KBP846.2
4258 Fraud
Offenses against public order and convenience
4305 General works
4307 Inciting insubordination
4310 Inciting crime
4320 Disrupting the peace of the community
4330 Crimes against the security of legal and monetary transactions and documents
Including forgery and counterfeiting
Cf. KBP846 Torts
4351.A-Z Other, A-Z
Crimes involving danger to the community. Terrorism
4351.5 General works
4354 Arson
4364 Poisoning wells or soil
4368 Biological terrorism
Including spreading communicable diseases, morbific agents, or parasites
4377 Crimes aboard aircraft. Air piracy
Crimes affecting traffic
4380 Dangerous interference with rail, ship, or air traffic
4384 Dangerous interference with street traffic. Motor vehicle offenses
4398 Riots
4400 Crimes against public health
Offenses against the peace. Political offenses
4415 General works
High treason and treason
4417 General works
4442 Espionage
4470 Offenses against national defense
4507.5 Chicanery and abuse of legal process
4514 Crimes involving communal employees. Corruption. Bribery
Including omission of official acts
Crimes against humanity
4538 General works

Furūʻ al-fiqh. Substantive law. Branches of law. فروع الفقه
Criminal law and procedure
Crimes and punishment
Individual offenses. Jarā'im. جرائم
Other offenses
Crimes against humanity -- Continued
4540 Genocide
4541 Torture
4543 Crimes against foreign states, supranational institutions, or international institutions
4545 War crimes
4550.A-Z Special topics, A-Z
Criminal procedure
For works on the reform of criminal procedure see KBP3790
For works on both criminal law and criminal procedure see KBP3791
4601 General (Comparative)
Administration of criminal justice. Courts see KBP1572
Procedural principles
4624 Accusation principle (no prosecution ex officio)
4630.A-Z Parties to action, A-Z
4630.A25 Accused. Person charged. Defendant
4630.A253 Accusers
Defendant see KBP4630.A25
4630.D43 Defense
Person charged see KBP4630.A25
4630.V52 Victim
Including victim's family
Witnesses see KBP4692
Pretrial procedures
4632 General works
4636 Investigation. Examination
For techniques of criminal investigation see HV8073+
For ḥisbah (office of the muḥtasib) see KBP1619.3
4648 Time periods. Deadlines
4650 Compulsory measures against the accused. Securing of evidence
Including arrest and detention before trial
Procedure at trial
4664 General works
4666 Jurisdiction
Including competence in subject matter and venue
4668 Action. Complaint. Charge
Including accusation by witnesses
4670 Exclusion and challenge of court members

KBP

Furūʻ al-fiqh. Substantive law. Branches of law. فروع الفقه
Criminal law and procedure
Criminal procedure
Procedure at trial -- Continued
Time periods and deadlines see KBP4648
Limitation of actions see KBP4038
Trial
4673 General works
Evidence. Burden of proof
4675 General works
Admission of evidence
4679 General works
4681 Confession. Iqrār. Self-incrimination. Entrapment. اقرار
Including withdrawing (rujūʻ) (رجوع) of confession
Cf. KBP816.7 Assumption of debt
4687 Physical examination
For forensic medicine see RA1001+
4689 Electronic listening and recording devices
Including wiretapping
4690 Previous testimony, police records, etc.
4692 Witnesses
Including qualification and number of witnesses, etc.
4700 Expert testimony
Cf. RA1001+ Medical jurisprudence
4702 Testimony of accused
4704 Documentary evidence
4709.A-Z Other, A-Z
4709.A45 Alibi
4709.C57 Circumstantial evidence
Oath see KBP4709.Y35
Retraction of evidence see KBP4709.R84
4709.R84 Rujūʻ. Retraction of evidence. الرجوع
4709.Y35 Yamīn. Oath. يمين
Including oath of witnesses and parties
Particular proceedings
4713 Proceedings against absentees and fugitives
4720 Procedure for juvenile delinquency
Judicial decisions. Judgments. Aḥkām. احكام
4736 General works
4740 Judicial discretion
Including opportunity and equity
4744 Acquittal
4746 Conviction
4750 Dismissal
4753 Correction or withdrawal of faulty decisions (errors)

Furūʻ al-fiqh. Substantive law. Branches of law. فروع الفقه
Criminal law and procedure
Criminal procedure
Procedure at trial
Trial
Judicial decisions. Judgments. Aḥkām. احكام -- Continued
4754 Res judicata
Cf. KBP1681 Courts and procedure
Special procedures
4769 Criminal proceedings by an irregular court
4770 Remedies
Execution of sentence
4795 General works
Ḥadd punishment see KBP3964
Exile. Banishment. Punitive deportation see KBP3997
Pardon see KBP4034
4855 Victimology. Victims of crimes
4860.A-Z Special topics, A-Z

History of canon law
Class here sources (collected and individual) and general works on the development of Canon law, covering all historic periods to late 19th cent.
For the codification period of Canon law, see subclass KBU
Bibliography
Including international and national bibliography
2 Bibliography of bibliography. Bibliographical concordances
3 General bibliography
Including works with consilia and rotal decisions
4 Indexes for periodical literature, society publications, collections, etc.
Subject bibliography
General (Collective)
see KBR3
Individual subjects and topics
see the subject
Early works, e. g. Repertoria
see the author in the appropriate period
6 Personal bibliography. Canonists. Writers on canon law (Collective or individual)
Catalogs, inventories and guides to manuscripts and incunabula collections in libraries or archives open to the public. By name of the library or archive
Including university, museum, cathedral, religious order and other institutional libraries or archives
9 General (Collective)
10.A-Z North America, A-Z
Including United States and Canada
12.A-Z Central and South American, A-Z
European
14.A-Z English, A-Z
14.5.A-Z French, A-Z
15.A-Z German, A-Z
15.5.A-Z Italian, A-Z
15.5.A73 Archivio Vaticano
15.5.B5 Biblioteca Apostolica Vaticana
16.A-Z Spanish and Portuguese, A-Z
17.A-Z Other European, A-Z
18.A-Z Asian and Pacific, A-Z
19.A-Z African, A-Z
<20> Periodicals
see subclass KB
21 Annuals. Yearbooks

22 Monographic series
e. g. Canon law studies; Theses as lauream in iure canonico (Pontificia Università lateranense); Monographias canonicas Penafort; Monumenta iuris canonici; Studia et documenta juris canonici; Annali di dottrina e giurisprudenza canonica; Österreichisches Archiv für Kirchenrecht
Kirchenrechtliche Abhandlungen see KB70.K57
Studia Gratiana
Official gazette of the Holy See
Cf. BX850+ Catholic Church
<25> Acta Sanctae Sedis (1865-1904)
Superceded by Acta Apostolicae Sedis
see KBU25
<26> Acta Apostolicae Sedis (1908-)
see KBU26
Official acts of the Holy See
Class here early or discontinued collections and compilations of apostolic constitutions, decrees, bulls, etc.
Including editions of papal registers
Regesta. Registers. Digests
27.A-Z General. By editor, A-Z
27.I53 Index bullarum, brevium, et constitutionum apostolicarum
27.J35 Jaffé, Philipp, 1819-1870. Regesta Pontificum romanorum: Ab condita ecclesia ad annum post Christum natum MCXVIII, 1885-88
Including indexes
27.P77 Potthast, August, 1824-1898. Regesta Pontificum romanorum inde ab A. post Christum natum MCXCVIII ad A. MCCCIV, 1874-75
Including indexes
27.5.A-Z By pope, A-Z
27.5.B46 Benedict XI (1303-1304)
27.5.B66 Boniface VIII (1294-1303)
27.5.N53 Nicholas IV (1288-1292)
Collections. Compilations. Selections
General
Class here comprehensive collections and compilations of pontifical acts, decrees, constitutions, and papal bulls, not relating to a specific historic period or pope, with or without ecclesiastical court decisions and acts/decisions of the Roman Curia, etc.
Including annotated editions and commentaries, and including topical collections
For individual acts, constitutiones, bulls, etc. see the subject
Cf. BX870 Catholic Church

Official acts of the Holy See
Collections. Compilations. Selections
General -- Continued

27.7 Agostinho Barbosa (1590-1649). Collectanea bvllarii, aliarvmve svmmorvm pontificvm constitvtionvm, necnon praicipuarum decisionum, qvae ab apostolica sede, et sacris congregationibus S. R. E. cardinalium Romae celebratis usque ad annum 1633 emanarunt

27.8 Acta pontificum Romanorum inedita (Julius von Pflugk-Harttung, 1848-1919, ed.)

28 Collectio diversarum constitutionum et litterarum Rom. Pont. a Gregorio VII usque ad sanctissimum D.N.D. Gregorium XIII ...

28.12 Bullae diuersorum pontificum incipiente a Ioanne XXII ...: ex bibliotheca R.P.D. Ludouici Gomes ... excerptae, & in vnum redactae ...

28.2 Summa constitutionum summorum pontificum et rerum in Ecclesia Romana gestarum a Gregorio IX usque ad Sixtum V ... per Petrum Matthaeum

28.3 Compendium constitutionum summorum Pontificum: quae extant a Gregorio VII usque ad Clementem VIII ... per ... Iocobum Castellanum ... collectum

(28.4) Constitutiones pontificiae et romanorum congregationum decisiones ad episcopos et abbates ... (Giovanni Battista Pittoni, d. 1748, comp.)
see KBR2792

28.42 Collectio constitutionum, chirographorum, et brevium diversorum Romanorum Pontificum ...

28.43 Bullarum privilegiorum, ac diplomatum romanorum pontificum amplissima collectio (Charles Cocquelines, d. 1758, ed.)

28.5 Bullarum, diplomatum et privilegiorum sanctorum romanorum pontificum taurinensis editio ... facta collectione novissima plurium brevium, epistolarum, decretorum actorumque s. Sedis a s. Leone Magno usque ad praesens ... (Charles Cocquelines, d. 1758 & Francesco Gaude, 1809-1860, et al., eds.)

28.52 Bullarum, diplomatum et privilegiorum sanctorum romanorum pontificum neapolitana editio

28.7 Bullarium, sive Nova collectio plurimarum apostolicarum diversorum Romanorum Pont. a beato Leone Primo usque ad ... Paulum Quintum (Laerzio Cherubini, d. ca. 1626, ed.)constitutionum multorum pontif. a Gregori Septimo usque ad s.d.m. sixtum quintum pontificem ...

Official acts of the Holy See
Collections. Compilations. Selections
General -- Continued

28.8 Bullarium Romanum novissimum: ab Leone Magno usque ad S.D.N. Urbanum VIII (Laerzio Cherubini, d. ca. 1626, and Angelo Maria Cherubini)

28.9 Magnum Bullarium Romanum: ab Urbano VIII usque ad S.D.N. Clementem X/ opus absolutissimum a ... Angelo a Lantusca, & Ioanne Paulo a Roma ...

29 Magnum bullarium romanum ab Leone Magno usque ad S.D.N. Innocentium X (Laerzio Cherubini, d. ca. 1626, & Angelo Maria Cherubini, eds.)

29.15 Bullarium Romanum seu novissima et accuratissima collectio apostolicarum constitutionum ... complectens constitutiones Clementis XI ab Anno XIII usque ad XXI Innocentii XIII, & Benedicti XIII Anno I editas

29.2 Bullarii romani continuatio summorum Pontificum Benedicti XIV, Clementis XIII ..., Pii VIII: constitutiones ... complectens

29.3 Canonici compendium bullarii/ A Laertio Cherubini patre; Flavii Cherubini (Laerzio Cherubini, d. ca. 1626, and Flavio Cherubini, comp.)

29.4 Summae bullarum, sive Apostolicarum constitutionum usu frequentiorum commentaria ... (Giovanni Antonio Novario, fl. 1631-1635)

Individual popes

Clement XI (Pope, 1700-1721)

30 General

30.12 Clementis undecimi Pont. Max. Bullarium

Benedict XIV (Pope, 1740-1758)

30.2 General

30.22 Benedicti Papae XIV bullarium ... in quo continentur constitutiones, epistolae, & ...

Clement XIII (Pope, 1758-1769)

30.23 General

30.24 Acta. Bullae, etc.

Clement XIV (Pope, 1769-1774)

30.25 General

30.26 Acta. Bullae, etc.

Gregory XVI (Pope, 1831-1846)

30.3 General

30.32 Acta Gregory XVI

Pius IX (Pope, 1846-1878)

30.4 General

30.42 Acta Pii IX

Leo XIII (Pope, 1878-1905)

Official acts of the Holy See
Collections. Compilations. Selections
Individual popes
Leo XIII (Pope, 1878-1905) -- Continued
30.5 General
30.52 Acta Leonis XIII
Pius X (Pope, 1903-1914)
30.6 General
30.62 Acta Pii X
Individual Apostolic constitutions and other particular acts
Class individual constitutions and acts by subject
Cf. BX870 Catholic Church
<32> By pope
Subarrange further by date of accession of pope
Litterae Encyclicae. Encyclicals see BX860
Epistolae. Litterae Pontificiae. Letters see BX863
Concordats
<38> Collections. Compilations. Selections
For collected concordats of a particular signatory jurisdiction, see secular ecclesiastical law in the appropriate K subclass for the jurisdiction, e. g. Germany, KK5520+
Class here universal collections not related to any particular jurisdiction
see KBU38
Individual
see the subject in the appropriate K subclass for the signatory jurisdiction
Decrees and decisions of the Curia Romana
<39> General (Collective)
Not including Papal documents
Signatura Gratiae. Signatura of Grace
39.2 Collections. Compilations. Selections. By editor, compiler, or title
Individual
see the subject
Camera Apostolica. Apostolic Chamber. Treasury
<39.3> Collections. Compilations. Selections. By editor, compiler, or title
Individual
see the subject
Secretaria Status. Secretariate of State of the Catholic Church
<39.4> Collections. Compilations. Selections. By editor, compiler, or title
Individual
see the subject
Secretaria Brevium

Official acts of the Holy See
Decrees and decisions of the Curia Romana
Secretaria Brevium -- Continued
<39.5> Collections. Compilations. Selections. By editor, compiler, or title
Individual
see the subject
Secretaria Memoralium
<39.6> Collections. Compilations. Selections. By editor, compiler, or title
Individual
see the subject
Roman congregations
40 Suprema Congregatio Sanctae Romanae et Universalis Inquisitionis. Supreme Congregation of the Holy Roman and Universal Inquisition (1542-1908) (Table KB1)
Cf. KBR2502+ Constitution of the Church
40.2 Congregatio Indicis. Congregation of the Index (1571-1917) (Table KB1)
<40.45> Congregation Sacrorum Rituum (1588-1969)
see KBU40.45
40.52 Congregatio super Consultationibus Regularium. Congregation for Consultations about Regulars (1586-1601) (Table KB1)
40.54 Congregatio super Consultationibus Episcoporum et Aliorum Praelatorum. Congregation for Consultations about Bishops and other Prelates (Table KB1)
40.55 Congregatio Episcoporum et Regularium. Congregation of Bishops and Regulars (Table KB1 modified)
Official records. Working documents
40.55.A35 Collectanea in usum secretariae S.C. Congregation episcoporum et regularium
<40.6> Congregatio pro Episcopis
see KBU40.6
<40.7> Congregatio de Propaganda Fide
see KBU40.7
<40.8> Congregatio Concilii (Congregatio Cardinalium Concilii Tridentini Interpretum) (to 1967)
see KBU40.8
41.2 Congregatio de Propaganda Fide pro Negotiis Ritus Orientalis (Congregatio super Correctione Librorum Ecclesiae Orientalis) (Table KB1 modified)
Official records. Working documents
Rules of proceedings of the organ and its committees, etc.

Official acts of the Holy See
Decrees and decisions of the Curia Romana
Roman congregations
Congregatio Specialis pro Negotiis Ritus Orientalis (Congregatio pro Corrigendis Libris Ecclesiae Orientalis)
Official records. Working documents
Rules of proceedings of the organ and its committees, etc. -- Continued
41.2.A45 Monographs. By date
e.g. Collectanea S.C. de Propaganda Fide, 1893, 1907
41.3 Congregatio Consistorialis (Congregation pro Erectione Ecclesiarum et Provisionibus Consistorialibus). Congregation of the Consistory (1588) (Table KB1)
41.32 Congregatio Signaturae Iustitiae (Table KB1)
41.33 Congregatio Ceremonialis. Congregation of Ceremonies (1588) (Table KB1)
41.34 Congregatio Visitationis Apostolicae. Congregation of the Visitation (1592) (Table KB1)
41.35 Congregationes super Disciplina Regulari and super Statu Regularium (Table KB1)
41.36 Congregatio Iurisdictionis et Immunitatis Ecclesiasticae (Table KB1)
41.4 Congregatio Indulgentiarum et Sacrarum Reliquiarum (Table KB1 modified)
Decisions. Decrees. Measures. Resolutions. Recommendations
Including opinions, consultations, etc.
For individual decisions, etc., see the subject
Collections. Selections
41.4.A6 Monographs. By date
41.4.A6 1668 Decreta authentica, 1668-1882
41.45 Congregatio pro Negotiis Ecclesiaticis Extraordinariis (Table KB1)
41.5 Congregatio Reverendae Fabricae Basilicae (Sancti Petri) (Table KB1)
41.7 Congregatio Boni Regiminis (Table KB1)
Decisions of ecclesiastical tribunals and courts, and related materials
Class here historic collections with or without annotations
For modern decisions, see subclass KBU
Collections. Compilations. Selections
42.A-Z General. By editor, compiler, or title, A-Z
Class here general collections not related to a particular court, with or without decisions of the Rota Romana.

Decisions of ecclesiastical tribunals and courts, and related materials
Collections. Compilations. Selections
General. By editor, compiler, or title, A-Z -- Continued
42.B44 Gilles de Bellemère (1342 or 3-1407) and Guilielmus Cassador (1477-1527 or 8?), comp. Sacrosanctae decisiones canonicae
Including decisiones Capellae Tolosanae and others
42.S63 Alessandro Sperelli, 1590-1671
By tribunal or court
Sacri Palatii auditorium. Rota Romana
43.A-Z Indexes and tables. Registra. Digests. By author or title, A-Z
Including indexes of the decisions of Rotal auditors with or without biographical notes
For indexes of decisions of an individual auditor, see the auditor at KBR43.2+
For the inventories of the Rota Archives see KBR15.5.A+
43.B37 Andrea Barberi
43.B53 Francesco Bianchi (fl. 1686). Elenchvs, sive index decisionvm Sacrae Rotae Romanae in libris impraessis ... & post indicem Ioannis Baptistae Cantalmaij aeditarum ..., 1687
43.C37 Guilielmus Cassador, 1477-1527 or 8?. Decisiones ac intelligentiae
43.C45 Emmanuele Cerchiari. Capellani papae et Apostolicae Sedis auditores causarum Sacri Palatii Apostolici, seu Sacra Romana Rota ab origine ad diem usque 20 Septembris 1870
43.C47 Aloisius Cerroti. Collectio omnium juris theorematum: quae in decisionibus S.Rotae Romannae ab anno MDCCXLI editis: continentur ... annuales indices, alphabetice digesta, 1846
43.C97 Controversiarum forensium liber primus[-tertius]: ... accesserunt decisiones aliquae Rotae Romanae nondum impressae ... (Franciscus Niger Cyriacus, fl. 1629, comp.)
43.I53 Index decisionum Sacrae Rotae Romanae que Anno 1751-1860?. Predierunt alphabetico conclusionum ordine digestus ...
43.N88 Johannes Balthassar Nuvoli, fl. 1841. Index generalis conclusionum rerumque notabilium quae continentur decisionibus a S. Romana Rota editis ab anno 1814 ad annum 1819 (and ab anno 1819 ad annum 1824)
43.15 Serials

KBR

Decisions of ecclesiastical tribunals and courts, and related materials
By tribunal or court
Sacri Palatii auditorium. Rota Romana -- Continued
Older (monographic) collections
Class here the early collections or compilations of Rota auditors, including collections with indexes, register, annotations and scholarly comment
For independently published commentaries (annotationes, additiones), etc. see KBR44.7.A+
43.2 Decisiones Thomae Falstoli (Thomas Falstolus, fl. 1338-1361)
43.3 Decisiones Antiquiores (Bernardus de Bosqueto, "Bisigneto," d. 1371)
43.4 Decisiones Antiquae (Gulielmus Gallici, comp.; continued by Guillelmus Horborch and Bonaguida Cremonensis)
43.5 Decisiones Aegidii Bellemère (Gilles de Bellemère, 1342 or 3-1407)
43.6 Decisiones novae (Conclusiones Dominorum de Rota) (Guillelmus Horborch, comp. et ed.)
Subsequent (comprehensive) collections. Compilations. Selections
Class here compilations that may include one or all of the earlier collections with or without annotation (additiones)
43.62 Novissimae decisiones (S. Rotae Romanae seu diversorum S. Palatii Apostolici auditorum)
43.64 Decisiones novae [et] antiquae
Including decisiones of earlier compilations by Guillelmus Horborch, Gulielmus Gallici, and Bonaguida Cremonensis
43.7 S. Rotae Romanae decisiones recentiores
43.72 S. Rotae Romanae decisiones recentiores in compendium redactae
43.74 Decisiones nuperrimae
43.75 Decisiones recentissimae
43.8 Rotae auditorum decisiones novae, antiquae, et antiquiores
Including decisions of earlier compilations by Thomas Falstolus, Bernardus de Bosqueto (Bisigneto), Gulielmus Gallici, Bonaguida Cremonensis, and Guillelmus Horborch
44.A-Z Other. By editor, compiler, or title, A-Z
44.A84 Ateneo di Milano
44.C37 Guilielmus Cassador, 1477-1527
44.C4 Luigi Cenci, d. 1637

Decisions of ecclesiastical tribunals and courts, and related materials
By tribunal or court
Sacri Palatii auditorium. Rota Romana
Subsequent (comprehensive) collections. Compilations. Selections
Other. By editor, compiler, or title, A-Z -- Continued

44.C6 Francesco Maria Constantini, 1639-1713
44.C74 Marcello Crescenzi, 1500?-1552
44.F37 Prospero Farinacci, 1554-1618
44.F72 Girolamo Francini
44.G73 Achilles de Grassis, 1498-1558
44.G74 Caesar de Grassis, fl. 1572-1591
44.M44 Camillus Melle, fl. 1550
44.M66 Benedetto Monaldi, 1588-1644
44.P38 Gianfrancesco Pavini
44.R43 Pierre Rebuffi, 1487-1557
44.R8 Paolo Rubeo
44.U22 Francesco Ubaldi, 1554-1626
44.5.A-Z Decisiones (Conclusiones) by auditors ("coram auditore") of the Rota. By auditor, A-Z
44.5.A54 Martin Andrés
44.5.A6 Ansaldo Ansaldi, 1651-1719
44.5.A7 Guttierez Arguelles
44.5.B3 Jacopo Balducci, 1657-1709
Gilles de Bellemère see KBR43.5
44.5.B4 Alexander Benincasa
44.5.B52 Celio Bichi, d. 1657
44.5.B8 Matteo Buratti, 1553-1657
44.5.C34 Alessandro Caprara
44.5.C35 Pedro Carrillo de Acuna, d. 1664
44.5.C36 Juan del Castillo Sotomayor, 1563-1640
44.5.C37 Giacomo Cavaliero
44.5.C38 Angelo Celso, fl. 1645-1668
44.5.C39 Serafino Cenci
44.5.C4 Carlo Cerri, d. 1690
44.5.C6 Giovanni Battista Coccino
44.5.C64 Ercole Consalvi, 1757-1824
44.5.C67 Cosimo Corsi, 1798-1870?
44.5.C74 Marcello Crescenzi, 1500?-1552
44.5.C75 Marcello Crescenzi, d. 1768
44.5.D42 Giovanni Battista De Luca, 1614-1683
44.5.D45 Giacomo del Pozzo (Puteus), 1508-1563
44.5.D75 Aimé du Nozet, d. 1657 (Amatus Dunozetus)
44.5.D76 Guilemus Du Nozet, d. 1626
44.5.D8 Pablo Durán, 1580-1651
44.5.E63 Joannes Emerix, d. 1669

Decisions of ecclesiastical tribunals and courts, and related materials
By tribunal or court
Sacri Palatii auditorium. Rota Romana
Decisiones (Conclusiones) by auditors ("coram auditore") of the Rota. By auditor, A-Z -- Continued

44.5.E64 Jacob Emerix de Matthiis, 1626-1696
44.5.F44 Alessandro Falconieri, 1657-1734
44.5.G73 Achilles de Grassis, 1498-1558
44.5.G74 Caesar de Grassis, fl. 1572-1591
44.5.H4 Juan de Herrera, 1661-1726
44.5.I76 Joachim Jean Xavier Isoard, 1766-1839
44.5.K3 Franz Karl von Kaunitz, 1676-1717
44.5.L35 Cyriacus Lancette
44.5.L8 Alessandro Ludovisi, 1554-1623 (Pope Gregory XV)
44.5.M34 Alexander Malvasia, 1740-1819
44.5.M36 Francesco Mantica, 1534-1614
44.5.M37 Alfonso Manzanedo de Quiñones
44.5.M47 Clemens Merlinus, d. 1642
44.5.M48 Teodolfo Mertel, 1806-1899
44.5.M5 Giovanni Garzia Millini, 17th cent.
44.5.M58 Joannes Mohedano, d. 1549
44.5.M6 José de Molinés, 1645-1717
44.5.O52 Bartolomeo Olivazzi, 1704 - ca. 1790?
44.5.O55 Seraphin Olivier, ca. 1533-1609
44.5.O8 Pietro Vito Ottoboni, 1610-1691 (Pope Alexander VIII)
44.5.P35 Giambattista Pamphili, 1574-1655 (Pope Innocent X)
44.5.P46 Francisco Peña, 1540-1612
44.5.P48 Christoph Peutinger
44.5.P74 Hieronymus Priolus, d. 1674
44.5.R38 Thomas Ratto, 1683-1738
44.5.R46 Johannes Baptist Rembold, 1580 or 2-1627
44.5.R49 Carlo Rezzonico, 1693-1769 (Pope Clement XIII)
44.5.R65 Francisco Rojas Borja y Aries, 1604-1684
44.5.R68 Aurelio Roverella, 1784-1812
44.5.T3 Alessandro Tanara, 1668-1754
44.5.U2 Felix Ubago y Rio, d. 1679 (Faelix Ubago et Rio)
44.5.V469 Paolo Emilio Veralli, d. 1577
44.5.V47 Joseph Alphonse de Veri, 1742-1799
44.5.V58 Giovanni Battista Visconti, d. 1756
44.6.A-Z Collections, compilations, or selections on particular subjects, A-Z
44.6.C38 Cathedral and collegiate chapter cases
Subarrange by date
44.6.C45 Church property
Subarrange by date
Including res sacrae and sacred utensils

Decisions of ecclesiastical tribunals and courts, and related materials
By tribunal or court
Sacri Palatii auditorium. Rota Romana
Collections, compilations, or selections on particular subjects, A-Z -- Continued
44.6.C58 Civil law
Subarrange by date
44.6.C66 Commercial law
Subarrange by date
44.6.C75 Criminal law
Subarrange by date
44.6.O75 Oriental Church
Subarrange by date
Res sacrae see KBR44.6.C45
Utensils, Sacred see KBR44.6.C45
44.7.A-Z Commentaries (Annotationes. Additiones) to decisiones. By author or title, A-Z
Including commentaries on collected decisions of an individual auditor or on comprehensive collections
44.7.C36 Giovanni Battista Cantalmagi, 17th cent. Selectanea rerum notabilium ad usum decisionum Sacrae Rotae Romanae
44.7.P36 Antonio Maria Papazzoni, 1501-1588. Aurea annotationes in Nouas Rotae decisiones, 1551.
44.7.R83 Theodosius Rubeus, fl. 1640. Singularia ex Sacrae Romanae decisionibus selectae
45 Tribunal of the Camera Apostolica
46 Signatura Apostolica
46.3 Signatura justitiae
47 Dataria Apostolica
48 Poenitentiaria Apostolica
Diocesan courts or tribunals
Class here decisions of ecclesiastical courts, tribunals and other authorities in a particular diocese or other ecclesiastical jurisdiction
Collections
<49> General
The Americas
Including territories, colonies, or states
<49.2> General (Collective)
North America
<49.5.A-Z> Canadian, A-Z
<50.A-Z> United States, A-Z
Central and South America
<50.2.A-Z> Mexican, A-Z
<50.3.A-Z> Other, A-Z

KBR

Decisions of ecclesiastical tribunals and courts, and related materials
By tribunal or court
Diocesan courts or tribunals
Collections -- Continued
Europe
<50.5.A-Z> Austrian, A-Z
Including the Austro-Hungarian Empire
<50.7.A-Z> Dutch, A-Z
<50.9.A-Z> English, A-Z
<51.A-Z> French and Belgian, A-Z
<51.T68> Archdiocese of Toulouse. Decisiones Capellae Tholosanae (Jean Corsier, fl. ca. 1392-1416, comp.; Etienne Aufreri, d. 1511, commentator)
<51.2.A-Z> German, A-Z
<51.3.A-Z> Hungarian, A-Z
<51.4.A-Z> Italian, A-Z
<51.5.A-Z> Polish, A-Z
<51.6.A-Z> Spanish and Portugese, A-Z
<51.7.A-Z> Other European countries, A-Z
Asia
Including territories, colonies, etc.
<52.A-Z> Middle East. By region or country, A-Z
<53.A-Z> Southeast Asia. By region or country, A-Z
Africa
Including territories, colonies, etc.
<54.A-Z> North Africa. By region or country, A-Z
<54.5.A-Z> Other, A-Z
56 Encyclopedias. Law dictionaries. Terms and phrases. Vocabularia
Including early works to the mid-16th century
For law dictionaries and vocabularies published after the mid-16th century see KB90.A+
For indexes and vocabularies on the corpus iuris canonici see KBR1564+
64 Directories
Including early works
64.E56 Nicolau Eimeric, 1320-1399. Directorium inquisitorium, 1587
64.R39 Petrus Ravennas, ca. 1448-1508 or 9. Alphabetum aureum famatissimi juris utriusque doctoris ...
Methodology see KBR190+
Auxiliary sciences
74 General works
75 Diplomatics
76 Paleography
e. g. Coloman E. Viola. Exercitationes paleographiae iuris canonici

Auxiliary sciences -- Continued
Papyrology see KBR190+
Linguistics. Semantics see KBR2203
78 Archaeology. Symbolism in law
Class here general works on various manifestations of legal symbolism
For early works including schemata, stemmata, arbores, etc., see the author in KBR1576+ or KBR1704+ e.g. Giovanni d'Andrea, KBR1775
Inscriptions. Epigraphy see KBR190+
83 Heraldry. Seals. Insignia, etc.
100.A-Z Proverbia. Legal maxims. Brocardica juris. Regulae juris. By author or title, A-Z
Including legal maxims, brocardica juris, etc. on both canon and Roman law
Cf. KJA100 Roman law
100.D36 Damasus, fl. 1210-1215 (Table K4 modified)
100.D36A3-.D36A39 Individual works. By title
Including unannotated and annotated editions, translations, particular manuscript editions, and including textual criticism
e.g. Brocarda, 1566
105.A-Z Formularies. Clauses and forms. Formularia. By author or title, A-Z
Including individual or collected formularies for notaries or trial lawyers, court and procedural practice before a particular office or court, e. g. the Rota Romana, Camera apostolica, Cancellaria apostolica, etc.
Including comparative works about formularies (Roman and canon law)
105.F64 Formularium instrumentorum, necnon artis notariatus
105.F65 Formularium instrumentorum ad usum Curiae Romanae
105.F66 Formularium instrumentorum et variorum processuum
105.F67 Formularium procuratorum (et advocatorum Curiae Romanae). Formularium variarum commissionum, articulorum, exceptionum ... sentiarum & appellationum
Formularium procuratorum
105.F68 Formularium terminorum Rotae Romanae
105.F69 Formularium terminorum seu registrorum noviter impressum & emendatum
Formularium variarum commissionum, articulorum, exceptionum ... sentiarum & appellationum see KBR105.F67
105.G66 Luis Gomez, d. 1542. Commentarii in judiciales regulas Cancellariae
Cf. KBR1925.G66 Sources

Formularies. Clauses and forms. Formularia. By author or title, A-Z -- Continued
105.M36 Quintiliano Mandosi, d. 1593. Praxis seu theoria commissionum ... ad causas decidendas quibuscunque iudicibus
105.M37 Antonio Massa, 16th cent. Ad formulam cameralis obligationis liber
105.N54 Dietrich von Nieheim, ca. 1340-1418. Stilus palatii abbreviatus
105.S85 Stil general des notaires apostoliques
105.S86 Stilus palatii
105.T53 Sallustius Tiberius. De modis procedendi in causis ... coram auditore Camerae
Repertoria. Summaria. Margaritae
General works see KBR2153
Comprehensive repertories, indexes, etc. By author see KBR2153.5.A+
Repertories, indexes, etc. for a particular work
see the title/author in the appropriate period
Repertories, indexes, etc. on the works of a particular author collectively
see the author in the appropriate period
Other forms/genre of contemporary legal literature see KBR2138.62+
Canon law and canonists in literature
see classes PB - PZ
Collective biography of canonists or jurists
Including decretists and decretalists
For individual biography see the canonist or jurist in the appropriate period
For early Christian biography (to ca. 600) see BR1720.A+
122 General
123 By school
e. g. 123.B65 Bologna
By country
see the subdivision for the country, e. g. KBR1850
124 Collections of portraits
Trials
127 Collections
Including criminal and civil trials
Criminal trials
Including inquisition trials
128 Collections
128.5.A-Z Individual. By defendant, plaintiff, or best known (popular) name, A-Z
Joan of Arc. Jeanne d'Arc see KJV130.J625
128.5.G35 Galilei, Galileo, 1564-1642

Trials -- Continued
Civil trials
129 Collections
129.5.A-Z Individual. By defendant, A-Z
Legal research. Legal bibliography. Methods of bibliographic research
130 General works
132 Systems of citation. Legal abbreviation. Modus legendi abbreviaturas
Including early works
Legal education. Study and teaching
For works on study and teaching of both Roman and canon law comparatively, e. g. Johannes Jacobus Canis (d. 1490), De modo studendi in utroque iure see KB133
133 General works
134.A-Z By school, A-Z
e. g.
134.B64 Bologna
The legal profession see KBR3822+
Societies. Associations. Academies, etc.
136.A-Z International, A-Z
National
138.A-Z North American, A-Z
Including United States and Canada
139.A-Z Central and South American, A-Z
European
141.A-Z English, A-Z
142.A-Z French, A-Z
143.A-Z German, A-Z
144.A-Z Italian, A-Z
145.A-Z Spanish and Portuguese, A-Z
146.A-Z Other European, A-Z
147.A-Z Asian and Pacific, A-Z
148.A-Z African, A-Z
150 Conferences. Symposia
160 General works
Class here modern introductions to the history of canon law
For studies on sources see KBR190+
For works on system and doctrinal devlopment of Canon law see KBR2160+
Canon law compared with other legal systems
Religious legal systems
see subclass KB
Roman law
General works
see subclass KB

KBR

Canon law compared with other legal systems
Roman law -- Continued
Comparison by subject
see the subject or the author in the appropriate period in subclass KBR
Comparative genre
see the genre in subclass KBR, e. g. Differentiae KBR2151; Vocabularia KBR56; Formularies KBR105; etc.
Civil law
see subclass KB
Sources
Studies on sources. By author
Including history of sources and methodology, e. g. papyrology, epigraphy, etc.
Class here collected or individual works of authors regardless of nationality or language
190 A - Hove
Subarrange each author by Table K4
190.B35 Ballerini, Pietro (1698-1769) (Table K4 modified)
190.B35A3-.B35A39 Individual works. By title
Including unannotated and annotated editions, translations, particular manuscript editions, and including textual criticism
e.g. De antiquis ... collectionibius et collectoribus canonum ad Gratianum usque, tractatus in quatuor partes distributus
190.C57 Cimetier, Francisque, 1880-1946 (Table K4 modified)
190.C57A3-.C57A39 Individual works. By title
Including unannotated and annotated editions, translations, particular manuscript editions, and including textual criticism
e.g. Les sources du droit ecclésiastique
190.F68 Fournier, Paul (1853-1935) and G. Le Bras (Table K4 modified)
190.F68A3-.F68A39 Individual works. By title
Including unannotated and annotated editions, translations, particular manuscript editions, and including textual criticism
e.g. Histoire des collections canoniques en Occident depuis les Fausses Décrétales jusquáu Décret de Gratien
190.F75 Friedberg, Emil (1837-1910) (Table K4 modified)

Sources
Studies on sources. By author
A - Hove
Friedberg, Emil (1837-1910) -- Continued

190.F75A3-.F75A39 Individual works. By title
Including unannotated and annotated editions, translations, particular manuscript editions, and including textual criticism
e.g. Die Canones-Sammlungen Zwischen Gratian und Bernhard von Pavia

190.3 Hove, A. van (Alphonse) (1872-1947) (Table K3 modified)

190.3.A3A-.A3Z Individual works. By title, A-Z
Including unannotated and annotated editions, translations, particular manuscript editions, and including textual criticism
e.g. Prolegomena ad codicem iuris canonici (Commentarium Lovaniense in codicem iuris canonici, 1-2)

190.4 Hove - Kuttner
Subarrange each author by Table K4

190.5 Kuttner, Stephan (1907-1996) (Table K3 modified)

190.5.A3A-.A3Z Individual works. By title, A-Z
Including unannotated and annotated editions, translations, particular manuscript editions, and including textual criticism
e.g. Medieval Councils, Decretals, and Collections of Canon Law: selected essays

190.6 Kuttner - Stickler
Subarrange each author by Table K4

190.6.L36 Landau, Peter, 1935- (Table K4)

190.6.M33 Maassen, Friedrich B.C. (1823-1900) (Table K4 modified)

190.6.M33A3-.M33A39 Individual works. By title
Including unannotated and annotated editions, translations, particular manuscript editions, and including textual criticism
e.g. Geschichte der Quellen und Literatur des Canonischen Rechts im Abendlande

190.6.S35 Schulte, Johann Friedrich von (1827-1914) (Table K4 modified)

190.6.S35A3-.S35A39 Individual works. By title
Including unannotated and annotated editions, translations, particular manuscript editions, and including textual criticism
e.g. Die Geschichte der Quellen und Literatur des canonischen Rechts von Gratian bis auf die Gegenwart

191 Stickler, Alphonsus M. (Table K3 modified)

Sources
Studies on sources. By author
Stickler, Alphonsus M. -- Continued
191.A3A-.A3Z Individual works. By title, A-Z
Including unannotated and annotated editions, translations, particular manuscript editions, and including textual criticism
e.g. Historia iuris Canonici Latini: institutiones Academiae, 1. Historia Fontium
191.3 Stickler - Z
Subarrange each author by Table K4
191.3.T28 Adolphe Tardif (1824-1890) (Table K4)
191.3.T54 Augustin Theiner (1804-1874) (Table K4 modified)
191.3.T54A3-.T54A39 Individual works. By title
Including unannotated and annotated editions, translations, particular manuscript editions, and including textual criticism
e.g. Disquisitiones criticae in praecipuas canonum et decretalium collectiones seu sylloges Gallandianae dissertationum de vetustis canonum collectionibus continuatio
191.3.V66 Vööbus, Arthus (Table K4 modified)
191.3.V66A3-.V66A39 Individual works. By title
Including unannotated and annotated editions, translations, particular manuscript editions, and including textual criticism
e.g. Syrische Kanonessammlungen; ein Beitrag zur Quellenkunde
191.3.W37 Wasserschleben, Hermann (1812-1893) (Table K4 modified)
191.3.W37A3-.W37A39 Individual works. By title
Including unannotated and annotated editions, translations, particular manuscript editions, and including textual criticism
e.g. Beiträge zur Geschichte der vorgratianischen Kirchenrechtsquellen
192 Classification of sources
Collections. Compilations. Selections
195 General
Class here comprehensive collections stemming from all historic periods of canon law
Including translations
For collections relating to a particular historic period or type of source, see the period or type of source, e. g. decretals, consilia, etc.

Sources
Collections. Compilations. Selections -- Continued
195.5 Indexes. Chronologies. Concordances
e. g. John Fulton (1834-1907). Index canonum: Containing the canons called apostolical, the canons of the ... general councils, and the canons of the provincial councils of Ancyra, Neo-Caesarea, Gangra ... with a complete digest of the whole code of canon law in the undivided primitive church, 1872
Pseudo-apostolic collections of canons, to ca. 400 A.D.
Class here collections of canonical legislation and church orders for the early church (ca. 30-600)
For general works see KBR190+
195.7 General collections. Selections
e.g. Reliquiae iuris ecclesiastici antiquissimae (Paul de Lagarde, 1827-1891, ed.)
196 Didache (Didachē tou Kyriou dia tōn Dōdeka Apostolōn tois Ethnesin. Teaching of the Twelve Apostles. Church order), between 1st and 3rd cent.? (Table K20b)
Cf. BS2940.T4+ New Testament apocryphal books
196.2 Traditio apostolica (Apostolikē paradosis) (Hippolytus, Antipope, ca. 170-235 or 6), 215? (Table K20b)
196.22 Canones Hippolyti (Canons of Hippolyt. Hippolytus, Antipope, ca. 170-235 or 6) (Table K20b)
196.3 Didascalia apostolorum (Catholic Teaching of the Twelve Apostles and Holy Disciples of Our Saviour). Syriac. 3rd cent. (Table K20b)
Canones apostolorum (Canones ecclesiastici sanctorum apostolorum. Apostolic canons) see KBR196.6
196.5 Constitutiones apostolorum (Diatagai tōn hagiōn apostolōn. Apostolic constitutions). Late 4th cent.? (Table K20b modified)
Also called Octateuchus Sancti Clementis
196.5.A22 Individual parts or sections. Selections. By title
Canones apostolorum see KBR196.6
Octoginta quinque regulae, seu canones apostolorum (Eighty-five ecclesiastical canons of the apostles) see KBR196.6
Canones Hippolyti see KBR196.22
Epitome libri VIII constitutionum apostolorum (Constitutiones per Hippolytum) see KBR196.7
196.6 Octoginta quinque regulae, seu canones apostolorum (Eighty-five ecclesiastical canons of the Apostles), early 4th cent.? (Table K20b)

KBR

Sources
Collections. Compilations. Selections
Pseudo-apostolic collections of canons, to ca. 400 A.D. -- Continued
196.7 Epitome libri VIII constitutionum apostolorum (Constitutiones per Hippolytum), 4th or 5th cent.? (Table K20b)
196.78 Horos kanonikos tōn hagiōn apostolōn (Canones poenitentiales apostolorum), 4th cent. (Table K20b)
196.9 Canones 9 synodi Antiochenae apostolorum (ascribed to the Synod of Antioch, 341)
Octateuchus Sancti Clementis
see KBR196.5
Didascalia (Arabic)
see KBR196.3
Didascalia (Ethiopian)
see KBR196.3
197.33 Testamentum Domini nostri Jesus Christi (Testament of Our Lord), 5th cent.? (Table K20b)
Cf. BS2960.T5+ New Testament apocryphal books
197.4 Liber canonum diversorum sanctorum patrum siue collectio in CLXXXIII titulos digesta
Jus ecclesiae Graecae seu Byzantinae. Greek-Byzantine collections, to ca. 1054 (Great Schism)
General works see KBR190+
197.45 Syntagmata canonum (Synodon conciliorum oecumenicorum) Chronological collection
Including decrees and canons of the early councils, beginning with the Council of Ancyra (314) to the Council of Chalcedon (451), and (since 6th cent.) the 85 Canones Apostolorum
197.5 Codex vetus Ecclesiae Universae, a Iustiniano Imperatore confirmatus ... ex Graecis codicibus editis & mss. collegit & emendavit. Latinum fecit (Christofle Iustel, 1580-1649, ed.)
197.6 Canones sanctorum Apostolorum, conciliorum generalium particularium, sanctorum patrum Dijonysij Alexandrini ... & alterum veterum theologorum: Photii Constantinopolitani Patriarchae praefixus est Nomocanon ..., de Graecis conversa ... (Gentian Hervet, 1499-1584, trans.) (Table K20b)
197.7 Codex Canonum ecclesiae primitivae (William Beveridge, 1637-1708, comp.) (Table K20b)
Systematic collections
197.8 Collectio sexaginta titulorum, ca. 535

Sources
Collections. Compilations. Selections
Jus ecclesiae Graecae seu Byzantinae. Greek-Byzantine collections, to ca. 1054 (Eastern Schism)
Systematic collections
197.9 Synagoge kanonon (Collectio quinquaginta titulorum) (John, Climacus, Saint. Joannes Scholasticus, 6th cent)
198 Synopsis [canonum], 6th cent. (Stephanus of Ephesus)
198.2 Epitome canonum (Simeon)
198.3 Collectio XXV capitulorum, 565-578
198.4 Collectio LXXXVII capitulorum, 565-578
198.6 Collectio tripartita (Collectio constitutionum ecclesiasticarum) (Table K20b)
Nomocanon collections
199 Nomocanon L titulorum (John, Climacus, Saint. Joannes Scholasticus, 6th cent.)
199.2 Nomocanon quatuordecim titulorum, ca. 630 (ascribed falsly to Photius I., Patriarch of Constantinople, ca. 820-ca. 891)
199.3 Second revision, 883
199.33 Third revision, 1198 (Theodore Balsamon, Patriarch of Antioch, 12th cent.)
Secular (Imperial Byzantine) law relating to the church
199.34 General (Comparative)
Theodorus Hermopolitanus, Scholasticus, fl. ca. 600 see KJA1462
Ecloge (Ecloge ton nomon; Leo III, 717-ca. 741), ca. 726 see KJA1362.2+
Prochiron (Procheiros nomos; Basileus I, Macedo, 867-886), ca. 870-879 see KJA1392.2+
Epanagoge tou nomou (Basileus I, Macedo, 876-886) see KJA1405
199.7.A-Z Canonists or jurists, A-Z
199.7.B47 Theodorus Bestes, 11th cent. (Table K4)
199.7.P76 Theodorus Prodromus, late 8th cent. (Table K4)
199.7.S96 Symeon, Metaphrastes (Symeon, Logothetes, fl. 10th cent.) (Table K4)
Canonical collections of councils and synods
Apostolic councils. Councils of the ancient church. 1st to 3rd centuries
199.8 General works
199.82 Council of Jerusalem, 45 (48?) (Table KB9)
199.83 Council of Jerusalem, 56 (55?) (Table KB9)
199.84 Council of Rome, 155 (Table KB9)
199.86 Council of Rome, 193 (Table KB9)
199.87 Council of Ephesus, 193 (Table KB9)

Sources
Collections. Compilations. Selections
Canonical collections of councils and synods
Apostolic councils. Councils of the ancient church. 1st to 3rd centuries -- Continued
199.9 Council of Carthage, 255 (Table KB9)
Councils (Concilia) and synods from the 4th century to 1054 (Great Schism)
Class here works on Eastern councils and Western councils (Frankish Church), including non-accepted councils
200.A-Z General (Collective). By author, editor, or title, A-Z
200.B35 Louis Bail, 1610-1669 (Table K4)
200.B36 Étienne Baluze, 1630-1718 (Table K4)
200.B48 William Beveridge, 1637-1708 (Table K4)
200.B56 Severin Binius, 1573-1641 (Table K4)
200.C37 Bartolomé Carranza, 1503-1576 (Table K4)
200.C66 Conciliorum omnium generalium et principalium collectio regia (1644)
200.C73 Pierre Crabbe, 1470-1553 (Table K4)
200.H37 Jean Hardouin (Table K4)
200.M36 Giovan Domenico Mansi, 1692-1769 (Table K4)
200.T36 Norman P. Tanner (Table K4)
205 General works
e. g. Peter L-Huillier, 1926- . The church of the ancient councils, 1995
Ecumenical or general councils
(209) Council of Elvira
see KBR244.3
210 1st Council of Nicea (1st Ecumenical), 325 (Table KB9)
(213) Council of Saragossa, 380
see KBR249 380
(214) Council of Aquileia, 381
see KBR249 381
215 1st Council of Constantinople (2nd Ecumenical), 381 (Table KB9)
220 Council of Ephesus (3rd Ecumenical), 431? or 449 (Table KB9)
225 Council of Chalcedon (4th Ecumenical), 451 (Table KB9)
230 2nd Council of Constantinople (5th Ecumenical), 553 (Table KB9)
235 3rd Council of Constantinople (6th Ecumenical), 680 (Table KB9)

Sources
Collections. Compilations. Selections
Canonical collections of councils and synods
Councils (Concilia) and synods from the 4th century to 1054 (Great Schism)
Ecumenical or general councils -- Continued
237 Council of Constantinople (Concilium Trullanum. Quinisext Synod), 692 (Table KB9)
Sequel council to the 5th and 6th Ecumenical Councils of Constantinople
240 2nd Council of Nicea (7th Ecumenical), 787 (Table KB9)
(242) Council of Frankfurt, 794
see KBR248
Provincial and national councils and synods
General (Collective) see KBR200.A+
General works see KBR205
Individual
244 Council of Carthage, 299
244.3 Council of Elvira, between 300? and 309?
244.5 Council of Carthage, 311
245 Council of Arles, 314
245.3 Council of Ancyra (Ankara), 314
245.5 Council of Neocaesarea (Niksar), 315
246 Council of Antioch (Antakya), 341
246.3 Council of Serdica (Sofia), 343 or 347?
246.5 Council of Gangra (Cankiri), 340? or 343
247 Council of Constantinople, 394
247.2 Council of Carthage, 398
247.5 Council of Carthage, 419
248 Council of Frankfurt, 794
Other
249 335 Council of Tyre, 335
249 380 Council of Sargossa, 380
249 381 Council of Aquileia, 381
249 401 Council of Turin, 401
249 553 Council of Aquileia, 553
249 553a Council of Carthage, 553
249 633 4th Council of Toledo, 633
(260.29) Council of Constantinople (Concilium Trullanum. Quinisext Synod), 692
see KBR237
Councils of the late 9th and 10th centuries
261 General (Collective)
Individual

KBR

Sources
Collections. Compilations. Selections
Canonical collections of councils and synods
Councils (Concilia) and synods from the 4th century to 1054 (Great Schism)
Councils of the late 9th and 10th centuries
Individual -- Continued
262 4th Council of Constantinople (Ignatian Council), 869 (Table KB9)
Contested by Eastern bishops
263 Council of Union (Photian Council), 879 (Table KB9)
Contested by Western bishops
264 [date] Other councils and synods. By date of opening
Provincial and national councils and synods
265 Council of Aachen, 809
266 Council of Worms, 868
General and ecumenical councils. 11th-21st centuries
Including post-schism and contested councils
820 General works
For general histories on the councils, synods, etc. see BX820+
General (Collective) see KBR200.A+
830 Individual councils. By date of opening
Cf. BX830 0809+ Catholic Church
830 1064 Council of Mantua, 1064 (Table KB9)
830 1095 Council of Clermont, 1095 (Table KB9)
830 1123 Lateran Council (1st), 1123 (Table KB9)
830 1139 Lateran Council (2nd), 1139 (Table KB9)
830 1179 Lateran Council (3rd), 1179 (Table KB9)
830 1215 Lateran Council (4th), 1215 (Table KB9)
830 1245 Council of Lyons (1st), 1245 (Table KB9)
830 1274 Council of Lyons (2nd), 1274 (Table KB9)
830 1311 Council of Vienne, 1311 (Table KB9)
830 1409 Council of Pisa (1st), 1409 (Table KB9)
830 1414 Council of Constance, 1414 (Table KB9)
830 1423 Council of Pavia-Siena, 1423 (Table KB9)
Council of Basel, 1431, and Ferrara, 1438 see KBR830 1439
830 1439 Council of Ferrara-Florence (Florentinum), 1439 (Table KB9)
830 1511 Council of Pisa (2nd), 1511 (Table KB9)
830 1512 Lateran Council (5th), 1512 (Table KB9)
830 1545 Council of Trent, 1545 (Table KB9)
Council of Brest-Litovsk see KBR830 1596
830 1596 Union of Brest, 1596 (Table KB9)
830 1869 Vatican Council (1st), 1869 (Table KB()

Sources
Collections. Compilations. Selections
Canonical collections of councils and synods
General and ecumenical councils. 11th-21st centuries
Individual councils. By date of opening -- Continued
830 1962 Vatican Council (2nd), 1962 (Table KB9)
Episcopal synods. Synodus episcoporum
830.5 General works
For general histories on the synods see BX831
831 Individual episcopal synods. By date of opening
Plenary councils. National councils
North America
United States
Cf. BX833+ Catholic plenary councils in the United States
833 General (Collective)
835 Individual. By date
835 1852 Plenary Council (1st), Baltimore, 1852
835 1866 Plenary Council (2nd), Baltimore, 1866
835 1884 Plenary Council (3d), Baltimore, 1884
Canada
Cf. BX837.C2 Catholic plenary councils in Canada
836 General (Collective)
837 Individual. By date
837 1909 Plenary Council (1st), Quebec, 1909
Central and South America
Cf. BX831.5+ Catholic plenary councils in Latin America
838 General (Collective)
For general histories on the plenary/national councils see BX832
839.A-Z Individual. By country, A-Z
Subarrange further by date of opening of the council
Europe
848 General (Collective)
849.A-Z Individual. By country, A-Z
Subarrange further by date of opening of the council
Asia
858 General (Collective)
Middle East. Southwest Asia
859 General (Collective)
860.A-Z Individual. By country, A-Z
Subarrange further by date of opening of the council
South Asia. Southeast Asia. East Asia
868 General (Collective)

Sources
Collections. Compilations. Selections
Canonical collections of councils and synods
Plenary councils. National councils
Asia
South Asia. Southeast Asia. East Asia -- Continued
869.A-Z Individual. By country, A-Z
Subarrange further by date of opening of the council
Africa
880 General (Collective)
882.A-Z Individual. By country, A-Z
Subarrange further by date of opening of the council
Pacific Area
903 General (Collective)
905 Australia. By date
910 New Zealand. By date
915.A-Z Other countries, A-Z
Subarrange further by date of opening of the council
Episcopal conferences. Conferencia episcoporum
Cf. BX837.5 Catholic episcopal conferences
935 General (Collective)
938 Individual. By ecclesiastical province
Subarrange further by date of opening of the conference
Provincial councils and diocesan synods
Including diocesan pastoral councils
Cf. BX838 Catholic diocesan synods
950 General (Collective)
The Americas
North American countries (and territories/colonies)
United States
953 General (Collective)
954 By province or diocese, and date of opening of synod or council
Canada
963 General (Collective)
964 By province or diocese, and date of opening of synod or council
Mexico, Central and South American countries
Subarrange by province or diocese, and date of opening of synod or council
Cf. BX831.5+ Catholic councils
973 General (Collective)
975 Mexico
Central American countries
979 Costa Rica
980 Guatemala
981 Honduras

Sources
Collections. Compilations. Selections
Canonical collections of councils and synods
Provincial councils and diocesan synods
The Americas
North American countries (and territories/colonies)
Mexico, Central and South American countries
Central American countries -- Continued
982 Nicaragua
983 Panama
984 El Salvador
985.A-Z Other, A-Z
South American countries
Subarrange by province or diocese, and date of opening of synod or council
987 General (Collective)
989 Argentina
990 Bolivia
991 Brazil
992 Chile
992.5 Colombia
993 Ecuador
993.5 Guiana
994.5 Paraguay
995 Uruguay
995.5 Venezuela
996.A-Z Other, A-Z
European countries
Subarrange each country by ecclesiastical jurisdiction, i.e., province or diocese, and date of opening of synod or council
998 General (Collective)
999 Austria. Austro-Hungarian Monarchy
Baltic countries
1001 General (Collective)
1001.2 Estonia
1001.5 Latvia
1001.6 Lithuania
1003 Belgium
1003.L54 Catholic Church. Diocese of Liege
1003.L542 Council of Aachen, 809
1003.M43 Catholic Church. Archidiocese of Mechelen
1003.3 Czechoslovakia
1003.5 Finland
1004 France
1004.T68 Catholic Church. Diocese of Toulouse. Statuta synodalia civitatis et diocesis Tholosanae

Sources
Collections. Compilations. Selections
Canonical collections of councils and synods
Provincial councils and diocesan synods
European countries -- Continued
1005 Germany
Great Britain
1005.5 General (Collective)
England. England and Wales (to ca. 1559)
For later periods of the Church of England see KD8624+
1006 General (Collective)
Catholic Church. Province of Canterbury
1006.2 General (Collective)
Class here constitutions of several provincial councils, with or without provincial statutes, e.g. Constitutiones provinciales ecclesiae Anglicanae (Provinciale, seu constitutiones Anglie)
1006.22.A-Z Individual, A-Z
1006.22.L43 Legatine Council, London, 1237 (Table KB9)
1006.22.L44 Legatine Council, London, 1268 (Table KB9)
1006.3 Scotland (to ca. 1560) (Table KB9)
For later periods of the Church of Scotland see KDC958+
1006.5 Greece
1007 Holland. The Netherlands
1008 Hungary
Cf. KBR999 Austro-Hungarian Monarchy
1009 Ireland. Éire
1010 Italy
1010.F56 Catholic Church. Province of Florence
1010.F562 Concilium 1517: Statuta Concilii Florentini
1010.F563 Concilium Provinciale Florentinum 1573: cum citationibus Decretorum & canonum
1010.M55 Catholic Church. Province of Milan
1010.V46 Catholic Church. Patriarchate of Venice
1010.V462 Synod of 1592
1010.V463 Synod of 1594 (1653, 1667, 1741, etc.)
1011 Poland
1012 Portugal
1012.5 Russia
Scandinavian countries
1013 General (Collective)
1013.2 Denmark
1013.3 Iceland
1013.5 Norway

Sources
Collections. Compilations. Selections
Canonical collections of councils and synods
Provincial councils and diocesan synods
European countries
Scandinavian countries -- Continued
1013.7 Sweden
1014 Spain
1014.T37 Catholic Church. Archdiocese of Tarragona
1014.T37 1704 Synod of 1704
1014.V35 Catholic Church. Diocese of Valencia
Southeast European countries. The Balkans
1015 General (Collective)
1015.2 Albania
1016 Bosnia and Hercegovina
1016.2 Bulgaria
1016.4 Croatia
1016.6 Cyprus
1017 Macedonia
1017.5 Montenegro
1017.6 Romania
1017.7 Serbia
1018 Turkey
1018.2 Yugoslavia
For Serbia see KBR1017.7
1018.5 Switzerland
1019.A-Z Other European countries, A-Z
Subarrange further by province or diocese, and date of opening of synod or council
Asian countries
1020 General (Collective)
Middle East. Southwest Asia
1022 General (Collective)
1023.A-Z By country, A-Z
Subarrange further by province or diocese, and date of opening of synod or council
South Asia. Southeast Asia. East Asia
1043 General (Collective)
1044 China
1045 India
1046 Indochina
1047 Indonesia
1048 Japan
1049 Malaysia
1050 Nepal
1051 Thailand
1052 Vietnam

Sources
Collections. Compilations. Selections
Canonical collections of councils and synods
Provincial councils and diocesan synods
Asian countries
South Asia. Southeast Asia. East Asia -- Continued
1053.A-Z Other South and East Asian countries, A-Z
Subarrange further by province or diocese, and date of opening of synod or council
African countries
1064 General (Collective)
1066 Algeria
1069 Egypt
1071 Ethiopia
1075 South Africa
1077 Tunisia
1080.A-Z Other African countries, A-Z
Subarrange further by province or diocese, and date of opening of synod or council
Pacific Area countries
1082 General (Collective)
1083 Australia
1084 New Zealand
1086.A-Z Other Pacific Area countries, A-Z
Subarrange further by province or diocese, and date of opening of synod or council
Latin (western) versions of Oriental canonical collections prior to pseudo-Isidoriana
Including collections of both canons of the early Oriental councils or synods, decrees and decretals
General works see KBR190+
Africa
1100 Summary of canons, Council of Hippo, 393
1110 Codex Canonum Ecclesiae Africanae, Christophorus Justellus ex mss. codicibus edidit. (Christofle Justel, 1580-1649, ed.)
1112 Corpus canonum Africanum, ca. 420
1120 Ferrandus, Fulgentius, fl. 523-ca. 546. Breviatio canonum, ca. 535
1130 Cresconius, African Bishop, 7th cent. Concordia canonum
1140 Athanasius, Saint, Patriarch of Alexandria, d. 373. Canons (Wilhelm Riedel, ed. and tr.), 1904
1145 Die Kirchenrechtsquellen des Patriarchats Alexandria (Wilhelm Riedel, ed. and tr., 1900)
Italy
1150 Collectio Prisca vel Itala, 5th cent.

Sources
Collections. Compilations. Selections
Latin (western) versions of Oriental canonical collections prior to pseudo-Isidoriana
Italy -- Continued
Collectio Isidoriana vel Hispana see KBR1255
1157 Collectio Vaticana, begin 6th cent.
Dionysius Exiguus, d. ca. 540
1159 General
1160 Collectio canonum (Collectio prima)
1162 Collectio XXXVIII decretalium (Collectio secunda)
Including Papal decretals from Siricius, 384-399, to Anastasius II, 496-498
1164 Collectio tertia
1166 Collectio Dionysiana (Collectio quarta), ca. 500
1170 Corpus codicis canonum
1175 (Collectio) Dionysio-Hadriana (Dionysiana. Hadriana); (Pope Adrian I, 772-795), before 774
1180 Theodosius, Diaconus. Collectio Theodosii diaconi, before 7th cent.
1182 Collectio Avellana, ca. 555
Gaul
Constitutiones Sirmondianae see KBR1268
1200 Collectio Vetus Gallica, between 585 and 626
1205 Quesnel, Paschasius. Collectio Quesnelliana (Codex canonum vetus Ecclesiae Romanae, end 5th to 6th cent.), 1675
1207 Collectio Remensis, 2nd half 6th cent.
1208 Collectio Hispana Gallica, end 7th cent.
1210 Statuta Ecclesiae antiqua (Statuta Ecclesiae unica. Statuta antiqua Orientis; ascribed to the Synod IV of Carthage, 398), late 5th or early 6th cent.
1215 Second recension, 7th cent.
Including canons of Gallic councils
1220 D'Archery, d. 1685. Collectio Dacheriana, ca. 800
1224 Collectio Hispana Gallica Augustodunensis, first half 9th cent.
1225 Quadripartitus (Antiqua canonum collectio ..., ed. E. L. Richter, 1844)
England and Ireland
1230 Theodore, Bp. of Canterbury. Collectio canonum Cantabrigiensis, 673
1235 Egbert, Saint, d. 766 (Egbert, Abp. of York). Collection, ca. 750
1240 Collectio Hibernensis, first half 8th cent.
1245 Liber ex lege Moysis, ca. 750
1247 Collectio Lanfranci, after 1059

Sources
Collections. Compilations. Selections
Latin (western) versions of Oriental canonical collections prior to pseudo-Isidoriana -- Continued
Spain
1250 Martin, of Braga, Saint, ca. 515-579 or 80. Collectio canonum (Collectio canonum Martini Bracarensis. Excerpta Martini. Capitula Martini Papae), 572
1255 Collectio Isidoriana seu Hispana (Corpus canonum. Codex canonum of Synod IV of Toledo; since 9th cent. ascribed to Isidore, of Seville, Saint, d 636), 7th ? cent.
1257 Epitome Hispana, between 598 and 619
Compilations of secular law pertaining to religious law
General works see KBR190+
Mosaicarum et Romanarum legum collatio
see subclass KB
Codex Theodosianus (Breviarium Alarici), 506 see KJA592.2+
1268 Constitutiones Sirmondianae (Jacques Sirmond, 1559-1651, ed.), between 425 and 438
1270 Lex Romana canonice compta (Capitula legis Romanae ad canones pertinentia), 9th cent.
Ansegisus, Saint, Abbot of Fontanelle, ca. 770-833. Capitularia see KJ322
Capitula episcoporum
Class here adaptations of provincial synodal canons to diocesan conditions
General works see KBR190+
1280 Theodolphus of Orleans, d. 821
1285 Haito of Basel, d. 836
1290 Herard of Tours, d. 870
Capitula Heraldi Archiepiscopi Turonensis, 858
Hincmar, Archbishop of Reims, ca. 806-882
1292 Collectio de ecclesiis et capellis
Pseudo-Isidoriana. 9th century
Cf. BX875.A2+ Forgeries of Catholic documents
1295 General works
e. g. Friedrich B.C. Maassen (1823-1900), Pseudoisidor-Studien II, 1885
1298 Isidorii Mercatoris falsarum decretalium collectio. Decretales pseudo-Isidorianae (Isidore, of Seville, Saint, d. 636), ca. 850
Benedictus, Levita, fl. 850
1305 Collectio capitularium, ca. 847-852
1308 Capitula Angilramni, ca. 850

Sources
Collections. Compilations. Selections -- Continued
Post Pseudo-Isidorian collections of canons and decretals, to 1140
1315 General works
Italy
Anselmo, Saint, Bishop of Lucca, 1036-1086
1320 Collectio canonum (Collectio Anselmi Lucani), after 1081
Atto, Bp. of Vercelli, 10th cent.
1325 Collectio canonum, mid 10th Cent.
Bonizo, Bp. of Sutri, ca. 1045-ca. 1096
1328 Liber de vita christiana, between 1089 and 1095
1330 Decretum
Deusdedit, Cardinal, d. ca. 1099
1332 Collectio canonum, 1083-1087
Gregory, Cardinal of San Crisogono, d. 1113
1335 Polycapurs, begin 12th cent.
1336 Collectio LXXIV titulorum
Germany
1337.92 Burchard, Bishop of Worms, ca. 965-1025
Decretum, between 1008 and 1012
1339 (Pseudo-) Remedius of Chur
Collectio canonum, after 880-895
Regino, Abbot of Prum, 840-915
1340 Libri duo de synodalibus causis et disciplinis ecclesiasticis, ca. 906 (Libri duo de ecclesiasticis disciplinis et religione christiana), ca. 906
Gaul
Abbo, of Fleury, Saint, ca. 945-1004
1342 Collectio canonum, between 988 and 996
Ivo, Saint, Bishop of Chartres, ca. 1040-1116
1345 Collectio trium partium (collectio tripartita), end 11th cent.
1347 Panormia, ca. 1094-1095
1349 Decretum (Decretum Ivonis Episcopi Carnutensis), after 1093
Alger, of Liège, ca. 1060-ca. 1132
1350 De misericordia et iustitia, between 1095 and 1121
Spain
1355 Collectio Tarreconensis, after 1085
1358 Collectio Caesaraugustana, 1110-1125

Sources
Collections. Compilations. Selections -- Continued
1362.2-1367 Decretum Gratiani. Concordia discordantium canonum (Gratian, 12th cent.), 1140 (Table K20a)
Add number from table to KBR1360
Including both unannotated editions and annotated editions (i.e. the marginal Glossa Ordinaria Decreti (Ordinary Gloss) of Johannes Teutonicus, d. 1245? and Bartolomeo da Brescia, d. 1258) and including "emendatio Decreti" editions (after 1582). For independently published related works such as the Gloss, additiones, summae, apparatus, etc. of a particular decretist or decretalist, see the canonist in the appropriate period
Collections. Compilations. Selections between 1140 and 1234 (Decretum Gratiani to Decretales Gregorii IX)
General
1410 Decretales ineditae saeculi XII (Walther Holtzman, 1891-1963; Stanley Chodorow and Charels Duggan, eds.)
1411 Summa constitutionum summorum pontificum et rerum in Ecclesia Romana gestarum a Gregorio IX vsque ad Sixtum V. (Pierre Matthieu, 1563-1621, ed.)
1412 Breviarium super totum Corpus iuris canonici (Paolo Attavanti, 1445?-1499, comp.)
Flores sive Decretorum compilationes
see KBR1362.22
1415 Collectio Farfensis (Gregorio, di Catino, fl. 1100, comp.), 12th cent.
1420 Appendix Concilii Lateranensis III (ascribed to Gilbertus, Anglicus), after 1181
1424 Collectio canonum Casinensis duodecimi seculi
1425 Collectio Compendiensis (Compiègne), ca. 1181-1185
1428 Collectio Lipsiensis (Leipzig), after 1181-1185
1430 Collectio Casselana (or Hesse-Casselana), ca. 1181-1185
1432 Collectio Parisiensis I, 1175-1179
1434 Collectio Parisiensis II (ascribed to Bernard, of Pavia), before 1179
1436 Collectio Brugensis, ca. 1187-1191
1438 Collectio Halensis, end 12th cent.
1440 Collectio Lucensis, end 12th cent.
1442 Compilations of Gilbertus, Anglicus, ca. 1205
1444 Compilatio of Alanus Anglicus, ca. 1208
1446 Collection of Bernard, Compostella, ca. 1208
1448 Rainerius, of Pomposa, 1201-1202

Sources
Collections. Compilations. Selections
Collections. Compilations. Selections between 1140 and 1234 (Decretum Gratiani to Decretales Gregorii IX) -- Continued
Quinque compilationes antiquae. The five compilations of decretales, 1188-1226
Including both unannotated editions and annotated editions (i.e. with glosses, summae, etc. by decretists or decretalists). For independently published related works such as additiones, glosses, summae, apparatus, etc. of a particular decretist or decretalist, see the canonist in the appropriate period

1450 Compilatio Prima (Breviarium extravagantium decretalium), ca. 1192
For Bernard, of Pavia, Summa (1191-1198), see KBR1700
For glossa ordinaria of Tancred see KBR1696.A3A+

1460 Compilatio Secunda (John of Wales, 13th cent.), 1210-1212
For glossa ordinaria of Tancred see KBR1696.A3A+

1470 Compilatio Tertia (Petrus, of Benevent; Collivaccinus), ca. 1209-1210
For glossa ordinaria of Tancred see KBR1696.A3A+

1480 Compilatio Quarta (Joannes, Teutonicus, d. 1245?), ca. 1216-1217
Cf. KBR1697 Individual canonists

1490 Compilatio Quinta (Johannes, Teutonicus, d. 1245?), 1226
For Jacobus de Albenga, d. 1274, Apparatus, see KBR1699

1502.2-1507 Liber Extra. Decretales Gregorii IX (Gregory IX, Pope, 1227-1241), 1234 (Table K20a)
Add number from table to KBR1500
Including both unannotated editions and annotated editions (i.e. with glosses, summae, etc. by decretists or decretalists). For independently published related works such as additiones, glosses, summae, apparatus, etc. of a particular decretist or decretalist, see the canonist in the appropriate period

1510 Novellae constitutiones, 1234-1298
1510.2 Collection of Innocent IV, Pope, 1243-1254
1510.3 Collection of Gregory X, Pope, 1271-1276
1512.4 Collection of Nicolaus III, Pope, 1277-1280

KBR

Sources

Collections. Compilations. Selections -- Continued

1532.2-1537 Liber Sextus decretalium. Sext (Boniface VIII, Pope, 1294-1303), 1298 (Table K20a)

Add number from table to KBR1530

Including both unannotated editions and annotated editions (i.e. with glosses, summae, etc. by decretists or decretalists). For independently published related works such as additiones, glosses, summae, apparatus, etc. of a particular decretist or decretalist, see the canonist in the appropriate period

1542.2-1547 Clementinae Constitutiones (Clement V, Pope, 1305-1315), 1317 (Table K20a)

Add table number to KBR1540

Including both unannotated editions and annotated editions (i.e. with glosses, summae, etc, by decretists or decretalists). For independently published related works such as additiones, glosses, summae, apparatus, etc. of a particular decretist or decretalist, see the canonist in the appropriate period

1552.2-1557 Extravagantes Joannis XXII (John XXII, Pope, 1316-1334), end 15th cent. (Table K20a)

Add number from table to KBR1550

Including both unnanotated editions and annotated editions (i.e. with glosses, summae, etc. by decretists or decretalists). For independently published related works such as additiones, glosses, summae, apparatus, etc. of a particular decretist or decretalist, see the canonist in the appropriate period

1562.2-1567 Extravagantes communes, end 15th cent. (Table K20a)

Add number from table to KBR1560

Including both unannotated editions and annotated editions (i.e. with glosses, summae, etc. by decretists or decretalists). For independently published related works such as additiones, glosses, summae, apparatus, etc. of a particular decretist or decretalist, see the canonist in the appropriate period

Sources
Collections. Compilations. Selections -- Continued
Corpus iuris canonici
Class here the editions of the body of church law in force until 1917 (enactment of the Codex Iuris Canonici), beginning with the authenticated Rome edition of the Corpus (comprising the six compilations, i.e., Decretum Gratiani; Decretales Gregorii IX; Liber Sextus Bonifacii VIII; Clementinae; Extravagantes Joannis XXII, and Extravagantes communes) as promulgated by Pope Gregory XIII in his brief, Cum pro munere pastorali (1580)
Including collections predating 1580 under the title "Corpus Iuris Canonici", already adopted by the Council of Basel in 1441
Cf. KBR1360+
1564 Indexes. Vocabularies. Glossaries to the corpus iuris canonici
e. g. Francis Germovnik, Indices ad corpus iuris canonici
1565 Particular editions. By date
1565 1500 Jean Chappuis (fl. 1500), Paris 1500-1501
1565 1554 Charles Du Moulin (Molinaeus, 1500-1566), Lyon 1554, etc.
1565 1570 Antoine Leconte (Contius, 1517-1586), Antwerp, 1570
1565 1582 Editio Romana (Correctores Romani), 1582
For the emendatio Decreti Gratiani see KBR1362.2+
1565 1687 Pierre et François Pithou (Pithoeus), 1687, etc.
1565 1728 Christoph Heinrich Freiesleben (d. ca. 1733), Prag 1728
1565 1747 Justus Henning Boehmer (1674-1749), Halle 1747
1565 1839 Aemilius Ludwig Richter (1808-1864), Leipzig 1839
1565 1879 Emil Friedberg, Leipzig 1879-81
Canonists and jurists
By period
12th to mid 16th centuries
Class here works produced by the early canonical jurisprudence (canonics) between Decretum Gratiani and Tridentinum (ca. 1140 to 1545)
Cf. KJA1630+ Individual jurists (6th to 15th cent. Post-Justinian periods. Jus Romanun Medii Aevi)
1570 General works
1573 Collections. Compilations. Selections
Paolo Attavanti Breviarium
see KBR1412

KBR

Sources
Canonists and jurists
By period
12th to mid 16th centuries -- Continued
Decretists and early decretalists
Class here works of canonists on the Decretum Gratiani, and works of canonists on the Quinque compilationes antiquae (collection decretalists), ca. 1140-ca. 1234
Including the school of Bologna, the French, Rheinish and Anglo-Normanic schools, etc.
General works see KBR1570
Particular types of contemporary legal literature (including auxiliary literature)
see KBR2139+
Collections see KBR1573
Individual titles or canonists
1575 In primis hominibus (12th cent.) (Table K20b)
1576 Paucapalea. Summa, before 1148 (Table K3)
1580 Stroma Rolandi, before 1148 (Table K20b)
1584 Rufinus, Bp. of Assissi, fl. 1157-1179 (Table K3 modified)
1584.A3A-.A3Z Individual works. By title, A-Z
Including unannotated and annotated editions, translations, particular manuscript editions, and textual criticism
e.g. Summa decretorum, ca. 1157-59
1586 Stephen, of Tournai (Stephanus Tornacensis), 1128-1203 (Table K3 modified)
1586.A3A-.A3Z Individual works. By title, A-Z
Including unannotated and annotated editions, translations, particular manuscript editions, and textual criticism
e.g. Summa, ca. 1160
1587 Distinctiones Monacenses ("Si Mulier eadem hora"), ca. 1168-1171 (Table K20b)
1588 Ordinaturus, ca. 1180-1182 (Table K3)
1590 Summa Coloniensis ("Summa Elegantius in iure diuino seu Coloniensis") (Gérard Fransen and Stephan Kuttner, eds., 1969) (Table K20b)
1592 Summa Parisiensis ("Magister Gratianus in hoc opere"), 1160 or 1170 (Table K20b)
1594 Johannes Faventinus, d. 1190 (Table K3)
Summa, after 1171
1598 Summa Monacensis ("Imperatorie maiestati"), 1175-1178 (Table K20b)

Sources
Canonists and jurists
By period
12th to mid 16th centuries
Decretists and early decretalists
Individual titles or canonists -- Continued

1600 Raymond, of Peñafort, Saint, 1175?-1275 (Table K3 modified)
1600.A3A-.A3Z Individual works. By title, A-Z
Including unannotated and annotated editions, translations, particular manuscript editions, and textual criticism
e.g. Summa de poenitentia et matrimonio
Decretales dni. pape Gregorij ... emendate
see KBR1500
1605 Simon de Bisignano (Table K3 modified)
1605.A3A-.A3Z Individual works. By title, A-Z
Including unannotated and annotated editions, translations, particular manuscript editions, and textual criticism
e.g. Summa, between 1177-1179
1610 Sicardus, Bishop of Cremona, d. 1215 (Table K3 modified)
1610.A3A-.A3Z Individual works. By title, A-Z
Including unannotated and annotated editions, translations, particular manuscript editions, and textual criticism
e.g. Summa, between 1179-1181
1620 Permissio quaedam (Summa), between 1179-1187 (Table K20b)
1630 Et est sciendum (Glossae Stuttgardienses), ca. 1181-1185 (Table K20b)
1635 Notae Atrebatenses, ca. 1182 (Table K20b)
1640 Summa Lipsiensis ("Omnis qui iuste iudicat"), ca. 1186 (Table K20b)
1645 De iure canonico tractaturus, ca. 1185-1190 (Table K20b)
1648 Honorius (Table K3 modified)
1648.A3A-.A3Z Individual works. By title, A-Z
Including unannotated and annotated editions, translations, particular manuscript editions, and textual criticism
e.g. Summa quaestionum decretalium, 1186-1190
1653 Summa ("Circa ius naturale"), 1186-1187 (Table K20b)
1655 Summa brevis, ca. 1196-1198 (Table K20b)
1660 Alanus Anglicus (Table K3 modified)

Sources
Canonists and jurists
By period
12th to mid 16th centuries
Decretists and early decretalists
Individual titles or canonists
Alanus Anglicus -- Continued
1660.A3A-.A3Z Individual works. By title, A-Z
Including unannotated and annotated editions, translations, particular manuscript editions, and textual criticism
e.g. Glossa ordinaria ("Ius naturale"), 1205 (1192); Ecce vicit Leo (Apparatus), after 1202
1665 Summa Bambergensis ("Animal est substantia"), 1206-1210 (Table K20b)
1670 Laurentius Hispanus, Bp., d. 1248 (Table K3 modified)
1670.A3A-.A3Z Individual works. By title, A-Z
Including unannotated and annotated editions, translations, particular manuscript editions, and textual criticism
e.g. Apparatus, between 1210-1215
1680 Burchardus Anerbe, de Argentina, 13th cent. (Table K3 modified)
1680.A3A-.A3Z Individual works. By title, A-Z
Including unannotated and annotated editions, translations, particular manuscript editions, and textual criticism
e.g. Summa de paenitentia seu de casibus conscientiae, between 1300 and 1350
1685 Glossa Palatina, ca. 1210-1215
1691 Vincentius Hispanus, 13th cent. (Table K3 modified)
1691.A3A-.A3Z Individual works. By title, A-Z
Including unannotated and annotated editions, translations, particular manuscript editions, and textual criticism
e.g. Apparatus 1209/10-1215
1696 Tancred, ca. 1185-1236? (Tancredus Bononiensis) (Table K3 modified)
Cf. KJA1696 Roman law

Sources
Canonists and jurists
By period
12th to mid 16th centuries
Decretists and early decretalists
Individual titles or canonists
Tancred, ca. 1185-1236? (Tancredus Bononiensis) -- Continued

1696.A3A-.A3Z Individual works. By title, A-Z
Including unannotated and annotated editions, translations, particular manuscript editions, and textual criticism
e.g. Glossa ordinaria on Compilatio decretalium prima and secunda, 1210-1215, 1220; on Compilatio tertia decretalium, 1216-1220

1697 Joannes, Teutonicus, d. 1245? (Table K3 modified)

1697.A3A-.A3Z Individual works. By title, A-Z
Including unannotated and annotated editions, translations, particular manuscript editions, and textual criticism
e.g. Glossa ordinaria on Compilatio quarta decretalium, 1216-1217

1698 Bartolomeo, da Brescia, d. 1258 (Table K3)

1699 Jacobus de Albenga, d. 1274 (Table K3 modified)

1699.A3A-.A3Z Individual works. By title, A-Z
Including unannotated and annotated editions, translations, particular manuscript editions, and textual criticism
e.g. Apparatus on Compilatio quinta decretalium, after 1226

1700 Bernard, of Pavia (Bernardus Balbus) (Table K3 modified)

1700.A3A-.A3Z Individual works. By title, A-Z
Including unannotated and annotated editions, translations, particular manuscript editions, and textual criticism
e.g. Ambrosius (revised edition, ca. 1215); Damasus (revised edition, ca. 1215); Flores sive Decretorum compilationes, 126-?; Summa on Compilatio prima decretalium, between 1191-1198

Decretalists and commentators (consiliators), to 1545
General works see KBR1570
Collections see KBR1573
Individual titles or canonists

1704 Peter Lombard, Bishop of Paris, ca. 1100-1160 (Table K3 modified)

Sources
Canonists and jurists
By period
12th to mid 16th centuries
Decretalists and commentators (consiliators), to 1545
Individual titles or canonists
Peter Lombard, Bishop of Paris, ca. 1100-1160 -- Continued

1704.A3A-.A3Z Individual works. By title, A-Z
Including unannotated and annotated editions, translations, particular manuscript editions, and textual criticism
e.g. Sententiarum libri IV

1705 Innocent III, Pope, 1160 or 61-1216 (Table K3)

1706 Innocent IV, Pope, ca. 1200-1254 (Table K3 modified)

1706.A3A-.A3Z Individual works. By title, A-Z
Including unannotated and annotated editions, translations, particular manuscript editions, and textual criticism
e.g. Apparatus super libros Decretalium

1707 Bernardo Bottoni (Bernardus de Botone Parmensis), d. 1266 (Table K3 modified)

1707.A3A-.A3Z Individual works. By title, A-Z
Including unannotated and annotated editions, translations, particular manuscript editions, and textual criticism
e.g. Casus longus super quinque libros decretalium

1708 Henricus, de Segusio, Cardinal, ca. 1200-1271 (Table K3 modified)

1708.A3A-.A3Z Individual works. By title, A-Z
Including unannotated and annotated editions, translations, particular manuscript editions, and textual criticism
e.g. Summa Hostiensis

1709 Vivianus Tuscus, 13th cent. (Table K3)
Cf. KJA1709 Roman law

1710 Alberto Gandino, 13th cent. (Table K3 modified)
Cf. KJA1710 Roman law

1710.A3A-.A3Z Individual works. By title, A-Z
Including unannotated and annotated editions, translations, particular manuscript editions, and textual criticism
e.g. Tractatus maleficiorum (1494)

1748 Guillaume Durand, ca. 1230-1296 (Table K3 modified)
Cf. KJA1748 Roman law

Sources
Canonists and jurists
By period
12th to mid 16th centuries
Decretalists and commentators (consiliators), to 1545
Individual titles or canonists
Guillaume Durand, ca. 1230-1296 -- Continued

1748.A3A-.A3Z Individual works. By title, A-Z
Including unannotated and annotated editions, translations, particular manuscript editions, and textual criticism
e.g. Breviarium aureum; Repertorium aureum iuris canonici; Speculum iudiciale

1748.A4A-.A4Z Indexes. Repertories. Margaritae, etc., A-Z
e.g. Bérenger Frédol, d. 1323, Inventarium Speculi iudicialis

1748.5 Goffredo, da Trani, d. 1245 (Table K3 modified)

1748.5.A3A-.A3Z Individual works. By title, A-Z
Including unannotated and annotated editions, translations, particular manuscript editions, and textual criticism
e.g. Summa super rubricis Decretalium

1748.7 Bartholomew, of San Concordio (Bartolommeo de Granchi da San Concordio, Pisano), 1262-1347 (Table K3 modified)

1748.7.A3A-.A3Z Individual works. By title, A-Z
Including unannotated and annotated editions, translations, particular manuscript editions, and textual criticism
e.g. Summa de casibus conscientiae

1748.9 Tancredus, de Corneto, fl. 1298-1310 (Table K3)

1749 Gilbertus Anglicus, fl. 1250 (Table K3)

1749.3 Innocentius Hispanus (Table K3)

1749.5 Jacobus de Albenga, d. 1274 (Table K3)

1749.6 Martinus Polonus, d. 1279 (Table K3)

1749.8 Guido, de Baysio (da Baisio), d. 1313 (Table K3)

1749.8.A3A-.A3Z Individual works. By title, A-Z
Including unannotated and annotated editions, translations, particular manuscript editions, and textual criticism
e.g. Rosarium

1750 Rolandinus, de Passageriis, d. 1300 (Table K3)
Cf. KJA1750 Roman law

1753 Dinus, de Mugello, 1245-ca. 1300 (Table K3 modified)
Cf. KJA1753 Roman law

Sources
Canonists and jurists
By period
12th to mid 16th centuries
Decretalists and commentators (consiliators), to 1545
Individual titles or canonists
Dinus, de Mugello, 1245-ca. 1300 -- Continued

1753.A3A-.A3Z Individual works. By title, A-Z
Including unannotated and annotated editions, translations, particular manuscript editions, and textual criticism
e.g. Commentarius in regulas iuris pontificij: cum additionibus Nicolai Boerij et. al.

1762 Pietro, da Unzola, d. 1312 (Table K3)
Cf. KJA1762 Roman law

1769 Oldrado da Ponte, d. 1335 (Table K3)
Cf. KJA1769 Roman law

1769.5 Gulielmus de Monte Lauduno, d. 1343 (Table K3)

1772 Cino da Pistoia, 1270?-1336 or 7 (Table K3)
Cf. KJA1772 Roman law

1774 Joannes de Anguissola (Table K3 modified)
Cf. KBR3112+ Marriage law

1774.A3A-.A3Z Individual works. By title, A-Z
Including unannotated and annotated editions, translations, particular manuscript editions, and textual criticism
e.g. De sponsalibus

1775 Giovanni d'Andrea, ca. 1270-1348 (Table K3)
Cf. KJA1775 Roman law

1775.A3A-.A3Z Individual works. By title, A-Z
Including unannotated and annotated editions, translations, particular manuscript editions, and textual criticism
e.g. Novella super secundo decretalium; Novella super I-V decretalium; Novella super VI decretalium; Novella super tit. de Regulis juris; Super arboribus consanguinitatis (Cf. KBR2237+ Consanguinity); Summa de sponsalibus et matrimoniis (Cf. KBR3112+ Marriage law); Quaestiones mercuriales super regulis iuris

1775.A4A-.A4Z Indexes. Repertories. Margaritae, etc., A-Z
e.g. Lucas Panaetius, Repertorium Novellarum Joannis Andree ... (Cf. KBR2153.5.A+ Repertoria)

1776 Albericus, de Rosate, 1290-1360 (Table K3)
Cf. KJA1776 Roman law

Sources
Canonists and jurists
By period
12th to mid 16th centuries
Decretalists and commentators (consiliators), to 1545
Individual titles or canonists -- Continued

1777 Bartolo, of Sassoferrato, 1314-1357 (Table K3)
Cf. KJA1777 Roman law

1777.5 Johannes Calderinus, d. 1365 (Table K3 modified)
1777.5.A3A-.A3Z Individual works. By title, A-Z
Including unannotated and annotated editions, translations, particular manuscript editions, and textual criticism
e.g. Repertorium iuris

1782 Goffredus, Saligniacus, fl. ca. 1373 (Table K3)
Cf. KJA1782 Roman law

1784 Baldo degli Ubaldi, 1327?-1400 (Table K3)
Cf. KBR2139 Glossae (Contemporary legal literature)
Cf. KJA1784 Roman law

1786.3 Adam Coloniensis, d. 1408 (Table K3 modified)
1786.3.A3A-.A3Z Individual works. By title, A-Z
Including unannotated and annotated editions, translations, particular manuscript editions, and textual criticism
e.g. Summula (Summula Raymundi)

1786.4 Pietro, d'Ancarano, 1330-1416 (Table K3 modified)
1786.4.A3A-.A3Z Individual works. By title, A-Z
Including unannotated and annotated editions, translations, particular manuscript editions, and textual criticism
e.g. Lectura super Sexto decretalium

1786.6 Giovanni, da Legnano, d. 1383 (Table K3 modified)
1786.6.A3A-.A3Z Individual works. By title, A-Z
Including unannotated and annotated editions, translations, particular manuscript editions, and textual criticism
e.g. De pluralitate beneficiorum ecclesiasticorum (Cf. KBR2358+ Constitution of the Church)

1787 Gilles de Bellemère (Aegidius Bellemera), 1342 or 3-1407 (Table K3 modified)
For his decisiones see KBR43.5

Sources
Canonists and jurists
By period
12th to mid 16th centuries
Decretalists and commentators (consiliators), to 1545
Individual titles or canonists
Gilles de Bellemère (Aegidius Bellemera), 1342 or 3-1407 -- Continued

1787.A3A-.A3Z Individual works. By title, A-Z
Including unannotated and annotated editions, translations, particular manuscript editions, and textual criticism
e.g. In primam primi[-tertiam secundi] Decretalium libri partem praelectiones; De permutatione beneficiorum

1788 Bartholomeo da Saliceto, d. 1412 (Table K3)
Cf. KJA1788 Roman law

1791 Joannes de Imola, d. 1436 (Table K3)
Cf. KJA1791 Roman law

1791.5 Francesco Zabarella, 1360-1417 (Table K3 modified)

1791.5.A3A-.A3Z Individual works. By title, A-Z
Including unannotated and annotated editions, translations, particular manuscript editions, and textual criticism
e.g. Lectura super Clementinis

1792 Libellus de modo confitendi et penitendi, 1488 (Table K3)

1796 Marianus Socinus, 1401-1467 (Table K3)
Cf. KJA1796 Roman law

1796.5 Joannes, de Anania, d. 1457 (Table K3 modified)

1796.5.A3A-.A3Z Individual works. By title, A-Z
Including unannotated and annotated editions, translations, particular manuscript editions, and textual criticism
e.g. Super primo Decretalium; Super secundo et tertio Decretalium; Super quinto decretalium; Index ... rerum ac sententiarum quae in lectura domini Ioannis de Anania super Decretalibus continentur

1798 Alessandro Tartagni, 1424-1477 (Table K3 modified)
Cf. KJA1798 Roman law

Sources
Canonists and jurists
By period
12th to mid 16th centuries
Decretalists and commentators (consiliators), to 1545
Individual titles or canonists
Alessandro Tartagni, 1424-1477 -- Continued

1798.A3A-.A3Z Individual works. By title, A-Z
Including unannotated and annotated editions, translations, particular manuscript editions, and textual criticism
e.g. Lectura super rubrica de translatione episcoporum

1798.5 Niccolò, de' Tudeschi (Panormitanus, Abbas Siculus) Archbishop, 1386-1445 (Table K3 modified)

1798.5.A3A-.A3Z Individual works. By title, A-Z
Including unannotated and annotated editions, translations, particular manuscript editions, and including textual criticism
e.g. Lectura super tertio Decretalium; Commentaria primae partis in primum Decretalium librum; Lectura super secundam partem libri secundi Decretalium; Commentaria in quartum et quintum Decretalium librum; Lectura super rubrica de translatione episcoporum

1798.5.A4A-.A4Z Indexes, etc., A-Z
e. g. Alonso Díaz de Montalvo, 1405-1499, Repertorium Quaestionum super Nicolaum de Tudeschis (Cf. KBR2153.5.A+ Repertoira); Antonio Corsetti (ca. 1450-1503), Repertorium in opera Nicolai de Tudeschis (Cf. KBR2153.5.A+ Repertoria)

1799 Bartolomeo Cipolla, d. 1477 (Table K3)
Cf. KJA1799 Roman law

1800 Francesco Accolti (Franciscus de Accoltis; Francesco Aretio), 1416 or 17-1488 (Table K3)
Cf. KJA1800 Roman law

1802 Giovanni Battista Caccialupi, d. 1496 (Table K3 modified)
Cf. KBR2360+ Union and incorporation of benefices
Cf. KJA1802 Roman law

Sources
Canonists and jurists
By period
12th to mid 16th centuries
Decretalists and commentators (consiliators), to 1545
Individual titles or canonists
Giovanni Battista Caccialupi, d. 1496 -- Continued
1802.A3A-.A3Z Individual works. By title, A-Z
Including unannotated and annotated editions, translations, particular manuscript editions, and textual criticism
e.g. De unionibus ecclesiarum et beneficiorum tractatus
1805 Lancelotto Decio, d. 1503 (Table K3)
Cf. KJA1805 Roman law
1806 Bartholomaeus Raimundus, fl. 1506 (Table K3)
Cf. KJA1806 Roman law
1806.5 Joannes Antonius de Sancto Georgio (Sangiorgi) (Table K3)
1807.5 Juan de Torquemada (Ioannis de Turre Cremata), 1388-1468 (Table K3 modified)
1807.5.A3A-.A3Z Individual works. By title, A-Z
Including unannotated and annotated editions, translations, particular manuscript editions, and textual criticism
e.g. Super toto Decreto; In primum volumen causarum; Super secundo volumine Causarum
1809.5 Nicholas, of Osimo,d. 1453 (Table K3 modified)
1809.5.A3A-.A3Z Individual works. By title, A-Z
Including unannotated and annotated editions, translations, particular manuscript editions, and textual criticism
e.g. Supplementum Summae Pisanellae
1814 Filippo Decio, 1454-1536 or 7 (Table K3)
Cf. KJA1814 Roman law
1817 Angelo Carletti, 1411-1495 (Table K3 modified)
1817.A3A-.A3Z Individual works. By title, A-Z
Including unannotated and annotated editions, translations, particular manuscript editions, and textual criticism
e.g. Summa Angelica de casibus conscientiae
1819 Battista, da Sambagio, ca. 1425-1492 (Table K3 modified)

Sources
Canonists and jurists
By period
12th to mid 16th centuries
Decretalists and commentators (consiliators), to 1545
Individual titles or canonists
Battista, da Sambagio, ca. 1425-1492 -- Continued
1819.A3A-.A3Z Individual works. By title, A-Z
Including unannotated and annotated editions, translations, particular manuscript editions, and textual criticism
e.g. Varii tractatus juridici
Compendium iuris canonici see KBR2154.3
English and Scottish canonists
1820 General works
1820.2 Collections. Compilations. Selections
1820.3 Odo of Dover. Decreta minora (1160-1170) (Table K3)
1820.4 Langton, Stephen, d. 1228 (Table K3)
1821 Richardus, Anglicus (Richard of Mores), d. 1252 (Table K3 modified)
1821.A3A-.A3Z Individual works. By title, A-Z
Including unannotated and annotated editions, translations, particular manuscript editions, and textual criticism
e.g. Summa quaestionum decretalium; Distinctiones (1196-1198)
1821.2 Peckham, John, d. 1292 (Table K3)
1821.3 Rolle, Richard, of Hampole, 1290?-1349 (Table K3)
1821.4 Stratford, John, d. 1348 (Table K3)
1822 William, of Pagula, ca. 1290-1332 (Table K3)
1822.12 William Lyndwood, 1375?-1446 (Table K3)
For his Provinciale, seu constitutiones Anglie see KBR1006.2
1822.2 Fliscus, Stephanus (Table K3)
1822.4 Robert, of Flamborough (Table K3 modified)
Cf. KBR2154.5 Penitentials
1822.4.A3A-.A3Z Individual works. By title, A-Z
Including unannotated and annotated editions, translations, particular manuscript editions, and textual criticism
e.g. Liber poenitentialis
French canonists
1822.5 General works
1823 Collections. Compilations. Selections

Sources
Canonists and jurists
By period
12th to mid 16th centuries
Decretalists and commentators (consiliators), to 1545
Individual titles or canonists
English and Scottish canonists

1824 John, of Salisbury, Bishop of Chartres, d. 1180 (Table K3)

1825 Alanus, de Insulis (Alain de Lille), d. 1202 (Table K3 modified)
Cf. KBR2154.5 Penitentials

1825.A3A-.A3Z Individual works. By title, A-Z
Including unannotated and annotated editions, translations, particular manuscript editions, and textual criticism
e.g. Liber poenitentialis

1828 Jacques, de Révigny (Jacobus de Ravennis), d. 1296 (Table K3)
Cf. KJA1828 Roman law

1830 Guide de Cumis, 13th cent. (Table K3)
Cf. KJA1830 Roman law

1832 Simon de Paris, 13th cent. (Table K3)
Cf. KJA1832 Roman law

1833 Zenzelinus de Cassanis (Jesselin de Cassagnes), d. ca. 1350 (Table K3)

1835 Henri Bohic (Boyk, Voich), 1310-ca. 1390 (Table K3 modified)

1835.A3A-.A3Z Individual works. By title, A-Z
Including unannotated and annotated editions, translations, particular manuscript editions, and textual criticism
e.g. Opus ... super quinque libris decretalium

1846 Joannes Faber (Jean Faure), 14th cent. (Table K3)
Cf. KJA1846 Roman law

1847 Pierre Rebuffi, 1487-1557 (Table K3 modified)

1847.A3A-.A3Z Individual works. By title, A-Z
Including unannotated and annotated editions, translations, particular manuscript editions, and textual criticism
e.g. Praxis beneficiorum; Commentaria super titulos ... Decretalium ...

1847.5 Dietrich von Nieheim, ca. 1340-1418 (Table K3 modified)

Sources
Canonists and jurists
By period
12th to mid 16th centuries
Decretalists and commentators (consiliators), to 1545
Individual titles or canonists
French canonists
Dietrich von Nieheim, ca. 1340-1418 -- Continued
1847.5.A3A-.A3Z Individual works. By title, A-Z
Including unannotated and annotated editions, translations, particular manuscript editions, and textual criticism
Stilus palatii abbreviatus see KBR105.N54
Spanish and Portugues canonists
1850 General works
1850.2 Collections. Compilations. Collections
1863 Diego de Covarrubias y Leyva, 1512-1577 (Table K3)
1864 Alonso Diaz de Montalvo, (Alphonsus Didaci), 1405-1499 (Table K3)
Cf. KJA1864 Roman law
1864.2 Juan Bernardo Díaz de Luco, d. 1556 (Table K3)
Practica criminalis canonica
1874 João de Deus (Deogratia), ca. 1190-1267 (Table K3)
Cf. KJA1874 Roman law
1875 Martín de Azpilcueta, 1492?-1586 (Table K3 modified)
1875.A3A-.A3Z Individual works. By title, A-Z
Including unannotated and annotated editions, translations, particular manuscript editions, and textual criticism
e.g. Tractado de las rentas de los beneficios ecclesiasticos
1877 Juan López de Palacios Rubios, 1450-1524 (Table K3 modified)
1877.A3A-.A3Z Individual works. By title, A-Z
Including unannotated and annotated editions, translations, particular manuscript editions, and textual criticism
e.g. Repetitio rubricae et capituli Per vestras
German canonists
1882 General works
1884 Collections. Compilations. Selections
1885 Henricus Merseburgensis (Heinrich von Merseburg), d. after 1276 (Table K3)

Sources
Canonists and jurists
By period
12th to mid 16th centuries
Decretalists and commentators (consiliators), to 1545
Individual titles or canonists
German canonists -- Continued

1887 Johannes, de Erfordia (von Erfurt), ca. 1250-ca. 1325 (Table K3 modified)
Cf. KBR2154.5 Penitentials

1887.A3A-.A3Z Individual works. By title, A-Z
Including unannotated and annotated editions, translations, particular manuscript editions, and textual criticism
e.g. Summa confessorum

Tabula utriusque iuris see KBR56

1887.3 Johannes, von Freiburg, d. 1314 (Table K3 modified)
Cf. KBR2154.5 Penitentials

1887.3.A3A-.A3Z Individual works. By title, A-Z
Including unannotated and annotated editions, translations, particular manuscript editions, and textual criticism
e.g. Summa confessorum

1887.5 Berthold von Freiburg, fl. 1304 (Table K3 modified)

1887.5.A3A-.A3Z Individual works. By title, A-Z
Including unannotated and annotated editions, translations, particular manuscript editions, and textual criticism
e.g. Summa Johannis

1889 Balduinus Brandenburgensis (Balduin von Brandenburg) (Table K3 modified)

1889.A3A-.A3Z Individual works. By title, A-Z
Including unannotated and annotated editions, translations, particular manuscript editions, and textual criticism
e.g. Summa titulorum

1891 Nicolaus Stör, d. 1424 (Table K3)
Expositio officii Missae sacrique Canonis

1893 Johann von Breitenbach, d. ca. 1507 (Table K3 modified)

1893.A3A-.A3Z Individual works. By title, A-Z
Including unannotated and annotated editions, translations, particular manuscript editions, and textual criticism
e.g. Repetitio

Sources
Canonists and jurists
By period
12th to mid 16th centuries
Decretalists and commentators (consiliators), to 1545
Individual titles or canonists
German canonists -- Continued

1894 Nicasius de Voerda, d. 1492 (Table K3)
Cf. KJA1894 Roman law
1895 Konrad Summenhart, 1465-1511 (Table K3)
1895.5 Johann Freiberger, ca. 1470-1541 (Table K3 modified)
1895.5.A3A-.A3Z Individual works. By title, A-Z
Including unannotated and annotated editions, translations, particular manuscript editions, and textual criticism
e.g. De pluralitate beneficiorum

Dutch canonists
1905 General works
1907 Collections. Compilations. Selections
1920 Johannes de Turnhout, d. 1492
Cf. KJA1920 Roman law

1925.A-Z Other canonists or jurists, A-Z
For Jurists of the 14th and 15th centuries see KJA1925.A+
1925.A39 Albericus, de Maletis (Table K4)
1925.A42 Pietro Albignani (Petrus Albignanus Trecius) (Table K4)
1925.A44 Alexander, Anglus (Alexander, Carpentarius, fl. 1429) (Table K4)
1925.A48 Jacopo Alvarotti, 1385-1453 (Table K4)
1925.A57 Antonio, da Cannara (Table K4)
1925.A77 Paolo Attavanti, 1445?-1499 (Table K4)
1925.A78 Astesano (Astesanus de Ast), d. 1330? (Table K4 modified)
Cf. KBR2154.5 Penitentials
1925.A78A3-.A78A39 Individual works. By title
Including unannotated and annotated editions, translations, particular manuscript editions, and textual criticism
e.g. Summa de casibus conscientiae
1925.A96 Johannes Auerbach(Urbach), fl. 1405 (Table K4 modified)
Cf. KJA1925.A96 Roman law

KBR

Sources
Canonists and jurists
By period
12th to mid 16th centuries
Decretalists and commentators (consiliators), to 1545
Individual titles or canonists
Other canonists or jurists, A-Z
Johannes Auerbach(Urbach), fl. 1405 -- Continued

1925.A96A3-.A96A39 Individual works. By title
Including unannotated and annotated editions, translations, particular manuscript editions, and textual criticism
e.g. Processus judiciarius

1925.B36 Andrea Barbazza, ca. 1410-1480 (Table K4)

1925.B37 Battista, da Sambagio, ca. 1425-1492 (Table K4 modified)

1925.B37A3-.B37A39 Individual works. By title
Including unannotated and annotated editions, translations, particular manuscript editions, and textual criticism
e.g. Varii tractatus juridici

1925.B42 Benedicto Capra de Benedictis (Table K4)

1925.B43 Jean Barbier (Johannes Berberius), 15th cent. (Table K4)

1925.B47 Bertachini, Giovanni, b. ca. 1448 (Table K4)

1925.B65 Nicolas de Bohier, 1469-1539 (Table K4 modified)
Cf. KBR4076+ Foreign affairs of the Holy See

1925.B65A3-.B65A39 Individual works. By title
Including unannotated and annotated editions, translations, particular manuscript editions, and textual criticism
Tractatus ... de officio et potestate ... de latere legati see KBR4083.B65

1925.B85 Antonius de Butrio, 1338-1408 (Table K4)

1925.C32 Vitalis de Cambanis, 15th cent. (Table K4)

1925.C35 Giovanni Campeggi (Joannes Campegius), 1448-1511 (Table K4)

1925.C63 Joannes Jacobus Canis, d. 1490 (Table K4)

1925.C64 Guilielmus Cassador, 1477-1527 (Table K4)

1925.C65 Johannes de Castellione, 15th cent. (Table K4)

1925.C66 Paolo Cittadino, d. 1525 (Table K4)

1925.C67 Stephanus Costa, 15th cent. (Table K4)

1925.C675 Emanuel Costa, d. 1564 (Table K4)

1925.C68 Antonio Corsetti, ca. 1450-1503 (Table K4)

1925.C82 Jerónimo Cucalón, 16th cent. (Table K4)

Sources
Canonists and jurists
By period
12th to mid 16th centuries
Decretalists and commentators (consiliators), to 1545
Individual titles or canonists
Other canonists or jurists, A-Z -- Continued

1925.C83 Marco Antonio Cucchi, 1506-1567 (Table K4)
1925.C86 Nicolaus Cusanus (Table K4)
1925.D44 Pietro del Monte, d. 1457 (Table K4)
1925.D65 Dominicus, de Sancto Geminiano, ca. 1375-1424 (Table K4)
1925.F34 Enea Falconi (Table K4)
1925.F48 Johannes Ferrarius, 1485 or 6-1558 (Table K4)
1925.F54 Filippo Franchi, d. 1471 (Table K4 modified)
Cf. KJA1925.F54 Roman law
1925.F54A3-.F54A39 Individual works. By title
Including unannotated and annotated editions, translations, particular manuscript editions, and textual criticism
e.g. Lectura super titulo De Appellationibus
1925.F55 Marcello Francolini, 1533-1591 (Table K4)
1925.G33 Antonio Gabrieli, d. 1555 (Table K4)
1925.G35 Angelo Gambiglioni, 15th cent. (Table K4 modified)
Cf. KJA1925.G35 Roman law
1925.G35A3-.G35A39 Individual works. By title
Including unannotated and annotated editions, translations, particular manuscript editions, and textual criticism
e.g. Tractatus de maleficiis
1925.G36 Pietro Andrea Gammaro, 1480-1528 (Table K4 modified)
1925.G36A3-.G36A39 Individual works. By title
Including unannotated and annotated editions, translations, particular manuscript editions, and textual criticism
Tractatus de officio atque auctoritate legati de latere see KBR4083.G36
1925.G37 Martino Garrati, 15th cent. (Table K4 modified)
1925.G37A3-.G37A39 Individual works. By title
Including unannotated and annotated editions, translations, particular manuscript editions, and textual criticism
e.g. De primogenitura
1925.G55 Girolamo Giganti, d. 1560 (Table K4)

KBR

Sources
Canonists and jurists
By period
12th to mid 16th centuries
Decretalists and commentators (consiliators), to 1545
Individual titles or canonists
Other canonists or jurists, A-Z -- Continued

1925.G66 Louis Gomez (Ludovicus Gomesius), d. 1542 or 3 (Table K4 modified)

1925.G66A3-.G66A39 Individual works. By title

Including unannotated and annotated editions, translations, particular manuscript editions, and textual criticism

Commentarii in iudicales regulas Cancellariae see KBR105.G66

1925.J62 Johannes, Monachus (Jean le Moine), d. 1313 (Table K4)

1925.L36 Cesare Lambertini, d. 1550 (Table K4)

1925.L37 Bernardino da Landrino, 15th/16th cent. (Table K4)

1925.L56 Johannes Lindholz, d. 1535 (Table K4 modified)

1925.L56A3-.L56A39 Individual works. By title

Including unannotated and annotated editions, translations, particular manuscript editions, and textual criticism

e. g. Arbores consanguinitatis, affinitatis, cognationis spiritualis atque legalis

1925.M5 Joannes Nicolaus Milis, 15th cent. (Table K4 modified)

1925.M5A3-.M5A39 Individual works. By title

Including unannotated and annotated editions, translations, particular manuscript editions, and textual criticism

e. g. Repertorium iuris

1925.M66 Lodovico Montalto, d. ca. 1533 (Table K4)

1925.N36 Thomas Naogeorg, 1511-1563 (Table K4)

1925.N48 Antonius Nicellus (Table K4 modified)

1925.N48A3-.N48A39 Individual works. By title

Including unannotated and annotated editions, translations, particular manuscript editions, and textual criticism

e.g. Concordantiae glossarum iuris canonici et civilis

1925.N5 Alessandro Nievo (Alexander de Nevo), d. 1484 (Table K4)

Sources
Canonists and jurists
By period
12th to mid 16th centuries
Decretalists and commentators (consiliators), to 1545
Individual titles or canonists
Other canonists or jurists, A-Z -- Continued

1925.P36 Guy de La Pape, ca. 1402-ca. 1487 (Table K4 modified)
Cf. KJA1925.P36 Roman law

1925.P36A3-.P36A39 Individual works. By title
Including unannotated and annotated editions, translations, particular manuscript editions, and textual criticism
e.g. Super decretales

1925.P38 Paulus, de Roma (15th cent.) (Table K4 modified)

1925.P38A3-.P38A39 Individual works. By title
Including unannotated and annotated editions, translations, particular manuscript editions, and textual criticism
e.g. Tractatus de pensione ecclesiastica

1925.P48 Petrus Ravennas (Peter Tomasi), d. 1502 (Table K4)

1925.P54 Pietro, d'Ancarano, 1330-1416 (Table K4)

1925.P65 Ludovico Pontano, 1409-1439 (Table K4)
Cf. KJA1925.P65 Roman law

1925.P73 Ioannis de Prato (Table K4)

1925.P88 Paris de Puteo, ca. 1413-1493 (Table K4)

1925.R42 Jacobus Rebuffi (of Montpellier), d. 1428 (Table K4)

1925.R53 Gregorius Rhamnusius, fl. 16th cent. (Table K4)

1925.R58 Gianfrancesco Riva di San Nazarro, d. 1535 (Table K4)

1925.R68 Antonius Rosellus (of Arezzo), 1466 (Table K4)

1925.R75 Caspar de Rossi, d. 1455 (Table K4 modified)

1925.R75A3-.R75A39 Individual works. By title
Including unannotated and annotated editions, translations, particular manuscript editions, and textual criticism
e.g. Tractatus de reservationibus beneficiorum

1925.S27 Felino Maria Sandeo, 1444-1503 (Table K4 modified)

Sources
Canonists and jurists
By period
12th to mid 16th centuries
Decretalists and commentators (consiliators), to 1545
Individual titles or canonists
Other canonists or jurists, A-Z
Felino Maria Sandeo, 1444-1503 -- Continued
1925.S27A3-.S27A39 Individual works. By title
Including unannotated and annotated editions, translations, particular manuscript editions, and textual criticism
e.g. Lectura super I, II, IV, et V Decretalium; Commentaria in quinque Decretalium libros
1925.S27A4-.S27A49 Indexes. Repertories. Margaritae, etc., A-Z
e.g. Benedetto Vadi (16th cent.) Repertorium Felini Sandei Commentarios ad quinque Decretalium libros (Cf. KBR2153+ Repertoria)
1925.S45 Jean de Selve, fl. ca. 1500 (Table K4 modified)
1925.S45A3-.S45A39 Individual works. By title
Including unannotated and annotated editions, translations, particular manuscript editions, and textual criticism
e.g. Tractatus beneficiales
1925.S89 Johannes de Stynna, fl. 1327-1342 (Table K4 modified)
1925.S89A3-.S89A39 Individual works. By title
Including unannotated and annotated editions, translations, particular manuscript editions, and textual criticism
e.g. Speculator abbreviatus
1545 (Council of Trent) to 19th century
Class here works of the post-Tridentine period of canonical jurisprudence
1928 General works
1929 Collections. Compilations. Selections
By nationality
English
see subclass KD
French and Belgian
Cf. KJA1942+ Roman law
1942 General works
1944 Collections. Compilations. Selections
Individual canonists and jurists (commentators)

Sources
Canonists and jurists
By period
1545 (Council of Trent) to 19th century
By nationality
French and Belgian
Individual canonists and jurists (commentators) -- Continued

1950 André Alciat (Andreas Alciatus), 1492-1550 (Table K3)
Cf. KJA1950 Roman law

1950.2 Antoine de Mouchy (Antonius Demochares), 1491-1574 (Table K3)

1953 Jean Quintin, 1500-1561 (Table K3)

1954 Francois Baudouin (Balduinus), 1520-1573 (Table K3)
Cf. KJA1954 Roman law

1956 Barnabe Brisson, 1531-1591 (Table K3)
Cf. KJA1956 Roman law

1956.2 Ioannes a Costa (de Lacoste), 1560-1637 (Table K3)

1957 Pierre Grégoire, 1540-1617 (Table K3 modified)

1957.A3A-.A3Z Individual works. By title, A-Z
Including unannotated and annotated editions, translations, particular manuscript editions, and textual criticism
e.g. Commentaria et annotationes in Decretalium Proemium ...

1959 Jean Chappuis, fl. 1500 (Table K3)

1966 Jacques Cujas, 1522-1590 (Table K3 modified)
Cf. KJA1966 Roman law

1966.A3A-.A3Z Individual works. By title, A-Z
Including unannotated and annotated editions, translations, particular manuscript editions, and textual criticism
e.g. Recitationes ad librum secundum Decretalium Gregorii IX

1967 Jean Doujat (Joannes Dovatius), 1609-1688 (Table K3)

1970 Hugo Doneau (Donellus), 1527-1591 (Table K3)
Cf. KJA1970 Roman law

1970.5 François Douaren, 1509-1559 (Table K3)
Cf. KJA1970.5 Roman law

1972 Charles Du Moulin (Carolus Molinaeus), 1500-1566 (Table K3)
Cf. KJA1972 Roman law

Sources
Canonists and jurists
By period
1545 (Council of Trent) to 19th century
By nationality
French and Belgian
Individual canonists and jurists (commentators)
Charles Du Moulin (Carolus Molinaeus), 1500-1566 -- Continued
In regulas Cancellariae romanae
see KBR2430
1974 Antoine Dadin d'Hauteserre (Antonius Alteserra), 1602-1682 (Table K3)
1975 Flavin-francois de Hautesere de Salvaizon (Flavius Alteserra), 16th/17th cent. (Table K3)
1979 Pierre Pithou, 1539-1596 (Table K3)
1979.3 Francois Pithou, 1543-1621 (Table K3)
1982 François Hotman (Hotomanus), 1524-1590 (Table K3)
1985 Philippe Labbé, 1607-1667 (Table K3)
1986 Jean de Launoy, 1603-1678 (Table K3)
1987 Antoine Le Conte (Antonius Contius), 1517-1586 (Table K3)
1988 Jean Majoret (Joannes Majoretus), fl. 1676 (Table K3)
1989.5.A-Z Other canonists and jurists, A-Z
1989.5.A72 Valerius Andreas, 1588-1655 (Table K4)
1989.5.B35 Etienne Baluze, 1630-1718 (Table K4)
1989.5.B54 Antoine Fabrice Bleynianus, 1520-1573 (Table K4)
1989.5.B56 David Blondel, 1591-1655 (Table K4)
1989.5.C33 Jean Cabassut, 1604-1685 (Table K4)
1989.5.C53 Barthelemy de Chasseneuz, (1480-1541) (Table K4 modified)
1989.5.C53A3-.C53A39 Individual works. By title, A-Z
Including unannotated and annotated editions, translations, particular manuscript editions, and textual criticism
e.g. Catalogus gloriae mundi
1989.5.C68 Pierre Coustant, d. 1721 (Table K4)
1989.5.D37 Jean Dartis, 1572-1651 (Table K4)
1989.5.D44 André Delvaux, 1569-1636 (Table K4)
1989.5.D86 Louis Ellies Dupin, 1657-1719 (Table K4)
1989.5.D88 André Duval, d. 1638 (Table K4)
1989.5.F44 Claude Joseph de Ferrière, d. ca. 1748 (Table K4)
1989.5.F54 Claude Fleury, 1640-1723 (Table K4)

Sources
Canonists and jurists
By period
1545 (Council of Trent) to 19th century
By nationality
French and Belgian
Other canonists and jurists, A-Z -- Continued

1989.5.G53 Jean Pierre Gilbert, 1660-1736 (Table K4)
1989.5.G67 Gabriel Gossart, 17th cent. (Table K4)
1989.5.G74 Pierre Grégoire (Gregorius Tolosanus), 1540-1597 (Table K4)
1989.5.H35 Francois Hallier, 1595-1659 (Table K4)
1989.5.M37 Pierre de Marca, 1594-1662 (Table K4)
1989.5.M57 Celestine Mirebeau (Mirbellus), fl. 1668 (Table K4)
1989.5.M67 Jean Morin, 1591-1659 (Table K4)
1989.5.T56 Louis Thomassin, 1619-1695 (Table K4)
1989.5.T66 Pierre Francois de Tonduti, 1583-1669 (Table K4)

Italian, Spanish, and Portuguese
Cf. KJA1990+ Roman law

1990 General works
1992 Collections. Compilations. Selections
Individual canonists and jurists (commentators)
1994 Giovanni Paolo Lancelotti, 1522-1590 (Table K3 modified)
1994.A3A-.A3Z Individual works. By title, A-Z
Including unannotated and annotated editions, translations, particular manuscript editions, and textual criticism
e.g. Institutiones iuris canonici
2000 Antonio Augustin, 1517-1586 (Table K3 modified)
Cf. KJA2000 Roman law
2000.A3A-.A3Z Individual works. By title, A-Z
Including unannotated and annotated editions, translations, particular manuscript editions, and textual criticism
De Pontifice Maximo: De Patriarchis & Primatibus see KBR2803
De Archiepiscopis & Metropolitanis see KBR2803
2002 Agostinho Barbosa, 1590-1649 (Table K3 modified)
Cf. KJA2002 Roman law

Sources
Canonists and jurists
By period
1545 (Council of Trent) to 19th century
By nationality
Italian, Spanish, and Portuguese
Individual canonists and jurists (commentators)
Agostinho Barbosa, 1590-1649 -- Continued
2002.A3A-.A3Z Individual works. By title, A-Z
Including unannotated and annotated editions, translations, particular manuscript editions, and textual criticism
e.g. Juris ecclesiastici universi libri tres
2004 Diego Covarrubias y Leyva, 1512-1577 (Table K3 modified)
Cf. KJA2004 Roman law
2004.A3A-.A3Z Individual works. By title, A-Z
Including unannotated and annotated editions, translations, particular manuscript editions, and textual criticism
e.g. In quartum Decretalium librum epitome; De regulis juris libri sexti relectio
2005 Antonio Gómez, b. 1501 (Table K3)
Cf. KJA2005 Roman law
2009 Prospero Fagnani, 1588-1678 (Table K3 modified)
2009.A3A-.A3Z Individual works. By title, A-Z
Including unannotated and annotated editions, translations, particular manuscript editions, and textual criticism
e.g. Commentaria in primum-quintum librum Decretalium
2054 Prospero Farinacci, 1554-1618 (Table K3)
Cf. KJA2054 Roman law
2057 Alberico Gentili, 1552-1606 (Table K3)
Cf. KJA2057 Roman law
2066.5 Lorenzo Ridolfi (Table K3)
Cf. KJA2066.5 Roman law
2066.6 Prospero Lambertini (Benedict XIV, Pope), 1675-1758 (Table K3)
2074.A-Z Other jurists, A-Z
2074.A53 Mattia degli Alberti, d. 1575 (Table K4)
2074.A55 Alonso de la Vera Cruz, fray, ca. 1507-1584 (Table K4)
2074.A57 Lelio Altogradi, 16th/17th cent. (Table K4)
2074.A68 Giovanni Carlo Antonelli, d. 1694 (Table K4 modified)

Sources
Canonists and jurists
By period
1545 (Council of Trent) to 19th century
By nationality
Italian, Spanish, and Portuguese
Individual canonists and jurists (commentators)
Other jurists, A-Z
Giovanni Carlo Antonelli, d. 1694 -- Continued

2074.A68A3-.A68A39	Individual works. By title Including unannotated and annotated editions, translations, particular manuscript editions, and textual criticism e.g. Tractaus posthumus de juribus & onoribus clericorum
2074.B35	Girolamo Ballerini, 1702-1781 (Table K4)
2074.B37	Giovanni Bartoli, 1695-1776 (Table K4)
2074.B47	Carlo Sebastiano Berardi, 1719-1768 (Table K4 modified)
2074.B47A3-.B47A39	Individual works. By title Including unannotated and annotated editions, translations, particular manuscript editions, and textual criticism e.g. Commentaria in jus canonicum universum
2074.B62	Virginio Boccacci, d. 1596 (Table K4)
2074.B65	Martino Bonacina, d. 1631 (Table K4)
2074.C36	Giovanni Battista Cantalmagi, 17th cent. (Table K4 modified)
2074.C36A3-.C36A39	Individual works. By title Including unannotated and annotated editions, translations, particular manuscript editions, and textual criticism e.g. Selecta nea rerum notabilium ad usum decisionum Sacrae Rotae Romanae
2074.C46	Pedro Cenedo, d. 1609 (Table K4)
2074.C66	Antonio Concioli, 17th cent. (Table K4)
2074.D37	Estaban Daoiz, d. 1619 (Table K4)
2074.D42	Giovanni Battista de Luca, 1614-1683 (Table K4)
2074.D48	Giovanni Devoti, 1744-1820 (Table K4)
2074.E76	Boetius Epo, 1529-1599 (Table K4)
2074.F38	Fatinellus de Fatinellis, 1627-1719 (Table K4)
2074.F46	Lucius Ferraris, d. 1760 (Table K4)
2074.G37	Nicolaus Garcia, d. 1645 (Table K4 modified)

Sources
Canonists and jurists
By period
1545 (Council of Trent) to 19th century
By nationality
Italian, Spanish, and Portuguese
Individual canonists and jurists (commentators)
Other jurists, A-Z
Nicolaus Garcia, d. 1645 -- Continued

2074.G37A3-.G37A39 Individual works. By title
Including unannotated and annotated editions, translations, particular manuscript editions, and textual criticism

2074.G57 Ubaldo Giraldi di San Cajetano, 1692-1775 (Table K4)

2074.G66 Manuel González Téllez, d. 1649 (Table K4)

(2074.M36) Giovanni Domenico Mansi
see KBR200.M36

2074.M37 Marco Mantova Benavides, 1489-1582 (Table K4)

2074.M44 Sebastiano Medici, d. 1595 (Table K4)

2074.M87 Pedro Murillo Velarde, 1696-1753 (Table K4)

2074.P37 Flaminicus Parisius, d. 1603 (Table K4)

2074.P38 Pietro Maria Passerini, 1594-1677 (Table K4)

2074.P39 Melchior Adam Pastorius, 1624-1702 (Table K4)

2074.P55 Giacomo Pignatelli, 1625-1698 (Table K4)

2074.P57 Francesco Pitoni, d. 1729 (Table K4)

2074.R55 Giovanni Lorenzo Riganti, 1661-1735 (Table K4)

2074.R56 Giovanni Domenico Rinaldi, 1628-1713 (Table K4)

2074.R64 Guglielmo Rodano, d. 1573 (Table K4 modified)

2074.R64A3-.R64A39 Individual works. By title
Including unannotated and annotated editions, translations, particular manuscript editions, and textual criticism

Tractatus de spoliis ecclesiasticis see KBR3374

2074.R65 Nicolas Rodriguez Hermosino, 1605-1669 (Table K4 modified)

2074.R65A3-.R65A39 Individual works. By title
Including unannotated and annotated editions, translations, particular manuscript editions, and textual criticism
e.g. Tractatus primus criminalium

Sources
Canonists and jurists
By period
1545 (Council of Trent) to 19th century
By nationality
Italian, Spanish, and Portuguese
Individual canonists and jurists (commentators)
Other jurists, A-Z -- Continued

2074.S36 Tomás Sanchez, 1550-1610 (Table K4 modified)

2074.S36A3-.S36A39 Individual works. By title
Including unannotated and annotated editions, translations, particular manuscript editions, and textual criticism
De Sancto matrimonii scramento disputationum Tomi I see KBR3110.A7+

2074.S37 Mauro Sarti, 1709-1766 (Table K4)

2074.S43 Giovanni Giacomo Scarfontoni, 1674-1748 (Table K4)

2074.S56 Diego Simancas, d. 1583 (Table K4)

2074.S59 Brunoro a Sole, 16th cent. (Table K4)

2074.S67 Domingo de Soto, 1494-1560 (Table K4)

2074.S73 Giovanni Stafileo, 1472-1528 (Table K4)

2074.S84 Francisco Súarez, 1548-1617 (Table K4)

2074.T66 Giacomo Filippo Tomasini, 1595-1655 (Table K4)

2074.U77 Domenico Ursaya, fl. 1729 (Table K4)

2074.V45 Gabriel de Vega, 16th/17th cent. (Table K4)

2074.V55 Francisco Torreblanca Villalpando, d. 1645 (Table K4)

2074.V74 Guiseppe Vredi, d. 1698 (Table K4)

2074.Z33 Francesco Antonio Zaccaria, 1714-1795 (Table K4)

German and Austrian
Cf. KJA2075+ Roman law

2075 General works

2077 Collections. Compilations. Selections

Individual canonists and jurists (commentators)

2077.3 Augustin von Alveldt, 16th cent. (Table K3)

2077.7 Jacob Ayrer, fl. 1593-1603 (Table K3)

2079 Justus Henning Böhmer, 1674-1749 (Table K3)
Cf. KJA2079 Roman law

2079.3 Georg Ludwig Böhmer, 1715-1797 (Table K3)

2079.5 Heinrich Canisius, 1548-1610 (Table K3 modified)

KBR

Sources
Canonists and jurists
By period
1545 (Council of Trent) to 19th century
By nationality
German and Austrian
Individual canonists and jurists (commentators)
Heinrich Canisius, 1548-1610 -- Continued

2079.5.A3A-.A3Z Individual works. By title, A-Z
Including unannotated and annotated editions, translations, particular manuscript editions, and textual criticism
e.g. Summa iuris canonici

2082.4 Ludwig Engel, d. 1674 (Table K3 modified)

2082.4.A3A-.A3Z Individual works. By title, A-Z
Including unannotated and annotated editions, translations, particular manuscript editions, and textual criticism
e.g. Universum jus canonicum

2094 Johann Gottlieb Heineccius, 1681-1741 (Table K3)
Cf. KJA2094 Roman law

2098.4 Paul Laymann, 1574-1635 (Table K3 modified)

2098.4.A3A-.A3Z Individual works. By title, A-Z
Including unannotated and annotated editions, translations, particular manuscript editions, and textual criticism
Quaestiones canonicae de praelatorum ecclesiasticorum electione ... see KBR2775

2098.5 Heinrich Linck, 1642-1696 (Table K3 modified)

2098.5.A3A-.A3Z Individual works. By title, A-Z
Including unannotated and annotated editions, translations, particular manuscript editions, and textual criticism
e.g. Commentarius in Decretales

2114 Christian Thomasius, 1655-1728 (Table K3)
Cf. KJA2114 Roman law

2115 Nicolaus Vigel, 1529-1600 (Table K3)
Cf. KJA2115 Roman law

2119 Kaspar Ziegler, 1621-1690 (Table K3 modified)

2119.A3A-.A3Z Individual works. By title, A-Z
Including unannotated and annotated editions, translations, particular manuscript editions, and textual criticism
e.g. Praelectiones publicae in Decretales

2119.5.A-Z Other jurists, A-Z

Sources
Canonists and jurists
By period
1545 (Council of Trent) to 19th century
By nationality
German and Austrian
Individual canonists and jurists (commentators)
Other jurists, A-Z -- Continued

2119.5.A66 Eusebius Amort, 1692-1723 (Table K4 modified)

2119.5.A66A3-.A66A39 Individual works. By title

Including unannotated and annotated editions, translations, particular manuscript editions, and textual criticism

e.g. Elementa juris canonici veteris et moderni

2119.5.A72 Valerius Andreas, 1588-1655 (Table K4)

2119.5.K55 Melchior Kling, 1504-1571 (Table K4)

2119.5.L47 Peter Leuren, 1646-1723 (Table K4 modified)

2119.5.L47A3-.L47A39 Individual works. By title

Including unannotated and annotated editions, translations, particular manuscript editions, and textual criticism

e.g. Forum ecclesiasticum

2119.5.P53 Vitus Pichler, 1670-1736 (Table K4)

2119.5.P56 Ehrenreich Pirhing, b. 1606 (Table K4 modified)

2119.5.P56A3-.P56A39 Individual works. By title

Including unannotated and annotated editions, translations, particular manuscript editions, and textual criticism

e.g. Jus canonicum in V libros decretalium, distributum

2119.5.R43 Anaklet Reiffenstuel, 1642 or 3-1703 (Table K4)

2119.5.S35 Franz Schmalzgrueber, 1663-1735 (Table K4)

2119.5.S36 Franz Schmier, 1680-1728 (Table K4 modified)

2119.5.S36A3-.S36A39 Individual works. By title

Including unannotated and annotated editions, translations, particular manuscript editions, and textual criticism

e.g. Jurisprudentia canonico-civilis

Dutch

Cf. KJA2120+ Roman law

2120 General works

2122 Collections. Compilations. Selections

Individual canonists and jurists (commentators)

2122.7 Arnoldus Corvinus, d. ca. 1680 (Table K3)

Cf. KJA2122.7 Roman law

2131 Gerardus van Aalst Schouten (Table K3)

Sources
Canonists and jurists
By period
1545 (Council of Trent) to 19th century
By nationality
Dutch
Individual canonists and jurists (commentators) -- Continued
2138.5.A-Z Other jurists, A-Z
Subarrange each by Table K4
Particular forms of contemporary legal literature
Including auxiliary literature
Dictionaria. Vocabularia see KBR56
Directoria see KBR64
Formularia see KBR105.A+
Glossae. Apparatus
2139 General works
By jurist or title
see the jurist or title in the appropriate period
Summae. Summulae
2140 General works
By jurist or title
see the jurist or title in the appropriate period
Rubricae
2141 General works
2141.5 Collections. Compilations. Selections (General)
By individual jurist or title
see the jurist or title in the appropriate period, e. g.
Rubricae sive summae capitulorum iuris canonici, see KBR1925.N36
Lecturae. Commenta. Commentaria. Repetitiones
2142 General works
2142.3 Collections. Compilations. Selections (General)
Primum volumen Repetitionum diuersorum doctorum in iure canonico ... including: Repertorium seu tabula Hieronymi de marliano ...
By individual jurist or title
see the jurist or title in the appropriate period
Additiones
2142.5 General works
By jurist or title
see the jurist or title in the appropriate period
Quaestiones. Distinctiones. Observationes
2143 General works
By jurist or title
see the jurist or title in the appropriate period

Sources
Particular forms of contemporary legal literature -- Continued
Decisiones and conclusiones of the Rota Romana auditores (S.R.R. decisiones dominorum auditorum) see KBR42+
Allegationes see KBR2145+
Dissensiones. Disputationes
2144 General works
By jurist or title
see the jurist or title in the appropriate period
Consilia. Responsa
Including allegationes and including all periods
2145 General works
2147 Collections. Compilations. Selections (General)
Including consilia collections of both Roman and canon law
2150.A-Z Individual canonists and jurists (commentators), A-Z
Including individual and collected consilia of an individual author
2150.A23 Francesco Accolti, 1416 or 17-1488 (Table K4)
2150.A42 Andrea Alciati, 1492-1550 (Table K4)
2150.A43 Silvestro Aldobrandini, 1499-1558 (Table K4)
2150.A96 Martin de Azpilcueda, 1492?-1586 (Table K4)
2150.B45 Gilles de Bellemère, 1342 or 3-1407 (Table K4)
2150.B46 Niccolò Bellone, d. 1552 (Table K4)
2150.B47 Giuseppe Bertacchini, fl. 1698 (Table K4)
2150.B65 Lodovico Bolognini, 1446-1508 (Table K4)
2150.B68 Giovanni Botta (Table K4)
2150.B78 Johann Brunneman, 1608-1672 (Table K4)
2150.B87 Antonius de Butrio, 1338-1408 (Table K4)
Cf. KJA2150.B87 Roman law
2150.C66 Antonio Concioli, 17th cent. (Table K4)
2150.D42 Giuseppe De Rosa, 1617-1671 (Table K4)
2150.D43 Filippo Decio, 1454-1536 or 7 (Table K4)
2150.D45 Giacomo del Pozzo (Puteus), 1508-1563 (Table K4)
2150.E74 Cesare Erione, b. 1767 (Table K4)
2150.F37 Prospero Farinacci, 1554-1618 (Table K4)
2150.F47 Giambattista Ferreti, 16th cent. (Table K4)
2150.G53 Hieronymus Giacharius, 16th cent. (Table K4)
2150.G54 Girolamo Giganti, d. 1560 (Table K4)
2150.G56 Orazio Giovagnoni, d. 1624 (Table K4)
2150.G58 Ludovico Giunti, 1529-1602 (Table K4)
2150.G73 Jacobus de Graffiis, 1548-1620 (Table K4)
2150.G88 Juan Gutierrez, d. 1618 (Table K4)
2150.L33 Guy de la Pape, ca. 1402-ca. 1487 (Table K4)
2150.M46 Giacomo Menochio, 1532-1607 (Table K4)
2150.M96 Joachim Mynsinger von Frundeck, 1514-1588 (Table K4)

Sources
Particular forms of contemporary legal literature
Consilia. Responsa
Individual canonists and jurists (commentators), A-Z -- Continued

2150.N48 Niccolò, de' Tudeschi, Archbishop, 1386-1445 (Table K4)
2150.N5 Alessandro Nievo, d. 1484 (Table K4)
2150.N66 Thobias Nonius, 1528-1570 (Table K4)
2150.O43 Oldrado da Ponte, d. 1335 (Table K4)
Cf. KJA2150.O43 Roman law
2150.O64 Giovanni Vincenzo Ondedeo, d. 1603 (Table K4)
2150.P33 Pietro Pacioni, 17th cent. (Table K4)
2150.P35 Michelangelo Paleoli, b. ca. 1710 (Table K4)
2150.P36 Pier Paolo Parisio, 1473-1545 (Table K4)
2150.P37 Prospero Pasetti, 16th cent. (Table K4)
2150.P54 Pietro d'Ancarano, 1330-1416 (Table K4)
2150.P55 Giacomo Pignatelli, 1625-1698 (Table K4)
Carmine Tommaso Pascucci (1653-1701), Compendium et index ad consultationes canonicas D. Iacobi Pignatelli
2150.P73 Simon de Praetis (Table K4)
2150.R35 José Ramón, 17th cent. (Table K4)
2150.R43 Pierre Rebuffi, 1487-1557 (Table K4)
2150.R49 Johann Daniel Reyser, 1640-1712 (Table K4)
2150.R58 Gianfrancesco Riva di San Nazarro, d. 1535 (Table K4)
2150.R63 Francesco Rocco, 1605-1676 (Table K4)
(2150.R68) Gianantonio Rossi, 1489-1544
see KJA2150.R673
2150.R85 Carlo Ruini, 1456-1530 (Table K4)
2150.S26 Felino Maria Sandeo, 1444-1503 (Table K4)
2150.S37 Marcantonio Savelli, 17th cent. (Table K4)
2150.S38 Ludolf Schrader, 1531-1589 (Table K4)
2150.S39 Hieronymus Schurff, 1480-1554 (Table K4)
2150.S45 Federico Scotti, 1522-1590 (Table K4)
2150.S52 Johannes Sichardt, 1499-1552 (Table K4)
2150.S54 Lorenzo Silvano, 16th cent. (Table K4)
2150.S58 Mariano Socini, 1482-1556 (Table K4)
2150.S59 Brunoro a Sole, 16th cent. (Table K4)
2150.S63 Giovanni Battista Spada, 1597-1675 (Table K4)
2150.T46 Jakob Thoming, 1524-1576 (Table K4)
2150.T67 Cristoforo Torniola, fl. 1547-1590 (Table K4)
2150.T673 Fabio Torretti, d. 1595 (Table K4)
2150.T73 Francesco Antonio Tranchedini (Table K4)
2150.T74 Alessandro Trentacinque, d. 1599 (Table K4)
2150.U23 Baldo degli Ubaldi, 1327?-1400 (Table K4)
2150.U73 Giuseppe Urceoli, d. 1698 (Table K4)

Sources
Particular forms of contemporary legal literature
Consilia. Responsa
Individual canonists and jurists (commentators), A-Z -- Continued

2150.V33 Juan Bautista Valenzuela Velázquez (Table K4)
2150.V34 Thomé Vallasco, 1553-ca. 1612 (Table K4)
2150.V35 Rolandus a Valle, 16th cent. (Table K4)
2150.V39 Alvaro Vaz, 1526-1593 (Table K4)
2150.V47 Giovanni Maria Vermiglioli, 1570-1657 (Table K4)
2150.W36 Johannes Wamesius, 1524-1590 (Table K4)
Cf. KJA2150.W36 Roman law
2150.W47 Matthaeus Wesenbeck, 1531-1586 (Table K4)
2150.Z33 Francesco Zabarella, 1360-1357 (Table K4)
2150.Z34 Paolo Zacchia, 1584-1659 (Table K4)

Differentiae
2150.5 General works
2151.A-Z By jurist or title, A-Z
2151.B37 Bartolo, of Sassoferrato, 1313-1357 (Table K4)
De differentiis inter ius canonicum et ius civile
2151.C36 Heinrich Canisius (1548-1610) (Table K4)
De differentiis iuris canonici et civilis, 1594
2151.D43 Ioannes de Molina (Table K4)
Tractatus differentiarum inter ius canonicum et regium

Brocardica see KBR100.A+

Casus literature
Including casūs longi and casūs breves decretalium
2151.5 General works
2152.A-Z By jurist or title, A-Z
2152.C3 Casus papales, episcopales et abbatiales, 1477-80
2152.C32 Casus summarii Decretalium (Casūs breves Decretalium Sexti Clementinorum)

Repertoria. Inventaria. Repertories. Inventories. Indexes
2153 General works

KBR

Sources
Particular forms of contemporary legal literature
Repertoria. Inventaria. Repertories. Inventories. Indexes -- Continued
2153.5.A-Z Comprehensive repertories, indexes, etc. By jurist or title, A-Z
Class here repertories, indexes, etc. of broad application, i.e. covering more than one particular author, work, or period
Including repertories on both canon and Roman law
For repertories of a particular author, or on a particular work, see the author or title in the appropriate period. For example, for Martinus Polonus, d. 1279, Margarita see KBR1749.6; for Baldo degli Ubaldi, 1327?-1400, Margarita see KBR1784; for Lucas Panaetius, Repertorium Novellarum Joannis Andree see KBR1775.A4A+ for Bérenger Frédol, d. 1323, Inventarium Speculi iudicialis see KBR1748.A4A+ for Antonio Corsetti, ca. 1450-1503, Repertorium in opera Nicolai de Tudeschis see KBR1798.5.A4A+ for Benedetto Vadi, 16th cent., Index ... in Felini Sandei Commentarios ad quinque Decretalium libros see KBR1925.S27A4+ for Repertorium locupletissimum in omnia opera ... Ioannis Francisci Ripae a S. Nazario see KBR1925.R58; for Index alphabeticus Commentariorum, Interpretationum, Tractus de peste, ac Responsorum ... Domini Ioann. Francisci de Ripa see KBR1925.R58; for Abbatis Panormitani repertorium ... Decretalium see KBR1798.5.A4A+
For indexes and vocabularies to the corpus iuris canonici see KBR1564+
2153.5.B47 Giovanni Bertachini, b. ca. 1448- (Table K4)
Repertorium iuris utriusque
Joannes Calderinus, d. 1365
Repertorium iuris see KBR1777.5
Guillaume Durand, ca. 1230-1296
Repertorium aureum iuris canonici see KBR1748
Joannes Nicolaus Milis, 15th century
Repertorium iuris see KBR1925.M5A3+
Exceptiones. Excerpta. Flores legum
2154 General works
By jurist or title
see the jurist or title in the appropriate period
2154.3 Compendia. Compends, syllabi, etc.

Sources
Particular forms of contemporary legal literature
Repertoria. Inventaria. Repertories. Inventories. Indexes -- Continued
2154.5 Penitentials
For early (pre-Tridentine) works, see the jurist or title in the appropriate period, e.g. KBR1660 , Raymond, of Peñafort, Saint, 1175?-1275; KBR1887 , Johannes, de Erfordia, ca. 1250-ca. 1325; KBR1887.3 , Johannes, von Freiburg, d. 1314; KBR1925.A78 , Astesano, d. 1330?; KBR1817 , Angelo Carletti, 1411-1495; etc.
Cf. KBR48 Poenitentiaria Apostolica (Penitentiary)
Cf. KBR3090+ Penitential discipline. Paenitentia
Cf. KBR3526+ Penal (Criminal) law
Canon law compared with other religious legal systems see KB162+
Canon law and other disciplines or subjects
2155 Canonical jurisprudence and theology. Law and gospel
Cf. BT79 Doctrinal theology
2155.2 Canon law and moral theology. Casuistry. Cases of conscience, etc.
Cf. BJ1188+ Religious ethics
2155.4 Canonical jurisprudence and general philosophy
Canon law and education see KBR3050+
2156 Canon law and criminal law
2157 Canon law and social legislation
Canonical jurisprudence. Canonical science
Class here comprehensive theoretical works on system and doctrinal development of Canon law, including contemporary and recent criticism on such works
For works on the Ius canonum of a particular period, and on authors or category of literature, see the period, author, or type of literature
For studies on sources in general see KBR190+
General works
2160.A-Z English and North American jurists, A-Z
Including Canadian jurists
2162.A-Z French and Belgian jurists, A-Z
2162.A63 Jean Francois André, 1809-1881 (Table K4)
2162.A65 Michael André, 1803-1878 (Table K4)
2162.B37 Michel Bargilliat, 1853-1926 (Table K4)
2162.B66 Dominique Bouix, 1808-1870 (Table K4)
Tractatus de principiis juris canonici (1853)
2162.B73 Pierre de Brabandere, 1828-1895 (Table K4)
Juris canonici et juris canonico-civilis compendium ... (1903)
2162.G68 Thomas M.J. Gousset, 1792-1866 (Table K4)

Canonical jurisprudence. Canonical science
General works
French and Belgian jurists, A-Z
Thomas M.J. Gousset, 1792-1866 -- Continued
Exposition des principes du droit canonique, 1859
2162.I33 Henri Joseph Icard, 1805-1893 (Table K4)
2162.T37 Adolphe Francois Lucien Tardif, 1824-1890 (Table K4)
Italian jurists
2163 A - Gasparri
2163.A75 Filippo de Angelis, 1824-1881 (Table K4)
2163.A76 Joseph d'Annibale, d. 1892 (Table K4)
2163.C36 Joseph de Camillis, 1828-1860 (Table K4)
2164 Pietro Gasparri, 1852-1934 (Table K3)
2165 Gasparri - Nardi
2165.G46 Casimiro Gennari, 1839-1914 (Table K4)
2165.L66 Carlo Lombardi, d. 1908 (Table K4)
2165.L83 Mariano de Luca, d. 1904 (Table K4)
2166 Francesco Nardi, 1808-1877 (Table K3)
2167 Nardi - Z
2167.N52 Laurentius Vigilius de Nicollis, d. 1745. Praxis canonica (Table K4)
2167.S43 Guglielmo Sebastianelli, d. 1920 (Table K4)
2167.V43 Septimio Vecchiotti, d. 1870 (Table K4)
2170.A-Z Spanish and Portuguese jurists, A-Z
Including Central and South American jurists
2170.D66 Iusto Donoso-Silva, d. 1868 (Table K4)
German jurists
Including Austrian and Swiss jurists
2172 A - Friedberg
2172.B56 Anton Joseph Binterim, 1779-1855 (Table K4)
2172.E53 Karl Friedrich Eichhorn, 1781-1854 (Table K4)
2172.F44 Hans Erich Alfred Feine, 1890-1965 (Table K4)
2173 Emil (Albert) Friedberg, 1837-1910 (Table K3)
2174 Friedberg - Kahl
2174.H56 Paul Hinschius, 1835-1898 (Table K4)
2177 Wilhelm Kahl, 1849-1932 (Table K3)
2178 Kahl - Phillips
2178.L34 Hugo Laemmer, 1835-1918 (Table K4)
2178.P47 Franz Michael Permaneder, 1794-1862 (Table K4)
2179 Georg Phillips, 1804-1872 (Table K3)
2180 Phillips - Sohm
2180.R52 Ämilius Ludwig Richter, 1808-1864 (Table K4)
2180.S35 Johann Friedrich von Schulte, 1827-1914 (Table K4)
2180.S43 Emil Seckel, 1864-1924 (Table K4)
2182 Rudolf Sohm, 1841-1917 (Table K3)
2183 Sohm - Z
2183.S89 Ulrich Stutz, 1868-1938 (Table K4)

Canonical jurisprudence. Canonical science
General works
German jurists
Sohm - Z -- Continued
2183.T54 Augustin Theiner, 1804-1874 (Table K4)
2185.A-Z Dutch jurists, A-Z
2185.B47 Henricus van den Berghe, b. 1848 (Table K4)
2185.F49 Hendrik Jan Feye, 1820-1894 (Table K4)
2185.V47 Arthur Vermeersch, 1858-1936 (Table K4)
2188.A-Z Other nationals, A-Z
Subarrange each by Table K4
The concept of law
2189 General works
2189.2 Authority
2189.4 Conciliar principle
Effectiveness of law. Validity and nullity of law see KBR2196
Sources and relationships of canon law
Class here theoretical treatises on the source (legal foundation) of Canon law
For particular sources or groups of sources, as well as works on a specific source see KBR190+
2190 Natural law and divine law. Canonical tradition. Ius naturale et ius divinum. Canonica traditio
Cf. K440+ Early Christian natural law
Canons and constitutions. Canones et constitutiones
2191 General works
2191.2 Apostolic constitutions and canons. Decretals (Constitutiones et canones apostolorum. Litterae decretales, constitutiones apostolicae, etc.)
2191.3 Conciliar canons and decrees (Jus canonum)
Including conciliar/synodal canons and decrees of the provincial councils and synods
For particular sources or groups of sources, as well as works on a specific source see KBR190+
2192 Custom. Consuetudo
2196 Validity, nullity, and effectiveness of law
Applicability (Territorial and temporal) of laws
2197 General works
2199.A-Z Conflict of laws. By topic, A-Z
2199.C59 Civil law
e. g. Hagemeier, De auctoritate iuris civilis et canonici (1663)
Ius civile see KBR2199.C59
Methodology
2200 General works
2202 Legal hermeneutics. Interpretation and construction

Canonical jurisprudence. Canonical science
Methodology -- Continued
2203 Legal semantics. Legal language
Particular schools
2204 General works
2204.3 Anglo-Norman school
2204.5 Rhenish school
Influence of other legal systems on Canon law
2205 General works
2206 Roman law. Civil law (Reception)
2206.3 Germanic law
2207 Law reform and policies. Criticism
2208.A-Z General concepts and principles, A-Z
Ius ecclesiasticum privatum
Persons. De personis
2224 General works
Natural persons. De personis physicis
2225 General (Table KB2)
2226 Birth. Birth rights
Including primogeniture
Baptism and church membership. De baptismo et eius effectu
2227 General (Table KB2)
2229.A-Z Special topics, A-Z
2229.A54 Age
Change (Transfer) to another ritual church see KBR2229.R57
2229.C55 Children. Infantes
e. g. Ascription to Latin Church
Choice of rites see KBR2229.R57
Conversion to another ritual church see KBR2229.R57
Infantes see KBR2229.C55
2229.N38 Natus
Patrini see KBR3079
2229.R57 Rites
Including choice and change of rites, e. g. to conjugal rites; children of mixed marriages, etc.
Ritus see KBR2229.R57
Sponsores see KBR3079
Legal capacity and incapacity
2231 General (Table KB2)
2232.A-Z Special topics, A-Z
2232.D42 Death
Infans (non sui compos) see KBR2232.I65
2232.I65 Infants (under seven years of age)
2232.I67 Insanity

Ius ecclesiasticum privatum
Persons. De personis
Natural persons. De personis physicis
Legal capacity and incapacity
Special topics, A-Z -- Continued
2232.M35 Majority
2232.M56 Minority
Quintiliano Mandosio (d. 1593), Tractatus de aetate minori
Persona maior see KBR2232.M35
Persona minor see KBR2232.M56
Pubertas see KBR2232.P83
2232.P83 Puberty, Age of
Legal acts and facts affecting persons
Domicile. Quasi-domicile. Domicilium. Quasi-domicilium
Including residents, temporary residents and travelers (incolae, advenae, and peregrini)
2235 General (Table KB2)
2236.A-Z Special topics, A-Z
2236.C55 Children (Place of origin)
Including illegitimate or poshhumous children
2236.D56 Diocesan domicile
Domicilium coniugale see KBR2236.S66
Domicilium dioecesanum see KBR2236.D56
Domicilium paroeciale see KBR2236.P37
Domicilium tutoris vel curatoris see KBR2236.T87
Filii (Locus originis) see KBR2236.C55
2236.F86 Funeral
Cf. KBR3190+ Ecclesiastical funeral rites
2236.I67 Institutes (Religious), Members of
2236.P37 Parochial domicile
Sepultura see KBR2236.F86
Sodales institutorum religiosorum see KBR2236.I67
2236.S66 Spouses, Domicile of
2236.T87 Tutor or curator, Domicile of
Consanguinity. Consanguinitas (Cognatio naturalis)
2237 General (Table KB2)
Giovanni d'Andrea. Super arboribus consanguinitatis see KBR1775
2238 Lineage and degree. Linea. Gradus
Including direct line (linea recta) and collateral line (linea obliqua; linea transversa), and computatio graduum
Cf. KBR1775 Giovanni d'Andrea (ca. 1270-1348), Super arboribus consanguinitatis
2239.A-Z Special topics, A-Z

Ius ecclesiasticum privatum
Persons. De personis
Natural persons. De personis physicis
Legal acts and facts affecting persons
Consanguinity. Consanguinitas (Cognatio naturalis)
Special topics, A-Z -- Continued
Adoptio see KBR2243
2239.C65 Cognatio legalis
2239.C66 Cognatio spiritualis
2239.I55 Illegitimacy
Gabriele Palotti, 1524-1597. De nothis spuriisque filiis
Affinity. Affinitas
Including lineage and computation of degrees
2240 General (Table KB2)
2242 By valid marriage. Matrimonium validum (Copula carnalis)
2243 Adoption. Adopted children. Adoptio. Filii adoptivi
Including adoptio perfecta (arrogatio) and adoptio imperfecta
Guardian and ward. Tutor. Curator
Including guardianship over minors and adults with mental disabilities
2245 General (Comparative)
2246.A-Z Special topics, A-Z
Inheritance and succession. Successio mortis causa
Including testate and intestate succession
2248 General (Comparative)
Testamentary succession. Last will. Testamentum. Ultima voluntas
2249 General (Comparative)
Testaments of the clergy. Facultas testandi clericorum see KBR3360+
2250.A-Z Special topics, A-Z
Juristic persons. De personis iuridicis
2253 General works
2254 Legal personality. Personalitas iuridica
Including juristic persons of public law and private law, i.e. by law, decree or statute
Collegiate juristic persons. Corporations. Universitas personarum
2256 General (Table KB2)
2257 Collegial acts, elections, etc. Actus collegiales, electiones, etc.
Associations. De christifidelium consociationibus
Including universal (international) and national organizations

Ius ecclesiasticum privatum
Persons. De personis
Juristic persons. De personis iuridicis
Collegiate juristic persons. Corporations. Universitas personarum
Associations. De christifidelium consociationibus -- Continued
2260 General (Table KB2)
2262 Public associations. Juristic persons of public law. Consociationes publicae. Personae iuridicae publicae
Including erection, statutes, administration, etc.
2266 Private associations. Juristic persons of private law. Consociationes privatae. Personae iuridicae privates
Including personalitas iuridica, and including erection, statutes, administration, etc.
2271.A-Z Special topics, A-Z
Non-collegiate juristic persons (Aggregate of property and resources). Universitas rerum
2273 General (Table KB2)
2276.A-Z Particular kinds of juristic persons, A-Z
2276.C53 Charitable uses, trusts, and foundations. Endowments
2280 Extinction. Division. Dismemberment
2282 Perpetuity
Legal transactions. De actibus iuridicis
2286 General (Comparative)
Validity. Void and voidable transactions. Validas actus iuridici
2288 General (Table KB2)
2290 Error. Ignorance
2292 Fraud. Duress. Necessity. Dolus. Vis. Metus gravis
2293 Consent or counsil. Consensus et consilium alicuius
2294 Liability. Damages. Obligatio dammum illatum reparandi
2295 Computation of time. Supputatio temporis
Including tempus continuum, tempus utile (available) and spatium (period)
Constitution of the Church
2310 General (Table KB2)
Obligations and rights of the Christian faithful. De obligationibus et iuribus christifidelium
2312 General works
2314.A-Z Special topics, A-Z
Support of the Church see KBR3384+
Obligations and rights of the laity. De obligationibus et iuribus laicorum

KBR

Constitution of the Church
Obligations and rights of the laity. De obligationibus et iuribus laicorum -- Continued
2316 General (Table KB2)
2318.A-Z Special topics, A-Z
The Clergy. The hierarchical order. De Ministris Sacris seu de Clericis. Hierarchia ordinis
Cf. BX1930+ Catholic Church
2320 General (Table KB2)
Formation, education of clerics. Institutio clericorum
2322 General (Table KB2)
2324 Seminaries and other institutions. Seminaria. Institutiones sacerdotales
2328 Administration and governance of the seminaries. Rectors and directors
Disporitiones ad ordines. Prerequisits
2329 Prima tonsura
Ordination. Sacra ordinatio
2330 General works
2331 Incapacity and irregularity. Irregularitas (Table KB2 modified)
Including irregularitas ex defectu and ex delicto
2331.A7-.Z79 General works
e.g. Simeone Maiolo (ca. 1520-1597?), De irregularitatibus et aliis canonicis impedimentis
2332 Title. Titulus
Including titulus beneficii, patrimonii, and titulus pensionis
Cf. KBR2357 Typology of benefices, etc.
Incardination of clerics. Adscriptio seu incardinatio clericorum
Including incardination to a particular church, personal prelature, religious institute or society of apostolic life
2333 General (Table KB2)
2334 Excardination of clerics. Excardinatio
Rights and obligations of clerics. De iuribus et oneribus clericorum
2336 General (Table KB2)
Legal status. Status clericalis
2337 General works
Praecedentia and praeeminentia iurisdictionis see KBR2355+
2338.A-Z Particular obligations, A-Z
2338.B74 Breviary, Praying of
2338.C45 Celibacy
2338.C53 Chastity
Ecclesiastical privileges and immunities. Privilegia clericalia. Immunitas a iure civili

Constitution of the Church
The Clergy. The hierarchical order. De Ministris Sacris seu de Clericis. Hierarchia ordinis
Incardination of clerics. Adscriptio seu incardinatio clericorum
Ecclesiastical privileges and immunities. Privilegia clericalia. Immunitas a iure civili -- Continued
2339 General (Table KB2)
2340.A-Z Special topics, A-Z
2340.P75 Privilegium canonis
2340.P76 Privilegium competentiae
2340.P77 Privilegium fori
2340.P78 Privilegium immunitatis
2342 Personal prelatures. De prelaturis personalibus
Loss of clerical state. Amissio status clericalis
2344 General (Table KB2)
2346.A-Z Special topics, A-Z
Ecclesiastical offices and benefices in general. De officiis ecclesiasticis et beneficiis
Including res temporales and res spirituales
Cf. BX1955 Catholic Church
2350 General (Table KB2 modified)
2350.A7-.Z79 General works
e.g. Carlo Gagliardi, 1710-1779. De beneficiis ecclesiasticis commentarius; Giovanni Battista de Luca, 1614-1683. Commentaria ad Constitutionem ... de statuariis successionibus ...: accedit De pensionibus ecclesiasticis; Nicolaus Garcia, d. 1645. Tractatus de beneficiis amplissimus; Pierre Grégoire, 1540-1617. Institutiones breves et nouae rei beneficiariae ecclesiasticae; Francisco Sarmiento de Mendoza, d. 1595. De reditibus ecclesiasticis; Paolo Sarpi, 1552-1623. Trattato delle materie beneficiarie; Ulrich Stutz. 1868-1938. Geschichte des kirchlichen Benefizialwesens von seinem Anfaengen bis auf die Zeit Alexanders III
Giovanni Battista Caccialupi, d. 1496. De pensionibus tractatus see KBR1802
Martin de Azpilcueda, 1492?-1586. Apologia libri de reditibus ecclesiasticis (Tractado de las rentas de los beneficios ecclesiasticos) see KBR1875
François Douaren, 1509-1559 see KBR1970.5
Pierre Rebuffi, 1487-1557. Praxis beneficiorum see KBR1847
2351 Erection. Creatio
2352 Incompatibility. Officia incompatibilia (Table KB2 modified)

Constitution of the Church
Ecclesiastical offices and benefices in general. De officiis ecclesiasticis et beneficiis
Incompatibility. Officia incompatibilia -- Continued
2352.A7-.Z79 General works
e.g. Alonso Hojeda de Mendoza, fl. 1579. De beneficiorum incompatibilitate atque compatibilitate tractatus
Rank and honors. De dignitatibus ecclesiasticis
2355 General (Table KB2)
Maioritas and ius praecedentiae
2356 General (Table KB2 modified)
2356.A7-.Z79 General works
e.g. Michael Manrique Ferro. Tractatus de praecedentiis et praelationibus ecclesiasticis; Andreas Jakob Crusius, 1636-1680. De praeeminentia, sessione, praecedentia ...; Jacques Godefroy, 1587-1652. De iure praecedentiae
Barthelemy de Chasseneuz, 1480-1541. Catalogus gloriae mundi see KBR1989.5.C53
2357 Typology of benefices, prebends, pensions, etc. Beneficia, praebenda, pensiones, etc.
Changes and loss of ecclesiastical office. Innovatio and amissio officii ecclesiastici
Including division (dismemberment), transfer (translatio, remotio), resignatio (renuntiatio), etc.
2358 General (Table KB2 modified)
2358.A7-.Z79 General works
e.g. Fatinellus de Fatinellis, 1627-1719. Tractatus de translatione pensionis (Cf. KBR3615.A+ Penalties peculiar to the clergy)
Gilles de Bellemere, 1342 or 3-1407. Tractatus de permutatione beneficiorum see KBR1787
Accumulation of benefices or prebends. Pluralitas beneficiorum
2359 General (Table KB2 modified)
2359.A7-.Z79 General works
Giovanni, da Legnano, d. 1383. De pluralitate beneficiorum ecclesiasticorum see KBR1786.6
Johann Freiberger, ca. 1470-1541. De pluralitate beneficiorum see KBR1895.5
Union and incorporation of benefices
2360 General (Table KB2 modified)
2360.A7-.Z79 General works
e.g. Iustus Richard Foesser. De unione speciatim de incorporatione beneficiorum; D. Lindner. Die Lehre von der Inkorporation in ihrer geschichtlichen Entwicklung

Constitution of the Church
Ecclesiastical offices and benefices in general. De officiis ecclesiasticis et beneficiis
Union and incorporation of benefices
General
General works -- Continued
Giovanni Battista Caccialupi, d. 1496. De unionibus ecclesiarum [et] beneficio[rum] tractatus see KBR1802
Patronage. Ius patronatus (reale and personale)
Cf. KBR4032 Church and feudal institutes
2361 General (Table KB2 modified)
2361.A7-.Z79 General works
e.g. Tractatus de iure patronatus clarissimorum omnium V.I.C. qui hactenus ... tractarunt materiam; Francois de Roye, d. 1686. Ad titulum de ivre patronatvs libro tertio. Eivsdem De ivribus honorificis in ecclesia; Carlo Gagliardi, 1710-1779. De jure patronatus commentarius; Ulrich Stutz, 1868-1938. Ausgewaehlte Kapitel aus der Geschichte der Eigenkirche und ihres Rechtes; Joern Sieglerschmidt. Territorialstaat und Kirchenregiment: Studien zur Rechtsdogmatik des Kirchenpatronatsrechts im 15. und 16. Jahrhundert
Hincmar, Archbishop of Reims, ca. 806-882. Collectio de ecclesiis et capellis see KBR1292
2362 Foundation (creation). Fundatio. Aedificatio. Dotatio (Table KB2)
Typology
Including ius patronatus ecclesiasticum (clericale), ius patronatus laicale, ius patronatus gentilitium (Family patronage), etc.
2362.2 General works
2362.4 Ius patronatus regium. Patronage of the state
Including secularization
Cf. KBR4043 Secularization
2362.6 Right of presentation. Praesentatio
2362.7 Extinction
Organs of government. Hierarchy. De ecclesiae constitutione hierarchica
Cf. BX1800+ Catholic Church
2363 General works

Constitution of the Church
Organs of government. Hierarchy. De ecclesiae constitutione hierarchica -- Continued
2364 Power of governance. Jurisdiction. De potestate regiminis. Hierarchia iuridictionis
Including potestas regiminis legislativa, executiva and iudicialis (external and internal fora); including delegation of powers (Potestas delegata, subdelegata), and further, extinction of powers (extinctio potestatis) by fulfillment of mandate, cessation, revocation, expiration, suspension, etc.
The Pope. The Roman Pontiff
Cf. BX1805+ Catholic Church
2366 General works
Primacy (Supremacy). Primatus jurisdictionis. Authority and jurisdiction
Including metropolitan and diocesan authority
2367 General works
e. g. Friedrich B.C. Maassen, 1823-1900. Der Primat des Bischofs von Rom und die alten Patriarchalkirchen. Geschichte der Hierarchie
Particular powers, rights, and privileges
Cf. BX1810 Catholic Church
Cf. KBR4000+ Church and state
2368 General (Comparative)
2370 Privileges. Honors. Primatus honoris
Legislative power. Potestas legislativa
2372 General works
2373.A-Z Special topics, A-Z
2375 Judicial and administrative powers. Potestas iudicialis. Potestas exsecutiva
2377 Treaty making power
For foreign and international relations of the Holy See see KBR4076+
2380 Convocation of an ecumenical council. Convocatio. Praesidium
Including agenda, transfer, suspension, dissolution of the council and approval of decrees
2383 Right to nominate legates. Ius legatos nominandi
2384 Power to dispose of episcopates and dioceses
2384.3 Confirmation and suspension of religious orders
2385 Granting of benefices
2386 Tax power
2390 Election. Election procedures. Enthronement (Table KB2)
2392 Vacancy of the Holy See
Including abdication

Constitution of the Church
Organs of government. Hierarchy. De ecclesiae constitutione hierarchica -- Continued
2412 Cardinalium Collegium. The College of Cardinals
Cf. BX1815 Catholic Church
The Curia Romana
Cf. BX1818+ Catholic Church
2420 General works
e.g. Dominique Bouis (1808-1870). Tractatus de Curia Romana, seu de Cardinalibus, Romanis Congrationibus, legatis, nuntiis, vicariis et protonotariis; Giovanni Battista De Luca (1614-1683), Tractatus de officiis venalibus vacabilibus Romanae Curiae; Formularium Procuratorum et Advocatorum Curiae Romanae see KBR105.F67
Particular tribunals and offices
Cancellaria Apostolica. Apostolic Chancery
Cf. BX1872 Catholic Church
2430 General (Table KB6 modified)
2430.A18 Constituent law and rules governing the organization. By date
e.g. Regulae, ordinationes, et constitutiones Cancellarie; Liber cancellariae apostolicae
Signatura gratiae see KBR2445
2435 Dataria Apostolica. Apostolic Datary (Table KB6)
Cf. BX1875 Catholic Church
Paenitentiaria Apostolica
Cf. BX1862 Catholic Church
General see KBR3812
Decisions see KBR48
Rota Romana
Cf. BX1865 Catholic Church
General see KBR3816
Signatura Apostolica see KBR3819+
2445 Signatura gratiae (Table KB6)
2455 Camera Apostolica. Apostolic Chamber. Treasury (Table KB6)
Cf. BX1878 Catholic Church
Secretaria Status. Secretariate of State
Cf. BX1881 Catholic Church
2470 General (Table KB6)
2477 Secretaria Literarum ad Principes (Memorialium). Secretariate of Briefs to Princes (Table KB6)
Cf. BX1884 Catholic Church
2480 Secretaria Literarum Latinarum. Secretariate of Latin Letters (Table KB6)
Cf. BX1887 Catholic Church

Constitution of the Church
Organs of government. Hierarchy. De ecclesiae constitutione hierarchica
The Curia Romana
Particular tribunals and offices -- Continued
Papal legates. Legati. Nuntii. Vicarii apostolici. Missi apostolicae sedis
Including permanent or temporary missions, e. g. legates to councils or church provinces, etc., and including all periods to ca. 1900
Cf. BX1908 Catholic Church
2482 General (Table KB6)
Particular see KBR4070
Roman congregations
Class here pre-Tridentine congregations established after the Tridentium
Cf. BX1820+ Catholic Church
2500 General works
Suprema Congregatio Sanctae Romanae et Universalis Inquisitionis. Supreme Congregation of the Holy Roman and Universal Inquisition (1542-1908)
2502 General (Table KB6)
2507.A-Z Special topics, A-Z
Congregatio Indicis. Congregation of the Index (1571 to 1917)
2511 General (Table KB6)
Index librorum prohibitorum see Z1020+
2513.A-Z Special topics, A-Z
Congregatio de Propaganda Fide pro Negotiis Ritus Orientalis (Congregatio super Correctione Librorum Ecclesiae Orientalis)
2515 General (Table KB6)
2515.5 Collectanea S.C. de Propaganda Fide, 1893, 1907
<2545> Congregatio Sacrorum Rituum (1588-1969)
see KBU2545+
<2555> Congregatio pro Episcopis
see KBU2555+
Congregatio super Consultationibus Regularium. Congregation for Consultations about Regulars (1586-1601)
Incorporated in 1601 into the Congregation pro consultationibus episcoporum et aliorum praelatorum
2570 General (Table KB6)
2572.A-Z Special topics, A-Z
Congregatio super Consultationibus Episcoporum et Aliorum Praelatorum. Congregation for Consultations about Bishops and other Prelates

Constitution of the Church
Organs of government. Hierarchy. De ecclesiae constitutione hierarchica
The Curia Romana
Roman congregations
Congregatio super Consultationibus Episcoporum et Aliorum Praelatorum. Congregation for Consultations about Bishops and other Prelates -- Continued
2575 General (Table KB6)
2577.A-Z Special topics, A-Z
Congregatio Episcoporum et Regularium. Congregation of Bishops and Regulars
2580 General (Table KB6)
2582.A-Z Special topics, A-Z
Congregatio Consistorialis (Congregatio pro Erectione Ecclesiarum et Provisionibus Consistorialibus). Congregation of the Consistory (1588)
2585 General (Table KB6)
2587.A-Z Special topics, A-Z
Congregatio Signaturae Iustitiae
2589 General (Table KB6)
2591.A-Z Special topics, A-Z
Congregatio Ceremonialis. Congregation of Ceremonies (1588)
2593 General (Table KB6)
2595.A-Z Special topics, A-Z
Congregatio Visitationis Apostolicae. Congregation of the Visitation (1592)
2610 General (Table KB6)
2612.A-Z Special topics, A-Z
<2635> Congregatio de Propaganda Fide
see KBU2635+
<2640> Congregatio Concilii (Congregatio Cardinalium Concilii Tridentini Interpretum) (to 1967)
see KBU2640+
<2660> Congregatio pro Universitate Studi Romani (1588-1908)
see KBU2668+
<2668> Congregatio Studiorum (1824-1908)
see KBU2668+
2674 Congregatio super Disciplina Regulari and super Statu Regularium (Table KB6)
2676 Congregatio Iurisdictionis et Immunitatis Ecclesiasticae (Table KB6)
2678 Congregatio Indulgentiarum et Sacrarum Reliquiarum (Table KB6)

Constitution of the Church
Organs of government. Hierarchy. De ecclesiae constitutione hierarchica
The Curia Romana
Roman congregations -- Continued
2680 Congregatio pro Negotiis Ecclesiasticis Extraordinariis (Table KB6)
2682 Congregatio Reverendae Fabricae Basilicae (Sancti Petri) (Table KB6)
2683 Congregatio Boni Regiminis (Table KB6)
Commission of cardinals
Cf. BX1890+ Catholic Church
2730 General (Table KB6)
2732.A-Z Particular commissions, A-Z
2775 Praelati Curiae Romanae. Prelatures (Table KB6)
Paul Laymann (1574-1635), Quaestiones canonicae de praelatorum ecclesiasticorum electione ...
Other offices or organizations of the Curia Romana
2778 Capella papalis (Table KB6)
Particular churches and groups of churches. De ecclesiis particularibus
Cf. BX1905 Catholic Church
2790 General works
Territorial division and episcopal jurisdiction
2792 Bishops in general. Episcopate and apostolate. De episcopis in genere
Including appointment, promotion, privileges, resignation, etc.
Ecclesiastical Provinces. Ecclesiastical Regions. Provinciae ecclesiasticae. Regiones ecclesiasticae
2796 General works
2798 Juristic personality. Personalitas iuridica
Organization and organs
2800 General (Comparative)
Metropolitans. De metropolitis
Including titles (patriarch or primate)
2803 General (Table KB2 modified)
Cf. KBR2000 Sources
2803.A7-.Z79 General works. Treatises
e.g. Antonio Augustin, 1517-1586. De Pontifice Maximo; De Patriarchis & Primatibus, De Archiepiscopis & Metropolitanis
2805 Jurisdiction. Powers, rights, privileges, etc.
Including prerogatives of honor
2807 The Metropolitan See. Sedes metropolitana
Including vacancy (de sede vacante)

Constitution of the Church
Organs of government. Hierarchy. De ecclesiae constitutione hierarchica
Particular churches and groups of churches. De ecclesiis particularibus
Territorial division and episcopal jurisdiction
Ecclesiastical Provinces. Ecclesiastical Regions. Provinciae ecclesiasticae. Regiones ecclesiasticae -- Continued
Regional and national councils, synods, etc.
For sources see KBR833+
2810 General works
2815 Plenary council. Concilium plenarium
2820 Provincial council. Concilium provinciale
e. g. Dominique Bouix, 1808-1870. Tractatus de concilio provinciali
Conference of Bishops (Episcopal conference). Conferentia episcoporum
For sources see KBR935+
Cf. BX837.5 Catholic Church
2825 General works
2827 Juristic personality. Personalitas iuridica
2829 Statute. President, etc. Statuta. Praeses, etc.
2830 Legislative power. Potestas legislativa
2832 Vote (deliberative and consultative). Suffragium deliberativum aut consultativum
Dioceses and diocesan bishop. Dioceses. Episcopus dioecesanus
2835 General (Comparative)
2837 Legislative, executive and judicial power. Potestas legislativa, exsecutiva vel iudicialis
2839 Residence. Residentia personalis in dioecesi
2840 Episcopal visitation. Visitatio episcopalis
Auxiliaries
2844 Coadjutor bishop. Auxiliary bishop. Episcopus coadiutor et episcopus auxiliaris
2846 Vacant or impeded episcopal see. De sede vacante et de sede impedita
Diocesan constitution and organs
Including territorial organization (partes seu paroeciae)
Cf. BX1911 Catholic Church
2850 General works
Diocesan synods see KBR2878+
Diocesan curia. Curia diocesana
Including administrative and judicial officers
For sources see KBR950+
2852 General works

Constitution of the Church
Organs of government. Hierarchy. De ecclesiae constitutione hierarchica
Particular churches and groups of churches. De ecclesiis particularibus
Territorial division and episcopal jurisdiction
Dioceses and diocesan bishop. Dioceses. Episcopus dioecesanus
Diocesan constitution and organs
Diocesan curia. Curia diocesana -- Continued
2854 Vicars general. Episcopal vicars. Vicarii generales vel episcopales (Table KB2 modified)
2854.A7-.Z79 General works
e.g. Giacomo Sbrozzi, 16th cent. Tractatus de vicario episcopi
2856 Chancellor and vice-chancellor. Notaries. Cancellarius and vice-cancellarius curiae. Notarii
2857.A-Z Particular offices, A-Z
2865 Presbyterate. Priests. Presbyterium. Sacerdotes
2868 Vicars forane. Vicarii foranei
2870 Seminary rectors. Rectores seminarii dioecesani
2872 Parish and pastor. Parochial vicar. Paroecia et parochus. Vicarius paroecialis
2874 Rectors of churches. Chaplains. Rectores ecclesiarum. Capellani
Diocesan councils, synods, etc.
Cf. KBR950+
2878 General (Table KB2)
2880 The diocesan synod. Synodus dioecesana
e.g. George Phillips, 1804-1872. Die Dioecesansynode
2882 The presbyterial council. Pastoral councils. Consilium presbyteriale. Consilium pastorale
2884 Chapter of canons (Cathedral or collegial). Capitulum canonicorum (cathedrale sive collegiale)
Including erection, statutes, chapter authority, etc.
Personnel of churches and ecclesiastical institutes
Cf. BX1919 Catholic Church
Cf. KBR3432+ Administration of church property
2886 General (Table KB2)
The clergy
2888 General works
Benefices. Prebends. Pensions, etc. of the clergy see KBR2350+
Officials and employees other than the clergy

Constitution of the Church
Organs of government. Hierarchy. De ecclesiae constitutione hierarchica
Personnel of churches and ecclesiastical institutes
Officials and employees other than the clergy -- Continued
2890 General works
2891 Wages. Mercedes iusta
Monasticism. Institutes of consecrated life and societies of apostolic life. De institutis vitae consecratae et de sociatatibus vitae apostolicae
Including religious institutes and societies of common life without public vows
Cf. Secular eccleasiastical law in K subclasses, e. g. KK5538+; KJV4244; KJ-KKZ1 2698+; etc.
For history see BX2460+
Erection. Founders. Constitutions (fundamental codes). Erectio. Fundatores. Constitutiones (codices fundamentales)
2892 General (Table KB2)
2893 Status of institutes. Clerical or lay institute. Institute of pontifical or diocesan right. Institutum clericale, laicale. Institutum iuris pontificii. Institutum iuris dioecesani
Jurisdiction. Governance (external and internal forum). Potestas regiminis (pro foro tam externo quam interno)
Cf. BX2433+ Catholic Church
2894 General works
2895 Exemption from jurisdiction of local ordinaries. Ab Ordinariorum loci regimine exemptio
2896 Equality of sexes. Quae statuuntur, pari iure de utroque sexu valent
2897 Division. Merger and unions of institutions. Divisio in partes. Fusiones et uniones
Religious institutes. Religious houses. Monasteris. De institutis religiosis
Including erection, consent of diocesan bishop, obligations and rights of the institute, etc.
2899 General (Table KB2)
Society and membership. Religious community. Societas. Sodales. Communitas religiosa
2902 General works
2903 Separation of members from the institute. Separatio sodalium
Including transitus, exclaustratio, dimissio, etc.

KBR

Constitution of the Church
Monasticism. Institutes of consecrated life and societies of apostolic life. De institutis vitae consecratae et de sociatatibus vitae apostolicae
Religious institutes. Religious houses. Monasteris. De institutis religiosis -- Continued
2906 Autonomy. Governance. Autonomia vitae et regiminis
For monastic rules see BX2436+
2908 Autonomous monasteries. Monasteria sui iuris
2909 Community (society) of persons without vows. Societas sine votis
Governance of institutes. De institutorum regimine
2912 General (Table KB2)
Superiors. Councils. Supreme moderators. Superiores. Consilia. Supremus Moderator
Including appointment, election, term (temporis spatium), removal, residence, etc.
2914 General (Table KB2)
2915 Major superior. Abbot primate. Superior maior. Abbas Primas
Including jurisdiction
2916 Provinces (Grouping and governance of several houses). Provinciae (plurium domorum coniunctio)
Chapters. Capitula
Including organs (organa) and authority
2918 General (Table KB2)
2919 General chapter. Capitulum generale
2920 Conferences of Major superiors. Conferentiae seu concilia
Temporal goods. Bona temporalia see KBR3370
Novitiate. Admission and formation of novices. Novitiatus. Admissio et novitiorum institutio
2922 General (Table KB2)
2923.A-Z Special topics, A-Z
2924 Public vows. Vota publica (perpetua vel temporaria)
Cf. BX2435 Monastic life. Vows. Discipline, etc.
2925 Secular institutes. De institutis saecularibus
2927.A-Z Special topics, A-Z
Castitas see KBR2927.C53
2927.C53 Chastity
2927.D69 Dowery
2927.M46 Membership. Admission into religious association
2927.O34 Obedience
Oboedientia see KBR2927.O34
Paupertas see KBR2927.P68
2927.P68 Poverty

Constitution of the Church
Monasticism. Institutes of consecrated life and societies of apostolic life. De institutis vitae consecratae et de sociatatibus vitae apostolicae
Religious institutes. Religious houses. Monasteris. De institutis religiosis
Special topics, A-Z -- Continued
2927.P75 Privileges
<2930-2978> Individual orders of men
see KBU2930+
<2980-3026> Individual orders of women
see KBU2980+
The teaching office of the church. Magisterium. De ecclesiae munere docendi
3040 General (Table KB2)
3046 Heresy and apostasy (Definition). Haeresis pertinax. Apostasia
Cf. KBR3628+ Penal (Criminal) law
3048 Catechetics and preaching. Catechetica. Dei verbum predicatio
Education and training of the clergy see KBR2322+
3049 Missionary activity. Actio ecclesiae missionalis
Education (General). Catholic religious education. Educatio catholica religiosa
3050 General (Table KB2)
3052 Right to establish and supervise schools. Ius ecclesiae scholas condendi ac moderandi
3054 Catholic universities. Institutions of higher education. Universitates catholicae. Studiorum superiorum instituta
3060 Ecclesiastical universities and faculties. Universitates vel facultates ecclesiasticae
Literature. Publishing and censorship
Including books in particular, newspapers, periodicals, etc. (In specie de libris)
Cf. BV4730 Prohibited books
Cf. KBR2511+ Congretatio Indicis
Cf. KBR3656+ Prohibited books
3064 General (Table KB2)
3068.A-Z Special topics, A-Z
3068.C46 Censors. Censorship
Commissio censorum see KBR3068.C46
Commission of censors see KBR3068.C46
3068.D46 Denunciation of bad books
Index librorum prohibitorum see Z1020+
Prohibited books see KBR3064+
3070 Profession of faith. Fidei professio

KBR

Sacraments. Administration of sacraments. De sacramentis et administratione
3075 General (Table KB2)
Cf. BX2200 Catholic Church
Baptism. De baptismo
Including adults and infants
Cf. BX2205 Catholic Church
3077 General (Table KB2)
3079 Sponsor. God parent. Patrinus
3082 Proof and records. Registration. De probatione et adnotatione. Regesta baptizatorum
Including registration of adopted children or those born of an unwed mother
Confirmation. De sacramento confirmationis
Cf. BX2210 Catholic Church
3083 General (Table KB2)
3084.A-Z Special topics, A-Z
The Most Holy Eucharist. Holy Communion. Lord's Supper. De Sanctissima Eucharistia
Cf. BX2215+ Catholic Church
3085 General (Table KB2)
Celebration of the mass
Including observation of rites, e.g. liturgical and communion rites
3087 General (Table KB2)
3088 Particular masses
e.g. Nuptial mass
Penance. Penitential discipline. De sacramento paenitentiae
Including sacramental confession
Cf. BX2260+ Catholic Church
3090 General (Table KB2)
3092 Sacremental seal. Sacramentale sigillum
3094.A-Z Special topics, A-Z
3094.I64 Indulgences
The Anointing of the Sick. De sacramento unctionis infirmorum
Cf. BX2292 Catholic Church
3096 General (Table KB2)
3098.A-Z Special topics, A-Z
Holy Orders. De ordine
Including episcopacy, presbyterate, and diaconate
Cf. BX2240 Catholic Church
3102 General (Table KB2)
3104 Candidate for ordination. Requirements. Prerequisites. Candidatus. De requisitis in ordinandis. De praerequisitis ad ordinationem
Irregularities and other impediments see KBR2331

Sacraments. Administration of sacraments. De sacramentis et administratione
Holy Orders. De ordine -- Continued
3106 Documents. Examination. Testimonial. Documenta requisita. Scrutinium de qualitatibus. Testimonium
3107 Registration and certification of ordination. adnotatio ac testimonium peractae ordinationis
Marriage. Marriage law. De matrimonio
For secular marriage law (civil law), see the K subclasses for individual countries
For marital property and regime see KBR3113
For matrimonial actions see KBR3885+
3109 General works
Class here comprehensive and comparative works on all periods of canon law
By period
Early to mid-16th century
see the canonist in the appropriate period, e. g. Tancred, ca. 1185-1236? Summa de matrimonio, KBR1696; Bernhard, of Pavia. Summa de matrimonio, KBR1700
3110 1545 (Council of Trent) to 1900 (Table KB2 modified)
3110.A7-.Z79 General works
e.g. Tomás Sanchez, 1550-1610. De Sancto matrimonii sacramento Disputationum Tomi II
1900- see KBU3110
Sponsalia. Promissio matrimonii. Betrothal. Promise of marriage
Including validitas sponsaliorum
3112 General (Table KB2 modified)
3112.A7-.Z79 General works
Joannes de Anguissola. De sponsalibus see KBR1774
Giovanni d'Andrea, ca. 1270-1348. De sponsalibus et matrimoniis see KBR1775
3112.2 Typology
3113 Antenuptial contracts. Marriage settlements
Including dower, marital property, dowry (dos), etc.
3114 Ratification and consummation. Matrimonium ratum et consummatum (Table KB2)
Unity. Indissolubility. Unitas. Indissolubilitas see KBR3155+
3116 Canon law and civil jurisdiction. Ius canonicum et competentia civilis potestatis
For matrimonial actions see KBR3889
3117 Marriage banns. Premarital examinations. Bannus nuptialis (Edicta matrimonialia). De examine sponsorum (Table KB2)
Impediments to marriage. Impedimenta matrimonii

Sacraments. Administration of sacraments. De sacramentis et administratione
Marriage. Marriage law. De matrimonio
Impediments to marriage. Impedimenta matrimonii -- Continued
3120 General works (Table KB2)
3121 Typology
3122.A-Z Mere prohibitive impediments. Impedimenta prohibentia (impedientia), A-Z
3122.C46 Censure
Matrimonium filii minoris see KBR3122.M56
Matrimonium vagorum see KBR3122.T73
3122.M56 Minor without parental consent
3122.T73 Transients
Diriment impediments. Impedimenta dirimentia
3124 General works
3128.A-Z Particular impediments, A-Z
3128.A34 Abduction. Detention of a woman
3128.A39 Adultery
Aetas see KBR3128.M37
Affinitas in linea recta see KBR3128.A44
3128.A44 Affinity (direct line)
Including adoption
Cf. KBR2240+ Canon law
Age of consent see KBR3128.M37
3128.B66 Bond, Existing
Child marriage see KBR3128.M37
3128.C66 Consanguinity (direct line and collateral line)
Cf. KBR2237+ Canon law
Constituti in sacris ordinibus see KBR3128.O74
3128.C85 Cult, Disparity of
Cultus disparitas see KBR3128.C85
3128.D87 Duress
3128.E77 Error
3128.H66 Homicide. Uxoricide
3128.I66 Impotence (antecedent and perpetual)
Impotentia see KBR3128.I66
3128.L55 Ligamen
Linea recta and linea collatoralis consanguinitatis see KBR3128.C66
3128.M37 Marriage age
Mors coniugis see KBR3128.H66
3128.O74 Holy orders
Raptus. Retentio mulieris see KBR3128.A34
Vinculum prioris matrimonii see KBR3128.B66
Vis. Metus see KBR3128.D87
Vota publica perpetua castitatis see KBR3128.V69

Sacraments. Administration of sacraments. De sacramentis et administratione
Marriage. Marriage law. De matrimonio
Impediments to marriage. Impedimenta matrimonii
Diriment impediments. Impedimenta dirimentia
Particular impediments, A-Z -- Continued
3128.V69 Vows of chastity, Public perpetual
3130 Dispensation from impediments. Dispensatio ab impedimentis (Table KB2)
Including local ordinary (ordinarius loci) and Holy See
3131 Rehabilitation. Revalidatio (Rehabilitatio) matrimonii
Including revalidatio ordinaria, and sanatio in radice
Matrimonial consent. Contract. Mutuus consensus. Contractus
3132 General (Table KB2)
Validity of consent. Consensus validus (Validitas sponsaliorum)
3133 General (Table KB2)
3134 Incapable persons. Incapaces matrimonii contrahendi
3135 Ignorance. Error in persona. Fraud. Duress. Ignorantia. Error in persona. Dolus. Metus gravis. Vis
3136 Conditions. Condiciones
Including conditions de futuro, de praeterito vel de praesente
3138 Emergency celebration. Deathbed marriage
3140 Invalid consent. Invalid marriage. Consensus invalidus. Matrimonium irritum
Including putative marriage (matrimonium putativum), defect of consent (defectum consensus), defect of form (defectum formae), and diriment impediment (impedimentum dirimens)
Performance of marriage. Celebration. De forma celebrationis matrimonii
Including marriage celebrants
3144 General (Table KB2)
Defects of form see KBR3140
3145 Witnesses. Testes
3146 Marriage registers. Regesta matrimoniorum
Including registration of death of a spouse, or divorce, and entry in the baptismal register of spouses (regesta baptizatorum)
Interfaith marriage. Mixed marriages. De matrimoniis mixtis
3148 General (Table KB2)
3150 Children of mixed marriages. Filii e matrimonio mixto nati

KBR

Sacraments. Administration of sacraments. De sacramentis et administratione
Marriage. Marriage law. De matrimonio
Performance of marriage. Celebration. De forma celebrationis matrimonii -- Continued
Clandestinity of marriage celebration. Clandestinitas. Clandestina coniugia
3152 General (Table KB2 modified)
Statutes. Papal constitutions. Treaties and concordats. Decrees. Privileges, etc.
3152.A4 Tam Etsi decree
3153 Morganatic marriages. Marriages of royalty and nobility
Marriage bond. Vinculum inter coniuges perpetuum et exclusivum. Husband and wife
Including right and duty to conjugal living (officium et ius servandi convictum coniugalem)
3155 General (Table KB2)
3157 Children. Presumption of legitimacy. Legitimi praesumuntur filii
Including legitimization by subsequent marriage
Dissolution of the bond. De dissolutione vinculi
Including non-consummated marriage or non-baptized parties (privilegium Paulinum)
3159 General (Table KB2)
3160 Remarriage. Ius novas nuptias contrahendi
Separation of the spouses. De separatione coniugum
3163 General (Table KB2)
3165 Adultery and condonation. Adulterium. Condonatio (Table KB2)
Including tacit condonation
Sacramentals. Sacramentalia
Including the right to establishing, interpreting and abolishing sacramentals
Cf. BX2295+ Catholic Church
3180 General (Table KB2)
3181 Consecrations. Dedications
3182.A-Z Particular sacramentals, A-Z
Other acts of divine worship. De ceteris actibus Cultus Divini
3184 Liturgy of the hours. Observation. Obligatio liturgiae horarum
Including obligation to celebrate the liturgy by clerics and members of institutes of consecrated life and societies of apostolic life
Cf. BX1970+ Catholic Church
Ecclesiastical funeral rites. Exequiae ecclesiasticae
For burial and cemetery laws of a particular jurisdiction, see the appropriate K subclasses
3190 General (Table KB2)

Other acts of divine worship. De ceteris actibus Cultus Divini
Ecclesiastical funeral rites. Exequiae ecclesiasticae -- Continued
3192 Granting or denying funeral rites. Exequiae ecclesiasticae concedendae aut denegandae
3193 Registration of internment. Inscriptio in librum defunctorum
3194.A-Z Special topics, A-Z
Veneration of Saints, sacred images, and relics. Cultus sanctorum, sacrarum imaginum et reliquiarum
Cf. BX2325+ Catholic Church
3200 General (Table KB2)
3202 Veneration through public cult. Veneratio cultu publico
Including permission of display, and other regulations
3204 Regulations concerning images valuable because of age, art or cult. Imagines pretiosae (vetustate, arte, aut cultu)
Including restoration of art works and removal (transfer)
For alienation (sale, auction, exchange, etc.) see KBR3332+
Vow and oath. Votum et iusiurandum
3210 General principles concerning vows
Including attributes of vows, e. g. public, solemn, simple, personal (real or mixed), etc.
3212 Suspension of obligation of vows. Potestas voti obligationem suspendendi
3214 Dispensation from private vows. Dispensandi potestas
3218 General principles concerning oaths
3220 Obligation from the oath. Obligatio iureiurando inducta
Including cesstion of obligation because of change of conditions, purpose, circumstances, etc.
3225 Dispensation or commutation of oath. Iurisiurandi dispensatio et commutatio
Sacred places and times. De locis et temporibus sacris
Sacred place. Loca sacra
Including decoration, furnishings, utensils, etc.
3230 General (Table KB2)
3232 Performance of dedication and blessing. Dedicatio vel benedictio
Including documentation of the event
3234 Violation of destruction of sacred places. Violatio per actiones graviter iniuriosas. Destructio
Including loss of dedication or blessing by decree or de facto
3236 Place and right of asylum
3238.A-Z Particular buildings, structures, etc., A-Z
Altaria sive fixa sive mobilia see KBR3238.A58
3238.A58 Altars (fixed or movable)

Other acts of divine worship. De ceteris actibus Cultus Divini
Sacred places and times. De locis et temporibus sacris
Sacred place. Loca sacra
Particular buildings, structures, etc., A-Z -- Continued
3238.C46 Cemeteries
3238.C53 Chapels, Private
3238.C58 Churches
Coemeteriae see KBR3238.C46
Ecclesiae see KBR3238.C58
Oratoria see KBR3238.O73
3238.O73 Oratories
3238.R45 Relics
Reliquiae Martyrum aliorumve Sanctorum see KBR3238.R45
Sacella privata see KBR3238.C53
Sanctuaria see KBR3238.S67
3238.S67 Shrines
Fasts and feasts (Church year). Tempora sacra
Including the right to establish, transfer, abolish feast days and days of penance
3242 General (Table KB2)
Sunday and other feasts. Dies dominica. Dies festi
3244 General (Table KB2)
3246.A-Z Particular feast days, A-Z
Days of penance. Dies et tempora paenitentialia
3250 General (Table KB2)
3252 Law of fast. Lex abstinentiae
3254 Processions. Pilgrimages (Table KB2)
Cf. BX2323+ Pilgrimages (Catholic Church)
Cf. BX2324+ Processions (Catholic Church)
3256.A-Z Special topics, A-Z
Social work of the Church. Public welfare. Caritas
Class here works on social service and welfare activities of the church, including work of religious and secular institutes, and societies of apostolic life
Cf. BV1120 Practical theology
Cf. KBR3460 Church property (Hospitals, etc.)
3264 General (Table KB2)
3270 Measures against contagious and infectious diseases
3273 Burials. Sepultura
3274.A-Z Public health hazards and measures, A-Z
3275.A-Z Particular institutions, A-Z
3275.H67 Hospitals and asylums
3275.O76 Orphanages
3280.A-Z Particular groups of people, A-Z
3280.A54 Aged. Older people
3280.E65 Epileptics

Social work of the Church. Public welfare. Caritas
Particular groups of people, A-Z -- Continued
3280.F73 Frail elderly
3280.I63 Incurables
3280.L46 Leprosy patients
3280.M46 Mentally ill
Older people see KBR3280.A54
3280.P46 People with disabilities
3280.P55 Pilgrims
3280.P66 Poor
3280.W37 War veterans, Disabled
Church property. Church economics and finance.
Administration
Cf. BV770+ Practical theology
3320 General (Table KB2)
Res sacrae. Res consecratae vel benedictae. Res extra commercium see KBR3405
Temporal goods of the Church. De bonis ecclesiasticis temporalibus
3328 General (Table KB2)
Acquisition and alienation of property. Acquisitio et alienatio bonorum
Including res mobiles and res immobiles
3332 General (Table KB2)
3340 Prescription
Gifts and legacies ad pias causas
Including donations mortis causa and inter vivos
3348 General (Table KB2)
Executor of pious wills see KBR3370
3350.A-Z Special topics, A-Z
3350.N69 Novices
3350.P76 Professed religious
Testaments. Testamenta. Ultima voluntas
3355 General (Table KB2)
3358 Change of last wills and testaments
Testaments of clerics. Testamenta clericorum
Including facultas testandi clericorum
3360 General (Table KB2)
3362 Peculium patrimoniale
Including bona patrimonialia (family property and inheritance), bona industrialia (earnings, stipends, donationes gratuitae, etc.), and bona parsimonialia (savings)
3364 Peculium clericale
Including bona ecclesiastica seu beneficialia
3366.A-Z Special topics, A-Z
Ius spolii see KBR3374

Church property. Church economics and finance.
Administration
Temporal goods of the Church. De bonis ecclesiasticis temporalibus
Acquisition and alienation of property. Acquisitio et alienatio bonorum
Testaments. Testamenta. Ultima voluntas
Testaments of clerics. Testamenta clericorum
Special topics, A-Z -- Continued
3366.S33 Sacra utensilia
3370 Executors of pius wills and gifts inter vivos
3374 Intestate succession and ius spolii of the Church
Guglielmo Rodano, d. 1573. Tractatus de spoliis ecclesiasticis
3378.A-Z Special topics, A-Z
Particular sources of revenue for support of the Church.
Church taxes
For state regulation of church taxation typical for a particular jurisdiciton, see the jurisdiction (Secular ecclesiastical law)
3384 General (Table KB2)
3386 Tithes. First fruit. Decimae clericales
3388 Cathedraticum
3390 Mass stipends
3392 Stole fees. Remuneration. Gratuities. Special levies. Stolae
Including stolae pro funeralibus
Privileges and immunities. Exemptions
Including taxes (immunitas realis), obligatory services (munera sordida), etc.
3400 General (Table KB2)
Secularization see KBR4043
3402.A-Z Special topics, A-Z
Types of property
3405 Res sacrae. Res consecratae vel benedictae. Res extra commercium
Guglielmo Rodano, d. 1573. De rebus Ecclesiae non alienandis
Real property. Land holdings (Church lands). Res immobiles
Including personal and real rights and claims (iura et actiones sive personales sive reales)
3410 General (Comparative)
3415 Restrictions
3417 Church buildings. Building and construction. Maintenance. Fabricae (Table KB2)
Including building laws

Church property. Church economics and finance.
Administration -- Continued
Administration and use of church property
Including organization (ecclesiastical organs), administrators and supervision
3432 General works
3440 Duties and obligations of administrators
Juristic (moral) persons and non-collegiate institutes
3450 General (Table KB2)
3452 Charitable uses, trusts, and foundations. Endowments. Fundationes piae. Fideicommissa
Other non-collegiate institutes
Including institutes owned, operated or supervised by the church
3456 General (Table KB2)
3458 Ecclesiastical benefices and other institutes. Beneficia ecclesiastica
Cf. KBR2350+ Ecclesiastical offices and benefices in general
3460 Loca pia. Hospitals. Orphanages. Schools, etc.
Cf. KBR3275.A+ Social work of the Church
Penal (Criminal) law. De lege poenali
3500 Bibliography
General works. By period
Class here comprehensive and comparative works on the development of penal law
Including general works on both penal law and penal (criminal) procedure
Early to mid 16th century
see the canonist in the appropriate period
3504 1545 (Council of Trent) to 19th century (Table KB2 modified)
3504.A7-.Z79 General works
e.g. Lega, Michele, 1860-1935
Penal laws and precepts. Applicability and validity
Including territorial and temporal applicability, and personal applicability (immunity)
3510 General (Table KB2)
3512 Poena latae sententiae (automatically incurred by law) and poena ferendae sententiae (by court decision)
3514 Ex post facto laws and retroactivity
Including appliction of the more favorable law or cessation of penalty
Classification of penal sanctions. Sanctiones poenales
3518 General (Table KB2)

Penal (Criminal) law. De lege poenali
Classification of penal sanctions. Sanctiones poenales -- Continued
Poenae medicinales. Medicinal penalties
Including poenae latae sententiae and poenae ferendae sententiae
3520 General works
Censures see KBR3604+
Poenae expiatoriae. Expiatory (vindictive) penalties
3522 General works
Particular penalties see KBR3611.2+
Remedia poenalis (Praecavenda). Paenitentia. Preventive penal remedies
3526 General (Table KB2)
Particular remedies see KBR3617.2+
Violation of law or precept. Criminal offense. Violatio legis vel praecepti
3533 General (Table KB2)
Imputability (Liability). Guilt. Dolus. Culpa
3537 General works
Incapacity. Delicti incapaces
3539 General works
3542 Insane persons. Qui rationis usu carent
3544 Minors under the sixteenth year of age. Minores
Justification of illegal acts. Exculpating or extenuating circumstances
3548 General (Table KB2)
3550 Necessity. Grave fear. Necessitas. Vis. Metus gravis
3552 Self-defense or defense of another. Legitimae tutelae causa contra iniustum agere
3553 Putative necessity
3554 Putative self-defense and exceeding self-defense. Sine debito moderamine
3555 Minors under the sixteenth year of age. Minores
3556 Limited capacity. Omissio debitae diligentiae
Incapacity see KBR3539+
3557 Ignorance about prohibition. Sine culpa ignorantia
3559.A-Z Special topics, A-Z
Aestus passionis, Gravis see KBR3559.D58
Affect see KBR3559.D58
3559.D58 Distemper. Passion. Affect
Ebrietas see KBR3559.I68
3559.I68 Intoxication
Passion see KBR3559.D58
3562 Error
Criminal act. Commission. Ommission. Actus vel ommissiones

Penal (Criminal) law. De lege poenali
Violation of law or precept. Criminal offense. Violatio legis vel praecepti
Criminal act. Commission. Ommission. Actus vel ommissiones -- Continued
3564 General (Table KB2)
3566 Attempt. Desistere ab incepta delicti exsecutione
Including active repentance, and inherently ineffective acts
Cf. KBR3590+ Causes barring execution
3570 Principals and accomplices. Auctores principales. Complices
Sentencing. Application of penalties. De poenis applicandis
3574 General (Table KB2)
Sentencing. Commensurateness of guilt and punishment
3576 General works
Judicial discretion
3577 General works
3578 Indeterminate penalty
Circumstances influencing measure of penalty
3580 General works
Exempting, aggravating and extenuating circumstances
3582 General works
3586.A-Z Special topics, A-Z
Causes barring execution
Including suspensive effect (effectus suspensivus) of appeal or recourse
3590 General (Table KB2)
3592 Active repentance
Including previous warning (admonition)
Cessation of penalties. Remission. Cessatio poenarum. Remissio poenae
3594 General works
3596 Power of remission. Potestas remittendi
Including reservation of the right
3598.A-Z Special topics, A-Z
Particular penalties and measures of rehabilitation. De poenis aliisque punitionibus
3600 Banishment. Bannum
Censures. De censuris
Including censurae iuris and censurae hominis
3602 General (Table KB2)
Excommunication. Effects of excommunication. Excommunicatio
Including excommunicatio minor and maior (Anathema)
3604 General (Table KB2)
3606.A-Z Special topics, A-Z
3606.A38 Absolution

Penal (Criminal) law. De lege poenali
Particular penalties and measures of rehabilitation. De poenis aliisque punitionibus
Censures. De censuris -- Continued
3607 Interdict. Effects of interdict. Interdictum (Table KB2)
Including interdictum locale and personale, and further interdictum generale and speciale
Suspension of clerics. Suspensio
Including suspensio ab ordine, ab officio, and a beneficio
3608 General (Table KB2)
3608.A-Z Special topics, A-Z
3609 Effect of suspension
Including suspensio totalis or specialis, and suspensio generalis or partialis
Expiatory (vindictive) penalties. De poenis expiatoriis
General see KBR3522
3612 Effects of expiatory penalties
3613.A-Z Common vindictive penalties, A-Z
3613.I53 Infamia. Infamy
3615.A-Z Vindictive penalties peculiar to the clergy, A-Z
3615.D43 Degradatio
3615.D45 Depositio
3615.P74 Privatio beneficii
3615.S94 Suspensio
3615.T73 Translatio pensionis
Penal remedies and penance. De remediis poenalibus et paenitentiis
General works see KBR3526
3618 Admonition and rebuke. Monitio vel correptio
3620.A-Z Special topics, A-Z
Individual offenses. De poenis in singula delicta
3625 General (Collective)
Including delicta mere ecclesiastica, delicta communia (laity and clergy), and delicta mixti fori or delicta mixta (civil and ecclesiastical jurisdiction)
Apostasy. The apostate. Apostasia a fide
3628 General (Table KB2)
3632.A-Z Special topics, A-Z
Heresy. The heretic. Haeresis formalis. Haeresis pertinax
3636 General (Table KB2)
3638.A-Z Special topics, A-Z
Schism. The schismatics. Schisma
3640 General (Table KB2)
3642.A-Z Special topics, A-Z
3644 Participation in forbidden rites. Idololatria
Including pagan (Germanic) rites
Superstition. Witchcraft. Sorcery. Superstitio

Penal (Criminal) law. De lege poenali
Individual offenses. De poenis in singula delicta
Superstition. Witchcraft. Sorcery. Superstitio -- Continued
3646 General (Table KB2)
3648.A-Z Particular offenses, A-Z
3648.A78 Astrologia iudiciaria
3648.M35 Magia superstitiosa seu diabolica
3648.N43 Necromantia
3648.P59 Phylacteria
3648.S67 Sortilegium
Blasphemy. Blasphemia
Including blasphemia haereticalis and simplex
3652 General (Table KB2)
3654.A-Z Special topics, A-Z
Publication of prohibited books
Cf. BV4730 Practical theology
Cf. KBR3064+ Literature, publishing
3656 General (Table KB2)
3658.A-Z Special topics, A-Z
Sacrilege. Sacrilegium (reale, personale, locale)
Including sacrilegium carnale
For delicta carnis (Offenses against morals) see KBR3752+
3660 General (Table KB2)
3662.A-Z Particular offenses, A-Z
3664 Profanation of the consecrated species. Abicere species consecratas (Table KB2)
3668 Perjury. Periurium (Table KB2)
Including iuramentum vanum and iuramentum iniustum
Offenses against ecclesiastical authorities. De delictis contra ecclesiasticas auctoritates
3670 General (Collective)
Offenses in connection with offices, benefices, or dignities see KBR3713
3696 Profanation of a movable or immovable sacred thing. Profanare rem sacram, mobilem vel immobilem (Table KB2)
3698 Alienation of ecclesiastical goods (Table KB2)
Abuse of ecclesiastical function or office. De munerum ecclesiasticorum usurpatione deque delictis in iis exercendis
Including abuse of ecclesiastical power
3700 General (Collective)
Simony. Simonia
Including simonia iuris divini and somonia iuris humani sive ecclesiastici
3709 General (Collective)

Penal (Criminal) law. De lege poenali
Individual offenses. De poenis in singula delicta
Abuse of ecclesiastical function or office. De munerum ecclesiasticorum usurpatione deque delictis in iis exercendis
Simony. Simonia -- Continued
3710 Simony in administration or reception of sacraments (Table KB2)
3711 Simony in connection with sacramentals
3713 Simony in connection with offices, benefices, or dignities (Table KB2)
3722 Solicitation or attempted bribe of officials in the Church
3724 Violation of the seal of confession. Violatio sacramentalis sigilli (Table KB2)
Falsehood. De crimine falsi
3730 General (Table KB2)
3734 Forgery and suppression of ecclesiastical documents
Including fabrication, change, or destruction of authentic documents, the use of false or altered documents, and including false statements made in public documents
Offenses of clerics or religious against particular obligations. De delictis contra speciales obligationes
3738 General (Collective)
3740 Unlawful trading or commerce by clerics or religious. Clerici vel religiosi mercaturam vel negotiationem exercentes contra canonum praescripta (Table KB2)
3742 Attempted marriage of a cleric. Clericus matrimonium, etiam civiliter tantum, attentans (Table KB2)
3744 Attempted marriage of a religious in perpetual vows. Religiosus a votis perpetuis, matrimonium etiam civiliter tantum, attentans) (Table KB2)
3746 Concubinage of a cleric. Clericus concubinarius (Table KB2)
3751 Other external sins (clericus in alio peccato externo) (Table KB2)
Including lewd acts, fornication, etc.
Offenses against human life, freedom and morals. De delictis contra hominis vitam et libertatem
3752 General (Collective)
Homicide. Delictum homicidii
3755 General (Table KB2)
3756 Abortion. Abortum procurare (Table KB2)
3759.A-Z Other offenses, A-Z
3759.D84 Dueling. Monomachia
3759.S85 Suicide. Suicidium
3759.T67 Torneamentum

Penal (Criminal) law. De lege poenali
Individual offenses. De poenis in singula delicta
Offenses against human life, freedom and morals. De delictis contra hominis vitam et libertatem -- Continued
3760 Abduction. Raptus (intuitu matrimonii vel explendae libidinis causa) (Table KB2)
Including abduction by violence and elopment
3762 Abduction of minors of either sex. Raptus impuberum alterutrius sexus (Table KB2)
Including abduction by force or deceit
3763 Slave trade. Delictum venditionis hominis (plagium) (Table KB2)
Including abduction by force or deceit
3764 Rape. Stuprum violentum (Table KB2)
3765 Detention. False imprisonment (fraudulently or with force). Hominem detinere (Table KB2)
3768 Mutilation. Assault and battery. Mutilare. Graviter vulnerare (Table KB2)
3770 Bigamy (Table KB2)
3774.A-Z Other offenses, A-Z
3774.A48 Adultery
3774.F67 Fornication
3774.I63 Incest
3774.L49 Lewd acts
3774.R63 Robbery. Rapina
3774.S64 Sodomy
Stuprum see KBR3774.L49
3774.U78 Usury
Judiciary. Ecclesiastical courts and procedure. De processibus
For works on both criminal law and criminal procedure see KBR3500+
3780 Bibliography
General works. By period
Early to mid 16th cent.
see the title or canonist in the appropriate period, e. g. KBR1600, Reymond, of Penafort, Saint, 1175?-1275. Summa de casibus poenitentiae; or KBR1925.A96, Johannes Auerbach (Urbach), fl. 1405. Processus judiciarius
3782 1545 (Council of Trent) to 19th cent. (Table KB2 modified)
3782.A7-.Z79 General works
e.g. Agostinho Barbosa, 1590-1649. De episcoporum Vicariis; Gomez Bayo, fl. 1627-1640. Praxis ecclesiastica, et secvlaris; Lega, Michele, 1860-1935

Judiciary. Ecclesiastical courts and procedure. De processibus -- Continued

Jurisdiction of ecclesiastical courts (General). The competent forum. De foro competente

Including forum externum and forum internum

For criminal jurisdiction see KBR3937

3784 Iurisdictio ordinaria vel delegata. Iurisdictio mandata

3785 Prorogation

Jurisdiction over persons or groups of persons

3786 The clergy

Including privilegium fori

3787.A-Z Other groups, A-Z

3787.C78 Crusaders

3787.I85 Itinerants

3787.J49 Jews

3787.P47 Personae miserabiles

Including widows, orphans, the poor, etc.

Competence in subject matter. Causae spirituales et spirituales annexae

3789 General (Table KB2)

3793 Actions concerning the administration of sacraments, vows, censures, elections, privileges, benefices and iuspatronatus, etc.

3795.A-Z Other subjects (causae civiles), A-Z

3795.C55 Children

3795.C66 Contracts (Breach of contracts)

Infantes see KBR3795.C55

3795.I66 Immobilia (Real rights)

Matrimonial actions see KBR3885+

3795.M63 Mobilia

3795.T47 Testaments

Venue. Place of court. Forum (commune or universale)

3797 General (Comparative)

3798 Particular fora

Including forum domicilii, forum rei sitae, forum contractus, etc.

3803 Judicial review of ecclesiastical administrative acts

3804 Conflict of jurisdictions. Conflictus competentiae inter tribunalia

Including civil and ecclesiastical courts

The tribunals. Court organization. De variis tribunalium gradibus et speciebus

General works see KBR3782

The tribunals (diocesan) of first and second instance. Tribunalia primae et secundae instantiae

Including single judge tribunals and collegiate tribunals

3806 General works

Judiciary. Ecclesiastical courts and procedure. De processibus
The tribunals. Court organization. De variis tribunalium gradibus et speciebus
The tribunals (diocesan) of first and second instance. Tribunalia primae et secundae instantiae -- Continued
Jurisdiction. Competence see KBR3783.92+
Judges and other court officials
Including officiales (officiales generales), vicarii, assessores, etc. and including iudices delegati
3807 General (Table KB2)
3807.5.A-Z Other, A-Z
3807.5.A39 Advocatus
3807.5.A93 Audientiarius
3807.5.A94 Auditor
3807.5.P76 Procurator
3807.5.R43 Receptor actorum
3807.5.R45 Registrator
The tribunals of the Apostolic See. Apostolicae Sedis tribunalia
3810 General works
The Sacred Penitentiary. Paenitentiaria Apostolica
Cf. BX1862 Catholic Church
3812 General (Table KB6)
3813 Jurisdiction. Competence (Forum internum)
3814.A-Z Special topics, A-Z
Rota Romana
Originally audientia sacri palatii
Cf. BX1865 Catholic Church
3816 General (Table KB6)
Ordo iudiciarius qui in Romana Curia consuevit
Stilus palatii see KBR105.A+
Dietrich von Nieheim (ca. 1340-1418), Stilus palatii abbreviatus see KBR105.N54
Judges and other court officials
Including auditores generales (causarum sacri palatii apostolici), coauditores, procuratores, advocati, etc.
3816.5 General works
For indexes of the decisions of Rotal auditors, with or without biographical notes see KBR43.A+
Formularium Procuratorum et Advocatorum Curiae Romanae see KBR105.F67
3817 Principles of collegiality
3817.3 Deliberating and voting. Secrecy. Legal opinions
3818 Court decorum. Court order. Proceedings
3818.5 Terms of court. Festa et ordo terminorum Sacri Palatii Apostolici

KBR

Judiciary. Ecclesiastical courts and procedure. De processibus
The tribunals. Court organization. De variis tribunalium gradibus et speciebus
The tribunals of the Apostolic See. Apostolicae Sedis tribunalia -- Continued
Tribunal of the Apostolic Signatura. Signatura Apostolica
Previously Signatura Justitiae
Cf. BX1868 Catholic Church
3819 General (Table KB6)
3820 Jurisdiction. Competence
The legal profession in general
3822 General works
3822.5 Legal education
Judges. Auditores. Advocates and procurators, etc.
3823 General (Comparative)
Judges and court officials at a a particular court
see the court, e. g. KBR3816.5
Notaries. Notarii
3823.5 General (Table KB2)
Formularium instrumentorum, necnon artis notariatus see KBR105.F64
Stil general des notaires apostoliques see KBR105.S85
3824.A-Z Special topics, A-Z
Procedural principles and court order. De disciplina in tribunalibus servanda
3825 Due process of law
3826 Speedy trial. De breviandis litibus
3827 Disqualification of judge or court officers. Conflict of interests
Including consanguinity, affinity, profit, etc.
3828.A-Z Other, A-Z
Deadlines see KBR3828.T56
Delays see KBR3828.T56
Dilationes see KBR3828.T56
Fatalia legis see KBR3828.T56
Iusiurandum de munere rite et fideliter implendo see KBR3828.O27
3828.O27 Oath of participants in trial
3828.O74 Order of adjudication (Docket)
Ordo terminorum see KBR3828.O74
3828.S43 Secrecy of office and deliberations
Termini see KBR3828.T56
3828.T56 Time. Deadlines. Delays
Parties to action. De partibus in causa
3830 General works
Juristic persons see KBR3833.J87

Judiciary. Ecclesiastical courts and procedure. De processibus
Parties to action. De partibus in causa -- Continued
Petitioner and respondent. Plaintiff and defendant. De actore et de parte conventa
3831 General works
Capacity to sue and to be sued
3832 General works
3833.A-Z Particular, A-Z
3833.J87 Juristic persons
Including legitimate representatives
3833.M56 Minors and people with mental disabilities
Including guardians and curators of such persons
People with mental disabilities see KBR3833.M56
Personae iuridicae see KBR3833.J87
3834 Procurators and advocates. Procuratores ad lites et advocati
Pretrial procedures see KBR3839.5
Actions and defenses. Exceptions. De actionibus et exceptionibus
3835 General works
3836 Joinder of actions
3837.A-Z Particular, A-Z
3837.C68 Counterclaim
Inhibitio exercitii iuris see KBR3837.S46
3837.L57 Lis pendens
Reconventio see KBR3837.C68
3837.R47 Res iudicata
3837.R48 Restraining order
Sequestratio see KBR3837.S46
3837.S46 Sequestration
The contentious trial. De iudicio contentioso
3838 General (Comparative)
Pretrial procedures
3839 Introductory petition. Libellus litis introductorius
Including form requirements
3839.5 Summons. Subpoena. Decretum citationis in iudicium
Procedure at first instance. Prima instantia
3840 General works
Jurisdiction. The competent forum
Including competence in subject matter and venue
3840.5 General works
3841.A-Z Special topics, A-Z
Actions and defenses. Exceptions. De actionibus et exceptionibus
3841.2 Joinder of actions
3841.3 Lis pendens
3841.5 Joinder of issue. Contestatio litis

Judiciary. Ecclesiastical courts and procedure. De processibus
The contentious trial. De iudicio contentioso
Procedure at first instance. Prima instantia -- Continued
3842.A-Z Particular proceedings, A-Z
3842.A33 Abatement of trial
Absens pars a iudicio see KBR3842.J84
3842.C53 Change of party
Including death
3842.I67 Intervention of third party
Interventus tertii in causa see KBR3842.I67
3842.J84 Judgment by default
Peremptum iudicium see KBR3842.A33
Settlement out of court see KBR3918
Evidence. Burden of proof. Probatio. Onus probandi
3843 General (Table KB2)
3844 Facts and presumptions. Facta et quae ab ipsa lege praesumuntur
Instrumenta probandi
3846 Declaration (testimony) of parties. Partium declarationes
Including party oath (iusiurandum partium de veritate dicenda) and judicial confession (confessio iudicialis)
3847 Documentary evidence. Probatio per documenta
3848 Witnesses. Testes et qui testes esse possint
Including capacity and incapables (incapaces) and including examination of witnesses (testium examen)
3849 Expert evidence. Experts. Periti
3850 Access and judicial inspection. Accessus et recognitio (inspectio) iudicialis
Presumptions see KBR3844
Incidental case (Causa incidens) see KBR3858
Intervention by third party see KBR3842.I67
Judicial decisions. Pronuntiationes iudicis
Including publication of decisions
3854 General (Table KB2)
3857 Sentences. Judgements. Sententiae definitivae
3858 Interlocutory decisions. Sententiae interlocutoriae
3859 Judicial decrees. Decreta iudicis
Judgement by default see KBR3842.J84
Remedies. De impugnatione sententiae
3861 General works
3863 Complaint of nullity. Querela nullitatis contra sententiam
3865 Appeal. Appellatio
3869 Res iudicata

Judiciary. Ecclesiastical courts and procedure. De processibus
The contentious trial. De iudicio contentioso
Procedure at first instance. Prima instantia -- Continued
3872 Restitutio in integrum
3874 Court costs. Expensae iudiciales
3876 Execution of sentence and executory decree. Exsecutio sententiae. Exsecutorium iudicis decretum
Including provisional execution (exsecutio provisoria) before res iudicata
The oral contentious process. De processu contentioso orali
3878 General works
3881.A-Z Special topics, A-Z
3882 Summary procedure. Summatim cognoscere (Table KB2)
3883 Non-contentious jurisdiction (Table KB2)
Special procedures. De quibusdam processibus specialibus
Matrimonial actions. De processibus matrimonialibus
3885 General (Table KB2)
Jurisdiction. Competence. Competens forum in causis matrimonialibus
Including competence in causis de matrimonii nullitate
3887 General works
3889 Jurisdiction of the civil courts. Causae pertinentes ad civilem magistratum
3890 Parties to action. Partes
Including spouses (coniuges) and promotor of justice (promotor iustitiae)
3893 Evidence. Burden of proof . Probatio. Onus probandi
3895 Sentence. Appellate procedure. Sententia et appellatio
Nullity of marriage (Summary procedures). Annullatio matrimonii
Cf. KBR3882 Contentious trial
3897 General (Table KB2)
3899 Documentary process. Processus documentalis
Separation. Divorce. Causae separationis coniugum. Divortium
Including separatio (quoad thorum et mensam) perpetua and temporaria
3901 General (Table KB2)
Deferral of the case to the civil court (Causa ad forum civile deferre) see KBR3889
3905.A-Z Special topics, A-Z
Adulterium see KBR3905.A48
3905.A48 Adultery
3905.A77 Assault and battery
3905.D87 Duress
3905.P75 Privilegium Petrinum

Judiciary. Ecclesiastical courts and procedure. De processibus
Special procedures. De quibusdam processibus specialibus
Matrimonial actions. De processibus matrimonialibus
Separation. Divorce. Causae separationis coniugum. Divortium
Special topics, A-Z -- Continued
Saevitia. Periculum animae seu corporis see KBR3905.A77
Vis. Metus see KBR3905.D87
Dispensation of ratified and non-consummated marriage. Dispensatio super. Matrimonio rato et non consummato
3907 General works
3908 Jurisdiction of the Apostolic See . Una Sedes Apostolica cognoscit de facto inconsummationis matrimonii
3909 Parties to action. Spouses. Coniuges
3910 Rescript of dispensation. Rescriptum dispensationis
Including entry in the registers of marriage and baptism
3912 Procedure in presumption and declaration of death of a spouse. Processus praesumptae mortis coniugis (Table KB2)
3914 Declaration of nullity of sacred ordination. De causis ad sacrae ordinationis nullitatem declarandam (Table KB2)
Including observation of canons on trials (general) and contentious trial
3916 Procedures in beatification and canonization (Table KB2)
3918 Settlement out of court. Arbitration. Compromise. Transactio seu reconciliatio. Iudicium arbitrale. Compromissum (Table KB2)
Noncontentious jurisdiction see KBR3883
Penal (Criminal) procedures. Processus poenalis iudicialis
3920 General (Table KB2)
3922 Denunciation procedure
3923 Accusation principle
Inquisition principle see KBR3942+
Parties to action. De partibus in causa
3926 Promoter of justice (petitioner). Promotor iustitiae
3927 Accused. Accusatus
3928 Advocates. Advocati
Pre-trial procedure
3930 General works
3931 Summons. Decretum citationis
3932 Complaints (petitions). Libelli iudicii
3933 Criminal investigation. De praevia investigatione
Including opening and closing decrees of the ordinary
Procedure at first instance. Prima instantia

Judiciary. Ecclesiastical courts and procedure. De processibus
Penal (Criminal) procedures. Processus poenalis iudicialis
Procedure at first instance. Prima instantia -- Continued
3936 General (Table KB2)
3937 Jurisdiction. The competent forum
Including forum externum and internum
Evidence. Burden of proof. Probatio. Onus probandi
3940 General works
Inquisition procedure. Investigation ex officio. Inquisitio generalis (praeparatoria; processus pro informatione curiae)
Including defamation (diffamatio) and verification
For particular inquisition processes (e. g. witchcraft trials) before the regular courts in a particular country, see the subclass for the jurisdiction, e. g. Germany KK95; and KK850+ (Witchcraft trials)
For history of the inquisition see BX1700+
3942 General works
3943.A-Z Special topics, A-Z
3943.C65 Confession (or self-incrimination) of the infamatus
3943.O38 Oath
3943.O73 Ordeal
3943.T67 Torture
3943.W58 Witnesses
Judicial decisions. Sentences. Sententiae
3944 General works
3946 Acquittal. Absolutio
3947 Res iudicata
Remedies. De impugnatione sententiae
3949 General works
3951 Appeal. Appellatio
Judicial review of administrative acts. Administrative remedies. De ratione procedendi in recursibus administrativis, i.e. Review of administrative acts issued in the external forum (in foro externo extra iudicium)
3960 General works
3961.A-Z Special topics, A-Z
Removal and transfer of pastors. De procedura in parochis amovendis vel transferendis
3973 General works
3975 Particular reasosn. Causae
3978 Resignation by pastor. Renuntiatio a parocho
3980 Decree of transfer. Decretum translationis
3983 Recourse against decree of removal. Recursus adversus amotionis decretum

KBR

Church and state relationships. De relationibus inter ecclesiam et status. Ius publicum ecclesiae
Class here works on competing jurisdiction of state and church
For the civil law impacting on ecclesiastical authority, see the K subclasses for individual countries, e. g. KK5519+ Secular ecclesiastical law in Germany
For collections of concordats with a particular country, see the K subclass for the country; for individual concordats, see the subject in the K subclass for the country
Cf. BX1790+ Catholic Church and the state
4000.A-Z General. By author, A-Z
4000.A85 Guilelmus Audisio (1802-ca. 1882). Diritto publico della Chiesa e delle genti cristiane, 1864
4000.G75 Hugo Grotius (1583-1645). De imperio summarum potestatum circa sacra
4000.H47 Joseph Hergenroether (1820-1890). Katholische Kirche und christlicher Staat, 1872
4000.L53 Matthaeus Liberatore (1810-1892). La Chiesa e lo stato cristiano, 1871
4000.M37 Wilhelm Martens (1831-1902). Die Beziehung der Ueberordnung, Nebenordnung und Unterordnung zwischen Kirche und Staat, 1877
4000.T37 Camillus Tarquini (1810-1874). Institutiones iuris publici ecclesiastici, 1860
4000.V46 Ioachimus Ventura (1792-1861). De iure publico ecclesiastico commentaria, 1826
Relation of papacy (primacy) to monarchic government (divine right of kings)
4010 General works
Early Church and Roman Empire. Byzantine Empire (to ca. 8th cent.)
4012 General works
4014 Constitutum Constantini. Donatio Constantini, 8th cent. (5th cent., Legenda s. Silvestri)
Cf. BX875.D6+ Donation of Constantine (Catholic Church)
Frankish (Germanic) Empire. Holy Roman Empire (Sacrum Imperium Romanum) (to ca. end 15th cent.)
Cf. BX1175 Catholic Church
4020 General works
4022 Carolingian theocracy. State church. Proprietary church (Eigenkirchenrecht)
4024 Potestas indirecta in temporalia (Gregory VII, 1073-1085)
4026 Potestas directa in temporalia (Bonifaz VIII, 1294-1303). Bulla "Unam sanctam"
Investiture struggle
4028 General works

Church and state relationships. De relationibus inter ecclesiam et status. Ius publicum ecclesiae
Frankish (Germanic) Empire. Holy Roman Empire (Sacrum Imperium Romanum) (to ca. end 15th cent.)
Investiture struggle -- Continued
4030 Concordate of Worms, 1122 (Table K22)
4032 Church and feudal institutes
For ius patronatus see KBR2361+
Cf. KJC4435+ Feudal law in Europe
Renaissance and Reformation (16th cent.)
4034 General works
Schism. Reform and restoration. Counter reformation
Cf. BX1270+ Catholic Church
4035 General works
4036 The reform councils. Conciliar theory
4037 Theory of ius circa sacra (Superiority of the state over the church)
4038.A-Z By region or country, A-Z
Absolutism. Enlightenment. Modernism (17th to end 19th cent.)
Cf. BX1330+ History of the Catholic Church
4040 General works
4042 Parity (Equality) of different cults (denominations.) Legal status and state protection
4043 Secularization
<4047> Separation of church and state
see KBU4047+
4050 Authority. Competence. Spiritual and temporal jurisdiction (Causae mere ecclesiasticae, causae civiles and causae mixtae)
4052 Conflict of jurisdictions
For courts see KBR3804
Legal and internatonal status of the Holy See
4064 General works
4068 Sovereignty
4070 Territory. Vatican. Papal States (to 1870)
For the Congregatio Boni Regiminis (Congregation for administration of Papal States), see KBR41.7 and KBR2683
For territorial divisions of the church see KBR2796+
Foreign and international relations of the Holy See
4076 General works
Papal legation. Diplomacy. De relationibus diplomaticis
4078 General works

KBR

Church and state relationships. De relationibus inter ecclesiam et status. Ius publicum ecclesiae
Foreign and international relations of the Holy See
Papal legation. Diplomacy. De relationibus diplomaticis -- Continued
Papal envoys. Legati. Nuntii. Internuntii
Including admission and accreditation by secular authority (State), and rank of legates or nuncios
Cf. BX1908 Organization of the Catholic Church
4080 General (Table KB2)
Legati a latere
4083.A-Z General. By author, A-Z
4083.B65 Nicolas de Bohier, 1469-1539 (Table K4)
4083.G36 Pietro Andrea Gammaro (Table K4)
Jurisdiction. Potestas (General)
4084 General works
4086 Legati missi and nuntii apostolici
Legati nati
4087 General works
4088 Jurisdiction. Potestas
4090 Synods of legates

Law of the Roman Catholic Church. The Holy See
Class here sources (individual and collected) and general works on codified canon law, including the codification period
For the cardinalitial commission of codification (1904-1917) see KBU2210
Bibliography
Including international and national bibliography
2 Bibliography of bibliography. Bibliographical concordances
3 General bibliography
4 Indexes for periodical literature, society publications, collections, etc.
Subject bibliography
5 General (Collective)
Individual subjects and topics
see the subject
Early works, e. g. Repertoria
see the author in the appropriate period
7 Personal bibliography. Writers on Canon law (Collective or individual)
Catalogs, inventories and guides to manuscripts and incunabula collections in libraries or archives open to the public. By name of the library or archive
Including university, museum, cathedral, religious order and other institutional libraries or archives
<9> General (Collective)
<10.A-Z> North American, A-Z
Including United States and Canada
<12.A-Z> Central and South American, A-Z
European
<14.A-Z> English, A-Z
<14.5.A-Z> French, A-Z
<15.A-Z> German, A-Z
<15.5.A-Z> Italian, A-Z
<15.5.B53> Biblioteca Apostolica Vaticana
<16.A-Z> Spanish and Portuguese, A-Z
<17.A-Z> Other European, A-Z
<18.A-Z> Asian and Pacific, A-Z
<19.A-Z> African, A-Z
<20> Periodicals
see subclass KB
21 Annuals. Yearbooks
e. g. L'année canonique

22 Monographic series
e. g. Kirchenrechtliche Abhandlungen; Theses ad lauream in iure canonico (Pontificia Università Lateranense); Monographias canonicas Penafort; Österreichisches Archiv für Kirchenrecht; Studia Gratiana
Official gazette of the Holy See
25 Acta Sanctae Sedis (1865-1904)
Superseded by Acta Apostolicae Sedis
Cf. BX850+ Catholic Church
26 Acta Apostolicae Sedis (1909-)
Official acts of the Holy See
Including Apostolic constitutions, and decrees of the Roman Curia (Curia Romana)
26.8 Bibliography
Early or discontinued collections and compilations
<27> Regesta. Registers. Digests
see KBR27
<28> General
see KBR28+
<29> Bullaria. Bullaries
see KBR29+
Individual popes
<30> To Pius X (Pope, 1903-1914)
see KBR30+
Collections. Compilations. Selections
30.5 Indexes. Registers. Digests
31 General
Including unannotated and annotated editions
32 Individual popes. By date of accession of pope
32 1914 Benedict XV (Pope, 1914-1922)
32 1922 Pius XI (Pope, 1922-1939)
32 1939 Pius XII (Pope, 1939-1958)
32 1958 John XXIII (Pope, 1958-1963)
32 1963 Paul VI (Pope, 1963-1978)
32 1978 John Paul I (Pope, 1978)
32 1978a John Paul II (Pope, 1978-)
Individual apostolic constitutions and other particular acts
34 By pope and date of accession of pope
Subarrange further by date
Cf. BX870 Catholic Church
34 1914 Benedict XV (Pope, 1914-1922)
34 1922 Pius XI (Pope, 1922-1939)
34 1939 Pius XII (Pope, 1939-1958)
34 1958 John XXIII (Pope, 1958-1963)
34 1963 Paul VI (Pope, 1963-1978)
34 1978 John Paul I (Pope, 1978)

Official acts of the Holy See
Individual apostolic constitutions and other particular acts
By pope and date of accession of pope -- Continued
34 1978a John Paul II (Pope, 1978-)
Litterae Encyclicae. Encyclicals see BX860
Epistolae. Litterae Pontificiae. Letters see BX863
38 Concordats (Collections. Compilations. Selections)
For collected concordats of a particular signatory jurisdiciton, see secular ecclesiastical law in the appropriate K subclass for the jurisdiciton, e. g. Germany, KK5520+ for individual concordats, see the subject in the appropriate K subclass for the signatory jurisdiction
Decrees and decisions of the Curia Romana
39 General (Collective)
Not including Papal documents
39.2 Cancellaria Apostolica
39.3 Camera Apostolica
Secretaria Status
39.5 Secretaria brevium
39.6 Secretaria Memorialium
Roman congregations
<40> Suprema Congregatio Sanctae Romanae et Universalis Inquisitionis. Supreme Congregation of the Holy Roman and Universal Inquisition (1542-1908)
see KBR40
Congregatio Sancti Officii. Holy Office see KBU40.25
<40.2> Congregatio Indicis. Congregation of the Index (1571 to 1917)
see KBR40.2
40.25 Congregatio pro Doctrina Fidei. Congregation for the Doctrine of the Faith (1967-) (Table KB1)
Cf. KBU2502+ Curia Romana
40.3 Congregatio de Disciplina Sacramentorum. Congregation for the Discipline of the Sacraments (1908-1975) (Table KB1)
Cf. KBU2531+ Curia Romana
40.32 Congregatio pro Cultu Divino. Congregation for Divine Worship (1969-1975) (Table KB1)
Cf. KBU2531+ Curia Romana
40.34 Congregatio pro Sacramentis et Cultu Divino. Congregation for the Sacraments and Divine Worship (1975-1984) (Table KB1)
40.4 Congregatio de Cultu Divino et Disciplina Sacramentorum. The Congregation for Divine Worship and the Discipline of the Sacraments (1988-) (Table KB1)

Official acts of the Holy See
Decrees and decisions of the Curia Romana
Roman congregations -- Continued

40.45 Congregatio Sacrorum Rituum (1588-1969) (Table KB1)
Cf. KBU2545+ Curia Romana

40.5 Congregatio pro Causis Sanctorum. Congregation for the Causes of Saints (1969-) (Table KB1)

<40.52> Congregatio super Consultationibus Regularium. Congregation for Consultations about Regulars (1586-1601)
see KBR40.52

<40.54> Congregatio super Consultationibus Episcoporum et Aliorum Praelatorum. Congregation for Consultations about Bishops and other Prelates
see KBR40.54

<40.55> Congregatio Episcoporum et Regularium. Congregation of Bishops
see KBR40.55

40.6 Congregatio pro Episcopis (Table KB1)
Cf. KBU2555+ Curia Romana

40.7 Congregatio pro Gentium Evangelizatione. Congregation for Evangelization of Peoples (1967-) (Table KB1)

40.8 Congregatio pro Clericis. Congregation for the Clergy (1967-) (Table KB1)

40.9 Congregatio pro Institutis Vitae Consecratae et Societatibus Vitae Apostolicae. Congregation for Institutes of Consecrated Life and Societies of Apostolic Life (1988-) (Table KB1)

41 Congregatio pro Institutione Catholica. Congregation for Catholic Education (Table KB1)

<41.2> Congregatio de Propaganda Fide pro Negotiis Ritus Orientalis (Congregatio super Correctione Librorum Ecclesiae Orientalis)
see KBR41.2

<41.3> Congregatio Consistorialis (Congregatio pro Erectione Ecclesiarum et Provisionibus Consistorialibus). Congregation of the Consistory (1588)
see KBR41.3

<41.32> Congregatio Signaturae Iustitiae
see KBR41.32

<41.33> Congregatio Ceremonialis. Congregation of Ceremonies (1588)
see KBR41.33

<41.34> Congregatio Visitationis Apostolicae. Congregation of the Visitation (1592)
see KBR41.34

Official acts of the Holy See
Decrees and decisions of the Curia Romana
Roman congregations -- Continued
<41.35> Congregationes super Disciplina Regulari and super Statu Regularium
see KBR41.35
<41.36> Congregatio Iurisdictionis et Immunitatis Ecclesiasticae
see KBR41.36
<41.4> Congregatio Indulgentiarum et Sacrarum Reliquiarum
see KBR41.4
<41.45> Congregatio pro Negotiis Ecclesiasticis Extraordinariis
see KBR41.45
<41.5> Congregatio Reverendae Fabricae Basilicae (Sancti Petri)
see KBR41.5
Decisions of ecclesiastical tribunals and courts, and related materials
42 General collections
Class here universal collections not related to a particular court
By tribunal or court
Rota Romana
Previously Sacri Palatii Auditorium
43 Indexes and tables. Repertories. Digests
For repertories to a particular work, see the author or title
Collections. Compilations. Selections
Including collections with annotations and scholarly comment
43.15 Serials
44.A-Z Monographs. By editor, compiler, or title, A-Z
44.5.A-Z Decisions by individual auditores of the Rota. By auditor, A-Z
44.6.A-Z Collections, compilations, or selections on particular subjects, A-Z
44.6.C45 Church property
Including res sacrae and sacred utensils
Res sacrae see KBU44.6.C45
Utensils, Sacred see KBU44.6.C45
44.7 Works on the Rota
e. g. Carolus Holboeck. Tractatus de jurisprudentiae S. Romanae Rotae
45 Tribunal of the Camera Apostolica (Table K19)
46.5 Signatura Apostolica (Supremum Signaturae Apostolicae Tribunal) (Table K19)
For decisions of the predecessor see KBR46
47 Dataria Apostolica (Table K19)
48 Paenitentiaria Apostolica (Table K19)

Decisions of ecclesiastical tribunals and courts, and related materials
By tribunal or court -- Continued
Diocesan courts or tribunals
Class here decisions of ecclesiastical courts, tribunals and other authorities in a particular diocese or other ecclesiastical jurisdiction
Including historic collections
49 Collections (General)
The Americas
Including territories, colonies, or states
49.2 General (Collective)
North America
49.5.A-Z Canadian. By name of court, A-Z
50.A-Z United States. By name of court, A-Z
Central and South America
50.2.A-Z Mexican. By name of court, A-Z
50.3.A-Z Other, A-Z
Do not subarrange further (by form)
European
50.5.A-Z Austrian. By name of court, A-Z
Including the Austro-Hungarian Empire
50.7.A-Z Dutch. By name of court, A-Z
50.9.A-Z English. By name of court, A-Z
51.A-Z French and Belgian. By name of court, A-Z
51.2.A-Z German. By name of court, A-Z
51.3.A-Z Hungarian. By name of court, A-Z
51.4.A-Z Italian. By name of court, A-Z
51.5.A-Z Polish. By name of court, A-Z
51.6.A-Z Spanish and Portuguese. By name of court, A-Z
51.7.A-Z Other European countries, A-Z
Do not subarrange further (by form)
Asian
Including territories, colonies, etc.
52.A-Z Middle East. By country, A-Z
Do not subarrange further (by form)
53.A-Z Southeast Asia. By country, A-Z
Do not subarrange further (by form)
African
Including territories, colonies, etc.
54.A-Z North Africa. By country, A-Z
Do not subarrange further (by form)
54.5.A-Z Other African countries, A-Z
Do not subarrange further (by form)
56 Encyclopedias

56.5	Dictionaries. Terms and phrases. Vocabularies
	For early works see KBR56
64	Directories
	Auxiliary sciences
	see KBR74+
<74>	General works
<75>	Diplomatics
<76>	Paleography
	Papyrology see KBR190+
	Legal semantics see KBU2203
<78>	Archaeology. Legal symbolism
	Inscriptions. Epigraphy see KBR190+
<83>	Heraldry. Seals. Insignia, etc.
100	Proverbs. Legal maxims
102	Form books. Clauses and forms
	Including individual or collected formularies for notaries or trial lawyers, court and procedural practice before a particular office or court, e. g. the Rota Romana, Camera apostolica, Cancellaria apostolica, etc.
<122>	Collective biography
	see KBR122+
	For individual biography see the canonist or jurist in the appropriate period
	Trials
127	Collections
	Including criminal and civil trials
	Criminal trials
	Including inquisition trials
128	Collections
128.5	Individual. By defendant, plaintiff, or best known (popular) name
	Civil trials
129	Collections
129.5	Individual. By defendant
	Legal research. Legal bibliography. Methods of bibliographic research
130	General works
132	Systems of citation. Legal abbreviation. Modus legendi abbreviaturas
133	Legal education. Study and teaching
	The legal profession see KBU3822+
	Societies. Associations
136.A-Z	International, A-Z
	National
138.A-Z	North American, A-Z
	Including United States and Canada

Societies. Associations
National -- Continued
139.A-Z Central and South American, A-Z
European
141.A-Z English, A-Z
142.A-Z French, A-Z
143.A-Z German, A-Z
144.A-Z Italian, A-Z
145.A-Z Spanish and Portuguese, A-Z
146.A-Z Other European, A-Z
147.A-Z Asian and Pacific, A-Z
148.A-Z African, A-Z
149 Academies. Institutes
150 Conferences. Symposia
Canon law compared with other religious legal systems
see subclass KB
160 General works
Including festschriften
For studies on sources see KBR190+
For works on system and doctrinal development (History) see KBR2160+
180.A-Z Works on diverse aspects of a particular subject and falling within several branches of the law. By subject, A-Z
History and study of sources
Including methodology, e. g. papyrology, epigraphy, etc.
<190> General. By author
see KBR190+
<192> Classification of sources
Collections. Compilations. Selections
<195> General
Class here comprehensive collections stemming from all periods of canon law
Including translations
For collections relating to a particular historic period or type of source, see the period or type of source (e. g. decretals, consilia, etc.)
<195.5> Indexes. Chronologies. Concordances
<196-197.4> Pseudo-apostolic collections of canons, to ca. 400 A.D.
<197.45-199.33> Jus ecclesiae Graecae seu Byzantinae. Greek-Byzantine collections, to ca. 14th cent.
Canonical collections of councils and synods
For general histories see BR200+
200.A-Z General (Collective). By author, A-Z
<200.B35> Louis Bail, 1610-1669. Summa conciliorum omnium (1659)

Collections. Compilations. Selections
Canonical collections of councils and synods
General (Collective). By author, A-Z -- Continued
<200.B36> Étienne Baluze, 1630-1718. Nova collectio conciliorum (1683)
<200.B48> William Beveridge, ed., 1637-1708. Synodikon (1672)
<200.B56> Severinus Binius. Concilia generalia et provincialia
<200.C37> Bartolomé Carranza, 1503-1576
<200.C66> Conciliorum omnium generalium et principalium collectio regia (1644)
<200.H37> Jean Hardouin. Conciliorum collectio regia maxima (1715)
<200.M36> J.D. Mansi. Sacrorum conciliorum nova et amplissima collectio ... (1901)
200.T36 Norman P. Tanner. Conciliorum oecumenicorum decreta (1990)
Early councils. Concilia. To end 9th century
Including general and ecumenical councils
205 General works
For general histories on the councils and synods see BR205+
By date of opening
<210> Council of Nicea (1st), 325
<213> Council of Saragossa, 380
<214> Council of Aquileia, 381
<215> Council of Constantinople (1st), 381
<220> Council of Ephesus, 449
<225> Council of Chalcedon, 451
<230> Council of Constantinople (2nd), 553
<235> Council of Constantinople (3rd), 680
<237> Quinisext Synod (Constantinople; Concilium Trullanum), 692
<240> Council of Nicea (2nd), 787
<242> Council of Frankfurt, 794
Provincial councils
Including provincial synods
<245> General works
General (Collective) see KBU200.A+
Individual
<260.2> Carthage, 255
<260.22> Ancyra (Ankara), 314
<260.23> Neocaesarea (Niksar), 315
<260.24> Antioch (Antakya), 341 (and Sardica (Sofia), 343)
<260.25> Gangra (Cankiri), 343
<260.26> Constantinople, 394
<260.27> Carthage, 398

Collections. Compilations. Selections
Canonical collections of councils and synods
Early councils. Concilia. To end 9th century
Provincial councils
Individual. By date of opening
<260.28> Carthage, 419
Cf. KBR1110 Codex Canonum Ecclesiae Africanae
<260.29> Constantinople, 861
<260.3> Constantinople, 879
General and ecumencial councils. From end 9th century
Including post-schism and contested councils
820 General works
For general histories on the councils, synods, etc. see BX820+
General (Collective) see KBU200.A+
<830> Individual councils. By date of opening
<830 0869> Council of Constantinople (4th), 869
<830 0879> Council of Union, 879
<830 1064> Council of Mantua, 1064
<830 1095> Council of Clermont, 1095
<830 1123> Lateran Council (1st), 1123
<830 1139> Lateran Council (2nd), 1139
<830 1179> Lateran Council (3rd), 1179
<830 1215> Lateran Council (4th), 1215
<830 1245> Council of Lyons (1st), 1245
<830 1274> Council of Lyons (2nd), 1274
<830 1311> Council of Vienne, 1311
<830 1409> Council of Pisa (1st), 1409
<830 1414> Council of Constance, 1414
<830 1423> Council of Pavia-Siena, 1423
Council of Basel, 1431, and Ferrara, 1438 see KBU830 1439
<830 1439> Council of Ferrara-Florence (Florentinum), 1439
<830 1511> Council of Pisa (2nd), 1511
<830 1512> Lateran Council (5th), 1512
<830 1545> Council of Trent, 1545
Council of Brest-Litovsk see KBU830 1596
<830 1596> Union of Brest, 1596
<830 1869> Vatican Council (1st), 1869
<830 1962> Vatican Council (2nd), 1962
Episcopal synods. Synodus episcoporum
830.5 General (Collective)
For general histories on the synods see BX831
831 Individual episcopal synods. By date of opening

Collections. Compilations. Selections
Canonical collections of councils and synods -- Continued
Plenary councils. National councils. By region or country
Under each country, include the diocesan and provincial councils in the order of jurisdictional hierarchy
The Americas
North America
United States
Cf. BX833+ Catholic Church
833 General (Collective)
Individual
<835> Plenary Council (1st), Baltimore, 1852
<835.2> Plenary Council (2nd), Baltimore, 1866
<835.3> Plenary Council (3d), Baltimore, 1884
Canada
Cf. BX837.C2 Catholic Church
836 General (Collective)
Individual
837 Plenary Council (1st), Quebec, 1909
Central and South America
Cf. BX831.5+ Catholic Church
838 General (Collective)
For general histories on the plenary/national councils see BX832
839.A-Z Individual. By country, A-Z
Subarrange further by date of opening of the council
Europe
848 General (Collective)
849.A-Z By country, A-Z
Subarrange further by date of opening of the council
Asia
858 General (Collective)
Middle East. Southwest Asia
General (Collective)
860.A-Z By country, A-Z
Subarrange further by date of opening of the council
South Asia. Southeast Asia. East Asia
868 General (Collective)
869.A-Z By country, A-Z
Subarrange further by date of opening of the council
Africa
880 General (Collective)
882.A-Z By country, A-Z
Subarrange further by date of opening of the council
Pacific Area
903 General (Collective)

Collections. Compilations. Selections
Canonical collections of councils and synods
Plenary councils. National councils. By region or country
Pacific Area -- Continued
905 Australia. By date
910 New Zealand. By date
915.A-Z Other countries, A-Z
Subarrange further by date of opening of the council
Conference of Bishops (Episcopal conference). Conferencia episcoporum
Cf. BX837.5 Catholic Church
925 General (Collective)
930.A-Z Individual. By country or ecclesiastical province, A-Z
Subarrange further by date of opening of the conference
Provincial councils and diocesan synods
Including diocesan pastoral councils
Cf. BX838 Catholic Church
950 General (Collective)
The Americas
North American countries (and territories)
United States
953 General (Collective)
954 By province or diocese, and date of opening of synod or council
Canada
963 General (Collective)
964 By province or diocese, and date of opening of synod or council
Central and South American countries
Subarrange by province or diocese, and date of opening of synod or council
Cf. BX831.5+ Catholic Church
973 General (Collective)
975 Mexico
979 Costa Rica
980 Guatemala
981 Honduras
982 Nicaragua
983 Panama
984 El Salvador
985.A-Z Other, A-Z
South American countries
Subarrange by province or diocese, and date of opening of synod or council
987 General (Collective)
989 Argentina

Collections. Compilations. Selections
Canonical collections of councils and synods
Provincial councils and diocesan synods
The Americas
Central and South American countries
South American countries -- Continued
990 Bolivia
991 Brazil
992 Chile
992.5 Colombia
993 Ecuador
993.5 Guiana
994.5 Paraguay
995 Uruguay
995.5 Venezuela
996.A-Z Other, A-Z
European countries
Subarrange each country by ecclesiastical jurisdictions (i.e. diocese or province) and date of opening of synod or council
998 General (Collective)
999 Austria. Austro-Hungarian Monarchy
Baltic countries
1001 General (Collective)
1001.2 Estonia
1001.5 Latvia
1001.6 Lithuania
1003 Belgium
1003.3 Czechoslovakia
1003.5 Finland
1004 France
1005 Germany
1006 Great Britain
1006.5 Greece
1007 Holland. The Netherlands
1008 Hungary
For Austro-Hungarian Monarchy see KBU999
1009 Ireland. Eire
1010 Italy
1011 Poland
1012 Portugal
1012.5 Russia
Scandinavia
1013 General (Collective)
1013.2 Denmark
1013.3 Iceland

Collections. Compilations. Selections
Canonical collections of councils and synods
Provincial councils and diocesan synods
European countries
Scandinavia -- Continued

1013.5 Norway
1013.7 Sweden
1014 Spain
Southeast European countries. The Balkans
1015 General (Collective)
1015.2 Albania
1016 Bosnia and Hercegovina
1016.2 Bulgaria
1016.4 Croatia
1016.6 Cyprus
1017 Macedonia
1017.3 Montenegro
1017.5 Romania
1017.7 Serbia
1018 Turkey
1018.2 Yugoslavia
For Serbia see KBU1017.7
1018.5 Switzerland
1019.A-Z Other European countries, A-Z
Subarrange further by province or diocese and date of opening of synod or council
Asian countries
1020 General (Collective)
Middle East. Southwest Asia
1022 General (Collective)
1023.A-Z By country, A-Z
Subarrange further by province or diocese, and date of opening of synod or council
South Asia. Southeast Asia. East Asia
1043 General (Collective)
1044 China
1046 Indochina
1047 Indonesia
1048 Japan
1049 Malaysia
1050 Nepal
1051 Thailand
1052 Vietnam
1053.A-Z Other countries, A-Z
Subarrange further by province or diocese, and date of opening of synod or council

Collections. Compilations. Selections

Canonical collections of councils and synods

Provincial councils and diocesan synods -- Continued

African countries

1064 General (Collective)

1066 Algeria

1069 Egypt

1071 Ethiopia

1075 South Africa

1077 Tunisia

1080.A-Z Other African countries, A-Z

Subarrange further by province or diocese, and date of opening of synod or council

Pacific Area

1082 General (Collective)

1083 Australia

1084 New Zealand

1086.A-Z Other Pacific Area countries, A-Z

<1100-1257> Latin (occidental) versions of Oriental canonical collections prior to pseudo-Isidoriana

Including collections of both canons of the early Oriental councils or synods, and decrees and decretals

<1268-1292> Compilations of secular law pertaining to religious law

<1295-1308> Pseudo-Isidoriana. 9th century

Cf. BX875.A2+ Forgeries (Catholic Church)

<1315-1358> Post Pseudo-Isidorian collections of canons and decretals, to 1140

<1360> Decretum Gratiani. Concordia discordantium canonum (Gratian, 12th cent.), 1140

<1510-1565> Collections. Compilations. Selections between 1140 and 1234 (Decretum to Gregory IX) (1500)

Liber extra. Decretales Gregorii IX (Gregory IX, Pope, 1227-1241), 1234

<1510> Novellae constitutiones, 1234-1298

<1530> Liber Sextus decretalium (Boniface VIII, Pope, 1294-1303), 1298

<1540> Clementinae Constitutiones (Clement V, Pope, 1305-1315), 1317

<1550> Extravagantes Joannis XXII (John XXII, Pope, 1316-1334), end 15th cent.

<1560> Extravagantes communes, end 15th cent.

<1565> Corpus iuris canonici. By date of edition

Including all editions under the title "Corpus Iuris Canonici"

Canonists and jurists

Canonists and jurists -- Continued
12th to mid 16th centuries
Class here works produced by the early canonical jurisprudence (canonics) between Decretum Gratiani and Tridentinum (ca. 1140 to 1545), including particular forms of contemporary (early) legal literature
Cf. KJA1630+ Individual jurists (6th to 15th cent. Post-Justinian periods. Jus Romanum Medii Aevi)
<1576-1702> Decretists and early decretalis
<1704-1925> Decretalists and commentators (consiliators), to 1545
1545 (Council of Trent) to 19th century
<1928-2138.5> By nationality
<2139-2154.5> Particular forms of early/contemporary legal literature
Canon law and other disciplines or subjects
2155 Canonical jurisprudence and theology. Law and gospel
Cf. BT79 Doctrinal theology
2156 Canon law and moral theology. Casuistry. Cases of conscience, etc.
Cf. BX1757.A1+ Catholic Church
Canon law and medical legislation see KBU3282+
2157 Canon law and social legislation
Canonical jurisprudence. Theory and science of canon law
General (Comparative). By canonist or jurist
2160 English and North American jurists
Including Canadian jurists
2162 French and Belgian jurists
2163 Italian jurists
2170 Spanish and Portuguese jurists
Including Central and South American jurists
2172 German jurists
2185 Dutch jurists
2188.A-Z Other nationals, A-Z
The concept of law
2189 General works
Effectiveness of law. Validity and nullity of law see KBU2196
2189.3.A-Z Special topics, A-Z
2189.3.M47 Mercy, Legal concept of
Miserecordia see KBU2189.3.M47
Sources and relationships of law
2190 Natural law and divine law. Canonical tradition. Ius naturale et ius divinum. Canonica tratitio
Canons and constitutions. Canones et constitutiones
2191 General works
<2191.2> Apostolic constitutions and canons

Canonical jurisprudence. Theory and science of canon law
The concept of law
Sources and relationships of law
Canons and constitutions. Canones et constitutiones -- Continued
<2191.3> Conciliar canons and decrees
Including conciliar/synodal canons and decrees of the provincial councils and synods
2192 Custom. Consuetudo
2193 General decrees and instructions. De decretis generalibus et instructionibus
Including decreta generalia executoria
Administrative acts. De actibus administrativis singularibus
Including acts issued motu proprio, and acts relating to the forum externum
2193.3 General works
2193.5 Individual decrees and precepts. Decreta et praecepta singularia
2194 Rescripts. Rescripta
2194.3 Privileges. Acquired rights. Privilegia. Iura quaesita
2194.5 Dispensations. Dispensationes
2195 Statutes and rules of order. De statutis et ordinibus
2196 Validity, nullity, and effectiveness of law
2196.3 Legal certainty
Applicability (Territorial and temporal) of laws
2197 General works
2198 Retroactivity. Non-retroactivity
2199 Conflict of laws
Class here general works on conflicts of canon law and civil law
For conflict of jurisdictions see KBU3804
Methodology
2200 General works
For studies on sources see KBR190+
2202 Legal hermeneutics. Interpretation and construction. Lacunae
Including interpretatio authentica
2203 Legal semantics. Legal language
2204 Particular schools
Influence of other legal systems on canon law
2205 General (Comparative)
2206 Roman law. Civil law (Reception)
2207 Law reform and policies. Criticism
2208.A-Z Concepts applying to several branches of the law, A-Z
The codes of canon law
2210 Codex Iuris Canonici (CIC), 1917 (Table KB7)

The codes of canon law -- Continued
2212 Codex Iuris Canonici (CIC), 1983 (Table KB7)
General norms and principles. De normis generalibus
For ecclesiastical offices in general see KBU2350+
2215 General works
Universal ecclesiastical laws. Leges ecclesiasticae universales
2216 General works
2218 Promulgation. Publicity. Promulgatio
Retroactivity. Non-retroactivity see KBU2198
2219 Ignorance or error. Ignorantia vel error
2220 Abrogation. Derogation. Revocation. Abrogatio. Derogatio. Revocatio
Authentic interpretation see KBU2202
Persons. De personis
2224 General works
Natural persons. Personarum physicarum condicio canonica
2225 General works
2226 Personality
Church membership. Adscriptio ecclesiae
For laity see KBU2316+
2227 General works
Baptism. Baptismus
2228 General works
2229.A-Z Special topics, A-Z
Change (Transfer) to another Ritual Church see KBU2229.R57
2229.C55 Children. Infants
e. g. Ascription of infants to Latin Church
Choice of rites see KBU2229.R57
Conversion to another Ritual Church see KBU2229.R57
2229.R57 Rites
Including choice and change of rites, e. g. to conjugal Ritual Church; children of mixed marriages, etc.
Ritual Church see KBU2229.R57
Ritus see KBU2229.R57
Legal capacity and incapacity
2230 General (Table KB2)
2232.A-Z Special topics, A-Z
Dementia see KBU2232.I67
Infans (non sui compos) see KBU2232.I65
2232.I65 Infants
2232.I67 Insanity
2232.M35 Majority

General norms and principles. De normis generalibus
Persons. De personis
Natural persons. Personarum physicarum condicio canonica
Legal capacity and incapacity
Special topics, A-Z -- Continued
2232.M56 Minority
Persona maior see KBU2232.M35
Persona minor see KBU2232.M56
Pubertas see KBU2232.P83
2232.P83 Puberty, Age of
Legal acts and facts affecting persons
Domicile. Quasi-domicile. Domicilium. Quasi-domicilium
Including residents, temporary residents and travelers. Incolae. Advenae. Peregrini
2235 General (Table KB2)
2236.A-Z Special topics, A-Z
2236.C55 Children (Place of origin)
Including illegitimate or posthumous children
2236.D56 Diocesan domicile
Domicilium coniugale see KBU2236.S66
Domicilium dioecesanum see KBU2236.D56
Domicilium paroeciale see KBU2236.P37
Filii (Locus originis) see KBU2236.C55
2236.I67 Institutes (religious), Members of
2236.P37 Parochial domicile
Sodales institutorum religiosorum see KBU2236.I67
2236.S66 Spouses, Domicile of
2236.T87 Tutor or curator, Domicile of
Tutoris vel curatoris domicilium see KBU2236.T87
Consanguinity. Consanguinitas
2237 General (Table KB2)
2238 Lineage and degree. Linea. Gradus
Including direct line (linea recta) and collateral line (linea obliqua)
2239.A-Z Special topics, A-Z
Affinity. Affinitas
2240 General (Table KB2)
2242 By valid marriage. Matrimonium validum (Copula carnalis)
Adopted children. Filii adoptivi
2243 General works
2244.A-Z Special topics, A-Z

General norms and principles. De normis generalibus
Persons. De personis
Natural persons. Personarum physicarum condicio canonica
Legal acts and facts affecting persons -- Continued
Guardian and ward. Tutor. Curator
Including guardianship over minors and adults with mental disabilities
2245 General (Table KB2)
2246.A-Z Special topics, A-Z
Inheritance and succession. Successio mortis causa
Including testate and intestate succession
2248 General (Table KB2)
Testamentary succession. Last will. Testamentum. Ultima voluntas
2249 General (Comparative)
2250.A-Z Special topics, A-Z
Juristic (moral) persons. De personis iuridicis
2253 General works
2254 Legal personality. Personalitas iuridica
Constitution of juristic persons
2255 Moralis persona by divine law
e. g. Catholic Church and Holy See
Juristic persons of public law (persona iuridica publica), or of private law (persona iuridica privata)
i.e. by law, decree or statute
Collegiate juristic persons. Corporations. Universitas personarum
2256 General works
2257 Collegial acts, elections, etc. Actus collegiales, electiones, etc.
Associations. De christifidelium consociationibus
Including universal (international) and national organizations
Class here canonically recognized associations, including those that admit non-Catholics (ecumenical or interreligious associations)
For ecumenical societies, associations, etc., in general see BX2+
For societies of apostolic life see KBU2892+
2260 General works
Public associations. Juristic persons of public law. Consociationes publicae. Personae iuridicae publicae
2262 General works

General norms and principles. De normis generalibus
Persons. De personis
Juristic (moral) persons. De personis iuridicis
Constitution of juristic persons
Juristic persons of public law (persona iuridica publica), or of private law (persona iuridica privata)
Collegiate juristic persons. Corporations. Universitas personarum
Associations. De christifidelium consociationibus
Public associations. Juristic persons of public law. Consociationes publicae. Personae iuridicae publicae -- Continued
2264 Erection. Statutes. Administration. Erectio. Statuta. Administratio
Private associations. Juristic persons of private law. Consociationes privatae. Personae iuridicae privatae
Including personalitat iuridica
2266 General works
2268 Erection. Statutes. Administration. Erectio. Statuta. Administratio
2271.A-Z Special topics, A-Z
Non-collegiate juristic persons (Aggregate of property and resources). Universitas rerum
2273 General works
2276.A-Z Particular kinds of juristic persons, A-Z
2276.C53 Charitable uses, trusts, and foundations. Endowments
2280 Extinction. Division. Dismemberment
2282 Perpetuity
2284.A-Z Particular persons or groups of persons, A-Z
2284.E33 Ecclesiastical estates
2284.O74 Orders of knighthood and chivalry, Papal (Members)
Legal transactions. De actibus iuridicis
2286 General (Comparative)
Validity. Void and voidable transactions. Validitas actus iuridici
2288 General works
2290 Error. Ignorance
2292 Fraud. Duress. Necessity. Dolus. Vis. Metus gravis
2293 Consent or counsil. Consensus et sonsilium alicuius
2294 Liability. Damages. Obligatio damnum illatum reparandi
2295 Computation of time. Supputatio temporis
Including tempus continuum, tempus utile (available) and spatium (period)

General norms and principles. De normis generalibus -- Continued
Power of governance. Jurisdiction. De potestate regiminis. Hierarchia iuridictionis
Including potestas regiminis legislativa, executiva and iudicialis
2298 General works
2300 Interpretation and construction
Delegation of powers. Subdelegation. Potestas delegata, subdelegata
2302 General works
2304 Delegation to several persons in solidum. Delegatio in solidum
2306 Extinction of powers. Extinctio potestatis
Including fulfillment of mandate, cessation, revocation, expiration, sustension, etc.
2308.A-Z Special topics, A-Z
Constitution of the Church
2310 General works
The people of the God. De populo Dei
Obligations and rights of the Christian faithful. De obligationibus et iuribus christifidelium
2312 General works
2314.A-Z Special topics, A-Z
Support of the Church see KBU3384+
Obligations and rights of the laity. De obligationibus et iuribus laicorum
2316 General works
2318.A-Z Special topics, A-Z
The clergy. The hierarchical order. De ministris sacris seu de clericis. Hierarchia ordinis
2320 General works
Formation, education of clerics. Institutio clericorum
Including philosophical and theological training
For state supervision (degrees), see secular ecclesiastical law in particular K subdivisions, e. g. KK5541.5
2322 General works
2324 Seminaries and other institutions. Seminaria. Institutiones sacerdotales
2326 Juristic personality of seminaries. Personalitas iuridica
2328 Administration and governance of the seminaries. Rectors and directors
Including episcopal supervision
2330 Ordination. Sacra ordinatio

Constitution of the Church
The people of God. De populo Dei
The clergy. The hierarchical order. De ministris sacris seu de clericis. Hierarchia ordinis -- Continued
Incardination of clerics. Adscriptio seu incardinatio clericorum
Including incardination to a particular church, personal prelature, religious institute or society of apostolic life
2333 General works
2334 Excardination of clerics. Excardinatio
Legal status. Rights and obligations of clerics. De clericorum iuribus et obligatonibus. Status clericalis
2336 General works
2338 Particular obligations
Ecclesiastical privileges and immunities. Privilegia clericalia. Immunitas
2339 General works
2340.A-Z Special topics, A-Z
2340.P77 Privilegium fori
2340.R47 Residence
2340.T66 Tonsure. Prima tonsura
2342 Personal prelatures. De praelaturis personalibus
Loss of clerical state. Amissio status clericalis
2344 General works
2346.A-Z Special topics, A-Z
Ecclesiastical offices (General). De officiis ecclesiasticis
Cf. BX1955 Catholic Church
2350 General works
2351 Presentation. Appointment call and election. Praesentatio. Electio
Including condition and revocation
2352 Incompatibility. Officia incompatibilia
2353 Free conferral. Libera collatio
2354 Postulation. Postulatio
2355 Salaries. Pensions, etc.
2358 Loss of ecclesiastical office. Amissio officii ecclesiastici
Including resignation, relocation, removal, privation, etc. Renuntiatio, translatio, amotio, privatio, etc.
Organs of government. Hierarchy. De ecclesiae constitutione hierarchica
2363 General works
Power of governance. Jurisdiction see KBU2298+
Supreme authority of the Church. Suprema ecclesiae auctoritas
2364.5 General works

Constitution of the Church
Organs of government. Hierarchy. De ecclesiae constitutione hierarchica
Supreme authority of the Church. Suprema ecclesiae auctoritas -- Continued
2365 The Roman Pontiff and the College of bishops. Romanus Pontifex et Collegium Episcoporum (General)
The Pope. The Roman Pontiff. Chief of State
Cf. BX1805+ Catholic Church
2366 General works
Primacy (Supremacy). Authority and jurisdiction. Primatus iurisdictionis
Including supreme power in the Universal Church and principate in the particular churches (metropolitan and diocesan authority)
2367 General works
Particular powers, rights, and privileges
2368 General (Comparative)
The teaching office of the Pope see KBU3040+
2370 Privileges. Honors. Primatus honoris
Legislative power. Potestas legislativa
Cf. KBU2396+ The College of Bishops
2372 General works
2373.A-Z Special topics, A-Z
Appellatio non datur see KBU2373.F56
2373.F56 Finality of papal decisions and decrees
Recursus non datur see KBU2373.F56
2375 Judicial power
2377 Treaty making power
For foreign and international relations of the Holy See see KBU4076+
2380 Convocation of an ecumenical council. Convocatio. Praesidium
Including agenda, transfer, suspension, dissolution of the council and approval of decrees
2382 Convocation of the synod of bishops
Including agenda, presidium, conclusion, transfer, suspension, etc. of the synod
2383 Right to nominate legates. Ius legatos nominandi
Including right to send, transfer, and recall legates
2384 Right to dispose of episcopates and dioceses
2384.3 Confirmation and suspension of religious orders
2385 Granting of benefices
2386 Tax power
2390 Election. Election procedures (Table KB2)

Constitution of the Church
Organs of government. Hierarchy. De ecclesiae constitutione hierarchica
Supreme authority of the Church. Suprema ecclesiae auctoritas
The Pope. The Roman Pontiff. Chief of State
Primacy (Supremacy). Authority and jurisdiction. Primatus iurisdictionis -- Continued
2392 Vacancy of the Holy See
Including abdication
Collegium Episcoporum. The College of Bishops
2395 General works
Power. Right and duty. Potestas. Ius et officum
2396 General works
2397 Ecumencial council, Participation in. Voting. Suffragium deliberativum
2398 Confirmation and promulgation of conciliar decrees under authority of the Pontiff
Synodus Episcoporum. The Synod of Bishops
2402 General works
2404 Members. Sodales
Including election, designation and nomination (Sodalium electio, designatio, nominatio)
Convocation and conclusion of session see KBU2382
2408 General secretary. Permanent general secretariat. Secretarius generalis. Secretaria generalis permanens
Collegium Cardinalium. College of Cardinals
Cf. BX1815 Catholic Church
2412 General works
2414 Ranks. Titles. Ordines. Tituli
2415 Creation of cardinals by the Pontiff. Creatio Cardinalium decreto
2416 Rights and duties
Including election of the Pope
2418 Dean and assistant dean. Decanus vel subdecanus
The Curia Romana
Including dicasteries and officials of the Holy See (State of Vatican City)
For the older offices see KBR2420+
Cf. BX1818+ Catholic Church
2420 General works
2430 Cancellaria Apostolica. Apostolic Chancery (Table KB6)
The tribunals of the Apostolic See. Apostolicae Sedis tribunalia
Paenitentiaria Apostolica. The Sacred Penitentiary

Constitution of the Church
Organs of government. Hierarchy. De ecclesiae constitutione hierarchica
The Curia Romana
The tribunals of the Apostolic See. Apostolicae Sedis tribunalia
Paenitentiaria Apostolica. The Sacred Penitentiary -- Continued
General see KBU3812
Decisions see KBU48
Rota Romana
General see KBU3816
Decisions see KBU44.A+
Supremum Signaturae Apostolicae Tribunal. The Supreme Tribunal of the Apostolic Signatura
General see KBU3819
Decisions see KBU46.5
2455 Camera Apostolica. Apostolic Chamber. Treasury (Table KB6)
Secretaria Status seu Papalis. Secretariat of State (Papal Secretariat)
2470 General (Table KB6)
2477 Secretaria Memorialium. Secretariate of Briefs to Princes (Table KB6)
2480 Secretaria Brevium. Secretariate of Latin Letters (Table KB6)
Pontifical legates and legation. Nuncios
2482 General (Table KB2)
Particular see KBU4080+
Roman Congregations
Cf. BX1820+ Catholic Church
2500 General (Collective)
Congregatio pro Doctrina Fidei. Congregation for the Doctrine of the Faith (1967-)
Instituted in 1542 as Supreme Congregation of the Holy Roman and Universal Inquisition (Suprema Congregatio Sanctae Romanae et Universalis Inquisitionis); from 1908 to 1967, Congregation of the Holy Office (Congregatio Sancti Officii). Absorbed the Congregation of the Index in 1917
Cf. KBR2511+ Congregation of the Index
2502 General (Table KB6)
2503 Foundation. Jurisdiction, etc.
2505.A-Z Particular commissions, A-Z
2507.A-Z Special topics, A-Z
Index librorum prohibitorum see Z1020+

Constitution of the Church
Organs of government. Hierarchy. De ecclesiae constitutione hierarchica
The Curia Romana
Roman Congregations -- Continued
Congregatio Sancti Officii. Holy Office (1908-1967) see KBU2502+
Congregatio Indicis see KBR2511+
Congregatio de Propaganda Fide pro Negotiis Ritus Orientalis (Congregatio super Correctione Librorum Ecclesiae Orientalis) see KBR2515+
Congregatio pro Ecclesiis Orientalibus. Congregation for the Oriental Churches
2517 General (Table KB6)
2518 Foundation. Jurisdiction, etc.
2520.A-Z Special topics, A-Z
Congregatio de Disciplina Sacramentorum. Congregation for the Discipline of the Sacraments (1908-1975)
Cf. KBU2531+ Congregatio pro Sacramentis et Cultu Divino
2525 General (Table KB6)
2526.A-Z Special topics, A-Z
Congregatio pro Cultu Divino. Congregation for Divine Worship (1969-1975)
Cf. KBU2531+ Congregatio pro Sacramentis et Cultu Divino
2528 General (Table KB6)
2529.A-Z Special topics, A-Z
Congregatio pro Sacramentis et Cultu Divino. Congregation for the Sacraments and Divine Worship (1975-1984)
Formed by the merger of the Congregatio de Discipline Sacramentorum and Congregatio pro Cultu Divino
2531 General (Table KB6)
2533.A-Z Special topics, A-Z
Congregatio de Cultu Divino et Disciplina Sacramentorum. The Congregation for Divine Worship and the Discipline of the Sacraments (1988-)
Formed 1988 by merger of the Congregatio pro Cultu Divino and Congregatio de Sacramentis (Congregation of the Sacraments)
2535 General (Table KB6)
2537 Foundation. Jurisdiction, etc.
2539.A-Z Special topics, A-Z

Constitution of the Church
Organs of government. Hierarchy. De ecclesiae constitutione hierarchica
The Curia Romana
Roman Congregations -- Continued
Congregatio Sacrorum Rituum. Congregation of Rites (1588-1969)
Cf. KBU2549+ Congregatio pro Causis Sanctorum
2545 General (Table KB6)
2547.A-Z Special topics, A-Z
Congregatio de Causis Sanctorum. Congregation for the Causes of Saints (1969-)
Created 1588 as Congregatio Sacrorum Rituum; 1969 divided into two congregations, the Congregatio pro Cultu Divino and Congregatio pro Causis Sanctorum
2549 General (Table KB6)
Decreta autentica, 1898, 1912, 1927
2551 Foundation. Jurisdiction, etc.
2553.A-Z Special topics, A-Z
Congregatio pro Episcopis. Congregation for Bishops
2555 General (Table KB6)
2557 Foundation. Jurisdicition, etc.
2559.A-Z Special topics, A-Z
Congregatio de Propaganda Fide. Congregation for the Propagation of the Faith (1622-1967) see KBU2635+
Congregatio pro Gentium Evangelizatione. Congregation for Evangelization of Peoples (1967-)
Previously Congregatio de Propaganda Fide
2635 General (Table KB6)
Collectanea S.C. de Propaganda Fide, 1893, 1907
2637 Foundation. Jurisdiction, etc.
2639.A-Z Special topics, A-Z
Congregatio Concilii (Congregatio Cardinalium Concilii Tridentini Interpretum). Congregation of the Council see KBU2640+
Congregatio pro Clericis. Congregation for the Clergy (1967-)
Previously Congregatio Concilii
2640 General (Table KB6)
2642 Foundations. Jurisdiction, etc.
2644.A-Z Special topics, A-Z
Congregatio de religiosis. Congregation for Religious (1908-1967) see KBU2660+

Constitution of the Church
Organs of government. Hierarchy. De ecclesiae constitutione hierarchica
The Curia Romana
Roman Congregations -- Continued
Congregatio pro Religiosis et Institutis Saecularibus. Congregation for Religious and Saecular Institutes (1967-1988) see KBU2660+
Congregatio pro Institutis Vitae Consecratae et Societatibus Vitae Apostolicae. Congregation for Institutes of Consecrated Life and Societies of Apostolic Life (1988-)
Previously Congregatio de religiosis (1908-1967) and Congregatio pro religiosis et institutis saecularibus (1967-1988)
2660 General (Table KB6)
2662 Foundation. Jurisdiction, etc.
2664.A-Z Special topics, A-Z
2666 Congregatio de Seminariis et Studiorum. Universitatibus (1908-1967)
Formed 1908 by merger of the Congregatio pro Universitate Studii Romani (1588-1908) and Congregatio Studiorum (1824-1908)
see KBU2668+
Congregatio de Institutione Catholica. Congregation for Catholic Education
Previously Congregatio de Seminarris et Studiorum Universitatibus (1908-1967)
2668 General (Table KB6)
2670 Foundation. Jurisdiction, etc.
2672.A-Z Special topics, A-Z
Pontifical councils
2695 General (Collective)
2698 Pontificium Consilium pro Laicis. Pontifical Council for the Laity (1967-) (Table KB6)
2700 Pontificium Consilium ad Christianorum Unitatem Fovendam. Pontifical Council for Promoting Christian Unity (1966-) (Table KB6)
Commission for Religious Relations with the Jews see KBU2742
2705 Pontificium Consilium pro Familia. Pontifical Council for the Family (1981-) (Table KB6)
Previously Committee for the Family (1973-1981)
2708 Pontificium Consilium de Justitia et Pace. Pontifical Council for Justice and Peace (Table KB6)

Constitution of the Church
Organs of government. Hierarchy. De ecclesiae constitutione hierarchica
The Curia Romana
Pontifical councils -- Continued
2712 Pontificium Consilium "Cor Unum" (1971-) (Table KB6)
Previously Pontifica Commissio Cor Unum
2715 Pontificium Consilium de Spirituali Migrantium atque Itinerantium Cura. Pontifical Council for the Pastoral care of Migrants and Itinerant People (Table KB6)
Previously Pontifical Commission for the Pastoral Care of Migrants and Itinerant Peoples (Pontificia Commissio de Spirituali Migratorum atque Itinerantium Cura)
2716 Pontificium Consilium de Apostolatu pro Valetudinis Administris. Pontifical Council for Pastoral Assistance to Health Care Workers (1988-) (Table KB6)
Previously Pontifical Commission for the Apostolate of Health Care Workers (1985-1988)
2720 Pontificium Consilium de Legum Textibus Interpretandis. Pontifical Council for Interpretation of Legislative Texts (Table KB6)
2722 Pontificium Consilium pro Dialogo inter Religiones. Pontifical Council for Interreligious Dialogue (1988-1993) (Table KB6)
Previously Secretariatus pro Non Christianis
Merged 1993 with the Pontifical Council for Culture
2724 Pontificium Consilium de Cultura. Pontifical Council for Culture (Table KB6)
2728 Pontificium Consilium de Communicationibus Socialibus. Pontifical Council for Social Communications (1988-) (Table KB6)
Commission of Cardinals
Cf. BX1890+ Catholic Church
2730 General works
Particular commissions
2732 Pontificia Commissio Codicis Iuris Canonici Recognoscendi. Pontifical Commission for the Revision of the Code of Canon Law (1963) (Table KB6)
Pontifical commissions
2740 General (Collective)
2742 Commission for Religious Relations with the Jews (1974-) (Table KB6)
2747 Pontifical Commission "Ecclesia Dei" (1988-) (Table KB6)

Constitution of the Church
Organs of government. Hierarchy. De ecclesiae constitutione hierarchica
The Curia Romana
Pontifical commissions -- Continued
2750 Commission for Cultural Heritage of the Church (1993-) (Table KB6)
2754 Commissio ad Catechismum Redigendum pro Ecclesia Universali. Commission for the Preparation of a Catechism for the Universal Church (1986-) (Table KB6)
Pontificia Commissio Iustitia et Pax. Pontifical Commission for Justice and Peace see KBU2708
2758 Consilium ad Exsequendam Constitutionem de Sacra Liturgia. Commission for Implementation of the Constitution on the Sacred Liturgy (Table KB6)
2760 Pontificium Consilium Centrale pro Arte Sacra in Italia. Pontifical Central Commission for Sacred Art in Italy (Table KB6)
Pontifical Commission for Social Communications see KBU2728
Pontificia Commissio de Spirituali Migratorum atque Itinerantium Cura. Pontifical Commission for the Pastoral Care of Migrants and Itinerant Peoples see KBU2715
Pontificium Consilium "Cor Unum" (1971-) see KBU2712
2765 Pontificia Commissio ad Redigendum Codicem Iuris Canonici Orientalis. Pontifical Commission for the Redaction of the Code of Oriental Canon Law (Table KB6)
Previously Pontificia Commissio ad Redigendum Codicem Iuris Canonici Orientalis. Pontifical Commission for the Redaction of the Code of Oriental Canon Law
Pontifical Commission for the Apostolate of Health Care Workers see KBU2716
2768 Pontificia Commissio pro America Latina. Pontifical Commission for Latin America (Table KB6)
2775 Praelati Curiae Romanae. Prelatures
Other offices or organizations of the Curia Romana
2780 Labor Office of the Holy See (Table K15)
2785 Institutions connected with the Holy See
Particular churches and groups of churches. De ecclesiis particularibus deque earundem coetibus
2790 General works

Constitution of the Church
Organs of government. Hierarchy. De ecclesiae constitutione hierarchica
Particular churches and groups of churches. De ecclesiis particularibus deque earundem coetibus -- Continued
Territorial divisions and episcopal jurisdiction in general
2792 Bishops in general. Episcopate and apostolate. De episcopis in genere
Including appointment, promotion, privileges, resignation, etc.
Supra-diocesan groupings and jurisdiction
Ecclesiastical Provinces. Ecclesiastical Regions. Provinciae ecclesiasticae. Regiones ecclesiasticae
2796 General works
2798 Juristic personality. Personalitas iuridica
Organization and organs
2800 General works
Metropolitans. De metropolitanis
Including titles (patriarch or primate)
2803 General works
2805 Jurisdiction. Powers, rights, privileges, etc.
Including prerogatives of honor
2807 The Metropolitan See. Sedes metropolitana
Including vacancy (de sede vacante)
Regional and national councils, synods, etc.
For sources, collected and individual see KBU833+
2810 General works
2815 Plenary council. Concilium plenarium
2820 Provincial council. Concilium provinciale
Conference of Bishops. Conferentia episcoporum
For sources, collected and individual see KBU925+
2825 General works
2827 Juristic personality. Personalitas iuridica
2829 Statute. President, etc. Statuta. Praeses, etc.
2830 Legislative power. Potestas legislativa
2832 Vote (deliberative and consultative). Suffragium deliberativum aut consultativum
Dioceses and diocesan bishop. Dioeceses. Episcopus dioecesanus
2835 General works
2837 Legislative, executive and judicial power. Potestas legislativa, exsecutiva vel iudicialis
2839 Residence. Residentia personalis in dioecesi

Constitution of the Church
Organs of government. Hierarchy. De ecclesiae constitutione hierarchica
Particular churches and groups of churches. De ecclesiis particularibus deque earundem coetibus
Territorial divisions and episcopal jurisdiction in general
Dioceses and diocesan bishop. Dioeceses. Episcopus dioecesanus -- Continued
2840 Episcopal visitation. Visitatio episcopalis
Auxiliaries
2844 Coadjutor bishop. Auxiliary bishop. Episcopus coadiutor et episcopus auxiliaris
2846 Vacant or impeded episcopal see. De sede vacante et de sede impedita
Diocesan constitution and organs
Including territorial organization (partes seu paroeciae)
2850 General works
Diocesan synods see KBU2878+
Diocesan curia. De curia dioecesana
Including administrative and judicial officers
2852 General works
2854 Vicars general. Episcopal vicars. Vicarii generales vel episcopales
Chancelor and vice-chancelor. Notaries. Cancellarius and vice-cancellarius curiae. Notarii
2856 General works
2857 Archives and secret archives. Safes. Archivum vel armarium secretum
2860 Finance council. Consilium a rebus oeconomicis
Including finance officer (oeconomus)
2865 Presbyterate. Priests. Presbyterium. Sacerdotes
2868 Vicars forane. Vicarii foranei
2870 Seminary rectors. Rectores seminarii dioecesani
2872 Parish and pastor. Parochial vicar. Paroecia et parochus. Vicarius paroecialis
2874 Rectors of churches. Chaplains. Rectores ecclesiarum. Capellani
Diocesan councils, synods, etc.
For sources, collected or individual see KBU950+
2878 General works
2880 The diocesan synod. Synodus dioecesana
2882 The presbyterial council. Pastoral councils. Consilium presbyteriale. Consilium pastorale

Constitution of the Church
Organs of government. Hierarchy. De ecclesiae constitutione hierarchica
Particular churches and groups of churches. De ecclesiis particularibus deque earundem coetibus
Territorial divisions and episcopal jurisdiction in general
Dioceses and diocesan bishop. Dioeceses. Episcopus dioecesanus
Diocesan councils, synods, etc. -- Continued
2884 Chapter of canons (Cathedral or collegial). Capitulum canonicorum (cathedrale sive collegiale)
Including errection, statutes, chapter authority, etc.
Personnel of churches and ecclesiastical institutes
Cf. KBU3432+ Administration of Church property
2886 General (Table KB2)
The clergy
2888 General works
Salaries and pensions of the clergy (including social policy) see KBU2355
Officials and employees other than the clergy
Including labor contract and social legislation
2890 General (Table KB2)
2891 Wages. Mercedes iusta
Monasticism. Institutes of consecrated life and societies of apostolic life. De institutis vitae consecratae et de societatibus vitae apostolicae
Cf. Secular ecclesaistical law in K subclasses, e. g. KK5538+; KJV4244; etc.
For history see BX2460+
General norms. Normae communes
Erection. Founders. Constitutions (fundamental codes). Erectio. Fundatores. Constitutiones (codices fundamentales)
2892 General (Table KB2)
2893 Status of institutes. Clerical or lay institute. Institute of pontifical or diocesan right. Institutum clericale, laicale. Institutum iuris pontificii. Institutum iuris dioecesani
Iurisdiction. Governance (external and internal forum). Potestas regiminis (pro foro tam externo quam interno)
Cf. BX2433+ Government and administration
2894 General works
2895 Exemption from jurisdiction of local ordinaries. Ab Ordinariorum loci regimine exemptio

Constitution of the Church
Monasticism. Institutes of consecrated life and societies of apostolic life. De institutis vitae consecratae et de societatibus vitae apostolicae
General norms. Normae communes
Erection. Founders. Constitutions (fundamental codes). Erectio. Fundatores. Constitutiones (codices fundamentales)
Iurisdiction. Governance (external and internal forum). Potestas regiminis (pro foro tam externo quam interno) -- Continued
2896 Equality of sexes. Quae statuuntur, pari iure de utroque sexu valent
2897 Division. Merger and unions of institutions. Divisio in partes. Fusiones et uniones
Religious institutes. Religious houses. Monasteries. De institutis religiosis. De domibus religiosis et monasteriei
Including erection, consent of diocesan bishop, obligations and rights of the institute, etc.
2899 General (Table KB2)
Society and membership. Religious community. Societas. Sodales. Communitas religiosa
2902 General (Table KB2)
2903 Separation of members from the institute. Separatio sodalium
Including transitus, exclaustratio, dimissio, etc.
2906 Autonomy. Governance. Autonomia vitae et regiminis
For monastic rules see BX2436+
2908 Autonomous monasteries. Monasteria sui iuris
2909 Community (society) of persons without vows. Societas sine votis
Governance of institutes. De institutorum regimine
2912 General (Table KB2)
Superiors. Councils. Supreme moderators. Superiores. Consilia. Supremus Moderator
Including appointment, election, term (temporis spatium), removal, residence, etc.
2914 General works
2915 Major superior. Abbot primate. Superior maior. Abbas Primas
Including jurisdiction
2916 Provinces (Grouping of several houses). Provinciae (plurium domorum coniunctio)
Including governance of provinces
Chapters. Capitula
Including organs (organa) and authority

Constitution of the Church
Monasticism. Institutes of consecrated life and societies of apostolic life. De institutis vitae consecratae et de societatibus vitae apostolicae
Religious institutes. Religious houses. Monasteries. De institutis religiosis. De domibus religiosis et monasteriis
Governance of institutes. De institutorum regimine
Chapters. Capitula -- Continued
2918 General works
2919 General chapter. Capitulum generale
2920 Conferences of major superiors. Conferentiae seu concilia
Temporal goods. Bona temporalia see KBU3410+
Novitiate. Admission and formation of novices. Novitatus. Admissio et novitiorum institutio
2922 General works
2923.A-Z Special topics, A-Z
2924 Public vows. Vota publica (perpetua vel temporaria)
Cf. BX2435 Monastic life. Vows. Discipline, etc.
2925 Secular institutes. De institutis saecularibus
2927.A-Z Special topics, A-Z
2927.C53 Chastity. Castitas
2927.C56 Cloistered women
2927.D69 Dowery
2927.M46 Membership. Admission into religious association
2927.O34 Obedience. Oboedientia
2927.P66 Property
2927.P68 Poverty. Paupertas
2927.P75 Privileges
Sodales institutionis see KBU2927.M46
Individual orders of men
Cf. BX2890+ Religious orders (Catholic Church)
<2930> Augustinians. Augustinian Eremites (Table KB8)
<2933> Benedictines (Table KB8)
<2935> Capuchins (Table KB8)
<2940> Carmelites. White Friars (Table KB8)
<2945> Carthusians (Table KB8)
<2950> Cistercians. Bernardines (Table KB8)
<2955> Dominicans. Friars Preachers. Black Friars (Table KB8)
<2960> Franciscans. Minorites. Grey Friars (Table KB8)
<2965> Jesuits. Society of Jesus. Societas Iesu (Table KB8)
<2970> Premonstratensians. White Canons. Norbertines (Table KB8)
<2974> Trappist (Table KB8)
<2978.A-Z> Other orders, A-Z

Constitution of the Church
Monasticism. Institutes of consecrated life and societies of apostolic life. De institutis vitae consecratae et de societatibus vitae apostolicae
Religious institutes. Religious houses. Monasteries. De institutis religiosis. De domibus religiosis et monasteriis -- Continued
Individual orders of women
Cf. BX4260+ Religious orders (Catholic Church)
<2980> Augustinian Eremites (Second Order) (Table KB8)
<2983> Benedictine Nuns (Table KB8)
<2985> Birgittines (Table KB8)
<2990> Capuchin Nuns (Table KB8)
<2992> Carmelites (Second Order) (Table KB8)
<2994> Dominican Sisters. Dominican Nuns (Table KB8)
<2996> Franciscans (Second Order). Poor Clares (Table KB8)
<2999> Institute of the Blessed Virgin Mary (Table KB8)
<3005> Little Sisters of the Poor (Table KB8)
<3008> Premonstratensians (Second Order) (Table KB8)
<3012> Society of the Sacred Heart (Table KB8)
<3014> School Sisters of Notre Dame (Table KB8)
<3016> Sisters of Charity of St. Vincent de Paul (Table KB8)
<3018> Sisters of Mercy. Sisters of Mercy of the Union in the USA. Institut of the Sisters of Mercy of the Americas (Table KB8)
<3020> Sisters of St. Joseph (Table KB8)
<3022> Sisters, Servants of the Immaculate Heart of Mary (Table KB8)
<3024> Ursulines (Table KB8)
<3025> Visitation Order (Table KB8)
<3026.A-Z> Other orders, A-Z
The teaching office of the Church. Magisterium. De ecclesiae munere docendi
3040 General works
3042 Infallible teaching authority. Infallibilitas in magisterio
3046 Heresy and apostasy, etc. Definitions. Haeresis pertinax. Apostasia
3048 Catechetics and preaching. Catechetica. Dei verbum praedicare
Education and training of the clergy see KBU2322+
3049 Missionary activity. Actio ecclesiae missionalis
Catholic religious education. Educatio catholica religiosa
For state regulation of prayer and religious education in public schools, see the law of education in K subclasses for individual countries
Cf. BV1606.2+ Practical theology

The teaching office of the Church. Magisterium. De ecclesiae munere docendi
Catholic religious education. Educatio catholica religiosa -- Continued
3050 General (Comparative)
3052 Right to establish and supervise schools. Ius ecclesiae scholas condendi ac moderandi
3054 Catholic universities. Institutions of higher education. Universitates catholicae. Studiorum superiorum instituta
3060 Ecclesiastical universities and faculties. Universitates vel facultates ecclesiasticae
Media of social communication. Mass media. De instrumentis communicationis socialis
3064 General (Table KB2)
3065 Literature. Books in particular. Scripta, in specie de libris
Including newspapers, periodicals, magazines, the press in general, etc.
3066 Radio communication. Telecommunication. Radiophonica aut televisifica
3068.A-Z Special topics, A-Z
3068.C46 Censors. Censorship
3068.D46 Denunciation of bad books
Index librorum prohibitorum see Z1020+
Prohibited books see KBU3065
3070 Profession of faith. Fidei professio
Sacraments. Administration of sacraments. De sacramentis et administratione
3075 General concepts and principles
Baptism. Confirmation. De baptismo. De sacramento confirmationis
Including adults and infants
3077 General (Table KB2)
3079 Sponsor. God parent. Patrinus
3082 Proof and records. Registration. De probatione et adnotatione
Including civil registry in case of children either born of an unwed mother, or adopted
Confirmation. De sacramento confirmationis
3083 General (Table KB2)
3084.A-Z Special topics, A-Z
The Most Holy Eucharist. Holy Communion. Lord's Supper. De Sanctissima Eucharistia
3085 General (Table KB2)

Sacraments. Administration of sacraments. De sacramentis et administratione
The Most Holy Eucharist. Holy Communion. Lord's Supper. De Sanctissima Eucharistia -- Continued
Celebration of the mass
Including observation of rites, e.g. liturgical and communion rites
3087 General (Table KB2)
3088 Particular masses
e.g. Nuptial mass
Penance. Penitential discipline. De sacramento paenitentiae
Including sacramental confession
Cf. KBU3510+ Punishment of offenses in general
3090 General (Table KB2)
3092 Sacremental seal. Sacramentale sigillum
3094.A-Z Special topics, A-Z
3094.I64 Indulgences
The Anointing of the Sick (Extreme unction). De sacramento unctionis infirmorum
3096 General (Table KB2)
3098.A-Z Special topics, A-Z
Orders. De ordine
Including episcopacy, presbyterate, and diaconate
3102 General (Table KB2)
3104 Candidate for ordination. Requirments. Prerequisites. Candidatus. De requisitis in ordinandis. De praerequisitis ad ordinationem
Irregularities and other impediments. De irregularitatibus aliisque impedimentis
3105 General (Table KB2)
3107 Documents. Examination. Testimonial. Documenta requisita. Scrutinium de qualitatibus. Testimonium
3108 Registration and certification of ordination. Adnotatio ac testimonium peractae ordinationis
Marriage. Marriage law. De matrimonio
For secular (civil) marriage law, see the K subclasses for individual countries
For marital property and regime see KBU3113
For matrimonial actions see KBU3885+
3110 General works
For comprehensive and comparative works on all periods of canon law see KBR3109
3110.2 Requirement of Baptism
3112 Betrothal. Promise of marriage. Promissio matrimonii. Sponsalia de futuro

KBU

Sacraments. Administration of sacraments. De sacramentis et administratione
Marriage. Marriage law. De matrimonio -- Continued
Matrimonial consent. Consensus matrimonialis see KBU3132+
3113 Antenuptial contracts. Marriage settlements
Including dower, marital property, etc.
3114 Ratification and consummation. Matrimonium ratum et consummatum
Unity. Indissolubility. Unitas. Indissolubilitas see KBU3155+
3116 Canon law and civil jurisdiction. Ius canonicum et competentia civilis potestatis
For interaction of secular (civil) law and ecclesiastical law, see the K subclasses for individual countries, e. g. Germany, KK1183
3117 Premarital examinations. Marriage banns. De examine sponsorum. De publicationibus matrimonialibus ad investigationes
Impediments to marriage. De impedimentis
3120 General (Table KB2)
3122.A-Z Mere prohibition of marriage, A-Z
3122.C46 Censure
Matrimonium filii minoris see KBU3122.M56
Matrimonium per procuratorem ineundum see KBU3122.P76
Matrimonium vagorum see KBU3122.T73
3122.M56 Minor without parental consent
3122.P76 Proxy, Marriage by
Cf. KBU3137 Matrimonial consent
3122.T73 Transients
Diriment impediments. Impedimenta dirimentia
3124 General (Table KB2)
3128.A-Z Particular impediments, A-Z
3128.A34 Abduction. Detention of a woman
Aetas see KBU3128.M37
Affinitas in linea recta see KBU3128.A44
3128.A44 Affinity (direct line)
Including adoption
Age of consent see KBU3128.M37
3128.B66 Bond, Existing
Child marriage see KBU3128.M37
3128.C66 Consanguinity (direct line and collateral line)
Constituti in sacris ordinibus see KBU3128.O74
3128.C85 Cult, Disparity of (Catholic baptized and non-Catholic)
3128.H66 Homicide. Uxoricide
3128.I66 Impotence (antecedent and perpetual)

Sacraments. Administration of sacraments. De sacramentis et administratione
Marriage. Marriage law. De matrimonio
Impediments to marriage. De impedimentis
Diriment impediments. Impedimenta dirimentia
Particular impediments, A-Z -- Continued
Impotentia see KBU3128.I66
Linea recta and linea collatoralis consanguinitatis see KBU3128.C66
3128.M37 Marriage age
Mors coniugis see KBU3128.H66
3128.O74 Orders, Holy
Persona baptizata in ecclesia catholica et altera non baptizata see KBU3128.C85
Raptus. Retentio mulieris see KBU3128.A34
Vinculum prioris matrimonii see KBU3128.B66
Vota publica perpetuae castitatis see KBU3128.V69
3128.V69 Vows of chastity, Public perpetual
3130 Dispensation from impediments. Dispensatio ab impedimentis
Including local ordinary (ordinarius loci) and Holy See
Matrimonial consent. De consensu matrimoniale
3132 General works
Validity of consent. Consensus validus
3133 General works
Incapable persons. Incapaces matrimonii contrahendi
3134 General works
3134.5 Incapacity due to mental illness
3135 Ignorance. Error in persona. Fraud. Duress. Ignorantia. Error in persona. Dolus. Metus gravis. Vis
3136 Conditions. Condiciones
Including conditions de futuro, de praeterito vel de praesente
3137 Marriage by proxy. Matrimonium per procuratorem
Cf. KBU3122.P76 Impediments to marriage
3138 Emergency celebration. Deathbed marriage
3140 Invalid consent. Invalid marriage. Consensus invalidus. Matrimonium irritum
Including putative marriage (matrimonium putativum), defect of consent (defectus consensus), defect of form (defectus formae), and diriment impediment (impedimentum dirimens)
3142 Convalidation. Radical sanitation. Convalidatio simplex. Sanatio in radice

Sacraments. Administration of sacraments. De sacramentis et administratione
Marriage. Marriage law. De matrimonio -- Continued
Performance of marriage. Celebration. De forma celebrationis matrimonii
Including marriage celebrants
3144 General (Table KB2)
Defects of form see KBU3140
3145 Witnesses. Testes
3146 Marriage registers. Regesta curiae matrimoniorum
Including registration of death of a spouse, or divorce, and entry in the baptismal register of spouses (regesta baptizatorum)
Interfaith marriage. Mixed marriages. De matrimoniis mixtis
3148 General (Table KB2)
3150 Children of mixed marriages. Filii e matrimonio mixto nati
Clandestinity of marriage celebration. De matrimonio secreto celebrando. Clandestinum matrimonium
3152 General (Table KB2)
Statutes. Papal constitutions. Treaties and concordats. Decrees. Privileges, etc.
3152.A4 "Ne Temere" decree
Marriage bond. Vinculum inter coniuges perpetuum et exclusivum. Husband and wife
Including right and duty to conjugal living (officium et ius servandi convictum coniugalem)
3155 General works
3157 Children. Presumption of legitimacy. Legitimi praesumuntur filii
Including legitimization by subsequent marriage
Dissolution of the bond. De dissolutione vinculi
Including non-consummated marriage or non-baptized parties (privilegium paulinum)
3159 General works
3160 Remarriage. Ius novas nuptias contrahendi
Separation of the spouses. De separatione coniugum
3163 General works
3165 Adultery and condonation. Adulterium. Condonatio
Including tacit condonation
Sacramentals. Sacramentalia
Including the right to establishing, interpreting and abolishing sacramentals
3180 General works
3181 Consecrations. Dedications

Sacramentals. Sacramentalia -- Continued
3182.A-Z Particular sacramentals, A-Z
Other acts of divine worship. De ceteris actibus Cultus Divini
3184 Liturgy of the hours. Observation. Obligatio liturgiae horarum
Including obligation to celebrate the liturgy by clerics and members of institutes of consecrated life and societies of apostolic life
Cf. BX1970+ Liturgy (Catholic Church)
Ecclesiastical funeral rites. Exequiae ecclesiasticae
For burial and cemetary laws of a particular jurisdiction, see the appropriate K subclasses
3190 General (Table KB2)
3192 Granting or denying funeral rites. Exequiae ecclesiasticae concedendae aut denegandae
3193 Registration of internment. Inscriptio in librum defunctorum
3194.A-Z Special topics, A-Z
Veneration of saints, sacred images and relics. Cultus sanctorum, sacrarum imaginum et reliquiarum
3200 General works
3202 Veneration through public cult. Veneratio cultu publico
Including permission of display, and other regulations
3204 Regulations concerning images valuable because of age, art or cult. Imagines pretiosae (vetustate, arte, aut cultu)
Including restoration of art works and removal (transfer)
For alienation (sale, auction, exchange, etc.) see KBU3405
Vow and oath. Votum et iusiurandum
3210 General principles concerning vows and oath
Including attributes of vows, e. g. public, solemn, simple, personal (real or mixed), etc.
3212 Suspension of obligation of vows. Potestas voti obligationem suspendendi
3214 Dispensation from private vows. Dispensandi potestas
3220 Obligation from the oath. Obligatio iureiurando inducta
Including cessation of obligation because of change of conditions, purpose, circumstances, etc.
3225 Dispensation or commutation of oath. Iurisiurandi dispensatio et commutatio
Sacred places and times. De locis et temporibus sacris
Sacred places. Loca sacra
Including decoration, furnishings, utensils, etc.
3230 General (Table KB2)

Other acts of divine worship. De ceteris actibus Cultus Divini
Sacred places and times. De locis et temporibus sacris
Sacred places. Loca sacra -- Continued
3232 Performance of dedication and blessing. Dedicatio vel benedictio
Including documentation of the event
Cf. KBU3181 Sacramentals
3234 Violation or destruction of sacred places. Violatio per actiones graviter iniuriosas. Destructio
Including loss of dedication or blessing by decree or de facto
Maintenance and repair see KBU3432+
3238.A-Z Particular buildings, structures, etc., A-Z
Altaria sive fixa sive mobilia see KBU3238.A58
3238.A58 Altars (fixed or movable)
3238.C46 Cemeteries
3238.C53 Chapels, Private
3238.C58 Churches
Coemeteriae see KBU3238.C46
Ecclesiae see KBU3238.C58
Oratoria see KBU3238.O73
3238.O73 Oratories
3238.R45 Relics
Reliquiae Martyrum aliorumve Sanctorum see KBU3238.R45
Sacella privata see KBU3238.C53
Sanctuaria see KBU3238.S67
3238.S67 Shrines
Sacred times. Fasts and feasts (Church year). Tempora sacra
Including the right to establish, transfer, abolish feast days and days of penance
3242 General (Table KB2)
Sunday and other feasts. Dies dominica. Dies festi
3244 General (Table KB2)
3246.A-Z Particular feast days, A-Z
Days of penance. Dies et tempora paenitentialia
3250 General (Table KB2)
3252 Law of fast. Lex abstinentiae
3254 Processions. Pilgrimages
3256.A-Z Special topics, A-Z
Social work of the Church. Public welfare. Caritas
Class here works on social service and welfare activities of the church
3264 General (Table KB2)
3270 Measures against contagious and infectious diseases

Social work of the Church. Public welfare. Caritas -- Continued
3273 Burials. Sepultura
3274.A-Z Public health hazards and measures, A-Z
3275.A-Z Particular institutions, A-Z
3275.A88 Asylums
Catholic hospitals see KBU3286
3275.O76 Orphanages
3280.A-Z Particular groups of people, A-Z
3280.A54 Aged. Older people
3280.E65 Epileptics
3280.F73 Frail elderly
3280.I63 Incurables
3280.L46 Leprosy patients
3280.M46 Mentally ill
3280.M53 Migrant labor
Older people see KBU3280.A54
3280.P46 People with disabilities
3280.P55 Pilgrims
3280.P66 Poor
3280.W37 War veterans, Disabled
Medical ethics and legislation. Church policy
3282 General (Table KB2)
3284 Catholic health organizations
3286 Catholic hospitals and other medical institutions or health services
Biomedical engineering. Medical technology
3290 General (Table KB2)
3292 Transplantation of organs, tissues, etc. (Table KB2)
3298 Human reproductive technology (Table KB2)
Including artificial insemination and fertilization in vitro
3300.A-Z Special topics, A-Z
3300.C65 Confidential communications
Experiments with the human body see KBU3290
Genetics, Medical see KBU3290
3300.I54 Informed consent
3304 Eugenics. Sterilization and castration (Table KB2)
3306 Euthanasia (Table KB2)
Cf. KBU3752+ Offenses against human life
Birth control. Family planning
3308 General (Table KB2)
3310.A-Z Special topics, A-Z
Church property. Church economics and finance
3320 General works

Church property. Church economics and finance -- Continued
Temporal goods of the Church. De bonis ecclesiasticis temporalibus
Including right and capacity to acquire, retain, administer, and alienate temporal goods
3328 General principles
Acquisition and alienation of property. De acquisitione et alienatione bonorum
Including res mobiles and res immobiles
3332 General (Comparative)
Including civil law and natural law
Contractual acquisition and alienation. De contractibus ac de alienatione
3334 General works
3336 Alienation of church property. Alienatio bonorum
Including requirements, permission, safeguards, and invalid alienation
3338 Loans and leases. Locatio bonorum
3340 Prescription. Praescriptio
3342 Ownership. Dominium bonorum
Obligation of the Christian faithful to support the Church. De obligatione christifidelium subveniendi Ecclesiae
Cf. KBU2312+ Constitution of the Church
3344 General (Table KB2)
3346 Collections. Fund raising. Offerings. Stips specialis. Stips quaesita. Oblationes
For special taxes and fees see KBU3384+
Gifts and legacies ad pias causas
Including donations mortis causa and inter vivos
3348 General works
Executors of pious wills see KBU3370
3350.A-Z Special topics, A-Z
Testaments. Last will. Testamenta. Ultima voluntas
3355 General (Comparative)
3358 Change in last wills and testaments
3370 Executors of pious wills (pia voluntas) and gifts inter vivos
3374 Intestate succession and ius spolii of the church
3376 Inheritance and heir. Hereditas et heres
Including heres necessarius, voluntarius, and legalis
Church taxes. Stole fees. Gratuities. Taxae and tributa. Subventiones rogatae. Exactiones
For state regulation of church taxation typical for a particular jurisdiction, see the jurisdiction (Secular ecclesiastical law)
3384 General (Table KB2)

Church property. Church economics and finance
Temporal goods of the Church. De bonis ecclesiasticis temporalibus
Obligation of the Christian faithful to support the Church. De obligatione christifidelium subveniendi Ecclesiae
Church taxes. Stole fees. Gratuities. Taxae and tributa. Subventiones rogatae. Exactiones -- Continued
Tithes and first fruits (Local custom) see KBR3386
Cathedraticum see KBR3388
3392.A-Z Other, A-Z
3392.C68 Court fees
3392.F86 Funeral taxes
3392.M37 Marriage dispensation
3392.M38 Mass stipends
3400 Privileges. Immunity. Privilegia. Immunitas
Including exemption from taxes, obligatory services (munera sordida), etc.
Types of property
3405 Res sacrae. Res consecratae vel benedictae. Res extra commercium
Including regulations for evaluation, sale or exchange
Cf. KBU3204 Regulations concerning images
Real property. Land holdings (Church lands). Res immobiles
Including personal and real rights and claims (iura et actiones sive personales sive reales)
3410 General (Comparative)
3413 Mortgages
3415 Restrictions
Church buildings. Building and construction. Maintenance and restoration
3417 General works
3419 Building laws
Administration and administrators of property. De administratione bonorum
Including hierarchy of organization, application of civil law, including labor and social policy (observantia legum civilium), and state supervision
3432 General works
Diocesan institutes for collection of goods and offerings (bona and oblationes)
3435 General works
3437 Funds. Massa communis
Duties and obligations of administrators
3440 General (Table KB2)
3444.A-Z Special topics, A-Z

Church property. Church economics and finance
Temporal goods of the Church. De bonis ecclesiasticis temporalibus
Administration and administrators of property. De administratione bonorum
Duties and obligations of administrators
Special topics, A-Z -- Continued
3444.B84 Budget (Annual)
3444.C54 Clergy, Support of
3444.I69 Inventories
Labor law for employees (non clergy) see KBU2890+
Mercedes iusta see KBU2891
Securitas socialis clericorum see KBU3444.S64
3444.S63 Social policy
3444.S64 Social security (for clerics)
Sustentatio clericorum see KBU3444.C54
Wages for employees (non clergy) see KBU2891
Juristic persons of public or private law. Personae iuridicae publicae vel privatae
3450 General works
Non-collegiate institutes
Charitable uses, trusts and foundations. Endowments. Fundationes piae. Fideicommissa
Including both piae fundationes autonomae and non autonomae
3452 General works
3454 Mass obligations or legacies. Onera missarum. Legata
Other non-collegiate institutes and institutions
Including institutes both owned or spiritually supervised by the church
3456 General works
3458 Ecclesiastical benefices
For the older law of erectionm, creation, etc. see KBR2350+
For the ius patronatus see KBR2361+
3460 Loca pia
Including hospitals, orphanages, schools, etc.
Medical ethics and legislation see KBU3282+
Sanctions in the Church. Criminal law. De sanctionibus in Ecclesia. De lege poenali
Including general works on both criminal law and procedure
3500 Bibliography
Punishment of offenses in general. De delictorum punitione generatim
Including the Christian faithful, laity, and the clergy

Sanctions in the Church. Criminal law. De sanctionibus in Ecclesia. De lege poenali
Punishment of offenses in general. De delictorum punitione generatim -- Continued
Penal laws and precepts. Applicability and validity
Including territorial and temporal applicability, and personal applicability (immunity)
3510 General works
3512 Poena latae sententiae (automatically incurred by law) and poena ferendae sententiae (by court decision)
3513 Uniformity of law application. Uniformes ferantur poenales leges
3514 Ex post facto laws and retroactivity
Including application of the more favorable law or cessation of penalty
Classification of penal sanctions. Sanctiones poenales
Including both layity and clergy
3518 General (Table KB2)
Poenae medicinales. Medicinal penalties
Including poenae latae sententiae and poenae ferendae sententiae
3520 General works
Censures see KBU3602+
Poenae expiatoriae. Expiatory (vindictive) penalties
3522 General works
Particular penalties see KBU3613.A+
Remedia poenalis (Praecavenda). Paenitentia. Preventive penal remedies and penance
3526 General (Table KB2)
Particular remedies see KBU3618
Violation of law or precept. Criminal offense. Violatio legis vel praecepti
3533 General works
Imputability (Liability). Guilt. Dolus. Culpa
3537 General works
Incapacity. Delicti incapaces
3539 General works
3542 Insane persons. Qui rationis usu carent
3544 Minors under the sixteenth year of age. Minores
Justification of illegal acts. Exculpating or extenuating circumstances
3548 General works
3550 Necessity. Grave fear. Necessitas. Vis. Metus gravis
3552 Self-defense or defense of another. Legitimae tutelae causa contra iniustum agere
3553 Putative necessity

Sanctions in the Church. Criminal law. De sanctionibus in Ecclesia. De lege poenali
Violation of law or precept. Criminal offense. Violatio legis vel praecepti
Imputability (Liability). Guilt. Dolus. Culpa
Justification of illegal acts. Exculpating or extenuating circumstances -- Continued
3554 Putative self-defense and exceeding self-defense. Sine debito moderamine
3555 Minors (below the sixteenth year of age). Minores
3556 Limited capacity. Omissio debitae diligentiae
Incapacity see KBU3539+
3557 Ignorance about prohibition. Sine culpa ignorantia
3559.A-Z Special topics, A-Z
Aestus passionis, Gravis see KBU3559.D58
Affect see KBU3559.D58
3559.D58 Distemper. Passion. Affect
Ebrietas see KBU3559.I68
3559.I68 Intoxication
Passion see KBU3559.D58
3562 Error
Criminal act. Commission. Ommission. Actus vel ommissiones
3564 General works
3566 Attempt. Desistere ab incepta delicti exsecutione
Including active repentance, and inherently ineffective acts
Cf. KBU3592 Sentencing
Compound offenses. Continuing crimes. Recidivism see KBU3588
3570 Principals and accomplices. Auctores principales. Complices
Sentencing. Application of penalties. De poenis applicandis
3574 General works
Sentencing. Commensurateness of guilt and punishment
3576 General works
Judicial discretion
3577 General works
3578 Indeterminate penalty
Circumstances influencing measure of penalty
3580 General works
Exempting, aggravating and extenuating circumstances
3582 General works
3586.A-Z Special topics, A-Z
3588 Compound punishment
Causes barring execution
3590 General works

Sanctions in the Church. Criminal law. De sanctionibus in Ecclesia. De lege poenali
Sentencing. Application of penalties. De poenis applicandis
Causes barring execution -- Continued
3592 Active repentance
Including previous warning (admonition)
Cessation of penalties. Remission. Cessatio poenarum. Remissio poenae
3594 General works
3596 Power of remission. Potestas remittendi
Including reservation of the right
3597 Suspensive effect of appeal or recourse. Effectus suspensivus
3598.A-Z Special topics, A-Z
Particular penalties and measures of rehabilitation. De poenis aliisque punitionibus
Including both laity and clergy
Censures. De censuris
3602 General (Collective)
3604 Excommunication. Effects of excommunication. Excommunicatio (Table K22)
3606 Interdict. Effects of interdict. Interdictum (Table K22)
3608 Suspension of clerics. Effect of suspension. Suspensio (Table K22)
Including suspension from order, office or benefice, and dismissal from clerical state. Dimittere e statu clericali
3610.A-Z Special topics, A-Z
3610.A38 Absolutio
Expiatory (vindictive) penalties. De poenis expiatoriis
General works see KBU3522
3612 Effects of expiatory penalties
Including effects in perpetuity, for a prescribed or indeterminate time
3613.A-Z Common vindictive penalties, A-Z
3615.A-Z Vindictive penalties peculiar to the clergy, A-Z
Penal remedies and penance. De remediis poenalibus et paenitentiis
General works see KBU3526
3618 Admonition and rebuke. Monitio vel correptio
3620.A-Z Special topics, A-Z
Individual offenses and prescribed penalties. De poenis in singula delicta
Offenses against religion and the unity of the Church. De delictis contra religionem et ecclesiae unitatem
3625 General (Collective)
Particular offenses

Sanctions in the Church. Criminal law. De sanctionibus in Ecclesia. De lege poenali
Individual offenses and prescribed penalties. De poenis in singula delicta
Offenses against religion and the unity of the Church. De delictis contra religionem et ecclesiae unitatem
Particular offenses -- Continued
Apostasy. The apostate. Apostata a fide
3628 General works
3632.A-Z Special topics, A-Z
Heresy. The heretic. Haereticus
Cf. KBU3678 Teaching of doctrines condemned by the Roman Pontiff
3636 General works
3638.A-Z Special topics, A-Z
Schism. The schismatic. Schismaticus
3640 General works
3642.A-Z Special topics, A-Z
3644 Prohibited participation in sacred rites. Vetita communicatio in sacris
3650 Baptizing and educating children out of faith. Baptismus liberorum vel educaio in religione acatholica
3652 Blasphemy. Use of the media (of social communications) to blaspheme and damage good morals, or for inciting hatred or contempt against religion or Church. Instrumentis communicationis socialis blasphemiam proferre aut bonos mores graviter laedere ... vel odium contemptumve excitare
3664 Profanation of the consecreted species. Sacrilege. Abicere species consecratas aut in sacrilegium finem retinere
3668 Perjury. Periurium coram ecclasiastica auctoritate
Offenses against ecclesiastical authorities and the freedom of the Church. De delictis contra ecclesiasticas auctoritates et ecclesiae libertatem
3670 General (Collective)
3672 Use of physical force against the Roman Pontiff. Adhibere vim physicam in Romanum Pontificem
3674 Use of physical force against a person with episcopal character. Adhibere vim physicam in eum cum episcopali charactere
3676 Use of physical force against a cleric or religious (contempt for faith, church, ecclesiastical power, etc.) Adhibere vim physicam in clericum vel religiosum

Sanctions in the Church. Criminal law. De sanctionibus in Ecclesia. De lege poenali
Individual offenses and prescribed penalties. De poenis in singula delicta
Offenses against ecclesiastical authorities and the freedom of the Church. De delictis contra ecclesiasticas auctoritates et ecclesiae libertatem -- Continued

3678 Teaching of doctrines condemned by the Roman Pontiff or ecumenical council
Cf. KBU3636+ Heresy

Recourse against an act of the Roman Pontiff to ecumenical council or college of bishops. Recursus contra Romani Pontificis actum ad Concilium Oecumenicum vel ad Episcoporum collegium

3680 General works

3682 Inciting in public hatred against the Holy See or an ordinary. Excitare publice vel odia adversus Sedem Apostolicam vel Ordinarium

3686 Disobedience to ecclesiastical authority. Non obtemperare Sedi Apostolicae, Ordinario, vel Superiori legitime praecipienti vel prohibenti
Including inciting disobedience against ecclesiastical authority

3688 Affiliation with societies conspiring against the Church. Nomen dare consociationi, quae contra Ecclesiam machinatur

Impeding freedom of ecclesiastical ministri, election, or jurisdiction. Impedire libertatem ministerii vel electionis vel potestatis ecclesiasticae

3690 General works

3692 Impeding legitimate use of sacred or other ecclesiastical goods. Impedire legitimum bonorum sacrorum aliorumve ecclesiasticorum usum

3694 Intimidation of an elector, the elected, ecclesiastical ministry or authority. Perterre electorem vel electum vel eum qui potestatem vel ministerium ecclesiasticum exercuit

3696 Profanation of a movable or immovable sacred thing. Profanare rem sacram, mobilem vel immobilem

3698 Alienation of ecclesiastical goods. Sine licentia bonorum ecclesiasticorum alienatio

Usurpation of ecclesiastical functions. De munerum ecclesiasticorum usurpatione deque delictis in iis exercendis
Including offenses while performing functions

3700 General (Collective)

Sanctions in the Church. Criminal law. De sanctionibus in Ecclesia. De lege poenali
Individual offenses and prescribed penalties. De poenis in singula delicta
Usurpation of ecclesiastical functions. De munerum ecclesiasticorum usurpatione deque delictis in iis exercendis -- Continued
3702 Absolving an accomplice in peccato. Absolutio complicis in peccato
3704 Attempted administration of the Eucharistic Sacrifice. Attentare liturgicam eucharistici Sacrificii actionem
3706 Giving absolution beyond own jurisdiction. Sacramentalem absolutionem dare valide nequire
Including hearing of confession (sacramentalem confessionem audire)
3708 Simulation of administration of a sacrament. Qui sacramentum se administrare simulat
3710 Simony in administration or reception of sacraments. Per simoniam sacramentum celebrare vel recipere
3712 Usurpation of ecclesiastical office. Usurpatio officii ecclesiastici
3714 Consecration of someone as a bishop without apostolic mandate. Sine pontificio mandato aliquem consecrare in Episcopum
3716 Ordination by a bishop of a person not under his jurisdiction (without dimissorial letters). Alienum subditum sine legitimis litteris dimissoriis ordinare
3718 Illegitimate performance of priestly functions or other sacred ministries. Illegitime exsequi sacerdotale munus vel aliud sacrum ministerium
3720 Illegitimately profiteering from a Mass stipend. Quaestum illegitime facere ex Missae stipe
3722 Solicitation or attempted bribe of officials in the Church
3724 Violation of the seal of confession. Violatio sacramentalis sigilli
Including confessor (confessarius) or interpretr (interpres)
3726 Abuse of ecclesiastical power or function. Ecclesiastica potestate vel munere abuti
3728.A-Z Other, A-Z
Falsehood. De crimine falsi
3730 General (Table KB2)
3732 Denunciation of solicitation against confessor before an ecclesiastical superior. Denuntiare confessarium de delicto sollicitationis apud ecclesiasticum Superiorem

Sanctions in the Church. Criminal law. De sanctionibus in Ecclesia. De lege poenali
Individual offenses and prescribed penalties. De poenis in singula delicta
Falsehood. De crimine falsi -- Continued
3734 Forgery and suppression of ecclesiastical documents
Including fabrication, change, or destruction of authentic documents, the use of false or altered documents, and including false statements made in public documents
Offenses against particular obligations. De delictis contra speciales obligationes
3738 General (Table KB2)
3740 Unlawful trading or commerce by a cleric or religious. Clerici vel religiosi mercaturam vel negotiationem exercentes contra canonum praescripta
3742 Attempted marriage of a cleric. Clericus matrimonium, etiam civiliter tantum, attentans
3744 Attempted marriage of a religious in perpetual vows. Religiosus a votis perpetuis, matrimonium etiam civiliter tantum, attentans
3746 Concubinage of a cleric. Clericus concubinarius
Including other external sins (clericus in alio peccato externo)
3750 Grave violation of obligation of residence. Residentiae obligationem graviter violare
Offenses against human life and freedom. De delictis contra hominis vitam et libertatem
3752 General works
Homicide. Homicidium
3755 General (Table KB2)
3756.A-Z Particular offenses, A-Z
3756.A36 Abortion. Abortum procurare (Table KB3)
3760 Abduction. Kidnapping. Raptus (Fraudulently or with force). Raptus, vi aut fraude
3764 Rape. Stuprum violentum
3764.5 Child sexual abuse
3765 Detention. False imprisonment (Fraudulently or with force). Hominem detinere
3768 Mutilation. Assault and battery. Mutilare. Graviter vulnerare
3774.A-Z Other offenses, A-Z
Courts and procedure. De processibus
3780 Bibliography
3782 General (Table KB2)
Administration of justice. The tribunals. De variis tribunalium gradibus et speciebus

Courts and procedure. De processibus
Administration of justice. The tribunals. De variis tribunalium gradibus et speciebus -- Continued
General works see KBU3782
Jurisdiction of ecclesiastical courts (General). The competent forum. De foro competenti
Including competence in subject matter and venue
For criminal jurisdiction see KBU3937
General works see KBU3782
3785 Prorogation
3789 Competence in subject matter. Causae spirituales et spirituales annexae
Venue. Place of court. Forum
3797 General (Table KB2)
3798 Particular fora
e. g. forum domicilii
3803 Judicial review of ecclesiastical administrative acts
Cf. KBU3803 Courts and procedure
3804 Conflict of jurisdictions. Conflictus competentiae inter tribunalia
3806 The tribunals (diocesan) of first instance. Tribunalis primae instantiae
Including single judge tribunals and collegiate tribunals
3808 The tribunals of second instance. Tribunalia secundae instantiae
Including oversight by the conference of bishops
The tribunals of the Apostolic See. Apostolicae Sedis tribunalia
For decisions see KBU43.15+
3810 General (Comparative)
3811 Iudex supremus. Supreme judge for the Catholic World. The Roman Pontiff
Including jurisdiction and delegated jurisdiction
Paenitentiaria Apostolica. The Sacred Penitentiary
Cf. BX1862 Catholic Church
3812 General (Table KB6)
3813 Jurisdicition (internal forum)
3814.A-Z Special topics, A-Z
Rota Romana (Tribunal ordinarium)
Cf. BX1865 Catholic Church
3816 General (Table KB6)
3816.3 Jurisdiction. Competence
Including 1st, 2nd, 3rd and further instances
3816.5 Judges and other court officials
Including auditores, procuratores, advocati, etc.
3817 Principle of collegiality

Courts and procedure. De processibus
Administration of justice. The tribunals. De variis tribunalium gradibus et speciebus
The tribunals of the Apostolic See. Apostolicae Sedis tribunalia
Rota Romana (Tribunal ordinarium) -- Continued
3818 Court decorum. Court order. Proceedings
Supremum Signaturae Apostolicae Tribunal. The Supreme Tribunal of the Apostolic Signatura. Court of cassation
3819 General (Table KB6)
3820 Jurisdiction (judicial, administrative, and disciplinary power)
Including recourse against rotal sentences, conflicts of competence between courts or dicasteries of the Roman Curia, judicial review of ecclesiastical administrative acts, etc., and including oversight over the administration of justice
The legal profession in general
3822 General (Comparative)
3822.5 Legal education
Judges and other court officials
Including auditors, advocates and procurators, etc. Iudices et ministri tribunalis
3823 General (Comparative)
Judges and court officials of a particular court
see the court
3823.3 Promoters of justice. Defenders of the bond. Promotores iustitiae. Defensores vinculi
Notaries. Notarii
3823.5 General (Table KB2)
3824.A-Z Special topics, A-Z
3825 Procedure in general
Including contentious and non-contentious procedures, matrimonial actions, and criminal procedures
Procedural principles and court order. De disciplina in tribunalibus servanda
3825.5 Due process of law
3826 Speedy trial
3827 Disqualification of judge or court officers. Conflict of interests
Including consanguinity, affinity, profit, etc.
3828.A-Z Other, A-Z
Album see KBU3828.O74
3828.D43 Deadline
Delays see KBU3828.T56

Courts and procedure. De processibus
Procedural principles and court order. De disciplina in tribunalibus servanda
Other, A-Z -- Continued
Dilationes see KBU3828.T56
Docket see KBU3828.O74
Fatalia legis see KBU3828.D43
Iusiruandum de munere rite et fideliter implendo see KBU3828.O27
3828.O27 Oath of participants in trial
3828.O74 Order of adjudication. Docket
Ordo cognitionum see KBU3828.O74
3828.P55 Place of the court
3828.S43 Secrecy of office and deliberations
Sedes tribunalis see KBU3828.P55
Termini see KBU3828.T56
3828.T56 Time limits. Delays
Parties to action. De partibus in causa
3830 General (Table KB2)
Juristic persons see KBU3833.J87
Petitioner and respondent. Plaintiff and defendant. De actore et parte conventa
3831 General works
Capacity to sue and to be sued
3832 General works
3833.A-Z Particular, A-Z
3833.J87 Juristic persons
Including legitimate representives
3833.M56 Minors and people with mental disabilities
Including guardians and curators of such persons
People with mental disabilities see KBU3833.M56
Personae iuridicae see KBU3833.J87
3834 Procurators and advocates. Procuratores ad lites et advocati (Table KB2)
Pretrial procedures see KBU3839+
Actions and defenses. Exceptions. De actionibus et exceptionibus
3835 General (Table KB2)
3836 Joinder of actions
3837.A-Z Particular, A-Z
3837.C68 Counterclaim
Inhibitio exercitii iuris see KBU3837.S46
3837.L57 Lis pendens
Reconventio see KBU3837.C68
3837.R47 Res iudicata
3837.R48 Restraining order

Courts and procedure. De processibus
Actions and defenses. Exceptions. De actionibus et exceptionibus
Particular, A-Z -- Continued
Sequestratio see KBU3837.S46
3837.S46 Sequestration
The contentious trial. De iudicio contentioso
3838 General works
Pretrial procedures
3839 Introductory petition. Libellus litis introductorius
Including form requirements
3839.5 Summons. Citation. Subpoena. Decretum citationis in iudicium
Procedure at first instance. Prima instantia
3840 General (Table KB2)
Jurisdiction. The competent forum
Including competence in subject matter and venue
3840.5 General works
3841.A-Z Particular, A-Z
3841.D65 Domicile
3841.F67 Forum rei sitae
3841.P75 Prorogation
Actions and defenses. Exceptions. De actionibus et exceptionibus
3841.2 Joinder of actions
3841.3 Lis pendens
3841.5 Joinder of issue. Contestatio litis
3842.A-Z Particular proceedings, A-Z
3842.A33 Abatement of trial
Absens pars a iudicio see KBU3842.J84
3842.C53 Change of party
Including death
3842.I67 Intervention of third party
Interventus tertii in causa see KBU3842.I67
3842.J84 Judgments by default
Peremptum iudicium see KBU3842.A33
Settlement out of court see KBU3918
Evidence. Burden of proof. Probatio. Onus probationis
3843 General (Table KB2)
3844 Facts and presumptions. Facta et quae ab ipsa lege praesummuntur
3845 Admission of evidence. Probationes adducere
3846 Declaration (testimony) of parties. Partium declarationes
Including party oath (iusiurandum partium de veritate dicenda) and judicial confession (confessio iudicialis)

Courts and procedure. De processibus
The contentious trial. De iudicio contentioso
Procedure at first instance. Prima instantia
Evidence. Burden of proof. Probatio. Onus probationis -- Continued
3847 Documentary evidence. Probatio per documenta (Table KB2)
Including public ecclesiastical and public civil documents, and vis probandi
3848 Witnesses. Testes et qui testes esse possint (Table KB2)
Including capacity and incapables (incapaces) and including examination of witnesses (testium examen)
3849 Expert evidence. Experts. Periti
3850 Access and judicial inspection. Accessus et recognitio (inspectio) iudicialis
Presumptions see KBU3844
Incidental case (Causa incidens) see KBU3858
Publication of acts. Conclusion and discussion of case. Actorum publicatio. Conclusio in causa et discussio causae
3851 General works
3852 Presentation of defense. Temporis spatium ad defensiones et animadversiones exhibendas
Intervention by third party see KBU3842.I67
Judicial decisions. De pronuntiationibus iudicis
Including publication of decisions
3854 General works
3855 Injunctions
3857 Sentences. Judgements. Sententiae definitivae
3858 Interlocutory decisions. Sententiae interlocutoriae
3859 Judicial decrees. Decreta iudicis
Judgement by default see KBU3842.J84
Remedies. Challenge of the sentence. De impugnatione sententiae
3861 General (Table KB2)
3863 Complaint of nullity. Querela nullitatis contra sententiam
3865 Appeal. Appellatio
3869 Res iudicata
3872 Restitutio in integrum
3874 Court costs. Expensae iudiciales
3876 Execution of sentence and executory decree. Exsecutio sententiae. Exsecutorium iudicis decretum
Including provisional execution (exsecutio provisoria) before res iudicata

Courts and procedure. De processibus -- Continued
The oral contentious process. De processu contentioso orali
3878 General (Table KB2)
3881.A-Z Special topics, A-Z
3883 Non-contentious jurisdiction
Particular procedures. De quibusdam processibus specialibus
Matrimonial actions. De processibus matrimonialibus
3885 General (Table KB2)
Jurisdiction. The competent forum. De foro competenti
Including competens tribunal in causis de matrimonii nullitate
3887 General (Comparative)
3889 Jurisdiction of the civil courts. Causae pertinentes ad civilem magistratum
3890 Parties to action (Partes habiles ad impugnandi matrimonium)
Including spouses (coniuges) and promotor of justice (promotor iustitiae)
3893 Evidence. Burden of proof. Probatio. Onus probandi
3895 Sentence. Appellate procedure. Sententia et appellatio
Nullity of marriage. Causae ad matrimonii nullitatem declarandam. Annulment
3897 General (Table KB2)
3899 Documentary process. Processus documentalis
Separation. Divorce. Causae separationis coniugum. Divortium
3901 General works
Deferral of case to the civil court. Causam ad forum civile deferre see KBU3889
3902 Custody and education of children
3905.A-Z Special topics, A-Z
3905.A48 Adultery
3905.P75 Privilegium Petrinum
Dispensation of ratified and non-consummated marriage. Dispensatio super matrimonio rato et non consummato
3907 General (Table KB2)
3908 Jurisdiction of the Apostolic See. Una Sedes Apostolica cognoscit de facto inconsummationis matrimonii
3909 Parties to action. Spouses. Coniuges
3910 Rescript of dispensation. Rescriptum dispensationis
Including entry in the registers of marriage and baptism
3912 Procedure in presumption and declaration of death of a spouse. Processus praesumptae mortis coniugis

Courts and procedure. De processibus
Particular procedures. De quibusdam processibus specialibus -- Continued
3914 Declaration of nullity of sacred ordination. De causis ad sacrae ordinationis nullitatem declarandam
Including observation of canons on trials (general) and contentious trial
3918 Settlement out of court. Arbitration. Compromise. Transactio seu reconciliatio. Iudicium arbitrale. Comprommisum
Penal (Criminal) procedure. De processu poenali
3920 General (Comparative)
3921 Procedural principles
Parties to action. De partibus in causa
3926 Promoter of justice (petitioner). Promotor iustitiae
3927 Accused. Accusatus
3928 Advocates. Advocati
Pre-trial procedure
Including opening and closing decrees of the Ordinary
3930 General (Table KB2)
3931 Summons. Decretum citationis
3932 Libellus of accusation. Libellus accusationis
3933 Investigation. De praevia investigatione
3934 Decree without trial. Decretum extra iudicium
Procedure at first instance. Prima instantia
3936 General (Table KB2)
3937 Jurisdiction. The competent forum
3938 Joinder of issue. Contestatio litis
3939.A-Z Particular proceedings, A-Z
Actio ad damna reparanda see KBU3939.D36
3939.D36 Damages, Reparation of
3939.I67 Intervention of third party
Interventus tertii in causa see KBU3939.I67
3940 Evidence. Burden of proof. Probatio. Onus probandi
3945 Renunciation (of instance) by the promoter of justice. Renuntiatio instantiae a promotore iustitiae
Judicial decisions. Sentence. Sententia
3947 General works
3949 Acquittal. Absolutio
3952 Res iudicata
3954 Restitutio in integrum
Remedies
3956 General (Table KB2)
3958 Appeal. Appellatio
Action for reparation of damages see KBU3939.D36

Courts and procedure. De processibus -- Continued
Judicial review of administrative acts. Administrative remedies. De ratione procedendi in recursibus administrativis
3964 General (Table KB2)
3966 Peremptory time period (available time). Terminus peremptorius (tempus utile)
3968 Gravamen
3969 Revocation of emendation of decree. Revocatio vel emendatio decreti
Recourse. Recursus
3970 General works
3972 Suspension of the execution (of a decree). Suspensio exsecutionis
Removal and transfer of pastors. De procedura in parochis amovendis vel transferendis
3975 General (Table KB2)
3977 Particular reasons. Causae
3979 Resignation by pastor. Renuntiatio a parocho
3982 Decree of transfer. Decretum translationis
3985 Recourse against decree of removal. Recursus adversus amotionis decretum
Church and state relationships. De relationibus inter ecclesiam et status. Ius publicum ecclesiae
Cf. BV629+ Practical theology
4000 General (Comparative)
Relation of papacy to monarchic government (divine right of kings)
4010 General (Comparative)
<4012> Early Church and Roman Empire. Byzantine Empire (to ca. 8th cent.)
see KBR4012+
<4020> Frankish and Holy Roman Empire (to ca. end 15th cent.)
see KBR4020+
<4034> Renaissance and Reformation (16th cent.)
see KBR4034+
<4040> Absolutism. Enlightenment. Modernism (17th to end 19th cent.)
see KBR4040+
Relation of the Church to democratic government
4045 General (Comparative)
Separation of Church and state. De separatione ecclesiae a statu

Church and state relationships. De relationibus inter ecclesiam et status. Ius publicum ecclesiae
Relation of the Church to democratic government
Separation of Church and state. De separatione ecclesiae a statu -- Continued
Authority. Competence. Spiritual and temporal jurisdiction. Causae mere ecclesiasticae, causae civiles and causae mistae
For secular ecclesiastical law, i.e. secular (civil) law affecting the church, see the K subclasses for individual countries, e. g. KK5520+ Secular ecclesiastical law in Germany
4050 General (Comparative)
4052 Conflict of jurisdiction (General)
For immunity of clergy (Privilegium fori) see KBU2340.P77
For courts see KBU3804
4057 Jurisdiction over marriage and civil marriage law
Cf. KBU3116 Marriage law
Human and civil rights and the Church
4059 General (Table KB2)
4060.A-Z Particular rights and freedom, A-Z
4060.F72 Freedom of assembly, association and demonstration
4060.F73 Freedom of expression
4060.F75 Freedom of information (press and radio communication)
4060.F77 Freedom of religion and conscience
4060.F78 Freedom of thought and speech
4060.I53 Individual freedom
4060.R53 Right to life
4062 Jurisdiction over education and the state's cultural mandate (Table KB2)
Including religious instruction in schools
Cf. KBU3050+ Catholic religious education
Legal and international status of the Holy See (State of Vatican City, 1929-)
For periods before 1929 see KZ4187
Treaties. Concordates
4064 Lateran Treaty (1929) (Table K5)
4066 General works
4068 Sovereignty
4070 Territory. Boundaries of Vatican City
4072 Extraterritoriality of Vatican City
4074 Papal independence from civil powers
Foreign and international relations of the Holy See
4076 General works

Church and state relationships. De relationibus inter ecclesiam et status. Ius publicum ecclesiae
Foreign and international relations of the Holy See -- Continued
Papal legation. Diplomacy. De relationibus diplomaticis
4078 General (Table KB2)
Papal envoys. Legates. Nuncios. Papal vicars. Legati pontificii. Nuntii
4080 General works
4082 Headquarters of Pontifical legation. Sedes legationis pontificiae
Including extraterritoriality
4084 Jurisdiction
Concordats. De concordatis
4095 General (Comparative)
Collections (General) see KBU38
Collections by country
see the appropriate K subclass for the country
Individual
see the subject in the appropriate K subclass for the country
4097 Peace efforts of the Holy See. The Pope as arbiter
Local Church government
By region or country
The Americas
4112 General works
4113 United States of America (Table KB4)
4114 Canada (Table KB4)
4115 Greenland (Table KB4)
Latin America
Including Mexico, Central and South America
4116 General works
4117 Mexico (Table KB4)
Central America
4118 General works
4119 Belize (Table KB4)
4120 Costa Rica (Table KB4)
4121 Guatemala (Table KB4)
4122 Honduras (Table KB4)
4123 Nicaragua (Table KB4)
4124 Panama (Table KB4)
4125 El Salvador (Table KB4)
West Indies. Carribean area
Including Federation of the West Indies, 1958-1962
4128 General works
4129 Cuba (Table KB4)

Local Church government
By region or country
The Americas
Latin America
West Indies. Carribean area -- Continued
4130 Haiti (Table KB4)
4131 Dominican Republic (Table KB4)
4132 Puerto Rico (Table KB4)
4133 Virgin Islands of the United States. Danish West Indies (Table KB4)
4134 British West Indies (Table KB4)
Including Guyana
Danish West Indies see KBU4133
4136 Netherlands Antilles. Dutch West Indies (Table KB4)
Including Curaçao
For Suriname (Dutch Guiana) see KBU4150
4137 French West Indies (Table KB4)
Including Guadeloupe and Martinique
For French Guiana see KBU4152
South America
4140 General works
4141 Argentina (Table KB4)
4142 Bolivia (Table KB4)
4144 Brazil (Table KB4)
4145 Chile (Table KB4)
4146 Colombia (Table KB4)
4147 Ecuador (Table KB4)
4148 Falkland Islands (Table KB4)
Guiana
4149 General works
Guyana. British Guiana see KBU4134
4150 Suriname. Dutch Guiana (Table KB4)
4152 French Guiana (Table KB4)
4153 Paraguay (Table KB4)
4154 Peru (Table KB4)
4155 Uruguay (Table KB4)
4156 Venezuela (Table KB4)
Europe
4160 General works
4161 Albania (Table KB4)
4162 Andorra (Table KB4)
4164 Austria. Austro-Hungarian Monarchy (Table KB4)
4166 Belarus (Table KB4)
4168 Belgium (Table KB4)
4170 Bosnia and Hercegovina (Table KB4)
4172 Bulgaria (Table KB4)

Local Church government
By region or country
Europe -- Continued
4173 Corsica (Table KB4)
4174 Croatia (Table KB4)
4177 Cyprus (Table KB4)
4180 Czechoslovakia (to 1993) (Table KB4)
4182 Czech Republic (1993-) (Table KB4)
4184 Estonia (Table KB4)
4186 Finland (Table KB4)
4188 France (Table KB4)
4192 Germany (Table KB4)
Including the Federal Republic of Germany (to 1990)
4194 Germany (Democratic Republic) (to 1990) (Table KB4)
4196 Great Britain. United Kingdom (Table KB4)
4197 Greece (Table KB4)
Holland see KBU4230
4198 Hungary (Table KB4)
4200 Ireland. Éire (Table KB4)
4203 Italy (Table KB4)
4205 Latvia (Table KB4)
4210 Liechtenstein (Table KB4)
4212 Lithuania (Table KB4)
4217 Luxembourg (Table KB4)
4218 Macedonia (Republic) (Table KB4)
4220 Malta (Table KB4)
4224 Moldova (Table KB4)
4226 Monaco (Table KB4)
4228 Montenegro (Table KB4)
4230 The Netherlands. Holland (Table KB4)
Including individual provinces and historic (defunct) jurisdictions
4232 Poland (Table KB4)
4234 Portugal (Table KB4)
4236 Romania (Table KB4)
4238 Russia (Table KB4)
4240 San Marino (Table KB4)
Scandinavia
4243 General works
4244 Denmark (Table KB4)
4246 Iceland (Table KB4)
4247 Norway (Table KB4)
4248 Sweden (Table KB4)
4250 Serbia (Table KB4)
4252 Slovakia (1993-) (Table KB4)
4254 Slovenia (Table KB4)

Local Church government
By region or country
Europe -- Continued
4258 Spain (Table KB4)
4260 Switzerland (Table KB4)
4262 Turkey (Table KB4)
4264 Ukraine (Table KB4)
4266 Yugoslavia (to 1992) (Table KB4)
Asia
Middle East. Southwest Asia
4270 General works
Caucasus
4272 Azerbaijan (Table KB4)
4273 Armenia (Table KB4)
4275 Bahrain (Table KB4)
Gaza see KBU4282
4278 Iran (Table KB4)
4280 Iraq (Table KB4)
4282 Israel. Palestine (Table KB4)
4284 Jerusalem (Table KB4)
4286 Jordan (Table KB4)
West Bank (Territory under Israeli occupation, 1967-) see KBU4282
4290 Kuwait (Table KB4)
4292 Lebanon (Table KB4)
4294 Oman (Table KB4)
Palestine (to 1948) see KBU4282
4297 Qatar (Table KB4)
4299 Saudi Arabia (Table KB4)
Southern Yemen see KBU4307
4301 Syria (Table KB4)
4303 United Arab Emirates (Table KB4)
4305 Yemen (Table KB4)
4307 Yemen (People's Democratic Republic) (to 1960) (Table KB4)
Previously Southern Yemen
Central Asia
4320 General works
4322 Kazakhstan (Table KB4)
4324 Kyrgyzstan (Table KB4)
4326 Tajikistan (Table KB4)
4328 Turkmenistan (Table KB4)
4330 Uzbekistan (Table KB4)
South Asia. Southeast Asia. East Asia
4335 General works
4337 Afghanistan (Table KB4)

Local Church government
By region or country
Asia
South Asia. Southeast Asia. East Asia -- Continued
4339 Bangladesh (Table KB4)
4341 Bhutan (Table KB4)
4343 Brunei (Table KB4)
4345 Burma. Myanmar (Table KB4)
4347 Cambodia (Table KB4)
China (to 1949)
4350 General (Table KB4)
4360.A-Z Provinces, A-Z
4360.A63 An-tung sheng
4360.C53 Ch'a-ha-erh sheng
Fukien Province. Fuijan sheng see KBU4378.A+
4360.H64 Ho-Chiang sheng
4360.H75 Hsi-k'ang sheng
4360.H76 Hsing-an sheng
4360.J44 Je-ho sheng
Kwangsi Province. Kuang-hsi see KBU4378.A+
Kwangtung Province. Guangdong sheng see KBU4378.A+
4360.L53 Liao-pei sheng
4360.N46 Neng-Chiang sheng
4360.N56 Ning-hsia sheng
4360.P56 Pin-Chiang sheng
Sikang Province see KBU4378.A+
4360.S85 Sui-yuan sheng
4360.S87 Sung-Chiang sheng
4360.T35 T'ai-wan sheng
4372 China (Republic, 1949-). Taiwan (Table KB4)
China (People's Republic, 1949-)
4376 General (Table KB4)
4378.A-Z Provinces, autonomous regions and municipalities, A-Z
4378.H66 Hong Kong
India
4400 General (Table KB4)
States, Union Territories, etc., and defunct jurisdictions
4402 Andaman and Nicobar Islands (Table KB4)
4404 Andrah Pradesh (Table KB4)
4405 Arunchal Pradesh (Table KB4)
4407 Assam (Table KB4)
4409 Bihar (Table KB4)
4411 Calcutta/Bengal Presidency (Table KB4)

Local Church government
By region or country
Asia
South Asia. Southeast Asia. East Asia
India
States, Union Territories, etc., and defunct jurisdictions -- Continued
4413 Chandighar (Table KB4)
4415 Dadra and Nagar Haveli (Table KB4)
4417 Delhi (Table KB4)
4419 Goa, Daman, and Diu (Table KB4)
4421 Gujarat (Table KB4)
4423 Haryana (Table KB4)
4425 Himachal Pradesh (Table KB4)
4425.5 Hyderabad (Table KB4)
4428 Jaipur (Table KB4)
4430 Jammu and Kashmir (Table KB4)
4432 Karnataka (Table KB4)
4435 Kerala (Table KB4)
4436 Kumaon (Table KB4)
4437 Lakshadweep (Table KB4)
4439 Madhya Pradesh (Table KB4)
4441 Madras Presidency (Table KB4)
4443 Maharashtra (Table KB4)
4445 Manipur (Table KB4)
4447 Meghalaya (Table KB4)
4449 Mizoram (Table KB4)
Mysore see KBU4467
4451 Nagaland (Table KB4)
4453 Orissa (Table KB4)
4455 Pondicherry (Table KB4)
4457 Punjab (Table KB4)
4459 Rajasthan (Table KB4)
4461 Sikkim (Table KB4)
4463 Tamil Nadu (Table KB4)
4465 Tripura (Table KB4)
4467 Uttar Pradesh (Table KB4)
4469 West Bengal (Table KB4)
4475 French Indochina (Table KB4)
Indonesia
4477 General (Table KB4)
4477.5.A-Z Provinces, A-Z
4477.5.T56 Timor. Timur
4479 Japan (Table KB4)
4483 South Korea (Table KB4)
4486 North Korea (Table KB4)

Local Church government
By region or country
Asia
South Asia. Southeast Asia. East Asia -- Continued
4488 Korea (to 1945) (Table KB4)
4490 Laos (Table KB4)
4492 Macau (Table KB4)
Malaysia
4494 General (Table KB4)
4495.A-Z Individual states, A-Z
4495.F44 Federated Malay States (1896-1942)
4495.M35 Malaya (1948-1962)
4495.M36 Malayan Union (1946-1947)
4495.S87 Straits Settlements (to 1942)
States of East and West Malaysia (1957-)
Brunei see KBU4343
4496 Federal Territory (Kuala Lumpur) (Table KB4)
4496.5 Johor (Table KB4)
4497 Kedah (Table KB4)
4497.5 Kelantan (Table KB4)
4498 Malacca (Table KB4)
4498.5 Negeri Sembilan (Table KB4)
4499 Pahang (Table KB4)
4499.5 Pinang (Table KB4)
4500 Perak (Table KB4)
4500.5 Perlis (Table KB4)
4501 Sabah (Table KB4)
Previously North Borneo
4501.5 Sarawak (Table KB4)
4502 Selangor (Table KB4)
4503 Terengganu (Table KB4)
4504 Labuan (Table KB4)
4506 Maldives (Table KB4)
4507 Mongolia (Table KB4)
Myanmar see KBU4345
4509 Nepal (Table KB4)
4511 Pakistan (Table KB4)
4513 Philippines (Table KB4)
4515 Singapore (Table KB4)
4518 Sri Lanka. Ceylon (Table KB4)
4520 Thailand (Table KB4)
4525 Vietnam (1976-) (Table KB4)
Including the periods up through 1945
4528 Vietnam (Republic). South Vietnam (1946-1975) (Table KB4)

Local Church government
By region or country
Asia
South Asia. Southeast Asia. East Asia -- Continued
4530 Vietnam (Democratic Republic). North Vietnam (1946-1975) (Table KB4)
Africa
4540 General works
4542 Algeria (Table KB4)
4544 Angola (Table KB4)
4546 Benin (Table KB4)
4550 Botswana (Table KB4)
4552 British Central Africa Protectorate (Table KB4)
4555 British Indian Ocean Territory (Table KB4)
4556 British Somaliland (Table KB4)
4560 Burkina Faso (Table KB4)
4562 Burundi (Table KB4)
4565 Cameroon (Table KB4)
4567 Cape Verde (Table KB4)
4569 Central African Republic (Table KB4)
4573 Chad (Table KB4)
4576 Comoros (Table KB4)
4580 Congo (Brazzaville) (Table KB4)
4582 Côte d'Ivoire. Ivory Coast (Table KB4)
4584 Djibouti (Table KB4)
4586 East Africa Protectorate (Table KB4)
4588 Egypt (Table KB4)
4589 Eritrea (Table KB4)
4590 Ethiopia (Table KB4)
4592 French Equatorial Africa (Table KB4)
4593 French West Africa (Table KB4)
4595 Gabon (Table KB4)
4597 Gambia (Table KB4)
4599 German East Africa (Table KB4)
4600 Ghana (Table KB4)
4604 Guinea (Table KB4)
4606 Guinea-Bissau (Table KB4)
4608 Equatorial Guinea (Table KB4)
4610 Ifni (Table KB4)
4612 Italian East Africa (Table KB4)
4614 Italian Somaliland (Table KB4)
4616 Kenya (Table KB4)
4618 Lesotho (Table KB4)
4620 Liberia (Table KB4)
4622 Libya (Table KB4)
4624 Madagascar (Table KB4)

Local Church government
By region or country
Africa -- Continued
4626 Malawi (Table KB4)
4628 Mali (Table KB4)
4630 Mauritania (Table KB4)
4633 Mauritius (Table KB4)
4635 Mayotte (Table KB4)
4637 Morocco (Table KB4)
4639 Mozambique (Table KB4)
4643 Namibia (Table KB4)
4645 Niger (Table KB4)
4650 Nigeria (Table KB4)
4653 Réunion (Table KB4)
4655 Rwanda (Table KB4)
4657 Saint Helena (Table KB4)
4660 Sao Tome and Principe (Table KB4)
4664 Senegal (Table KB4)
4666 Seychelles (Table KB4)
4668 Sierra Leone (Table KB4)
4670 Somalia (Table KB4)
South Africa, Republic of
4680 General (Table KB4)
4682.A-Z Provinces and self-governing territories, A-Z
Including former independent homelands
4682.B66 Bophuthatswana
4682.C36 Cape of Good Hope. Kaapland (to 1994)
4682.C57 Ciskei
4682.E36 Eastern Cape
Eastern Transvaal see KBU4682.M68
4682.F74 Free State. Orange Free State
4682.G38 Gauteng
4682.K93 KwaZula-Natal. Natal
Including former KwaZula Homeland areas
4682.M68 Mpulamanga. Eastern Transvaal
Natal see KBU4682.K93
4682.N64 North West
4682.N65 Northern Cape
4682.N67 Northern Province. Northern Transvaal
Northern Transvaal see KBU4682.N67
Orange Free State. Oranje Vrystaat see KBU4682.F74
4682.T73 Transkei
4682.T74 Transvaal
4682.V46 Venda
4682.W47 Western Cape

Local Church government
By region or country
Africa -- Continued
4700 Spanish West Africa (to 1958) (Table KB4)
4702 Spanish Sahara (to 1975) (Table KB4)
4704 Sudan (Table KB4)
4706 Swaziland (Table KB4)
4708 Tanzania (Table KB4)
4710 Togo (Table KB4)
4712 Tunisia (Table KB4)
4714 Uganda (Table KB4)
4716 Zaire. Congo (Democratic Republic) (Table KB4)
4720 Zambia (Table KB4)
4722 Zanzibar (to 1964) (Table KB4)
4724 Zimbabwe (Table KB4)
Pacific Area
Australia
States and territories
4738 Australian Capital Territory (Table KB4)
4740 Northern Territory (Table KB4)
4742 New South Wales (Table KB4)
4744 Queensland (Table KB4)
4746 South Australia (Table KB4)
4748 Tasmania (Table KB4)
4750 Victoria (Table KB4)
4752 Western Australia (Table KB4)
4760 New Zealand (Table KB4)
Other Pacific Area jurisdictions
4770 American Samoa (Table KB4)
4772 British New Guinea (Territory of Papua) (Table KB4)
4774 Cook Islands (Table KB4)
4776 Easter Island (Table KB4)
4778 Fiji (Table KB4)
4780 French Polynesia (Table KB4)
4782 German New Guinea (to 1914) (Table KB4)
4784 Guam (Table KB4)
4788 Kiribati (Table KB4)
4790 Marshall Islands (Table KB4)
4792 Micronesia (Federated States) (Table KB4)
4794 Midway Islands (Table KB4)
4796 Nauru (Table KB4)
4798 Netherlands New Guinea (to 1963) (Table KB4)
4800 New Caledonia (Table KB4)
4802 Niue (Table KB4)
4803 Northern Mariana Islands (Table KB4)
4804 Pacific Islands (Trust Territory) (Table KB4)

Local Church government
By region or country
Pacific Area
Other Pacific Area jurisdictions -- Continued
4805 Palau (Table KB4)
4806 Papua New Guinea (Table KB4)
4807 Pitcairn Island (Table KB4)
Samoa see KBU4820
4808 Solomon Islands (Table KB4)
4810 Tonga (Table KB4)
4812 Tuvalu (Table KB4)
4814 Vanuatu (Table KB4)
4816 Wake Island (Table KB4)
4818 Wallis and Futuna Islands (Table KB4)
4820 Samoa. Western Samoa (Table KB4)

Official records. Working documents
.A3 Indexes and tables. Digests
For indexes and tables to a particular publication, see the publication
.A35 Rules of order. Rules of procedure
Rules of proceedings of the organ and its committees, etc.
.A4 Serials
.A45 Monographs. By date
Decisions. Decrees. Measures. Resolutions. Recommendations
Including opinions, consultations, etc.
For individual decisions, etc., see the subject
.A47 Indexes and tables. Digests
Collections. Selections
.A5 Serials
.A6 Monographs. By date

TABLES

Statutes. Papal constitutions. Treaties and concordats. Decrees. Privileges, etc.

.A12 Indexes and tables. Digests

.A2 Collections. Selections

.A4 Individual laws

Including unannotated and annotated editions (Glosses)

.A55 Court decisions. Advisory opinions (Consilia). Dooms

For decisiones of the Rota Romana, see KBR43+

.A7-.Z79 General works. Treatises

TABLES

Statutes. Papal constitutions. Treaties and concordats. Decrees. Privileges, etc.

.xA12 Indexes and tables. Digests

.xA2 Collections. Selections

.xA4 Individual laws. By date

Including unannotated and annotated editions (Glosses)

.xA55 Court decisions. Advisory opinions (Consilia). Dooms. By date

For decisiones of the Rota Romana, see KBR43+

.xA7-.xZ79 General works. Treatises

.A12 Periodicals
Concordats (Collected or individual)
see the appropriate K subclass for the country
Documents
For documents on special subjects see KB4 .A7
Collections. Selections (General)
.A2 Serials
.A3 Monographs. By date
National councils and synods
see KBR/KBU833+
Provincial councils and diocesan synods (including diocesan pastoral councils)
see KBR/KBU953+
<.A4> Collections. Selections
<.A6> General works. Treatises
.A7 General works. Treatises
Including works and documents on special topics
.A8-.Z7 Individual archdioceses and dioceses, A-Z
Subarrange each by KB5

.xA12 Periodicals

Documents

For documents on special subjects see KB5 .xA8

.xA2 General. Collective

.xA3 Episcopal letters. Decrees. Ordinances

.xA4 Diocesan curia. Chancery office

.xA5 Chancery court

.xA6 Matrimonial court

.xA7 School board

.xA8 General works. Treatises

Including works and documents on special subjects, e. g. election of bishops

.xA9-.xZ7 Individual parishes, A-Z

.A12	Bibliography
.A15	Periodicals
	Including gazettes, yearbooks, bulletins, etc.
.A18	Constituent law and rules governing the organization. By date
.A7	Annual (official) reports
	Yearbooks see KB6 .A15
.A9-.Z9	General works on the congregation, commission, etc.

.A12 Indexes and tables. By date

Legislative documents and related works

.A14 Drafts. By date

Including records of proceedings and minutes of evidence

.A32 Documents of code commissions and revision commissions. Reports. Memoranda. By date

Including commentaries on drafts

Contemporary (private) criticism and comment on drafts see KB7 .A6+

.A52 Text of the code. Unannotated editions. By date

Including official editions with or without annotations; and including bilingual editions

.A6-.Z8 Annotated editions. Commentaries. General works

Including "interpretationes authenticae"

Constitution. By laws

<.A12> Text

<.A2> Translations

<.A3> Commentary

General works

see BX2890+ (for men) and BX4260+ (for women)

.A12 Indexes and tables. Registers

.A2 Collections. Selections

Including both unannotated editions and annotated editions (i.e. scholarly comment), with or without indexes, registers, etc.

Individual documents

Including bulls of intimation (convocation)

.A45 Text. By date

.A5 Annotated editions. Commentaries

General works on the document see KB9 .A5

General works on the council

see the council in BR205+ and BX820+

	ʻAbodah zarah (Avodah zarah)
<.A15>	Original texts (Hebrew or Aramaic). By date
<.A15A-.A15Z>	Translations. By language, A-Z
	e.g.
<.A15E5>	English
<.A15E65>	English paraphrases
<.A16>	Selections. By date
<.A17>	Criticism. Commentaries, etc.
	Aboth (Avot)
<.A2>	Original texts (Hebrew or Aramaic). By date
<.A2A-.A2Z>	Translations. By language, A-Z
<.A2A1>	Polyglot. By date
<.A22>	Selections. By date
<.A23>	Criticism. Commentaries, etc.
	Ahilot see KBM1 .O3+
	Arakhin
<.A7>	Original texts (Hebrew or Aramaic). By date
<.A7A-.A7Z>	Translations. By language, A-Z
<.A72>	Selections. By date
<.A73>	Criticism. Commentaries, etc.
	Avodah zarah see KBM1 .A15+
	Avot see KBM1 .A2+
	Bavot
<.B15>	Original texts (Hebrew or Aramaic). By date
<.B15A-.B15Z>	Translations. By language, A-Z
<.B16>	Selections. By date
<.B17>	Criticism. Commentaries, etc.
	Bava kamma
<.B2>	Original texts (Hebrew or Aramaic). By date
<.B2A-.B2Z>	Translations. By language, A-Z
<.B22>	Selections. By date
<.B23>	Criticism. Commentaries, etc.
	Bava meẓia
<.B3>	Original texts (Hebrew or Aramaic). By date
<.B3A-.B3Z>	Translations. By language, A-Z
<.B32>	Selections. By date
<.B33>	Criticism. Commentaries, etc.
	Bava batra
<.B4>	Original texts (Hebrew or Aramaic). By date
<.B4A-.B4Z>	Translations. By language, A-Z
<.B42>	Selections. By date
<.B43>	Criticism. Commentaries, etc.
	Beḥirta see KBM1 .E3+
	Bekhorot
<.B5>	Original texts (Hebrew or Aramaic). By date

	Bekhorot -- Continued
<.B5A-.B5Z>	Translations. By language, A-Z
<.B52>	Selections. By date
<.B53>	Criticism. Commentaries, etc.
	Berakhot
<.B6>	Original texts (Hebrew or Aramaic). By date
<.B6A-.B6Z>	Translations. By language, A-Z
<.B62>	Selections. By date
<.B63>	Criticism. Commentaries, etc.
	Beẓah
<.B7>	Original texts (Hebrew or Aramaic). By date
<.B7A-.B7Z>	Translations. By language, A-Z
<.B72>	Selections. By date
<.B73>	Criticism. Commentaries, etc.
	Bikkurim
<.B8>	Original texts (Hebrew or Aramaic). By date
<.B8A-.B8Z>	Translations. By language, A-Z
<.B82>	Selections. By date
<.B83>	Criticism. Commentaries, etc.
	Demai
<.D3>	Original texts (Hebrew or Aramaic). By date
<.D3A-.D3Z>	Translations. By language, A-Z
<.D4>	Selections. By date
<.D5>	Criticism. Commentaries, etc.
	Eduyyot. Beḥirta
<.E3>	Original texts (Hebrew or Aramaic). By date
<.E3A-.E3Z>	Translations. By language, A-Z
<.E4>	Selections. By date
<.E5>	Criticism. Commentaries, etc.
	Eruvin
<.E7>	Original texts (Hebrew or Aramaic). By date
<.E7A-.E7Z>	Translations. By language, A-Z
<.E8>	Selections. By date
<.E9>	Criticism. Commentaries, etc.
	Gittin
<.G5>	Original texts (Hebrew or Aramaic). By date
<.G5A-.G5Z>	Translations. By language, A-Z
<.G52>	Selections. By date
<.G53>	Criticism. Commentaries, etc.
	Ḥagigah
<.H3>	Original texts (Hebrew or Aramaic). By date
<.H3A-.H3Z>	Translations. By language, A-Z
<.H32>	Selections. By date
<.H33>	Criticism. Commentaries, etc.
	Ḥallah

	Ḥallah -- Continued
<.H4>	Original texts (Hebrew or Aramaic). By date
<.H4A-.H4Z>	Translations. By language, A-Z
<.H42>	Selections. By date
<.H43>	Criticism. Commentaries, etc.
	Horayot
<.H5>	Original texts (Hebrew or Aramaic). By date
<.H5A-.H5Z>	Translations. By language, A-Z
<.H6>	Selections. By date
<.H7>	Criticism. Commentaries, etc.
	Ḥullin
<.H8>	Original texts (Hebrew or Aramaic). By date
<.H8A-.H8Z>	Translations. By language, A-Z
<.H82>	Selections. By date
<.H83>	Criticism. Commentaries, etc.
	Kelim
<.K2>	Original texts (Hebrew or Aramaic). By date
<.K2A-.K2Z>	Translations. By language, A-Z
<.K22>	Selections. By date
<.K23>	Criticism. Commentaries, etc.
	Keritot
<.K3>	Original texts (Hebrew or Aramaic). By date
<.K3A-.K3Z>	Translations. By language, A-Z
<.K32>	Selections. By date
<.K33>	Criticism. Commentaries, etc.
	Ketubbot
<.K4>	Original texts (Hebrew or Aramaic). By date
<.K4A-.K4Z>	Translations. By language, A-Z
<.K42>	Selections. By date
<.K43>	Criticism. Commentaries, etc.
	Kiddushin
<.K5>	Original texts (Hebrew or Aramaic). By date
<.K5A-.K5Z>	Translations. By language, A-Z
<.K52>	Selections. By date
<.K53>	Criticism. Commentaries, etc.
	Kilayim
<.K6>	Original texts (Hebrew or Aramaic). By date
<.K6A-.K6Z>	Translations. By language, A-Z
<.K62>	Selections. By date
<.K63>	Criticism. Commentaries, etc.
	Kinnim
<.K7>	Original texts (Hebrew or Aramaic). By date
<.K7A-.K7Z>	Translations. By language, A-Z
<.K72>	Selections. By date
<.K73>	Criticism. Commentaries, etc.

	Kodashim (Order)
<.K8>	Original texts (Hebrew or Aramaic). By date
<.K8A-.K8Z>	Translations. By language, A-Z
<.K82>	Selections. By date
<.K83>	Criticism. Commentaries, etc.
	Ma‘aser sheni
<.M13>	Original texts (Hebrew or Aramaic). By date
<.M13A-.M13Z>	Translations. By language, A-Z
<.M14>	Selections. By date
<.M15>	Criticism. Commentaries, etc.
	Ma‘aserot
<.M17>	Original texts (Hebrew or Aramaic). By date
<.M17A-.M17Z>	Translations. By language, A-Z
<.M18>	Selections. By date
<.M19>	Criticism. Commentaries, etc.
	Makhshirin. Mashkim
<.M2>	Original texts (Hebrew or Aramaic). By date
<.M2A-.M2Z>	Translations. By language, A-Z
<.M22>	Selections. By date
<.M23>	Criticism. Commentaries, etc.
	Makkot
<.M3>	Original texts (Hebrew or Aramaic). By date
<.M3A-.M3Z>	Translations. By language, A-Z
<.M32>	Selections. By date
<.M33>	Criticism. Commentaries, etc.
	Mashkim see KBM1 .M2+
	Mashkin see KBM1 .M8+
	Megillah
<.M4>	Original texts (Hebrew or Aramaic). By date
<.M4A-.M4Z>	Translations. By language, A-Z
<.M42>	Selections. By date
<.M43>	Criticism. Commentaries, etc.
	Me‘ilah
<.M44>	Original texts (Hebrew or Aramaic). By date
<.M44A-.M44Z>	Translations. By language, A-Z
<.M45>	Selections. By date
<.M46>	Criticism. Commentaries, etc.
	Menaḥot
<.M47>	Original texts (Hebrew or Aramaic). By date
<.M47A-.M47Z>	Translations. By language, A-Z
<.M48>	Selections. By date
<.M49>	Criticism. Commentaries, etc.
	Middot
<.M5>	Original texts (Hebrew or Aramaic). By date
<.M5A-.M5Z>	Translations. By language, A-Z

	Middot -- Continued
<.M52>	Selections. By date
<.M53>	Criticism. Commentaries, etc.
	Mikva'ot
<.M6>	Original texts (Hebrew or Aramaic). By date
<.M6A-.M6Z>	Translations. By language, A-Z
<.M62>	Selections. By date
<.M63>	Criticism. Commentaries, etc.
	Minor tractates
	see KBM506.4
	Mo'ed (Order)
<.M7>	Original texts (Hebrew or Aramaic). By date
<.M7A-.M7Z>	Translations. By language, A-Z
<.M72>	Selections. By date
<.M73>	Criticism. Commentaries, etc.
	Mo'ed katan. Mashkin
<.M8>	Original texts (Hebrew or Aramaic). By date
<.M8A-.M8Z>	Translations. By language, A-Z
<.M82>	Selections. By date
<.M83>	Criticism. Commentaries, etc.
	Nashim (Order)
<.N2>	Original texts (Hebrew or Aramaic). By date
<.N2A-.N2Z>	Translations. By language, A-Z
<.N22>	Selections. By date
<.N23>	Criticism. Commentaries, etc.
	Nazir
<.N3>	Original texts (Hebrew or Aramaic). By date
<.N3A-.N3Z>	Translations. By language, A-Z
<.N32>	Selections. By date
<.N33>	Criticism. Commentaries, etc.
	Nedarim
<.N4>	Original texts (Hebrew or Aramaic). By date
<.N4A-.N4Z>	Translations. By language, A-Z
<.N42>	Selections. By date
<.N43>	Criticism. Commentaries, etc.
	Nega'im
<.N5>	Original texts (Hebrew or Aramaic). By date
<.N5A-.N5Z>	Translations. By language, A-Z
<.N52>	Selections. By date
<.N53>	Criticism. Commentaries, etc.
	Nezikin (Order)
<.N6>	Original texts (Hebrew or Aramaic). By date
<.N6A-.N6Z>	Translations. By language, A-Z
<.N62>	Selections. By date
<.N63>	Criticism. Commentaries, etc.

	Niddah
<.N7>	Original texts (Hebrew or Aramaic). By date
<.N7A-.N7Z>	Translations. By language, A-Z
<.N72>	Selections. By date
<.N73>	Criticism. Commentaries, etc.
	Oholot (Ahilot)
<.O3>	Original texts (Hebrew or Aramaic). By date
<.O3A-.O3Z>	Translations. By language, A-Z
<.O4>	Selections. By date
<.O5>	Criticism. Commentaries, etc.
	Orlah
<.O6>	Original texts (Hebrew or Aramaic). By date
<.O6A-.O6Z>	Translations. By language, A-Z
<.O7>	Selections. By date
<.O8>	Criticism. Commentaries, etc.
	Parah
<.P2>	Original texts (Hebrew or Aramaic). By date
<.P2A-.P2Z>	Translations. By language, A-Z
<.P3>	Selections. By date
<.P4>	Criticism. Commentaries, etc.
	Pe'ah
<.P5>	Original texts (Hebrew or Aramaic). By date
<.P5A-.P5Z>	Translations. By language, A-Z
<.P6>	Selections. By date
<.P7>	Criticism. Commentaries, etc.
	Pesaḥim
<.P8>	Original texts (Hebrew or Aramaic). By date
<.P8A-.P8Z>	Translations. By language, A-Z
<.P82>	Selections. By date
<.P83>	Criticism. Commentaries, etc.
	Pirkei Avot see KBM1 .A2+
	Rosh ha-Shanah
<.R5>	Original texts (Hebrew or Aramaic). By date
<.R5A-.R5Z>	Translations. By language, A-Z
<.R6>	Selections. By date
<.R7>	Criticism. Commentaries, etc.
	Sanhedrin
<.S2>	Original texts (Hebrew or Aramaic). By date
<.S2A-.S2Z>	Translations. By language, A-Z
<.S22>	Selections. By date
<.S23>	Criticism. Commentaries, etc.
	Shabbat
<.S25>	Original texts (Hebrew or Aramaic). By date
<.S25A-.S25Z>	Translations. By language, A-Z
<.S26>	Selections. By date

	Shabbat -- Continued
<.S27>	Criticism. Commentaries, etc.
	Shebi'it (Shevi'it)
<.S3>	Original texts (Hebrew or Aramaic). By date
<.S3A-.S3Z>	Translations. By language, A-Z
<.S32>	Selections. By date
<.S33>	Criticism. Commentaries, etc.
	Shebu'ot (Shevu'ot)
<.S4>	Original texts (Hebrew or Aramaic). By date
<.S4A-.S4Z>	Translations. By language, A-Z
<.S42>	Selections. By date
<.S43>	Criticism. Commentaries, etc.
	Sheḥitat kodashim see KBM1 .Z5+
	Shekalim
<.S5>	Original texts (Hebrew or Aramaic). By date
<.S5A-.S5Z>	Translations. By language, A-Z
<.S52>	Selections. By date
<.S53>	Criticism. Commentaries, etc.
	Shevi'it see KBM1 .S3+
	Shevu'ot see KBM1 .S4+
	Sotah
<.S7>	Original texts (Hebrew or Aramaic). By date
<.S7A-.S7Z>	Translations. By language, A-Z
<.S72>	Selections. By date
<.S73>	Criticism. Commentaries, etc.
	Sukkah
<.S9>	Original texts (Hebrew or Aramaic). By date
<.S9A-.S9Z>	Translations. By language, A-Z
<.S92>	Selections. By date
<.S93>	Criticism. Commentaries, etc.
	Ta'anit
<.T2>	Original texts (Hebrew or Aramaic). By date
<.T2A-.T2Z>	Translations. By language, A-Z
<.T22>	Selections. By date
<.T23>	Criticism. Commentaries, etc.
	Tamid
<.T3>	Original texts (Hebrew or Aramaic). By date
<.T3A-.T3Z>	Translations. By language, A-Z
<.T32>	Selections. By date
<.T33>	Criticism. Commentaries, etc.
	Tebul yom (Tevul yom)
<.T4>	Original texts (Hebrew or Aramaic). By date
<.T4A-.T4Z>	Translations. By language, A-Z
<.T42>	Selections. By date
<.T43>	Criticism. Commentaries, etc.

	Temurah
<.T5>	Original texts (Hebrew or Aramaic). By date
<.T5A-.T5Z>	Translations. By language, A-Z
<.T52>	Selections. By date
<.T53>	Criticism. Commentaries, etc.
	Terumot
<.T6>	Original texts (Hebrew or Aramaic). By date
<.T6A-.T6Z>	Translations. By language, A-Z
<.T62>	Selections. By date
<.T63>	Criticism. Commentaries, etc.
	Tevul yom see KBM1 .T4+
	Tohorot (Order)
<.T7>	Original texts (Hebrew or Aramaic). By date
<.T7A-.T7Z>	Translations. By language, A-Z
<.T72>	Selections. By date
<.T73>	Criticism. Commentaries, etc.
	Tohorot
<.T8>	Original texts (Hebrew or Aramaic). By date
<.T8A-.T8Z>	Translations. By language, A-Z
<.T82>	Selections. By date
<.T83>	Criticism. Commentaries, etc.
	Ukẓin
<.U5>	Original texts (Hebrew or Aramaic). By date
<.U5A-.U5Z>	Translations. By language, A-Z
<.U6>	Selections. By date
<.U7>	Criticism. Commentaries, etc.
	Yadayim
<.Y2>	Original texts (Hebrew or Aramaic). By date
<.Y2A-.Y2Z>	Translations. By language, A-Z
<.Y3>	Selections. By date
<.Y4>	Criticism. Commentaries, etc.
	Yevamot
<.Y5>	Original texts (Hebrew or Aramaic). By date
<.Y5A-.Y5Z>	Translations. By language, A-Z
<.Y6>	Selections. By date
<.Y7>	Criticism. Commentaries, etc.
	Yoma
<.Y8>	Original texts (Hebrew or Aramaic). By date
<.Y8A-.Y8Z>	Translations. By language, A-Z
<.Y82>	Selections. By date
<.Y83>	Criticism. Commentaries, etc.
	Zavim
<.Z2>	Original texts (Hebrew or Aramaic). By date
<.Z2A-.Z2Z>	Translations. By language, A-Z
<.Z3>	Selections. By date

Zavim -- Continued

<.Z4> Criticism. Commentaries, etc.

Zebaḥim (Zevaḥim). Sheḥitat kodashim

<.Z5> Original texts (Hebrew or Aramaic). By date

<.Z5A-.Z5Z> Translations. By language, A-Z

<.Z6> Selections. By date

<.Z7> Criticism. Commentaries, etc.

Zera'im (Order)

<.Z8> Original texts (Hebrew or Aramaic). By date

<.Z8A-.Z8Z> Translations. By language, A-Z

<.Z82> Selections. By date

<.Z83> Criticism. Commentaries, etc.

Zevaḥim see KBM1 .Z5+

<.x>	General works
<.x2A-.x2Z>	Individual synagogues or congregations, A-Z

<.x>	General works
<.x2A-.x2Z>	Individual synagogues or congregations. By place, A-Z

TABLES

	Texts
<.xA05>	Facsimiles. By date
<.xA1>	Original language. By date
	Translations
<.xA2>	Hebrew. By date
<.xA3>	English. By date
<.xA4>	French. By date
<.xA5>	German. By date
<.xA61-.xA619>	Other languages. By language, alphabetically, and date
<.xA7-.xZ>	History and criticism

	This table is used with the alternative classification numbers provided in the schedule. It is not used at the Library of Congress
	Texts
	Including selections
<0.2>	Polyglot. By date
	Hebrew
<0.25A-.25Z>	Printed texts. By editor, A-Z, or date
	Manuscripts
<0.27>	General works
	Individual manuscripts
<0.275A-.275Z>	By name, A-Z
<0.277>	By number
	English
<0.35A-.35Z>	Printed texts. By version, translator, or editor, A-Z, or date
	Manuscripts
<0.37-.377>	General works
	Individual manuscripts
<0.375A-.375Z>	By name, A-Z
<0.377>	By number
<0.4A-.4Z>	Other languages, A-Z
	Subarrange each language by version, translator, or editor, A-Z
	Criticism, commentaries, etc.
<0.5>	Early through 1950
	1955-2000
<0.52>	Criticism
<0.53>	Commentaries
<0.54>	Sermons. Meditations. Devotions
<0.55>	Other
	2001-
<0.552>	Criticism
<0.553>	Commentaries
<0.554>	Sermons. Meditations. Devotions
<0.555>	Other
<0.556A-.556Z>	Special topics, A-Z

	This table is used with the alternative classification numbers provided in the schedule. It is not used at the Library of Congress
	Texts
<.x2>	Polyglot. By date
	Hebrew
<.x25A-.x25Z>	Printed texts. By editor, A-Z, or date
	Manuscripts
<.x27>	General works
	Individual manuscripts
<.x275A-.x275Z>	By name, A-Z
<.x277>	By number
	English
<.x35A-.x35Z>	Printed texts. By version, translator, or editor, A-Z
	Manuscripts
<.x37>	General works
	Individual manuscripts
<.x375A-.x375Z>	By name, A-Z
<.x377>	By number
<.x4A-.x4Z>	Other languages, A-Z
	Subarrange each language by version, translator, or editor, A-Z
	Criticism, commentaries, etc.
<.x5>	Early through 1950
	1951-2000
<.x52>	Criticism
<.x53>	Commentaries
<.x54>	Sermon. Meditations. Devotions
<.x55>	Other
	2001-
<.x552>	Criticism
<.x553>	Commentaries
<.x554>	Sermons. Meditations. Devotions
<.x555>	Other
<.x56A-.x56Z>	Special topics, A-Z

This table is used with the alternative classification numbers provided in the schedule. It is not used at the Library of Congress

	Texts
<.xA1>	Polyglot. By date
<.xA3>	English. By date
<.xA5-.xZ>	Other languages, A-Z Subarrange each language by date
<.x2>	History, criticism, etc. Including works on manuscripts

TABLES

Unaffiliated authors
Class here works of authors not affiliated with a particular school
Early period (1st and 2nd cent. A.H.)
Including companions and successors
0.2 General (Collective)
0.22.A-Z Individual authors, A-Z
For author Cutter numbers see KBP250+
Middle period (to ca. 1920)
Including non-Muslims, or Muslims treating Islamic law as a contemporary academic discipline
0.23 General (Collective)
0.25.A-Z Individual authors, A-Z
For author Cutter numbers see KBP250+
Late period (ca. 1920-)
Including non-Muslims, or Muslims treating Islamic law as a contemporary academic discipline
0.3 General (Collective)
0.32.A-Z Individual authors, A-Z
For author Cutter numbers see KBP250+
Authors affiliated with a particular school
Sunnī schools
0.35 General (Collective and comparative)
Including works on several schools; or on several authors belonging to different Sunnī schools (branches)
For works comparing Sunnī law with Shīʻī law see KBP1 0.95
Ḥanafī. Ḥanafīyah. حنفي. حنفية
0.4 General (Collective)
0.43.A-Z Individual authors, A-Z
For author Cutter numbers see KBP250+
Ḥanbalī. Ḥanbalīyah. حنبلي. حنبلية
0.45 General (Collective)
0.5.A-Z Individual authors, A-Z
For author Cutter numbers see KBP250+
Mālikī. Mālikīyah. مالكي. مالكية
0.53 General (Collective)
0.55.A-Z Individual authors, A-Z
For author Cutter numbers see KBP250+
Shāfiʻī. Shāfiʻīyah. شافعي. شافعية
0.6 General (Collective)
0.62.A-Z Individual authors, A-Z
For author Cutter numbers see KBP250+
Ẓāhirī. Ẓāhirīyah. ظاهري. ظاهرية
0.63 General (Collective)
0.64.A-Z Individual authors, A-Z
For author Cutter numbers see KBP250+

Authors affiliated with a particular school
Sunnī schools -- Continued
Mixed. Comparative see KBP1 0.35
Shīʻī schools. Shīʻah. شيعة
0.65 General (Collective and comparative)
Including works on several schools; or on several authors belonging to different Shīʻī schools (branches)
For works comparing Sunnī law with Shīʻī law see KBP1 0.95
Ismāʻīlī. اسماعيلي
0.7 General (Collective)
0.72.A-Z Individual authors, A-Z
For author Cutter numbers see KBP250+
Jaʻfarīs. Ithnaʻasharis. جعفري. اثناء عشري
0.74 General (Collective)
0.76.A-Z Individual authors, A-Z
For author Cutter numbers see KBP250+
Zaydī. Zaydīyah. زيدي. زيدية
0.8 General (Collective)
0.82.A-Z Individual authors, A-Z
For author Cutter numbers see KBP250+
Mixed. Comparative see KBP1 0.65
ʻIbāḍī. اباضي
0.85 General (Collective)
0.9.A-Z Individual authors, A-Z
For author Cutter numbers see KBP250+
0.93.A-Z Other schools, A-Z
0.95 Mixed. Comparative
Class here works comparing authors affiliated with different schools (e.g. Sunnī and Shīʻī schools or branches thereof)

TABLES

	Unaffiliated authors
	Class here works of authors not affiliated with a particular school
	Early period (1st and 2nd cent. A.H.)
	Including companions and successors
.A2	General (Collective)
.A22A-.A22Z	Individual authors, A-Z
	For author Cutter numbers see KBP250+
	Middle period (to ca. 1920)
	Including non-Muslims, or Muslims treating Islamic law as a contemporary academic discipline
.A23	General (Collective)
.A25A-.A25Z	Individual authors, A-Z
	For author Cutter numbers see KBP250+
	Late period (ca. 1920-)
	Including non-Muslims, or Muslims treating Islamic law as a contemporary academic discipline
.A3	General (Collective)
.A32A-.A32Z	Individual authors, A-Z
	For author Cutter numbers see KBP250+
	Authors affiliated with a particular school
	Sunnī schools
.A35	General (Collective and comparative)
	Including works on several authors belonging to different Sunnī schools (branches)
	For works comparing Sunnī law with Shīʻī law see KBP2 .A95
	Ḥanafī. Ḥanafīyah. حنفي. حنفية
.A4	General (Collective)
.A43A-.A43Z	Individual authors, A-Z
	For author Cutter numbers see KBP250+
	Ḥanbalī. Ḥanbalīyah. حنفي. حنفية
.A45	General (Collective)
.A5A-.A5Z	Individual authors, A-Z
	For author Cutter numbers see KBP250+
	Mālikī. Mālikīyah. مالكي. مالكية
.A53	General (Collective)
.A55A-.A55Z	Individual authors, A-Z
	For author Cutter numbers see KBP250+
	Shāfiʻī. Shāfiʻīyah. شافعي. شافعية
.A6	General (Collective)
.A62A-.A62Z	Individual authors, A-Z
	For author Cutter numbers see KBP250+
	Ẓāhirī. Ẓāhirīyah. ظاهري. ظاهرية
.A63	General (Collective)
.A64A-.A64Z	Individual authors, A-Z
	For author Cutter numbers see KBP250+

Authors affiliated with a particular school
Sunnī schools -- Continued
Mixed. Comparative see KBP2 .A35
Shīʻī schools. Shīʻah. شيعة
.A65 General (Collective and comparative)
Including works on authors belonging to different Shīʻī schools (branches)
Ismāʻīlī. اسماعيلي
.A7 General (Collective)
.A72A-.A72Z Individual authors, A-Z
For author Cutter numbers see KBP250+
Jaʻfarīs. Ithnaʻasharis. جعفري. اثناء عشري
.A74 General (Collective)
.A76A-.A76Z Individual authors, A-Z
For author Cutter numbers see KBP250+
Zaydī. Zaydīyah. زيدي. زيدية
.A8 General (Collective)
.A82A-.A82Z Individual authors, A-Z
For author Cutter numbers see KBP250+
Mixed. Comparative see KBP2 .A65
ʻIbāḍī. اباضي
.A85 General (Collective)
.A9A-.A9Z Individual authors, A-Z
For author Cutter numbers see KBP250+
.A93A-.A93Z Other schools, A-Z
.A95 Mixed. Comparative
Class here works comparing authors affiliated with different schools (e.g. Sunnī and Shīʻī schools)

Unaffiliated authors
Class here works of authors not affiliated with a particular school
Early period (1st and 2nd cent. A.H.)
Including companions and successors
.xA2 General (Collective)
.xA22A-.xA22Z Individual authors, A-Z
For author Cutter numbers see KBP250+
Middle period (to ca. 1920)
Including non-Muslims, or Muslims treating Islamic law as a contemporary academic discipline
.xA23 General (Collective)
.xA25-.xZ299 Individual authors, A-Z
For author Cutter numbers see KBP250+
Late period (ca. 1920-)
Including non-Muslims, or Muslims treating Islamic law as a contemporary academic discipline
.xA3 General (Collective)
.xA32-.xZ349 Individual authors, A-Z
For author Cutter numbers see KBP250+
Authors affiliated with a particular school
Sunnī schools
.xA35 General (Collective and comparative)
Including works on several authors belonging to different Sunnī schools (branches)
For works comparing Sunnī law with Shīʻī law see KBP3 .xA95
Ḥanafī. Ḥanafīyah. حنفي. حنفية
.xA4 General (Collective)
.xA43-.xZ449 Individual authors, A-Z
For author Cutter numbers see KBP250+
Ḥanbalī. Ḥanbalīyah. حنبلي. حنبلية
.xA45 General (Collective)
.xA5-.xZ529 Individual authors, A-Z
For author Cutter numbers see KBP250+
Mālikī. Mālikīyah. مالكي. مالكية
.xA53 General (Collective)
.xA55-.xZ599 Individual authors, A-Z
For author Cutter numbers see KBP250+
Shāfiʻī. Shāfiʻīyah. شافعي. شافعية
.xA6 General (Collective)
.xA62-.xZ649 Individual authors, A-Z
For author Cutter numbers see KBP250+
Mixed. Comparative see KBP3 .xA35
Shīʻī schools. Shīʻah. شيعة

	Authors affiliated with a particular school
	Shīʻī schools. Shīʻah. شيعة -- Continued
.xA65	General (Collective and comparative)
	Including works on authors belonging to different Shīʻī schools (branches)
	Ismāʻīlī. اسماعيلي
.xA7	General (Collective)
.xA72-.xZ739	Individual authors, A-Z
	For author Cutter numbers see KBP250+
	Jaʻfarīs. Ithnaʻasharis. جعفري. اثناء عشري
.xA74	General (Collective)
.xA76-.xZ779	Individual authors, A-Z
	For author Cutter numbers see KBP250+
	Zaydī. Zaydīyah. زيدي. زيدية
.xA8	General (Collective)
.xA82-.xZ849	Individual authors, A-Z
	For author Cutter numbers see KBP250+
	Mixed. Comparative see KBP3 .xA65
	ʻIbāḍī. اباضي
.xA85	General (Collective)
.xA9-.xZ929	Individual authors, A-Z
	For author Cutter numbers see KBP250+
.xA93-.xZ949	Other schools, A-Z
.xA95	Mixed. Comparative
	Class here works comparing authors affiliated with different schools (e.g. Sunnī and Shīʻī schools)

.A2 Original text

Including facsimiles or originals; and including typographical reproductions of the text entirely in non-Roman or ancient type, or transliterated in Roman characters; and including bilingual editions

Arrange chronologically from the earliest to the latest (recent) editions

Translations

.A3A-.A3Z English. By translator, A-Z

.A4A-.A4Z Other languages, A-Z

.A5-.Z Commentaries. Criticism

For philological studies, see PJ

A

A hwāl shakh sīyah: KBP524+
Aachen, Council of, 809: KBR265
Abandonment
  Ownership
    Islamic law: KBP673
Abandonment of a child
  Islamic law: KBP4190
  Jewish law: KBM4190
Abatement of trial
  Canon law: KBR3842.A33
  Roman Catholic law: KBU3842.A33
Abbas Primas
  Canon law: KBR2915
Abbot primate
  Canon law: KBR2915
  Roman Catholic law: KBU2915
'Abd: KBP529.3+
Abdication
  The Pope
    Canon law: KBR2392
    Roman Catholic law: KBU2392
Abduction
  Canon law: KBR3760
  Islamic law: KBP4125
  Jewish law: KBM4125
  Marriage impediments
    Canon law: KBR3128.A34
    Roman Catholic law: KBU3128.A34
  Roman Catholic law: KBU3760
Abduction for lewd acts
  Islamic law: KBP4206
Abduction of a minor from legal custodian
  Jewish law: KBM4188
Abduction of minors
  Canon law: KBR3762
Abicere species consecratas
  Penal (Criminal) law
    Canon law: KBR3664
Abicere species consecratas aut in sacrilegium finem retinere
  Roman Catholic law: KBU3664
Ablutions
  Islamic law: KBP184.46+
Abortion
  Abortion without consent of father
    Islamic law: KBP4070
  Canon law: KBR3756
  Criminal law
    Comparative religious law: KB4070
    Jewish law: KBM4070
  Family planning
    Islamic law: KBP3125.A36
  Forced abortion for population control
    Comparative religious law: KB3125.A36
    Jewish law: KBM3125.A36
  Medical legislation
    Jewish law: KBM3119.A36
  Roman Catholic law: KBU3756.A36
  Voluntary abortion
    Comparative religious law: KB3125.A36
Abortum procurare
  Canon law: KBR3756
  Roman Catholic law: KBU3756.A36
Abrogating hadith and abrogated hadith
  Islamic law: KBP136.78
Abrogatio
  Ecclesiastical laws
    Roman Catholic law: KBU2220
Abrogation
  Ecclesiastical laws
    Roman Catholic law: KBU2220
Abrogation, Theory of
  Islamic law: KBP463
Absent persons
  Comparative religious law: KB524.8
  Islamic law: KBP524.8
Absentees, Proceedings against
  Criminal procedure
    Comparative religious law: KB4710
    Islamic law: KBP4713
Absolutio
  Canon law: KBR3946
  Roman Catholic law: KBU3610.A38
Absolution
  Penal (Criminal) law
    Canon law: KBR3606.A38

Absolutism
  Church and state
    Canon law: KBR4040+
Abstinence (Mandatory) from alcohol
  Islamic law: KBP184.9.A27
Abuse of a child
  Islamic law: KBP4190
  Jewish law: KBM4190
Abuse of ecclesiastical function
  Canon law: KBR3700+
  Roman Catholic law: KBU3726
Abuse of legal process
  Islamic law: KBP4507.5
Abutting property
  Water resources
    Islamic law: KBP3047
Academic freedom
  Comparative religious law: KB3137.5
  Jewish law: KBM3137.5
Academies
  Cultural affairs
    Comparative religious law: KB3161
    Islamic law: KBP3160
    Jewish law: KBM3161
Acceptable impurity
  Islamic law: KBP184.43
Acceptance
  Betrothal
    Islamic law: KBP543.952
  Contracts
    Comparative religious law: KB869.3+
    Islamic law: KBP869.3+
    Jewish law: KBM869.3+
Access and judicial inspection
  Trials
    Canon law: KBR3850
Access to children
  Family law
    Comparative religious law: KB602
    Islamic law: KBP602
Access to public records
  Jewish law: KBM3042
Accessions
  Ownership
    Islamic law: KBP659
Accessus et recognitio (inspectio) iudicialis
  Trials
    Canon law: KBR3850
Accidents
  Torts
    Jewish law: KBM842.3
Accomplices
  Criminal act
    Jewish law: KBM3920
Accord and satisfaction
  Insolvency procedures
    Comparative religious law: KB1932
    Islamic law: KBP1932
Accountants
  Jewish law: KBM3517
Accounting
  Business
    Jewish law: KBM923
  Merchant enterprise
    Jewish law: KBM923
Accusation by witnesses
  Criminal procedure
    Islamic law: KBP4668
Accusation principle
  Criminal procedure
    Comparative religious law: KB4624
    Islamic law: KBP4624
  Penal (criminal) procedures
    Canon law: KBR3923
Accusatus
  Criminal procedures
    Canon law: KBR3927
Accused
  Compulsory measures against
    Islamic law: KBP4650
    Jewish law: KBM4650
  Criminal procedure
    Islamic law: KBP4630.A25
    Jewish law: KBM4630.A25
    Roman Catholic law: KBU3927
  Criminal procedures
    Canon law: KBR3927
  Duty to warn before commission of the crime
    Jewish law: KBM4621

Accused
  Testimony of
    Comparative religious law: KB4709.T47
    Islamic law: KBP4702
    Jewish law: KBM4702
Accusers
  Criminal procedure
    Comparative religious law: KB4630.A253
    Islamic law: KBP4630.A253
Acquisitio et alienatio bonorum
  Canon law: KBR3332+
Acquisition and alienation of property
  Canon law: KBR3332+
Acquisition and loss
  Property
    Comparative religious law: KB655+
  Real property
    Comparatiave religious law: KB687.5+
Acquisition and loss of ownership
  Jewish law: KBM655+
  Real property
    Islamic law: KBP687.5+
Acquisition and transfer of possession and ownership
  Comparative religious law: KB648+
  Jewish law: KBM648+
Acquisition of fruits and parts of things
  Comparative religious law: KB663
  Islamic law: KBP663
  Jewish law: KBM663
Acquisition of ownership
  Land law
    Jewish law: KBM687.5+
Acquisition of possession and ownership
  Islamic law: KBP648+
Acquittal
  Canon law: KBR3946
  Criminal procedure
    Comparative religious law: KB4742.A27+
    Islamic law: KBP4744
    Jewish law: KBM4744
Acquittal
  Penal (Criminal) procedure
    Roman Catholic law: KBU3949
Acquittance
  Obligations
    Comparative religious law: KB817
    Islamic law: KBP817.5
    Jewish law: KBM818+
Actio ecclesiae missionalis
  Canon law: KBR3049
Action
  Criminal procedure
    Islamic law: KBP4668
    Jewish law: KBM4668
Actions and defenses
  Courts and procedure
    Comparative religious law: KB1666+
    Islamic law: KBP1666+
    Jewish law: KBM1666+
  Judiciary
    Canon law: KBR3835+
  Procedure at first instance
    Roman Catholic law: KBU3841.2+
  Trial
    Canon law: KBR3841.2+
Active repentance
  Criminal law
    Comparative religious law: KB4023.A25
    Islamic law: KBP4023.T38
Acts of communal agencies
  Administrative law
    Jewish law: KBM2732
Acts of government
  Administrative law
    Jewish law: KBM2732
  Administrative process
    Islamic law: KBP2732
Adab al-qāḍī: KBP1595
'Adam al-kaf': KBP524.7+
'Ādāt: KBP455
Additives, Food
  Islamic law: KBP3379
Adjoining landowners: KBM700+
  Building and construction
    Islamic law: KBP3069

INDEX

Adjoining landowners
  Comparative religious law: KB700
  Land law
    Islamic law: KBP700+
  Public land law
    Jewish law: KBM3069
'Adl: KBP524.7+
Administration
  Auxiliary court personnel
    Islamic law: KBP1623
  Environmental law
    Comparative religious law: KB3128
    Islamic law: KBP3128
Administration and use of church property
  Canon law: KBR3432+
Administration of church property
  Canon law: KBR3320+
  Roman Catholic law: KBU3432+
Administration of justice: KBM1572+
  Comparative religious law: KB1572+
  Endangering the
    Jewish law: KBM4484+
  Islamic law: KBP1572
  Roman Catholic law: KBU3782.52+
Administration of sacraments
  Canon law: KBR3075+
Administration of the seminaries
  Canon law: KBR2328
Administrative acts
  Roman Catholic law: KBU2193.3+
Administrative and constitutional law
  Comparative religious law: KB2101+
Administrative law
  Communal agencies
    Jewish law: KBM2711+
Administrative organization
  Islamic law: KBP2860+
Administrative process
  Communal agencies
    Jewish law: KBM2711+
  Government
    Islamic law: KBP2730+
Administrative sanctions
  Islamic law: KBP2757
  Jewish law: KBM2757
Administrators of estate
  Islamic law: KBP635.954
  Jewish law: KBM635.4
Admission into religious association
  Religious institutes
    Canon law: KBR2927.M46
Admission of evidence
  Criminal procedure
    Comparative religious law: KB4675+
    Islamic law: KBP4679+
    Jewish law: KBM4679+
Admonition and rebuke
  Criminal law
    Canon law: KBR3618
Adopted children
  Roman Catholic law: KBU2243+
Adopted persons
  Natural persons
    Canon law: KBR2243
Adoptio imperfecta
  Natural persons
    Canon law: KBR2243
Adoptio perfecta (arrogatio)
  Natural persons
    Canon law: KBR2243
Adoption
  Comparative religious law: KB609
  Islamic law: KBP609
  Jewish law: KBM609
  Marriage impediments
    Canon law: KBR3128.A44
    Roman Catholic law: KBU3128.A44
  Natural persons
    Canon law: KBR2243
Adscriptio ecclesiae
  Roman Catholic law: KBU2227+
Adscriptio seu incardinatio clericorum
  Canon law: KBR2333+
  Roman Catholic law: KBU2333+
Adult education
  Islamic law: KBP3158
  Jewish law: KBM3158.5
Adulteration of food
  Islamic law: KBP3379
  Jewish law: KBM3377+

Adulterium
  Canon law: KBR3165
Adultery: KBM4184
  Family law
    Jewish law: KBM544.7
  Grounds for divorce
    Jewish law: KBM559.8
  Impediments to marriage
    Canon law: KBR3128.A39
  Islamic law: KBP4184
  Matrimonial actions
    Canon law: KBR3905.A48
  Penal (Criminal) law
    Canon law: KBR3774.A48
  Roman Catholic law: KBU3905.A48
Adultery and condonation
  Canon law: KBR3165
  Roman Catholic law: KBU3165
Adults
  Capacity and disability
    Islamic law: KBP525.5
  Guardianship
    Comparative religious law: KB627
Advertising
  Regulation of industry, trade, and commerce
    Comparative religious law: KB3280
    Islamic law: KBP3280
    Jewish law: KBM3280
  Unfair competition
    Islamic law: KBP1237
    Jewish law: KBM1237
Advisory opinions
  Courts and procedure
    Comparative religious law: KB1679.3
    Islamic law: KBP1679.3
    Jewish law: KBM1679.3
Advocates
  Penal (Criminal) procedure
    Roman Catholic law: KBU3928
  Penal (criminal) procedures
    Canon law: KBR3928
  The legal profession
    Canon law: KBR3823+
Advocati
  Penal (criminal) procedures
    Canon law: KBR3928
Advocatus
  Court officials
    Canon law: KBR3807.5.A39
Affect
  Defense
    Criminal law
      Roman Catholic law: KBU3559.D58
  Justification of illegal acts
    Canon law: KBR3559.D58
Affinitas
  Natural persons
    Canon law: KBR2240+
    Roman Catholic law: KBU2240+
Affinity
  Domestic relations
    Islamic law: KBP583+
  Family law
    Comparative religious law: KB583+
    Jewish law: KBM583+
  Marriage impediments
    Canon law: KBR3128.A44
    Comparative religious law: KB544.2
    Islamic law: KBP544.955
    Jewish law: KBM544.2
    Roman Catholic law: KBU3128.A44
  Natural persons
    Canon law: KBR2240+
    Roman Catholic law: KBU2240+
Affreightment
  Maritime law
    Comparative religious law: KB971
    Islamic law: KBP971
    Jewish law: KBM971
Afrād: KBP524.6+
'Afw: KBP4034
Age
  Baptism
    Canon law: KBR2229.A54
Age, Marriage
  Marriage impediments
    Canon law: KBR3128.M37
    Roman Catholic law: KBU3128.M37

Agency
  Contracts
    Comparative religious law: KB861
    Islamic law: KBP861+
    Jewish law: KBM861+
Agency and prokura
  Jewish law: KBM924
Agent of the qāḍī
  Islamic law: KBP1622
Aggravated theft
  Ḥadd crimes
    Islamic law: KBP4046.2
Aggravating circumstances
  Criminal law
    Comparative religious law: KB4023.A35
    Islamic law: KBP4020+
  Offenses against public order and convenience
    Jewish law: KBM4305+
Agricultural cooperatives
  Comparative religious law: KB3314
  Islamic law: KBP3316
  Jewish law: KBM3316+
Agriculture
  Regulation
    Comparative religious law: KB3294.22+
    Islamic law: KBP3293+
    Jewish law: KBM3293+
Agunahs
  Jewish law: KBM550.5
Aḥkām: KBP4736+
Aḥkām sulṭānīyah: KBP1572
Ahl al-dhimmah: KBP1588.7
Ahlīyah: KBP524.7+
Ahlīyat al-adā': KBP524.7+
Ahlīyat al-wujūb: KBP524.7+
AIDS (Disease)
  Public health
    Islamic law: KBP3082.A53
    Jewish law: KBM3082.A53
  Public health laws
    Comparative religious law: KB3082.A53
Air and space above ground
  Ownership
    Islamic law: KBP696
    Jewish law: KBM696
Air law
  Islamic law: KBP3467
  Jewish law: KBM3467
Air piracy
  Comparative religious law: KB4377
  Islamic law: KBP4377
  Jewish law: KBM4396
Air pollution
  Copmparative religious law: KB3130.5
  Islamic law: KBP3130.5
  Jewish law: KBM3130.5
Air traffic, Dangerous interference with
  Islamic law: KBP4380
Aircraft, Crimes aboard
  Islamic law: KBP4377
  Jewish law: KBM4396
Ajīr: KBP892.6
Ajīr khāṣṣ: KBP892.6
Akhlāqīyah: KBP444
Alcoholic beverages
  Islamic law: KBP184.42+
  Public health
    Jewish law: KBM3097
Alcoholic preparations
  Islamic law: KBP184.42+
Aleatory contracts
  Comparative religious law: KB899
  Islamic law: KBP899
  Jewish law: KBM899+
Aleatory obligations
  Islamic law: KBP814
Alibi
  Criminal trial
    Comparative religious law: KB4709.A45
    Islamic law: KBP4709.A45
    Jewish law: KBM4706
Alien property
  Emergency measures
    Islamic law: KBP3712
Alienation of church property
  Roman Catholic law: KBU3336

Alienation of ecclesiastical goods
  Roman Catholic law: KBU3698
Aliens
  Registration
    Islamic law: KBP1865
Alimony
  Dissolved marriage
    Islamic law: KBP567
  Domestic relations
    Islamic law: KBP584
  Jewish law: KBM567
Almsgiving
  Islamic law: KBP180
  Property tax
    Islamic law: KBP3620+
Altaria sive fixa sive mobilia
  Canon law: KBR3238.A58
Altars
  Canon law: KBR3238.A58
  Roman Catholic law: KBU3238.A58
Amah: KBP529.3+
Amānah: KBP889+
Amīn: KBP1622
Amir: KBP2532+
Amissio officii ecclesiastici
  Roman Catholic law: KBU2358
Amissio status clericalis
  Canon law: KBR2344+
  Roman Catholic law: KBU2344+
Amnesty
  Tax and customs crimes
    Islamic law: KBP3705
Amputation of limbs
  Criminal law punishment
    Islamic law: KBP3980.A46
Amr ʻāmm: KBP462.A57
Amulets
  Islamic law: KBP186.97.A58
Analogical deduction
  Islamic law: KBP452
Ancient legal systems and Jewish law:
  KBM524.36
Ancyra, Council of, 314: KBR245.3
Androginos
  Natural persons
    Jewish law: KBM529.7.H47
Anglo-Norman school
  Canon law: KBR2204.3
Animal experimentation
  Jewish law: KBM3123.2
Animal experimentation and research
  Islamic law: KBP3123.2
Animal protection
  Comparative religious law: KB3123+
  Islamic law: KBP3123+
  Jewish law: KBM3123+
Animal research
  Jewish law: KBM3123.2
Animal rights
  Comparative religious law: KB3123+
  Islamic law: KBP3123+
  Jewish law: KBM3123+
Animal welfare
  Comparative religious law: KB3123+
  Islamic law: KBP3123+
  Jewish law: KBM3123+
Animals
  Taxable income
    Islamic law: KBP3620.3.A54
Annullatio matrimonii
  Canon law: KBR3897+
Annulment
  Matrimonial actions
    Islamic law: KBP557
    Roman Catholic law: KBU3897+
Anointing of the Sick
  Roman Catholic law: KBU3096+
  Sacraments
    Canon law: KBR3096+
Antenuptial contracts
  Canon law: KBR3113
  Islamic law: KBP543.952
  Jewish law: KBM572
  Marital property and regime
    Islamic law: KBP572
  Marriage law
    Roman Catholic law: KBU3113
Antioch, Council of, 341: KBR246
Antitrust law
  Islamic law: KBP3242
  Jewish law: KBM3242
Apiculture
  Comparative religious law: KB3334

Apiculture
Islamic law: KBP3334
Jewish law: KBM3334
Apikoros: KBM4418
Apostasia
Canon law: KBR3046
Apostasia a fide
Canon law: KBR3628+
Apostasy
Canon law: KBR3628+
Criminal law
Islamic law: KBP4172
From Islam of a spouse
Islamic law: KBP557.3
Roman Catholic law: KBU3628+
Apostolic Chamber
Organs of government
Canon law: KBR2455
Roman Catholic law: KBU2455
Apostolic Chancery: KBR2430+
Roman Catholic law: KBU2430
Apostolic councils: KBR199.8+
Apostolic Datary
Canon law: KBR2435
Apostolic See, Jurisdiction of the
Dispensation of ratified and non-consummated marriage
Canon law: KBR3908
Apostolicae Sedis tribunalia
Canon law: KBR3810+
Roman Catholic law: KBU3810+
Apotropos
Jewish law: KBM622+
Appeal
Penal (Criminal) procedure
Roman Catholic law: KBU3958
Penal (criminal) procedures
Canon law: KBR3951
Procedure in general
Islamic law: KBP1687
Trials
Roman Catholic law: KBU3865
Appeal from one court to another
Islamic law: KBP1586
Jewish law: KBM1586
Appellate procedure
Matrimonial actions
Canon law: KBR3895
Roman Catholic law: KBU3895
Procedure in general
Jewish law: KBM1687
Appellate procedures
Procedure in general
Comparative religious law: KB1687
Appellatio
Penal (criminal) procedures
Canon law: KBR3951
Trials
Canon law: KBR3865
Applicability and validity of the law
Criminal law
Jewish law: KBM3825+
Applicability of laws
Roman Catholic law: KBU2197+
Applicability of the law
Islamic law: KBP501+
Applicability (Territorial and temporal) of laws
Canon law: KBR2197+
Appointment of arbitrator
Islamic law: KBP1619
Apprentices, Artisans'
Comparative religious law: KB3427
Islamic law: KBP3427
Jewish law: KBM3427
Appropriation of land by the state
Islamic law: KBP2825+
'Aqār: KBP683+
'Āqilah: KBP1040+
'Aql: KBP448.A74
Aquilea, Council of, 381: KBR249 381
Aquileia, Council of, 553: KBR249 553
Arāḍī al-dawlah: KBP3056+
Arāmil: KBP550+
Arbitration
Court procedure
Comparative religious law: KB1829
Jewish law: KBM1829
Courts
Roman Catholic law: KBU3918
Courts and procedure
Islamic law: KBP1829+

Arbitration
  Courts and tribunals
    Jewish law: KBM1588
  Ecclesiastical courts
    Canon law: KBR3918
Arbitrator
  Judges
    Islamic law: KBP1619
Arbitrators
  Judges
    Jewish law: KBM1619
Archaeological sites
  Islamic law: KBP3183+
  Jewish law: KBM3183
Archaeology
  Religious law: KB78.A+
Archaeology and canon law: KBR78
Architectural landmarks
  Comparative religious law: KB3183
  Islamic law: KBP3183+
  Jewish law: KBM3183
Archives
  Comparative religious law: KB3177
  Islamic law: KBP3177
  Jewish law: KBM3177
  Organs of government
    Roman Catholic law: KBU2857
Archivio Vaticano
  Bibliographies: KBR15.5.A73
'Āriyah: KBP879.4
Arles, Council of, 314: KBR245
Armed forces
  Comparative religious law: KB3738+
  Islamic law: KBP3738+
Armed Forces
  Jewish law: KBM3738+
Arson
  Criminal law
    Comparative religious law: KB4354
    Islamic law: KBP4354
  Jewish law: KBM4351.5
Artificial insemination
  Family law
    Islamic law: KBP619.T34
    Jewish law: KBM619.A77
  Medical legislation
    Comparative religious law: KB3117
Artificial insemination
  Medical legislation
    Islamic law: KBP3117
    Jewish law: KBM3117
  Roman Catholic law: KBU3298
Artisans
  Comparative religious law: KB3426+
  Islamic law: KBP3426+
  Jewish law: KBM3426+
Artisans' apprentices
  Jewish law: KBM3427
Artisans' partnership
  Comparative religious law: KB1048
  Islamic law: KBP1048
  Jewish law: KBM1048
Arts
  Islamic law: KBP3168+
Arts, The
  Comparative religious law: KB3168+
  Jewish law: KBM3160+
Ascription of infants
  Roman Catholic law: KBU2229.C55
Ascription to Latin Church
  Canon law: KBR2229.C55
Ashkhāṣ: KBP524.6+
'Āshūrā': KBP186.3
Aṣīl: KBP811, KBP900
Asmakhta: KBM524.34
Assassination by order of Bet din:
  KBM3965
Assault and battery
  Matrimonial actions
    Canon law: KBR3905.A77
  Penal (Criminal) law
    Canon law: KBR3768
  Roman Catholic law: KBU3768
Assessment
  Income tax
    Public finance
      Jewish law: KBM3576
    Stock companies
      Islamic law: KBP3597.3
  Property tax
    Jewish law: KBM3619
  Utilities
    Islamic law: KBP3065
    Jewish law: KBM3065

Assistance in emergencies
  Jewish law: KBM524.5
Assisted reproduction
  Family law
    Jewish law: KBM619.A77
  Islamic law: KBP619.T34
Assisting suicide
  Comparative religious law: KB4058
  Islamic law: KBP4058
  Jewish law: KBM4056
Associations
  Artisans
    Jewish law: KBM3429
  Contracts
    Comparative religious law: KB1040+
    Islamic law: KBP1040+
    Jewish law: KBM1040+
  Juristic persons
    Canon law: KBR2260+
    Jewish law: KBM530
    Roman Catholic law: KBU2260+
Assumption of debt
  Islamic law: KBP816.7
Assumption of obligations
  Comparative religious law: KB816
  Islamic law: KBP816+
  Jewish law: KBM816
Assumption of risk
  Criminal offense
    Comparative religious law: KB3861
    Islamic law: KBP3861
Astrologia iudiciaria
  Penal (Criminal) law
    Canon law: KBR3648.A78
Asylum
  Criminal procedure
    Jewish law: KBM4826.5
Asylum, Right of
  Constitution of the state
    Islamic law: KBP2485.5
  Constitutional and administrative law
    Comparative religious law: KB2485.5
  Sacred places
    Canon law: KBR3236
Asylums
  Canon law: KBR3275.H67
  Roman Catholic law: KBU3275.A88
Attachment and garnishment
  Courts and procedure
    Jewish law: KBM1888
Attempt
  Criminal act
    Comparative religious law: KB3854
    Islamic law: KBP3854
    Jewish law: KBM3854
  Violation of law or precept
    Penal (Criminal) law
      Canon law: KBR3566
Attorneys
  Islamic law: KBP1637
  Jewish law: KBM1630
Auction houses
  Islamic law: KBP3423.5.A82
  Jewish law: KBM3423.5.A82
Auctioneers
  Comparative religious law: KB930
  Jewish law: KBM930
Auctions
  Islamic law: KBP878.A93
  Jewish law: KBM930
Audientia sacri palatii
  Canon law: KBR3816+
Audientiarius
  Court officials
    Canon law: KBR3807.5.A93
Auditor
  Court officials
    Canon law: KBR3807.5.A94
Auditores
  The legal profession
    Canon law: KBR3823+
Auditors
  Jewish law: KBM3518
Author and publisher
  Copyright
    Islamic law: KBP1185
  Jewish law: KBM1185
Authority
  Church and state
    Roman Catholic law: KBU4050+

Authority and jurisdiction
  The Pope
    Canon law: KBR2367+
    Roman Catholic law: KBU2367+
Authorization
  Agency
    Islamic law: KBP861.3
Automobile emission control
  Comparative religious law: KB3130.5
  Islamic law: KBP3130.5
  Jewish law: KBM3130.5
Automobiles
  Retail trade
    Islamic law: KBP3422.A88
    Jewish law: KBM3422.A88
Automotive transportation
  Islamic law: KBP3442+
  Jewish law: KBM3442+
Autonomous monasteries
  Canon law: KBR2908
Autonomy
  Communal agencies
    Jewish law: KBM2724
  Monasticism
    Canon law: KBR2906
  Municipal government
    Islamic law: KBP2938
Autopsy
  Medical legislation
    Jewish law: KBM3119.A88
Auxiliaries
  Dioceses
    Canon law: KBR2844+
Auxiliary bishop
  Canon law: KBR2844
Auxiliary medical professions
  Comparative religious law: KB3104+
  Islamic law: KBP3104+
  Jewish law: KBM3104+
Auxiliary personnel
  The legal profession
    Islamic law: KBP1620+
    Jewish law: KBM1620+
Auxiliary services during war or emergency
  Military law
    Jewish law: KBM3749
Avenger
  Criminal procedure
    Jewish law: KBM4630.V52
Average
  Maritime law
    Comparative religious law: KB979
    Islamic law: KBP978+
    Jewish law: KBM978+
Aviation
  Jewish law: KBM3467
'Awl: KBP633.952.A84
'Ayn: KBP642.3+
'Azīmah/Rukhṣah: KBP501.5

B

Ba'ale teshuvah
  Equality before the law
    Jewish law: KBM2467.B32
Baalei Tseuvah
  Education of children
    Jewish law: KBM3143.4
Bahai
  Islamic law: KB255.B34
Bailiffs
  Islamic law: KBP1624
  Jewish law: KBM1624
Bālīgh: KBP525.5
Banishment
  Criminal law
    Comparative religious law: KB3993.B35
    Islamic law: KBP3997
    Jewish law: KBM3997
  Criminal procedure
    Jewish law: KBM4826+
  Penal (Criminal) law
    Canon law: KBR3600
Banking
  Jewish law: KBM940+
Banking transactions: KBP951+
  Comparative religious law: KB940.A+
  Excise taxes
    Comparative religious law: KB3640.B35
    Islamic law: KBP3640.B35
  Jewish law: KBM951+

Bankruptcy
  Comparative religious law: KB1942
  Islamic law: KBP1942
  Jewish law: KBM1942
Banks
  Jewish law: KBM940+
Banks and banking
  Comparative religious law: KB940.A+
  Islamic law: KBP940+
Bannum
  Penal (Criminal) law
    Canon law: KBR3600
Baptism
  Canon law: KBR3077+
  Marriage law
    Roman Catholic law: KBU3110.2
  Roman Catholic law: KBU2228+, KBU3077+
Baptism and church membership
  Canon law: KBR2227+
Baptismus
  Roman Catholic law: KBU2228+
Baptismus liberorum vel educaio in religione acatholica
  Roman Catholic law: KBU3650
Baptizing and educating children out of faith
  Roman Catholic law: KBU3650
Barter
  Comparative religious law: KB879
  Jewish law: KBM879+
Baths, Public
  Ablutions
    Islamic law: KBP184.47.P82
Battery
  Criminal law
    Comparative religious law: KB4076
    Islamic law: KBP4076+
    Jewish law: KBM4076
Bay': KBP874+
Bay' al-dayn bi-al-dayn: KBP856
Bay' al-'īnah: KBP877.3
Bayyinah: KBP1672+
Beatification, Procedures in
  Canon law: KBR3916
Beekeeping
  Comparative religious law: KB3334
Beekeeping
  Islamic law: KBP3334
  Jewish law: KBM3334
Beheading
  Criminal law punishment
    Comparative religious law: KB3980.B43
    Islamic law: KBP3980.B43
Beis din
  Criminal proceeding by: KBM4613
Benediction
  Oraḥ ḥayim law: KBM523.3.B4
Benefices, Granting of
  The Pope
    Canon law: KBR2385
    Roman Catholic law: KBU2385
Benefices, prebends, penions, etc
  Ecclesiastical offices
    Canon law: KBR2357
Beneficiaries of social service
  Jewish law: KBM1528+
Benefits
  Social insurance
    Islamic law: KBP1476
    Jewish law: KBM1476
Benevolence
  Yoreh de'ah law: KBM523.5.B4
Berat gecesi: KBP186.38
Bet David
  Constitutional principles
    Jewish law: KBM2130
Bet din: KBM1582
Betrothal
  Comarative religious law: KB543+
  Islamic law: KBP543+
  Jewish law: KBM543+
  Marriage law
    Roman Catholic law: KBU3112
Betting
  Aleatory contracts
    Jewish law: KBM899.3
Beverages
  Regulation
    Islamic law: KBP3395+
    Jewish law: KBM3395+
Bi'ah
  Jewish law: KBM546.16

Bibliographic research, Methods of
  Religious law in general: KB130+
Biblioteca Apostolica Vaticana:
  KBU15.5.B53
  Bibliographies: KBR15.5.B5
Bid'ah: KBP448.B53
Bigamy
  Family law
    Jewish law: KBM544.6
  Islamic law: KBP4186
  Penal (Criminal) law
    Canon law: KBR3770
Ḅikr: KBP528.B54
Bill of divorce
  Jewish law: KBM562.3
Bill paying services
  Islamic law: KBP961
Bills of exchange
  Islamic law: KBP938
  Jewish law: KBM938
Biographical dictionaries
  Islamic law: KBP253
Biography
  Historians
    Islamic law: KBP49.5
  Legal scholars
    Islamic law: KBP253
  Scholars
    Islamic law: KBP49.5
Biological terrorism
  Comparative religious law: KB4368
  Islamic law: KBP4368
Biomedical engineering
  Islamic law: KBP3115+
  Medical legislation
    Jewish law: KBM3115+
  Roman Catholic law: KBU3290+
Birds
  Conservation
    Comparative religious law: KB3135
    Islamic law: KBP3135
Birth
  Canon law: KBR2226
  Comparative religious law: KB524.72,
    KB524.8
  Persons
    Islamic law: KBP524.72
Birth
  Registration
    Comparative religious law: KB1862
    Islamic law: KBP1862
Birth control
  Comparative religious law: KB3124+
  Islamic law: KBP3124+
  Jewish law: KBM3124+
  Roman Catholic law: KBU3308+
Birth rights
  Canon law: KBR2226
Bishops, Coadjutor and auxiliary
  Organs of government
    Law of the Roman Catholic Church:
      KBU2844
Bishops (General)
  Canon law: KBR2792
Blasphemia
  Penal (Criminal) law
    Canon law: KBR3652+
Blasphemy
  Criminal law
    Islamic law: KBP4172
    Jewish law: KBM4172
  Penal (Criminal) law
    Canon law: KBR3652+
  Roman Catholic law: KBU3652
Blessing of sacred places
  Canon law: KBR3232
Blind
  Social service
    Islamic law: KBP1534.B54
    Jewish law: KBM1534.B54
Blood as food or medicine
  Islamic law: KBP184.9.B45
Blood banks
  Comparative religious law:
    KB3110.3.56
  Islamic law: KBP3112
  Jewish law: KBM3112
Blood money
  Qiṣāṣ punishment
    Islamic law: KBP3976
Blood sacrifices
  Islamic law: KBP184.6+

Blood tests
  Criminal procedure
    Jewish law: KBM4687
Blood transfusion
  Islamic law: KBP3119.B55
Bond, Existing
  Impediments to marriage
    Canon law: KBR3128.B66
  Marriage impediments
    Roman Catholic law: KBU3128.B66
Bonds
  Corporate finance
    Jewish law: KBM1064
  Excise taxes
    Islamic law: KBP3640.S42
  Stock corporations
    Islamic law: KBP1064
Bookdealers
  Islamic law: KBP3504.5
  Jewish law: KBM3504.5
Books, Denunciation of bad
  Canon law: KBR3068.D46
Books, Prohibited
  Roman Catholic law: KBU3065
Books, Prohibited, Publication of
  Penal (Criminal) law
    Canon law: KBR3656+
Boundaries of Vatican City
  Roman Catholic law: KBU4070
Branches of law
  Islamic law: KBP490+
Breach of contract
  Comparative religious law: KB826
  Jewish law: KBM826
  Obligations
    Islamic law: KBP824+
Breach of duty of assistance to a pregnant woman
  Islamic law: KBP4194
Breach of duty of support
  Criminal law
    Islamic law: KBP4192
    Jewish law: KBM4192
Breach of trust
  Criminal law
    Jewish law: KBM4266
Breaking the fast at the end of Ramaḍān: KBP186.45
Breviary, Praying of
  Clergy
    Canon law: KBR2338.B74
Brewing
  Jewish law: KBM3395
Bribe, Attempted, of officials in the Church
  Penal (Criminal) law
    Canon law: KBR3722
Bribery
  Communal employees
    Comparative law: KB4514
    Islamic law: KBP4514
  Crimes against communal employees
    Jewish law: KBM4520
  Of officials of secular authority
    Jewish law: KBM2023
Bridegroom, Equal birth of
  Islamic law: KBP543.957
Bringing false complaint
  Criminal law
    Jewish law: KBM4498
Broadcasting
  Jewish law: KBM3495
Brocardica juris and canon law: KBR100.A+
Brokerage
  Comparative religious law: KB929
  Islamic law: KBP929
  Jewish law: KBM929
Budget
  Administration of church property
    Roman Catholic law: KBU3444.B84
Building and construction
  Church buildings
    Roman Catholic law: KBU3417+
  Public property
    Jewish law: KBM3067+
  Regional planning
    Islamic law: KBP3067+
Building and construction industry
  Islamic law: KBP3402
  Jewish law: KBM3402

Building laws
Church buildings
Canon law: KBR3417
Roman Catholic law: KBU3419
Building safety and control
Jewish law: KBM3071
Buildings
Taxable income
Islamic law: KBP3620.3.B84
Buildings, Church
Canon law: KBR3417
Roman Catholic law: KBU3417+
Buildings, Historic
Islamic law: KBP3183+
Bulūgh: KBP525.6.B84
Burden of proof
Canon law: KBR3843+
Criminal procedure
Comparative religious law: KB4675+
Islamic law: KBP4675+
Jewish law: KBM4675+
Matrimonial actions
Canon law: KBR3893
Roman Catholic law: KBU3893
Penal (criminal) procedures
Canon law: KBR3940+
Procedure at first instance
Penal (Criminal) procedure
Roman Catholic law: KBU3940
Procedure at trial
Comparative religious law: KB1672+
Islamic law: KBP1672+
Jewish law: KBM1672+
Trials
Roman Catholic law: KBU3843+
Burial and cemetery laws
Islamic law: KBP3078
Jewish law: KBM3078+
Burial service
Islamic law: KBP184.55
Burial society
Jewish law: KBM3078.5
Burials
Canon law: KBR3273
Roman Catholic law: KBU3273
Burning to death
Criminal law punishment
Jewish law: KBM3964.3
Business associations
Taxation
Jewish law: KBM3592
Business enterprise
Jewish law: KBM921+
Business enterprises
Property tax
Islamic law: KBP3616+, KBP3663
Business expenses
Income tax
Jewish law: KBM3582.3.B88
Business tax
Local finance
Islamic law: KBP3674+
Local revenue
Comparative religious law: KB3674+
National revenue
Comparative religious law: KB3674+
By-laws
Sources of fiqh
Islamic law: KBP458.L35
Byzantine Empire (to ca. 8th cent.) and Early Church
Church and state
Canon law: KBR4012+

C

Cabinet, The
Constitution of the state
Islamic law: KBP2580
Cadaster
Jewish law: KBM758
Cadastral surveys
Jewish law: KBM758
Call to prayer
Islamic law: KBP184.3+
Camera Apostolica
Curia Romana: KBU39.3
Organs of government
Canon law: KBR2455
Roman Catholic law: KBU2455

Campgrounds
  Public safety
    Jewish law: KBM3034.5
Cancellaria Apostolica
  Canon law: KBR2430+
  Curia Romana: KBU39.2
  Roman Catholic law: KBU2430
Cancellarius and vice-cancellarius curiae
  Diocesan constitution and organs
    Canon law: KBR2856
Cancellation of contract
  Comparative religious law: KB873.8
  Islamic law: KBP873.8
  Jewish law: KBM873.8
Candidate for ordination
  Holy Orders
    Canon law: KBR3104
  Roman Catholic law: KBU3104
Candidatus
  Holy Orders
    Canon law: KBR3104
Canon law
  Compared with civil law and Roman law: KB215+
Canon Law: KBR2+
Canon law and civil jurisdiction
  Marriage: KBR3116
  Marriage law
    Roman Catholic law: KBU3116
Canon law and criminal law: KBR2156
Canon law and moral theology: KBR2155.2
  Roman Catholic law: KBU2156
Canon law and other disciplines or subjects: KBR2155+
Canon law and other legal systems: KBR2205+
Canon law and social legislation: KBR2157
  Roman Catholic law: KBU2157
Canon law, Early
  Influence on Islamic law: KBP469
Canon law (Greek-Byzantine and post-schismatic)canon law and Roman law: KB245.A+
Canon law (Occidental) and common law: KB243.A+
Canon law of Eastern churches: KBS3+
Canonica traditio: KBR2190
Canonica tratitio
  Roman Catholic law: KBU2190
Canonical collections of councils and synods (Sources)
  Canon law: KBR199.8+
Canonical jurisprudence: KBR2160+
  Roman Catholic law: KBU2160+
Canonical jurisprudence and general philosophy: KBR2155.4
Canonical jurisprudence and theology: KBR2155
  Roman Catholic law: KBU2155
Canonical science
  Canon law: KBR2160+
Canonical tradition: KBR2190
  Roman Catholic law: KBU2190
Canonists and jurists
  Canon law: KBR1570+
Canonization, Procedures in
  Canon law: KBR3916
Canons and constitutions
  Canon law: KBR2191+
Capacity
  Criminal liability
    Comparative religious law: KB3882+
    Islamic law: KBP3882+
    Jewish law: KBM3880+
Capacity and disability
  Persons
    Islamic law: KBP524.7+
Capacity and incapacity
  Natural persons
    Canon law: KBR2231+
    Jewish law: KBM524.7+
Capacity and incapacity, Legal
  Natural persons
    Roman Catholic law: KBU2230+
Capacity to sue and to be sued
  Roman Catholic law: KBU3832+
Capella papalis
  Organs of government
    Canon law: KBR2778

Capellani
  Diocesan constitution and organs
    Canon law: KBR2874
Capital
  Limited partnership
    Islamic law: KBP1047.4
  Personal companies
    Jewish law: KBM1047.4
  Silent partnership
    Islamic law: KBP1049.4
    Jewish law: KBM1049.4
  Taxation
    Jewish law: KBM3616+
    National revenue
      Islamic law: KBP3616+
  Taxation of
    Local revenue
      Islamic law: KBP3663
    National revenue
      Islamic law: KBP3663
Capital gains tax
  Income tax
    Jewish law: KBM3578.5.P75
  Local finance
    Islamic law: KBP3672
  Local revenue
    Comparative religious law: KB3623
  National revenue
    Comparative religious law: KB3623
    Islamic law: KBP3623
  Public finance
    Jewish law: KBM3623
Capital investment
  Income tax
    Islamic law: KBP3588
Capital punishment
  Criminal procedure
    Jewish law: KBM4612
  Jewish law: KBM3964+
Capital stock
  Stock companies
    Jewish law: KBM1062
  Stock corporations
    Islamic law: KBP1062
Capitulum canonicorum (cathedrale sive collegiale)
  Canon law: KBR2884
Capitulum canonicorum (cathedrale sive collegiale)
  Roman Catholic law: KBU2884
Cardinalium Collegium
  Canon law: KBR2412
Cardinals, Commission of
  Canon law: KBR2730+
Care for the child
  Family law
    Islamic law: KBP602.5
Caritas
  Canon law: KBR3264+
  Roman Catholic law: KBU3264+
Carolingian theocracy
  Canon law: KBR4022
Carriage of goods and passengers
  Jewish law: KBM3455
  Road traffic
    Islamic law: KBP3455+
Carriage of goods at sea and inland waters
  Affreightment
    Comparative religious law: KB971
    Islamic law: KBP971
    Jewish law: KBM971
Carriage of passengers and goods
  Coastwise and inland shipping
    Islamic law: KBP3478
  Comparative religious law: KB931
  Contracts
    Islamic law: KBP931
    Jewish law: KBM931
Carriage of passengers at sea and inland waters
  Comparative religious law: KB976
  Maritime law
    Islamic law: KBP976
    Jewish law: KBM976
Cartels
  Islamic law: KBP3225+
Carthage, Council of, 255: KBR199.9
Carthage, Council of, 299: KBR244
Carthage, Council of, 311: KBR244.5
Carthage, Council of, 398: KBR247.2
Carthage, Council of, 491: KBR247.5
Carthage, Council of, 553: KBR249
  553a

Castitas
  Monasticism
    Roman Catholic law: KBU2927.C53
Castration
  Comparative religious law: KB3121+
  Medical legislation
    Islamic law: KBP3121+
    Jewish law: KBM3121
  Roman Catholic law: KBU3304
Casuistry
  Canon law and moral theology: KBR2155.2
  Roman Catholic law: KBU2156
Catechetica
  Canon law: KBR3048
Catechetics and preaching
  Canon law: KBR3048
  Teaching office of the Church
    Roman Catholic law: KBU3048
Cathedral and collegiate chapter cases
  Canon law
    Rota Romana: KBR44.6.C38
Cathedraticum
  Canon law: KBR3388
Catholic health organizations
  Roman Catholic law: KBU3284
Catholic hospitals
  Roman Catholic law: KBU3286
Catholic religious education
  Canon law: KBR3050+
Catholic universities
  Canon law: KBR3054
  Roman Catholic law: KBU3054
Causae pertinentes ad civilem magistratum
  Matrimonial actions
    Canon law: KBR3889
Causae separationis coniugum
  Matrimonial actions
    Canon law: KBR3901+
  Roman Catholic law: KBU3901+
Causation
  Criminal act
    Islamic law: KBP3851
    Jewish law: KBM3851
  Jewish law: KBM524.4.C38
Celebration
  Marriage
    Canon law: KBR3144+
Celebration of marriage
  Comparative religious law: KB546
Celebration of the mass
  Canon law: KBR3087+
  Roman Catholic law: KBU3087+
Celibacy
  Clergy
    Canon law: KBR2338.C45
Cemeteries
  Roman Catholic law: KBU3238.C46
  Sacred places
    Canon law: KBR3238.C46
Cemetery laws
  Comparative religious law: KB3080+
  Islamic law: KBP3078
Censors
  Canon law: KBR3068.C46
  Roman Catholic law: KBU3068.C46
Censorship
  Arts
    Comparative religious law: KB3168+
  Arts, The
    Islamic law: KBP3168+
  Canon law: KBR3068.C46
  Mass media
    Comparative religious law: KB3483
    Islamic law: KBP3483
    Jewish law: KBM3483
  Prohibition of
    Comparative religious law: KB2478
    Islamic law: KBP2478
    Jewish law: KBM2478
  Roman Catholic law: KBU3068.C46
Censorship and publishing
  Canon law: KBR3064+
Censure
  Marriage impediments
    Canon law: KBR3122.C46
  Mere prohibition of marriage
    Roman Catholic law: KBU3122.C46
Censures
  Penal (Criminal) law
    Canon law: KBR3602+

Censures
  Penalties
    Roman Catholic law: KBU3602+
Cereal products
  Islamic law: KBP3380
Cereals and cereal products
  Jewish law: KBM3380
Certainty, Legal
  Jewish law: KBM524.26
  Roman Catholic law: KBU2196.3
Certification
  Courts and procedure
    Jewish law: KBM1847
  Notaries
    Comparative religious law: KB1847
    Islamic law: KBP1847
Chalcedon, Council of, 451
  Canon law: KBR225
Challenge of court members
  Islamic law: KBP4670
  Jewish law: KBM4670
Challenge of the sentence
  Law of the Roman Catholi Church:
    KBU3861+
Chancellor and vice-chancellor
  Diocesan constitution and organs
    Canon law: KBR2856
Chancelor and vice-chancelor
  Organs of government
    Roman Catholic law: KBU2856+,
      KBU2856
Change of parties
  Procedure at trial
    Islamic law: KBP1668.C53
Change of party
  Procedure at first instance
    Roman Catholic law: KBU3842.C53
  Trials
    Canon law: KBR3842.C53
Chapels, Private
  Roman Catholic law: KBU3238.C53
  Sacred places
    Canon law: KBR3238.C53
Chaplains
  Diocesan constitution and organs
    Canon law: KBR2874
Chaplains
  Organs of government
    Roman Catholic law: KBU2874
Chapter of canons (Cathedral or
  collegial)
  Canon law: KBR2884
  Roman Catholic law: KBU2884
Chapters
  Religious institutes
    Canon law: KBR2918+
Charge
  Criminal procedure
    Islamic law: KBP4668
Charges brought against a person
  Pretrial criminal procedure
    Jewish law: KBM4634
Charitable gifts
  Income tax
    Jewish law: KBM3580
  Inheritance and succession
    Comparative religious law: KB636.3
  Islamic law: KBP636.3
  Jewish law: KBM636.3
Charitable or educational gifts and
  contributions
  Income tax
    Islamic law: KBP3580
Charitable uses
  Church property
    Canon law: KBR3452
  Islamic law: KBP637+
  Juristic persons
    Canon law: KBR2276.C53
Charitable uses, trusts, and foundations
  Non-collegiate juristic persons
    Roman Catholic law: KBU2276.C53
Charities
  Comparative religious law: KB1468+
  Islamic law: KBP1520+
Chastity
  Clergy
    Canon law: KBR2338.C53
  Monasticism
    Roman Catholic law: KBU2927.C53
  Religious institutes
    Canon law: KBR2927.C53

Chastity, Vows of
Impediments to marriage
Canon law: KBR3128.V69
Marriage impediments
Roman Catholic law: KBU3128.V69
Chicanery
Islamic law: KBP4507.5
Chief of State (The Pope)
Roman Catholic law: KBU2366+
Child labor
Comparative religious law: KB1278.C45
Islamic law: KBP1422
Jewish law: KBM1422
Child marriage
Islamic law: KBP543.955
Jewish law: KBM543.5
Marriage impediments
Canon law: KBR3128.M37
Roman Catholic law: KBU3128.M37
Child sexual abuse
Law of the Roman Catholic Church: KBU3764.5
Childbirth
Ablutions
Islamic law: KBP184.47.C45
Children
Access to
Islamic law: KBP602
Baptism
Canon law: KBR2229.C55
Roman Catholic law: KBU2229.C55
Capacity and disability
Islamic law: KBP525
Child of an incestuous or adulterous relationship, Legal status of
Jewish law: KBM613
Children of a female slave
Islamic law: KBP529.54
Claiming a slave child
Islamic law: KBP529.5
Domicile
Roman Catholic law: KBU2236.C55
Equality before the law
Jewish law: KBM2467.C48
Family law
Comparative religious law: KB589
Children
Family law
Jewish law: KBM589+
Illegitimate children
Islamic law: KBP612+
Jurisdiction of ecclesiastical courts
Canon law: KBR3795.C55
Lewd acts with
Islamic law: KBP4208
Marriage bond
Canon law: KBR3157
Roman Catholic law: KBU3157
Obligation of parents to educate their children
Comparative religious law: KB3139.3
Islamic law: KBP3139.3
Raising a child not one's own
Jewish law: KBM609
Resulting from unlawful intercourse
Islamic law: KBP612+
Right to education
Jewish law: KBM3139.3
Slaves
Comparative religious law: KB529.5.C45
Social laws
Comparative religious law: KB1540
Social service
Islamic law: KBP1542+
Jewish law: KBM1542+
Children, Custody and education of
Separation and divorce
Roman Catholic law: KBU3902
Children from defective or divorced marriages
Jewish law: KBM589+
Children of Baalei Tseuvah, Education of
Jewish law: KBM3143.4
Children of converts to Judaism, Education of
Jewish law: KBM3143.4
Children of mixed marriages
Baptism
Canon law: KBR2229.R57
Canon law: KBR3150

Children of mixed marriages
  Roman Catholic law: KBU3150
Children (Place of origin)
  Natural persons
    Canon law: KBR2236.C55
Children with disabilities
  Education
    Comparative religious law: KB3143
    Islamic law: KBP3143+
Children with mental disabilities
  Education
    Comparative religious law: KB3143
    Islamic law: KBP3143.6
Children with physical disabilities
  Education
    Islamic law: KBP3143.6
Children with social disabilities
  Education
    Islamic law: KBP3143.4
Choice of law
  Comparative religious law: KB482
  Islamic law: KBP482+
Choice of residence
  Husband and wife
    Islamic law: KBP548
Christian law and international law:
  KB265
Chronology
  Islamic law: KBP54
Church and democratic government
  Roman Catholic law: KBU4045+
Church and feudal institutes
  Canon law: KBR4032
Church and state relationships
  Canon law: KBR4000+
  Roman Catholic law: KBU4000+
Church buildings
  Canon law: KBR3417
  Roman Catholic law: KBU3417+
Church economics and finance
  Canon law: KBR3320+
Church lands
  Roman Catholic law: KBU3410+
Church membership
  Roman Catholic law: KBU2227+
Church property
  Canon law: KBR3320+
Church property
  Canon law
    Rota Romana: KBR44.6.C45
  Roman Catholic law: KBU3320+
    Rota Romana: KBU44.6.C45
Church taxes
  Canon law: KBR3384+
  Roman Catholic law: KBU3384+
Churches
  Roman Catholic law: KBU3238.C58
  Sacred places
    Canon law: KBR3238.C58
Churches and groups of churches
  Organs of government
    Canon law: KBR2790+
Churches, Particular, and groups of
  churches
  Roman Catholic law: KBU2790+
Circumcision
  Comparative religious law:
    KB3119.C57
  Islamic law: KBP184.8
  Medical legislation
    Islamic law: KBP3119.C57
    Jewish law: KBM3119.C57
Circumcision, Female
  Medical legislation
    Islamic law: KBP3119.F45
Circumstances influencing measures of
  penalty
  Criminal law
    Islamic law: KBP4020+
Circumstantial evidence
  Criminal procedure
    Comparative religious law:
      KB4709.C57
    Islamic law: KBP4709.C57
    Jewish law: KBM4705
Citation
  Roman Catholic law: KBU3839.5
Cities of refuge
  Criminal procedure
    Jewish law: KBM4826.5
Citizenship
  Comparative religious law: KB529.72
  Individual and state
    Islamic law: KBP2430+

Citizenship
Persons
Islamic law: KBP529.72
City planning and redevelopment
Islamic law: KBP3062+
Jewish law: KBM3062+
Civil and political rights
Comparative religious law: KB2460+
Islamic law: KBP2460+
Jewish law: KBM2460+
Civil courts, Jurisdiction of
Matrimonial actions
Roman Catholic law: KBU3889
Civil defense
Jewish law: KBM3752
Civil disobedience
Jewish law: KBM2486
Civil duties
Jewish law: KBM2460+
Civil jurisdiction
Marriage law
Roman Catholic law: KBU3116
Civil jurisdiction and canon law
Marriage: KBR3116
Civil law
Canon law
Rota Romana: KBR44.6.C58
Comparative religious law: KB491
Compared with canon law and Roman law: KB215+
Compared with Jewish law and Roman law: KB201+
Conflict of laws
Canon law: KBR2199.C59
Jewish law: KBM524.44
Civil law (Reception) and Canon law: KBR2206
Civil law (Reception) and law of the Roman Catholic Church: KBU2206
Civil marriages, Validity of
Jewish law: KBM546.18
Civil obligations
Islamic law: KBP814
Jewish law: KBM814
Civil procedure
Jewish law: KBM1650+
Civil register
Comparative religious law: KB1854+
Civil rights and the Church
Roman Catholic law: KBU4059+
Civil rights, Loss of
Criminal law punishment
Jewish law: KBM4004
Civil service
Comparative religious law: KB2870
Islamic law: KBP2970
Jewish law: KBM2970
Civil status
Registration
Comparative religious law: KB1856+
Islamic law: KBP1856+
Civil suit, Victim's
Criminal proceedings
Jewish law: KBM4767
Civil trials
Canon law: KBR129+
Roman Catholic law: KBU129+
Claimant
Courts
Comparative religious law: KB1655
Procedure in general
Islamic law: KBP1657
Claims against estate
Islamic law: KBP633.952.T37
Jewish law: KBM633+
Claims and actions resulting from ownership
Property
Comparative religious law: KB675
Islamic law: KBP675
Jewish law: KBM675
Clandestinitas
Marriage
Canon law: KBR3152+
Clandestinity of marriage celebration
Canon law: KBR3152+
Roman Catholic law: KBU3152+
Clauses
Contracts
Comparative religious law: KB870
Islamic law: KBP870
Jewish law: KBM870

Clergy
Constitution
Roman Catholic law: KBU2320+
Organs of government
Roman Catholic law: KBU2888+
Clergy, Support of
Administration of church property
Roman Catholic law: KBU3444.C54
Clergy, The
Canon law: KBR2320+
Jurisdiction of ecclesiastical courts
Canon law: KBR3786
Personnel of churches and ecclesiastical institutes
Canon law: KBR2888+
Clericus concubinarius
Penal (Criminal) law
Canon law: KBR3746
Roman Catholic law: KBU3746
Clericus matrimonium
Penal (Criminal) law
Canon law: KBR3742
Clerks to the court
Islamic law: KBP1621
Clitoridectomy
Islamic law: KBP3119.F45
Cloistered women
Roman Catholic law: KBU2927.C56
Clothing
Islamic law: KBP184.9.C45
Co-ownership
Land
Islamic law: KBP694
Property
Comparative religious law: KB674
Islamic law: KBP674
Jewish law: KBM674
Land
Comparative religious law: KB694
Co-ownership of land
Jewish law: KBM694
Coadjutor bishop
Canon law: KBR2844
Coastal zone management
Islamic law: KBP3053
Coastwise and inland shipping
Islamic law: KBP3478
Code
Sources of fiqh
Islamic law: KBP458.Q36
Codex Iuris Canonici (CIC), 1917
Roman Catholic law: KBU2210
Codex Iuris Canonici (CIC), 1983
Roman Catholic law: KBU2212
Coemeteriae
Sacred places
Canon law: KBR3238.C46
Coercion
Criminal law
Jewish law: KBM3823.F67
Coffee
Islamic law: KBP3396
Cognatio legalis
Natural persons
Canon law: KBR2239.C65
Cognatio spiritualis
Natural persons
Canon law: KBR2239.C66
Cohabitation, Unmarried
Jewish law: KBM546.17
Cohanim, Restrictions on
Jewish law: KBM544.5
Collaborating
Criminal law
Jewish law: KBM4442
Collectanea in usum secretariae S.C. Congregation episcoporum et regularium: KBR40.55.A35
Collectanea S.C. de Propaganda Fide, 1893, 1907
Organs of government
Canon law: KBR2515.5
Collection
Tax administration
Islamic law: KBP3560+
Collective farming
Islamic law: KBP3316
Jewish law: KBM3316+
Collective patrimony
Islamic law: KBP686
Land law
Jewish law: KBM685.5
College of Bishops
Roman Catholic law: KBU2395+

INDEX

College of Cardinals
Canon law: KBR2412
Roman Catholic law: KBU2412+
Collegiality, Principles of
Judges
Rota Romana
Canon law: KBR3817
Collegiate chapter cases
Canon law
Rota Romana: KBR44.6.C38
Collegiate juristic persons
Canon law: KBR2256+
Roman Catholic law: KBU2256+
Collegium Cardinalium
Roman Catholic law: KBU2412+
Collegium Episcoporum
Roman Catholic law: KBU2395+
Collision at sea
Islamic law: KBP980
Jewish law: KBM980
Combinations
Associations
Islamic law: KBP1137+
Jewish law: KBM1137+
Combinations in restraint of trade
Economic law
Comparative religious law: KB3220
Commercial agents
Jewish law: KBM927
Commercial contracts
Formation
Comparative religious law: KB869+
Jewish law: KBM869+
Commercial employees
Jewish law: KBM924
Commercial investments
Banks and banking
Islamic law: KBP1049+
Jewish law: KBM961.5
Commercial law
Canon law
Rota Romana: KBR44.6.C66
Islamic law: KBP920+
Jewish law: KBM920+
Commercial merchandise
Taxable income
Islamic law: KBP3620.3.M47
Commercial partnerships
Contracts
Jewish law: KBM1043+
Islamic law: KBP1043+
Commercial sale
Jewish law: KBM926+
Commercial transactions
Islamic law: KBP920+
Jewish law: KBM920+
Commissio ad Catechismum Redigendum pro Ecclesia Universali
Roman Catholic law: KBU2754
Commission for Cultural Heritage of the Church
Roman Catholic law: KBU2750
Commission for Implementation of the Constitution on the Sacred Liturgy
Roman Catholic law: KBU2758
Commission for Religious Relations with the Jews
Roman Catholic law: KBU2742
Commission for the Preparation of a Catechism for the Universal Church
Roman Catholic law: KBU2754
Commission merchant
Jewish law: KBM928
Commission of cardinals
Canon law: KBR2730+
Commission of Cardinals
Roman Catholic law: KBU2730+
Commitment to medical or psychiatric facilities
Criminal law
Jewish law: KBM3982+
Commodatum
Comparative religious law: KB890
Pecuniary transactions without countervalue
Islamic law: KBP879.4
Commodity exchanges
Comparative religious law: KB962.8
Islamic law: KBP962.8
Jewish law: KBM962.8
Common law and Canon law (Occidental): KB243.A+
Common law marriages
Jewish law: KBM546.17

Common use
Water resources
Islamic law: KBP3046.5
Jewish law: KBM3046.5
Commonage and pasture
Comparative religious law: KB708
Islamic law: KBP708
Jewish law: KBM708
Commons
Use without shares in ownership
Comparative religious law: KB686
Communal agencies
Administrative law and process
Jewish law: KBM2711+
Employees
Comparative religious law: KB2870
Jewish law: KBM2970
Liability
Islamic law: KBP2840
Jewish law: KBM2840
Communal employees, Crimes against
Jewish law: KBM4514+
Communal employees, Crimes involving
Islamic law: KBP4514
Communal employees,Crimes involving
Comparative religious law: KB4514
Communal fundraising
Taxation
Jewish law: KBM3540+
Communal leaders, Jewish: KBM2532
Communal legislation
Jewish law: KBM2510+
Communal property
Islamic law: KBP686
Jewish law: KBM3040.5+
Communal religious activities
Islamic law: KBP190
Communal-sponsored militias
Jewish law: KBM3007
Communal-sponsored police patrols
Jewish law: KBM3007
Communal taxation
Jewish law: KBM3540+
Communicable diseases, Spreading of
Criminal law
Comparative religious law: KB4368
Islamic law: KBP4368
Communication
Comparative religious law: KB3482+
Islamic law: KBP3482+
Jewish law: KBM3482+
Communion, Admission to the Holy
Roman Catholic law: KBU3087
Communion, Holy, Admission to the
Canon law: KBR3087
Communitas religiosa
Monasticism
Canon law: KBR2902+
Community defense
Jewish law: KBM3738+
Community of property
Marital property
Jewish law: KBM574
Community-operated publishing activities
Jewish law: KBM3504
Community-owned business enterprises
Jewish law: KBM3217
Companionate marriage
Islamic law: KBP546.955
Comparative religious law: KB2+
Compensation
Divorce for a compensation
Islamic law: KBP563.4
Qisas punishment
Islamic law: KBP3976
Compensation for damages
Emergency measures
Jewish law: KBM3727+
Compensation for maintenance and improvement
Islamic law: KBP822
Jewish law: KBM822
Competence
Matrimonial actions
Judiciary
Canon law: KBR3887+
Tribunal of the Apostolic Signatura
Canon law: KBR3820
Competence (Forum internum)
Tribunals of the Apostolic See
Canon law: KBR3813

Competence in subject matter and venue
  Criminal courts and procedure
    Jewish law: KBM4666
  Criminal procedure
    Comparative religious law: KB4666
    Islamic law: KBP4666
  Procedure in general
    Comparative religious law: KB1664
    Islamic law: KBP1664
    Jewish law: KBM1664
Competent court
  Comparative religious law: KB1664
  Islamic law: KBP1664
  Jewish law: KBM1664
Competent forum
  Penal procedures
    Canon law: KBR3937
  Trial
    Canon law: KBR3840.5+
Competition rules
  Comparative religious law: KB3220
  Islamic law: KBP3220+
  Jewish law: KBM3220+
Complaint
  Criminal procedure
    Islamic law: KBP4668
    Jewish law: KBM4668
Complaint of nullity
  Trials
    Canon law: KBR3863
Complaints (petitions)
  Penal (criminal) procedures
    Canon law: KBR3932
Complicity
  Criminal act
    Comparative religious law: KB3922
    Islamic law: KBP3922
Compound offenses
  Jewish law: KBM3940
Compound punishment
  Jewish law: KBM3940
Compromise
  Courts
    Roman Catholic law: KBU3918
  Ecclesiastical courts
    Canon law: KBR3918
Compromise
  Obligations
    Islamic law: KBP817.2+
  Procedure at trial
    Comparative religious law: KB1668.S48
    Islamic law: KBP1668.S88
Compromissum
  Ecclesiastical courts
    Canon law: KBR3918
Compulsory education
  Jewish law: KBM3139.4
Compulsory labor
  Emergency measures
    Islamic law: KBP3715
Compulsory measures against the accused
  Criminal procedure
    Islamic law: KBP4650
    Jewish law: KBM4650
Computation of time
  Ius ecclesiasticum privatum
    Canon law: KBR2295
Computers
  Jewish law: KBM524.4.C65
Concept of law
  Canonical jurisprudence: KBR2189+
  Jewish law: KBM524.12+
Concessions
  Police and public safety
    Jewish law: KBM3002
Conciliar theory
  Counter reformation
    Canon law: KBR4036
Concilium plenarium
  Ecclesaistical Provinces
    Canon law: KBR2815
Concilium provinciale
  Ecclesaistical Provinces
    Canon law: KBR2820
Concilium Trullanum, 692
  Canon law: KBR237
Concordate of Worms, 1122
  Canon law: KBR4030
Concordats
  Foreign relations of the Holy See
    Roman Catholic law: KBU4095+

Concordia discordantium canonum
(Gratian, 12th cent.)
Canon law: KBR1362.2+
Concubinage
Islamic law: KBP546.17
Jewish law: KBM546.17
Concubinage of a cleric
Penal (Criminal) law
Canon law: KBR3746
Roman Catholic law: KBU3746
Conditional repudiation
Matrimonial actions
Islamic law: KBP562.954
Conditional sale
Islamic law: KBP877+
Jewish law: KBM877+
Conditions
Contracts
Comparative religious law: KB870
Islamic law: KBP870
Jewish law: KBM870
Islamic law concepts: KBP505
Marriage consent
Roman Catholic law: KBU3136
Conditions of divorce
Islamic law: KBP558+
Conditions of trading
Comparative religious law: KB3418
Jewish law: KBM3419
Retail trade
Islamic law: KBP3419
Condonation
Matrimonial actions
Jewish law: KBM560
Confectionary industry
Islamic law: KBP3382
Jewish law: KBM3382
Conference of Bishops
Ecclesiastical Provinces
Canon law: KBR2825+
Roman Catholic law: KBU2825+
Conference of Bishops (Episcopal
conference)
Roman Catholic law: KBU925+
Conferences of Major superiors
Religious institutes
Canon law: KBR2920
Conferencia episcoporum
Roman Catholic law: KBU925+
Conferentia episcoporum
Ecclesiastical Provinces
Canon law: KBR2825+
Organs of government
Roman Catholic law: KBU2825+
Conferentiae seu concilia
Religious institutes
Canon law: KBR2920
Confession
Criminal procedure
Comparative religious law:
KB4675+
Islamic law: KBP4681
Criminal trial
Jewish law: KBM4681
Confession (or self-incrimination) of the
infamatus
Inquisition
Canon law: KBR3943.C65
Confession, Sacramental
Canon law: KBR3090+
Roman Catholic law: KBU3090+
Confession, Violation of the seal of
Penal (Criminal) law
Canon law: KBR3724
Roman Catholic law: KBU3724
Confidential communication
Courts and procedure
Islamic law: KBP1676
Procedure in general
Jewish law: KBM1676
Confidential communications
Biomedical engineering
Roman Catholic law: KBU3300.C65
Confirmaition
Canon law: KBR3083+
Confirmation
Roman Catholic law: KBU3077+
Confirmation and suspension of
religious orders
The Pope
Canon law: KBR2384.3
Confiscation of property
Criminal law punishment
Islamic law: KBP4006

Confiscation of property
  Criminal law punishment
    Jewish law: KBM4006
Confiscations
  Emergency measures
    Jewish law: KBM3712
  War damage compensation
    Jewish law: KBM3728.R47
Conflict of conscience
  Jihād
    Islamic law: KBP182+
Conflict of equivalent testimony
  Islamic law: KBP1677.T35
Conflict of interests
  Constitution of the state
    Islamic law: KBP2275
  Constitutional and administrative law
    Comparative religious law: KB2275
  Constitutional law
    Jewish law: KBM2275
  Judges
    Canon law: KBR3827
Conflict of jurisdiction (General)
  Church and state
    Roman Catholic law: KBU4052
Conflict of jurisdictions
  Church and state
    Canon law: KBR4052
  Courts
    Roman Catholic law: KBU3804
  Ecclesiastical courts
    Canon law: KBR3804
Conflict of laws
  Canon law: KBR2199.A+
  Comparative religious law: KB480+
  Criminal law
    Jewish law: KBM3835
  Islamic law: KBP480+
  Jewish law: KBM524.43
Conflict-related groups
  Social laws
    Comparative religious law:
      KB1537+
  Social service
    Islamic law: KBP1537+
    Jewish law: KBM1537+
Conflictus competentiae inter tribunalia
  Ecclesiastical courts
    Canon law: KBR3804
Conformism, Legal
  Sources of fiqh
    Islamic law: KBP454
Confusion of rights
  Obligations
    Comparative religious law: KB823
    Islamic law: KBP823
    Jewish law: KBM823
Conganguinity
  Marriage impediments
    Roman Catholic law: KBU3128.C66
Congregatio Boni Regiminis: KBR41.7
Congregatio Boni Reiminis
  Organs of government
    Canon law: KBR2683
Congregatio Ceremonialis: KBR41.33
  Organs of government
    Canon law: KBR2593+
Congregatio Consistorialis (Congregatio
  pro Erectione Ecclesiarum et
  Provisionibus Consistorialibus)
  Organs of government
    Canon law: KBR2585+
Congregatio Consistorialis
  (Congregation pro Erectione
  Ecclesiarum et Provisionibus
  Consistorialibus): KBR41.3
Congregatio de Causis Sanctorum
  Roman Catholic law: KBU2549+
Congregatio de Cultu Divino et
  Disciplina Sacramentorum
  Roman Catholic law: KBU40.4,
    KBU2535+
Congregatio de Disciplina
  Sacramentorum
  Roman Catholic law: KBU40.3,
    KBU2525+
Congregatio de Institutione Catholica
  Roman Catholic law: KBU2668+
Congregatio de Propaganda Fide pro
  Negotiis Ritus Orientalis: KBR41.2
  Organs of government
    Canon law: KBR2515+

Congregatio Episcoporum et
  Regularium: KBR40.55
  Organs of government
    Canon law: KBR2580+
Congregatio Indicis: KBR40.2
  Organs of government
    Canon law: KBR2511+
Congregatio Indulgentiarum et
  Sacrarum Reliquiarum: KBR41.4
  Organs of government
    Canon law: KBR2678
Congregatio Iurisdictionis et Immunitatis
  Ecclesiasticae: KBR41.36
  Organs of government
    Canon law: KBR2676
Congregatio pro Causis Sanctorum
  Roman Catholic law: KBU40.5
Congregatio pro Clericis
  Roman Catholic law: KBU40.8,
    KBU2640+
Congregatio pro Cultu Divino
  Roman Catholic law: KBU40.32,
    KBU2528+
Congregatio pro Doctrina Fidei
  Roman Catholic law: KBU40.25,
    KBU2502+
Congregatio pro Ecclesiis Orientalibus
  Roman Catholic law: KBU2517+
Congregatio pro Episcopis
  Roman Catholic law: KBU40.6,
    KBU2555+
Congregatio pro Gentium
  Evangelisatione
  Roman Catholic law: KBU40.7
Congregatio pro Gentium
  Evangelizatione
  Roman Catholic law: KBU2635+
Congregatio pro Institutione Catholica
  Roman Catholic law: KBU41
Congregatio pro Institutis Vitae
  Consecratae et Societatibus Vitae
  Apostolicae
  Roman Catholic law: KBU40.9,
    KBU2660+
Congregatio pro Negotiis Ecclesiasticis
  Extraordinariis
  Organs of government
    Canon law: KBR2680
Congregatio pro Negotiis Ecclesiaticis
  Extraordinariis: KBR41.45
Congregatio pro Sacramentis et Cultu
  Divino
  Roman Catholic law: KBU40.34,
    KBU2531+
Congregatio Reverendae Fabricae
  Basilicae (Sancti Petri): KBR41.5
  Organs of government
    Canon law: KBR2682
Congregatio Sacrorum Rituum
  Roman Catholic law: KBU40.45,
    KBU2545+
Congregatio Signaturae Iustitiae:
  KBR41.32
  Organs of government
    Canon law: KBR2589+
Congregatio super Consultationibus
  Episcoporum et Aliorum Praelatorum:
  KBR40.54
  Organs of government
    Canon law: KBR2575+
Congregatio super Consultationibus
  Regularium
  Organs of government
    Canon law: KBR2570+
Congregatio super Disciplina Regulari
  and super Statu Regularium
  Organs of government
    Canon law: KBR2674
Congregatio Visitationis Apostolicae:
  KBR41.34
  Organs of government
    Canon law: KBR2610+
Congregation for Bishops
  Roman Catholic law: KBU2555+
Congregation for Catholic Education
  Roman Catholic law: KBU41,
    KBU2668+
Congregation for Consultations about
  Bishops and other Prelates:
  KBR40.54

Congregation for Consultations about
  Bishops and other Prelates
  Organs of government
    Canon law: KBR2575+
Congregation for Consultations about
  Regulars: KBR40.52
  Organs of government
    Canon law: KBR2570+
Congregation for Divine Worship
  Roman Catholic law: KBU40.32,
    KBU2528+
Congregation for Divine Worship and
  the Discipline of the Sacraments
  Roman Catholic law: KBU40.4,
    KBU2535+
Congregation for Evangelization of
  Peoples
  Roman Catholic law: KBU40.7,
    KBU2635+
Congregation for Institutes of
  Consecrated Life and Societies of
  Apostolic Life
  Roman Catholic law: KBU40.9,
    KBU2660+
Congregation for the Causes of Saints
  Roman Catholic law: KBU40.5,
    KBU2549+
Congregation for the Clergy
  Roman Catholic law: KBU40.8,
    KBU2640+
Congregation for the Discipline of the
  Sacraments
  Roman Catholic law: KBU40.3,
    KBU2525+
Congregation for the Doctrine of the
  Faith
  Roman Catholic law: KBU40.25,
    KBU2502+
Congregation for the Oriental Churches
  Roman Catholic law: KBU2517+
Congregation for the Sacraments and
  Divine Worship
  Roman Catholic law: KBU40.34,
    KBU2531+
Congregation of Bishops and Regulars:
  KBR40.55
Congregation of Bishops and Regulars
  Organs of government
    Canon law: KBR2580+
Congregation of Ceremonies
  Organs of government
    Canon law: KBR2593+
Congregation of Ceremonies (1588):
  KBR41.33
Congregation of Rites
  Roman Catholic law: KBU2545+
Congregation of the Consistory
  Organs of government
    Canon law: KBR2585+
Congregation of the Consistory (1588):
  KBR41.3
Congregation of the Index: KBR40.2
  Organs of government
    Canon law: KBR2511+
Congregation of the Visitation
  Organs of government
    Canon law: KBR2610+
Congregation of the Visitation (1592):
  KBR41.34
Congregation super Consultationibus
  Regularium: KBR40.52
Congregationes super Disciplina
  Regulari and super Statu Regularium:
  KBR41.35
Coniuges
  Dispensation of marriage
    Roman Catholic law: KBU3909
  Dispensation of ratified and non-
    consummated marriage
    Canon law: KBR3909
Consanguinitas
  Natural persons
    Canon law: KBR2237+
    Roman Catholic law: KBU2237+
Consanguinity
  Domestic relations
    Islamic law: KBP583+
  Family law
    Comparative religious law: KB583+
    Jewish law: KBM583+
  Marriage impediments
    Jewish law: KBM544.2

Consanguinity
Natural persons
Canon law: KBR2237+
Roman Catholic law: KBU2237+
Consanguinity and affinity
Marriage impediments
Comparative religious law: KB544.2
Islamic law: KBP544.955
Consanguinity (direct line and collateral line)
Impediments to marriage
Canon law: KBR3128.C66
Conscience, Cases of
Canon law and moral theology: KBR2155.2
Conscience, Conflict of
Jihād
Islamic law: KBP182+
Conscientious objection
Jewish law: KBM3740.C65
Consecration of someone as a bishop without apostolic mandate
Roman Catholic law: KBU3714
Consecrations
Canon law: KBR3181
Consensus
Sources of fiqh
Islamic law: KBP451
Consensus et consilium alicuius
Legal transactions
Ius ecclesiasticum privatum: KBR2293
Roman Catholic law: KBU2293
Consensus invalidus
Canon law: KBR3140
Marriage
Law of the Roman Cathoic Church: KBU3140
Consent
Betrothal
Islamic law: KBP543.952
Contracts
Islamic law: KBP869.6
Consent, Matrimonial
Canon law: KBR3132+
Roman Catholic law: KBU3132+
Consent of the injured party
Criminal offense
Comparative religious law: KB3861
Islamic law: KBP3861
Jewish law: KBM3861
Consent or counsil
Legal transactions
Ius ecclesiasticum privatum: KBR2293
Roman Catholic law: KBU2293
Conservation
Agricultural and forestry lands
Islamic law: KBP3299
Energy policy
Islamic law: KBP3431.2
Environmental resources
Comparative religious law: KB3129
Islamic law: KBP3129
Fishery
Islamic law: KBP3135
Water resources
Islamic law: KBP3049
Conservation of agricultural and forestry lands
Comparative religious law: KB3299
Conservation of environmental resources
Jewish law: KBM3129
Consignation
Sale
Jewish law: KBM926.2.C65
Consignment
Jewish law: KBM928
Consignment shops
Regulation
Jewish law: KBM3423.5.C64
Consilia
Religious institutes
Canon law: KBR2914+
Consilium a rebus oeconomicis
Organs of government
Roman Catholic law: KBU2860
Consilium ad Exsequendam Constitutionem de Sacra Liturgia
Roman Catholic law: KBU2758
Consilium pastorale
Canon law: KBR2882

Consilium presbyteriale
  Canon law: KBR2882
Consociationes privatae
  Juristic persons
    Canon law: KBR2266
Consociationes publicae
  Juristic persons
    Canon law: KBR2262
Consortium
  Industrial trusts
    Islamic law: KBP1138
    Jewish law: KBM1138
Constantinople, Council of, 1st, 381
  Canon law: KBR215
Constantinople, Council of, 2nd, 553
  Canon law: KBR230
Constantinople, Council of, 394: KBR247
Constantinople, Council of, 3rd, 680
  Canon law: KBR235
Constantinople, Council of, 4th, 869: KBR262
Constantinople, Council of, 692
  Canon law: KBR237
Constitution
  Roman Catholic law: KBU2310+
Constitution and organs, Diocesan
  Canon law: KBR2850+
Constitution of juristic persons
  Roman Catholic law: KBU2255+
Constitution of Medina: KBP2200.D86
Constitution of the Church: KBR2310+
Constitution of the state
  Islamic law: KBP2101+
Constitutional and administrative law
  Comparative religious law: KB2101+
Constitutional history
  Jewish law: KBM2085+
Constitutional history, Comparative
  Islamic law: KBP2101+
Constitutional law
  Jewish law: KBM2070+
Constitutional principles of the Jewish community: KBM2070+
  Constitutional history
    Jewish law: KBM2129+
Constitutions and canons
  Canon law: KBR2191+
Constitutions and religion
  Comparative religious law: KB2101+
constitutions (fundamental codes)
  Monasticism
    Canon law: KBR2892+
Constitutum Constantini
  Canon law: KBR4014
Construction
  Engineering
    Islamic law: KBP3519
  Public property
    Jewish law: KBM3067+
  Regional planning
    Islamic law: KBP3067+
Construction industry
  Islamic law: KBP3402
  Regulation
    Jewish law: KBM3402
Construction profession
  Jewish law: KBM3519+
Consuetudo
  Canon law: KBR2192
  Roman Catholic law: KBU2192
Consultation
  Constitution of the state
    Islamic law: KBP2255
Consumer protection
  Islamic law: KBP3276
  Jewish law: KBM3276
Consummation
  Marriage
    Comparative religious law: KB546
    Islamic law: KBP546.16
  Roman Catholic law: KBU3114
Consummation of marriage
  Jewish law: KBM546.16
Contagious and infectious diseases
  Public health
    Comparative religious law: KB3080+
    Islamic law: KBP3080+
    Jewish law: KBM3080+
Contagious diseases, Measures against
  Canon law: KBR3270
  Roman Catholic law: KBU3270

Containers
  Economic law
    Comparative religious law: KB3257
    Islamic law: KBP3257+
    Jewish law: KBM3257+
Contempt of court
  Criminal law
    Jewish law: KBM4510
Contentious trial
  Canon law: KBR3838+
  Roman Catholic law: KBU3838+
Contestatio litis
  Trial
    Canon law: KBR3841.5
Continental shelf and its resources
  Islamic law: KBP3347
Contract
  Marriage
    Canon law: KBR3132+
Contract for service and labor
  Jewish law: KBM892+
Contract for work and labor
  Islamic law: KBP893+
  Jewish law: KBM893+
Contract law
  Comparative religious law: KB858+
  Islamic law: KBP858+
  Jewish law: KBM858+
Contract of manufacture
  Islamic law: KBP877.4
Contracts
  Aleatory contracts
    Islamic law: KBP899
  Antenuptial contracts
    Islamic law: KBP543.952
  Building and construction industry
    Islamic law: KBP3402
  Comparative religious law: KB810+
  Government
    Islamic law: KBP2754
  Illegal contracts
    Islamic law: KBP868+
  Jewish law: KBM801+
  Labor contract and employment
    Islamic law: KBP1279+
  Licensing contracts
    Islamic law: KBP3237
Contracts
  Obligations
    Islamic law: KBP810+
  Public works
    Jewish law: KBM3073
  Standardized forms of contract
    Islamic law: KBP3239
Contracts and breach of contracts
  Jurisdiction of ecclesiastical courts
    Canon law: KBR3795.C66
Contracts and combinations in restraint of trade, Control of
  Islamic law: KBP3220+
  Jewish law: KBM3220+
Contracts by adhesion
  Islamic law: KBP869.55
  Jewish law: KBM869.55
Contracts for service and labor
  Comparative religious law: KB892+
  Islamic law: KBP892+
Contracts for work and labor
  Comparative religious law: KB893+
Contracts of pledging
  Comparative religious law: KB726, KB737
  Property
    Islamic law: KBP726+
    Jewish law: KBM726+
Contractual emancipation
  Slaves
    Islamic law: KBP529.5
Contractus
  Marriage
    Canon law: KBR3132+
Control of contracts
  Economic law
    Comparative religious law: KB3220
Control of hazardous materials and processes
  Jewish law: KBM3009
Control of individuals
  Public safety
    Comparative religious law: KB3022
    Islamic law: KBP3022+
    Jewish law: KBM3022

Control of property
  Emergency measures
    Islamic law: KBP3712
    Jewish law: KBM3712
Control of social activities
  Public safety
    Comparative religious law: KB3034
    Islamic law: KBP3034+
    Jewish law: KBM3034+
Control of subversive activities or groups
  Comparative religious law: KB2490
  Constitution of the state
    Islamic law: KBP2490
  Constitutional law
    Jewish law: KBM2490
Control of unemployment
  Jewish law: KBM3714
Convalidation
  Marriage
    Law of the Roman Cathoic Church: KBU3142
Conversion to Judaism
  Jewish law: KBM2448
Converts to Judaism
  Education of children
    Jewish law: KBM3143.4
  Equality before the law
    Jewish law: KBM2467.C64
Conviction
  Criminal procedure
    Comparative religious law: KB4742.C66
    Islamic law: KBP4746
    Jewish law: KBM4746
Convocatio
  Ecumenical council
    Canon law: KBR2380
Convocation of an ecumenical council
  The Pope
    Roman Catholic law: KBU2380
Convocation of the synod of bishops
  The Pope
    Roman Catholic law: KBU2382
Cooperative associations
  Comparative religious law: KB3429
Cooperative retail trade
  Jewish law: KBM3421
Cooperative societies
  Artisans
    Islamic law: KBP3429
  Comparative religious law: KB1120.A+
  Economic law
    Islamic law: KBP3250
  Islamic law: KBP1120+
  Jewish law: KBM1120+
Cooperatives
  Income tax
    Islamic law: KBP3595+
Copyright
  Comparative religious law: KB1160
  Islamic law: KBP1160+
  Jewish law: KBM1160+
Cor Unum
  Roman Catholic law: KBU2712
Corporate finance
  Jewish law: KBM1061+
  Stock corporations
    Islamic law: KBP1061+
Corporate reorganization
  Islamic law: KBP1147
  Jewish law: KBM1147
Corporate representation
  Artisans
    Islamic law: KBP3429
  Cooperative associations
    Comparative religious law: KB3429
  Guilds
    Comparative religious law: KB3429
Corporate structure
  Energy policy
    Islamic law: KBP3431.4
Corporation tax
  Income tax
    Comparative religious law: KB3592
    Islamic law: KBP3592+
Corporations
  Contracts
    Comparative religious law: KB1040+
    Islamic law: KBP1040+
    Jewish law: KBM1040+

Corporations
Juristic persons
Canon law: KBR2256+
Jewish law: KBM530
Roman Catholic law: KBU2256+
Taxation
Jewish law: KBM3592
Corpus iuris canonici
Canon law: KBR1564+
Correction of faulty decisions
Criminal procedure
Comparative religious law: KB4753
Islamic law: KBP4753
Jewish law: KBM4753
Correction of judicial error
Procedure in general
Jewish law: KBM1679.5
Corruption
Communal employees
Comparative religious law: KB4514
Islamic law: KBP4514
Jewish law: KBM4516+
Corruption of prayer
Islamic law: KBP184.33.C67
Costs, Court
Roman Catholic law: KBU3874
Trials
Canon law: KBR3874
Council of Aachen, 809: KBR265
Council of Ancyra, 314: KBR245.3
Council of Antioch, 341: KBR246
Council of Aquilea, 381: KBR249 381
Council of Aquileia, 553: KBR249 553
Council of Arles, 314: KBR245
Council of Carthage, 255: KBR199.9
Council of Carthage, 299: KBR244
Council of Carthage, 311: KBR244.5
Council of Carthage, 398: KBR247.2
Council of Carthage, 419: KBR247.5
Council of Carthage, 553: KBR249 553a
Council of Chalcedon, 451
Canon law: KBR225
Council of Constantinople, 1st, 381
Canon law: KBR215
Council of Constantinople, 2nd, 553
Canon law: KBR230
Council of Constantinople, 394: KBR247
Council of Constantinople, 3rd, 680
Canon law: KBR235
Council of Constantinople, 4th, 869: KBR262
Council of Constantinople, 692
Canon law: KBR237
Council of Elvira, between 300? and 309?: KBR244.3
Council of Ephesus, 193: KBR199.87
Council of Ephesus, 431? or 449
Canon law: KBR220
Council of Frankfurt, 794: KBR248
Council of Gangra, 340? or 343: KBR246.5
Council of Jerusalem, 45 (48?): KBR199.82
Council of Jerusalem, 56 (55?): KBR199.83
Council of Ministers
Islamic law: KBP2585
Council of Neocaesarea, 315: KBR245.5
Council of Nicea, 1st, 325
Canon law: KBR210
Council of Nicea, 2nd, 787
Canon law: KBR240
Council of Rome, 155: KBR199.84
Council of Rome, 193: KBR199.86
Council of Sargossa, 380: KBR249 380
Council of Serdica, 343 or 347?: KBR246.3
Council of Toledo, 4th, 633: KBR249 633
Council of Turin, 401: KBR249 401
Council of Tyre, 335: KBR249 335
Council of Union, 879: KBR263
Council of Worms, 868: KBR266
Councils
Religious institutes
Canon law: KBR2914+
Councils and synods (11th-21st centuries)
Canon law: KBR820+
Counter reformation
Canon law: KBR4035+

Counterclaim
Courts
Roman Catholic law: KBU3837.C68
Judiciary
Canon law: KBR3837.C68
Obligations
Islamic law: KBP817.3
Procedure at trial
Islamic law: KBP1667.T33
Counterfeiting
Legal and monetary transactions
Comparative religious law: KB4330
Jewish law: KBM4330
Legal and monetary transactions and documents
Islamic law: KBP4330
Court administration
Jewish law: KBM1623
Court costs
Roman Catholic law: KBU3874
Trials
Canon law: KBR3874
Court decorum and discipline
Islamic law: KBP1595
Jewish law: KBM1595
Court decorum and order
Rota Romana
Canon law: KBR3818
Rota Romana (Tribunal ordinarium)
Roman Catholic law: KBU3818
Court fees
Church taxes and fees
Roman Catholic law: KBU3392.C68
Court of cassation
Roman Catholic law: KBU3819+
Court organization
Canon law: KBR3805.2+
Islamic law: KBP1580
Court personnel
Comparative religious law: KB1600+
Jewish law: KBM1600+
Court records
Court procedure
Islamic law: KBP1623
Jewish law: KBM1623
Courts and procedure
Comparative religious law: KB1572+
Courts and procedure
Islamic law: KBP1572+
Jewish law: KBM1572+
Military law
Comparative religious law: KB3770+
Islamic law: KBP3770
Jewish law: KBM3770
Roman Catholic law: KBU3780+
Courts and procedure, Ecclesiastical
Canon law: KBR3780+
Courts and tribunals
Comparative religious law: KB1580+
Courts of special jurisdiction
Islamic law: KBP1588+
Jewish law: KBM1588
Coverage and benefits
Social insurance
Islamic law: KBP1476
Jewish law: KBM1476
Creatio
Ecclesiastical offices
Canon law: KBR2351
Credit
Banks and banking
Islamic law: KBP955+
Jewish law: KBM955+
Credit cooperatives
Islamic law: KBP1133.S35
Creditor
Contracts
Jewish law: KBM811
Creditors, Defeating rights of
Jewish law: KBM4270
Crimes
Islamic law: KBP3946+
Crimes aboard aircraft
Comparative religious law: KB4377
Islamic law: KBP4377
Jewish law: KBM4396
Crimes affecting traffic
Comparative religious law: KB4380+
Islamic law: KBP4380+
Jewish law: KBM4380+
Crimes against communal employees
Jewish law: KBM4514+

Crimes against foreign states
  Comparative religious law: KB4543
  Islamic law: KBP4543
Crimes against humanity
  Comparative religious law: KB4538+
  Islamic law: KBP4538+
  Jewish law: KBM4538
Crimes against inchoate life
  Islamic law: KBP4070
  Jewish law: KBM4070
Crimes against incohate life
  Comparative religious law: KB4070
Crimes against international institutions
  Comparative religious law: KB4543
  Islamic law: KBP4543
Crimes against national defense
  Comparative religious law: KB4470
Crimes against personal freedom
  Comparative religious law: KB4116+
  Islamic law: KBP4116+
  Jewish law: KBM4116+
Crimes against physical inviolability
  Comparative religious law: KB4074+
  Islamic law: KBP4074+
  Jewish law: KBM4074+
Crimes against property
  Comparative religious law: KB4230+
  Islamic law: KBP4230+
Crimes against public health
  Islamic law: KBP4400
  Jewish law: KBM4400+
Crimes against security of legal and monetary transactions
  Comparative religious law: KB4330
  Jewish law: KBM4330
Crimes against supranational institutions
  Comparative religious law: KB4543
  Islamic law: KBP4543
Crimes against the environment
  Jewish law: KBM4351.5
Crimes against the person
  Islamic law: KBP842.2+
Crimes against the security of legal and monetary transactions and documents
  Islamic law: KBP4330
Crimes involving communal employees
  Comparative law: KB4514
Crimes involving communal employees
  Islamic law: KBP4514
Crimes involving danger to the community
  Comparative religious law: KB4351.5+
  Islamic law: KBP4351.5+
  Jewish law: KBM4351.5
Criminal act
  Comparative religious law: KB3840+
  Islamic law: KBP3840+
  Jewish law: KBM3840+
  Penal (Criminal) law
    Canon law: KBR3564+
  Roman Catholic law: KBU3564+
Criminal act, Form of
  Islamic law: KBP3852+
Criminal court
  Islamic law: KBP1588.3
Criminal intent
  Comparative religious law: KB3867
  Islamic law: KBP3867+
  Jewish law: KBM3867
Criminal investigation
  Penal (criminal) procedures
    Canon law: KBR3933
Criminal judge
  Jewish law: KBM4630.C74
Criminal justice and the press
  Islamic law: KBP3507
Criminal law: KBM3790+
  Canon law: KBR3500+
    Rota Romana: KBR44.6.C75
  Comparative religious law: KB3790+
  Islamic law: KBP3790+
  Roman Catholic law: KBU3500+
Criminal law and canon law: KBR2156
Criminal law and psychology
  Jewish law: KBM3819
Criminal law and society
  Jewish law: KBM3818
Criminal laws issued by secular authority
  Jewish law: KBM2024
Criminal liability
  Comparative religious law: KB3878+
  Islamic law: KBP3878+

Criminal liability
  Jewish law: KBM3878+
Criminal liability of agents and principals
  Jewish law: KBM861.2
Criminal offense
  Comparative religious law: KB3840+
  Islamic law: KBP3840+
  Jewish law: KBM3840+
  Penal (Criminal) law
    Canon law: KBR3533+
  Roman Catholic law: KBU3533+
Criminal procedure
  Comparative religious law: KB4601+
  Islamic law: KBP4601+
  Jewish law: KBM4610+
Criminal provisions
  Government measures, etc
    Comparative religious law: KB3726
Criminal registers
  Jewish law: KBM4845
Criminal trials
  Canon law: KBR128+
  Roman Catholic law: KBU128+
Crisis relief
  Jewish law: KBM3717
Criticism, Law
  Islamic law: KBP470
Crops
  Taxable income
    Islamic law: KBP3620.3.C75
Crown privilege
  Comparative religious law: KB2554
  Islamic law: KBP2554
Crucifixion
  Criminal law punishment
    Comparative religious law: KB3980.B78
    Islamic law: KBP3980.C78
Cruelty to animals
  Prevention
    Jewish law: KBM3123+
Crusaders
  Jurisdiction of ecclesiastical courts
    Canon law: KBR3787.C78
Culpa
  Criminal law
    Roman Catholic law: KBU3537+
Culpa
  Obligations
    Comparative religious law: KB824+
    Jewish law: KBM824.5
  Violation of criminal law
    Canon law: KBR3537+
Culpa in contrahendo
  Comparative religious law: KB825.5
  Islamic law: KBP825.5
Culpability
  Criminal offense
    Comparative religious law: KB3878+
    Islamic law: KBP3878+
Cult, Disparity of
  Impediments to marriage
    Canon law: KBR3128.C85
Cult, Disparity of (Catholic baptized and non-Catholic)
  Marriage impediments
    Roman Catholic law: KBU3128.C85
Cultural affairs
  Comparative religious law: KB3137+
  Islamic law: KBP3137+
  Jewish law: KBM3137+
Cultural policy
  Comparative religious law: KB3137.7
  Jewish law: KBM3137.7
Culture
  Human rights
    Islamic law: KBP2468.L36
    Jewish law: KBM2468.L36
Cultus sanctorum, sacrarum imaginum et reliquiarum
  Canon law: KBR3200+
  Roman Catholic law: KBU3200+
Cupping
  Medical legislation
    Islamic law: KBP3119.C87
Curator
  Natural persons
    Roman Catholic law: KBU2245+
Curator or tutor, Domicile of
  Natural persons
    Canon law: KBR2236.T87

Curatorship
Family law
Islamic law: KBP622+
Jewish law: KBM622+
Curia diocesana
Canon law: KBR2852+
Curia Romana
Canon law: KBR2420+
Organs of government
Roman Catholic law: KBU2420+
Curia Romana, Decrees and decisions of the
Roman Catholic law: KBU39+
Custody
Parent and child
Comparative religious law: KB602
Islamic law: KBP602
Custody and education of children
Separation and divorce
Roman Catholic law: KBU3902
Custody of children
Jewish law: KBM602
Custom
Canon law: KBR2192
Jewish law: KBM524.3
Roman Catholic law: KBU2192
Sources of fiqh
Islamic law: KBP455
Customary co-ownership
Land
Comparative religious law: KB694
Islamic law: KBP694
Customary co-ownership of land
Jewish law: KBM694
Customary law: KB2340
Islamic law: KBP2340
Jewish law: KBM2340
Customs
Comparative religious law: KB3681
Islamic law: KBP3681
Customs crimes
Jewish law: KBM3693+

D

Dā'in wa-madyūn: KBP811
Dairy farming
Regulation
Jewish law: KBM3329+
Dairy farming and industry
Regulation
Islamic law: KBP3329+
Dairy products
Islamic law: KBP3388
Jewish law: KBM3388
Damage compensation
Emergency measures
Jewish law: KBM3727+
Damages
Legal transactions
Ius ecclesiasticum privatum: KBR2294
Roman Catholic law: KBU2294
Obligations
Comparative religious law: KB834+
Islamic law: KBP834+
Jewish law: KBM842+
Damages and indemnification
Economic law
Islamic law: KBP3247
Jewish law: KBM3247
Damages, Reparation of
Procedure at first instance
Penal (Criminal) procedure
Roman Catholic law: KBU3939.D36
Ḍamān: KBP839+
Dangerous criminals
Protective custody
Jewish law: KBM3992
Dangerous interference with air traffic
Comparative religious law: KB4380
Islamic law: KBP4380
Jewish law: KBM4380
Dangerous interference with rail traffic
Comparative religious law: KB4380
Islamic law: KBP4380
Jewish law: KBM4380
Dangerous interference with ship traffic
Comparative religious law: KB4380
Islamic law: KBP4380
Jewish law: KBM4380

Dangerous interference with street traffic
Comparative religious law: KB4384
Islamic law: KBP4384
Jewish law: KBM4384
Ḍarūrah: KBP509
Dataria Apostolica: KBR47
Canon law: KBR2435
Decisions of ecclesiastical tribunals
Roman Catholic law: KBU47
Day care centers for infants and children
Jewish law: KBM3114.D39
Day of sacrifice
Islamic law: KBP186.6
Days of penance
Canon law: KBR3250+
Roman Catholic law: KBU3250+
Dayyanim: KBM1610+
De actibus administrativis singularibus
Roman Catholic Church: KBU2193.3+
De actibus iuridicis
Ius ecclesiasticum privatum: KBR2286+
Roman Catholic law: KBU2286+
De actionibus et exceptionibus
Judiciary
Canon law: KBR3835+
Procedure at first instance
Roman Catholic law: KBU3841.2+
Trial
Canon law: KBR3841.2+
De actore et de parte conventa
Judiciary
Canon law: KBR3831+
De actore et parte conventa
Courts
Roman Catholic law: KBU3831+
De baptismo
Canon law: KBR3077+
Roman Catholic law: KBU3077+
De baptismo et eius effectu
Canon law: KBR2227+
De bonis ecclesiasticis temporalibus
Canon law: KBR3328+
Roman Catholic law: KBU3328+
De breviandis litibus
Canon law: KBR3826
De causis ad sacrae ordinationis nullitatem declarandam
Canon law: KBR3914
De censuris
Penal (Criminal) law
Canon law: KBR3602+
De christifidelium consociationibus
Canon law: KBR2260+
Juristic persons
Roman Catholic law: KBU2260+
De clericorum iuribus et obligationibus
Roman Catholic law: KBU2336+
De concordatis
Foreign relations of the Holy See
Roman Catholic law: KBU4095+
De consensu matrimoniale
Roman Catholic law: KBU3132+
De crimine falsi
Penal (Criminal) law
Canon law: KBR3730+
Roman Catholic law: KBU3730+
De curia dioecesana
Roman Catholic law: KBU2852+
De delictis contra ecclesiasticas auctoritates
Penal (Criminal) law
Canon law: KBR3670+
De delictis contra ecclesiasticas auctoritates et ecclesiae libertatem
Roman Catholic law: KBU3670+
De delictis contra hominis vitam et libertatem
Penal (Criminal) law
Canon law: KBR3752+
De delictis contra religionem et ecclesiae unitatem
Roman Catholic law: KBU3625+
De delictis contra speciales obligationes
Penal (Criminal) law
Canon law: KBR3738+
De dignitatibus ecclesiasticis
Canon law: KBR2355+
De dissolutione vinculi
Marriage bond
Canon law: KBR3159+
Roman Catholic law: KBU3159+

De ecclesiae constitutione
  Roman Catholic law: KBU2363+
De ecclesiae constitutione hierarchica
  Canon law: KBR2363+
De ecclesiae munere docendi
  Canon law: KBR3040+
De ecclesiis particularibus
  Organs of government
    Canon law: KBR2790+
De examine sponsorum
  Canon law: KBR3117
  Marriage law
    Roman Catholic law: KBU3117
De-facto marriage
  Islamic law: KBP546.17
De forma celebrationis matrimonii
  Canon law: KBR3144+
De foro competente
  Ecclesiastical courts
    Canon law: KBR3783.92+
De impugnatione sententiae
  Penal (criminal) procedure
    Canon law: KBR3949+
  Trials
    Canon law: KBR3861+
De institutis religiosis
  Monasticism
    Canon law: KBR2899+
De institutis saecularibus
  Canon law: KBR2925
De institutis vitae consecratae et de sociatatibus vitae apostolicae
  Canon law: KBR2892+
De institutis vitae consecratae et de societatibus vitae apostolicae
  Roman Catholic law: KBU2892+
De institutorum regimine
  Monasticism
    Canon law: KBR2912+
De instrumentis communicationis socialis
  Roman Catholic law: KBU3064+
De iudicio contentioso
  Canon law: KBR3838+
  Roman Catholic law: KBU3838+
De iuribus et oneribus clericorum
  Canon law: KBR2336+
De lege poenali
  Canon law: KBR3500+
  Roman Catholic law: KBU3500+
De locis et temporibus sacris
  Canon law: KBR3230+
  Law of the Roman Cathoic Church: KBU3230+
De matrimoniis mixtis
  Canon law: KBR3148+
  Roman Catholic law: KBU3148+
De matrimonio
  Canon law: KBR3109+
  Roman Catholic law: KBU3109.2+
De metropolitanis
  Roman Catholic law: KBU2803+
De metropolitis
  Canon law: KBR2803+
De ministris sacris seu de clericis
  Roman Catholic law: KBU2320+
De Ministris Sacris seu de Clericis
  Canon law: KBR2320+
De munerum ecclesiasticorum usurpatione deque delictis in iis exercendis
  Canon law: KBR3700+
  Roman Catholic law: KBU3700+
De obligatione christifidelium subveniendi
  Roman Catholic law: KBU3344+
De obligationibus et iuribus christifidelium
  Canon law: KBR2312+
  Roman Catholic law: KBU2312+
De obligationibus et iuribus laicorum
  Canon law: KBR2316+
  Roman Catholic law: KBU2316+
De officiis ecclesiasticis
  Roman Catholic law: KBU2350+
De officiis ecclesiasticis et beneficiis
  Canon law: KBR2350+
De ordine
  Canon law: KBR3102+
De partibus in causa
  Courts
    Roman Catholic law: KBU3830+
  Judiciary
    Canon law: KBR3830+

De partibus in causa
  Penal (criminal) procedures
    Canon law: KBR3926+
De personis
  Canon law: KBR2224+
  Roman Catholic law: KBU2224+
De personis iuridicis
  Canon law: KBR2253+
  Roman Catholic law: KBU2253+
De personis physicis
  Canon law: KBR2225+
De poenis expiatoriis
  Penal (Criminal) law
    Canon law: KBR3611.2+
  Roman Catholic law: KBU3611.2+
De populo Dei
  Roman Catholic law: KBU2312+
De potestate regiminis
  Canon law: KBR2364
  Roman Catholic law: KBU2298+
De praelaturis personalibus
  Roman Catholic law: KBU2342
De praevia investigatione
  Penal (Criminal) procedure
    Roman Catholic law: KBU3933
  Penal (criminal) procedures
    Canon law: KBR3933
De prelaturis personalibus
  Canon law: KBR2342
De procedura in parochis amovendis vel
  transferendis
  Penal (criminal) procedures
    Canon law: KBR3973+
  Roman Catholic law: KBU3975+
De processibus
  Canon law: KBR3780+
  Roman Catholic law: KBU3780+
De processibus matrimonialibus
  Courts
    Roman Catholic law: KBU3885+
  Judiciary
    Canon law: KBR3885+
De processu contentioso orali
  Courts
    Roman Catholic law: KBU3878+
  Trials
    Canon law: KBR3878+
De processu poenali
  Roman Catholic law: KBU3920+
De pronuntiationibus iudicis
  Roman Catholic law: KBU3854+
De relationibus diplomaticis
  Roman Catholic law: KBU4078+
  The Holy See
    Canon law: KBR4078+
De relationibus inter ecclesiam et status
  Canon law: KBR4000+
  Roman Catholic law: KBU4000+
De remediis poenalibus et paenitentiis
  Criminal law
    Roman Catholic law: KBU3617.2+
De sacramentis et administratione
  Canon law: KBR3075+
  Roman Catholic law: KBU3075+
De sacramento confirmationis
  Canon law: KBR3083+
  Roman Catholic law: KBU3077+
De sacramento paenitentiae
  Canon law: KBR3090+
  Roman Catholic law: KBU3090+
De sacramento unctionis infirmorum
  Canon law: KBR3096+
  Roman Catholic law: KBU3096+
De Sanctissima Eucharistia
  Canon law: KBR3085+
  Roman Catholic law: KBU3085+
De separatione coniugum
  Canon law: KBR3163+
  Roman Catholic law: KBU3163+
De separatione ecclesiae a statu
  Roman Catholic law: KBU4047+
De statutis et ordinibus
  Roman Catholic law: KBU2195
De variis tribunalium gradibus et
  speciebus: KBR3805.2+
  Roman Catholic law: KBU3782.52+
Dead, Disposal of the
  Islamic law: KBP3078
Deadlines
  Courts
    Jewish law: KBM1662.T56
    Roman Catholic law: KBU3828.D43
  Pretrial criminal procedures
    Comparative religious law: KB4648

Deadlines
Pretrial criminal procedures
Islamic law: KBP4648
Jewish law: KBM4648
Pretrial procedure
Islamic law: KBP1662.T56
Deaf-mute
Social service
Islamic law: KBP1534.D42
Jewish law: KBM1534.D42
Death
Capacity and disability
Islamic law: KBP524.8
Capacity and incapacity
Canon law: KBR2232.D42
Emancipation depending on
Islamic law: KBP529.5
Registration
Comparative religious law: KB1862
Islamic law: KBP1864
Death by wrongful act
Torts
Jewish law: KBM842.6
Death, Definition of
Medical legislation
Jewish law: KBM3119.D43
Death of a spouse, Procedure in presumption and declaration of
Matrimonial actions
Canon law: KBR3912
Death of party
Procedure at trial
Islamic law: KBP1668.C53
Death penalty
Constitutional law
Jewish law: KBM2484.5
Death, Presumption of
Islamic law: KBP524.8
Death, Unintentional, by wrongful act
Torts
Islamic law: KBP842.6
Deathbed marriage
Canon law: KBR3138
Roman Catholic law: KBU3138
Debt, Assumption of
Islamic law: KBP816.7
Debtor
Contracts
Jewish law: KBM811
Debtor and creditor
Contracts
Comparative religious law: KB811
Obligations
Islamic law: KBP811
Debtor and guarantor
Contracts
Comparative religious law: KB900
Islamic law: KBP900
Jewish law: KBM900
Debtor, Detention of
Islamic law: KBP1913
Debts of estate
Islamic law: KBP634.957
Jewish law: KBM634.7
Decapitation
Criminal law punishment
Jewish law: KBM3964.2
Decapitation by the sword
Criminal law punishment
Comparative religious law: KB3980.B43
Islamic law: KBP3980.B43
Decedents' estates
Inheritance and succession
Comparative religious law: KB633
Islamic law: KBP633+
Jewish law: KBM633+
Deceit
Torts
Islamic law: KBP846
Jewish law: KBM846
Decimae clericales
Canon law: KBR3386
Declaration of consent
Contracts
Islamic law: KBP869.6
Jewish law: KBM869.6
Declaration of intention
Contracts
Comparative religious law: KB860+
Jewish law: KBM860+

Declaration of nullity of sacred
ordination
Canon law: KBR3914
Declaration (testimony) of parties
Trials
Canon law: KBR3846
Roman Catholic law: KBU3846
Decrease of share
Decedents' estates
Islamic law: KBP633.952.A84
Decree law of Muslim rulers
Sources of fiqh
Islamic law: KBP458.N59
Decree law versus ijtihhād
Islamic law: KBP2516
Decree of transfer
Penal (criminal) procedures
Canon law: KBR3980
Decree of transfer of pastor
Roman Catholic law: KBU3982
Decree without trial
Penal (Criminal) procedure
Roman Catholic law: KBU3934
Decreta iudicis
Trials
Canon law: KBR3859
Decretalists and commentators
(consiliators), to 1545
Canon law: KBR1703.82+
Decretists and early decretalists
Canon law: KBR1574.2+
Decretum citationis
Penal (Criminal) procedure
Roman Catholic law: KBU3931
Penal (criminal) procedures
Canon law: KBR3931
Decretum citationis in iudicium
Canon law: KBR3839.5
Roman Catholic law: KBU3839.5
Decretum extra iudicium
Penal (Criminal) procedure
Roman Catholic law: KBU3934
Decretum Gratiani
Canon law: KBR1362.2+
Decretum translationis
Penal (criminal) procedures
Canon law: KBR3980
Dedication and blessing of sacred
places
Canon law: KBR3232
Dedications
Sacramentals
Canon law: KBR3181
Deductions
Income tax
Islamic law: KBP3579+
Jewish law: KBM3579+
Defamation
Comparative religious law: KB4147
Islamic law: KBP4147
Default
Obligations
Comparative religious law: KB827.5
Jewish law: KBM827.5
Pretrial procedure
Islamic law: KBP1662.T56
Pretrial procedures
Jewish law: KBM1662.T56
Default of buyer
Jewish law: KBM926.2.D43
Defeating rights of creditors
Jewish law: KBM4270
Defect of goods sold
Islamic law: KBP876
Defective marriage
Comparative religious law: KB556+
Islamic law: KBP556+
Jewish law: KBM556
Defective marriage, Settlement of claims
from
Comparative religious law: KB567
Defects of goods sold
Jewish law: KBM876
Defendant
Courts
Comparative religious law: KB1655
Criminal procedure
Islamic law: KBP4630.A25
Jewish law: KBM4630.A25
Procedure in general
Islamic law: KBP1657
Surety
Islamic law: KBP1925.S87

Defense
  Criminal procedure
    Comparative religious law: KB4630.D43
    Islamic law: KBP4630.D43
Defense attorney
  Jewish law: KBM4630.D43
Defense forces, Organized
  Jewish law: KBM3738+
Defense of another
  Criminal offense
    Islamic law: KBP3856
    Jewish law: KBM3856
Defense, Presentation of
  Trials
    Roman Catholic law: KBU3852
Degradatio
  Clergy
    Canon law: KBR3615.D43
Dei verbum predicatio
  Canon law: KBR3048
Delay
  Limitation of actions
    Islamic law: KBP508
Delays
  Courts
    Roman Catholic law: KBU3828.T56
Delegation of powers
  Constitution of the state
    Islamic law: KBP2270
  Constitutional and administrative law
    Comparative religious law: KB2270
  Roman Catholic law: KBU2302+
Deliberate intent
  Criminal intent
    Islamic law: KBP3868
Deliberating and voting
  Judges
    Rota Romana
      Canon law: KBR3817.3
Delicti incapaces
  Criminal law
    Roman Catholic law: KBU3539+
  Violation of criminal lal
    Canon law: KBR3539+
Delicts
  Obligations
    Comparative religious law: KB834+
    Islamic law: KBP834+
    Jewish law: KBM834+
Delictum homicidii
  Penal (Criminal) law
    Canon law: KBR3755+
Delictum venditionis hominis (plagium)
  Penal (Criminal) law
    Canon law: KBR3763
Democratic government and Church
  Roman Catholic law: KBU4045+
Democratic government and Islam, Compatibility of
  Islamic law: KBP2035
Democratic government and religion, Compatibility of
  Comparative religious law: KB2035
Demonstrations
  Public safety
    Jewish law: KBM3036.5.D45
Dentists
  Jewish law: KBM3103.D45
Denunciation of bad books
  Canon law: KBR3068.D46
  Roman Catholic law: KBU3068.D46
Denunciation procedure
  Penal (criminal) procedures
    Canon law: KBR3922
Dependent work
  Contracts
    Comparative religious law: KB892.5
    Islamic law: KBP892.5+
    Jewish law: KBM892.5+
Deportation
  Criminal law
    Jewish law: KBM3997
  Punitive deportation
    Jewish law: KBM4826+
Deportation, Punitive
  Comparative religious law: KB3993.B35
  Criminal procedure
    Islamic law: KBP3997

Deposit
Contracts
Islamic law: KBP896
Jewish law: KBM896
Depositio
Clergy
Canon law: KBR3615.D45
Deprivation of liberty, Measures entailing
Criminal law
Jewish law: KBM3982+
Dereliction
Ownership
Islamic law: KBP673
Derogatio
Ecclesiastical laws
Roman Catholic law: KBU2220
Derogation
Ecclesiastical laws
Roman Catholic law: KBU2220
Desertion
Military law
Islamic law: KBP3760.D46
Jewish law: KBM3760.D46
Deserts
Wilderness preservation
Comparative religious law: KB3134+
Islamic law: KBP3134+
Desistere ab incepta delicti exsecutione
Violation of law or precept
Penal (Criminal) law
Canon law: KBR3566
Destitute
Comparative religious law: KB1528
Social services
Islamic law: KBP1528
Jewish law: KBM1528
Destructio
Sacred places
Roman Catholic law: KBU3234
Destruction of property
Torts
Islamic law: KBP842.8
Destruction of property and conversion
Comparative religious law: KB4256
Islamic law: KBP4256
Destruction of property and conversion
Jewish law: KBM4256
Destruction of sacred places
Canon law: KBR3234
Detention and false imprisonment
Canon law: KBR3765
Roman Catholic law: KBU3765
Detention of a woman
Marriage impediments
Canon law: KBR3128.A34
Roman Catholic law: KBU3128.A34
Detention of debtor
Comparative religious law: KB1913
Islamic law: KBP1913
Development and conservation of water resources
Islamic law: KBP3049
Development gains
Capital gains tax
Islamic law: KBP3672
Developmentally disabled people
Institutions for
Jewish law: KBM3113
Dhawū al-furūḍ: KBP633.955+
Dhimmah: KBP810+
Dhimmīyūn
Capacity and disability
Islamic law: KBP529.6
Constitution of the state
Islamic law: KBP2449
Dhū al-yad: KBP646+
Diamonds
Retail trade
Jewish law: KBM3422.D52
Diaspora
Constitutional history
Jewish law: KBM2106+
Dichotomy of halakhah: KBM524.17
Dies dominica
Canon law: KBR3244+
Dies dominica and dies festi
law of the Roman Catholic Church: KBU3244+
Dies et tempora paenitantialia
Roman Catholic law: KBU3250+
Dies et tempora paenitentialia
Canon law: KBR3250+

Dies festi
Canon law: KBR3244+
Dietary laws
Islamic law: KBP184.9.D54
Difā' 'an al-nafs: KBP509
Dignity
Human rights
Comparative religious law: KB2462
Islamic law: KBP2462
Dina de-malkhuta dina: KBM524.24
Dine nefshot: KBM4612
Dinei mamonot: KBM639+
Diocesan constitution and organs
Canon law: KBR2850+
Diocesan councils, synods
Canon law: KBR2878+
Diocesan councils, synods, etc
Organs of government
Roman Catholic law: KBU2878+
Diocesan courts or tribunals
Roman Catholic law: KBU49+
Diocesan curia
Canon law: KBR2852+
Roman Catholic law: KBU2852+
Diocesan domicile
Natural persons
Canon law: KBR2236.D56
Roman Catholic law: KBU2236.D56
Diocesan synod, The
Canon law: KBR2880
Diocesan synods
Roman Catholic law: KBU950+
Dioceses
Canon law: KBR2835+
Dioceses and diocesan bishop
Canon law: KBR2835+
Organs of government
Roman Catholic law: KBU2835+
Diplomacy
Roman Catholic law: KBU4078+
The Holy See
Canon law: KBR4078+
Diplomatics and canon law: KBR75
Diriment impediments
Marriage
Roman Catholic law: KBU3124+
Disabilities, People with
Equality before the law
Jewish law: KBM2467.D58
Social service
Islamic law: KBP1532+
Jewish law: KBM1532+
Disability insurance
Jewish law: KBM1508
Social security
Islamic law: KBP1508
Disabled children
Education
Jewish law: KBM3143+
Disabled people
Equality before the law
Islamic law: KBP2467.D58
Social laws
Comparative religious law: KB1534.A+
Social work
Roman Catholic law: KBU3280.P46
Disabled war veterans
Social work
Canon law: KBR3280.W37
Roman Catholic law: KBU3280.W37
Disaster control
Islamic law: KBP3037
Jewish law: KBM3037
Disaster relief
Islamic law: KBP3037
Jewish law: KBM3037
Disciplinary power
Teachers
Jewish law: KBM3140.7
Discipline
Judges
Islamic law: KBP1614
Jewish law: KBM1614
Discord
Grounds for divorce
Islamic law: KBP559.952
Discrimination
Violation of price regulations
Jewish law: KBM4290

Diseases, Contagious and infectious, Measures against
Canon law: KBR3270
Disenfranchisement
Criminal law punishment
Jewish law: KBM4004
Disinheritance
Comparative religious law: KB636
Jewish law: KBM636
Dismemberment
Juristic persons
Canon law: KBR2280
Roman Catholic law: KBU2280
Dismissal
Criminal procedure
Comparative religious law: KB4742.57
Islamic law: KBP4750
Jewish law: KBM4750
Disobedience
Grounds for divorce
Islamic law: KBP559.953
Disobedience to ecclesiastical authority
Roman Catholic law: KBU3686
Disparity of cult
Impediments to marriage
Canon law: KBR3128.C85
Disparity of cult (Catholic baptized and non-Catholic)
Marriage impediments
Roman Catholic law: KBU3128.C85
Dispensandi potestas
Canon law: KBR3214
Dispensatio ab impedimentis
Marriage
Canon law: KBR3130
Dispensatio super
Canon law: KBR3907+
Dispensation from impediments
Marriage
Roman Catholic law: KBU3130
Dispensation from marriage impediments
Canon law: KBR3130
Dispensation from private vows
Canon law: KBR3214
Dispensation of ratified and non-consummated marriage
Canon law: KBR3907+
Roman Catholic law: KBU3907+
Dispensations
Roman Catholic law: KBU2194.5
Disposal of the dead
Islamic law: KBP3078
Jewish law: KBM3078+
Dispose of episcopates and dioceses, Power to
The Pope
Canon law: KBR2384
Dispositiones ad ordines
Canon law: KBR2329+
Dispossession
Jewish law: KBM651
Property
Comparative religious law: KB651
Islamic law: KBP651
Disqualification of judge
Roman Catholic law: KBU3827
Disqualification of judges
Canon law: KBR3827
Disrupting the peace of the community
Islamic law: KBP4320
Jewish law: KBM4320
Dissection
Animal experimentation
Islamic law: KBP3123.2
Dissolution
Cooperative societies
Islamic law: KBP1134
Jewish law: KBM1134
Marriage
Islamic law: KBP555+
Silent partnership
Islamic law: KBP1049.7
Jewish law: KBM1049.7
Stock companies
Jewish law: KBM1085
Stock corporations
Islamic law: KBP1085
Dissolution of marriage
Comparative religious law: KB555+
Jewish law: KBM555+

Dissolution of the marriage bond
  Canon law: KBR3159+
  Roman Catholic law: KBU3159+
Dissolved marriage, Settlement of claims from
  Comparative religious law: KB567
Distemper
  Defense
    Criminal law
      Roman Catholic law: KBU3559.D58
  Incapacity
    Criminal liability
      Jewish law: KBM3892.D58
  Justification of illegal acts
    Canon law: KBR3559.D58
Distribution of estate: KBM633+
  Comparative religious law: KB635.2
  Islamic law: KBP633.952.T37
  Wills
    Jewish law: KBM635.2
Disturbing a religious observance
  Criminal law
    Jewish law: KBM4174
  Islamic law: KBP4174
Disturbing the peace of the dead
  Criminal law
    Jewish law: KBM4176
  Islamic law: KBP4176
Divider of inheritance
  Courts and procedure
    Islamic law: KBP1622.2
Divine law
  Jewish law: KBM524.2+
Divine law and natural law: KBR2190
Divine right of kings and papacy
  Canon law: KBR4010+
  Roman Catholic law: KBU4010+
Division
  Juristic persons
    Canon law: KBR2280
Divorce
  Comparative religious law: KB558+
  Islamic law: KBP558+
  Jewish law: KBM558+
  Matrimonial actions
    Canon law: KBR3901+
Divorce
  Roman Catholic law: KBU3901+
Divortium
  Matrimonial actions
    Canon law: KBR3901+
  Roman Catholic law: KBU3901+
Divre ha-rav: KBM3900
Divre ha-talmid: KBM3900
Dīwān: KBP1623
Dīyah: KBP3976
Docket
  Courts
    Roman Catholic law: KBU3828.O74
Documentary evidence
  Criminal procedure
    Comparative religious law: KB4709.D63
    Islamic law: KBP4704
    Jewish law: KBM4704
  Procedure in general
    Comparative religious law: KB1676.7
    Islamic law: KBP1676.7
    Jewish law: KBM1676.7
  Trials
    Canon law: KBR3847
    Roman Catholic law: KBU3847
Documentary process
  Nullity or marriage
    Canon law: KBR3899
Dolus
  Criminal law
    Roman Catholic law: KBU3537+
  Legal transactions
    Ius ecclesiasticum privatum: KBR2292
    Roman Catholic law: KBU2292
  Obligations
    Comparative religious law: KB824+
    Jewish law: KBM824.5
  Torts
    Comparative religious law: KB839
    Islamic law: KBP839+
    Jewish law: KBM834.9+
  Violation of criminal law
    Canon law: KBR3537+

Domestic and foreign correspondents
  Islamic law: KBP3504.3
Domestic relations
  Comparative religious law: KB531+
  Islamic law: KBP540+
  Jewish law: KBM531+
Domestic trade
  Comparative religious law: KB3415+
  Islamic law: KBP3415+
Domicile
  Jurisdiction
    Procedure at first instance
      Roman Catholic law: KBU3841.D65
  Natural persons
    Canon law: KBR2235+
    Roman Catholic law: KBU2235+
Domicilium
  Natural persons
    Canon law: KBR2235+
    Roman Catholic law: KBU2235+
Dominium bonorum
  Church property
    Roman Catholic law: KBU3342
Donatio Constantini, 8th cent
  Canon law: KBR4014
Donation of organs, tissues, etc
  Medical legislation
    Comparative religious law: KB3116
    Islamic law: KBP3116
    Jewish law: KBM3116
Donations
  Islamic law: KBP636.3
  Jewish law: KBM636.3
Donations mortis causa and inter vivos
  Temporal goods of the Church
    Canon law: KBR3348+
Doraita: KBM3810, KBM3948
Dower
  Betrothal
    Islamic law: KBP543.953+
  Canon law: KBR3113
  Comparative religious law: KB543.3
  Dissolved marriage
    Islamic law: KBP567
  Marriage law
    Roman Catholic law: KBU3113
Dowery
  Monasticism
    Roman Catholic law: KBU2927.D69
  Religious institutes
    Canon law: KBR2927.D69
Dowry
  Jewish law: KBM567
Dowry (Dos)
  Canon law: KBR3113
Draft evasion
  Military law
    Jewish law: KBM3760.D73
Dress
  Islamic law: KBP184.9.C45
  Muslim women
    Islamic law: KBP528.H54
Drinking
  Islamic law: KBP184.9.D74
Drinking water standards
  Comparative religious law: KB3089
  Islamic law: KBP3089
  Jewish law: KBM3089
Driving while intoxicated
  Jewish law: KBM4384
Drug laws
  Comparative religious law: KB3090+
  Islamic law: KBP3090+
  Jewish law: KBM3090+
Drugs, Force by the use of
  Criminal law
    Jewish law: KBM3823.F67
Drugs of abuse
  Comparative religious law: KB3090+
  Islamic law: KBP3090+
Due process of law
  Constitution of the state
    Islamic law: KBP2484
  Constitutional and administrative law
    Comparative religious law: KB2484
  Constitutional law
    Jewish law: KBM2484
  Courts
    Islamic law: KBP1651
    Jewish law: KBM1651
  Criminal procedure
    Jewish law: KBM4620

Due process of law
  Judiciary
    Canon law: KBR3825
  Roman Catholic law: KBU3825.5
Due process sof law
  Courts
    Comparative religious law: KB1651
Dueling
  Penal (Criminal) law
    Canon law: KBR3759.D84
Dukhūl: KBP546.16
Duress
  Criminal liability
    Islamic law: KBP3897.I47
  Impediments to marriage
    Canon law: KBR3128.D87
  Legal transactions
    Ius ecclesiasticum privatum: KBR2292
    Roman Catholic law: KBU2292
  Marriage consent
    Roman Catholic law: KBU3135
  Matrimonial actions
    Canon law: KBR3905.D87
  Void and voidable contracts
    Comparative religious law: KB867.5
    Islamic law: KBP867.5
    Jewish law: KBM867.5
Duress %b Criminal law
  Comparative religious law: KB3897
Dustūr al-Madīnah: KBP2200.D86
Duties of leaders
  Constitution of the state
    Islamic law: KBP2250.3
  Constitutional and administrative law
    Comparative religious law: KB2250.3
Duty of husband to support wife
  Islamic law: KBP548.3
Duty of pilgrimage
  Islamic law: KBP184.7+
Duty to act
  Criminal offense
    Comparative religious law: KB3859
    Islamic law: KBP3859
    Jewish law: KBM3859
Dynastic rules
  Constitutional and administrative law
    Comparative religious law: KB2535.D96, KB2535.S92
  Constitutionof the state
    Islamic law: KBP2535.Y37
Dynasty
  Constitution of the state
    Islamic law: KBP2532+

E

Early Church and Byzantine Empire (to ca. 8th cent.)
  Church and state
    Canon law: KBR4012+
Early Church and Roman Empire
  Church and state
    Canon law: KBR4012+
Eastern churches and Roman Catholic Church: KB165.A+
Eastern churches, Canon law of: KBS3+
Eating customs
  Islamic law: KBP184.9.D54
Ecclesiae
  Sacred places
    Canon law: KBR3238.C58
Ecclesiastical benefices
  Non-collegiate institutes
    Juristic persons
      Roman Catholic law: KBU3458
Ecclesiastical courts and procedure
  Canon law: KBR3780+
Ecclesiastical estates
  Persons
    Roman Catholic law: KBU2284.E33
Ecclesiastical funeral rites
  Canon law: KBR3190+
Ecclesiastical offices and benefices
  Canon law: KBR2350+
Ecclesiastical offices (General)
  Roman Catholic law: KBU2350+
Ecclesiastical privileges and immunities
  Clergy
    Canon law: KBR2339+
    Roman Catholic law: KBU2339+

Ecclesiastical Provinces
  Canon law: KBR2796+
Ecclesiastical Provinces and Regions
  Roman Catholic law: KBU2796+
Ecclesiastical Regions
  Canon law: KBR2796+
Ecclesiastical universities and faculties
  Canon law: KBR3060
Ecological aspects
  Fishery
    Islamic law: KBP3135
Economic and financial advisors
  Jewish law: KBM3517+
Economic assistance
  Agriculture
    Islamic law: KBP3321
  Islamic law: KBP3206
Economic crisis, Government measures in time of
  Islamic law: KBP3709+
Economic crisis, Measures in time of
  Jewish law: KBM3709+
Economic law
  Comparative religious law: KB3190+
  Islamic law: KBP3190+
  Jewish law: KBM3190+
Economic recovery measures
  Emergency measures
    Islamic law: KBP3720
    Jewish law: KBM3720
Economics, Church
  Canon law: KBR3320+
  Roman Catholic law: KBU3320+
Ecumenical council, Convocation of The Pope
    Canon law: KBR2380
Ecumenical councils (11th-21st centuries)
  Canon law: KBR820+
'Ed eḥad: KBM1676.5
'Edim: KBM4630.W56
Educatio catholica religiosa
  Canon law: KBR3050+
  Roman Catholic law: KBU3050+
Education: KBM3138+
  Children's right to education
    Jewish law: KBM3139.3
Education
  Comparative religious law: KB3138+
  Compulsory education
    Jewish law: KBM3139.4
  Criminal law punishment
    Jewish law: KBM3956
  Health professions
    Islamic law: KBP3100+
    Jewish law: KBM3100+
  Islamic law: KBP3138+
  Parents obligation to educate their children
    Jewish law: KBM3139.3
  Teachers
    Islamic law: KBP3140.5
Education and training of teachers
  Jewish law: KBM3140.5
Education (General)
  Canon law: KBR3050+
Education, Legal
  Canon law: KBR133+, KBR3822.5
  Comparative religious law: KB133
  Roman Catholic law: KBU133, KBU3822.5
Education of clerics
  Canon law: KBR2322+
Education, Religious
  Roman Catholic law: KBU3050+
Educational expenses
  Income tax
    Jewish law: KBM3582.3.E38
Educational gifts and contributions
  Income tax
    Jewish law: KBM3580
  Income tax deductions
    Islamic law: KBP3580
Effect of marriage
  Islamic law: KBP546.2
Effect of registration
  Property
    Jewish law: KBM745
Effectiveness of law
  Canon law: KBR2196
  Jewish law: KBM524.24
Egg products
  Islamic law: KBP3386

Elderly, Frail
  Social work
    Canon law: KBR3280.F73
    Roman Catholic law: KBU3280.F73
Election
  The Pope
    Roman Catholic law: KBU2390
Election of the Pope
  Canon law: KBR2390
Electricity
  Islamic law: KBP3432
Electronic funds transfers
  Islamic law: KBP961
Electronic listening and recording devices
  Criminal trial
    Comparative religious law: KB4689
    Islamic law: KBP4689
    Jewish law: KBM4689
Elementary education
  Comparative religious law: KB3141+
  Islamic law: KBP3141+
  Jewish law: KBM3141
Elvira, Council of, between 300? and 309?: KBR244.3
Emancipation
  Slaves
    Comparative religious law: KB529.5.E52
    Islamic law: KBP529.5
Embezzlement
  Comparative religious law: KB4250
  Islamic law: KBP4250
  Jewish law: KBM4234
Emergency celebration
  Marriage consent
    Roman Catholic law: KBU3138
  Validity of consent for marriage
    Canon law: KBR3138
Emergency management
  Islamic law: KBP3037
  Jewish law: KBM3037
Emergency medical services
  Jewish law: KBM3114.E43
Eminent domain
  Comparative religious law: KB2824+
  Islamic law: KBP2824+
Emotional distress, Liability for
  Jewish law: KBM853.E47
Emotionally disabled people
  Social laws
    Comparative religious law: KB1534.A+
Employees
  Commercial employees
    Jewish law: KBM924
  Communal agencies
    Comparative religious law: KB2870
  Communal agency employees
    Jewish law: KBM2970
  Communal employees, Crimes against
    Jewish law: KBM4514+
  Contracts
    Islamic law: KBP892.6
    Jewish law: KBM892.6
  Religious corporations
    Comparative religious law: KB2870
  State agencies
    Comparative religious law: KB2870
Employees of communal agencies
  Islamic law: KBP2970
Endangering the administration of justice
  Jewish law: KBM4484+
Endangering the welfare of the community
  Jewish law: KBM4432
Endowments
  Church property
    Canon law: KBR3452
  Islamic law: KBP637+
  Non-collegiate juristic persons
    Roman Catholic law: KBU2276.C53
Enemy property
  Islamic law: KBP3712
Energy policy
  Islamic law: KBP3431+
  Jewish law: KBM3431+
Enforcement
  Administrative law
    Jewish law: KBM2757
  Administrative process
    Islamic law: KBP2757

Enforcement
  Obligations
    Islamic law: KBP822.5
    Jewish law: KBM822.5
  Tax administration
    Islamic law: KBP3560+
Enforcement of orders
  Military discipline
    Comparative religious law: KB3780
    Islamic law: KBP3782
    Jewish law: KBM3782
Engineering
  Energy policy
    Islamic law: KBP3431.7
Engineering and construction
  Islamic law: KBP3519
  Jewish law: KBM3519+
Engineers
  Islamic law: KBP3519
  Jewish law: KBM3519
Enlightenment
  Church and state
    Canon law: KBR4040+
Enthronement of the Pope
  Canon law: KBR2390
Entrapment
  Criminal trial
    Islamic law: KBP4681
    Jewish law: KBM4681
Environmental crimes
  Jewish law: KBM4351.5
Environmental damages
  Torts
    Comparative religious law: KB840.E58
    Jewish law: KBM852.4
Environmental law
  Comparative religious law: KB3127+
  Islamic law: KBP3127+
  Jewish law: KBM3127+
Environmental planning
  Comparative religious law: KB3129
  Islamic law: KBP3129
  Jewish law: KBM3129
Environmental pollution
  Comparative religious law: KB3130+
  Islamic law: KBP3130+
Environmental pollution
  Jewish law: KBM3130+
Ephesus, Council of, 193: KBR199.87
Ephesus, Council of, 431? or 449
  Canon law: KBR220
Epileptics
  Social work
    Canon law: KBR3280.E65
    Roman Catholic law: KBU3280.E65
Episcopal conference
  Ecclesaistical Provinces
    Canon law: KBR2825+
Episcopal synods
  Roman Catholic law: KBU830.5+
Episcopal vicars
  Diocesan constitution and organs
    Canon law: KBR2854
  Roman Catholic law: KBU2854
Episcopal visitation
  Canon law: KBR2840
  Dioceses and diocesan bishop
    Roman Catholic law: KBU2840
Episcopus coadiutor et episcopus auxiliaris
  Canon law: KBR2844
Episcopus dioecesanus
  Canon law: KBR2835+
Epistemology
  Islamic law: KBP430
Equal shares
  Unlimited commercial partnership
    Islamic law: KBP1045.4
    Jewish law: KBM1045.4
Equal status of bridegroom
  Islamic law: KBP543.957
Equality
  Jewish law: KBM524.4.E65
  Taxation and tax exemption
    Jewish law: KBM3553+
  Women
    Islamic law: KBP528.K33
Equality before the law
  Comparative religious law: KB2465+
  Islamic law: KBP2465+
  Jewish law: KBM2465+

Equality of different denominations
Church and state
Canon law: KBR4042
Equality of sexes
Monasticism
Canon law: KBR2896
Equity
Jewish law: KBM524.13
Judicial discretion
Criminal procedure
Islamic law: KBP4740
Jewish law: KBM4740
Uṣūl al-fiqh
Islamic law: KBP446
Erection
Ecclesiastical offices
Canon law: KBR2351
Monasticism
Canon law: KBR2892+
Erosion control
Islamic law: KBP3299
Error
Criminal law
Canon law: KBR3562
Roman Catholic law: KBU3562
Criminal offense
Comparative religious law: KB3902
Islamic law: KBP3902
Jewish law: KBM3902
Impediments to marriage
Canon law: KBR3128.E77
Judicial decisions
Comparative religious law: KB4753
Islamic law: KBP4753
Jewish law: KBM4753
Legal transactions
Ius ecclesiasticum privatum: KBR2290
Roman Catholic law: KBU2290
Void and voidable contracts
Comparative religious law: KB867.3
Islamic law: KBP867.3
Jewish law: KBM867.3
Erusin: KBM543+
Espionage
Treasonable espionage
Comparative religious law: KB4442
Espionage
Treasonable espionage
Islamic law: KBP4442
Estate
Distribiution of
Comparative religious law: KB635.2
Estate, Debts of
Islamic law: KBP634.957
Estate, Distribution of
Jewish law: KBM635.2
Estate taxes
Jewish law: KBM3621
Local revenue
Comparative religious law: KB3621
National revenue
Comparative religious law: KB3621
Islamic law: KBP3621
Estates, Ecclesiastical
Persons
Roman Catholic law: KBU2284.E33
Estates of decedents: KBP633+
Ethics
Concept of Jewish law: KBM524.14
Health professions
Islamic law: KBP3100+
Judges
Islamic law: KBP1614
Jewish law: KBM1614
Medical ethics
Jewish law: KBM3098.5
Uṣūl al-fiqh
Islamic law: KBP444
Ethics in government
Constitution of the state
Islamic law: KBP2275
Constitutional and administrative law
Comparative religious law: KB2275
Constitutional law
Jewish law: KBM2275
Ethics, Professional
Comparative religious law: KB3522
Ethiopian Jews
Marriage
Jewish law: KBM546.3.E86
Eucharist
Canon law: KBR3085+
Roman Catholic law: KBU3085+

Eugenics
  Comparative religious law: KB3121+
  Islamic law: KBP3121+
  Jewish law: KBM3121
  Roman Catholic law: KBU3304
Euthanasia
  Criminal law
    Comparative religious law: KB4058
  Islamic law: KBP4058
  Medical legislation
    Comparative religious law: KB3121.7
    Jewish law: KBM3121.7
  Roman Catholic law: KBU3306
Evidence
  Canon law: KBR3843+
  Circumstantial evidence
    Islamic law: KBP4709.C57
    Jewish law: KBM4705
  Criminal procedure
    Comparative religious law: KB4675+
    Islamic law: KBP4675+
    Jewish law: KBM4675+
  Documentary evidence
    Islamic law: KBP4704
    Jewish law: KBM4704
  Matrimonial actions
    Canon law: KBR3893
    Roman Catholic law: KBU3893
  Penal (criminal) procedures
    Canon law: KBR3940+
  Procedure at first instance
    Penal (Criminal) procedure
      Roman Catholic law: KBU3940
  Procedure at trial
    Comparative religious law: KB1672+
    Islamic law: KBP1672+
    Jewish law: KBM1672+
  Retraction of
    Islamic law: KBP4709.R84
  Securing of
    Islamic law: KBP4650
    Jewish law: KBM4650
  Trials
    Roman Catholic law: KBU3843+
Ex post facto laws and retroactivity
  Canon law: KBR3514
  Roman Catholic law: KBU3514
Ex-prisoners of war
  Social service
    Islamic law: KBP1539
    Jewish law: KBM1539
Exactiones
  Roman Catholic law: KBU3384+
Examination
  Criminal procedure
    Islamic law: KBP4636
  Pretrial procedures
    Comparative religious law: KB4636
Examinations, Premarital
  Canon law: KBR3117
Excardinatio
  Clergy
    Canon law: KBR2334
Excardination of clerics
  Canon law: KBR2334
  Roman Catholic law: KBU2334
Exceptions
  Islamic law: KBP462.I78
  Judiciary
    Canon law: KBR3835+
  Trial
    Canon law: KBR3841.2+
Excess profits tax
  Jewish law: KBM3625
Exchange
  Contracts
    Comparative religious law: KB879
    Islamic law: KBP879+
    Jewish law: KBM879+
Excise taxes
  Comparative religious law: KB3627+
  Islamic law: KBP3627+
  Jewish law: KBM3627+
Exclusion from inheritance
  Comparative religious law: KB634.6
  Islamic law: KBP634.956
  Jewish law: KBM634.6
Exclusion of court members
  Islamic law: KBP4670
  Jewish law: KBM4670

Excommunication
  Penal (Criminal) law
    Canon law: KBR3604+
  Roman Catholic law: KBU3604
Exculpating circumatances
  Criminal liability
    Comparative religious law: KB3897
Exculpating circumstances
  Criminal liability
    Islamic law: KBP3897.A+
    Jewish law: KBM3897
Exculpating or extenuating circumstances
  Criminal law
    Law of the Roman Catholic Church: KBU3548+
Execution
  Insolvency
    Islamic law: KBP1888+
    Jewish law: KBM1888
  Other than after formal proceedings
    Jewish law: KBM3965
  Taxation
    Islamic law: KBP3570
Execution for payment due
  Insolvency
    Comparative religious law: KB1888+
Execution of judgment
  Courts
    Jewish law: KBM1690
  Courts and procedure
    Comparative religious law: KB1690
    Islamic law: KBP1690, KBP1883
Execution of sentence
  Criminal procedure
    Comparative religious law: KB4795+
    Islamic law: KBP4795+
    Jewish law: KBM4795+
Execution of sentence and executory decree
  Roman Catholic law: KBU3876
  Trials
    Canon law: KBR3876
Executive branch
  Comparative religious law: KB2577+
Executive branch
  Islamic law: KBP2577+
  Jewish law: KBM2577+
Executive power
  Dioceses
    Canon law: KBR2837
  Dioceses and diocesan bishop
    Roman Catholic law: KBU2837
Executors of estate
  Islamic law: KBP635.954
  Jewish law: KBM635.4
Executors of gifts inter vivos
  Canon law: KBR3370
Executors of pius wills
  Canon law: KBR3370
Exemptions
  Income tax
    Islamic law: KBP3578+
    Jewish law: KBM3578+
  Property tax
    Jewish law: KBM3620
  Temporal goods of the Church
    Canon law: KBR3400+
Exequiae ecclesiasticae
  Canon law: KBR3190+
  Roman Catholic law: KBU3190+
Exercise of rights
  Islamic law: KBP509+
Exilarch: KBM2107
Exile
  Criminal law
    Comparative religious law: KB3993.B35
    Jewish law: KBM3997
  Criminal procedure
    Islamic law: KBP3997
    Jewish law: KBM4826+
Expensae iudiciales
  Roman Catholic law: KBU3874
  Trials
    Canon law: KBR3874
Expenses and losses
  Income tax deductions
    Islamic law: KBP3582.3.A+
    Jewish law: KBM3582+

Expert evidence
  Trials
    Canon law: KBR3849
    Roman Catholic law: KBU3849
Expert testimony
  Criminal procedure
    Comparative religious law: KB4700
    Islamic law: KBP4700
    Jewish law: KBM4700
  Procedure in general
    Comparative religious law: KB1676
    Islamic law: KBP1676
    Jewish law: KBM1676
Experts and expert witnesses
  Criminal procedure
    Islamic law: KBP4700
    Jewish law: KBM4700
  Islamic law: KBP1626+
  Jewish law: KBM1626+
Expiation
  Criminal law punishment
    Islamic law: KBP3979
Expiatory (vindictive) penalties
  Criminal law
    Roman Catholic law: KBU3522+
  Penal (Criminal) law
    Canon law: KBR3522+,
      KBR3611.2+
  Roman Catholic law: KBU3611.2+
Export sales
  Excise taxes
    Islamic law: KBP3640.E96
Export trade
  Regulation
    Comparative religious law: KB3410
    Islamic law: KBP3410
Expropriation
  Comparative religious law: KB2824+
  Emergency measures
    Islamic law: KBP3720
    Jewish law: KBM3720
Expropriation of land by the state
  Islamic law: KBP2825+
Expulsion
  Criminal law
    Islamic law: KBP3997
    Jewish law: KBM3997
Exsecutio sententiae
  Roman Catholic law: KBU3876
  Trials
    Canon law: KBR3876
Exsecutorium iudicis decretum
  Trials
    Canon law: KBR3876
Extenuating circumstances
  Criminal law
    Comparative religious law:
      KB4023.A35
    Islamic law: KBP4020+
Extinctio potestatis
  Roman Catholic law: KBU2306
Extinction
  Ecclesiastical offices
    Canon law: KBR2362.7
  Juristic persons
    Canon law: KBR2280
    Roman Catholic law: KBU2280
Extinction of employment
  Islamic law: KBP1303
  Jewish law: KBM1303
Extinction of obligation
  Comparative religious law: KB817
  Islamic law: KBP817+
  Jewish law: KBM817+
Extinction of powers
  Roman Catholic law: KBU2306
Extortion
  Jewish law: KBM4264
Extortionate kidnapping
  Comparative religious law: KB4120
  Islamic law: KBP4120
  Jewish law: KBM4120
Extra-contractual liability
  Delicts and torts
    Islamic law: KBP839+
Extractive industries
  Regulation
    Comparative religious law:
      KB3294.22+
    Islamic law: KBP3293+,
      KBP3293.212+
    Jewish law: KBM3293+
Extraterritoriality of Vatican City
  Roman Catholic law: KBU4072

Extreme unction
  Roman Catholic law: KBU3096+

F

Fabricae
  Church buildings
    Canon law: KBR3417
Facta et quae ab ipsa lege praesummuntur
  Trials
    Roman Catholic law: KBU3844
Facta et quae ab ipsa lege praesumuntur
  Canon law: KBR3844
Facts and presumptions
  Trials
    Canon law: KBR3844
    Roman Catholic law: KBU3844
Faḍl māl bi-lā ʻiwaḍ: KBP854+
Fairness
  Taxation and tax exemption
    Jewish law: KBM3553+
Fairs
  Retail trade
    Jewish law: KBM3420.M37
Faith
  Islamic law: KBP184.9.F34
Faith, Profession of
  Canon law: KBR3070
False accusation
  Criminal law
    Jewish law: KBM4496
False accusation of unlawful intercourse
  Ḥadd crimes
    Islamic law: KBP4044
False imprisonment
  Canon law: KBR3765
  Jewish law: KBM4118
  Roman Catholic law: KBU3765
False testimony
  Criminal law
    Jewish law: KBM4484
Falsehood
  Penal (Criminal) law
    Canon law: KBR3730+
  Roman Catholic law: KBU3730+
Falsehood
  Uṣūl al-fiqh
    Islamic law: KBP448.F35
Falsus procurator
  Comparative religious law: KB861
  Islamic law: KBP862
  Jewish law: KBM862
Families, Large
  Social service
    Islamic law: KBP1531
Family
  Large families, Social service to
    Jewish law: KBM1531
  Offenses against marriage, family, and family status
    Jewish law: KBM4180+
  Victim's family
    Jewish law: KBM4630.V52
Family law
  Comparative religious law: KB531+
  Islamic law: KBP540+
  Jewish law: KBM531+
Family name
  Jewish law: KBM549
Family names
  Registration
    Comparative religious law: KB1857
    Islamic law: KBP1857
Family planning
  Comparative religious law: KB3124+
  Islamic law: KBP3124+
  Jewish law: KBM3124+
  Roman Catholic law: KBU3308+
Family theft
  Criminal law
    Comparative religious law: KB4235
  Islamic law: KBP4235
Farāʼiḍ: KBP632+
Faskh: KBP557, KBP873.8
Fast-breaking at the end of Ramaḍān: KBP186.45
Fast, Law of
  Canon law: KBR3252
Fasting
  Islamic law: KBP184.5+
  Pillars of Islam
    Islamic law: KBP179

INDEX

Fasts and feasts (Church year)
  Canon law: KBR3242+
  Roman Catholic law: KBU3242+
Fatwas
  Islamic law: KBP491+
Fear, Grave
  Justification
    Criminal law
      Roman Catholic law: KBU3550
Feast of breaking the Ramadan fast: KBP184.54.I32
Fees
  National revenue
    Islamic law: KBP3540.3
Female circumcision
  Comparative religious law: KB3119.F45
  Medical legislation
    Islamic law: KBP3119.F45
Female slave
  Capacity and disability
    Islamic law: KBP529.3+
Female slaves
  Comparative religious law: KB529.3+
Fertilization in vitro
  Medical legislation
    Comparative religious law: KB3117
    Islamic law: KBP3117
    Jewish law: KBM3117
  Roman Catholic law: KBU3298
Fetus
  Natural persons
    Jewish law: KBM529.7.U53
Feudal institutes and church
  Canon law: KBR4032
Fictions
  Jewish law: KBM524.4.F52
Fidei professio
  Canon law: KBR3070
  Teaching office of the Church
    Roman Catholic law: KBU3070
Fideicommissa
  Church property
    Canon law: KBR3452
Fiduciary transactions
  Contracts
    Comparative religious law: KB859, KB889
    Islamic law: KBP859
    Jewish law: KBM889+
  Jewish law: KBM859
  Trust and trustee
    Islamic law: KBP889+
Field irrigation
  Islamic law: KBP3299
Filii adoptivi
  Natural persons
    Canon law: KBR2243
  Roman Catholic law: KBU2243+
Filii e matrimonio mixto nati
  Canon law: KBR3150
  Roman Catholic law: KBU3150
Filius nullius
  Islamic law: KBP612+
Final divorce
  Islamic law: KBP562.953
Finance
  Mining industry
    Islamic law: KBP3353
  Public finance
    Comparative religious law: KB3526+
    Islamic law: KBP3526+
    Jewish law: KBM3526+
Finance, Church
  Canon law: KBR3320+
  Roman Catholic law: KBU3320+
Finance council
  Organs of government
    Roman Catholic law: KBU2860
Financial advisors
  Jewish law: KBM3517+
Financial obligations, Divorce with mutual waiving of
  Islamic law: KBP563.2
Fine arts
  Comparative religious arts: KB3169
  Islamic law: KBP3169
  Jewish law: KBM3169

Fines
  Criminal law
    Jewish law: KBM3976
  National revenue
    Islamic law: KBP3540.3
  Qisas punishment
    Islamic law: KBP3976
Fiqh: KBP1+
  Disputed sources: KBP452+
  Sources: KBP449+
Fiqh and siyāsah, Dichotomy of: KBP445
Fire
  Jewish law: KBM853.F57
Fire prevention and control
  Jewish law: KBM3016
Fish
  Conservation
    Comparative religious law: KB3135
    Islamic law: KBP3135
Fish industry
  Regulation
    Jewish law: KBM3392
Fishery
  Comparative religious law: KB3340
  Islamic law: KBP3340+
  Jewish law: KBM3340
Fishery products
  Islamic law: KBP3392
Fishing rights
  Comparative religious law: KB699
  Ownership of land
    Islamic law: KBP699
    Jewish law: KBM699
Five compilations of decretales, 1188-1226
  Canon law: KBR1450+
Five duties of a Muslim, The
  Islamic law: KBP176+
Flagellation
  Criminal law punishment
    Comparative religious law: KB3980.F57
    Islamic law: KBP3980.F57
Flogging
  Criminal law penalty
    Jewish law: KBM3980.F55
Flogging
  Criminal law punishment
    Comparative religious law: KB3980.F57
Food
  Forbidden food
    Islamic law: KBP184.9.D54
  Islamic law: KBP184.9.D54
Food additives
  Islamic law: KBP3379
  Jewish law: KBM3377+
Food processing industries
  Comparative religious law: KB3377
  Islamic law: KBP3377+
  Jewish law: KBM3377+
Food products
  Comparative religious law: KB3377
  Islamic law: KBP3377+
  Jewish law: KBM3377+
Forbidden food
  Islamic law: KBP184.9.D54
Forbidden rites
  Canon law: KBR3644
Force
  Criminal law
    Jewish law: KBM3823.F67
Forced labor
  Emergency measures
    Islamic law: KBP3715
Foreign and international relations of the Holy See
  Roman Catholic law: KBU4076+
Foreign corporations
  Income tax
    Islamic law: KBP3614+
Foreign correspondents
  Islamic law: KBP3504.3
Foreign exchange violations
  Jewish law: KBM4292
Foreign investments
  Income tax
    Islamic law: KBP3588
  Taxation
    Islamic law: KBP3553.3
Foreign Office
  Islamic law: KBP2604

Foreign relations
Islamic law: KBP2400+
Foreign relations and the judiciary
Jewish law: KBM1574
Foreign relations of the Holy See
Canon law: KBR4076+
Foreign states, Crimes against
Comparative religious law: KB4543
Islamic law: KBP4543
Foreign stockholders
Corporation tax
Islamic law: KBP3614+
Foresight
Criminal offense
Jewish law: KBM3874
Forestry
Islamic law: KBP3293+, KBP3336
Jewish law: KBM3293+
Regulation
Jewish law: KBM3336
Forests
Wilderness preservation
Comparative religious law: KB3134+
Islamic law: KBP3134+
Jewish law: KBM3134
Forfeiture
Criminal law punishment
Jewish law: KBM4010
Forgery
Legal and monetary transactions
Comparative religious law: KB4330
Jewish law: KBM4330
Torts
Islamic law: KBP846
Jewish law: KBM846
Forgery and suppression of ecclesiastical documents
Penal (Criminal) law
Canon law: KBR3734
Roman Catholic law: KBU3734
Forgery of legal and monetary transactions and documents
Islamic law: KBP4330
Forgery of seals, stamps, etc
Tax crimes
Islamic law: KBP3699
Form requirements
Contracts
Jewish law: KBM866
Contracts and transactions
Islamic law: KBP866
Procedure at trial
Islamic law: KBP1667.F67
Formal charge
Criminal procedure
Jewish law: KBM4668
Formalities
Contracts
Comparative religious law: KB872.5
Islamic law: KBP872.5
Jewish law: KBM872.5
Formation, education of clerics
Canon law: KBR2322+
Formation of contract
Comparative religious law: KB869+
Labor contracts
Islamic law: KBP1295
Formation of contracts: KBM869+
Islamic law: KBP869+
Labor laws
Jewish law: KBM1295
Forms
Substantive law
Islamic law: KBP496.3
Formularies
Canon law: KBR105.A+
Fornication
Offenses of clerics
Penal (Criminal) law
Canon law: KBR3751
Penal (Criminal) law
Canon law: KBR3774.F67
Forum
Ecclesiastical courts
Canon law: KBR3797+
Forum rei sitae
Jurisdiction
Procedure at first instance
Roman Catholic law: KBU3841.F67
Fosterage
Parent and child
Comparative religious law: KB610

Fosterage
  Parent and child
    Islamic law: KBP610.2
Foundations
  Islamic law: KBP637+
  Juristic persons
    Canon law: KBR2276.C53
    Jewish law: KBM530
Founders
  Monasticism
    Canon law: KBR2892+
Foundling
  Islamic law: KBP619.L34
Frail elderly
  Social work
    Canon law: KBR3280.F73
    Roman Catholic law: KBU3280.F73
Franchises
  Jewish law: KBM926.3.F72
Frankfurt, Council of, 794: KBR248
Frankish (Germanic) Empire
  Canon law: KBR4020+
Fraud
  Comparative religious law: KB4258
  Islamic law: KBP4258
  Jewish law: KBM4258
  Legal transactions
    Ius ecclesiasticum privatum: KBR2292
    Roman Catholic law: KBU2292
  Marriage consent
    Roman Catholic law: KBU3135
  Void and voidable contracts
    Comparative religious law: KB867.5
    Islamic law: KBP867.5
    Jewish law: KBM867.5
Free loan societies
  Jewish law: KBM955.2
Freedom
  Human rights
    Comparative religious law: KB2469+
    Islamic law: KBP2469+
    Jewish law: KBM2469+
Freedom of assembly
  Comparative religious law: KB2483
  Islamic law: KBP2483
Freedom of assembly, association and demonstration
  Roman Catholic law: KBU4060.F72
Freedom of association
  Comparative religious law: KB2483
  Islamic law: KBP2483
  Jewish law: KBM2483
Freedom of communication
  Islamic law: KBP3483
  Jewish law: KBM3483
Freedom of comunication
  Comparative religious law: KB3483
Freedom of demonstration
  Comparative religious law: KB2483
  Islamic law: KBP2483
Freedom of expression
  Comparative religious law: KB2470
  Islamic law: KBP2470
  Jewish law: KBM2470
  Roman Catholic law: KBU4060.F73
Freedom of information
  Comparative religious law: KB2476
  Islamic law: KBP2476
  Jewish law: KBM2476
Freedom of information (press and radio communication)
  Roman Catholic law: KBU4060.F75
Freedom of religion
  Comparative religious law: KB2472
  Islamic law: KBP2472
  Jewish law: KBM2472
Freedom of religion and conscience
  Roman Catholic law: KBU4060.F77
Freedom of science and the arts
  Cultural affairs
    Comparative religious law: KB3137.5
    Jewish law: KBM3137.5
Freedom of speech
  Human rights
    Comparative religious law: KB2474+
  Islamic law: KBP2474+
  Jewish law: KBM2474+
Freedom of the press
  Comparative religious law: KB3483
  Islamic law: KBP3483

Freedom of thought
  Islamic law: KBP2474+
  Jewish law: KBM2474+
Freedom of thought and speech
  Comparative religious law: KB2474+
  Roman Catholic law: KBU4060.F78
Freedom of worship
  Comparative religious law: KB2472
  Islamic law: KBP2472
  Jewish law: KBM2472
Freedom, Personal
  Married women
    Islamic law: KBP553.F73
Freight forwarders and carriers
  Comparative religious law: KB931
  Islamic law: KBP931
  Jewish law: KBM931
Friday prayer
  Islamic law: KBP184.32.F74
Fridays
  Islamic law: KBP186.15
Fringe benefits
  Income tax
    Jewish law: KBM3584
Fruits
  Taxable income
    Islamic law: KBP3620.3.C75
Fruits and vegetables
  Islamic law: KBP3381
  Jewish law: KBM3381
Fuḍūlī: KBP862
Fugitives, Proceedings against
  Comparative religious law: KB4710
  Islamic law: KBP4713
Functionaries, Religious
  Islamic law: KBP185
Fundationes piae
  Church property
    Canon law: KBR3452
Fundraising and taxation
  Local finance
    Jewish law: KBM3660
Funeral
  Natural persons
    Canon law: KBR2236.F86
Funeral procession prayers
  Islamic law: KBP184.55
Funeral rites
  Islamic law: KBP184.55
  Roman Catholic law: KBU3190+
Funeral rites, Ecclesiastical
  Canon law: KBR3190+
Funeral taxes
  Church taxes and fees
    Roman Catholic law: KBU3392.F86
Fungibles
  Comparative religious law: KB642.3
  Islamic law: KBP642.3
  Jewish law: KBM642.3
Furu' al-fiqh: KBP490+
Furūq Ashbāh wa-naẓā'ir, qawā'id:
  KBP497.2+
Futures
  Sale
    Jewish law: KBM926.2.F87

G

Gabai: KBM1624
Galileo
  Trial (Canon law): KBR128.5.G35
Galleries
  Comparative religious law: KB3182.5
  Islamic law: KBP3182.5
  Jewish law: KBM3182.5
Gambling
  Aleatory contracts
    Jewish law: KBM899.3
  Criminal law
    Jewish law: KBM4406
  Regulation
    Jewish law: KBM3036.5.G35
Game
  Wildlife conservation
    Comparative religious law: KB3135
    Islamic law: KBP3135
Game laws
  Comparative religious law: KB3336
  Islamic law: KBP3336
  Jewish law: KBM3336
Games of chance
  Control of
    Jewish law: KBM3036.5.G35

Gangra, Council of, 340? or 343:
  KBR246.5
Gas
  Energy policy
    Islamic law: KBP3433
  Regulation
    Islamic law: KBP3366+
Gas leases
  Islamic law: KBP3367
Gays
  Equality before the law
    Jewish law: KBM2467.G37
Gemach
  Jewish law: KBM955.2
Gemilut ḥasadim
  Yoreh de'ah law: KBM523.5.B4
Genealogy
  Islamic law: KBP54.5
Genetic engineering
  Medical legislation
    Islamic law: KBP3115.5
    Jewish law: KBM3115.5
  Medical technology
    Comparative religious law:
      KB3115.5
Genevah: KBM4234
Genocide
  Comparative religious law: KB4540
  Islamic law: KBP4540
Gentiles
  Natural persons
    Jewish law: KBM529.7.N65
Gerama
  Jewish law: KBM524.4.C38
Germanic law and Canon law:
  KBR2206.3
Gerushim
  Jewish law: KBM558+
Geṭ (Divorce)
  Jewish law: KBM562.3
Geṭ me'uśeh: KBM562.4
Gezelah: KBM4234
Ghā'ib: KBP524.8
Ghalta: KBP867.5
Ghalṭah: KBP867.3
Gharar: KBP866.5
Ghaṣb: KBP846.2
Gift taxes
  Jewish law: KBM3621
  Local revenue
    Comparative religious law: KB3621
  National revenue
    Comparative religious law: KB3621
    Islamic law: KBP3621
Gifts
  Inheritance and succession
    Comparative religious law: KB636.3
  Islamic law: KBP636.3
Gifts and legacies ad pias causas
  Church property
    Roman Catholic law: KBU3348+
  Temporal goods of the Church
    Canon law: KBR3348+
Gifts (Donations)
  Jewish law: KBM636.3
Gifts mortis causa
  Comparative religious law: KB636.2
  Islamic law: KBP636.2
  Jewish law: KBM636.2
Giyur: KBM2448
Glass, Recycling of
  Islamic law: KBP3264+
God parent
  Baptism
    Roman Catholic law: KBU3079
God's rule
  Islamic law: KBP2020+
  Public law
    Comparative religious law:
      KB2020+
Gold trading and gold standard
  Islamic law: KBP3537
  Jewish law: KBM3537
Good faith
  Jewish law: KBM524.4.G66
Gospel and law
  Canon law: KBR2155
  Roman Catholic law: KBU2155
Governance of institutes
  Monasticism
    Canon law: KBR2912+
Governance, Power of
  Canon law: KBR2364

Government
  Offenses against
    Comparative religious law:
      KB4415+
Government business enterprises
  Economic law
    Islamic law: KBP3217
Government contracts
  Islamic law: KBP2754
Government liability
  Islamic law: KBP2840
  Jewish law: KBM2840
Government measures in time of war, national emergency, or economic crisis
  Comparative religious law: KB3709+
  Islamic law: KBP3709+
Government property
  Comparative religious law:
    KB3040.5+
  Islamic law: KBP3040.5+
Government retail trade
  Comparative religious law: KB3418
Government rights
  Mining and quarrying
    Islamic law: KBP3345
    Jewish law: KBM3345
Goyim, Legal status of
  Natural persons
    Jewish law: KBM529.7.N65
Gradus
  Consanguinity
    Roman Catholic law: KBU2238
  Natural persons
    Canon law: KBR2238
Grammar and interpretation
  Islamic law: KBP461+
Granting of benefices
  The Pope
    Canon law: KBR2385
    Roman Catholic law: KBU2385
Gratuities
  Roman Catholic law: KBU3384+
  Support for the Church
    Canon law: KBR3392
Gravamen
  Judicial review of administrative acts
    Roman Catholic law: KBU3968
Grave fear
  Justification
    Criminal law
      Roman Catholic law: KBU3550
Graviter vulnerare
  Penal (Criminal) law
    Canon law: KBR3768
  Roman Catholic law: KBU3768
Grazing associations
  Comparative religious law: KB3314
  Islamic law: KBP3316
Grazing rights
  Comparative religious law: KB708
  Islamic law: KBP708
  Jewish law: KBM708
Grievance court
  Islamic law: KBP1588.4
Grounds for divorce
  Comparative religious law: KB559.A+
  Islamic law: KBP559+
Groundwater
  Jewish law: KBM3046+
Groundwater pollution
  Islamic law: KBP3131
  Jewish law: KBM3131
Group homes for the mentally ill and/or developmentally disabled
  Jewish law: KBM3113
Group lands
  Comparative religious law: KB686
  Islamic law: KBP686
Group prayer
  Islamic law: KBP184.32.G75
Guarantor
  Contracts
    Comparative religious law: KB900
    Islamic law: KBP900
    Jewish law: KBM900
Guardian and ward
  Comparative religious law: KB622+
  Islamic law: KBP622+
  Jewish law: KBM622+
  Natural persons
    Canon law: KBR2245+

Guardian and ward
  Natural persons
    Roman Catholic law: KBU2245+
Guardianship
  Comparative religious law: KB622+
  Islamic law: KBP622+
Guardianship over adults
  Comparative religious law: KB627
  Islamic law: KBP627+
  Jewish law: KBM627+
Guardianship over minors
  Comparative religious law: KB625
  Islamic law: KBP625
  Jewish law: KBM625
Guardianship over minors and adults
  with mental disabilities
  Natural persons
    Canon law: KBR2245+
Guardianship over the betrothed
  Islamic law: KBP543.954+
Guilds
  Artisans
    Islamic law: KBP3429
  Comparative religious law: KB3429
Guilt
  Criminal law
    Roman Catholic law: KBU3537+
  Criminal offense
    Comparative religious law:
      KB3878+
    Islamic law: KBP3878+
    Jewish law: KBM3878+
  Violation of criminal law
    Canon law: KBR3537+

H

Habitual criminals
  Protective custody
    Jewish law: KBM3992
Ḥabs: KBP731+, KBP894, KBP3992
Ḥadd crimes: KBP4041+
Ḥadd punishment: KBP3964
Hadith: KBP135.A1+
  Sources of fiqh: KBP450
Haeresis formalis
  Canon law: KBR3636+
Haeresis pertinax
  Canon law: KBR3046, KBR3636+
Ḥajj: KBP181
Hajr: KBP628
Ḥakam: KBP1619
Halakhah: KBM1+
  Jewish law: KBM520+
Halakhic jurisprudence: KBM524
Ḥalal: KBM544.5
Ḥalitsah: KBM563
Hallah
  Yoreh de'ah law: KBM523.5.H3
Ḥanafī school of thought: KBP295+
Ḥanbalī school of thought: KBP305+
Ḥaqq: KBP448.H37
Ḥarbīyūn
  Capacity and disability
    Islamic law: KBP529.6
  Constitution of the state
    Islamic law: KBP2449
Hatsalah: KBM3108.H36
Havarie grosse
  Comparative religious law: KB979
  Islamic law: KBP979
  Jewish law: KBM979
Ḥawālah: KBP816+
Ḥawālah and suftajah, Difference
  between: KBP938
Ḥazaḳah: KBM1677.H37
Hazardous articles and processes
  Public safety
    Islamic law: KBP3011+
Hazardous materials and processes,
  Control of
  Jewish law: KBM3009
Hazmanah: KBM1662.S86
Heads of state
  Comparative religious law: KB2530+
Healers
  Comparative religious law:
    KB3103.H42
  Islamic law: KBP3103.H42
  Jewish law: KBM3103.H42
Health insurance
  Social laws
    Jewish law: KBM1483

Health insurance
  Social legislation
    Islamic law: KBP1483
Health organizations
  Islamic law: KBP3108.A+
  Jewish law: KBM3108.A+
Health professions
  Comparative religious law: KB3100+
  Islamic law: KBP3100+
  Jewish law: KBM3100+
Health resorts and spas
  Jewish law: KBM3111
Health services, Catholic
  Roman Catholic law: KBU3286
Heat
  Energy policy
    Islamic law: KBP3435
Heavy industries
  Manufacturing
    Jewish law: KBM3372+
Hebrew language
  Jewish law: KBM3137.9
Heirs
  Islamic law: KBP633.955+
Heraldry and canon law: KBR83
Herbalists
  Jewish law: KBM3103.H42
Ḥerem: KBM3997
Ḥerem de-Rabenu Gershom:
  KBM531.5
Heresy
  Canon law: KBR3636+
  Criminal law
    Jewish law: KBM4418
  Roman Catholic law: KBU3636+
Heresy and apostasy
  Canon law: KBR3046
  Teaching office of the Church
    Roman Catholic law: KBU3046
Herev: KBM3964.2
Hermaphrodites
  Capacity and disability
    Islamic law: KBP529.7.H47
  Comparative religious law:
    KB529.7.H47
  Natural persons
    Jewish law: KBM529.7.H47
Heter me'ah rabanim: KBM562.7
Heter me’ah rabanim: KBM562.4
Ḥevra kaddisha: KBM3078.5
Hibah: KBP636.3
Ḥiḍānah: KBP602.5
Hierarchia iuridictionis
  Canon law: KBR2364
Hierarchia ordinis
  Canon law: KBR2320+
Hierarchical order
  Clergy
    Canon law: KBR2320+
Hierarchy
  Organs of government
    Canon law: KBR2363+
  Roman Catholic law: KBU2363+
High treason
  Comparative religious law: KB4417+
  Islamic law: KBP4417+
Higher education
  Comparative religious law: KB3147
  Islamic law: KBP3147+
  Jewish law: KBM3147+
Highway robbery with homicide
  Ḥadd crimes
    Islamic law: KBP4046
Highway safety
  Jewish law: KBM3448
Highways
  Islamic law: KBP3044.7
  Jewish law: KBM3044.7, KBM3046+
Ḥijāb
  Ritual law: KBP184.9.C45
  Substantive law: KBP528.H54
Ḥinuḳ: KBM3964.4
Hire
  Contracts
    Comparative religious law: KB892.5
    Islamic law: KBP892.5+
    Jewish law: KBM892.5+
Ḥisbah: KBP3034.3
Historic buildings and monuments
  Comparative religious law: KB3183
  Islamic law: KBP3183+
  Jewish law: KBM3183
Historic documents
  Comparative religious law: KB3177

Historic documents
  Islamic law: KBP3177
  Jewish law: KBM3177
History of Judaism
  Jewish law: KBM150+
Ḥiyal: KBP496
Hoarding
  Violation of price regulations
    Jewish law: KBM4290
Holiday laws
  Retail trade
    Islamic law: KBP3419
  Road traffic
    Islamic law: KBP3458
Holiday legislation
  Comparative religious law: KB3418
Holy Communion
  Canon law: KBR3085+
  Roman Catholic law: KBU3085+
Holy Communion, Admission to the
  Canon law: KBR3087
Holy orders
  Marriage impediments
    Roman Catholic law: KBU3128.O74
Holy Orders
  Canon law: KBR3102+
  Impediments to marriage
    Canon law: KBR3128.O74
Holy Roman Empire (Sacrum Imperium Romanum)
  Canon law: KBR4020+
Holy See, Foreign and international relations of the
  Canon law: KBR4076+
Holy See, Legal and international status of
  Roman Catholic law: KBU4064+
Holy See, Legal and international status of the
  Canon law: KBR4064+
Holy See, The: KBU2+
Homeless persons
  Social laws
    Comparative religious law: KB1536
  Social service
    Islamic law: KBP1536
    Jewish law: KBM1536
Homeopaths
  Jewish law: KBM3103.H42
Homicide
  Comparative religious law: KB4050+
  Highway robbery with
    Islamic law: KBP4046
  Impediments to marriage
    Canon law: KBR3128.H66
  Islamic law: KBP4050+
  Jewish law: KBM4050+
  Marriage impediments
    Roman Catholic law: KBU3128.H66
  Penal (Criminal) law
    Canon law: KBR3755+
  Roman Catholic law: KBU3755+
Homicidium
  Roman Catholic law: KBU3755+
Hominem detinere
  Canon law: KBR3765
  Roman Catholic law: KBU3765
Honors
  The Pope
    Canon law: KBR2370
Honors and rank
  Ecclesiastical offices
    Canon law: KBR2355+
Horticulture
  Comparative religious law: KB3335, KB3336
  Islamic law: KBP3335
  Jewish law: KBM3335
Hospitals
  Church property
    Canon law: KBR3460
  Juristic persons
    Roman Catholic law: KBU3460
  Medical legislation
    Comparative religious law: KB3110+
    Islamic law: KBP3110+
    Jewish law: KBM3110+
Hospitals and asylums
  Canon law: KBR3275.H67
Hospitals, Catholic
  Roman Catholic law: KBU3286

Hostels
  Public safety
    Jewish law: KBM3034.5
Hotels
  Regulation
    Islamic law: KBP3424.5
    Jewish law: KBM3424.5
House of David
  Constitutional principles
    Jewish law: KBM2130
Ḥukm: KBP447
Human dignity
  Jewish law: KBM2462
Human experimentation in medicine
  Medical legislation
    Comparative religious law:
      KB3115+
    Islamic law: KBP3115+
    Jewish law: KBM3115+
Human reproductive technology
  Medical legislation
    Comparative religious law: KB3117
    Islamic law: KBP3117
    Jewish law: KBM3117
  Roman Catholic law: KBU3298
Human rights
  Comparative religious law: KB2460+
  Islamic law: KBP2460+
  Jewish law: KBM2460+
Human rights and the Church
  Roman Catholic law: KBU4059+
Humanity, Crimes against
  Islamic law: KBP4538+
Ḥumash, Criminal law in the: KBM3810
Hunting rights
  Comparative religious law: KB699
  Islamic law: KBP699
  Ownership of land
    Jewish law: KBM699
Ḥuppah
  Jewish law: KBM546.14
Ḥuqūq wa-qawānīn al-mutazawwijāt:
  KBP550+
Husband
  Dissolution of marriage
    Islamic law: KBP562+
Husband
  Impotence or incurable diseases of
    Matrimonial actions
      Islamic law: KBP565
  Oath of on wife's unchastity
    Islamic law: KBP564.2.L52
  Repudiation of wife by
    Islamic law: KBP562+
Husband abuse
  Jewish law: KBM4077
Husband and wife
  Canon law: KBR3155+
  Comparative religious law: KB547+
  Islamic law: KBP547+
  Jewish law: KBM547+
  Roman Catholic law: KBU3155+
Hypnosis, Force by the use of
  Criminal law
    Jewish law: KBM3823.F67
Hypothecation
  Comparative religious law: KB717

I

ʻIbādāt: KBP184+
ʻIbāḍī: KBP390+
Ibrā': KBP817.5
ʻĪd al-Aḍḥā: KBP186.6
ʻĪd al-Fiṭr: KBP184.54.I32, KBP186.45
ʻIddah: KBP566
Idhn: KBP861.3
Idolatry
  Criminal law
    Islamic law: KBP4172
    Jewish law: KBM4418
  Yoreh deʻah law: KBM523.5.I3
Idololatria
  Canon law: KBR3644
Īfā': KBP817.2+
Iflās: KBP1942
Ignatian Council, 869: KBR262
Ignorance
  Criminal liability
    Comparative religious law: KB3896
  Legal transactions
    Ius ecclesiasticum privatum:
      KBR2290

Ignorance
  Legal transactions
    Roman Catholic law: KBU2290
  Marriage consent
    Roman Catholic law: KBU3135
Ignorance about prohibition
  Criminal law
    Roman Catholic law: KBU3557
  Justification of illegal acts
    Canon law: KBR3557
Ignorance of the law
  Islamic law: KBP500
Ignorance or error
  Ecclesiastical laws
    Roman Catholic law: KBU2219
Ignorantia vel error
  Ecclesiastical laws
    Roman Catholic law: KBU2219
Iḥtiyāṭ: KBP448.I38
Iḥyā' al-mawāt: KBP687.6
Ījāb and qabūl: KBP869.3+
Ijārah: KBP892.5+
Ijmā'
  Sources of fiqh: KBP451
Ijtihād: KBP453
Ijtihād al-ra'y: KBP453
Ijtihād versus Decree law
  Islamic law: KBP2516
Ikhtilāf: KBP465
Ikhtilās: KBP4235
Ikrāh: KBP867.5, KBP3897.I47
Īlā': KBP564
Illegal abortion
  Jewish law: KBM4070
Illegal contracts
  Comparative religious law: KB868+
  Islamic law: KBP868+
  Jewish law: KBM868+
Illegality and justification
  Military criminal law and procedure
    Jewish law: KBM3758.5
Illegitimacy
  Family law
    Jewish law: KBM612+
  Natural persons
    Canon law: KBR2239.I55
Illegitimacy
  Parent and child
    Comparative religious law: KB612
Illegitimate children
  Islamic law: KBP612+
Illegitimate performance of priestly
  functions
  Roman Catholic law: KBU3718
Illegitimately profiteering from a Mass
  stipend
  Roman Catholic law: KBU3720
Ilqá bi-al-ḥajar: KBP899
Imams: KBP185, KBP2532+
Immaterial rights
  Islamic law: KBP502.4
Immobilia (Real rights)
  Jurisdiction of ecclesiastical courts
    Canon law: KBR3795.I66
Immoral contracts
  Labor law
    Islamic law: KBP1302
    Jewish law: KBM1302
Immoral transactions
  Islamic law: KBP868+
  Void and voidable contracts
    Jewish law: KBM868+
Immovable property
  Islamic law: KBP683+
Immunitas a iure civili
  Clergy
    Canon law: KBR2339+
Immunities
  Criminal law
    Comparative religious law: KB3838
  Personal immunities
    Criminal law
      Islamic law: KBP3824.I55
Immunities of rulers
  Constitution of the state
    Islamic law: KBP2300
  Constitutional law
    Jewish law: KBM2300
Immunities, Personal
  Criminal law
    Jewish law: KBM3838.3

Immunization
  Public health laws
    Comparative religious law:
      KB3086.A+
  Public health measures
    Islamic law: KBP3086.A+
    Jewish law: KBM3085+
Impedimenta dirimentia
  Marriage
    Roman Catholic law: KBU3124+
Impedimenta matrimonii
  Canon law: KBR3120+
Impediments to inheritance
  Islamic law: KBP636
Impediments to marriage
  Canon law: KBR3120+
  Comparative religious law: KB544+
  Jewish law: KBM544+
  Marriage
    Islamic law: KBP544+
Implied consent
  Contracts
    Islamic law: KBP869.6
    Jewish law: KBM869.6
Import and export sales tax
  Islamic law: KBP3640.E96
Impotence
  Grounds for divorce
    Jewish law: KBM559.65
  Marriage impediments
    Roman Catholic law: KBU3128.I66
Impotence (antecedent and perpetual)
  Impediments to marriage
    Canon law: KBR3128.I66
Imprisonment
  Criminal law
    Comparative religious law:
      KB3993.I47
    Islamic law: KBP3992
    Jewish law: KBM3970
  Criminal procedure
    Jewish law: KBM4798
Improper driving
  Jewish law: KBM4384
Impugnatione sententiae
  Roman Catholic law: KBU3861+
Impurity
  Islamic law: KBP184.42+
Imputability (Liability)
  Criminal law
    Roman Catholic law: KBU3537+
  Violation of criminal law
    Canon law: KBR3537+
In Ḥumash: KBM3948
ʻĪnah: KBP955.4
Incapable persons
  Marriage consent
    Roman Catholic law: KBU3134+
  Validity of consent for marriage
    Canon law: KBR3134
Incapaces matrimonii contrahendi
  Canon law: KBR3134
Incapacity
  Criminal law
    Roman Catholic law: KBU3539+
  Violation of criminal law
    Canon law: KBR3539+
Incapacity and capacity
  Natural persons
    Canon law: KBR2231+
Incapacity and irregularity
  Clergy
    Canon law: KBR2331
Incapacity and limited capacity
  Criminal liability
    Comparative religious law:
      KB3882+
    Islamic law: KBP3882+
    Jewish law: KBM3882+
Incapacity due to mental illness
  Marriage consent
    Roman Catholic law: KBU3134.5
Incardination of clerics
  Canon law: KBR2333+
  Roman Catholic law: KBU2333+
Incest
  Criminal law
    Islamic law: KBP4182
    Jewish law: KBM4182
  Family law
    Jewish law: KBM544.2
  Penal (Criminal) law
    Canon law: KBR3774.I63

Incitement
  Military law
    Islamic law: KBP3760.I53
    Jewish law: KBM3760.I53
Inciting crime
  Islamic law: KBP4310
  Jewish law: KBM4310
Inciting insubordination
  Criminal law
    Islamic law: KBP4307
    Jewish law: KBM4307
Income tax
  Comparative religious law: KB3573+
  Islamic law: KBP3573+
  Jewish law: KBM3573+
Incompatibility
  Ecclesiastical offices
    Canon law: KBR2352
Incorporated business associations
  Corporation tax
    Islamic law: KBP3596+
  Islamic law: KBP1050+
  Jewish law: KBM1050+
Incurables
  Social work
    Canon law: KBR3280.I63
    Roman Catholic law: KBU3280.I63
Indemnification and damages
  Economic law
    Islamic law: KBP3247
    Jewish law: KBM3247
Indemnification for government acts
  Jewish law: KBM2824+
Independence of judges
  Islamic law: KBP1612
  Jewish law: KBM1612
Independent work
  Contracts
    Islamic law: KBP892.3
    Jewish law: KBM892.3
Indeterminate penalty
  Criminal law
    Roman Catholic law: KBU3578
Indirect causation
  Criminal act
    Islamic law: KBP3851
Indirect homicide
  Islamic law: KBP4054.5
Individual and state
  Comparative religious law: KB2430+
  Islamic law: KBP2430+
Individual freedom
  Roman Catholic law: KBU4060.I53
Individual reasoning
  Sources of fiqh
    Islamic law: KBP453.2
Individuals, Control of
  Public safety
    Islamic law: KBP3022+
    Jewish law: KBM3022
Indulgences
  Penance
    Canon law: KBR3094.I64
  Roman Catholic law: KBU3094.I64
Industrial property
  Comparative religious law: KB1155+
  Islamic law: KBP1155+
  Jewish law: KBM1155+
Industrial trusts
  Islamic law: KBP1137+
  Jewish law: KBM1137+
Industrial use of scarce materials, Prohibition of
  Islamic law: KBP3265
Infallible teaching authority
  Roman Catholic law: KBU3042
Infamia
  Vindictive penalties
    Canon law: KBR3613.I53
Infamy
  Criminal law
    Comparative religious law: KB3993.I54
    Islamic law: KBP4004
    Jewish law: KBM4004
  Vindictive penalties
    Canon law: KBR3613.I53
Infantes
  Baptism
    Canon law: KBR2229.C55
Infants
  Baptism
    Roman Catholic law: KBU2229.C55

Infants
  Capacity and incapacity
    Roman Catholic law: KBU2232.I65
  Comparative religious law: KB525
  Criminal liability
    Comparative religious law: KB3886
    Islamic law: KBP3886
    Jewish law: KBM3886
Infants (under seven years of age)
  Capacity and incapacity
    Canon law: KBR2232.I65
Infectious diseases
  Public health
    Comparative religious law: KB3080+
    Islamic law: KBP3080+
    Jewish law: KBM3080+
Infectious diseases, Measures against
  Canon law: KBR3270
  Roman Catholic law: KBU3270
Informed consent
  Biomedical engineering
    Roman Catholic law: KBU3300.I54
Informing
  Criminal law
    Jewish law: KBM4442
Inheritance
  Probate court
    Comparative religious law: KB1880
    Islamic law: KBP1880
Inheritance and heir
  Church property
    Roman Catholic law: KBU3376
Inheritance and succession
  Comparative religious law: KB632+
  Islamic law: KBP632+
  Jewish law: KBM632+
  Natural persons
    Canon law: KBR2248+
  Roman Catholic law: KBU2248+
Inheritance, Divider of
  Courts and procedure
    Islamic law: KBP1622.2
Inheritance procedure
  Probate court
    Jewish law: KBM1880
Inheritance taxes
  Jewish law: KBM3621
  Local revenue
    Comparative religious law: KB3621
  National revenue
    Comparataive religious law: KB3621
    Islamic law: KBP3621
Injunctions
  Trials
    Roman Catholic law: KBU3855
Injured party, Consent of the
  Criminal offense
    Jewish law: KBM3861
Inland shipping
  Islamic law: KBP3478
Innocent persons, Prosecuting
  Jewish law: KBM4507
Innovation
  Uṣūl al-fiqh
    Islamic law: KBP448.B53
Inquisition procedure
  Penal (criminal) procedures
    Canon law: KBR3942+
Inquisition trials
  Canon law: KBR128+
  Roman Catholic law: KBU128+
Insane persons
  Capacity and disability
    Islamic law: KBP529
  Comparative religious law: KB529
  Criminal law
    Roman Catholic law: KBU3542
  Criminal liability
    Comparative religious law: KB3884
    Islamic law: KBP3884
    Jewish law: KBM3884
  Incapacity
    Violation of criminal law
      Canon law: KBR3542
  Natural persons
    Jewish law: KBM529
Insanity
  Capacity and incapacity
    Canon law: KBR2232.I67
    Roman Catholic law: KBU2232.I67

Inscriptio in librum defunctorum
  Canon law: KBR3193
  Roman Catholic law: KBU3193
Insignia and canon law: KBR83
Insolvency
  Comparative religious law: KB1885+
  Islamic law: KBP1885+
  Jewish law: KBM1885+
Insolvent debtors
  Emergency measures
    Jewish law: KBM3717
Institutes
  Public policies in research
    Islamic law: KBP3160
Institutes of consecrated life and societies of apostolic life
  Canon law: KBR2892+
Institutes (religious), Members of
  Domicile
    Roman Catholic law: KBU2236.I67
Institutes (Religious), Members of
  Natural persons
    Canon law: KBR2236.I67
Institutio clericorum
  Canon law: KBR2322+
Institutiones sacerdotales
  Canon law: KBR2324
Institutions for the mentally ill
  Islamic law: KBP3113
Institutions for the mentally ill and/or developmentally disabled
  Jewish law: KBM3113
Institutions of higher education
  Canon law: KBR3054
Instrumenta probandi
  Trials
    Canon law: KBR3846+
Insubordination
  Military law
    Islamic law: KBP3760.I56
    Jewish law: KBM3760.I56
Insurance law
  Comparative religious law: KB998.A+
  Islamic law: KBP998+
  Jewish law: KBM998+
Intellectual and industrial property
  Comparative religious law: KB1155+
Intellectual and industrial property
  Islamic law: KBP1155+
  Jewish law: KBM1155+
Intelligentsia
  Comparative religious law: KB3515+
  Islamic law: KBP3515+
Intention
  Contracts
    Comparative religious law: KB860+
    Islamic law: KBP860+
    Jewish law: KBM860+
  Islamic law: KBP504.5
Interdict
  Penal (Criminal) law
    Canon law: KBR3607
  Roman Catholic law: KBU3606
Interdiction
  Guardianship
    Comparative religious law: KB628
    Islamic law: KBP628
  Jewish law: KBM628
Interdictum
  Penal (Criminal) law
    Canon law: KBR3607
Interest
  Loans
    Jewish law: KBM955.4
Interest device
  Banks and banking
    Islamic law: KBP955.4
Interfaith marriage
  Canon law: KBR3148+
  Islamic law: KBP546.952
  Jewish law: KBM546.2
  Roman Catholic law: KBU3148+
Interlocutory decisions
  Trials
    Canon law: KBR3858
    Roman Catholic law: KBU3858
Intermarriage
  Comparative religious law: KB546.2
International date line
  Oraḥ ḥayim law: KBM523.3.I5
International institutions, Crimes against
  Comparative religious law: KB4543
  Islamic law: KBP4543

International law and Jewish law:
KBM524.15
International relations of the Holy See
Canon law: KBR4076+
International trade
Comparative religious law: KB3405+
Islamic law: KBP3405+
Interpretation and construction
Canon law: KBR2202
Criminal law
Comparative religious law: KB3821
Islamic law: KBP3821
Jewish law: KBM3821
Jewish law development: KBM524.32
Interpretation and grammar
Islamic law: KBP461+
Interpreter of the qāḍī
Islamic law: KBP1622
Intervention
Procedure at trial
Comparative religious law:
KB1668.I68, KB1668.S48
Islamic law: KBP1668.I68
Intervention of third party
Procedure at first instance
Penal (Criminal) procedure
Roman Catholic law:
KBU3939.I67
Roman Catholic law: KBU3842.I67
Trials
Canon law: KBR3842.I67
Intestate succesion and ius spolii of the Church
Canon law: KBR3374
Intestate succession
Church property
Roman Catholic law: KBU3374
Natural persons
Canon law: KBR2248+
Roman Catholic law: KBU2248+
Intimidation of an elector, the elected, ecclesiastical ministry or authority
Roman Catholic law: KBU3694
Intoxicants
Islamic law: KBP184.42+
Intoxication
Criminal liability
Jewish law: KBM3892.I58
Defense
Criminal law
Roman Catholic law:
KBU3559.I68
Justification of illegal acts
Canon law: KBR3559.I68
Introductory petition
Courts
Roman Catholic law: KBU3839
Trials
Canon law: KBR3839
Invalid adults
Medical legislation
Jewish law: KBM3114.O42
Invalid consent and marriage
Roman Catholic law: KBU3140
Invalid marriage
Canon law: KBR3140
Comparative religious law: KB556+
Islamic law: KBP556+
Invalidity of originally valid marriage
Islamic law: KBP557.3
Inventories
Administration of church property
Roman Catholic law: KBU3444.I69
Investigation
Criminal procedure
Islamic law: KBP4636
Jewish law: KBM4636
Penal (Criminal) procedure
Roman Catholic law: KBU3933
Pretrial procedures
Comparative religious law: KB4636
Investigation, Criminal
Penal (criminal) procedures
Canon law: KBR3933
Investigation ex officio
Penal (criminal) procedures
Canon law: KBR3942+
Investments
Taxation
Islamic law: KBP3553.3

Iqrār
Assumption of debt
Islamic law: KBP816.7
Confession
Islamic law: KBP4681
Iqṭā': KBP3061
'Ire miḳlaṭ: KBM4826.5
Irregular court, Criminal proceedings by an
Islamic law: KBP4769
Jewish law: KBM4769
Irregularitas
Clergy
Canon law: KBR2331
Irrevocable divorce
Islamic law: KBP562.953
Irrigation zones, Public
Islamic law: KBP3058
Ishara ma'huda: KBP869.6
Ishtirāk: KBP674
Islam and democratic government, Compatibility of
Islamic law: KBP2035
Islam and the state: KBP173.6
Islamic law: KBP1+
Comparative religious law: KB185.A+
Islamic law and international law: KB260
Islamic law and Jewish law: KB190
Islamic law and society: KBP173.25
Islamic state
Islamic law: KBP2000+
Ismā'īlī: KBP355+
Istighlāl: KBP663
Istiḥsān: KBP454.3
Istīlā': KBP656
Istīlād: KBP529.5
Istinjā': KBP184.45
Istiṣḥāb: KBP457
Istiṣlāḥ: KBP456
Istiṣnā': KBP877.4
Istithnā': KBP462.I78
Isur hana'ah: KBM524.4.W75
I'tāq: KBP529.53
Ithbāt al-nasab: KBP619.I75
Ithna'asharis: KBP365+
Itinerants
Jurisdiction of ecclesiastical courts
Canon law: KBR3787.I85
Itlāf: KBP842.8
'Itq: KBP529.53
Iudex supremus
Roman Catholic law: KBU3811
Iudicium arbitrale
Ecclesiastical courts
Canon law: KBR3918
Iuramentum vanum and iuramentum iniustum
Penal (Criminal) law
Canon law: KBR3668
Iurisdictio mandata
Ecclesiastical courts
Canon law: KBR3784
Iurisdictio ordinaria vel delegata
Ecclesiastical courts
Canon law: KBR3784
Ius canonicum et competentia civilis potestatis
Marriage: KBR3116
Ius circa sacra, Theory of
Canon law: KBR4037
Ius civile
Conflict of laws
Canon law: KBR2199.C59
Ius ecclesiasticum privatum
Canon law: KBR2224+
Ius legatos nominandi
The Pope
Canon law: KBR2383
Ius naturale et ius divinum: KBR2190
Roman Catholic law: KBU2190
Ius novas nuptias contrahendi
Canon law: KBR3160
Roman Catholic law: KBU3160
Ius patronatus (reale and personale)
Ecclesiastical offices
Canon law: KBR2361+
Ius patronatus regium
Canon law: KBR2362.4
Ius publicum ecclesiae
Canon law: KBR4000+
Roman Catholic law: KBU4000+
'Iwaḍ: KBP879.3+

J

Jadal: KBP466
Ja'faris: KBP365+
Janīn: KBP524.72
Jānin
  Inheritance and succession
    Islamic law: KBP634.953.J35
Jarā'im: KBP4040.92+
Jerusalem, Council of, 45 (48?): KBR199.82
Jerusalem, Council of, 56 (55?): KBR199.83
Jewelry
  Islamic law: KBP184.9.J38
Jewish community
  Constitutional principles: KBM2070+
    Jewish law: KBM2129+
  Cooperation with secular state government: KBM2380
  Relations with non-Jews: KBM2400
Jewish councils in occupied Europe, 1939-1945: KBM2612.J83
Jewish law: KBM1+
  Comparative religious law: KB180.A+
  Compared with civil law and Roman law: KB201+
  Influence on Islamic law: KBP469
Jewish law and international law: KB259
Jewish law and Islamic law: KB190
Jewishness
  Natural persons
    Jewish law: KBM529.83
Jews
  Jurisdiction of ecclesiastical courts
    Canon law: KBR3787.J49
Ji'ālah: KBP895
Jihād: KBP182+
  Foreign relations
    Islamic law: KBP2416
Jizyah: KBP3680.J59
Joinder of actions
  Judiciary
    Canon law: KBR3836
  Procedure at first instance
    Roman Catholic law: KBU3841.2
Joinder of actions
  Trial
    Canon law: KBR3841.2
Joinder of issue
  Procedure at first instance
    Penal (Criminal) procedure
      Roman Catholic law: KBU3938
    Roman Catholic law: KBU3841.5
  Trial
    Canon law: KBR3841.5
Joint obligations
  Islamic law: KBP812
  Jewish law: KBM812
Joint ownership
  Property
    Comparative religious law: KB674
    Islamic law: KBP674
    Jewish law: KBM674
Joint ventures
  Industrial trusts
    Islamic law: KBP1139
    Jewish law: KBM1139
Journalists
  Comparative religious law: KB3500+
  Islamic law: KBP3504.3
Judenrat: KBM2612.J83
Judgements
  Trials
    Canon law: KBR3857
Judges
  Appointment of, for an ad hoc bet din: KBM1619
  Comparative religious law: KB1610
  Islamic law: KBP1610+
  Jewish law: KBM1610+
  Rota Romana (Tribunal ordinarium)
    Roman Catholic law: KBU3816.5
  The legal profession
    Canon law: KBR3823+
Judges and other court officials
  Canon law: KBR3807+
  Roman Catholic law: KBU3823+
  Rota Romana
    Canon law: KBR3816.5+

Judgment
  Courts and procedure
    Criminal procedure
      Islamic law: KBP4736+
      Jewish law: KBM4738
  Criminal procedure
    Comparative religious law:
      KB4738+
  Execution of
    Courts
      Jewish law: KBM1690
Judgment by default
  Trials
    Canon law: KBR3842.J84
Judgments by default
  Procedure at first instance
    Roman Catholic law: KBU3842.J84
Judicial and administrative powers
  The Pope
    Canon law: KBR2375
Judicial decisions
  Comparative religious law: KB1679+
  Criminal procedure
    Comparative religious law:
      KB4738+
    Islamic law: KBP4736+
    Jewish law: KBM4736+
  Islamic law: KBP1679+
  Jewish law: KBM1679+
  Penal (Criminal) procedure
    Roman Catholic law: KBU3947+
  Penal (criminal) procedures
    Canon law: KBR3944+
  Roman Catholic law: KBU3854+
  Trials
    Canon law: KBR3854+
Judicial decrees
  Trials
    Canon law: KBR3859
    Roman Catholic law: KBU3859
Judicial discretion
  Criminal law
    Roman Catholic law: KBU3577+
  Criminal procedure
    Comparative religious law:
      KB4738+
    Islamic law: KBP4740
Judicial discretion
  Criminal procedure
    Jewish law: KBM4740
  Penal (Criminal) law
    Canon law: KBR3577+
Judicial error
  Procedure in general
    Jewish law: KBM1679.5
Judicial independence
  Islamic law: KBP1612
  Jewish law: KBM1612
Judicial mistakes
  Procedure in general
    Jewish law: KBM1679.5
Judicial opinions
  Comparative religious law: KB1679.3
  Islamic law: KBP1679.3
  Jewish law: KBM1679.3
Judicial power
  Dioceses
    Canon law: KBR2837
  Dioceses and diocesan bishop
    Roman Catholic law: KBU2837
  The Pope
    Roman Catholic law: KBU2375
Judicial review of administrative acts
  Canon law: KBR3960+
  Roman Catholic law: KBU3964+
Judicial review of ecclesiastical
  administrative acts
  Canon law: KBR3803
  Roman Catholic law: KBU3803
Judiciary
  Canon law: KBR3780+
Judiciary and foreign relations
  Jewish law: KBM1574
Jum'ah: KBP186.15
Jura in re
  Comparative religious law: KB646+
Jurisdiction
  Abbot primate
    Roman Catholic law: KBU2915
  Apostolic See
    Dispensation of marriage
      Roman Catholic law: KBU3908
  Criminal procedure
    Comparative religious law: KB4666

Jurisdiction
  Criminal procedure
    Islamic law: KBP4666
    Jewish law: KBM4666
  Legati nati
    Canon law: KBR4088
  Matrimonial actions
    Courts
      Roman Catholic law: KBU3887+
    Judiciary
      Canon law: KBR3887+
  Metropolitans
    Canon law: KBR2805
  Organs of government
    Canon law: KBR2364
  Papal legation
    Canon law: KBR4084+
    Roman Catholic law: KBU4084
  Penal procedures
    Canon law: KBR3937
  Procedure at first instance
    Penal (Criminal) procedure
      Roman Catholic law: KBU3937
    Roman Catholic law: KBU3840.5+
  Procedure in general
    Comparative religious law: KB1664
    Islamic law: KBP1664
    Jewish law: KBM1664
  Rota Romana (Tribunal ordinarium)
    Roman Catholic law: KBU3816.3
  Sacred Penitentiary
    Roman Catholic law: KBU3813
  Supreme Tribunal of the Apostolic Signatura
    Roman Catholic law: KBU3820
  Trial
    Canon law: KBR3840.5+
  Tribunal of the Apostolic Signatura
    Canon law: KBR3820
  Tribunals of the Apostolic See
    Canon law: KBR3813
Jurisdiction of ecclesiastical courts
  Canon law: KBR3783.92+
Jurisdiction of ecclesiastical courts (General)
  Roman Catholic law: KBU3782.62+
Jurisdiction of the civil courts
  Matrimonial actions
    Canon law: KBR3889
Jurisdiction over education and the state's cultural mandate
  Roman Catholic law: KBU4062
Jurisdiction over marriage and civil marriage law
  Roman Catholic law: KBU4057
Jurisdiction, Spiritual and temporal
  Church and state
    Roman Catholic law: KBU4050+
Jurisdictions, Conflict of
  Church and state
    Canon law: KBR4052
Jurisprudence
  Religious law: KB2+
Jurisprudence, Canonical: KBR2160+
Juristic (moral) persons
  Roman Catholic law: KBU2253+
Juristic (moral) persons and non-collegiate institutes
  Canon law: KBR3450+
Juristic personality
  Conference of Bishops
    Canon law: KBR2827
    Roman Catholic law: KBU2827
  Ecclesiastical Provinces
    Canon law: KBR2798
  Ecclesiastical provinces and regions
    Roman Catholic law: KBU2798
Juristic personality of seminaries
  Roman Catholic law: KBU2326
Juristic persons
  Associations
    Islamic law: KBP1040+
  Canon law: KBR2253+
  Capacity to sue and to be sued
    Roman Catholic law: KBU3833.J87
  Capaticy to sue
    Canon law: KBR3833.J87
  Corporations
    Islamic law: KBP1040+
  Jewish law: KBM530
  Property tax
    Islamic law: KBP3616+, KBP3663

Juristic persons of private law
  Canon law: KBR2266
Juristic persons of public law
  Canon law: KBR2262
Juristic persons of public or private law
  Roman Catholic law: KBU2256+
Jurists and canonists
  Canon law: KBR1570+
Just price
  Economic law
    Comparative religious law: KB3210
Justice and law
  Jewish law: KBM524.12
  Uṣūl al-fiqh
    Islamic law: KBP442
Justification
  Military criminal law and procedure
    Jewish law: KBM3758.5
Justification of illegal acts
  Criminal law
    Roman Catholic law: KBU3548+
Justification of otherwise prohibited acts
  Comparative religious law: KB3855+
  Islamic law: KBP3855+
  Jewish law: KBM3855+
Juvenile delinquency
  Criminal procedure
    Comparative religious law: KB4720
    Islamic law: KBP4720
    Jewish law: KBM4720
Juveniles
  Criminal liability
    Comparative religious law: KB3886
    Islamic law: KBP3886
    Jewish law: KBM3886

K

Kafā'ah: KBP528.K33, KBP543.957
Kafālah: KBP609, KBP900
Kaffārah: KBP3979
Kāfil: KBP900
Karaites
  Marriage
    Jewish law: KBM546.3.K37
Kātib: KBP1621, KBP1846+
Kavanah
  Jewish law: KBM3867
Kawad: KBP3951
Kehillah: KBM2000+
Ḳeṭanim: KBM525
  Criminal liability
    Jewish law: KBM3886
Ketubah: KBM546.13
  Economic document: KBM572
Ketubah, Payment of
  Jewish law: KBM567
Khalīfah: KBP2532+
Khamr: KBP184.42+
Kharāj: KBP3670+
Khaṣm: KBP1655+
Khāṣṣ: KBP462.K45
Khatā': KBP3870
Khaṭa': KBP867.3
Khefiyah: KBM562.4
Khiyānah: KBP4250
Khiyār: KBP858.5.K45
Khul': KBP563.4
Khuṣūmah: KBP1666+
Khuṭubāh: KBP543+
Ḳiddushin
  Jewish law: KBM546.15
Kidnapping
  Extortionate kidnapping
    Jewish law: KBM4120
  Kidnapping for sale
    Jewish law: KBM4121
  Parental kidnapping
    Criminal law
      Jewish law: KBM4188
    Family law
      Jewish law: KBM602
  Roman Catholic law: KBU3760
Kidnapping, Extortionate
  Comparative religious law: KB4120
  Islamic law: KBP4120
Kidnapping for sale
  Comparative religious law: KB4121
  Islamic law: KBP4121
Kidnapping, Parental
  Family law
    Islamic law: KBP602
Ḳidushe ṭa'ut: KBM556

Killing on request
  Jewish law: KBM4056
Kimi: KBP643
Kings, princes, and rulers
  Comparative religious law: KB2532+
  Constitutional law
    Islamic law: KBP2532+
Kingship
  Constitutional history
    Jewish law: KBM2129+
Kinship
  Comparative religious law: KB583+
  Criminal law
    Islamic law: KBP4023.K56
  Jewish law: KBM583+
Ḳinyanim
  Jewish law: KBM524.4.K55
Kitābah: KBP529.5
Knasim: KBM3976
Koran: KBP100+
  Sources of fiqh: KBP449
Kosher food
  Excise taxes
    Jewish law: KBM3640.K66
Kosher meat
  Excise taxes
    Jewish law: KBM3640.K66

L

l Acquisition and oss of ownership
  Property
    Islamic law: KBP655+
Labeling
  Economic law
    Comparative religious law: KB3268
    Islamic law: KBP3268
    Jewish law: KBM3268
Labeling of processed food
  Jewish law: KBM3378
Labor contract and employment
  Islamic law: KBP1279+
  Jewish law: KBM1279+
Labor laws and legislation
  Comparative religious law: KB1270+
  Islamic law: KBP1270+
  Jewish law: KBM1270+
Labor Office of the Holy See
  Roman Catholic law: KBU2780
Lā'iḥah (Amendments)
  Sources of fiqh
    Islamic law: KBP458.L35
Laity, Obligations and rights of the
  Canon law: KBR2316+
Lakes
  Public property
    Comparative religious law: KB3046+
    Islamic law: KBP3046+
    Jewish law: KBM3046+
Land
  Expropriation or appropriation by the state
    Islamic law: KBP2825+
Land appropriation
  Comparative religious law: KB2829
Land development
  Comparative religious law: KB3056
  Islamic law: KBP3057+
Land grants, State
  Islamic law: KBP3061
Land holdings
  Church property
    Roman Catholic law: KBU3410+
Land holdings (Church lands)
  Canon law: KBR3410+
Land law
  Comparative religious law: KB683+
  Islamic law: KBP683+
  Jewish law: KBM683+
Land lease
  Comparative religious law: KB884.R43
  Islamic law: KBP884.R43
  Jewish law: KBM884.R43
Land ownership
  Comparative religious law: KB683+
Land policy
  Islamic law: KBP3056
Land policy legislation
  Jewish law: KBM3293
Land reform
  Public land law
    Islamic law: KBP3056

Land register
  Comparative religious law: KB737
  Islamic law: KBP737
  Jewish law: KBM737+
Land settlement
  Islamic law: KBP3060
Land systems legislation
  Islamic law: KBP3056
Land tax
  Islamic law: KBP3670+
  National and local revenue
    Comparative religious law: KB3670
Land tenancy
  Comparative religious law: KB683+
Land titles, Registration of
  Comparative religious law: KB737
Land use policy
  Islamic law: KBP3056
Landlord and tenant
  Comparative religious law: KB880+
  Islamic law: KBP880+
  Jewish law: KBM880+
Language
  Comparative religious law: KB3137.8
  Human rights
    Islamic law: KBP2468.L36
    Jewish law: KBM2468.L36
  Islamic law: KBP3137.9
  Jewish law: KBM3137.9+
Language, Legal
  Canon law: KBR2203
  Roman Catholic law: KBU2203
Laqīṭ: KBP619.L34
Larceny
  Comparative religious law: KB4235
  Islamic law: KBP4235
  Jewish law: KBM4234
Large families
  Social service
    Islamic law: KBP1531
    Jewish law: KBM1531
Lashing
  Criminal law punishment
    Comparative religious law:
      KB3980.F57
Last will
  Church property
    Roman Catholic law: KBU3355+
  Natural persons
    Canon law: KBR2249+
    Roman Catholic law: KBU2249+
Lateran Treaty
  Roman Catholic law: KBU4064
Law and gospel
  Canon law: KBR2155
  Roman Catholic law: KBU2155
Law and justice
  Jewish law: KBM524.12
  Uṣūl al-fiqh
    Islamic law: KBP442
Law criticism
  Comparative religious law: KB410
  Islamic law: KBP470
Law development, Methodology of
  Jewish law: KBM524.32+
Law enforcement
  Military law
    Comparative religious law: KB3780
    Islamic law: KBP3780+
    Jewish law: KBM3780+
Law, Islamic: KBP1+
Law, Jewish: KBM1+
Law-making power and process
  Comparative religious law: KB2510
Law of fast
  Canon law: KBR3252
  Roman Catholic law: KBU3252
Law of the Roman Catholic Church:
  KBU2+
Law reform: KBM524.38
  Criminal law
    Islamic law: KBP3790
    Jewish law: KBM3790
  Islamic law: KBP470
Law reform and policies
  Comparative religious law: KB410
Laylat al-Barā'ah: KBP186.38
Laylat al-Mi'rāj: KBP186.36
Laylat al-Qadr: KBP186.43
Leaders, Duties of
  Jewish law: KBM2250.3

Lease
  Contract for service and labor
    Islamic law: KBP892.5+
  Contracts
    Comparative religious law: KB880+
    Jewish law: KBM880+
  Landlord and tenant
    Islamic law: KBP880+
Legacies
  Comparative religious law: KB635.2
  Islamic law: KBP635.952
  Jewish law: KBM635.2
Legal and international status of the Holy See
  Canon law: KBR4064+
Legal archaeology
  Islamic law: KBP53.5
Legal artifices
  Substantive law
    Islamic law: KBP496
Legal aspects
  Observances and practice of Islam: KBP174+
Legal bibliography
  Religious law in general: KB130+
Legal capacity and disability
  Comparative religious law: KB524.7+
Legal certainty
  Roman Catholic law: KBU2196.3
Legal conformism
  Sources of fiqh
    Islamic law: KBP454
Legal disputation, Rules of
  Islamic law: KBP466
Legal education
  Canon law: KBR133+, KBR3822.5
  Comparative religious law: KB133, KB1600+
  Islamic law: KBP42+
  Roman Catholic law: KBU133, KBU3822.5
Legal effect of divorce
  Islamic law: KBP558+
Legal equality
  Jewish law: KBM2465+
Legal hermeneutics
  Canon law: KBR2202
Legal hermeneutics
  Comparative religious law: KB3821
  Criminal law
    Islamic law: KBP3821
    Jewish law: KBM3821
  Jewish law: KBM524.32
Legal implications of acts and facts
  Islamic law: KBP504
Legal instruments
  Courts and procedure
    Jewish law: KBM1847
  Notaries
    Comparative religious law: KB1847
    Islamic law: KBP1847
Legal language
  Canon law: KBR2203
  Jewish law: KBM524.33
Legal majority
  Persons
    Comparative religious law: KB525
    Islamic law: KBP525+
Legal maxims
  Roman Catholic law: KBU100
Legal maxims and canon law: KBR100.A+
Legal minority
  Persons
    Comparative religious law: KB525
    Islamic law: KBP525+
Legal opinions
  Rota Romana
    Canon law: KBR3817.3
Legal order
  Jewish law: KBM524.2+
Legal personality
  Juristic persons
    Canon law: KBR2254
  Roman Catholic law: KBU2254
Legal positivism and contemporary
  Jewish law: KBM524.17
Legal process, Abuse of
  Islamic law: KBP4507.5
Legal profession
  Comparative religious law: KB1600+
  Islamic law: KBP1600+
  Jewish law: KBM1600+

Legal profession in general
Canon law: KBR3822+
Roman Catholic law: KBU3822+
Legal qualification
Uṣūl al-fiqh
Islamic law: KBP447
Legal research
Islamic law: KBP41
Religious law in general: KB130+
Legal scholars, Religious
Islamic law: KBP185
Legal schools
Islamic law: KBP250+
Legal semantics
Canon law: KBR2203
Jewish law: KBM524.33
Legal sharers
Inheritance and succession
Comparative religious law: KB634
Legal status
Clergy
Canon law: KBR2337+
Roman Catholic law: KBU2336+
Dynasty (Heads of state)
Comparative religious law: KB2535.D96
Married women
Comparative religious law: KB549
Islamic law: KBP550+
Muslim women
Islamic law: KBP526+
Legal status of married women
Jewish law: KBM550+
Legal symbolism and canon law: KBR78
Legal transactions
Administrative process
Islamic law: KBP2754
Ius ecclesiasticum privatum: KBR2286+
Roman Catholic law: KBU2286+
Legality
Constitution of the state
Islamic law: KBP2250
Constitutional law
Jewish law: KBM2250
Legates
Roman Catholic law: KBU4080+
Legates, Right to nominate
The Pope
Canon law: KBR2383
Legati
Organs of government
Canon law: KBR2482+
Legati missi and nuntii apostolici
Canon law: KBR4086
Legati nati
Canon law: KBR4087+
Legati pontificii
Roman Catholic law: KBU4080+
Legislative power
Conference of Bishops
Canon law: KBR2830
Roman Catholic law: KBU2830
Dioceses
Canon law: KBR2837
Dioceses and diocesan bishop
Roman Catholic law: KBU2837
Islamic law: KBP2510+
Jewish law: KBM2510+
The Pope
Canon law: KBR2372+
Roman Catholic law: KBU2372+
Legislative power and process
Comparative religious law: KB2510
Legislative process
Islamic law: KBP2516
Jewish law: KBM2510+
Legislature
Comparative religious law: KB2510
Legitimacy
Blood sacrifices
Islamic law: KBP184.62.L43
Constitution of the state
Islamic law: KBP2240
Constitutional law
Jewish law: KBM2240
Legitimacy, Presumption of
Children
Marriage bond
Canon law: KBR3157

Legitimae tutelae causa contra iniustum agere
Criminal law
Roman Catholic law: KBU3552
Justification of illegal acts
Canon law: KBR3552
Legitimi praesumuntur filii
Marriage bond
Canon law: KBR3157
Leprosy patients
Social work
Canon law: KBR3280.L46
Roman Catholic law: KBU3280.L46
Lesbians
Equality before the law
Jewish law: KBM2467.G37
Letters
Non-governmental delivery of
Jewish law: KBM3485.7
Levies
Support for the Church
Canon law: KBR3392
Levirate marriage
Jewish law: KBM563
Lewd acts
Offenses of clerics
Penal (Criminal) law
Canon law: KBR3751
Penal (Criminal) law
Canon law: KBR3774.L49
Lewd acts with children
Islamic law: KBP4208
Lewd acts with persons incapable of resistance
Islamic law: KBP4204
Lex abstinentiae
Canon law: KBR3252
Roman Catholic law: KBU3252
Liability
Communal agencies
Islamic law: KBP2840
Contract for work and labor
Islamic law: KBP893.5
Jewish law: KBM893.5
Contracts for work and labor
Comparative religious law: KB893+
Liability
Criminal liability
Jewish law: KBM3878+
Delicts
Comparative religious law: KB839
Islamic law: KBP839+
Jewish law: KBM834.9+
Government liability
Islamic law: KBP2840
Health professions
Islamic law: KBP3100+
Jewish law: KBM3100+
Inheritance and succession
Islamic law: KBP634.957
Jewish law: KBM634.7
Legal transactions
Ius ecclesiasticum privatum: KBR2294
Roman Catholic law: KBU2294
Limited partnership
Islamic law: KBP1047.6
Jewish law: KBM1047.6
Torts
Islamic law: KBP839+
Unlimited commercial partnership
Islamic law: KBP1045.6
Jewish law: KBM1045.6
Liability for emotional distress
Jewish law: KBM853.E47
Liability for environmental damages
Jewish law: KBM852.4
Liability for sports accidents
Jewish law: KBM848
Liability for the torts of others
Islamic law: KBP839.7
Jewish law: KBM839.7
Liability of communal agencies
Jewish law: KBM2840
Liʻān: KBP564.2.L52
Libel and slander
Torts
Jewish law: KBM842.8
Libelli iudicii
Penal (criminal) procedures
Canon law: KBR3932

Libellus accusationis
  Penal (Criminal) procedure
    Roman Catholic law: KBU3932
Libellus litis introductorius
  Courts
    Roman Catholic law: KBU3839
  Trials
    Canon law: KBR3839
Libellus of accusation
  Penal (Criminal) procedure
    Roman Catholic law: KBU3932
Liberty of contract
  Comparative religious law: KB858.3
  Islamic law: KBP858.3
  Jewish law: KBM858.3
Librarians
  Comparative religious law: KB3179
  Islamic law: KBP3179
  Jewish law: KBM3179
Libraries
  Comparative religious law: KB3179
  Islamic law: KBP3179
  Jewish law: KBM3179
Licenses
  Police and public safety
    Jewish law: KBM3002
Licensing
  Artisans
    Jewish law: KBM3428
  Energy policy
    Islamic law: KBP3431.25
  Health professions
    Islamic law: KBP3100+
    Jewish law: KBM3100+
  Regulation of industry, trade, and commerce
    Islamic law: KBP3273
    Jewish law: KBM3273
  Trade within the Jewish community
    Jewish law: KBM3419
Licensing contracts
  Contracts and combinations in restraint of trade
    Islamic law: KBP3237
Liens
  Contract
    Work contract
      Jewish law: KBM894
  Contract for work and labor
    Islamic law: KBP894
  Landlord
    Comparative religious law: KB881.3
    Islamic law: KBP881.3
    Jewish law: KBM881.3
Life
  Constitution of the state
    Islamic law: KBP2484.5
Life annuity
  Contracts
    Comparative religious law: KB898.5
Ligamen
  Impediments to marriage
    Canon law: KBR3128.L55
Light industries
  Manufacturing
    Jewish law: KBM3372+
Limitation of actions
  Criminal law
    Comparative religious law: KB4038
    Islamic law: KBP4038
    Jewish law: KBM4038
  Islamic law: KBP507+
  Procedure at trial
    Islamic law: KBP1667.L55
Limited capacity
  Criminal law
    Roman Catholic law: KBU3556
  Criminal liability
    Comparative religious law: KB3882+
    Islamic law: KBP3882+
    Jewish law: KBM3882+
  Justification of illegal acts
    Canon law: KBR3556
Limited liability partnership
  Islamic law: KBP1047+
  Jewish law: KBM1047+
Limited partnership
  Islamic law: KBP1047+
  Jewish law: KBM1047+

Linea
  Consanguinity
    Roman Catholic law: KBU2238
  Natural persons
    Canon law: KBR2238
Lineage and degree
  Consanguinity
    Roman Catholic law: KBU2238
  Natural persons
    Canon law: KBR2238
Liquidation
  Cooperative societies
    Islamic law: KBP1134
    Jewish law: KBM1134
  Stock companies
    Jewish law: KBM1085
  Stock corporations
    Islamic law: KBP1085
Lis pendens
  Courts
    Roman Catholic law: KBU3837.L57
  Judiciary
    Canon law: KBR3837.L57
  Procedure at first instance
    Roman Catholic law: KBU3841.3
  Procedure at trial
    Islamic law: KBP1667.L58
  Trial
    Canon law: KBR3841.3
Literature
  Canon law: KBR3064+
Literature (books, magazines, the press, etc.)
  Roman Catholic law: KBU3065
Litigants
  Courts
    Jewish law: KBM1657
  Procedure in general
    Islamic law: KBP1657
Litigation
  Courts and procedure
    Comparative religious law: KB1666+
    Islamic law: KBP1666+
Liturgical objects and memorials
  Islamic law: KBP184.95+
Liturgical objects industry
  Jewish law: KBM3373.L57
Liturgy of the hours
  Canon law: KBR3184
  Roman Catholic law: KBU3184
Livestock industry
  Islamic law: KBP3327+
  Jewish law: KBM3327+
Living will
  Comparative religious law: KB3121.7
  Jewish law: KBM3121.7
Loan for use
  Contracts
    Comparative religious law: KB890
    Jewish law: KBM890
Loan of non-fungibles
  Islamic law: KBP879.4
  Jewish law: KBM879.23
Loans
  Banks and banking
    Islamic law: KBP955+
    Jewish law: KBM955+
Loans and leases
  Church property
    Roman Catholic law: KBU3338
Loans for consumption
  Contracts
    Islamic law: KBP891
Loca pia
  Church property
    Canon law: KBR3460
  Juristic persons
    Roman Catholic law: KBU3460
Loca sacra
  Canon law: KBR3230+
Local Church government
  Roman Catholic law: KBU4112+
Local finance
  Jewish law: KBM3655+
Local government
  Islamic law: KBP2920+
Local revenue
  Comparative religious law: KB3540+
Locatio conductio
  Comparative religious law: KB892.5
  Contracts for service and labor
    Islamic law: KBP892.5+

Logic
  Islamic law: KBP461+
Lord's Supper
  Canon law: KBR3085+
  Roman Catholic law: KBU3085+
Loss of civil rights
  Criminal law punishment
    Jewish law: KBM4004
Loss of clerical state
  Canon law: KBR2344+
  Roman Catholic law: KBU2344+
Loss of ecclesiastical office
  Roman Catholic law: KBU2358
Loss of ownership
  Land law
    Jewish law: KBM687.5+
  Property
    Comparative religious law: KB655+, KB673
    Islamic law: KBP673
    Jewish law: KBM672
    Real property
      Comparative religious law: KB687.5+
Losses
  Income tax deductions
    Islamic law: KBP3582.3.A+
    Jewish law: KBM3582+
Lost persons
  Inheritance and succession
    Islamic law: KBP634.953.L67
Lost profits
  Obligations
    Jewish law: KBM842+
Lost property
  Islamic law: KBP657
  Jewish law: KBM657
Lotteries
  Aleatory contracts
    Jewish law: KBM899.3
  Control of
    Jewish law: KBM3036.5.G35
Luqāṭah: KBP658

M

Ma'akeh
  Building and construction: KBM3072.R65
Madhāhib: KBP250+
Mafqūd: KBP524.8
Magen David adom: KBM3108.M33
Magia superstitiosa seu diabolica
  Penal (Criminal) law
    Canon law: KBR3648.M35
Magisterium
  Canon law: KBR3040+
  Roman Catholic law: KBU3040+
Maḥākim: KBP1580+
Maḥārim: KBP544+
Maḥḍar: KBP1623
Mahjurs
  Guardianship interdiction
    Islamic law: KBP628
Mahr: KBP543.953+
  Dissolved marriage: KBP567
Mail
  Non-governmental delivery of
    Jewish law: KBM3485.7
Mail-order businesses
  Trade regulation
    Jewish law: KBM3420.M34
Maintenace and restoration
  Church buildings
    Roman Catholic law: KBU3417+
Maintenance
  Church buildings
    Canon law: KBR3417
Maioritas and ius praecedentiae
  Canon law: KBR2356+
Majāz: KBP462.M35
Majnūn: KBP529
Major superior
  Religious institutes
    Canon law: KBR2915
Majority
  Capacity and incapacity
    Canon law: KBR2232.M35
    Roman Catholic law: KBU2232.M35

Majority, Legal
  Persons
    Comparative religious law: KB525
    Islamic law: KBP525+
Makot: KBM3980.F55
Māl: KBP640+
Māl manqūl: KBP643, KBP675
Male slave
  Capacity and disability
    Islamic law: KBP529.3+
Male slaves
  Comparative religious law: KB529.3+
Malik: KBP2532+
Mālik: KBP646+
Mālikī school of thought: KBP315+
Malingering
  Military law
    Islamic law: KBP3760.S44
    Jewish law: KBM3760.S44
Malpractice, Medical
  Islamic law: KBP3100.5
  Jewish law: KBM3100.5
Malshinim: KBM4442
Mamzer: KBM613, KBM619.P38
Mamzerim: KBM544.8
Mamzerut: KBM612+
Mandate
  Contracts
    Comparative religious law: KB864
    Islamic law: KBP864
    Jewish law: KBM864
Manfaʻah: KBP715
Manpower control
  Emergency measures
    Islamic law: KBP3714+
    Jewish law: KBM3714
Manslaughter
  Comparative religious law: KB4050+, KB4070
  Islamic law: KBP4050+
  Jewish law: KBM4054
Manufacturing industries
  Regulation
    Islamic law: KBP3372+
    Jewish law: KBM3372+
Manumission
  Comparative religious law: KB529.5.M35
  Islamic law: KBP529.53
Maqāṣid al-sharīʻah: KBP442
Mar'ah: KBP526+
Marine insurance
  Jewish law: KBM985
Marital bed, Separation from
  Matrimonial actions
    Islamic law: KBP564
Marital property
  Islamic law: KBP569+
Marital property and regime
  Comparative religious law: KB569+
  Jewish law: KBM569+
Maritime contracts
  Comparative religious law: KB970+
  Islamic law: KBP970+
  Jewish law: KBM970+
Maritime courts
  Islamic law: KBP984.5
  Jewish law: KBM984.5
Maritime law
  Comparative religious law: KB970+
  Islamic law: KBP970+
  Jewish law: KBM970+
Marketing cooperatives
  Jewish law: KBM3317
Marketing orders
  Agriculture
    Islamic law: KBP3320+
Markets
  Retail trade
    Jewish law: KBM3420.M37
Marriage
  Canon law: KBR3109+
  Comparative religious law: KB542+
  Islamic law: KBP542+
  Jewish law: KBM542+
  Offenses against marriage, family, and family status
    Jewish law: KBM4180+
  Registration
    Comparative religious law: KB1860
  Registration of
    Islamic law: KBP1860

Marriage
  Roman Catholic law: KBU3109.2+
Marriage age
  Comparative religious law: KB542+
  Islamic law: KBP543.955
  Marriage impediments
    Canon law: KBR3128.M37
    Roman Catholic law: KBU3128.M37
Marriage, Attempted, of a cleric
  Roman Catholic law: KBU3742
Marriage bond
  Canon law: KBR3155+
  Roman Catholic law: KBU3155+
Marriage contracts
  Islamic law: KBP572
Marriage dispensation
  Church taxes and fees
    Roman Catholic law: KBU3392.M37
Marriage law
  Canon law: KBR3109+
Marriage of a cleric, Attempted
  Penal (Criminal) law
    Canon law: KBR3742
Marriage registers
  Canon law: KBR3146
Marriage settlements
  Canon law: KBR3113
  Roman Catholic law: KBU3113
Marriage to non-Jews
  Jewish law: KBM546.2
Marriage, Valid
  Affinity
    Canon law: KBR2242
Married women
  Legal status
    Islamic law: KBP550+
Married women, Legal status of
  Comparative religious law: KB549
Martyrs
  Biography
    Islamic law history: KBP72
Maskan: KBP548
Maṣlaḥah: KBP442, KBP456
Mass
  Celebration of
    Canon law: KBR3087+
    Roman Catholic law: KBU3087+
Mass events
  Public safety
    Jewish law: KBM3035.5
Mass media
  Comparative religious law: KB3482+
  Islamic law: KBP3482+
  Jewish law: KBM3482+
  Roman Catholic law: KBU3064+
Mass obligations and legacies
  Roman Catholic law: KBU3454
Mass stipends
  Canon law: KBR3390
  Church taxes and fees
    Roman Catholic law: KBU3392.M38
Master and servant
  Comparative religious law: KB892+
  Contracts
    Islamic law: KBP892+
    Jewish law: KBM892+
Maternity
  Comparative religious law: KB616.5+
  Jewish law: KBM616.5+
Matrilineal ascendants and descendants
  Jewish law: KBM544.2
Matrilineal descendants
  Comparative religious law: KB616.5+
Matrimonial actions
  Comparative religious law: KB555+
  Courts
    Roman Catholic law: KBU3885+
  Islamic law: KBP555+
  Jewish law: KBM555+
  Judiciary
    Canon law: KBR3885+
Matrimonial consent
  Canon law: KBR3132+
  Roman Catholic law: KBU3132+
Matrimonial domicile
  Islamic law: KBP548
  Jewish law: KBM548
Matrimonio rato et non consummato
  Canon law: KBR3907+
Matrimonium irritum
  Canon law: KBR3140
Matrimonium per procuratorem
  Roman Catholic law: KBU3137

Matrimonium ratum et consummatum
Roman Catholic law: KBU3114
Matrimonium validum
Affinity
Canon law: KBR2242
Ma'tūh: KBP529
Mawānī: KBP636
Mawlid al-Nabī: KBP186.34
Maẓālim: KBP1588.4
Meat industry
Regulation
Islamic law: KBP3383
Jewish law: KBM3383
Meat products industry
Regulation
Jewish law: KBM3383
Media of social communication
Roman Catholic law: KBU3064+
Medical devices
Medical legislation
Islamic law: KBP3119.M43
Jewish law: KBM3119.M43
Medical ethics
Jewish law: KBM3098.5
Medical ethics and legislation
Roman Catholic law: KBU3282+
Medical instruments and apparatus
Medical legislation
Comparative religious law: KB3119.M43
Islamic law: KBP3119.M43
Jewish law: KBM3119.M43
Medical legislation
Comparative religious law: KB3098+
Islamic law: KBP3098+
Jewish law: KBM3098+
Medical personnel
Jewish law: KBM3100+
Medical professions, Auxiliary
Islamic law: KBP3104+
Jewish law: KBM3104+
Medical technology
Medical legislation
Islamic law: KBP3115+
Jewish law: KBM3115+
Roman Catholic law: KBU3290+
Medicinal penalties
Criminal law
Roman Catholic law: KBU3520+
Penal (Criminal) law
Canon law: KBR3520+
Medicine
Human experimentation in
Jewish law: KBM3115+
Membership
Cooperative societies
Islamic law: KBP1131
Jewish law: KBM1131
Monasticism
Roman Catholic law: KBU2927.M46
Religious institutes
Canon law: KBR2927.M46
The Jewish community
Jewish law: KBM2447+
Membership, Church
Roman Catholic law: KBU2227+
Mens rea
Criminal offense
Comparative religious law: KB3867
Islamic law: KBP3867+
Jewish law: KBM3867
Menstruation
Ablutions
Islamic law: KBP184.47.M45
Mental disabilities, People with
Equality before the law
Islamic law: KBP2467.D58
Jewish law: KBM2467.D58
Natural persons
Jewish law: KBM529
Social service
Islamic law: KBP1532+
Jewish law: KBM1532+
Mentally disabled children, Education of
Jewish law: KBM3143.6
Mentally disabled people
Social laws
Comparative religious law: KB1534.A+
Mentally ill
Institutions for
Islamic law: KBP3113

Mentally ill
Social work
Canon law: KBR3280.M46
Roman Catholic law: KBU3280.M46
Mentally ill people
Institutions for
Jewish law: KBM3113
Merchandise, Commercial
Taxable income
Islamic law: KBP3620.3.M47
Merchant and business enterprise
Jewish law: KBM921+
Mercy, Legal concept of
Roman Catholic law: KBU2189.3.M47
Metal rights incident to ownership of land
Comparative religious law: KB697
Islamic law: KBP697
Jewish law: KBM697
Metallurgy
Comparative religious law: KB3344, KB3377
Islamic law: KBP3344+
Jewish law: KBM3344+
Metals
Recycling of
Islamic law: KBP3264+
Retail trade
Islamic law: KBP3422.M48
Jewish law: KBM3422.M48
Taxable income
Islamic law: KBP3620.3.M48
Metals, Precious
Retail trade
Islamic law: KBP3422.P73
Jewish law: KBM3422.P73
Metaphor
Islamic law: KBP462.M35
Methodology
Canon law: KBR2200+
Methodology of law development
Jewish law: KBM524.32+
Metropolitan See, The
Canon law: KBR2807
Metropolitans
Canon law: KBR2803+
Roman Catholic law: KBU2803+
Metus gravis
Justification
Criminal law
Roman Catholic law: KBU3550
Legal transactions
Ius ecclesiasticum privatum: KBR2292
Roman Catholic law: KBU2292
Mezonot
Jewish law: KBM548.3
Mi Yehudi: KBM529.83
Mid-Sha‘bān, Night of: KBP186.38
Midot: KBM3257+
Midrash
Jewish law: KBM510+
Midwives
Comparative religious law: KB3104.3.M53
Islamic law: KBP3106
Jewish law: KBM3106
Migrant labor
Social work
Roman Catholic law: KBU3280.M53
Milḥemet Mitzvah: KBM3740.M54
Military criminal law and procedure
Comparative religious law: KB3758+
Islamic law: KBP3758+
Jewish law: KBM3758+
Military discipline
Comparative religious law: KB3780
Islamic law: KBP3780+
Jewish law: KBM3780+
Military law
Comparative religious law: KB3735+
Islamic law: KBP3738+
Jewish law: KBM3738+
Military requisitions from civilians in time of war, etc
Islamic law: KBP3710
Militias
Community defense
Jewish law: KBM3738+
Islamic law: KBP3748.M54
Militias, Communal-sponsored
Jewish law: KBM3007
Milk: KBP646+

Milk production
Islamic law: KBP3329+
Jewish law: KBM3329+
Minbars
Islamic law: KBP184.95+
Mineral resources, Rights to
Islamic law: KBP3350
Mineral rights incident to ownership of land
Comparative religious law: KB697
Islamic law: KBP697
Jewish law: KBM697
Mineral waters
Islamic law: KBP3399
Minerals
Taxable income
Islamic law: KBP3620.3.M55
Mines, Rights to
Islamic law: KBP3350
Minhag: KBM524.3
Mining and quarrying
Regulation
Comparative religious law: KB3344
Islamic law: KBP3344+
Jewish law: KBM3344+
Ministry
Constitution of the state
Islamic law: KBP2580
Minor without parental consent
Marriage impediments
Canon law: KBR3122.M56
Mere prohibition of marriage
Roman Catholic law: KBU3122.M56
Minores
Criminal law
Law of the Roman Cathoic Church: KBU3544
Roman Catholic law: KBU3555
Incapacity
Violation of criminal law
Canon law: KBR3544
Justification of illegal acts
Canon law: KBR3555
Minority
Capacity and incapacity
Canon law: KBR2232.M56
Roman Catholic law: KBU2232.M56
Minority disabled people
Equality before the law
Islamic law: KBP2467.D58
Minority, Legal
Persons
Comparative religious law: KB525
Islamic law: KBP525+
Minors
Capacity and disability
Islamic law: KBP525
Capacity to sue
Canon law: KBR3833.M56
Capacity to sue and to be sued
Roman Catholic law: KBU3833.M56
Criminal liability
Comparative religious law: KB3886
Islamic law: KBP3886
Jewish law: KBM3886
Guardianship
Comparative religious law: KB625
Islamic law: KBP625
Natural persons
Jewish law: KBM525
Minors (below the sixteenth year of age)
Criminal law
Roman Catholic law: KBU3555
Minors under the sixteenth year of age
Criminal law
Roman Catholic law: KBU3544
Incapacity
Violation of criminal law
Canon law: KBR3544
Justification of illegal acts
Canon law: KBR3555
Minutes of proceedings
Court proceedings
Islamic law: KBP1623
Mīrāth: KBP632+
Misconduct by husband
Jewish law: KBM559.6
Misconduct by wife
Jewish law: KBM559.3
Mishpat Ivri: KBM523.8+
Misrepresentation
Obligations (Torts)
Islamic law: KBP846

Misrepresentation
  Torts
    Jewish law: KBM846
Missi apostolicae sedis
  Organs of government
    Canon law: KBR2482+
Missing persons
  Comparative religious law: KB524.8
  Inheritance and succession
    Islamic law: KBP634.953.L67
  Islamic law: KBP524.8
Missionary activity
  Canon law: KBR3049
  Teaching office of the Church
    Roman Catholic law: KBU3049
Mistake
  Defective marriage
    Jewish law: KBM556
  Void and voidable contracts
    Comparative religious law: KB867.3
    Islamic law: KBP867.3
    Jewish law: KBM867.3
Mistake of law %b Criminal liability
  Comparative religious law: KB3896
Mistakes in prayer
  Islamic law: KBP184.33.M58
Misyār: KBP546.955
Mithlī: KBP642.3
Mitzvah connected to the land
  Land policy legislation
    Jewish law: KBM3293
Mixed marriage
  Canon law: KBR3148+
  Comparative religious law: KB546.2
Mobilia
  Jurisdiction of ecclesiastical courts
    Canon law: KBR3795.M63
Modernism (17th to end 19th cent.)
  Church and state
    Canon law: KBR4040+
Monarchic government
  Canon law: KBR4010+
Monarchic government and papacy
  Roman Catholic law: KBU4010+
Monasteria sui iuris
  Canon law: KBR2908
Monasteries
  Roman Catholic law: KBU2899+
Monasteris
  Monasticism
    Canon law: KBR2899+
Monasticism
  Canon law: KBR2892+
  Roman Catholic law: KBU2892+
  Sufis
    Islamic law: KBP189.68
Money
  Comparative religious law: KB3534
  Islamic law: KBP3534+
  Jewish law: KBM3534+
  Taxable income
    Islamic law: KBP3620.3.M65
Money, Exchange of
  Contracts
    Islamic law: KBP879.2.S27
Monitio vel correptio
  Criminal law
    Canon law: KBR3618
Monomachia
  Penal (Criminal) law
    Canon law: KBR3759.D84
Monopolies
  Islamic law: KBP3242
  Jewish law: KBM3242
Monuments, Historic
  Islamic law: KBP3183+
Moral theology and canon law:
  KBR2155.2
  Roman Catholic law: KBU2156
Moralis persona by divine law
  Roman Catholic law: KBU2255
Morality of law
  Jewish law: KBM524.14
Morbific agents, Spreading of
  Criminal law
    Comparative religious law: KB4368
    Islamic law: KBP4368
Moredet: KBM559.3
Mores of Islam
  Uṣūl al-fiqh
    Islamic law: KBP444
Morganatic marriages
  Canon law: KBR3153

INDEX

Mortgages
  Church property
    Roman Catholic law: KBU3413
Mosques
  Ablutions
    Islamic law: KBP184.47.M68
Most Holy Eucharist, The
  Canon law: KBR3085+
  Roman Catholic law: KBU3085+
Mother, Parental power of
  Jewish law: KBM607
Motion pictures
  Comparative religious law: KB3173
  Islamic law: KBP3173
  Jewish law: KBM3173
Motor vehicle offenses
  Comparative religious law: KB4384
  Islamic law: KBP4384
  Jewish law: KBM4384
Mu'āmalāt: KBP639+
Mu'āwaḍah mālīyah: KBP879+
Mubāra'ah: KBP563.2
Muḍārabah: KBP1049+
Mudda'á 'alayhī: KBP1657
Muddah al-qānūnīyah lil-da'wá:
  KBP507+
Mudda'ī: KBP1657
Mufāwaḍa: KBP1045+
Muflis: KBP1942
Muftis: KBP491
Muḥammad, Prophet: KBP75+
Muḥarram, First of
  Islamic law: KBP186.2
Muḥarram, Tenth of
  Islamic law: KBP186.3
Muḥtasib: KBP1619.3
Mukallaf: KBP525.5
Mukhāṭarah: KBP955.4
Mulāzamah: KBP1925.M85
Multi-national corporations
  Income tax
    Islamic law: KBP3615+
  Islamic law: KBP1116
Multiple-judge court
  Islamic law: KBP1585
Multiple marriage
  Comparative religious law: KB546.4
Multiple marriage
  Islamic law: KBP546.954
  Jewish law: KBM546.4
Munaffidh al-waṣīyah: KBP635.954
Municipal government
  Islamic law: KBP2920+
Municipal public services
  Islamic law: KBP2955+
Muqaradah: KBP1049+
Muqāṣṣah: KBP817.3
Murder
  Comparative religious law: KB4050+
  Islamic law: KBP4050+
  Jewish law: KBM4052
Museums and galleries
  Comparative religious law: KB3182.5
  Islamic law: KBP3182.5
  Jewish law: KBM3182.5
Mushā': KBP674
Music
  Cultural affairs
    Comparative religious law: KB3171
    Islamic law: KBP3171
    Jewish law: KBM3171
Musicians
  Comparative religious law: KB3171
  Islamic law: KBP3171
  Jewish law: KBM3171
Muta
  Islamic law: KBP546.955
Mut'ah: KBP546.955
Mutilare
  Penal (Criminal) law
    Canon law: KBR3768
  Roman Catholic law: KBU3768
Mutilation
  Animals
    Comparative religious law:
      KB3123.5.M88
    Islamic law: KBP3123.5.M88
  Criminal law penalty
    Jewish law: KBM3980.M87
  Criminal law punishment
    Comparative religious law:
      KB3980.M87
    Islamic law: KBP3980.M87

Mutilation
Penal (Criminal) law
Canon law: KBR3768
Roman Catholic law: KBU3768
Mutiny
Military law
Islamic law: KBP3760.I53
Jewish law: KBM3760.I53
Mutuum
Comparative religious law: KB891
Islamic law: KBP891
Mutuus consensus
Marriage
Canon law: KBR3132+
Muzāraʻah: KBP715
Muzāyadah: KBP878.A93
Mysticism
Islamic law: KBP188.5+

N

Nafaqah
Dissolved marriage: KBP567
Domestic relations: KBP584
Nafy: KBP3997
Nagid (Jewish communal leaders): KBM2532
Nahb: KBP4254
Narcotics
Comparative religious law: KB3092
Illegal use of, possession of, and traffic in
Jewish law: KBM4404
Islamic law: KBP3092
Jewish law: KBM3092
Nasab: KBP616.5+
Nasciturus
Comparative religious law: KB524.72
Islamic law: KBP524.72
Naskh: KBP463
National defense
Crimes against
Comparative religious law: KB4470
National defense, Offenses against
Islamic law: KBP4470
National emergency, Government measures in time of
Islamic law: KBP3709+
National emergency, Measures in time of
Jewish law: KBM3709+
National preserves
Comparative religious law: KB3054
Islamic law: KBP3054
National revenue
Comparative religious law: KB3540+
Islamic law: KBP3540+
Nationality
Islamic law: KBP2430+
Nationalization
Comparative religious law: KB2824+
Emergency measures
Islamic law: KBP3720
Jewish law: KBM3720
Islamic law: KBP2824+
Natural gas
Energy policy
Islamic law: KBP3433
Regulation
Islamic law: KBP3366+
Natural law and divine law: KBR2190
Roman Catholic law: KBU2190
Natural law and Jewish law: KBM524.15
Natural law and religious law: KB280
Natural monuments
Wilderness preservation
Comparative religious law: KB3134+
Islamic law: KBP3134+
Jewish law: KBM3134
Natural obligations
Aleatory contracts
Comparative religious law: KB899
Jewish law: KBM899+
Islamic law: KBP814
Jewish law: KBM814
Natural parents
Inheritance and succession
Islamic law: KBP634.955
Natural persons
Canon law: KBR2225+

Natural persons
  Jewish law: KBM524.692+
  Roman Catholic law: KBU2225+
Naturopaths
  Jewish law: KBM3103.H42
Natus
  Baptism
    Canon law: KBR2229.N38
"Ne Temere" decree
  Roman Catholic law: KBU3152.A4
Necessitas
  Justification
    Criminal law
      Roman Catholic law: KBU3550
Necessity
  Criminal offense
    Comparative religious law: KB3857
    Islamic law: KBP3857
    Jewish law: KBM3857
  Justification
    Criminal law
      Roman Catholic law: KBU3550
  Justification of illegal acts
    Canon law: KBR3550
  Legal transactions
    Ius ecclesiasticum privatum: KBR2292
    Roman Catholic law: KBU2292
  Protection of rights
    Islamic law: KBP509
Necromantia
  Penal (Criminal) law
    Canon law: KBR3648.N43
Neglect of a child
  Islamic law: KBP4190
  Jewish law: KBM4190
Negligence
  Criminal offense
    Jewish law: KBM3874
  Obligations
    Comparative religious law: KB824+
    Jewish law: KBM824.5
  Torts
    Comparative religious law: KB839
    Islamic law: KBP839+
    Jewish law: KBM834.9+
Negotiable instruments
  Islamic law: KBP937+
  Jewish law: KBM937+
Neocaesarea, Council of, 315: KBR245.5
Neutrality
  Foreign relations
    Islamic law: KBP2415
New trial
  Criminal procedure
    Jewish law: KBM4792
New Year's Day
  Islamic law: KBP186.2
Nicea, Council of, 1st, 325
  Canon law: KBR210
Nicea, Council of, 2nd, 787
  Canon law: KBR240
Night of mid-Sha'bān: KBP186.38
Nikāḥ: KBP542+
Nisā': KBP526+
Nissu'in: KBM542+
Nīyah: KBP504.5
  Contracts: KBP860+
  Ritual law: KBP184.12
Niẓām
  Sources of fiqh: KBP458.N59
Noise
  Pollution
    Comparative religious law: KB3132.5
    Islamic law: KBP3132.5
    Jewish law: KBM3132.5
Non-collegiate institutes
  Juristic persons
    Roman Catholic law: KBU3452+
Non-collegiate juristic persons
  Roman Catholic law: KBU2273+
Non-collegiate juristic persons (Aggregate of property and resources)
  Canon law: KBR2273+
Non-contentious jurisdiction
  Courts
    Roman Catholic law: KBU3883
  Judiciary
    Canon law: KBR3883
Non-fungibles
  Comparative religious law: KB642.3

Non-fungibles
  Islamic law: KBP642.3
  Jewish law: KBM642.3
Non-Jewish children of Jews
  Jewish law: KBM589.3
Non-Jewish law, Status of
  Jewish law: KBM524.24
Non-Jews
  Equality before the law
    Jewish law: KBM2467.N64
  Natural persons
    Jewish law: KBM529.7.N65
Non-Jews, Marriage to
  Jewish law: KBM546.2
Non-Muslim, Marriage to a
  Islamic law: KBP546.952
Non-Muslims
  Capacity and disability
    Islamic law: KBP529.6
  Constitution of the state
    Islamic law: KBP2449
Non-proprietary rights
  Islamic law: KBP502.4
Non-wage payments
  Income tax
    Jewish law: KBM3584
Noncash funds transfer
  Islamic law: KBP961
Nonperformance
  Obligations
    Comparative religious law: KB824+
    Islamic law: KBP824+
    Jewish law: KBM824+
Nonprofit associations and corporations
  Income tax
    Islamic law: KBP3593+
Norms
  Economic law
    Comparative religious law: KB3254+
    Islamic law: KBP3254+
    Jewish law: KBM3254+
Notarial practice and procedure
  Comparative religious law: KB1846+
Notaries
  Comparative religious law: KB1846+
Notaries
  Diocesan constitution and organs
    Canon law: KBR2856
  Islamic law: KBP1846+
  Jewish law: KBM1846+
  Organs of government
    Roman Catholic law: KBU2856+, KBU2856
  Roman Catholic law: KBU3823.5+
  The legal profession
    Canon law: KBR3823.5+
Notarii
  Diocesan constitution and organs
    Canon law: KBR2856
  Roman Catholic law: KBU3823.5+
  The legal profession
    Canon law: KBR3823.5+
Notice
  Contracts
    Jewish law: KBM866
  Contracts and transactions
    Islamic law: KBP866
Novices
  Temporal goods of the Church
    Canon law: KBR3350.N69
Novitiate
  Canon law: KBR2922+
  Religious institutes
    Roman Catholic law: KBU2922+
Novitiatus
  Canon law: KBR2922+
Noxious gases
  Comparative religious law: KB3130.5
  Islamic law: KBP3130.5
  Jewish law: KBM3130.5
Nuclear energy
  Islamic law: KBP3436
  Jewish law: KBM3436
Nuclear power
  Public safety
    Islamic law: KBP3012
Nulla poena sine lege
  Jewish law: KBM3826
Nullity
  Contracts
    Comparative religious law: KB867+
    Islamic law: KBP867+

INDEX

Nullity
  Contracts
    Jewish law: KBM867+
Nullity, Complaint of
  Trials
    Roman Catholic law: KBU3863
Nullity of law
  Canon law: KBR2196
  Jewish law: KBM524.24
  Roman Catholic law: KBU2196
Nullity of marriage
  Roman Catholic law: KBU3897+
Nullity of marriage (Summary procedures)
  Canon law: KBR3897+
Nullity of sacred ordination
  Roman Catholic law: KBU3914
Nullity of sacred ordination, Declaration of
  Canon law: KBR3914
Nullum crimen sine lege
  Jewish law: KBM3826
Nuncios
  Roman Catholic law: KBU2482+, KBU4080+
Nuntii
  Organs of government
    Canon law: KBR2482+
  Roman Catholic law: KBU4080+
Nuptial gifts
  Betrothal
    Islamic law: KBP543.953+
  Comparative religious law: KB543.3
Nurses and nursing
  Comparative religious law: KB3104.3.N87
  Islamic law: KBP3105
  Jewish law: KBM3105
Nursing homes
  Jewish law: KBM3114.O42
Nursing, Relationship by
  Parent and child
    Islamic law: KBP610.2
Nushūz: KBP559.953

O

Oath
  Courts and procedure
    Comparative religious law: KB1677.O23
    Islamic law: KBP1677.Y35
  Criminal procedure
    Comparative religious law: KB4709.O28
  Divine worship
    Canon law: KBR3210+
  Inquisition
    Canon law: KBR3943.O38
Oath of abstinence by husband
  Matrimonial actions
    Islamic law: KBP564
Oath of evidence
  Criminal trial
    Islamic law: KBP4709.Y35
Oath of participants in trial
  Canon law: KBR3828.O27
  Courts
    Roman Catholic law: KBU3828.O27
Oaths
  Procedure in general
    Jewish law: KBM1677.S53
Obedience
  Monasticism
    Roman Catholic law: KBU2927.O34
  Religious institutes
    Canon law: KBR2927.O34
Object and objective of law
  Uṣūl al-fiqh
    Islamic law: KBP442
Obligatio dammum illatum reparandi
  Legal transactions
    Ius ecclesiasticum privatum: KBR2294
Obligatio damnum illatum reparandi
  Legal transactions
    Roman Catholic law: KBU2294
Obligatio iureiurando inducta
  Private vows and oaths
    Canon law: KBR3220
Obligatio liturgiae horarum
  Canon law: KBR3184

Obligatio liturgiae horarum
  Roman Catholic law: KBU3184
Obligation for obligation, Prohibition of exchange of
  Islamic law: KBP856
Obligation from the oath
  Private vows and oaths
    Canon law: KBR3220
Obligation of the Christian failthful to support the Church
  Roman Catholic law: KBU3344+
Obligation to do or refrain from doing
  Islamic law: KBP815
Obligation to give
  Islamic law: KBP814.5
Obligation to serve
  Military law
    Comparative religious law: KB3739
    Islamic law: KBP3739+
    Jewish law: KBM3739+
Obligations
  Comparative religious law: KB810+
  Islamic law: KBP810+
  Jewish law: KBM801+
Obligations and rights of the Christian failthful
  Roman Catholic law: KBU2312+
Obligations and rights of the Christian faithful
  Canon law: KBR2312+
Obligations and rights of the laity
  Canon law: KBR2316+
  Roman Catholic law: KBU2316+
Obligations of clerics
  Canon law: KBR2336+
Obligations to do or refrain from doing
  Jewish law: KBM815
Obligations to give
  Jewish law: KBM814.5
Oboedientia
  Monasticism
    Roman Catholic law: KBU2927.O34
Observances and practice of Islam
  Legal aspects
    Islamic law: KBP174+
Observation
  Divine worship
    Canon law: KBR3184
Obstruction of justice
  Jewish law: KBM4484+
Occidental canon law and Roman law: KB230+
Occupancy of waste land by cultivator
  Comparative religious law: KB687.6
Occupation
  Property
    Comparative religious law: KB656
    Islamic law: KBP656
    Jewish law: KBM656
Occupation of waste land by cultivator
  Jewish law: KBM687.6
Offender, Acknowledgment by
  Criminal offense
    Jewish law: KBM3868
Offenses against ecclesiastical authorities
  Penal (Criminal) law
    Canon law: KBR3670+
Offenses against ecclesiastical authorities and the freedom of the Church
  Roman Catholic law: KBU3670+
Offenses against human life and freedom
  Roman Catholic law: KBU3752+
Offenses against human life, freedom and morals
  Penal (Criminal) law
    Canon law: KBR3752+
Offenses against marriage, family, and family status
  Islamic law
    Islamic law: KBP4180+
  Jewish law: KBM4180+
Offenses against national defense
  Islamic law: KBP4470
Offenses against private and public property
  Jewish law: KBM4230+
Offenses against public order and convenience
  Comparative religious law: KB4305+

Offenses against public order and convenience
Islamic law: KBP4305+
Jewish law: KBM4305+
Offenses against religion and the unity of the Church
Roman Catholic law: KBU3625+
Offenses against religious tranquility and the peace of the dead: KBP4170
Islamic law: KBP4170+
Jewish law: KBM4170+
Offenses against sexual integrity
Islamic law: KBP4200+
Jewish law: KBM4200+
Offenses against the government
Comparative religious law: KB4415+
Offenses against the national economy
Jewish law: KBM4286+
Offenses against the peace
Criminal law
Comparative religious law: KB4415+
Jewish law: KBM4415.7+
Islamic law: KBP4415+
Offenses against the person
Criminal law
Jewish law: KBM4048+
Offenses of clerics or religious against particular obligations
Penal (Criminal) law
Canon law: KBR3738+
Offer and acceptance
Betrothal
Islamic law: KBP543.952
Contracts
Comparative religious law: KB869.3+
Islamic law: KBP869.3+
Jewish law: KBM869.3+
Offer of reward
Contracts
Islamic law: KBP895
Officia imcompatibilia
Ecclesiastical offices
Canon law: KBR2352
Officials and employees other than the clergy
Personnel of churches and ecclesiastical institutes
Canon law: KBR2890+
Oil and gas leases
Islamic law: KBP3367
Oils and fats
Regulation of food processing
Islamic law: KBP3393
Old age homes
Jewish law: KBM3114.O42
Old age insurance
Jewish law: KBM1508
Social security
Islamic law: KBP1508
Older people
Social service
Islamic law: KBP1529
Jewish law: KBM1529
Social work
Canon law: KBR3280.A54
Roman Catholic law: KBU3280.A54
Oligopolies
Islamic law: KBP3242
Omissio debitae diligentiae
Criminal law
Roman Catholic law: KBU3556
Justification of illegal acts
Canon law: KBR3556
Omission
Criminal act
Jewish law: KBM3853
Onera missarum
Roman Catholic law: KBU3454
'Onés: KBM3823.F67
Onus probandi
Canon law: KBR3843+
Matrimonial actions
Canon law: KBR3893
Penal (criminal) procedures
Canon law: KBR3940+
Onus probationis
Trials
Roman Catholic law: KBU3843+

Opinion
Sources of fiqh
Islamic law: KBP453.2
Opinion of another, Relying upon
Sources of fiqh
Islamic law: KBP454
Opium
Drug laws
Comparative religious law: KB3092
Opium legislation
Islamic law: KBP3092
Opportunity
Judicial discretion
Islamic law: KBP4740
Jewish law: KBM4740
Option
Contracts
Islamic law: KBP858.5.K45
Jewish law: KBM858.5.O68
Oral contentious process
Courts
Roman Catholic law: KBU3878+
Trials
Canon law: KBR3878+
Oral law
Jewish law: KBM524.3
Oratoria
Sacred places
Canon law: KBR3238.O73
Oratories
Roman Catholic law: KBU3238.O73
Sacred places
Canon law: KBR3238.O73
Ordeal
Courts and procedure
Comparative religious law: KB1677.O73
Inquisition
Canon law: KBR3943.O73
Order of adjudication
Courts
Roman Catholic law: KBU3828.O74
Order of adjudication (Docket)
Canon law: KBR3828.O74
Order of succession
Comparative religious law: KB634
Islamic law: KBP634+
Order of succession
Jewish law: KBM634+
Orders and ordination
Roman Catholic law: KBU3102+
Orders, Holy
Impediments to marriage
Canon law: KBR3128.O74
Marriage impediments
Roman Catholic law: KBU3128.O74
Orders of knighthood and chivalry, Papal
Persons
Roman Catholic law: KBU2284.O74
Ordination
Canon law: KBR2330+
Clergy
Roman Catholic law: KBU2330
Ordination by a bishop of a person not under his jurisdiction (without dimissorial letters)
Roman Catholic law: KBU3716
Ordre public
Comparative religious law: KB481
Organ donation and transplantation
Medical legislation
Islamic law: KBP3116
Jewish law: KBM3116
Organization
Environmental law
Comparative religious law: KB3128
Judiciary
Comparative religious law: KB1572+
Organization and administration
Environmental law
Islamic law: KBP3128
Judiciary
Jewish law: KBM1572+
Organization and organs
Ecclesiastical Provinces
Canon law: KBR2800+
Organized defense forces
Islamic law: KBP3738+
Organized smuggling
Islamic law: KBP3698
Organs of government
Canon law: KBR2363+

Organs of government
Comparative religious law: KB2500+
Islamic law: KBP2500+
Jewish law: KBM2500+
Roman Catholic law: KBU2363+
Organs of state power and state administration
Comparative religious law: KB2500+
Organs, tissues, etc., Transplantation of
Roman Catholic law: KBU3292
Oriental Church
Canon law
Rota Romana: KBR44.6.O75
Orphanages
Canon law: KBR3275.O76
Church property
Canon law: KBR3460
Juristic persons
Roman Catholic law: KBU3460
Roman Catholic law: KBU3275.O76
Orphans
Education
Comparative religious law: KB3143
Islamic law: KBP3143.4
Jurisdiction of ecclesiastical courts
Canon law: KBR3787.P47
Outcasts (Children)
Education
Comparative religious law: KB3143
Islamic law: KBP3143.4
Outdoor swimming facilities
Public safety
Jewish law: KBM3034.5
Overselling prices established by government
Jewish law: KBM4290
Owner
Property
Comparative religious law: KB646+, KB648+
Islamic law: KBP646+
Jewish law: KBM646+
Ownership
Church property
Roman Catholic law: KBU3342
Commons for use without shares in
Comparative religious law: KB686
Ownership
Negotiable instruments
Islamic law: KBP937.3
Jewish law: KBM937.3
Property
Comparative religious law: KB646+
Islamic law: KBP646+
Jewish law: KBM646+
Ownership, Loss of
Property
Jewish law: KBM672

P

Paenitentia
Criminal law
Canon law: KBR3526+
Paenitentiaria Apostolica
Canon law: KBR3812+
Decisions of ecclesiastical tribunals
Roman Catholic law: KBU48
Roman Catholic law: KBU3812+
Pagan (Germanic) rites
Canon law: KBR3644
Painting
Islamic law: KBP184.9.P56
Paleography and canon law: KBR76
Pandering and pimping
Jewish law: KBM4224
Papacy and monarchic government
Canon law: KBR4010+
Roman Catholic law: KBU4010+
Papal envoys
Canon law: KBR4080+
Roman Catholic law: KBU4080+
Papal independence from civil powers
Roman Catholic law: KBU4074
Papal legates
Organs of government
Canon law: KBR2482+
Papal legation
Canon law: KBR4078+
Roman Catholic law: KBU4078+
Papal orders of knighthood and chivalry
Persons
Roman Catholic law: KBU2284.O74

Papal States (to 1870)
  Canon law: KBR4070
Papal vicars
  Roman Catholic law: KBU4080+
Paper, Recycling of
  Islamic law: KBP3264+
Paramedical professions
  Comparative religious law: KB3104+
  Islamic law: KBP3104+
  Jewish law: KBM3104+
Parasites, Spreading of
  Criminal law
    Comparative religious law: KB4368
    Islamic law: KBP4368
Parasitic diseases
  Public health
    Comparative religious law: KB3080+
    Islamic law: KBP3080+
    Jewish law: KBM3080+
Pardon
  Criminal law
    Comparative religious law: KB4034
    Islamic law: KBP4034
  Tax and customs crimes
    Islamic law: KBP3705
Parent and child
  Comparative religious law: KB587+
  Islamic law: KBP587+
  Jewish law: KBM587+
  Obligation of parents to educate their children
    Comparative religious law: KB3139.3
    Islamic law: KBP3139.3
    Jewish law: KBM3139.3
  Procedure in parent and child cases
    Islamic law: KBP1807
Parent and child cases
  Courts and procedure
    Comparative religious law: KB1807
Parental kidnapping
  Criminal law
    Jewish law: KBM4188
  Family law
    Islamic law: KBP602
    Jewish law: KBM602
Parental power
  Family law
    Comparative religious law: KB598+
  Islamic law: KBP598+
  Jewish law: KBM598+
Parish and pastor
  Diocesan constitution and organs
    Canon law: KBR2872
  Organs of government
    Roman Catholic law: KBU2872
Parity of different denominations
  Church and state
    Canon law: KBR4042
Parks
  Wilderness preservation
    Comparative religious law: KB3134+
    Jewish law: KBM3134
Parnas (Jewish communal leaders): KBM2532
Parochial domicile
  Natural persons
    Canon law: KBR2236.P37
  Roman Catholic law: KBU2236.P37
Parochial vicar
  Diocesan constitution and organs
    Canon law: KBR2872
  Organs of government
    Roman Catholic law: KBU2872
Paroecia et parochus
  Diocesan constitution and organs
    Canon law: KBR2872
Partes
  Matrimonial actions
    Canon law: KBR3890
Parties to action
  Courts
    Comparative religious law: KB1655
    Roman Catholic law: KBU3830+
  Criminal procedure
    Comparative religious law: KB4630.A+, KB4630.A25
    Islamic law: KBP4630.A+
    Jewish law: KBM4630.A+
  Dispensation of marriage
    Roman Catholic law: KBU3909

INDEX

Parties to action
  Dispensation of ratified and non-consummated marriage
    Canon law: KBR3909
  Judiciary
    Canon law: KBR3830+
  Matrimonial actions
    Roman Catholic law: KBU3890
  Penal (criminal) procedures
    Canon law: KBR3926+
    Roman Catholic law: KBU3926+
  Procedure in general
    Islamic law: KBP1655+
    Jewish law: KBM1655+
Parties to actions
  Matrimonial actions
    Canon law: KBR3890
Parties to contract
  Comparative religious law: KB873+
  Islamic law: KBP873+
  Jewish law: KBM873+
  Labor law
    Islamic law: KBP1300
Partition of estate
  Islamic law: KBP633.952.T37
  Jewish law: KBM633+
Partium declarationes
  Trials
    Canon law: KBR3846
Partners
  Personal companies
    Islamic law: KBP1043.3
    Jewish law: KBM1043.3
Partnerships
  Personal companies
    Islamic law: KBP1043+
    Jewish law: KBM1043+
Party autonomy
  Contracts
    Comparative religious law: KB858.3
    Islamic law: KBP858.3
    Jewish law: KBM858.3
Passion
  Defense
    Criminal law
      Roman Catholic law: KBU3559.D58
Passion
  Incapacity
    Criminal liability
      Jewish law: KBM3892.D58
  Justification of illegal acts
    Canon law: KBR3559.D58
Pastoral councils
  Canon law: KBR2882
Patent law and trademarks
  Comparative religious law: KB1194
  Islamic law: KBP1194
  Jewish law: KBM1194
Paternal ancestry
  Married women
    Islamic law: KBP553.P38
Paternity
  Comparative religious law: KB616.5+
  Islamic law: KBP616.5+
  Jewish law: KBM616.5+
  Proof of
    Islamic law: KBP619.I75
Paternity, Proof of
  Jewish law: KBM619.P38
Patriarch or primate
  Canon law: KBR2803+
Patrilineal and matrilineal descendants
  Comparative religious law: KB616.5+
Patrilineal ascendants and descendants
  Jewish law: KBM544.2
Patrols
  Community defense
    Jewish law: KBM3738+
Patrols (Militias)
  Islamic law: KBP3748.M54
Patronage
  Ecclesiastical offices
    Canon law: KBR2361+
  Slaves
    Comparative religious law: KB529.5.P38
    Islamic law: KBP529.52
Patronage of the state
  Ecclesiastical offices
    Canon law: KBR2362.4
Paupers (Children)
  Education
    Comparative religious law: KB3143

Paupers (Children)
Education
Islamic law: KBP3143.4
Paupertas
Monasticism
Roman Catholic law: KBU2927.P68
Pawnbrokers
Regulation
Jewish law: KBM3423.5.C64
Payment
Obligations
Comparative religious law: KB817
Islamic law: KBP817.2+
Jewish law: KBM818+
Payment of money debts
Islamic law: KBP820
Jewish law: KBM820
Peace efforts of the Holy See
Roman Catholic law: KBU4097
Peculium clericale
Canon law: KBR3364
Peculium patrimoniale
Canon law: KBR3362
Pecuniary transaction without countervalue
Comparative religious law: KB879.23+
Islamic law: KBP879.3+
Jewish law: KBM879.22+
Peddling
Retail trade
Jewish law: KBM3420.P43
Penal (Criminal) law
Canon law: KBR3500+
Penal (Criminal) procedure
Roman Catholic law: KBU3920+
Penal (criminal) procedures
Canon law: KBR3920+
Penal laws and precepts
Canon law: KBR3510+
Penal remedies and penance
Criminal law
Canon law: KBR3617.2+
Roman Catholic law: KBU3617.2+
Penal report
Pretrial criminal procedure
Jewish law: KBM4634
Penal sanctions, Classification of
Canon law: KBR3518+
Penalties
Criminal law
Jewish law: KBM3962+
Penance
Canon law: KBR3090+
Islamic law: KBP184.9.P45
Roman Catholic law: KBU3090+
Penance, Days of
Canon law: KBR3250+
Penitential discipline
Canon law: KBR3090+
Pensioners
Social service
Islamic law: KBP1530
Jewish law: KBM1530
Pensions
Ecclesiastical offices
Roman Catholic law: KBU2355
People of God
Roman Catholic law: KBU2312+
People with disabilities
Social work
Canon law: KBR3280.P46
Roman Catholic law: KBU3280.P46
People with mental disabilites
Comparative religious law: KB529
People with mental disabilities
Capacity and disability
Islamic law: KBP529
Capacity to sue
Canon law: KBR3833.M56
Capacity to sue and to be sued
Roman Catholic law: KBU3833.M56
Comparative religious law: KB529
Criminal liability
Comparative religious law: KB3884
Islamic law: KBP3884
Jewish law: KBM3884
People with physical disabilities
Capacity and disability
Islamic law: KBP529.7.P48
People with physical illness
Capacity and disability
Islamic law: KBP529.7.P48

Peremptory time period
  Judicial review of administrative acts
    Roman Catholic law: KBU3966
Performance
  Obligations
    Comparative religious law: KB817
    Islamic law: KBP817.2+
    Jewish law: KBM818+
Performance of marriage
  Canon law: KBR3144+
  Islamic law: KBP546+
  Jewish law: KBM546+
  Law of the Roman Cathoic Church:
    KBU3144+
Performing arts
  Comparative religious arts: KB3170+
  Islamic law: KBP3170+
  Jewish law: KBM3170+
Perfumes
  Islamic law: KBP184.42+
Periti
  Trials
    Canon law: KBR3849
Periurium
  Penal (Criminal) law
    Canon law: KBR3668
Periurium coram ecclasiastica auctoriate
  Roman Catholic law: KBU3668
Perjury
  Jewish law: KBM4484
  Penal (Criminal) law
    Canon law: KBR3668
  Roman Catholic law: KBU3668
Permits
  Police and public safety
    Jewish law: KBM3002
Perpetrators
  Criminal act
    Comparative religious law: KB3922
    Islamic law: KBP3922
    Jewish law: KBM3920
Perpetuity
  Juristic persons
    Canon law: KBR2282
    Roman Catholic law: KBU2282
Person charged
  Criminal procedure
    Islamic law: KBP4630.A25
    Jewish law: KBM4630.A25
Person of age
  Capacity and disability
    Islamic law: KBP525.5
Personable property
  Comparative religious law: KB643
Personae miserabiles
  Jurisdiction of ecclesiastical courts
    Canon law: KBR3787.P47
Personal applicability
  Criminal law
    Comparative religious law: KB3838
    Islamic law: KBP3824.I55
    Jewish law: KBM3838.3
Personal companies
  Income tax
    Islamic law: KBP3594+
  Islamic law: KBP1043+
  Jewish law: KBM1043+
Personal damages
  War damage compensation
    Jewish law: KBM3728.P47
Personal freedom
  Married women
    Islamic law: KBP553.F73
Personal freedom, Crimes against
  Jewish law: KBM4116+
Personal loans
  Contracts
    Comparative religious law: KB891
    Islamic law: KBP891
    Jewish law: KBM891
Personal (Movable) property
  Islamic law: KBP643
  Jewish law: KBM643
Personal names
  Islamic law: KBP529.8
  Natural persons
    Jewish law: KBM529.8
Personal prelatures
  Canon law: KBR2342
  Roman Catholic law: KBU2342

Personal property
  Pledges
    Islamic law: KBP728
Personal servitude
  Jewish law: KBM713
Personal servitudes
  Comparative religious law: KB713
  Islamic law: KBP713
Personalitas iuridica
  Conference of Bishops
    Canon law: KBR2827
  Ecclesiastical Provinces
    Canon law: KBR2798
  Juristic persons
    Canon law: KBR2254
  Private associations
    Juristic persons
      Canon law: KBR2266
  Roman Catholic law: KBU2254
Personality
  Comparative religious law: KB524.7+
  Islamic law: KBP524.7+
  Law of the Roman Catholic Church: KBU2226
  Natural persons
    Jewish law: KBM524.7+
Personality, Legal
  Juristic persons
    Canon law: KBR2254
Personality rights
  Islamic law: KBP529.8
  Natural persons
    Jewish law: KBM529.8
Personarum physicarum condicio canonica
  Roman Catholic law: KBU2225+
Personnel of churches and ecclesiastical institutes
  Canon law: KBR2886+
  Organs of government
    Roman Catholic law: KBU2886+
Persons
  Canon law: KBR2224+
  Comparative religious law: KB524+
  Islamic law: KBP524.6+
  Jewish law: KBM524.6+
  Roman Catholic law: KBU2224+
Persons of uncertain gender
  Natural person
    Jewish law: KBM529.7.H47
Perterre electorem vel electum vel eum qui potestatem vel ministerium ecclesiasticum exercuit
  Roman Catholic law: KBU3694
Petitioner and respondent
  Courts
    Roman Catholic law: KBU3831+
  Judiciary
    Canon law: KBR3831+
Petroleum
  Regulation
    Islamic law: KBP3366+
Philosophy
  Criminal law
    Jewish law: KBM3812+
  Public law
    Jewish law: KBM2015+
Philosophy and theory of religious law: KB270+
Philosophy (General) and canonical jurisprudence: KBR2155.4
Photian Council, 879: KBR263
Photography
  Islamic law: KBP184.9.P56
Phylacteria
  Penal (Criminal) law
    Canon law: KBR3648.P59
Physical disabilities, People with
  Equality before the law
    Islamic law: KBP2467.D58
    Jewish law: KBM2467.D58
  Social service
    Islamic law: KBP1532+
    Jewish law: KBM1532+
Physical education
  Adults
    Islamic law: KBP3159
    Jewish law: KBM3159
Physical examination
  Criminal procedure
    Comparative religious law: KB4687
    Islamic law: KBP4687
    Jewish law: KBM4687

Physical injuries
  Torts
    Islamic law: KBP842.2+
    Jewish law: KBM842.2+
Physical therapists
  Jewish law: KBM3107
Physically disabled children, Education of
  Jewish law: KBM3143.6
Physically disabled people
  Social laws
    Comparative religious law: KB1534.A+
Physicians
  Comparative religious law: KB3100
  Islamic law: KBP3100+
  Jewish law: KBM3100+
Physiognomy
  Islamic law: KBP619.I75
Pickpocketing
  Islamic law: KBP4235
Pidyon shevuyim: KBM1539
Pikku'ah nefesh: KBM3858
Pilegesh: KBM546.17
Pilgrimage to Mecca
  Islamic law: KBP181
Pilgrimages
  Canon law: KBR3254
  Islamic law: KBP184.7+
  Roman Catholic law: KBU3254
Pilgrims
  Islamic law: KBP184.7+
  Social work
    Canon law: KBR3280.P55
    Roman Catholic law: KBU3280.P55
Pillars of Islam
  Islamic law: KBP176+
Pimping
  Criminal law
    Jewish law: KBM4224
Pipelines
  Islamic law: KBP3466
Pit, Being tossed into a
  Criminal law punishment
    Jewish law: KBM3964.5
Place and right of asylum
  Sacred places
    Canon law: KBR3236
Place of court
  Ecclesiastical courts
    Canon law: KBR3797+
Place of the court
  Roman Catholic law: KBU3828.P55
Plaintiff
  Courts
    Comparative religious law: KB1655
  Procedure in general
    Islamic law: KBP1657
Plaintiff and defendant
  Canon law: KBR3831+
  Courts
    Roman Catholic law: KBU3831+
Planning
  Energy policy
    Islamic law: KBP3431.2
Plant protection
  Wilderness preservation
    Comparative religious law: KB3134.6
    Islamic law: KBP3134.6
Plastic surgery
  Medical legislation
    Comparative religious law: KB3119.P42
    Islamic law: KBP3119.P42
Pledge
  Personal property
    Comparative religious law: KB726
    Islamic law: KBP728
    Jewish law: KBM728
  Property
    Comparative religious law: KB726
    Jewish law: KBM726+
  Rights
    Comparative religious law: KB726
    Islamic law: KBP730
    Jewish law: KBM730
Pledges
  Property
    Islamic law: KBP726+

Plenary council
  Ecclesiastical Provinces
    Canon law: KBR2815
Plurality of debtor and creditor
  Jewish law: KBM812
Plurality of debtors and creditors
  Islamic law: KBP812
Plurality of laws conflict
  Jewish law: KBM524.43
Poena ferendae sententiae
  Canon law: KBR3512
Poena latae sententiae
  Canon law: KBR3512
  Roman Catholic law: KBU3512
Poenae expiatoriae
  Criminal law
    Roman Catholic law: KBU3522+
  Penal (Criminal) law
    Canon law: KBR3522+
Poenae medicinales
  Criminal law
    Roman Catholic law: KBU3520+
  Penal (Criminal) law
    Canon law: KBR3520+
Poenitentiaria Apostolica: KBR48
Poisoning
  Wells or soil
    Comparative religious law: KB4364
    Islamic law: KBP4364
Poisons
  Public safety
    Islamic law: KBP3014.A+
Police and public safety
  Comparative religious law: KB3000+
  Islamic law: KBP3000+
  Jewish law: KBM3000+
Police court
  Islamic law: KBP1588.3
Police force
  Jewish law: KBM3007
Police records
  Criminal procedure
    Islamic law: KBP4690
    Jewish law: KBM4690
Political offenses
  Criminal law
    Comparative religious law:
      KB4415+
    Islamic law: KBP4415+
    Jewish law: KBM4415.7+
Political rights
  Islamic law: KBP2460+
  Jewish law: KBM2460+
Poll tax
  Islamic law: KBP3680.J59
  Jewish law: KBM3626
Pollutants: KBM3131.5+
  Comparative religious law:
    KB3131.5+
  Islamic law: KBP3131.5+
  Water and groundwater pollution
    Comparative religious law: KB3131
    Islamic law: KBP3131
    Jewish law: KBM3131
Pollution, Environmental
  Comparative religious law: KB3130+
  Islamic law: KBP3130+
  Jewish law: KBM3130+
Polyandry
  Comparative religious law: KB546.4
  Islamic law: KBP546.954
Polygamy
  Comparative religious law: KB546.4
  Islamic law: KBP546.954
  Jewish law: KBM546.4
Pontifical Central Commission for
  Sacred Art in Italy
  Roman Catholic law: KBU2760
Pontifical Commission "Ecclesia Dei"
  Roman Catholic law: KBU2747
Pontifical Commission for Latin America
  Roman Catholic law: KBU2768
Pontifical Commission for the Redaction
  of the Code of Oriental Canon Law
  Roman Catholic law: KBU2765
Pontifical Commission for the Revision
  of the Code of Canon Law
  Roman Catholic law: KBU2732
Pontifical commissions
  Roman Catholic law: KBU2740+

Pontifical Council for Culture
Roman Catholic law: KBU2724
Pontifical Council for Interpretation of Legislative Texts
Roman Catholic law: KBU2720
Pontifical Council for Interreligious Dialogue
Roman Catholic law: KBU2722
Pontifical Council for Justice and Peace
Roman Catholic law: KBU2708
Pontifical Council for Pastoral Assistance to Health Care Workers
Roman Catholic law: KBU2716
Pontifical Council for Promoting Christian Unity
Roman Catholic law: KBU2700
Pontifical Council for Social Communications
Roman Catholic law: KBU2728
Pontifical Council for the Family
Roman Catholic law: KBU2705
Pontifical Council for the Laity
Roman Catholic law: KBU2698
Pontifical Council for the Pastoral care of Migrants and Itinerant People
Roman Catholic law: KBU2715
Pontifical councils
Roman Catholic law: KBU2695+
Pontifical legates and legation
Roman Catholic law: KBU2482+
Pontificia Commissio ad Redigendum Codicem Iuris Canonici Orientalis
Roman Catholic law: KBU2765
Pontificia Commissio Codicis Iuris Canonici Recognoscendi
Roman Catholic law: KBU2732
Pontificia Commissio pro America Latina
Roman Catholic law: KBU2768
Pontificium Consilium ad Christianorum Unitatem Fovendam
Roman Catholic law: KBU2700
Pontificium Consilium Centrale pro Arte Sacra in Italia
Roman Catholic law: KBU2760
Pontificium Consilium "Cor Unum"
Roman Catholic law: KBU2712
Pontificium Consilium de Apostolatu pro Valetudinis Administris
Roman Catholic law: KBU2716
Pontificium Consilium de Communicationibus Socialibus
Roman Catholic law: KBU2728
Pontificium Consilium de Justitia et Pace
Roman Catholic law: KBU2708
Pontificium Consilium de Legum Textibus Interpretandis
Roman Catholic law: KBU2720
Pontificium Consilium pro Cultura
Roman Catholic law: KBU2724
Pontificium Consilium pro Dialogo inter Religiones
Roman Catholic law: KBU2722
Pontificium Consilium pro Familia
Roman Catholic law: KBU2705
Pontificium Consilium pro Laicis
Roman Catholic law: KBU2698
Poor
Comparative religious law: KB1528
Jurisdiction of ecclesiastical courts
Canon law: KBR3787.P47
Restitution
Islamic law: KBP855
Social services
Islamic law: KBP1528
Jewish law: KBM1528
Social work
Canon law: KBR3280.P66
Roman Catholic law: KBU3280.P66
Poor persons
Equality before the law
Jewish law: KBM2467.P64
Pope as arbiter
Foreign relations of the Holy See
Roman Catholic law: KBU4097
Pope, The
Canon law: KBR2366+
Roman Catholic law: KBU2366+
Possession
Negotiable instruments
Islamic law: KBP937.3
Jewish law: KBM937.3

Possession
  Property
    Comparative religious law: KB646+, KB648+
    Islamic law: KBP646+
    Jewish law: KBM646+
Possessor
  Property
    Comparative religious law: KB646+
    Islamic law: KBP646+
    Jewish law: KBM646+
Possessory actions
  Islamic law: KBP652
  Jewish law: KBM652
Post-conviction remedies
  Criminal law and procedure
    Jewish law: KBM4790+
Postal services
  Islamic law: KBP3485+
  Jewish law: KBM3485+
Potestas
  Legati nati
    Canon law: KBR4088
Potestas delegata, subdelegata
  Roman Catholic law: KBU2302+
Potestas directa in temporalia (Bonifaz VIII)
  Canon law: KBR4026
Potestas exsecutiva
  The Pope
    Canon law: KBR2375
Potestas (General)
  Papal legation
    Canon law: KBR4084+
Potestas indirecta in temporalis (Gregory VII)
  Canon law: KBR4024
Potestas iudicialis
  The Pope
    Canon law: KBR2375
Potestas legislativa
  Conference of Bishops
    Canon law: KBR2830
    Roman Catholic law: KBU2830
  The Pope
    Canon law: KBR2372+
Potestas legislativa, exsecutiva vel iudicialis
  Dioceses
    Canon law: KBR2837
  Dioceses and diocesan bishop
    Roman Catholic law: KBU2837
Potestas regiminis legislativa
  Canon law: KBR2364
Poultry products
  Islamic law: KBP3384
  Jewish law: KBM3384
Poverty
  Monasticism
    Roman Catholic law: KBU2927.P68
  Religious institutes
    Canon law: KBR2927.P68
Power of governance
  Canon law: KBR2364
  Roman Catholic law: KBU2298+
Power supply
  Islamic law: KBP3431+
  Jewish law: KBM3431+
Power to dispose of episcopates and dioceses
  The Pope
    Canon law: KBR2384
Power to tax
  The Pope
    Canon law: KBR2386
Powers
  Metropolitans
    Canon law: KBR2805
Practice of Islam
  Legal aspects
    Islamic law: KBP174+
Practice of law
  Islamic law: KBP1630+
  Jewish law: KBM1630
Praelati Curiae Romanae
  Organs of government
    Canon law: KBR2775
  Roman Catholic law: KBU2775
Praesentatio
  Ecclesiastical offices
    Canon law: KBR2362.6

Praesidium
Ecumenical council
Canon law: KBR2380
Prayer
Ablutions
Islamic law: KBP184.47.P72
Ritual law
Islamic law: KBP184.3+
The five duties of a Muslim
Islamic law: KBP178
Prayers
Funeral procession prayers
Islamic law: KBP184.55
Praying of breviary
Clergy
Canon law: KBR2338.B74
Pre-emption, Right of
Jewish law: KBM716
Pre-trial procedure
Penal (Criminal) procedure
Roman Catholic law: KBU3930+
Penal (criminal) procedures
Canon law: KBR3930+
Precaution
Uṣūl al-fiqh
Islamic law: KBP448.I38
Precious metals
Retail trade
Islamic law: KBP3422.P73
Jewish law: KBM3422.P73
Precious metals, Exchange of
Contracts
Islamic law: KBP879.2.S27
Pregnancy
Islamic law: KBP528.P74
Pregnant woman, Breach of duty of assistance to a
Islamic law: KBP4194
Prelatures
Organs of government
Canon law: KBR2775
Roman Catholic law: KBU2775
Premarital examination
Islamic law: KBP545
Premarital examinations
Canon law: KBR3117
Premarital examinations
Marriage law
Roman Catholic law: KBU3117
Premiums
Unfair competition
Islamic law: KBP1250
Jewish law: KBM1250
Preparation
Criminal act
Jewish law: KBM3854
Prerequisits
Clergy
Canon law: KBR2329+
Prerogatives and powers
Constitutional and administrative law
Comparative religious law: KB2550+
Prerogatives of rulers
Constitution of the state
Islamic law: KBP2300
Constitutional law
Jewish law: KBM2300
Presbyterate
Diocesan constitution and organs
Canon law: KBR2865
Organs of government
Roman Catholic law: KBU2865
Presbyterial council, The
Canon law: KBR2882
Presbyterium
Diocesan constitution and organs
Canon law: KBR2865
Preschool education
Jewish law: KBM3140.9
Prescribed giving
Property tax
Islamic law: KBP3620+
Preservation of life
Criminal law
Jewish law: KBM3858
Justification of otherwise prohibited acts
Comparative religious law: KB3858
Islamic law: KBP3858
President, etc
Conference of Bishops
Canon law: KBR2829

Presidents
Comparative religious law: KB2540
Islamic law: KBP2540
Press and criminal justice
Comparative religious law: KB3500.7
Islamic law: KBP3507
Press law
Comparative religious law: KB3500+
Islamic law: KBP3500+
Jewish law: KBM3500+
Presumption of death
Comparative religious law: KB524.8
Presumption of preference
Sources of fiqh
Islamic law: KBP457
Presumptions
Courts and procedure
Comparative religious law: KB1677.P74
Islamic law: KBP1677.T35
Procedure in general
Jewish law: KBM1677.H37
Pretrial procedures
Canon law: KBR3839+
Courts
Comparative religious law: KB1660+
Criminal procedure
Comparative religious law: KB4632+
Islamic law: KBP4632+
Jewish law: KBM4632+
Procedure in general
Islamic law: KBP1660+
Jewish law: KBM1660+
Roman Catholic law: KBU3839+
Prevention of cruelty to animals
Islamic law: KBP3123+
Preventive or coercive measures
Criminal law
Comparative religious law: KB3982+
Islamic law: KBP3982+
Preventive penal remedies
Criminal law
Canon law: KBR3526+
Roman Catholic law: KBU3526+
Previous testimony
Criminal procedure
Islamic law: KBP4690
Jewish law: KBM4690
Price control
Economic law
Comparative religious law: KB3210
Emergency measures
Islamic law: KBP3724
Jewish law: KBM3724
Price fixing
Jewish law: KBM4290
Price norms
Islamic law: KBP3210
Price regulations
Violation of
Jewish law: KBM4290
Prices and price control
Economic law
Comparative religious law: KB3210
Islamic law: KBP3210
Jewish law: KBM3210
Priests
Diocesan constitution and organs
Canon law: KBR2865
Organs of government
Roman Catholic law: KBU2865
Prima instantia
Canon law: KBR3840+
Criminal procedure
Canon law: KBR3936+
Roman Catholic law: KBU3936+
Roman Catholic law: KBU3840+
Prima tonsura
Clergy
Canon law: KBR2329
Roman Catholic law: KBU2340.T66
Primacy
The Pope
Canon law: KBR2367+
Roman Catholic law: KBU2367+
Primary production
Comparative religious law: KB3294.22+
Islamic law: KBP3293.212+
Jewish law: KBM3293+

Primatus honoris
The Pope
Canon law: KBR2370
Primatus jurisdictionis
The Pope
Canon law: KBR2367+
Primogeniture
Canon law: KBR2226
Princes and rulers
Comparative religious law: KB2532+
Constitutional law
Islamic law: KBP2532+
Principle of collegiality
Rota Romana (Tribunal ordinarium)
Roman Catholic law: KBU3817
Prisoners of war
Social service
Islamic law: KBP1539
Jewish law: KBM1539
Privacy, Right of
Islamic law: KBP529.83
Jewish law: KBM524.4.P74
Private associations
Juristic persons
Canon law: KBR2266
Roman Catholic law: KBU2266+
Private chapels
Roman Catholic law: KBU3238.C53
Private international law
Comparative religious law: KB480+
Private law
Comparative religious law: KB479
Jewish law: KBM524.42
Private property
Offenses against
Jewish law: KBM4230+
Public restraint on
Comparative religious law: KB2824+
Islamic law: KBP2824+
Jewish law: KBM2824+
Requisition of for community use
Jewish law: KBM3710
Restraints on
Jewish law: KBM3040.5+
Privatio beneficii
Clergy
Canon law: KBR3615.P74
Privileged parties
Courts and procedure
Islamic law: KBP1656
Privileged witnesses
Criminal procedure
Jewish law: KBM4696
Procedure in general
Comparative religioius law: KB1676
Islamic law: KBP1676
Jewish law: KBM1676
Privileges
Metropolitans
Canon law: KBR2805
Monasticism
Roman Catholic law: KBU2927.P75
Religious institutes
Canon law: KBR2927.P75
The Pope
Canon law: KBR2370
Privileges and immunities
Temporal goods of the Church
Canon law: KBR3400+
Privileges and immunity
Church property
Roman Catholic law: KBU3400
Privileges of rulers
Constitution of the state
Islamic law: KBP2300
Constitutional law
Jewish law: KBM2300
Privilegia clericalia
Canon law: KBR2339+
Roman Catholic law: KBU2339+
Privilegium canonis
Clergy
Canon law: KBR2340.P75
Privilegium competentiae
Clergy
Canon law: KBR2340.P76
Privilegium fori
Clergy
Canon law: KBR2340.P77
Ecclesiastical courts
Canon law: KBR3786

Privilegium fori
  Roman Catholic law: KBU2340.P77
Privilegium immunitatis
  Clergy
    Canon law: KBR2340.P78
Privilegium Petrinum
  Matrimonial actions
    Canon law: KBR3905.P75
  Roman Catholic law: KBU3905.P75
Probate courts and procedure
  Comparative religious law: KB1880
  Courts and procedure
    Islamic law: KBP1880
  Jewish law: KBM1880
Probatio
  Canon law: KBR3843+
  Matrimonial actions
    Canon law: KBR3893
  Penal (criminal) procedures
    Canon law: KBR3940+
  Trials
    Roman Catholic law: KBU3843+
Probatio per documenta
  Trials
    Canon law: KBR3847
    Roman Catholic law: KBU3847
Procedural principles
  Courts and procedure
    Comparative religious law: KB1651+
    Islamic law: KBP1651+
    Jewish law: KBM1650.9+
  Criminal procedure
    Islamic law: KBP4624+
    Jewish law: KBM4620+
Procedure
  Courts and procedure
    Jewish law: KBM1650+
  Dissolution of marriage
    Islamic law: KBP562+
  Execution for payment due
    Islamic law: KBP1888+
  Matrimonial actions
    Comparative religious law: KB562
  Military criminal law
    Islamic law: KBP3758+
Procedure
  Military discipline
    Islamic law: KBP3780+
  Mines and mineral resources
    Islamic law: KBP3350
  Tax and customs crimes and delinquency: KBP3700.92+
  Trial procedure
    Islamic law: KBP1663+, KBP4664+
Procedure at first instance
  Canon law: KBR3840+
  Criminal procedure
    Canon law: KBR3936+
    Roman Catholic law: KBU3936+
  Roman Catholic law: KBU3840+
Procedure at trial
  Courts
    Comparative religious law: KB1663+
  Criminal procedure
    Comparative religious law: KB4664+
Processions
  Canon law: KBR3254
  Public safety
    Jewish law: KBM3036.5.D45
  Roman Catholic law: KBU3254
Processus documentalis
  Nullity of marriage
    Canon law: KBR3899
Processus poenalis iudicialis
  Canon law: KBR3920+
Processus praesumptae mortis coniugis
  Matrimonial actions
    Canon law: KBR3912
Procurator
  Court officials
    Canon law: KBR3807.5.P76
  Islamic law: KBP1637
  Jewish law: KBM4630.S73
Procuratores ad lites et advocati
  Canon law: KBR3834
  Courts
    Roman Catholic law: KBU3834
Procurators
  The legal profession
    Canon law: KBR3823+

INDEX

Procurators and advocates
Canon law: KBR3834
Courts
Roman Catholic law: KBU3834
Produce exchanges
Comparative religious law: KB962.8
Islamic law: KBP962.8
Jewish law: KBM962.8
Producers cooperatives
Jewish law: KBM3317
Profanare rem sacram, mobilem vel immobilem
Roman Catholic law: KBU3696
Profanation of a movable or immovable sacred thing
Roman Catholic law: KBU3696
Profanation of the consecrated species
Penal (Criminal) law
Canon law: KBR3664
Profanation of the consecreted species
Roman Catholic law: KBU3664
Professed religious
Temporal goods of the Church
Canon law: KBR3350.P76
Profession of faith
Canon law: KBR3070
Islamic law: KBP177
Teaching office of the Church
Roman Catholic law: KBU3070
Professional ethics
Comparative religious law: KB3522
Professions
Comparative religious law: KB3515+
Contracts
Islamic law: KBP892.3
Jewish law: KBM892.3
Islamic law: KBP3515+
Jewish law: KBM3515+
Prohibition against practicing
Criminal law
Jewish law: KBM4002
Profits
Income tax
Jewish law: KBM3578.5.P75
Limited partnership
Islamic law: KBP1047.4
Profits
Personal companies
Jewish law: KBM1047.4
Silent partnership
Islamic law: KBP1049.4
Jewish law: KBM1049.4
Programming
Radio and television broadcasting
Jewish law: KBM3495
Prohibited books
Roman Catholic law: KBU3065
Prohibited participation in sacred rites
Roman Catholic law: KBU3644
Prohibited work
Oraḥ ḥayim law: KBM523.3.P7
Prohibition against practicing a profession
Criminal law
Jewish law: KBM4002
Prohibition of censorship
Constitutional and administrative law
Comparative religious law: KB2478
Islamic law: KBP2478
Jewish law: KBM2478
Promissio matrimonii
Marriage law
Roman Catholic law: KBU3112
Promoter of justice (petitioner)
Penal (criminal) procedures
Canon law: KBR3926
Promotor iustitiae
Penal (criminal) procedures
Canon law: KBR3926
Promotor of justice
Matrimonial actions
Canon law: KBR3890
Promulgatio
Ecclesiastical laws
Roman Catholic law: KBU2218
Promulgation
Ecclesiastical laws
Roman Catholic law: KBU2218
Pronuntiationes iudicis
Trials
Canon law: KBR3854+
Proof of paternity
Islamic law: KBP619.I75

Property: KBM640+
Communal property
Jewish law: KBM3040.5+
Comparative religious law: KB640+
Control of
Emergency measures
Islamic law: KBP3712
Destruction of property and conversion
Jewish law: KBM4256
Islamic law: KBP640+
Monasticism
Roman Catholic law: KBU2927.P66
Property, Church
Canon law: KBR3320+
Roman Catholic law: KBU3320+
Property confiscation
Criminal law punishment
Islamic law: KBP4006
Jewish law: KBM4006
Property loss or damages
War damage compensation
Jewish law: KBM3728.P47
Property management
Parental power
Jewish law: KBM606
Property, Marital
Jewish law: KBM569+
Property regime
Married women
Islamic law: KBP553.P76
Property rights
Public restraint on
Islamic law: KBP3345
Property tax
Jewish law: KBM3616+
Local revenue
Comparative religious law: KB3616
Islamic law: KBP3663
National revenue
Comparative religious law: KB3616
Islamic law: KBP3616+, KBP3663
Proprietary church (Eigenkirchenrecht)
Canon law: KBR4022
Prorogation
Courts
Roman Catholic law: KBU3785
Prorogation
Ecclesiastical courts
Canon law: KBR3785
Jurisdiction
Procedure at first instance
Roman Catholic law: KBU3841.P75
Prosecuting innocent persons
Jewish law: KBM4507
Prostitution
Jewish law: KBM4224
Protection of children against obscenity
Islamic law: KBP1547
Jewish law: KBM1547
Protection of children in public
Islamic law: KBP1546
Jewish law: KBM1546
Protection of labor
Islamic law: KBP1408+
Jewish law: KBM1408+
Protection of ownership
Property
Comparative religious law: KB675
Islamic law: KBP675
Jewish law: KBM675
Protection of rights
Islamic law: KBP509+
Protective custody
Criminal law
Comparative religious law: KB3993.I47
Islamic law: KBP3992
Jewish law: KBM3992
Protective surveillance
Criminal law
Islamic law: KBP3995
Jewish law: KBM3995
Protestant Church and Roman Catholic Church: KB170.A+
Proverbia and canon law: KBR100.A+
Proverbs
Roman Catholic law: KBU100
Provinciae ecclesiasticae
Canon law: KBR2796+
Roman Catholic law: KBU2796+

Provincial council
  Ecclesiastical Provinces
    Canon law: KBR2820
Provincial councils
  Roman Catholic law: KBU950+
Proximate cause
  Jewish law: KBM524.4.C38, KBM3851
Proxy
  Marriage consent
    Roman Catholic law: KBU3137
Proxy, Marriage by
  Mere prohibition of marriage
    Roman Catholic law: KBU3122.P76
Psychologists
  Jewish law: KBM3103.P79
Psychology and criminal law
  Jewish law: KBM3819
Psychopharmaca
  Jewish law: KBM3092
Psychotherapists
  Jewish law: KBM3103.P79
Puberty
  Islamic law: KBP525.6.B84
Puberty, Age of
  Capacity and incapacity
    Canon law: KBR2232.P83
    Roman Catholic law: KBU2232.P83
Public associations
  Juristic persons
    Canon law: KBR2262
    Roman Catholic law: KBU2262+
Public baths
  Ablutions
    Islamic law: KBP184.47.P82
Public collections
  Cultural affairs
    Comparative religious law: KB3176+
    Islamic law: KBP3176+
    Jewish law: KBM3176+
Public defender
  Criminal procedure
    Jewish law: KBM4630.D43
Public finance
  Comparative religious law: KB3526+
  Islamic law: KBP3526+
Public finance
  Jewish law: KBM3526+
Public health
  Comparative religious law: KB3075+
  Crimes against
    Islamic law: KBP4400
    Jewish law: KBM4400+
  Islamic law: KBP3075+
  Jewish law: KBM3075+
Public health hazards
  Roman Catholic law: KBU3274.A+
Public health measures
  Contagious and infectious diseases
    Islamic law: KBP3084+
    Jewish law: KBM3084+
Public institutions
  Science and the arts
    Comparative religious law: KB3161
    Jewish law: KBM3161
Public irrigation zones
  Islamic law: KBP3058
Public land acquisition legislation
  Islamic law: KBP3057.3
Public land law
  Comparative religious law: KB3056
  Islamic law: KBP3056+
  Jewish law: KBM3061.92+
Public lands
  Comparative religious law: KB3056
  Islamic law: KBP3056+
Public law
  Comparative religious law: KB2000+
  Islamic law: KBP2000+
  Jewish law: KBM2000+
Public order
  Comparative religious law: KB481
  Islamic law: KBP481
  Offenses against
    Jewish law: KBM4305+
Public policies in research
  Jewish law: KBM3160+
Public policy
  Concept of Jewish law: KBM524.14
  Research
    Comparative religious law: KB3160+

Public policy
  Science and the arts
    Islamic law: KBP3160
  Unfair competition
    Islamic law: KBP1235
    Jewish law: KBM1235
Public property
  Comparative religious law:
    KB3040.5+
  Islamic law: KBP3040.5+
  Jewish law: KBM3040.5+
  Offenses against
    Jewish law: KBM4230+
Public restraint on private property
  Comparative religious law: KB2824+
  Islamic law: KBP2824+
  Jewish law: KBM2824+
Public restraint on property rights
  Mining and quarrying
    Islamic law: KBP3345
    Jewish law: KBM3345
Public safety
  Comparative religious law: KB3000+
  Islamic law: KBP3009+
  Jewish law: KBM3000+
Public services, Municipal
  Islamic: KBP2955+
Public utilities, Municipal
  Islamic law: KBP2955+
Public vows
  Religious institutes
    Canon law: KBR2924
Public welfare
  Canon law: KBR3264+
  Roman Catholic law: KBU3264+
Public works
  Jewish law: KBM3073
Public worship
  Islamic law: KBP184.32.G75
Publication of prohibited books
  Penal (Criminal) law
    Canon law: KBR3656+
Publicity
  Ecclesiastical laws
    Roman Catholic law: KBU2218
Publishers and publishing
  Copyright
    Islamic law: KBP1185
  Press law
    Comparative religious law:
      KB3500+
    Islamic law: KBP3500+
    Jewish law: KBM3503+
Publishing and censorship
  Canon law: KBR3064+
Punishment
  Criminal law
    Comparative religious law:
      KB3946+
    Islamic law: KBP3946+
    Jewish law: KBM3946+
  Determining the measure of
    Comparative religious law:
      KB4012+
    Islamic law: KBP4012+
    Jewish law: KBM4012
  Resemblance of to the committed act
    Islamic law: KBP3951
Punishment of offenses in general
  Criminal law
    Roman Catholic law: KBU3510+
Punitive deportation
  Criminal procedure
    Islamic law: KBP3997
    Jewish law: KBM4826+
Purification
  Islamic law: KBP184.44+
Purity
  Food processing
    Islamic law: KBP3379
    Jewish law: KBM3379
Purity of intention
  Islamic law: KBP184.12
Purity, Ritual
  Islamic law: KBP184.4+
Putative necessity
  Criminal law
    Roman Catholic law: KBU3553
  Justification of illegal acts
    Canon law: KBR3553

Putative self-defense
Justification of illegal acts
Canon law: KBR3554
Putative self-defense and exceeding self-defense
Criminal law
Roman Catholic law: KBU3554

Q

Qabūl: KBP869.3+
Qaḍā': KBP817.2+, KBP1679+
Qadhf: KBP4044, KBP4147
Qāḍī: KBP1610+
Assistant to
Islamic law: KBP1621
Dissolution of marriage pronounced by
Islamic law: KBP565
Qāḍī al-Quda: KBP1687
Qāḍī court
Islamic law: KBP1584
Qāḍī, Duty of
Islamic law: KBP1595
Qānūn
Sources of fiqh: KBP458.Q36
Qānūn al-baḥrīyah: KBP970+
Qānūn al-bunūk: KBP940+
Qānūn al-ta'mīn: KBP998+
Qarābah: KBP544.955
Criminal law
Islamic law: KBP4023.K56
Domestic relations: KBP583+
Qarḍ: KBP891
Qaṣd: KBP3868
Qasīm: KBP1622.2
Qāṣir: KBP622+
Qaṭ' al-ṭarīq: KBP4046
Qatl bi-sabab: KBP4054.5
Qawānīn al-khāṣṣah bi-al-nisā': KBP526+
Qīmī: KBP642.3
Qiṣāṣ punishment: KBP3975+
Qisṭ: KBP446
Qiyāfah: KBP619.I75
Qiyāṣ: KBP452
Quae statuuntur, pari iure de utroque sexu valent
Monasticism
Canon law: KBR2896
Qualification as heir
Comparative religious law: KB634
Jewish law: KBM633.5+
Qualification, Legal
Uṣūl al-fiqh
Islamic law: KBP447
Quality control
Economic law
Islamic law: KBP3255
Jewish law: KBM3255
Quality inspection
Food processing industries
Comparative religious law: KB3377
Islamic law: KBP3377+
Jewish law: KBM3377+
Quarantine
Public health
Comparative religious law: KB3087
Jewish law: KBM3087
Quarrying
Comparative religious law: KB3344
Regulation
Islamic law: KBP3344+
Jewish law: KBM3344+
Quasi-deliberate intent
Criminal intent
Islamic law: KBP3869
Quasi-domicile
Natural persons
Canon law: KBR2235+
Roman Catholic law: KBU2235+
Quasi-domicilium
Natural persons
Canon law: KBR2235+
Querela nullitatis contra sententiam
Trials
Canon law: KBR3863
Roman Catholic law: KBU3863
Questionable mamzerim: KBM544.8
Qui rationis usu carent
Criminal law
Law of the Roman Cathoic Church: KBU3542

Qui rationis usu carent
  Incapacity
    Violation of criminal law
      Canon law: KBR3542
Quinisext Synod, 692
  Canon law: KBR237
Quinque compilationes antiquae
  Canon law: KBR1450+
Qur'ān: KBP100+
  Sources of fiqh: KBP449
Qurbah: KBP544.955
Qurūḍ: KBP955+

R

Rabb al-māl: KBP1049.3
Rabbinate: KBM2200.R33
Rabbinical court
  Criminal proceeding by: KBM4613
Rabbinical Courts: KBM1582
Rabbinical literature
  Jewish law: KBM495+
Rabbinical seminaries
  Jewish law: KBM3147.7.A+
Rabbis: KBM2200.R33
Raḍā'
  Parent and child: KBP610.2
Radd: KBP633.952.R33
Radio broadcasting
  Comparative religious law: KB3491
  Islamic law: KBP3491
  Jewish law: KBM3491+
Radio communication
  Comparative religious law: KB3491
  Islamic law: KBP3491
  Jewish law: KBM3491+
  Roman Catholic law: KBU3066
Radioactive substances
  Pollution
    Comparative religious law: KB3132
    Islamic law: KBP3132
    Jewish law: KBM3132
Rafting
  Islamic law: KBP3478
Rahn: KBP726+
Rail traffic, Dangerous interference with
  Islamic law: KBP4380
Railroads
  Islamic law: KBP3459
  Jewish law: KBM3459
Rain prayer
  Islamic law: KBP184.32.R34
Raj'ah: KBP560
Ramadan: KBP186.4
Ramaḍān: KBP186.4
Ramadan fast: KBP184.54.R35
Rank and honors
  Ecclesiastical offices
    Canon law: KBR2355+
Ransoming of war or conflict captives
  Jewish law: KBM1539
Rape: KBP4202
  Jewish law: KBM4202
  Penal (Criminal) law
    Canon law: KBR3764
  Roman Catholic law: KBU3764
Rapina
  Penal (Criminal) law
    Canon law: KBR3774.R63
Raptus
  Roman Catholic law: KBU3760, KBU3764
Raptus impuberum alterutrius sexus
  Canon law: KBR3762
Raptus (intuitu matrimonii vel explendae libidinis causa)
  Canon law: KBR3760
Raqīq: KBP529.3+
Ratification and consummation
  Marriage law
    Roman Catholic law: KBU3114
Ratio utilitatis
  Sources of fiqh
    Islamic law: KBP456
Rationing
  Emergency measures
    Islamic law: KBP3724
    Jewish law: KBM3724
Ra'y: KBP453.2
Reactors, Nuclear
  Public safety
    Islamic law: KBP3012
Real property: KBM683+
  Canon law: KBR3410+

Real property
  Church property
    Roman Catholic law: KBU3410+
  Comparative religious law: KB683+
  Islamic law: KBP683+
  Lease
    Comparative religious law: KB884.R43
    Islamic law: KBP884.R43
    Jewish law: KBM884.R43
  Taxes
    Local finance
      Islamic law: KBP3670+
    Local revenue
      Comparative religious law: KB3670
    National revenue
      Comparative religious law: KB3670
Real rights
  Property
    Comparative religious law: KB646+
Real servitudes
  Comparative religious law: KB710
  Islamic law: KBP710
  Jewish law: KBM710
Reason
  Uṣūl al-fiqh
    Islamic law: KBP448.A74
Reasoning, Legal
  Sources of fiqh
    Islamic law: KBP457
Rebates
  Unfair competition
    Islamic law: KBP1250
    Jewish law: KBM1250
Rebellious wife
  Jewish law: KBM559.3
Rebelliousness
  Criminal law
    Jewish law: KBM3811
Receptor actorum
  Court officials
    Canon law: KBR3807.5.R43
Reconciliation
  Divorce
    Islamic law: KBP560
Reconciliation
  Matrimonial actions
    Comparative religious law: KB560
    Jewish law: KBM560
Recording
  Courts and procedure
    Comparative religious law: KB1850+
    Islamic law: KBP1850+
    Jewish law: KBM1850
Records management
  Public property
    Jewish law: KBM3042
Recourse
  Judicial review of administrative acts
    Roman Catholic law: KBU3970+
Recourse against decree of removal
  Penal (criminal) procedures
    Canon law: KBR3983
Recourse against decree of removal of pastor
  Roman Catholic law: KBU3985
Recreational drugs
  Comparative religious law: KB3090+
Rectores ecclesiarum
  Diocesan constitution and organs
    Canon law: KBR2874
Rectores seminarii diocesani
  Organs of government
    Roman Catholic law: KBU2870
Rectores seminarii dioecesani
  Diocesan constitution and organs
    Canon law: KBR2870
Rectors and directors
  Seminaries
    Canon law: KBR2328
Rectors of churches
  Diocesan constitution and organs
    Canon law: KBR2874
  Organs of government
    Roman Catholic law: KBU2874
Recursus adversus amotionis decretum
  Penal (criminal) procedures
    Canon law: KBR3983
Recycling of refuse
  Islamic law: KBP3264+

Red Crescent
  Islamic law: KBP3108.R42
Red Cross
  Islamic law: KBP3108.R43
  Jewish law: KBM3108.R43
Reform
  Law reform
    Criminal law
      Comparative religious law: KB3790
Reform and policies
  Roman Catholic law: KBU2207
Reform councils
  Counter reformation
    Canon law: KBR4036
Reform, Law: KBM524.38
  Criminal law
    Islamic law: KBP3790
    Jewish law: KBM3790
  Islamic law: KBP470
Reform, Law, and policies
  Canon law: KBR2207
Reformation
  Church and state
    Canon law: KBR4034+
Refuat shinayim
  Jewish law: KBM3103.D45
Refuge, Cities of
  Criminal procedure
    Jewish law: KBM4826.5
Refugees
  War refugees
    Social service
      Islamic law: KBP1538
      Jewish law: KBM1538
Refuse disposal
  Public health
    Islamic law: KBP3088.R43
    Jewish law: KBM3088.R43
Refuse, Recycling of
  Islamic law: KBP3264+
Regesta curiae matrimoniorum
  Roman Catholic law: KBU3146
Regesta matrimoniorum
  Canon law: KBR3146
Regional planning
  Islamic law: KBP3057+
Regiones ecclesiasticae
  Canon law: KBR2796+
  Roman Catholic law: KBU2796+
Registers, Criminal
  Jewish law: KBM4845
Registers, Marriage
  Roman Catholic law: KBU3146
Registration
  Artisans
    Jewish law: KBM3428
  Courts and procedure
    Comparative religious law: KB1850+
    Islamic law: KBP1850+
    Jewish law: KBM1850
  Land titles
    Islamic law: KBP737
  Mines and mineral resources
    Islamic law: KBP3350
Registration of civil status
  Islamic law: KBP1856+
Registration of internment
  Canon law: KBR3193
  Roman Catholic law: KBU3193
Registration of land titles
  Comparative religious law: KB737
  Jewish law: KBM737+
Registrator
  Court officials
    Canon law: KBR3807.5.R45
Regulation of industry, trade, and commerce
  Comparative religious law: KB3272+
  Islamic law: KBP3272+
  Jewish law: KBM3272+
Regulations
  Sources of fiqh
    Islamic law: KBP458.L35
Rehabilitation
  Criminal law measures
    Comparative religious law: KB3982+
  Criminal law punishment
    Jewish law: KBM3956
  Marriage
    Canon law: KBR3131

Rehabilitation measures
Criminal law
Islamic law: KBP3982+
Relics
Islamic law: KBP186.97+
Roman Catholic law: KBU3238.R45
Sacred places
Canon law: KBR3238.R45
Religion and constitutions
Comparative religious law: KB2101+
Religion and democratic government, Compatibility of
Comparative religious law: KB2035
Religious brotherhoods
Contracts
Comparative religious law: KB1040+
Religious community
Monasticism
Canon law: KBR2902+
Religious corporations
Employees
Comparative religious law: KB2870
Religious education
Roman Catholic law: KBU3050+
Teachers
Cornparative religious law: KB3140
Islamic law: KBP3140.5
Religious functionaries
Islamic law: KBP185
Religious houses
Monasticism
Canon law: KBR2899+
Religious institutes
Monasticism
Canon law: KBR2899+
Religious institutes and houses
Roman Catholic law: KBU2899+
Religious instruction in schools
Separation of Church and state
Roman Catholic law: KBU4062
Religious law and natural law: KB280
Religious law (General): KB2+
Religious legal scholars
Islamic law: KBP185
Religious minority court
Islamic law: KBP1588.7
Religious observance, Offenses against
Islamic law: KBP4174
Religious observances and rituals
Comparative religious law: KB400
Reliquiae Martyrum aliorumve Sanctorum
Sacred places
Canon law: KBR3238.R45
Remarriage
Canon law: KBR3160
Roman Catholic law: KBU3160
Remedia poenalis (Praecavenda)
Criminal law
Canon law: KBR3526+
Roman Catholic law: KBU3526+
Remedies
Courts and procedure
Comparative religious law: KB1686+
Islamic law: KBP1686+
Jewish law: KBM1686+
Criminal procedure
Comparative religious law: KB4770
Islamic law: KBP4770
Insolvency
Comparative religious law: KB1926
Islamic law: KBP1926
Jewish law: KBM1926
Penal (Criminal) procedure
Roman Catholic law: KBU3956+
Penal (criminal) procedures
Canon law: KBR3949+
Post-conviction remedies
Jewish law: KBM4790+
Roman Catholic law: KBU3861+
Trials
Canon law: KBR3861+
Removal and transfer of pastors
Penal (criminal) procedures
Canon law: KBR3973+
Roman Catholic law: KBU3975+
Remuneration
Support for the Church
Canon law: KBR3392
Renaissance
Church and state
Canon law: KBR4034+

Rent
  Contracts
    Servants and employees
      Jewish law: KBM892.6
Renunciation (of instance) by the promotor of justice
  Penal (Criminal) procedure
    Roman Catholic law: KBU3945
Renuntiatio a parocho
  Penal (criminal) procedures
    Canon law: KBR3978
Reopening a case
  Criminal procedure
    Jewish law: KBM4792
Reparation
  Victims of crimes
    Jewish law: KBM4767
Reparation of damages
  Procedure at first instance
    Penal (Criminal) procedure
      Roman Catholic law: KBU3939.D36
Reprimand
  Criminal law
    Jewish law: KBM3978
Reproductive choices
  Constitution of the state
    Islamic law: KBP2484.5
  Constitutional and administrative law
    Comparative religious law: KB2484.5
  Constitutional law
    Jewish law: KBM2484.5
Reproductive technology, Human
  Roman Catholic law: KBU3298
Repudiation of wife by husband
  Dissolution of marriage
    Islamic law: KBP562+
Requisition of private property for community use
  Jewish law: KBM3710
Requisitioned land in time of war
  Islamic law: KBP3710
Requisitions
  War damage compensation
    Jewish law: KBM3728.R47
Res consecratae vel benedictae
  Canon law: KBR3405
Res extra commercium
  Canon law: KBR3405
Res immobiles
  Canon law: KBR3410+
  Church property
    Roman Catholic law: KBU3410+
Res in commercio
  Comparative religious law: KB640+
  Islamic law: KBP640+
  Jewish law: KBM640+
Res iudicata
  Courts
    Roman Catholic law: KBU3837.R47
  Judiciary
    Canon law: KBR3837.R47
  Penal (Criminal) procedure
    Roman Catholic law: KBU3952
  Penal (criminal) procedures
    Canon law: KBR3947
  Roman Catholic law: KBU3869
  Trials
    Canon law: KBR3869
Res judicata
  Courts and procedure
    Islamic law: KBP1681
  Criminal procedure
    Comparative religious law: KB4754
    Islamic law: KBP4754
    Jewish law: KBM4754
Res sacrae
  Canon law: KBR3405
  Church property
    Canon law
      Rota Romana: KBR44.6.C45
    Roman Catholic law: KBU3405
      Rota Romana: KBU44.6.C45
Res spirituales
  Canon law: KBR2350+
Res temporales
  Canon law: KBR2350+
Resale
  Islamic law: KBP878.R47
  Jewish law: KBM878.R47

Rescript of dispensation
  Dispensation of ratified and non-consummated marriage
    Canon law: KBR3910
  Marriage
    Roman Catholic law: KBU3910
Rescriptum dispensationis
  Dispensation of ratified and non-consummated marriage
    Canon law: KBR3910
Research
  Public policies in research
    Comparative religious law: KB3160+
    Islamic law: KBP3160
Resh galuta: KBM2107
Residence
  Clergy
    Roman Catholic law: KBU2340.R47
  Dioceses
    Canon law: KBR2839
  Dioceses and diocesan bishop
    Roman Catholic law: KBU2839
Residentia personalis in diocesi
  Canon law: KBR2839
Resignation by pastor
  Penal (criminal) procedures
    Canon law: KBR3978
  Roman Catholic law: KBU3979
Respect for law
  Jewish law: KBM524.2+
Respect to parents and teachers
  Yoreh de'ah law: KBM523.5.R4
Restaurants
  Regulation
    Islamic law: KBP3424.5
    Jewish law: KBM3424.5
Restitutio in integrum
  Penal (Criminal) procedure
    Roman Catholic law: KBU3954
  Roman Catholic law: KBU3872
  Trials
    Canon law: KBR3872
Restitution
  Islamic law: KBP855
  Obligations
    Jewish law: KBM855
Restitution
  Pretrial procedure
    Islamic law: KBP1662.T56
  Pretrial procedures
    Jewish law: KBM1662.T56
Restoration of religious art works
  Roman Catholic law: KBU3204
Restraining order
  Courts
    Roman Catholic law: KBU3837.R48
  Judiciary
    Canon law: KBR3837.R48
Restraints on private property
  Jewish law: KBM3040.5+
Restrictions on cohanim
  Jewish law: KBM544.5
Retail trade
  Comparative religious law: KB3418
  Excise taxes
    Islamic law: KBP3640.R48
    Jewish law: KBM3640.R48
  Islamic law: KBP3418+
  Jewish community
    Jewish law: KBM3418+
Retaliation
  Criminal law punishment
    Comparative religious law: KB3952
  Measure of punishment
    Islamic law: KBP3951
  Punishment
    Criminal law
      Jewish law: KBM3952
Retention of ownership
  Conditional sale
    Islamic law: KBP877.2
    Jewish law: KBM877.2
Retention to secure a claim
  Property
    Islamic law: KBP731+
    Jewish law: KBM731
Retraction of evidence
  Criminal procedure
    Comparative religious law: KB4709.R48
  Criminal trial
    Islamic law: KBP4709.R84

Retribution
  Punishment
    Criminal law
      Jewish law: KBM3952
Retroactivity
  Islamic law concepts: KBP505
  Roman Catholic law: KBU2198
Return
  Decedents' estates
    Islamic law: KBP633.952.R33
Revenue for support of the Church
  Canon law: KBR3384+
Revenue service
  National and local revenue
    Comparative religious law: KB3558
  National revenue
    Islamic law: KBP3558+
Revocable divorce
  Islamic law: KBP562.953
Revocatio
  Ecclesiastical laws
    Roman Catholic law: KBU2220
Revocation
  Ecclesiastical laws
    Roman Catholic law: KBU2220
Revocation of emendation of decree
  Judicial review of administrative acts
    Roman Catholic law: KBU3969
Reward, Offer of
  Contracts
    Islamic law: KBP895
Rhenish school
  Canon law: KBR2204.5
Ribā: KBP868.2
Rida
  Declaration of consent: KBP869.6
Ridá
  Antenuptial contract: KBP543.952
Riddah
  Criminal law
    Islamic law: KBP4172
Right of asylum
  Constitution of the state
    Islamic law: KBP2485.5
  Constitutional and administrative law
    Comparative religious law:
      KB2485.5
Right of asylum
  Sacred places
    Canon law: KBR3236
Right of pre-emption
  Comparative religious law: KB716
  Islamic law: KBP716
  Jewish law: KBM716
Right of presentation
  Ecclesiastical offices
    Canon law: KBR2362.6
Right of privacy
  Islamic law: KBP529.83
  Jewish law: KBM524.4.P74
Right of recission
  Matrimonial actions
    Islamic law: KBP565
Right of rescission
  Contracts
    Comparative religious law:
      KB869.3+
    Islamic law: KBP869.3+
    Jewish law: KBM869.3+
  Defect of goods sold
    Islamic law: KBP876
  Sale
    Jewish law: KBM876
Right of way
  Real servitudes
    Comparative religious law: KB710
    Islamic law: KBP710
    Jewish law: KBM710
Right to die
  Comparative religious law: KB3121.7
  Jewish law: KBM3121.7
Right to draw water
  Real servitudes
    Comparative religious law: KB710
    Islamic law: KBP710
    Jewish law: KBM710
Right to information
  Press law
    Comparative religious law:
      KB3500.3
    Islamic law: KBP3500.3
    Jewish law: KBM3500.3

Right to life
  Constitution of the state
    Islamic law: KBP2484.5
  Constitutional and administrative law
    Comparative religious law:
      KB2484.5
  Constitutional law
    Jewish law: KBM2484.5
  Roman Catholic law: KBU4060.R53
Right to resistance against political
  authority
  Jewish law: KBM2486
Right to resistance against political
  authority or ideology
  Comparative religious law: KB2486
  Islamic law: KBP2486
Rights
  Exercise of
    Islamic law: KBP509+
  Islamic law: KBP502.4
  Metropolitans
    Canon law: KBR2805
  Pledges of rights (Property)
    Islamic law: KBP730
  Protection of
    Islamic law: KBP509+
Rights and duties
  Respect for law
    Jewish law: KBM524.22
Rights and obligations of clerics
  Canon law: KBR2336+
  Roman Catholic law: KBU2336+
Rights and obligations of the Christian
  faithful
  Canon law: KBR2312+
Rights and obligations of the laity
  Canon law: KBR2316+
Rights as to the use of another's land
  Comparative religious law: KB706+
  Islamic law: KBP706+
  Jewish law: KBM706+
Rights incident to ownership of land
  Comparative religious law: KB695+
  Islamic law: KBP695+
  Jewish law: KBM695+
Riots
  Criminal law
    Islamic law: KBP4398
    Jewish law: KBM4398
Riparian rights
  Comparative religious law: KB698
  Islamic law: KBP698
  Jewish law: KBM698
Risk
  Contracts
    Comparative religious law: KB866.5
    Islamic law: KBP866.5
    Jewish law: KBM866.5
Rites
  Baptism
    Canon law: KBR2229.R57
    Roman Catholic law: KBU2229.R57
Ritual bathing of the corpse
  Islamic law: KBP184.55
Ritual law
  Comparative religious law: KB400
  Islamic law: KBP184+
Ritual purity
  Islamic law: KBP184.4+
Ritual slaughtering
  Islamic law: KBP184.6+
Ritus
  Baptism
    Canon law: KBR2229.R57
Rivers
  Public property
    Comparative religious law:
      KB3046+
    Islamic law: KBP3046+
    Jewish law: KBM3046+
Road traffic
  Islamic law: KBP3442+
  Jewish law: KBM3442+
Roads and highways
  Islamic law: KBP3044.7
  Jewish law: KBM3044.7
Robbery
  Comparative religious law: KB4254
  Islamic law: KBP4254
  Penal (Criminal) law
    Canon law: KBR3774.R63

Roman Catholic Church and Eastern churches: KB165.A+
Roman Catholic Church and Protestant Church: KB170.A+
Roman Catholic Church, Law of the: KBU2+
Roman congregations
  Organs of government
    Canon law: KBR2500+
Roman Congregations
  Roman Catholic law: KBU2500+
Roman Empire and Early Church
  Church and state
    Canon law: KBR4012+
Roman law
  Compared with civil law, and canon law: KB215+
  Compared with civil law and Jewish law: KB201+
Roman law and Canon law: KBR2206
Roman law and Canon law (Greek-Byzantine and post-schismatic): KB245.A+
Roman law and law of the Roman Catholic Church: KBU2206
Roman law and Occidental canon law: KB230+
Roman Pontiff
  Tribunals of the Apostolic See
    Roman Catholic law: KBU3811
Roman Pontiff and the College of bishops (General)
  Roman Catholic law: KBU2365
Roman Pontiff, The
  Canon law: KBR2366+
  Roman Catholic law: KBU2366+
Romanus Pontifex et Collegium Episcoporum (General)
  Roman Catholic law: KBU2365
Rome, Council of, 155: KBR199.84
Rome, Council of, 193: KBR199.86
Roofs
  Building and construction
    Jewish law: KBM3072.R65
Rota Romana: KBR43+
  Decisions of ecclesiastical tribunals
    Roman Catholic law: KBU43+
Rota Romana
  Tribunals of the Apostolic See
    Canon law: KBR3816+
Rota Romana (Tribunal ordinarium)
  Roman Catholic law: KBU3816+
Rowdyism
  Criminal law
    Jewish law: KBM4309
Royalty and nobility, Marriages of
  Canon law: KBR3153
Rujūʻ
  Retraction of evidence
    Islamic law: KBP4709.R84
Rujūʼ
  Withdrawal of offer
    Islamic law: KBP869.3+
Rule-making power
  Municipal government
    Islamic law: KBP2938
Rule of law
  Public law
    Comparative religious law: KB2020+
    Islamic law: KBP2020+
    Jewish law: KBM2020+
Rulemaking power
  Communal agencies
    Jewish law: KBM2724
Rulers
  Constitutional law
    Islamic law: KBP2532+
  Constitutional principles
    Comparative religious law: KB2532+
  Privileges, prerogatives, and immunities
    Islamic law: KBP2300
    Jewish law: KBM2300
Rules of legal disputation
  Islamic law: KBP466
Rural law
  Comparative religious law: KB3294.22+
  Jewish law: KBM3293+
Rural laws
  Islamic law: KBP3293+

Rural planning
  Comparative religious law: KB3056
Rural planning and development zones
  Islamic law: KBP3059+
Rural schools
  Comparative religious law: KB3142
  Elementary education
    Islamic law: KBP3142
Rushd: KBP525+

S

Sabab: KBP544.955
  Domestic relations: KBP583+
Ṣabīy: KBP525
Sabotaging weapons, equipment, or
  means of defense
  Military law
    Islamic law: KBP3760.S32
    Jewish law: KBM3760.S32
Sacelli privati
  Sacred places
    Canon law: KBR3238.C53
Sacerdotes
  Diocesan constitution and organs
    Canon law: KBR2865
  Organs of government
    Roman Catholic law: KBU2865
Sacra ordinatio
  Canon law: KBR2330+
  Clergy
    Roman Catholic law: KBU2330
Sacra utensilia
  Canon law: KBR3366.S33
Sacramental confession
  Canon law: KBR3090+
Sacramental seal
  Penance
    Canon law: KBR3092
Sacramentale sigillum
  Penance
    Canon law: KBR3092
Sacramentalia
  Canon law: KBR3180+
Sacramentals
  Canon law: KBR3180+
  Roman Catholic law: KBU3180+
Sacraments
  Canon law: KBR3075+
  Roman Catholic law: KBU3075+
Sacred Penitentiary
  Canon law: KBR3812+
  Law of the Roman Cathoic Church:
    KBU3812+
Sacred places and times
  Canon law: KBR3230+
  Roman Catholic law: KBU3230+
Sacred times
  Roman Catholic law: KBU3242+
Sacred utensils
  Church property
    Canon law
      Rota Romana: KBR44.6.C45
    Roman Catholic law
      Rota Romana: KBU44.6.C45
Sacri Palatii auditorium: KBR43+
  Decisions of ecclesiastical tribunals
    Roman Catholic law: KBU43+
Sacrifices, Blood
  Islamic law: KBP184.6+
Sacrificial animal
  Islamic law: KBP184.62.S23
Sacrilege
  Penal (Criminal) law
    Canon law: KBR3660+
  Roman Catholic law: KBU3664
Sacrilegium carnale
  Penal (Criminal) law
    Canon law: KBR3660+
Sacrilegium (reale, personale, locale)
  Penal (Criminal) law
    Canon law: KBR3660+
Sadak: KBP543.954+
Ṣadaqah: KBP636.3
Sadd al-dharāʾiʻ: KBP457.3
Ṣadūqah: KBP543.953+
Safeguarding the social and political
  order
  Criminal law punishment
    Comparative religious law: KB3954
    Islamic law: KBP3950.2

Safeguarding the social and political system
  Criminal law punishment
    Jewish law: KBM3954
Safeḳ mamzerim: KBM544.8
Ṣaghīr: KBP525
Saint worship
  Sufism
    Islamic law: KBP189.585
Ṣakk: KBP1676.7
Salam contract
  Islamic law: KBP877.4
Salaries
  Ecclesiastical offices
    Roman Catholic law: KBU2355
  Income tax
    Jewish law: KBM3584
Sale
  Contracts
    Comparative religious law: KB874
    Islamic law: KBP874+
    Jewish law: KBM874+
Sale as slave as punishment for convicted criminals
  Jewish law: KBM4820
Sale on credit
  Islamic law: KBP877.3
  Jewish law: KBM877.3
Sales
  Excise taxes
    Islamic law: KBP3640.S25
Sales tax
  Comparative religious law: KB3627+
Sales taxes
  Islamic law: KBP3627+
Salvage
  Maritime law
    Comparative religious law: KB981
    Islamic law: KBP981
    Jewish law: KBM981
Samaritans
  Marriage
    Jewish law: KBM546.3.S36
Same-sex marriage
  Comparative religious law: KB546.6
Sanctiones poenales
  Canon law: KBR3518+
Sanctions
  Respect for law
    Jewish law: KBM524.22
Sanctuarii
  Sacred places
    Canon law: KBR3238.S67
Sanhedrin: KBM1587+
Sanhedrin, Trial by little or great: KBM4612
Sanitation
  City planning and redevelopment
    Islamic law: KBP3065
    Jewish law: KBM3065
  Food processing industries
    Comparative religious law
      Comparative religious law: KB3377
    Islamic law: KBP3377+
    Jewish law: KBM3377+
Ṣarf: KBP879.2.S27
Sargossa, Council of, 380: KBR249 380
Sariqah: KBP4235
Ṣawm: KBP179, KBP184.5+
Schism
  Canon law: KBR3640+
  Renaissance and Reformation
    Church and state
      Canon law: KBR4035+
  Roman Catholic law: KBU3640+
Schisma
  Canon law: KBR3640+
Schismatics, The
  Canon law: KBR3640+
School functionaries
  Islamic law: KBP3140+
  Jewish law: KBM3140+
School government
  Islamic law: KBP3138.55
  Jewish law: KBM3138.55
Schools
  Church property
    Canon law: KBR3460
  Juristic persons
    Roman Catholic law: KBU3460
Schools of thought
  Islamic law: KBP250+
Science and the arts: KBM3160+

Science and the arts
  Comparative religious law: KB3160+
  Freedom of
    Jewish law: KBM3137.5
  Islamic law: KBP3160+
Science, Canonical
  Canon law: KBR2160+
Science of religious law: KB270+
Scope of protection
  Copyright
    Islamic law: KBP1160.6
    Jewish law: KBM1160.6
Scribes, Jewish
  Jewish law: KBM1846.5
Seafood
  Regulation
    Islamic law: KBP3392
Seafood industry
  Regulation
    Jewish law: KBM3392
Seals and canon law: KBR83
Seclusion
  Islamic law: KBP184.5+
Secondary education
  Comparative religious law: KB3146
  Islamic law: KBP3146
  Jewish law: KBM3146
Secondhand trade
  Islamic law: KBP3423+
  Jewish law: KBM3423+
Secrecy
  Judges
    Rota Romana
      Canon law: KBR3817.3
Secrecy of office and deliberations
  Courts
    Roman Catholic law: KBU3828.S43
  Judiciary
    Canon law: KBR3828.S43
Secretaria Literarum ad Principes (Memorialium)
  Organs of government
    Canon law: KBR2477
Secretaria Literarum Latinarum
  Organs of government
    Canon law: KBR2480
Secretaria Status
  Organs of government
    Canon law: KBR2470+
Secretaria Status seu Papalis
  Roman Catholic law: KBU2470+
Secretariat of State (Papal Secretariat)
  Roman Catholic law: KBU2470+
Secretariate of Briefs to Princes
  Organs of government
    Canon law: KBR2477
Secretariate of Latin Letters
  Organs of government
    Canon law: KBR2480
Secretariate of State
  Organs of government
    Canon law: KBR2470+
Secular authorities, Obedience to the law issued by
  Jewish law: KBM2021+
Secular authority
  Bribery of officials of
    Jewish law: KBM2023
  Constitution of the state
    Islamic law: KBP2250.3
  Constitutional and administrative law
    Comparative religious law: KB2250.3
  Obligation of paying taxes to
    Jewish law: KBM2022
Secular authority and sharīʻah
  Islamic law: KBP2511
Secular authority to set and define law
  Jewish law: KBM524.2+
Secular courts
  Relationships with Jewish courts
    Jewish law: KBM1575
Secular (Imperial Byzantine) law relating to the church: KBR199.34+
Secular institutes
  Canon law: KBR2925
Secular laws, Violation of
  Jewish law: KBM3835
Secular state
  Relationship of the Jewish community (Kehillah) to: KBM2370+

Secularization
  Church and state
    Canon law: KBR4043
Secured transactions
  Comparative religious law: KB859
  Islamic law: KBP859
  Jewish law: KBM859
Securing evidence
  Criminal courts and procedure
    Jewish law: KBM4650
  Criminal procedures
    Islamic law: KBP4650
Securities
  Corporate finance
    Jewish law: KBM1064
  Stock corporations
    Islamic law: KBP1064
Securities and bonds
  Excise taxes
    Islamic law: KBP3640.S42
Security
  Contract for work and labor
    Islamic law: KBP894
  Contracts
    Comparative religious law: KB859
    Islamic law: KBP859
    Jewish law: KBM859
  Work contract
    Jewish law: KBM894
Sedes metropolitana
  Canon law: KBR2807
Seḳilah: KBM3964.1
Self-defense
  Criminal law
    Roman Catholic law: KBU3552
  Justification of illegal acts
    Canon law: KBR3552
  Protection of rights
    Islamic law: KBP509
Self-defense or defense of another
  Criminal offense
    Comparative religious law: KB3856
    Islamic law: KBP3856
    Jewish law: KBM3856
Self-government
  Jewish law: KBM2070+
Self-help
  Courts and procedure
    Islamic law: KBP1883
Self-incrimination
  Criminal trial
    Islamic law: KBP4681
    Jewish law: KBM4681
Self-mutilation
  Military law
    Islamic law: KBP3760.S44
    Jewish law: KBM3760.S44
Semantics, Legal
  Canon law: KBR2203
  Roman Catholic law: KBU2203
Seminaria
  Canon law: KBR2324
Seminaries
  Canon law: KBR2324
  Roman Catholic law: KBU2324
Seminaries, Teachers'
  Jewish law: KBM3147.8
Seminary rectors
  Diocesan constitution and organs
    Canon law: KBR2870
  Organs of government
    Roman Catholic law: KBU2870
Sentence
  Matrimonial actions
    Canon law: KBR3895
    Roman Catholic law: KBU3895
  Penal (Criminal) procedure
    Roman Catholic law: KBU3947+
Sentences
  Penal (criminal) procedures
    Canon law: KBR3944+
  Trials
    Canon law: KBR3857
    Roman Catholic law: KBU3857
Sentencing
  Criminal law
    Comparative religious law:
      KB4012+
    Islamic law: KBP4012+
    Jewish law: KBM4012
    Roman Catholic law: KBU3574+
  Penal (Criminal) law
    Canon law: KBR3574+

Sententia et appellatio
  Matrimonial actions
    Canon law: KBR3895
Sententiae
  Penal (criminal) procedures
    Canon law: KBR3944+
Sententiae definitivae
  Trials
    Canon law: KBR3857
Sententiae interlocutoriae
  Trials
    Canon law: KBR3858
Separation
  Matrimonial actions
    Canon law: KBR3901+
    Roman Catholic law: KBU3901+
Separation of Church and state
  Roman Catholic law: KBU4047+
Separation of powers
  Constitution of the state
    Islamic law: KBP2270
  Constitutional and administrative law
    Comparative religious law: KB2270
Separation of property
  Marital property
    Jewish law: KBM573
Separation of the spouses
  Canon law: KBR3163+
  Roman Catholic law: KBU3163+
Sepultura
  Canon law: KBR3273
  Roman Catholic law: KBU3273
Sequestration
  Courts
    Roman Catholic law: KBU3837.S46
  Judiciary
    Canon law: KBR3837.S46
Serdica, Council of, 343 or 347?:
  KBR246.3
Serefah: KBM3964.3
Servants
  Contracts
    Islamic law: KBP892.6
    Jewish law: KBM892.6
Service of process
  Pretrial procedures
    Criminal procedure
      Jewish law: KBM4646
Service trades
  Regulation
    Islamic law: KBP3424+
    Jewish law: KBM3424+
Servitudes
  Comparative religious law: KB709+
  Islamic law: KBP709+
  Jewish law: KBM709+
Set-off
  Procedure at trial
    Islamic law: KBP1667.T33
Settlement
  Claims from dissolved marriage
    Islamic law: KBP567
  Obligations
    Comparative religious law: KB817
    Jewish law: KBM818+
Settlement out of court
  Procedure at trial
    Comparative religious law:
      KB1668.S48
    Islamic law: KBP1668.S88
  Roman Catholic law: KBU3918
Settlement out or court in
  Canon law: KBR3918
Severely disabled people
  Social service
    Islamic law: KBP1534.S38
    Jewish law: KBM1534.S38
Sewage
  Municipal public services
    Islamic law: KBP2956
Sewage control
  Comparative religious law: KB3131
  Islamic law: KBP3131
  Jewish law: KBM3131
Sex
  Islamic law: KBP184.9.S38
Sex discrimination
  Comparative religious law: KB2467.5
  Islamic law: KBP2467.5
  Jewish law: KBM2467.5

Sexual behavior within marriage
  Jewish law: KBM552
Sexual etiquette
  Islamic law: KBP184.9.S38
Sexual integrity
  Offenses against
    Islamic law: KBP4200+
Sexual integrity, Offenses against
  Jewish law: KBM4200+
Sexual intercourse, Accusation of
  Islamic law: KBP4147
Sexually transmitted diseases
  Public health
    Islamic law: KBP3082.S47
    Jewish law: KBM3082.S47
  Public health laws
    Comparative religious law:
      KB3082.S47
Shaatnez
  Yoreh de'ah law: KBM523.5.S5
Shāfi'ī school of thought: KBP325+
Shahādah: KBP1675+
Shammash: KBM1624
Sharers
  Inheritance and succession
    Islamic law: KBP633.955+
Sharers (Heirs)
  Jewish law: KBM633.5+
Shares of decedents' estates: KBP633+
  Jewish law: KBM633+
Shares of estates
  Comparative religious law: KB633
Sharī'ah: KBP1+
Sharī'ah and secular authority
  Islamic law: KBP2511
Sharī'ah courts: KBP1580+
Sharīk: KBP1043.3
Sharikah: KBP1040+
Sharikat al-ṣanā'ī waal-taqabbul:
  KBP1048
Sharikat al-wujūh: KBP1133.S35
Sharikat 'aqd: KBP1043+
Sharikat 'inān: KBP1047+
Sharikat māl: KBP674
Shart al-khiyar: KBP869.3+
Shaving
  Yoreh de'ah law: KBM523.5.S53
Sheliaḥ bet din: KBM1624
Shelom bayit, Pursuit of
  Jewish law: KBM560
Shevuot: KBM1677.S53
Shibh al-'amd: KBP3869
Shiddukhin: KBM543+
Shīʻī schools of thought: KBP350+
Ship masters
  Maritime law
    Islamic law: KBP970.97
    Jewish law: KBM970.97
Ship traffic, Dangerous interference with
  Islamic law: KBP4380
Ships and ship owners
  Maritime law
    Islamic law: KBP970.97
    Jewish law: KBM970.97
Shipwreck
  Islamic law: KBP981
Shiqāq: KBP559.952
Shoḥad: KBM4520
Shore protection
  Islamic law: KBP3053
Shoṭeh: KBM529
Shrines
  Comparative religious law: KB3183
  Roman Catholic law: KBU3238.S67
  Sacred places
    Canon law: KBR3238.S67
Shroud
  Islamic law: KBP184.55
Shuhūd: KBP543.958
Shūrá: KBP2255
Shurb al-khamr: KBP4045
Shurṭah: KBP1588.3
Shurūṭ: KBP496.3
Sidur ha-geṭ: KBM562+
Signatura Apostolica: KBR46
  Canon law: KBR3819+
Signatura Apostolica (Supremum
  Signaturae Apostolicae Tribunal)
  Decisions of ecclesiastical tribunals
    Roman Catholic law: KBU46.5
Signatura justitiae
  Canon law: KBR46.3
Signatura Justitiae
  Canon law: KBR3819+

INDEX

Signaturae gratiae
Organs of government
Canon law: KBR2445
Sijill: KBP1679+
Silent partner
Personal companies
Islamic law: KBP1049.3
Jewish law: KBM1049.3
Silent partnership
Islamic law: KBP1049+
Personal companies
Jewish law: KBM1049+
Simonia
Penal (Criminal) law
Canon law: KBR3709+
Simony
Penal (Criminal) law
Canon law: KBR3709+
Simony in administration or reception of sacraments
Roman Catholic law: KBU3710
Sine culpa ignorantia
Criminal law
Roman Catholic law: KBU3557
Justification of illegal acts
Canon law: KBR3557
Sine debito moderamine
Criminal law
Roman Catholic law: KBU3554
Justification of illegal acts
Canon law: KBR3554
Sine licentia bonorum ecclesiasticorum alienatio
Roman Catholic law: KBU3698
Single-judge court
Islamic law: KBP1584
Single witness, Testimony by a
Jewish law: KBM1676.5
Siyar: KBP2400+
Siyāsah: KBP2730+, KBP3950.2
Siyāsah and fiqh, Dichotomy of: KBP445
Siyāsah sharīʿah: KBP2511
Siyāsah tribunals: KBP1580+
Slaughtering of animals
Comparative religious law: KB3123.3
Islamic law: KBP3123.3
Slaughtering, Ritual
Islamic law: KBP184.6+
Slave, Sale as
Criminal procedure
Jewish law: KBM4820
Slave trade
Penal (Criminal) law
Canon law: KBR3763
Slave traffic
Comparative religious law: KB4121
Islamic law: KBP4121
Jewish law: KBM4121
Slaves
Capacity and disability
Islamic law: KBP529.3+
Comparative religious law: KB529.3+
Criminal liability
Comparative religious law: KB3886.5
Islamic law: KBP3886.5
Liability for the torts of others
Islamic law: KBP839.7
Natural persons
Jewish law: KBM529.3
Small business
Islamic law: KBP3249
Smallpox
Immunization
Jewish law: KBM3086.S62
Smoking
Comparative religious law: KB3096.5
Public health
Islamic law: KBP3096.5
Jewish law: KBM3096.5
Smuggling
Tax crimes
Islamic law: KBP3698
Soccer
Public safety
Jewish law: KBM3036.S65
Social activities, Control of
Public safety
Comparative religious law: KB3034
Islamic law: KBP3034+
Jewish law: KBM3034+

Social disabilities, People with
  Equality before the law
    Islamic law: KBP2467.D58
    Jewish law: KBM2467.D58
  Social service
    Islamic law: KBP1532+
    Jewish law: KBM1532+
Social equality
  Jewish law: KBM2465+
Social insurance
  Islamic law: KBP1472+
  Jewish law: KBM1472+
Social laws and legislation
  Comparative religious law: KB1468+
  Jewish law: KBM1468+
Social legislation and canon law:
  KBR2157
  Roman Catholic law: KBU2157
Social policy
  Administration of church property
    Roman Catholic law: KBU3444.S63
Social reform and policies
  Islamic law: KBP1468
  Jewish law: KBM1468
Social security
  Islamic law: KBP1472+
  Jewish law: KBM1472+
Social security (for clerics)
  Administration of church property
    Roman Catholic law: KBU3444.S64
Social service
  Islamic law: KBP1520+
  Jewish law: KBM1520+
Social service and welfare activities of
  the church
  Canon law: KBR3264+
Social service beneficiaries
  Islamic law: KBP1528+
Social work of the church
  Canon law: KBR3264+
Social work of the Church
  Roman Catholic law: KBU3264+
Socially disabled children, Education of
  Jewish law: KBM3143.4
Societas
  Monasticism
    Canon law: KBR2902+
Societies
  Artisans
    Jewish law: KBM3429
Society and criminal law
  Comparative religious law: KB3818
  Islamic law: KBP3818
  Jewish law: KBM3818
Society and Islamic law: KBP173.25
Society and membership
  Monasticism
    Canon law: KBR2902+
Sociology of criminal procedure
  Jewish law: KBM4616
Sodales
  Monasticism
    Canon law: KBR2902+
Sodomy
  Comparative religious law: KB4172
  Islamic law: KBP4216
  Penal (Criminal) law
    Canon law: KBR3774.S64
Soferim: KBM1846.5
Soil conservation
  Islamic law: KBP3299
Soldiers
  Social service
    Islamic law: KBP1539
    Jewish law: KBM1539
Solicitation or attempted bribe of officials
  in the Church
  Penal (Criminal) law
    Canon law: KBR3722
Sorcery
  Penal (Criminal) law
    Canon law: KBR3646+
Sortilegium
  Penal (Criminal) law
    Canon law: KBR3648.S67
Sotah ritual
  Jewish law: KBM4184
Sound judgment
  Sources of fiqh
    Islamic law: KBP453.2
Sources
  Canon law: KBR190+
Sources of law
  Jewish law: KBM524.3

Sovereignty
Comparative religious law: KB2015
Holy See
Roman Catholic law: KBU4068
The Holy See
Canon law: KBR4068
Sovereignty questions
Islamic law: KBP2015
Sovereignty, Questions of
Jewish law: KBM2015
Space above ground
Ownership
Jewish law: KBM696
Space law
Islamic law: KBP3467
Jewish law: KBM3469
Spas
Jewish law: KBM3111
Specifications b Building and construction industry
Islamic law: KBP3402
Speedy trial
Canon law: KBR3826
Roman Catholic law: KBU3826
Sport fields
Torts
Jewish law: KBM848
Sport installations
Torts
Jewish law: KBM848
Sports
Islamic law: KBP3159
Jewish law: KBM3159
Torts
Jewish law: KBM848
Sports activities
Public safety
Jewish law: KBM3035+
Spouses
Dispensation of marriage
Roman Catholic law: KBU3909
Dispensation of ratified and non-consummated marriage
Canon law: KBR3909
Matrimonial actions
Canon law: KBR3890
Spouses, Domicile of
Natural persons
Canon law: KBR2236.S66
Roman Catholic law: KBU2236.S66
Spreading communicable diseases, morbific agents, or parasites
Comparative religious law: KB4368
Islamic law: KBP4368
Standard of conduct
Jewish law: KBM3874
Standardization
Economic law
Comparative religious law: KB3259+
Islamic law: KBP3259+
Jewish law: KBM3259+
Standardized forms of contract
Islamic law: KBP3239
Standards
Drinking water
Comparative religious law: KB3089
Economic law
Comparative religious law: KB3254+
Islamic law: KBP3254+
Jewish law: KBM3254+
State
Public law
Comparative religious law: KB2000+
State agencies
Employees
Comparative religious law: KB2870
State and church relationships
Canon law: KBR4000+
State and Church relationships
Roman Catholic law: KBU4000+
State and Islam: KBP173.6
State land grants
Islamic law: KBP3061
State prosecutor
Jewish law: KBM4630.S73
State protection of different denominations
Church and state
Canon law: KBR4042

State, The, and the Jewish community: KBM2000+
Stateless foreigners
  Registration
    Islamic law: KBP1865
Statue
  Conference of Bishops
    Canon law: KBR2829
Status clericalis
  Canon law: KBR2337+
Status, Legal, of married women
  Jewish law: KBM550+
Statute
  Sources of fiqh
    Islamic law: KBP458.Q36
Statutes and rules of order
  Roman Catholic law: KBU2195
Steam distributed by central plant
  Energy policy
    Islamic law: KBP3435
Stepchildren
  Jewish law: KBM608
Sterilization
  Roman Catholic law: KBU3304
Sterilization and castration
  Medical legislation
    Comparative religious law: KB3121+
    Islamic law: KBP3121+
    Jewish law: KBM3121
Stipulation
  Contracts
    Jewish law: KBM872
Stipulations
  Antenuptial contracts
    Islamic law: KBP543.952
  Blood sacrifices
    Islamic law: KBP184.62.S74
  Contracts
    Comparative religious law: KB872
    Islamic law: KBP872
Stock
  Stock corporations
    Islamic law: KBP1064
Stock companies
  Income tax
    Islamic law: KBP3596+
Stock companies
  Islamic law: KBP1050+
  Jewish law: KBM1050+
Stock corporations
  Islamic law: KBP1052+
Stock exchange transactions
  Excise taxes
    Islamic law: KBP3640.S76
Stocks
  Corporate finance
    Jewish law: KBM1064
Stolae
  Support for the Church
    Canon law: KBR3392
Stolae pro funeralibus
  Canon law: KBR3392
Stole fees
  Canon law: KBR3392
  Roman Catholic law: KBU3384+
Stoning
  Criminal law punishment
    Comparative religious law: KB3980.S85
    Islamic law: KBP3980.S85
Stoning to death
  Criminal law punishment
    Jewish law: KBM3964.1
Strangulation
  Criminal law punishment
    Jewish law: KBM3964.4
Street cleaning
  Public health
    Islamic law: KBP3088.S77
    Jewish law: KBM3088.S77
Street traffic, Dangerous interference with
  Islamic law: KBP4384
Students: KBM3139+
  Comparative religious law: KB3139+
  Higher education
    Comparative religious law: KB3147
    Islamic law: KBP3153
    Jewish law: KBM3153
  Islamic law: KBP3139+
Studiorum superiorum instituta
  Canon law: KBR3054

Stuprum
Penal (Criminal) law
Canon law: KBR3774.L49
Stuprum violentum
Penal (Criminal) law
Canon law: KBR3764
Roman Catholic law: KBU3764
Subpoena
Canon law: KBR3839.5
Criminal procedure
Jewish law: KBM4646
Roman Catholic law: KBU3839.5
Substantive law
Islamic law: KBP490+
Substituted performance
Obligations
Islamic law: KBP817.5
Subventiones rogatae
Roman Catholic law: KBU3384+
Subversive activities, Control of
Comparative religious law: KB2490
Subversive activities or groups, Control of
Constitution of the state
Islamic law: KBP2490
Constitutional law
Jewish law: KBM2490
Successio mortis causa
Natural persons
Canon law: KBR2248+
Roman Catholic law: KBU2248+
Succession
Comparative religious law: KB632+
Constitution of the state
Islamic law: KBP2535.S92
Islamic law: KBP632+
Jewish law: KBM632+
Kings, princes, and rulers
Comparative religious law: KB2535.S92
Succession, Order of
Islamic law: KBP634+
Jewish law: KBM634+
Sue, Capacity to
Canon law: KBR3832+
Suffragium deliberativum aut consultativum
Conference of Bishops
Canon law: KBR2832
Ṣūfī monastic orders: KBP189.68
Sufism: KBP188.5+
Suftajah: KBP938
Suicide
Penal (Criminal) law
Canon law: KBR3759.S85
Suicide, Assisting
Comparative religious law: KB4058
Islamic law: KBP4058
Jewish law: KBM4056
Suicidium
Penal (Criminal) law
Canon law: KBR3759.S85
Sulh
Courts: KBP1668.S88
Ṣulḥ
Contracts: KBP817.2+
Sultan
Constitution of the state
Islamic law: KBP2532+
Summary procedure
Trials
Canon law: KBR3882
Summatim cognoscere
Trials
Canon law: KBR3882
Summons
Canon law: KBR3839.5
Courts
Islamic law: KBP1662.S86
Jewish law: KBM1662.S86
Criminal procedure
Jewish law: KBM4646
Penal (Criminal) procedure
Roman Catholic law: KBU3931
Penal (criminal) procedures
Canon law: KBR3931
Roman Catholic law: KBU3839.5
Sunday and other feasts
Roman Catholic law: KBU3244+
Sundays
Canon law: KBR3244+
Sunna: KBP135.A1+

Sunna
  Sources of fiqh: KBP450
Sunnī schools of thought: KBP285+
Superior maior
  Religious institutes
    Canon law: KBR2915
Superior orders
  Military criminal law and procedure
    Jewish law: KBM3758.5
  Military discipline
    Islamic law: KBP3782
    Jewish law: KBM3782
  Military law
    Comparative religious law: KB3780
Superior orders and justification or excusation
  Jewish law: KBM3900
Superiores
  Religious institutes
    Canon law: KBR2914+
Superiority of the state over th church
  Canon law: KBR4037
Superiors
  Religious institutes
    Canon law: KBR2914+
Superiors, councils, etc
  Religious institutes
    Roman Catholic law: KBU2914+
Superstitio
  Penal (Criminal) law
    Canon law: KBR3646+
Superstition
  Penal (Criminal) law
    Canon law: KBR3646+
Superstitious practices
  Islamic law: KBP186.97+
Support
  Breach of duty of
    Islamic law: KBP4192
    Jewish law: KBM4192
  Consanguinity and affinity
    Jewish law: KBM584
  Domestic relations
    Islamic law: KBP584
Supputatio temporis
  Ius ecclesiasticum privatum
    Canon law: KBR2295
Supputatio temporis
  Roman Catholic law: KBU2295
Supranational institutions, Crimes against
  Comparative religious law: KB4543
  Islamic law: KBP4543
Suprema Congregatio Sanctae Romanae et Universalis Inquisitionis: KBR40
  Canon law: KBR2502+
Suprema ecclesiae auctoritas
  Roman Catholic law: KBU2364.5+
Supreme authority of the Church
  Roman Catholic law: KBU2364.5+
Supreme Congregation of the Holy Roman and Universal Inquisition: KBR40
  Canon law: KBR2502+
Supreme judge for the Catholic World
  Law of the Roman Cathoic Church: KBU3811
Supreme judicial authority
  Islamic law: KBP1591.5
Supreme moderators
  Religious institutes
    Canon law: KBR2914+
Supreme Tribunal of the Apostolic Signatura
  Roman Catholic law: KBU3819+
Supremum Signaturae Apostolicae Tribunal
  Roman Catholic law: KBU3819+
Supremus Moderator
  Religious institutes
    Canon law: KBR2914+
Surety for the defendant
  Islamic law: KBP1925.S87
Suretyship
  Contracts
    Comparative religious law: KB900
    Islamic law: KBP900
    Jewish law: KBM900
Surgical and other medical treatment, Criminal aspects of
  Jewish law: KBM4096

INDEX

Surrogate motherhood
Family law
Jewish law: KBM619.A77
Surtaxes
Jewish law: KBM3624+
National revenue
Islamic law: KBP3624
Surviving spouses
Inheritance and succession
Islamic law: KBP634.954
Survivors insurance
Jewish law: KBM1508
Survivors' insurance
Social security
Islamic law: KBP1508
Suspensio
Clergy
Canon law: KBR3615.S94
Penal (Criminal) law
Canon law: KBR3608+
Suspension
Insolvency
Islamic law: KBP1932
Insolvency claims enforcement
Comparative religious law: KB1932
Suspension of clerics
Penal (Criminal) law
Canon law: KBR3608+
Roman Catholic law: KBU3608
Suspension of religious orders
The Pope
Canon law: KBR2384.3
Suspension of the execution (of a decree)
Judicial review of administrative acts
Roman Catholic law: KBU3972
Suspensive conditions
Islamic law concepts: KBP505
Symbolism
Islamic law: KBP182.5
Symbolism in law
Islamic law: KBP53.5
Religious law: KB78.A+
Symbolism, Legal, and canon law: KBR78
Symbols
Islamic law: KBP182.5
Synod of Bishops
Roman Catholic law: KBU2402+
Synods of legates
Canon law: KBR4090
Synodus dioecesana
Canon law: KBR2880
Synodus episcoporum
Roman Catholic law: KBU830.5+
Synodus Episcoporum
Roman Catholic law: KBU2402+

T

Ta'addī: KBP834+
Ta'addud al-zawjāt: KBP546.954
Ta'āruḍ al-adillah: KBP460
Tacit condonation
Roman Catholic law: KBU3165
Tadbīr: KBP529.5
Tadfīn: KBP184.55
Tafrīq: KBP565
Tafwīḍ: KBP563
Taghṣīl: KBP184.55
Taḥāluf: KBP1667.T33
Ṭahārah: KBP184.4+
Tahātur: KBP1677.T35
Tahdīd: KBP867.5
Takfīn: KBP184.55
Takkanot ha-kahal: KBM2510+
Takkanot ha-Ḳahal: KBM570
Ṭalāq bā' in: KBP562.953
Ṭalāq divorce: KBP558+
Ṭalāq raj'ī: KBP562.953
Talion
Comparative religious law: KB3952
Islamic law: KBP3951
Ta'līq al-ṭalāq: KBP562.954
Talmudic literature
Jewish law: KBM497+
Talqīḥ basharī: KBP619.T34
Tanāzu' al-qawānīn: KBP480+
Tanẓīm: KBP470
Taqādum: KBP507+
Criminal law: KBP4038
Taqlīd: KBP454
Taqsīm al-tarikah: KBP633+, KBP633.952.T37

Tariff
  Comparative religious law: KB3681
  Islamic law: KBP3681
Tarikah: KBP633+
Tasbīb: KBP3851
Tashābuh: KBP3951
Tashmishe ḳodesh industry
  Jewish law: KBM3373.L57
Tasjīl 'aqārī: KBP737
Taṣyīr: KBP817.5
Taverns
  Regulation
    Islamic law: KBP3424.5
    Jewish law: KBM3424.5
Tawbah: KBP3868
  Criminal law
    Islamic law: KBP4023.T38
  Imprisonment aiming at repentance
    Islamic law: KBP3992
Tawrīth: KBP632+
Tawthīq 'aqārī: KBP737
Tax administration
  National and local revenue
    Comparative religious law: KB3558
  National revenue
    Islamic law: KBP3558+
  Public finance
    Jewish law: KBM3558
Tax and customs courts
  Comparative religious law: KB3682
  Islamic law: KBP3682+
Tax and customs crimes and delinquency
  Comparative religious law: KB3693+
  Islamic law: KBP3693+
  Jewish law: KBM3693+
Tax avoidance
  Comparative religious law: KB3694.T39
  Islamic law: KBP3695
  Jewish law: KBM3557
Tax collection
  National and local revenue
    Comparative religious law: KB3558
Tax enforcement
  National and local revenue
    Comparative religious law: KB3558
Tax evasion
  Comparative religious law: KB3694.T39
  Islamic law: KBP3695
Tax power
  The Pope
    Canon law: KBR2386
    Roman Catholic law: KBU2386
Tax saving
  Jewish law: KBM3557
Tax valuation
  Property tax
    Jewish law: KBM3617
Taxable income
  Islamic law: KBP3578+
  Jewish law: KBM3578+
Taxable property
  Jewish law: KBM3620
Taxae and tributa
  Roman Catholic law: KBU3384+
Taxation
  Local revenue
    Comparative religious law: KB3541+
  National revenue
    Comparative religious law: KB3541+
    Islamic law: KBP3541+
  Obligation of paying taxes to secular authority
    Jewish law: KBM2022
Taxation and fundraising
  Local finance
    Jewish law: KBM3660
Taxation of capital
  Jewish law: KBM3616+
  Local revenue
    Comparative religious law: KB3616
  National revenue
    Comparataive religious law: KB3616
    Islamic law: KBP3616+
Taxation per capita
  Jewish law: KBM3626
Taxes, Church
  Canon law: KBR3384+
  Roman Catholic law: KBU3384+

Taʻzīr punishment: KBP3965
Teachers: KBM3140+
  Comparative religious law: KB3140
  Elementary education
    Comparative religious law: KB3141+
    Islamic law: KBP3141+
    Jewish law: KBM3141
  Higher education
    Comparative religious law: KB3147
    Islamic law: KBP3152
    Jewish law: KBM3152
  Islamic law: KBP3140+
  Vocational education
    Islamic law: KBP3144.5
    Jewish law: KBM3144.5
Teaching of doctrines condemned by the Roman Pontiff or ecumenical council
  Roman Catholic law: KBU3678
Teaching office of the church
  Canon law: KBR3040+
Teaching office of the Church
  Roman Catholic law: KBU3040+
Telecommunication
  Islamic law: KBP3485+
  Jewish law: KBM3487
  Roman Catholic law: KBU3066
Telephone
  Jewish law: KBM3487
Television broadcasting
  Comparative religious law: KB3491
  Islamic law: KBP3491
  Jewish law: KBM3491+
Tempora sacra
  Canon law: KBR3242+
  Roman Catholic law: KBU3242+
Temporal goods of the Church
  Canon law: KBR3328+
  Roman Catholic law: KBU3328+
Temporary marriage
  Comparative religious law: KB546.5
  Islamic law: KBP546.955
  Jewish law: KBM546.5
Tempus continuum
  Ius ecclesiasticum privatum
    Canon law: KBR2295
Tenaim: KBM543+
Tenancy
  Islamic law: KBP683+
Tenant
  Lease
    Islamic law: KBP880+
Tenant and landlord
  Comparative religious law: KB880+
  Jewish law: KBM880+
Termination
  Cooperative societies
    Islamic law: KBP1134
    Jewish law: KBM1134
  Silent partnership
    Islamic law: KBP1049.7
    Jewish law: KBM1049.7
  Stock companies
    Jewish law: KBM1085
  Stock corporations
    Islamic law: KBP1085
Terminus peremptorius
  Judicial review of administrative acts
    Roman Catholic law: KBU3966
Terms
  Contracts
    Comparative religious law: KB870
    Islamic law: KBP870
    Jewish law: KBM870
  Islamic law concepts: KBP505
Terms of court
  Rota Romana
    Canon law: KBR3818.5
Terres communes
  Comparative religious law: KB686
  Islamic law: KBP686
Territory
  Constitution of the state
    Islamic law: KBP2390
  Holy See
    Roman Catholic law: KBU4070
Terrorism
  Comparative religious law: KB4351.5+
  Islamic law: KBP4351.5+
  Jewish law: KBM4351.5
Terrorist activity
  Jewish law: KBM4351.5

Testamenta clericorum
Canon law: KBR3360+
Testamentary bequests
Comparative religious law: KB635.2
Islamic law: KBP635.952
Jewish law: KBM635.2
Testamentary succession
Comparative religious law: KB635+
Islamic law: KBP635+
Jewish law: KBM635+
Natural persons
Canon law: KBR2249+
Roman Catholic law: KBU2249+
Testaments
Church property
Roman Catholic law: KBU3355+
Jurisdiction of ecclesiastical courts
Canon law: KBR3795.T47
Temporal goods of the Church
Canon law: KBR3355+
Testaments of clerics
Canon law: KBR3360+
Testamentum
Natural persons
Canon law: KBR2249+
Roman Catholic law: KBU2249+
Testate succession
Natural persons
Canon law: KBR2248+
Roman Catholic law: KBU2248+
Testes
Marriage
Canon law: KBR3145
Roman Catholic law: KBU3145
Testes et qui testes esse possint
Trials
Canon law: KBR3848
Roman Catholic law: KBU3848
Testimony
Conflict of equivalent testimony
Islamic law: KBP1677.T35
Procedure in general
Comparative religious law: KB1675+
Islamic law: KBP1675+
Jewish law: KBM1675+
Testimony of parties
Trials
Roman Catholic law: KBU3846
Testimony of the accused
Criminal procedure
Comparative religious law: KB4709.T47
Islamic law: KBP4702
Jewish law: KBM4702
Testimony, Previous
Criminal procedure
Jewish law: KBM4690
Theater
Cultural affairs
Comparative religious law: KB3172
Islamic law: KBP3172
Jewish law: KBM3172
Theft
Aggravated theft
Islamic law: KBP4046.2
Criminal law
Comparative religious law: KB4235
Islamic law: KBP4235
Jewish law: KBM4234
Torts
Jewish law: KBM846.2
Theocratic state, Islamic
Legal philosophy and theory
Islamic law: KBP2000+
Theology and canonical jurisprudence: KBR2155
Roman Catholic law: KBU2155
Theory
Public law
Jewish law: KBM2015+
Punishment
Criminal law
Jewish law: KBM3950+
Theory and science of canon law
Roman Catholic law: KBU2160+
Theory of knowledge
Islamic law: KBP430
Theory of punishment
Criminal law
Comparative religious law: KB3950+

Things
  Jewish law: KBM642.3+
  Property
    Comparative religious law:
      KB642.3+
Things (Property)
  Islamic law: KBP642.3+
Third parties
  Contracts
    Comparative religious law: KB873.3
    Islamic law: KBP873.3
    Jewish law: KBM873.3
  Courts
    Jewish law: KBM1657
Third party, Intervention of
  Procedure at first instance
    Penal (Criminal) procedure
      Roman Catholic law:
        KBU3939.I67
Threat
  Void and voidable contracts
    Comparative religious law: KB867.5
    Islamic law: KBP867.5
    Jewish law: KBM867.5
Thwarting criminal justice
  Jewish law: KBM4500
Ṭifl: KBP525
Timber laws
  Comparative religious law: KB3336
  Islamic law: KBP3336
  Jewish law: KBM3336
Time, Computation of
  Ius ecclesiasticum privatum
    Canon law: KBR2295
  Roman Catholic law: KBU2295
Time limits
  Courts
    Roman Catholic law: KBU3828.T56
Time of effectiveness
  Contracts
    Jewish law: KBM866
  Contracts and transactions
    Islamic law: KBP866
Time periods
  Courts
    Jewish law: KBM1662.T56
Time periods
  Criminal procedure
    Comparative religious law: KB4648
    Islamic law: KBP4648
    Jewish law: KBM4648
  Islamic law: KBP506
  Pretrial procedure
    Islamic law: KBP1662.T56
Tissue donation and transplantation
  Medical legislation
    Islamic law: KBP3116
    Jewish law: KBM3116
Tithes
  Canon law: KBR3386
Title
  Clergy
    Canon law: KBR2332
Titles of credit
  Islamic law: KBP937+
  Jewish law: KBM937+
Titulus
  Clergy
    Canon law: KBR2332
Tobacco
  Islamic law: KBP184.42+
Tobacco use
  Comparative religious law: KB3096.5
  Public health
    Islamic law: KBP3096.5
    Jewish law: KBM3096.5
Toledo, Council of, 4th, 633: KBR249
  633
Tombs, Visitation of
  Islamic law: KBP186.97.T65
Tonsure
  Clergy
    Roman Catholic law: KBU2340.T66
Torneamentum
  Penal (Criminal) law
    Canon law: KBR3759.T67
Torts
  Comparative religious law: KB834+
  Obligations
    Islamic law: KBP834+
    Jewish law: KBM834+

Torture
  Criminal procedure
    Comparative religious law: KB4541
    Islamic law: KBP4541
  Inquisition
    Canon law: KBR3943.T67
Tourism
  Public safety
    Islamic law: KBP3033
Toxic substances
  Public safety
    Islamic law: KBP3014.A+
Trade
  Trade with non-Jews
    Jewish law: KBM3405
  Trade within the Jewish community
    Jewish law: KBM3415+
Trade practices
  Food processing industries
    Comparative religious law: KB3377
    Islamic law: KBP3377+
Trademarks
  Comparative religious law: KB1194
  Islamic law: KBP1194
Tradition
  Jewish law: KBM524.3
Tradition, Canonical
  Roman Catholic law: KBU2190
Traditions
  Islamic law: KBP135.A1+
Traffic
  Crimes affecting
    Comparative religious law:
      KB4380+
Traffic noise
  Pollutants
    Islamic law: KBP3132.5
    Jewish law: KBM3132.5
Traffic regulations and enforcement
  Islamic law: KBP3448+
  Jewish law: KBM3448
Traffic,Crimes affecting
  Islamic law: KBP4380+
  Jewish law: KBM4380+
Trail
  Criminal procedure
    Comparative religious law:
      KB4673+
Training
  Teachers
    Islamic law: KBP3140.5
Transactio seu reconciliatio
  Ecclesiastical courts
    Canon law: KBR3918
Transactio seu recondiliatio
  Courts
    Roman Catholic law: KBU3918
Transactions
  Jewish law: KBM801+
  Obligations
    Islamic law: KBP810+
  Taxable income
    Islamic law: KBP3620.3.T72
Transfer
  Negotiable instruments
    Islamic law: KBP937.3
    Jewish law: KBM937.3
Transfer and assumption of obligations
  Comparative religious law: KB816
  Islamic law: KBP816+
  Jewish law: KBM816
Transfer of possession and ownership
  Comparative religious law: KB648+
  Islamic law: KBP648+
  Jewish law: KBM648+
Transients
  Marriage impediments
    Canon law: KBR3122.T73
  Mere prohibition of marriage
    Roman Catholic law: KBU3122.T73
Transit traffic
  Public safety
    Islamic law: KBP3033
Translatio pensionis
  Clergy
    Canon law: KBR3615.T73
Transplantation of organs, tissues, etc
  Medical legislation
    Comparative religious law: KB3116
    Islamic law: KBP3116
    Jewish law: KBM3116

Transplantation of organs, tissues, etc
Roman Catholic law: KBU3292
Transportation
Comparative religious law: KB3440+
Islamic law: KBP3440+
Jewish law: KBM3440+
Transportation of hazardous articles and processes by land
Public safety
Islamic law: KBP3011+
Travel
Islamic law: KBP184.9.T72
Traveler's prayer
Islamic law: KBP184.32.T72
Traveling and transit traffic
Public safety
Islamic law: KBP3033
Traveling salespeople
Agency and prokura
Jewish law: KBM924
Jewish law: KBM926.3.T73
Treason
Comparative religious law: KB4417+
Islamic law: KBP4417+
Treasure troves
Comparative religious law: KB658
Islamic law: KBP658
Jewish law: KBM658
Treasury
Organs of government
Canon law: KBR2455
Treaty making power
The Pope
Canon law: KBR2377
Roman Catholic law: KBU2377
Treatymaking power
Constitutional and administrative law
Comparative religious law: KB2558
Organs of government
Islamic law: KBP2558
Trees
Jewish law: KBM524.4.T73
Trial
Canon law: KBR3838+
Criminal law and procedure
Islamic law: KBP4664+
Jewish law: KBM4664+
Trial
Criminal procedure
Islamic law: KBP4673+
Jewish law: KBM4673+
Procedure in general
Islamic law: KBP1663+
Jewish law: KBM1663+
Trial, Contentious
Roman Catholic law: KBU3838+
Trials
Canon law: KBR127+
Roman Catholic law: KBU127+
Tribal law
Sources of fiqh
Islamic law: KBP458.T74
Tribunal of the Apostolic Signatura
Canon law: KBR3819+
Tribunal of the Camera Apostolica
Canon law: KBR45
Decisions of ecclesiastical tribunals
Roman Catholic law: KBU45
Tribunalia primae et secundae instantiae
Canon law: KBR3806+
Tribunals
Canon law: KBR3805.2+
Comparative religious law: KB1580+
Courts and procedure
Islamic law: KBP1588+
Jewish law: KBM1580+
Roman Catholic law: KBU3782.52+
Tribunals (diocesan) of first and second instance
Canon law: KBR3806+
Tribunals of first instance
Roman Catholic law: KBU3806
Tribunals of second instance
Roman Catholic law: KBU3808
Tribunals of the Apostolic See
Canon law: KBR3810+
Roman Catholic law: KBU3810+
Trullanum, Concilium, 692
Canon law: KBR237
Trust and trustee
Contracts
Comparative religious law: KB889

Trust investments
  Corporate finance
    Jewish law: KBM1064
  Stock corporations
    Islamic law: KBP1064
Trusts
  Juristic persons
    Canon law: KBR2276.C53
Trusts and trustee
  Contracts
    Islamic law: KBP889+
Trusts and trustees
  Contracts
    Jewish law: KBM889+
Truth
  Uṣūl al-fiqh
    Islamic law: KBP448.H37
Tuberculosis
  Public health
    Islamic law: KBP3082.T82
    Jewish law: KBM3082.T82
Turin, Council of, 401: KBR249 401
Tutor
  Natural persons
    Roman Catholic law: KBU2245+
Tutor or curator, Domicile of
  Natural persons
    Canon law: KBR2236.T87
  Roman Catholic law: KBU2236.T87
Twilight
  Oraḥ ḥayim law: KBM523.3.T9
Tyre, Council of, 335: KBR249 335

U

'Ubar
  Natural persons
    Jewish law: KBM529.7.U53
'Ulamā': KBP185
Ultima voluntas
  Natural persons
    Canon law: KBR2249+
    Roman Catholic law: KBU2249+
  Temporal goods of the Church
    Canon law: KBR3355+
'Ulūm al-ḥadīth: KBP135.6+
Umm walad: KBP529.5
Unauthorized agent
  Islamic law: KBP862
Unauthorized representation
  Agency
    Comparative religious law: KB861
  Contracts
    Jewish law: KBM862
Unborn child
  Comparative religious law: KB524.72
Unborn children
  Capacity and disability
    Islamic law: KBP524.72
  Inheritance and succession
    Islamic law: KBP634.953.J35
  Natural persons
    Jewish law: KBM529.7.U53
Unconscionable transactions
  Comparative religious law: KB868+
  Islamic law: KBP868+
  Void and voidable contracts
    Jewish law: KBM868+
Underground
  Ownership
    Comparative religious law: KB697
    Islamic law: KBP697
    Jewish law: KBM697
Underground water
  Ownership
    Comparative religious law: KB698
    Islamic law: KBP698
  Ownership of land
    Jewish law: KBM698
  Public property
    Comparative religious law: KB3046+
    Islamic law: KBP3046+
    Jewish law: KBM3046+
Underselling prices established by government
  Jewish law: KBM4290
Unemployment insurance
  Islamic law: KBP1512
  Jewish law: KBM1512
Unfair competition
  Comparative religious law: KB1234
  Islamic law: KBP1234+
  Jewish law: KBM1234+

Unincorporated business associations
Income tax
Islamic law: KBP3594+
Union, Council of, 879: KBR263
Universal ecclesiastical laws
Roman Catholic law: KBU2216+
Universitas personarum
Juristic persons
Canon law: KBR2256+
Roman Catholic law: KBU2256+
Universitas rerum
Juristic persons
Roman Catholic law: KBU2273+
Universitates catholicae
Canon law: KBR3054
Roman Catholic law: KBU3054
Universitates vel facultates ecclesiasticae
Canon law: KBR3060
Universities
Comparative religious law: KB3147
Islamic law: KBP3147+
Universities and colleges offering secular studies
Jewish law: KBM3147.5
Universities, Catholic
Canon law: KBR3054
Roman Catholic law: KBU3054
Unjust enrichment
Obligations
Comparative religious law: KB854+
Islamic law: KBP854+
Jewish law: KBM854+
Unlawful intercourse
Grounds for divorce
Islamic law: KBP559.958
Ḥadd crimes
Islamic law: KBP4043
Unlimited commercial partnership
Islamic law: KBP1045+
Jewish law: KBM1045+
Unmarried cohabitation
Comparative religious law: KB568.U56
Islamic law: KBP546.17
Jewish law: KBM546.17
Unworthiness of heir
Comparative religious law: KB636
Jewish law: KBM636
'Uqūd al-zawāj: KBP572
'Uqūd ghayr sharī'ah: KBP868+
'Urf: KBP455, KBP2340
Urine tests
Criminal procedure
Jewish law: KBM4687
Usufruct
Comparative religious law: KB715
Islamic law: KBP715
Jewish law: KBM715
Uṣūl al-fiqh
Concepts
Islamic law: KBP442+
Usura
Penal (Criminal) law
Canon law: KBR3774.U78
Usurious contracts
Comparative religious law: KB868.2
Islamic law: KBP868.2
Jewish law: KBM868.2
Usurpation of another's property
Torts
Islamic law: KBP846.2
Jewish law: KBM846.2
Usurpation of ecclesiastical functions
Roman Catholic law: KBU3700+
Usurpation of ecclesiastical office
Roman Catholic law: KBU3712
Usury
Criminal law
Jewish law: KBM4268
Penal (Criminal) law
Canon law: KBR3774.U78
Utensils, Sacred
Church property
Canon law
Rota Romana: KBR44.6.C45
Roman Catholic law
Rota Romana: KBU44.6.C45
Uxoricide
Impediments to marriage
Canon law: KBR3128.H66
Marriage impediments
Roman Catholic law: KBU3128.H66

V

Vacancy of the Holy See
  Canon law: KBR2392
  Roman Catholic law: KBU2392
Vacations
  Public safety
    Jewish law: KBM3034.5
Vaccination
  Public health laws
    Comparative religious law: KB3086.A+
  Public health measures
    Islamic law: KBP3086.A+
    Jewish law: KBM3085+
Valid marriage
  Islamic law: KBP546.2
Validas actus iuridici
  Legal transactions
    Ius ecclesiasticum privatum: KBR2288+
Validitas actus iuridici
  Roman Catholic law: KBU2288+
Validity
  Legal transactions
    Ius ecclesiasticum privatum: KBR2288+
    Roman Catholic law: KBU2288+
Validity and applicability of the law
  Criminal law
    Jewish law: KBM3825+
Validity of civil marriages
  Jewish law: KBM546.18
Validity of law
  Canon law: KBR2196
  Jewish law: KBM524.24
  Roman Catholic law: KBU2196
Validity of the law
  Islamic law: KBP501+
  Pre-Islamic law: KBP501.3
Valuation of real property
  Taxation
    Jewish law: KBM3617
Vandalism
  Criminal law
    Jewish law: KBM4309
Vatican
  Church and state
    Canon law: KBR4070
Vatican City, Legal and international status of
  Roman Catholic law: KBU4064+
Vatican Council (1st), 1869
  Canon law: KBR830 1869
Vatican Council (2nd), 1962
  Canon law: KBR830 1962
Vegetables
  Islamic law: KBP3381
  Jewish law: KBM3381
Vendor and purchaser
  Jewish law: KBM687.5+
Veneration
  Islamic law: KBP186.97+
Veneration of saints, sacred images and relics
  Roman Catholic law: KBU3200+
Veneration of Saints, sacred images, and relics
  Canon law: KBR3200+
Venereal diseases
  Public health
    Islamic law: KBP3082.S47
    Jewish law: KBM3082.S47
  Public health laws
    Comparative religious law: KB3082.S47
Venue
  Courts
    Roman Catholic law: KBU3797+
  Ecclesiastical courts
    Canon law: KBR3797+
Veterans
  Social service
    Islamic law: KBP1539
    Jewish law: KBM1539
Veterans, War, Disabled
  Social work
    Canon law: KBR3280.W37
Veterinary medicine
  Comparative religious law: KB3122
  Jewish law: KBM3122
Veterinary medicine and hygiene
  Islamic law: KBP3122

Veterinary public health
  Islamic law: KBP3122
Vetita communicatio in sacris
  Roman Catholic law: KBU3644
Vicarii apostolici
  Organs of government
    Canon law: KBR2482+
Vicarii foranei
  Diocesan constitution and organs
    Canon law: KBR2868
  Organs of government
    Roman Catholic law: KBU2868
Vicarii generales vel episcopales
  Diocesan constitution and organs
    Canon law: KBR2854
  Roman Catholic law: KBU2854
Vicarius paroecialis
  Diocesan constitution and organs
    Canon law: KBR2872
Vicars forane
  Diocesan constitution and organs
    Canon law: KBR2868
  Organs of government
    Roman Catholic law: KBU2868
Vicars general
  Diocesan constitution and organs
    Canon law: KBR2854
  Roman Catholic law: KBU2854
Victim
  Criminal procedure
    Comparative religious law: KB4630.V52
    Islamic law: KBP4630.V52
    Jewish law: KBM4630.V52
Victimology
  Comparative religious law: KB4855
  Islamic law: KBP4855
  Jewish law: KBM4855
Victim's family
  Criminal procedure
    Comparative religious law: KB4630.V52
    Islamic law: KBP4630.V52
    Jewish law: KBM4630.V52
Victims of crimes
  Comparative religious law: KB4855
Victims of crimes
  Compensation to
    Jewish law: KBM4767
  Islamic law: KBP4855
  Jewish law: KBM4855
Village settlement
  Comparative religious law: KB3056
  Islamic law: KBP3060
Vinculum inter coniuges perpetuum et exclusivum
  Canon law: KBR3155+
  Roman Catholic law: KBU3155+
Violatio legis vel praecepti
  Criminal law
    Roman Catholic law: KBU3533+
  Penal (Criminal) law
    Canon law: KBR3533+
Violatio per actiones graviter iniuriosas
  Canon law: KBR3234
  Roman Catholic law: KBU3234
Violatio sacramentalis sigilli
  Penal (Criminal) law
    Canon law: KBR3724
Violation of freedom
  Torts
    Islamic law: KBP842
    Jewish law: KBM842
Violation of integrity
  Torts
    Jewish law: KBM842.7+
Violation of law or precept
  Criminal law
    Roman Catholic law: KBU3533+
  Penal (Criminal) law
    Canon law: KBR3533+
Violation of price regulations
  Jewish law: KBM4290
Violation of privacy
  Torts
    Jewish law: KBM843
Violation of sacred places
  Canon law: KBR3234
Violation of secular laws
  Jewish law: KBM3835
Violation of the seal of confession
  Penal (Criminal) law
    Canon law: KBR3724

Violation or destruction of sacred places
Roman Catholic law: KBU3234
Virginity
Muslim women
Islamic law: KBP528.B54
Vis
Justification
Criminal law
Roman Catholic law: KBU3550
Legal transactions
Ius ecclesiasticum privatum: KBR2292
Roman Catholic law: KBU2292
Visitatio episcopalis
Canon law: KBR2840
Visitation of tombs
Islamic law: KBP186.97.T65
Viticulture
Jewish law: KBM3333
Vivisection
Animal experimentation
Islamic law: KBP3123.2
Viziers: KBP2580
Vocational education
Islamic law: KBP3144.5
Jewish law: KBM3144.5
Void and voidable contracts: KBM867+
Comparative religious law: KB867+
Islamic law: KBP867+
Labor law
Islamic law: KBP1302
Jewish law: KBM1302
Void and voidable legal transactions
Roman Catholic law: KBU2288+
Void and voidable transactions
Legal transactions
Ius ecclesiasticum privatum: KBR2288+
Void marriage
Islamic law: KBP556+
Void or voidable marriage
Jewish law: KBM556
Vota publica (perpetua vel temporaria)
Religious institutes
Canon law: KBR2924
Vote (deliberative and consultative)
Conference of Bishops
Canon law: KBR2832
Votum et iusiurandum
Roman Catholic law: KBU3210+
Vow and oath
Divine worship
Canon law: KBR3210+
Roman Catholic law: KBU3210+
Vows
Islamic law: KBP184.9.V68
Vows of chastity, Public perpetual
Impediments to marriage
Canon law: KBR3128.V69
Marriage impediments
Roman Catholic law: KBU3128.V69
Vows, Public
Religious institutes
Roman Catholic law: KBU2924

W

Waḍī'ah: KBP896
Wages
Church employees
Canon law: KBR2891
Contracts
Servants and employees
Jewish law: KBM892.6
Income tax
Jewish law: KBM3584
Labor law
Islamic law: KBP1330
Jewish law: KBM1330
Waiting period
Dissolution of marriage
Islamic law: KBP566
Waiver
Obligations
Islamic law: KBP817.5
Wakālah: KBP1630+
Wakīl: KBP1637
Walā': KBP529.52
Walad: KBP587+
Walad al-li'ān
Inheritance and succession: KBP634.953.W34

INDEX

Walad al-zinā': KBP612+
  Inheritance and succession:
    KBP634.953.W35
Walī: KBP622+
Wālī: KBP543.954+
Wālid: KBP587+
Wanted notice
  Pretrial criminal procedures
    Jewish law: KBM4646
Wantonness
  Criminal offense
    Jewish law: KBM3874
Waqf
  Charitable uses: KBP637+
  Social welfare
    Islamic law: KBP1522
Waqt: KBP506
War
  Government measures in time of
    Islamic law: KBP3709+
War and emergency powers
  Constitutional and administrative law
    Comparative religious law: KB2564
War crimes
  Comparative religious law: KB4545
  Islamic law: KBP4545
  Jewish law: KBM4545
War damage compensation
  Islamic law: KBP3727
War declared by a king, Obligation to
  serve in
  Jewish law: KBM3740.M54
War, Measures in time of
  Jewish law: KBM3709+
War profits tax
  Jewish law: KBM3625
War-related groups
  Social laws
    Comparative religious law:
      KB1537+
  Social service
    Islamic law: KBP1537+
    Jewish law: KBM1537+
War veterans, Disabled
  Social work
    Canon law: KBR3280.W37
War veterans, Disabled
  Social work
    Roman Catholic law:
      KBU3280.W37
Wara': KBP502.2
Warehousing
  Contracts
    Comparative religious law: KB930.3
  Jewish law: KBM930.3
Wārith: KBP633.955+
Warranty
  Contract for work and labor
    Islamic law: KBP893.5
    Jewish law: KBM893.5
  Contracts for work and labor
    Comparative religious law: KB893+
  Sale
    Islamic law: KBP875
    Jewish law: KBM875
Wartime measures
  Jewish law: KBM3717
Waṣīy: KBP635.954
Waṣīyah: KBP635+
Wasteland
  Occupancy of by cultivator
    Islamic law: KBP687.6
Water
  Municipal public services
    Islamic law: KBP2956
  Ritual purity
    Islamic law: KBP184.4+
Water and groundwater pollution
  Comparative religious law: KB3131
  Islamic law: KBP3131
  Jewish law: KBM3131
Water resources
  Public property
    Comparative religious law:
      KB3046+
    Islamic law: KBP3046+
    Jewish law: KBM3046+
Water rights
  Islamic law: KBP698, KBP3046.7
  Jewish law: KBM698
  Ownership
    Comparative religious law: KB698

Water rights
  Public property
    Comparative religious law:
      KB3046.7
Water transportation
  Islamic law: KBP3470+
  Jewish law: KBM3471
Watercourses
  Public property
    Comparative religious law:
      KB3046+
    Islamic law: KBP3046+
    Jewish law: KBM3046+
Wathīqah/wathā'iq: KBP1676.7
Wazīr: KBP2580
Wealth tax
  Jewish law: KBM3616+
Web-based businesses
  Trade regulation
    Jewish law: KBM3420.M34
Weights and measures
  Economic law
    Comparative religious law: KB3257
    Islamic law: KBP3257+
  Jewish law: KBM3257+
Welfare
  Comparative religious law: KB1468+
  Islamic law: KBP1520+
  Jewish law: KBM1520+
Welfare, Public
  Canon law: KBR3264+
Whipping
  Criminal law punishment
    Comparative religious law:
      KB3980.F57
    Islamic law: KBP3980.F57
Wholesale trade
  Jewish community
    Jewish law: KBM3416
  Regulation
    Islamic law: KBP3416
Widows
  Jurisdiction of ecclesiastical courts
    Canon law: KBR3787.P47
  Legal status
    Islamic law: KBP550+
Wife
  Dissolution of marriage
    Islamic law: KBP562+
  Power of to repudiate herself
    Islamic law: KBP563
  Retaining the repudiated wife
    Islamic law: KBP560
Wife abuse
  Jewish law: KBM4077
Wife and husband
  Jewish law: KBM547+
Wilderness preservation
  Comparative religious law: KB3134+
  Islamic law: KBP3134+
  Jewish law: KBM3134
Wildlife conservation
  Islamic law: KBP3135
Will, Last
  Church property
    Roman Catholic law: KBU3355+
  Natural persons
    Roman Catholic law: KBU2249+
Wills
  Comparative religious law: KB635+
  Islamic law: KBP635+
  Jewish law: KBM635+
Wine
  Drinking of wine
    Islamic law: KBP4045
  Islamic law: KBP184.9.W55
Wine and winemaking
  Yoreh de'ah law: KBM523.5.W5
Winemaking
  Jewish law: KBM3397
Wiretapping
  Criminal trial
    Islamic law: KBP4689
    Jewish law: KBM4689
  Criminal trials
    Comparative religious law: KB4689
Witchcraft
  Penal (Criminal) law
    Canon law: KBR3646+
Withdrawal of faulty decisions
  Criminal procedure
    Comparative religious law: KB4753
    Islamic law: KBP4753

Withdrawal of faulty decisions
  Criminal procedure
    Jewish law: KBM4753
Withdrawal of offer
  Contracts
    Comparative religious law:
      KB869.3+
    Islamic law: KBP869.3+
    Jewish law: KBM869.3+
Witnesses
  Accusation by
    Islamic law: KBP4668
  Criminal procedure
    Comparative religious law: KB4692
    Islamic law: KBP4692
    Parties to action
      Jewish law: KBM4630.W56
    Procedure at trial
      Jewish law: KBM4692+
  Inquisition
    Canon law: KBR3943.W58
  Marriage
    Canon law: KBR3145
    Islamic law: KBP543.958
    Roman Catholic law: KBU3145
  Procedure in general
    Comparative religious law:
      KB1675+
    Islamic law: KBP1675+
    Jewish law: KBM1675+
  Trials
    Canon law: KBR3848
    Roman Catholic law: KBU3848
Witnesses, Accusation by
  Pretrial criminal procedure
    Jewish law: KBM4634
Witnesses, Warning by
  Criminal offense
    Jewish law: KBM3868
Wizārah: KBP2580
Women
  Biography
    Islamic law history: KBP73
  Capacity and disability
    Islamic law: KBP526+
  Comparative religious law: KB526+
Women
  Court witnesses
    Islamic law: KBP1677.W65
  Labor
    Comparative religious law:
      KB1278.W65
    Jewish law: KBM1424
  Natural persons
    Jewish law: KBM526+
  Witnesses in court
    Islamic law: KBP1677.W65
Women judges
  Islamic law: KBP1611
  Jewish law: KBM1611
Women's labor
  Islamic law: KBP1424
Wood, Recycling of
  Islamic law: KBP3264+
Words
  Interpretation and grammar
    Islamic law: KBP461+
Work and labor, Contract for
  Islamic law: KBP893+
Worker's compensation
  Islamic law: KBP1495
  Jewish law: KBM1495
Worms, Council of, 868: KBR266
Worship
  Islamic law: KBP184+
Wounds, Surgical repetition of
  Criminal law punishment
    Islamic law: KBP3980.W68
Wrongful act, Prohibition of benefitting
  from
  Jewish law: KBM524.4.W75
Wuḍū': KBP184.46+

Y

Yad: KBP646+
Yadu'a ba-tsibur: KBM546.17
Yamīn: KBP1677.Y35, KBP4709.Y35
Yāsā
  Dynastic rules
    Islamic law: KBP2535.Y37
  Islamic law: KBP458.Y37
Yeshivot: KBM3147.7.A+

Yibum: KBM563
Yiḥus: KBM583+
Young adults
  Criminal liability
    Jewish law: KBM3886
Youth
  Equality before the law
    Jewish law: KBM2467.C48
  Social laws
    Comparative religious law: KB1540
  Social service
    Islamic law: KBP1542+
    Jewish law: KBM1542+
Youth labor
  Comparative religious law:
    KB1278.C45
  Islamic law: KBP1422
  Jewish law: KBM1422

Z

Ẓāhirī school of thought: KBP335+
Zakāh: KBP180, KBP3620+
Zakat: KBP180, KBP3620+
Zawāj: KBP542+
Zawāj bayna Muslim wa-ghayr
  Muslimah: KBP546.952
Zawj: KBP547+
Zawjah: KBP547+
Zaydī: KBP375+
Zaydīyah: KBP375+
Ẓihār: KBP563.6
Zinā': KBP559.958, KBP4043

INDEX

GPO U.S. GOVERNMENT PRINTING OFFICE: 2008–340–014/60031